The Other Balkan Wars

A 1913 Carnegie Endowment
Inquiry in Retrospect
with a New Introduction
and Reflections on the
Present Conflict by George F. Kennan

A CARNEGIE ENDOWMENT BOOK

Library of Congress Cataloging-in-Publication Data

International Commission to Inquire into the Causes and
    Conduct of the Balkan Wars.
        The other Balkan wars: 1914 Carnegie Endowment Report
    of the International Commission to Inquire into the
    Causes and Conduct of the Balkan Wars / introduction
    with reflections on the present conflict
    by George F. Kennan.
            p. cm.
      "A Carnegie Endowment book"
      Originally published: Report of the International Commission to
    Inquire into the Causes and Conduct of the Balkan Wars:
    The Endowment, 1914.
      ISBN 0-87003-032-9 (pbk.) $15.95
      1. Balkan Peninsula—History—War of 1912–1913.
    I. Kennan, George Frost, 1904– . II. International Commission to
    Inquire into the Causes and Conduct of the Balkan Wars. III. Title.
    DR46.I63 1993
    949.6—dc20

                              93-19720
                                CIP

Cover: Wickham & Associates, Inc.
Copy Editor: Stephanie Terry
Printing: Jarboe Printing Co., Inc.

For information regarding sales of this book, please contact:
Brookings Institution Publications
Dept. 029, Washington DC 20042-0029
or call 1-800-275-1447

The Carnegie Endowment for International Peace

The Carnegie Endowment was founded in 1910 by Andrew Carnegie to promote international peace and understanding. To that end the Endowment conducts programs of research, discussion, publication and education in international affairs and American foreign policy. The Endowment also publishes the quarterly journal *Foreign Policy*.

As a tax-exempt operating foundation, the endowment maintains a professional staff of Senior and Resident Associates who bring to their work substantial firsthand experience in foreign affairs. Through writing, public and media appearances, Congressional testimony, participation in conferences, and other means, the staff engages the major policy issues of the day in ways that reach both expert and general audiences. Accordingly the Endowment seeks to provide a hospitable umbrella under which responsible analysis and debate may be civilly conducted, and it encourages Associates to write and speak freely on the subjects of their work. The Endowment serves as a forum for discussion and debate, and policy consultation, and from time to time issues reports of commissions or study groups.

The Endowment normally does not take institutional positions on public policy issues and funds its activities principally from its own resources, supplemented by other non-governmental, philanthropic sources of support.

Preface

In November 1992, I read a "Letter from Bosnia" in the *New Yorker* magazine, which chronicled the horrors of Serbian "ethnic cleansing." The article led off with a quotation from a report that the Carnegie Endowment for International Peace released in 1914 on this century's first Balkan wars in 1912 and 1913. I knew about the report but had never read it.

I retrieved a copy from the Endowment's archives, along with other documentation indicating that *New York Times* dispatches and interviews in July 1913 described terrible atrocities occurring in the Balkans. Those accounts prompted Nicholas Murray Butler, one of the Endowment's leaders and president of Columbia University, to send an urgent telegram to the president of the Board of Trustees, Elihu Root, then a U.S. senator and formerly secretary of war and secretary of state. "Amazing charges of Bulgarian outrages attributed to the King of Greece," Butler told Root, "give us great opportunity for prompt action. If you approve I will send notable commission at once to Balkans to ascertain facts and to fix responsibility for prolonging hostilities and committing outrages. Please reply...today if possible."

Root approved by midnight. In a remarkably short span of little more than a month, an International Commission of Inquiry was on its way to Belgrade. When the second Balkan war ended a week later, the inquiry turned into a study of the "causes and conduct" of the two wars.

Reading that commission's report convinced me that others should also have an opportunity to read it. It is a document with many stories to tell us in this twilight decade of the twentieth century, when yet again a conflict in the Balkans torments Europe and the conscience of the international community, and when our willingness to act has not matched our capacity for moral outrage.

I do not know exactly why George Kennan agreed so readily when I asked him to give context and perspective to those stories by writing a new introduction to the original report. I know only that he did so with dispatch that rivals Elihu Root's, and that we all now benefit from his insight, his sure sense of history, and his felicitous literary style.

Kennan's introduction lifts our sights while lowering our expectations. In its final pages, he focuses our attention—as it must eventually be focused—not on tomorrow or the next day, but on what must be done in the former Yugoslavia after the present hostilities have come to an end. The "very ugly problem in this southeastern part of the European continent" will not go away, Kennan warns. Will we then muster the political will to do what we have been unable to do in the midst of conflict? Our expectations about the virulence of the postwar environment in the Balkans needs to be clear-headed. The ferocity of the present war will scar and embitter all peoples of the Balkans, already long burdened by the history that Kennan obliges us to remember.

Regrettably, the postwar problems that he trenchantly discusses may be some time coming. The first two Balkan wars, for all their savagery, were mercifully brief. But a malignant nationalism still dominates the leaders of the present Balkan states, much as it did their predecessors in the then new Balkan states eighty years ago. No one knows when the current Balkan war will end or whether it will spread. Many anticipate strife and simmering violence to continue until exhaustion or political upheavals transform Serbia and Croatia. The driving ambition to create a greater Serbia, a factor in those earlier wars, could again today engulf Macedonia and totally change Kosovo's ethnic makeup.

A staff member in Elihu Root's Endowment, after reading incoming drafts of this report, confided to a colleague that he was "feeling considerably depressed. It seems impossible that such things as are related...can have occurred in the 20th Century." Indeed, the illusions at that far end of this century seem simple in retrospect. But were they any simpler than the illusions accompanying the end of the Cold War, when even those who foresaw the breakup of Yugoslavia dared not imagine "in the twentieth century" that the breakup could be so incomprehensibly violent and tragic?

If contemporary readers are sobered and enlightened by what they read in this volume, then the Endowment will have done a service to its own history and, more important, to the ever-more relevant history of the Balkans. For it is here, and it is now, that the uphill task of building a better international order in Europe—and elsewhere—is being tested in European capitals and in Washington.

Morton Abramowitz
President
Carnegie Endowment for
International Peace
May 2, 1993

Introduction

THE BALKAN CRISES: 1913 AND 1993
GEORGE F. KENNAN

At the outset of the present century there emerged in the United States, England and other parts of northern Europe a vigorous movement for the strengthening and consolidation of world peace, primarily by the development of new legal codes of international behavior. The movement was given a significant fillip when Tsar Nicholas II of Russia in 1899 issued a call for an international conference on disarmament. This curious initiative, largely the product of the immature dilettantism of the Tsar himself and elaborated by the characteristic confusions of the Russian governmental establishment of the time, was not a serious one. But it was at once seized upon with enthusiasm by adherents of the peace movements and had consequences the Tsar himself had not anticipated. Of those, the most important were the two Hague Peace Conferences of 1899 and 1907, resulting in a modernization and renewed codification of international law and in a significant elaboration, in particular, of the laws of war. Beyond that there was, especially in the United States, a marked surge of interest and enthusiasm for the negotiation and adoption of treaties of arbitration and conciliation. And these governmental efforts were supported by a number of private institutional initiatives, one of the most lasting and notable of which was the founding, in 1910, of the Carnegie Endowment for International Peace. That institution was only one of the several creative initiatives of Andrew Carnegie on behalf of world peace, another being the erection of the great "Peace Palace" at the Hague.

It is both sad and ironic to reflect that these so far-seeing and commendable efforts on behalf of international peace were proceeding simultaneously with the intensive pursuit by the great European powers of what were, whether so intended or otherwise, preparations for the First World War. As recently as 1894 the French and the Russian general staffs had linked the fates of their countries in a secret treaty of alliance, so worded as almost to ensure that there could be no further minor complication in European affairs that would not lead to wider hostilities among the great powers. It was in 1898 that there had been inaugurated, for the first time in earnest, the unnecessary and dreadfully misguided effort of Kaiser Wilhelm II's Germany to compete with Great Britain in the development of naval power. And throughout all of it the great powers were busy with military preparations that, however defensively conceived, simply diminished whatever small possibility of avoiding a general conflagration might still have existed.

In the face of all the preparations, the strivings and enthusiasms of the peace movement of those first years of this century might appear, in today's retrospect, unrealistic, naive and pathetic. But they were, in addition to being—as we see today—profoundly prophetic and well justified in the concerns they reflected, deeply, almost desperately, believed in by those who experienced them. And they were not wholly without justification. Nearly a hundred years had then elapsed since the last great all-European military conflagration, that of the Napoleonic wars. An entire generation had intervened since the last great bilateral intra-European conflict, the Franco-Prussian War. Was there not then, people could ask themselves, a possibility that the great European powers could now be brought, with sufficient outside encouragement and pressure, to perceive the folly of war among highly industrialized powers in the modern age and then to retire at the brink?

It was in the entertainment of such hopes, fears and aspirations that the protagonists of the American and European peace movements were struggling along as Europe entered the second decade of the present century.

A hundred years before that time the entire Balkan Peninsula, from the Aegean Sea and the Turkish straits to the borders of the Russian and Austro-Hungarian empires, had been, with minor exceptions, embraced by the Turkish empire. But in the course of the nineteenth century the Turks had been compelled to withdraw southward and eastward, to a point where all that remained of their European dominions were the southernmost parts of the peninsula, primarily Thrace and Macedonia. By the beginning of the twentieth century a number of new states—notably Bulgaria, Serbia, Montenegro and Rumania—had sprung up in the area thus liberated from Turkish control. Those states were, without exception, monarchically governed; and the monarchs were, as a rule, somewhat more moderate and thoughtful than their subjects. But their dynasties were not well established. Their powers were usually disputed by inexperienced and unruly parliamentary bodies. Borders were in many instances vague and lacking in firm acceptance. The entire peninsula was, in short, devoid of international stability.

It was, of course, a time when the powerful forces of modern nationalism were achieving everywhere, but particularly in nations new to the experience of political independence, their greatest intensity. And nowhere did this have a more violent, intoxicating effect than on the politicians and military leaders of the newly founded Balkan countries. If, initially, the leading impulses for the expulsion of the Turks from European Russia had come from the neighboring great powers, Russia and Austria-Hungary, the political leaders of the newly established Balkan states were now beginning to take matters into their own hands. And it was hard for people who had recently achieved so much, and this so suddenly, to know where to stop. Dreams of new glories to flow from new territorial expansion bemused many minds. The air was clouded by visions of a greater this or that: a "greater Serbia," a "greater Bulgaria," and so on. And while the remaining areas of Turkish control in the southern Balkans, Thrace and Macedonia, were by no means the only objectives of such aspirations, it was no more than natural that they should have been the principal ones. Turkey was regarded, in the common phrase of the time, as "the sick man of Europe." If this "sick man" had now been expelled from most of the peninsula, was there any reason why he could not be similarly expelled from the remainder as well? For that, however, alliance and common action were required. "Let us unite to complete the expulsion of the Turks," was the general feeling. "And then, when we are free," as one Bulgarian revolutionary put it, "each shall have what belongs to him."

Vague impulses of that nature, hastily linked together by a flimsy patchwork of secret and poorly thought-out military engagements, led the Serbs, Bulgarians, Greeks and Montenegrins to launch conjointly, in the early autumn of 1912, a military action against the Turks. That was the first of the two Balkan wars of 1912 and 1913. The Turks, as it happened, proved to be considerably weaker than had been generally supposed. Within a few weeks they had been driven, primarily by the Bulgarians, to the gates of Constantinople, and the war was over.

But never, surely, did any coalition of powers launch a war on the basis of flimsier understandings among them about what it was they were fighting for than did the participants of this military action against the Turks. The relations among the supposed allies, and particularly the most prominent of them—Serbs, Bulgarians and Greeks—had, even before this, been of the worst kind, ridden by rivalries, suspicions and conflicting aims. The result was predictable. The defeat of the Turks ended with forces of Serbia, Bulgaria and Greece in occupation of portions of the helpless Macedonia. Each had aspirations with relation to that territory that could be satisfied only at the expense of the others. It was not surprising, therefore, that in June 1913 war broke out among them. It was this that was known as the second Balkan war.

The second fracas centered upon the fighting between the Serbs and the Bulgarians, long-standing rivals for preeminence in that southern part of the Balkans. Hostilities were furious but brief, lasting only over the midsummer of 1913. The Bulgarians, already over-extended by their action against the Turks, were decisively defeated. A species of peace treaty (like many such arrangements, in essence a provisorium) was signed in Bucharest on August 10, 1913.

The news that the first war had broken out in the Balkans, reaching the major Western countries in the early autumn of 1912, naturally came as a shock to the adherents of the European and American peace movements. The shock was modified, to be sure, by the fact that in Britain and America public opinion, and in particular the liberal opinion so prominently represented in the peace movements, had for years been strongly, sometimes fulsomely, sympathetic to the Balkan Slavs in their struggle for liberation from Turkey. Many well-meaning people in the West found it easy, in the light of their enthusiasm, to forget that the hostilities had been inaugurated in the first war by the Balkan Slavs themselves, in ways that constituted violations not only of international law but of existing contractual agreements of one sort or another.

In the case of the second war, the situation was different. The Turks (although they took advantage of the occasion to recover a small part of the territory they had lost) were no longer a principal party to the hostilities. Not only that, but reports were now coming in of the extreme savagery of the fighting that had marked the first war and of the many atrocities against war prisoners and innocent civilian populations that had accompanied it. It was becoming evident that by no means all of the atrocities had come from the Turkish side. Altogether, it was now being realized that the continuation of the Balkan hostilities constituted a serious challenge to the peace movements of the time.

By no institution in the West could that challenge have been more keenly felt than by the Carnegie Endowment for International Peace. Only three years had elapsed since its founding. What was happening was plainly in flagrant conflict with its commitment. But what could be done? What action could it take? Disturbing as the situation was, the information coming in from the area of hostilities was still for the most part fragmentary, indirect and unsatisfactory. Little of it was fully reliable. It was hard to know how to distinguish fact from fiction, reality from exaggeration, the known from the merely alleged. Before far-reaching decisions could be made, one had to gain a clearer picture of what was happening.

This was the background for the decision of the Carnegie Endowment, made immediately upon the outbreak of the second war, to set up a prestigious international commission and to charge it with the task of establishing the facts and giving to Western opinion a clear and reliable picture of what was going on in the affected region. Once this picture was available it would be easier, one felt, not just for the Endowment itself but for the many others as well who were committed to the cause of international peace to determine what might be done to set things to rights.

The commission, then, was duly established. It consisted of seven members: one each from the United States, Britain, Germany, Austria-Hungary and Russia, and two from France. They were all men of some prominence in their respective countries, chosen particularly for their interest in the peace movements. Their names and titles appear on the third sheet of the attached report. The presidency of the commission was exercised by a French senator, Baron d'Estournelles de Constant, a man of much eminence who had not only taken a prominent part in the peace movement, serving as the French representative to the Hague conferences, but had considerable familiarity with at least one area of the Balkans.

Four of the men were designated to serve as a special fact-finding subcommittee charged with visiting the region of the Balkan hostilities on behalf of the commission. Three included the American, Dr. Samuel T. Dutton, professor at Teacher's College, Columbia University; the French lawyer and member of the Chamber of Deputies, M. Justin Godart; and the well-known Russian professor, historian, writer and liberal political figure, Paul Milyukov (destined later to play so prominent a role in the Provisional Government of 1917). The fourth was a British journalist, a man whose distinction was also to reach its acme in later years: Henry N. Brailsford. A person of outstanding intelligence, literary talent and scholarly diligence, Brailsford would appear to have been the only one of the four who had extensive previous experience in the Balkans and was conversant with at least two of its languages. He had lived in both Greece and Macedonia and had written, some six years earlier, an excellent book on the Macedonia of that day.

These men set forth from Paris on August 2, 1913, shortly before the ending of the second of the two wars. Their journey took them, together or severally, to Belgrade, Salonica, Athens, Constantinople and Sofia. Although the commission's report includes no account of their experiences, reason tells us that it must have been, to say the least, an eventful journey; and that supposition is confirmed by several hints given us in Baron d'Estournelles's introduction to the report. From these hints we may conclude, for example, that the Serbian government, resenting (for different reasons in each case) the inclusion of Milyukov and Brailsford in the delegation, not only declined to give any official recognition to the commissioners but also was initially reluctant to assist them in practical ways. The commissioners persisted, however, and in the end the government provided them "with every facility for reaching the frontier and Salonica." The Greek government, similarly motivated, officially denied permission for Brailsford (who had once fought with the Greeks against the Turks but had later been critical of the Greeks in certain respects) to come to Kilkich, and limited his movements while he was in Salonica. As a result of these reactions, Milyukov curtailed his participation. But the other three commissioners, undismayed by the rebuffs, pushed on with their mission; and, after nearly eight weeks of strenuous travel, they returned to Paris on the 28th of September. They had seen little of the actual hostilities, which ended at roughly the same time the commissioners arrived. But they had seen much of their immediate aftermath, and had tapped the fresh memories of many survivors, military and civilian. That, in the circumstances, was quite enough.

The report of the commission as a whole follows this introduction. It consisted, as the reader will see, of seven chapters. There was first a long historical introduction leading up to the outbreak of the first war but no further—a document that becomes more complicated and more difficult to comprehend for the reader of this present age as it approaches its conclusion. There followed three chapters, comprising 135 of the report's long and finely printed pages, forming the very body of the document. Those chapters dealt exclusively with the excesses, and particularly the atrocities, that marked the hostilities and their aftermath: in short, the abundant evidences of violations not only of international law but of the minimum dictates of common humanity. While the final report, issued unanimously in the names of all the members of the commission, did not identify the authors of the various chapters, the Carnegie Endowment's archives clarify the matter, without indicating the degree of collaboration among the principal authors. The first chapter, the historical résumé, was written by Milyukov. The following three, concentrating on the atrocities, were from the pen of Brailsford (chapter two) or Milyukov (chapters three and four).

There followed a chapter on the precise relationship of the two wars to the principles and accepted provisions of international law—a document that also came from Milyukov's pen. A further chapter, on the economic consequences of the two wars, was written by the French authority, Godart. The brief final chapter of conclusions, written by Dutton, was a sad and penetrating document, not hesitating to recognize the two wars as "a ghastly chapter of horrors," declaring that the commission's members could "indulge in no optimism regarding the immediate political future of Macedonia" in particular, and confessing that for the region in general the case for the future seemed "well nigh hopeless" in the light of prevailing conditions.

Following the return of the three commissioners who visited the affected area, the report was rather laboriously put together—laboriously because the several members of the commission were living in widely dispersed geographical locations; and it was not completed and made public until the early summer of 1914. It was, of course, destined to be at once blanketed, in the attention and reactions of the world public, by the more sensational event of the outbreak of the First World War—a circumstance that offers all the more reason for its re-publication today, when the attention of world opinion is once more so unhappily drawn to the still unsolved problems of the region with which it dealt.

Examined from a distance of some eighty years, the report makes today, in some respects, an odd impression. There seems to be little unity among its various parts. In the narrative chapters, the ones describing the atrocities, no effort seems to have been made to relate the happenings to the political and military events that supplied the background for them—not even noting the beginnings and endings of hostilities in the various wars and regions. There was no attempt to analyze the political motivations of the various governments participating in the wars, or to suggest what might be done by the peace movements to prevent the wars' recurrence. But the document is replete with interesting and often penetrating passages on individual matters; and it may stand, in its entirety, as one of the most eloquent and compelling pleas for recognition of the folly of modern war and the essentiality of international peace, not just in the Balkans but everywhere in the civilized world.

All of the above having been said, the importance of this report for the world of 1993 lies primarily in the light it casts on the excruciating situation prevailing today in the same Balkan world with which it dealt. The greatest value of this report is to reveal to people of this age how much of today's problem has deep roots and how much does not. It will be easier to think of solutions when such realities are kept in mind.

The measure of historical continuity should not be exaggerated. There are significant differences between the Balkan situation of 1913 and that of the present day.

There has been since that time a revolution in weaponry. In 1913 even the machine gun was in its infancy. There was no air power. Motor vehicles were so scarce that they played no significant part in military transport. The atrocities recounted in the report were ones perpetrated for the most part by the bayonet, the rifle butt, the cudgel and the whiplash.

The revolution in communication, so predominant in daily life of our day and strongly affecting military affairs, would have been not only implausible but probably wholly unimaginable to the peoples and the soldiers of 1913. The outside world knew of the horrors and atrocities of that day only from the reports of itinerant journalists. The report of Carnegie's Balkan commission was, in its capacity as a thorough survey of at least one outstanding aspect of those wars, a unique phenomenon. Today the evidences of all the excesses, and in some instances the excesses themselves, are on the screens of hundreds of millions of homes across the globe. And the publicity has had much to do with the prominent involvement of Western governments and other outsiders in the hostilities, an involvement taking the form of the presence of many thousands of Westerners — U.N. and Red Cross personnel, reporters and photographers for the news media, representatives of private charitable organizations and official conciliators—at or near the scenes of hostilities. The commissioners of 1913 were almost alone in their effort to bring to the attention of the world the truly alarming aspects of Balkan violence. Today, they would have had a host of collaborators in such an effort.

But even more significant than those differences are the many and depressing evidences of similarity between what was occurring in the Balkans in 1913 and what is going on there today. There are too many to be listed here, but a few examples will suffice.

Let us take just the general manner in which warfare is being waged. The common feature of Balkan wars, it is said in the 1913 report, is that "war is waged not only by the armies but by the nations themselves....This is why these wars are so sanguinary, why they produce so great a loss in men, and end in the annihilation of the population and the ruin of whole regions." The object of armed conflict, the report continued, was "the complete extermination of an alien population." Villages were not just captured; they were in large part destroyed. The inhabitants were driven out (where they had not already fled), and their houses burned. Woe betided the man of military age, or the woman of "enemy" national identity, who were found alive in the conquered village. Rape was ubiquitous, sometimes murderous. Victims, now wholly dispossessed and homeless, were obliged to take to the roads or the mountain trails by the thousands, in a frantic search for places where they could at least lay their heads. Great streams of pathetically suffering refugees could be seen on many of the roads of the peninsula. Little pity was shown for the sick and the wounded. Prisoners of war, if not killed outright, were sometimes driven into outdoor compounds or ramshackle buildings and left there to die of hunger and exposure. There was in general a total hard-heartedness with relation to the defeated, whether military or civilian. Some of this was carried beyond just the level of neglect and indifference and into the realm of sickening and deliberate cruelty.

The similarity of all this with what is happening today is inescapable. And comparisons of who, statistically, committed the most atrocities are idle. A single person's painful death under such treatment is always alone a measureless tragedy. That there were any such horrors at all in the Balkan wars was an abomination. Very often, as the 1913 commissioners discovered, the rumors of the scale of the atrocities turned out, upon careful examination, to be exaggerations. But the commissioners were also obliged to point out, in many such instances, that the residue of reality discovered to lie behind the quantitative exaggerations was in itself enough to turn the stomach of any reasonably decent person.

It was often similarly charged in 1913 that those who ordered the excesses were not the regular governments and commanders—that the atrocities were perpetrated by armed bands of like political sympathies, but operating semi-independently under their own chieftains. The 1913 commissioners found this a lame excuse. If the behavior in question was not ordered by the regular commanders, they pointed out, it was certainly tolerated and winked at, sometimes actually encouraged, by them. Again, the comparison with what is going on today is obvious.

The 1913 commissioners found it hard, in investigating all the excesses, to distinguish comparative degrees of guilt among the various belligerents. The Serbs, indeed, figured as major offenders, particularly for the manner in which they treated the Macedonians in the liberated territory of which they were in occupation in the aftermath of the first of the two wars. But the Serbs happened to be, as they were destined to be in the hostilities of 1992–93, the strongest party. And who could say with certainty or even plausibility that other parties, had they been in the driver's seat, would have behaved any better? None, after all, were entirely innocent in that respect. It was emphasized, in the words of the commission's report, that "there is no clause in international law applicable to land war and to the treatment of the wounded, which was not violated, to a greater or lesser extent, by all the belligerents."

The question arose in the minds of the commissioners of how much of the ferocity of these hostilities could be properly attributed to religious fanaticism. That religion played a part at many points in the animosities that motivated the fighting was clearly recognized. This was particularly the case in the first of the wars, which found the other parties, mostly Christians, ranged together against the Muslim Turks. And similar situations had some part in the second war as well, there being Muslim elements in both the Bulgarian and Macedonian populations.

But the conclusion of the commissioners was that to see those differences as the principal cause of animosity would be to go too far. The Turks, for one thing, appear to have been, in the centuries of their one-time ascendancy in the Balkans, relatively tolerant in their treatment of non-Muslim religious institutions. Their treatment of such institutions was in any case not the leading grievance against them. And as the future was to demonstrate, the Christians were capable of being just as violent and savage in their conflicts with other Christians as they were with the Muslims. In the period of these Balkan wars, the Croats, as the only Roman Catholic people, were still, with very minor exceptions, living in areas belonging to, or under occupation of, the Austro-Hungarian Empire. They were not, therefore, directly involved in these two Balkan wars; and the Eastern Orthodox–Roman Catholic religious antagonisms that were to play so unfortunate a role in later years were not at that time prominently involved.

No, the strongest motivating factor involved in the Balkan wars was not religion but aggressive nationalism. But that nationalism, as it manifested itself on the field of battle, drew on deeper traits of character inherited, presumably, from a distant tribal past: a tendency to view the outsider, generally, with dark suspicion, and to see the political-military opponent, in particular, as a fearful and implacable enemy to be rendered harmless only by total and unpitying destruction. And so it remains today.

In attempting to reason with the respective governments about these matters, the 1913 commissioners found themselves up against blank walls. What was called in the report "the megalomania of the national ideal" had room for neither reason nor compromise. Statistics used to support a government's case were distorted to the point of sheer absurdity. Those invoked by different governments differed so widely as to afford no conceivable basis for reconciliation. Yet anyone who challenged a given government's version of the truth documented himself thereby, in the eyes of that government, as a committed enemy. "It is," wrote Baron d'Estournelles in his introduction to the report, "impossible to avoid the reproach of a party, if one does not take sides with it against the others, and conversely." In the face of extreme nationalistic self-admiration and suspicion of every neighbor, there was little room for anything resembling conciliation.

One cannot end this summary of the similarities between yesterday and today without noting some of the reminiscences and reflections of the president of the Balkan commission, Baron d'Estournelles, as recorded in his introduction to the report. He had served, many years before, as a member of the international commission set up to delineate, on the spot, the Balkan boundaries described in the Berlin Treaty of 1879–80. He had taken advantage of those duties to travel independently through much of Albania and Macedonia. Those countries were then very little known. They "were then, and are still, unlike Europe," he wrote, "more widely separated from her than Europe from America." Such were the impressions he had gained that he had, "as a matter of professional discretion," he said, "scarcely dared" to publish any of them.

Even then there had been hesitations about the desirability of sending a commission to investigate the circumstances of the Balkan wars. What if the commission should find "that the atrocities were inevitable, inseparable from the condition of war...? What an exposure of the powerlessness of civilization!" And would its efforts not merely stimulate the animosities? It was that anxiety, "the fear of compromise, the fear of displeasing one or another of the nations, the terror, in short, of intervening reasonably and in time, which has brought about a crisis, the gravity of which is not only of yesterday and of today, but also of tomorrow."

Others were saying, of course, why go further afield to seek troubles and duties? Have you not enough to do at home? "Yes," was his answer. "We have plenty to do at home." But "my own imperfection," he argued, "need not prevent me from doing my utmost to be useful." And, after all: "All this horror will not cease to exist as long as Europe continues to ignore it....The spectacle of destitute childhood in a civilized country is beginning to rouse the hardest hearts. What shall be said of the destitution of a whole people, of several nations, in Europe, in the Twentieth Century?" And then, this paragraph:

> This is the state of things which the Americans wish to help in ending. Let them be thanked and honored for their generous initiative. I have been appealing to it for a long time....We are only too happy today to combine our strength, too willing to raise with them a cry of protestation against the contempt of the skeptics and ill-wishers who will try to suppress it.

Well, here we are, in 1993. Eighty years of tremendous change in the remainder of Europe and of further internecine strife in the Balkans themselves have done little to alter the essence of the problem this geographic region presents for Europe, for our own country and for the United Nations. Obviously, it is a problem with very deep historical roots. Those roots reach back, clearly, not only into the centuries of Turkish domination but also into the Byzantine penetration of the Balkans even before that time.

One must not be too hard on the Turks. The atrocities attributed to them in this report were no worse than those that the Christian peoples were inflicting both on the Turks and on each other in these wars. The report makes reference to the fact that there were those in Macedonia, in the period of Greek and Serbian occupation, who began to long for the return of the Turks. But that this effective separation from Europe during three centuries of immensely significant development in the civilization of the remainder of the European continent had profound effects on the development of the Balkan peoples cannot be denied. The author of the first historical résumé, in the 1913 report, referred to the Turkish conquest as "leveling all the nationalities and preserving them all alike in a condition of torpor, in a manner comparable to the action of a vast refrigerator." And it is worth noting that the events of the second part of the present century, and outstandingly the thirty years of communist power, were not helpful in thawing out that congealment; in a sense, they may be said to have prolonged it. What we are up against is the sad fact that developments of those earlier ages, not only those of the Turkish domination but of earlier ones as well, had the effect of thrusting into the southeastern reaches of the European continent a salient of non-European civilization that has continued to the present day to preserve many of its non-European characteristics, including some that fit even less with the world of today than they did with the world of eighty years ago.

It will be argued that these states of mind are not peculiar to the Balkan peoples—that they can be encountered among other European peoples as well. True enough. But all these distinctions are relative ones. It is the undue predominance among the Balkan peoples of these particular qualities, and others that might have been mentioned, that seems to be decisive as a determinant of the troublesome, baffling and dangerous situation that marks that part of the world today.

What, then, can be done?

That question has already been the subject of much extensive discussion and altercation in Western opinion, and this introduction is not the place for any attempt at a definitive answer. But there are two or three observations that might serve as a suitable termination for this introduction:

First of all, let it be noted that while this Balkan situation is one to which the United States cannot be indifferent, it is primarily a problem for the Europeans.

It is their continent, not ours, that is affected. They have the physical and military resources with which to confront the problem. And if they claim, as many of them do, that they lack the political unity to confront it successfully, the answer is that perhaps this is one of those instances, not uncommon in the lives of nations as of individuals, when one has to rise to the occasion.

Second, it is clear that no one—no particular country and no group of countries—wants, or should be expected, to occupy the distracted Balkan region, to subdue its excited peoples and to hold them in order until they can calm down and begin to look at their problems in a more orderly way. Conceivably, it might be momentarily helpful; but even that is not certain; and in any case any effort along that line could be only the most tenuous and temporary of improvisations. In the long run, no region can solve any other region's problems. The best the outsider can do is to give occasional supplementary help in the pinches.

And finally, there is the question of the more distant future. When the present hostilities are ended (as someday they must be) there will still remain the question of how the Balkan peoples are to relate to each other in the years that lie ahead.

Let us glance at what will presumably be the formal international structure of the Balkan community in the post-hostilities period. We may start by leaving aside two of the possible actors on that scene: the Slovenes, who are really an alpine people and who will, let us hope, remain remote from Balkan political affairs; and the Montenegrins, who have so extensively identified themselves with the Serbs in the recent unpleasantness that we may regard them as effectively subsumed by the Serbian state. There will then presumably remain nine countries, including Yugoslavia, actively involved in Balkan problems: Greece, Albania, Macedonia, Serbia, Croatia, Rumania, Bulgaria and Bosnia (or as much of it as survives). That is three more than there were before the breakup of Yugoslavia.

If there is to be followed the modern custom of conferring upon any body politic of whatever size or quality that demands membership in the United Nations the status of a fully sovereign state, theoretically equal to every other state in its proud independent quality, then each of the Balkan states will presumably be given that status, if it does not already enjoy it. And each of them, we might note, will then have the right to develop whatever armed forces its resources and circumstances will permit.

Now, the practice of conferring that status on Balkan peoples is not new. The same practice was followed more than a century ago when the first of them were liberated from Turkish rule. Even then, the result was not a happy one, as is so clearly shown in the Carnegie report of 1914. It very soon became evident that the new states had great difficulty in relating to one another in a mature and peaceful manner. In a sense, there was more peace when they were still under Turkish rule than there was after they gained their independence. (That is not to say that the Turkish rule was in all other respects superior to what came after.)

Eighty years have now passed since the Carnegie commissioners paid their visit to that region. And this writer knows of no evidence that the ability of the Balkan peoples to interact peaceably with one another is any greater now than it was those eighty years ago. If proof of that were needed, it would be abundantly there in the appalling state of hostilities that now prevails in the region. And the difficulty of such interaction can only have been heightened by the fact that the number of players at this tragic game has now been significantly increased.

A further complication exists, in that connection, in the question of the future relationship of certain of those peoples, and particularly the Serbs, to the United Nations. The Serbs, just to take them as the leading example, have violated in every conceivable way the one and only requirement for membership in the United Nations as specified in its Charter: "to accept the obligations contained in the present Charter, and, in the judgement of the Organization, [to be] able and willing to carry out these obligations." Not only have the Serbs consistently and contemptuously flouted, for months on end, the obligations in question, but they have repeatedly exerted themselves to frustrate the U.N.'s efforts to relieve the sufferings of the civilian population in the region of hostilities. In some instances they would appear even to have opposed U.N. efforts by force of arms. And there could have been no behavior more fundamentally contrary to the first principles of the U.N. Charter, not to mention the provisions of international war and the laws of war, than the persistent artillery bombardment over weeks and months on end of the helpless civilian populations of entire cities. Something of the same could be said, no doubt, of the behavior of certain of the other parties; but if so, it would have been true in far lesser degree.

What account is to be taken of such conduct, one wonders, when it comes to a peace settlement and the determination of future international relationships in the region? To date, no one has suggested that the membership of Yugoslavia in the U.N. should even be suspended in the light of the behavior of the Serbs in the theater of hostilities. Are we to assume that when it comes to the designing of a post-hostilities settlement all this is to be forgotten and the Yugoslavs (read: the Serbs) and the other parties are to be welcomed back to their normal position and role in the United Nations, as though none of this had ever happened? And if so, what would that say to any other U.N. member that found itself in some sort of military conflict and thought it to its advantage to ignore and flout its obligations as a member of that organization? And what, indeed, would it say to the world as a whole about the U.N. as the only living and accepted symbol of the community of fate that links all the peoples of this planet? Are we to understand that membership in it involves no significant obligations at all? That the

Charter's provisions on membership are meaningless and that the persistent and contemptuous disregard of them has no effect on a country's membership?

Those are questions that are bound to present themselves when the necessity arises of devising some future status quo for international life in the Balkans to replace that which has now broken down so disastrously. If all these countries are to be established or re-established as fully independent and sovereign states, members of the United Nations, with no serious obligations to flow from U.N. membership and without any other significant restraints on their conduct, what are we to expect, on the record of the more remote past and of the immediate one, of their future interaction? Let us recall, as just one example of the potential instability, that at least three of them and possibly a fourth have political or territorial designs on one of their members, Macedonia—designs that are sure to come to the surface of their inter-relationships as soon as attention is withdrawn from the present hostilities.

It is relentlessly obvious that when the present military conflict is over, the international community, and particularly the European community, is going to find itself up against a very ugly problem in this southeastern part of the European continent. Two things will be necessary: the first, a new and clearly accepted territorial status quo; the second, certain greater and more effective restraints on the behavior of the states of the region. It would be naive to suppose that the first of those requirements—the designing of a new territorial status quo—could be met solely by negotiations among the various parties themselves. Their views should, of course, be heard and seriously considered; but it will take outside mediation, and in all probability outside force, to devise a reasonable settlement and to bring the various parties to accept and observe it. As for the second, the restraints on the Balkan parties in the exercise of what they view as their unlimited sovereignty and freedom of action will clearly have to be greater than those that are now normally applied in the international community.

There will, therefore, be two necessities to confront those who, from the outside, try to be helpful in the solution of this great problem. One will be a capacity for innovation with respect to the rights and duties implicit in the term "sovereignty." The other will be force—minimum force, of course, but force nevertheless—and the readiness to employ it where nothing else will do.

Those will, I repeat, be necessities confronting in the most immediate way the European community; but the wider international community will also have a serious interest in seeing them met. Is there any reason to believe that in either of those communities the necessary resolve to tackle this problem, and the necessary readiness to accept the attendant agonies of effort, will be forthcoming? The answer is that there is only one reason; and that is the fact that the alternatives, for anyone who looks realistically at the problem, will clearly be worse.

Carnegie Endowment for International Peace

DIVISION OF INTERCOURSE AND EDUCATION

Publication No. 4

REPORT

OF THE

INTERNATIONAL COMMISSION

To Inquire into the Causes and Conduct

OF THE

BALKAN WARS

PUBLISHED BY THE ENDOWMENT
WASHINGTON, D. C.
1914

PRESS OF BYRON S. ADAMS
WASHINGTON, D. C.

PREFACE

The circumstances which attended the Balkan wars of 1912 and 1913 were of such character as to fix upon them the attention of the civilized world. The conflicting reports as to what actually occurred before and during these wars, together with the persistent rumors often supported by specific and detailed statements as to violations of the laws of war by the several combatants, made it important that an impartial and exhaustive examination should be made of this entire episode in contemporary history. The purpose of such an impartial examination by an independent authority was to inform public opinion and to make plain just what is or may be involved in an international war carried on under modern conditions. If the minds of men can be turned even for a short time away from passion, from race antagonism and from national aggrandizement to a contemplation of the individual and national losses due to war and to the shocking horrors which modern warfare entails, a step and by no means a short one, will have been taken toward the substitution of justice for force in the settlement of international differences.

It was with this motive and for this purpose that the Division of Intercourse and Education of the Carnegie Endowment for International Peace constituted in July, 1913, an International Commission of Inquiry to study the recent Balkan wars and to visit the actual scenes where fighting had taken place and the territory which had been devastated. The presidency of this International Commission of Inquiry was entrusted to Baron d'Estournelles de Constant, Senator of France, who had represented his country at the First and Second Hague Conferences of 1899 and of 1907, and who as *Président Fondateur* of the *Conciliation Internationale,* has labored so long and so effectively to bring the various nations of the world into closer and more sympathetic relations. With Baron d'Estournelles de Constant there were associated men of the highest standing, representing different nationalities, who were able to bring to this important task large experience and broad sympathy.

The result of the work of the International Commission of Inquiry is contained in the following report. This report, which has been written without prejudice and without partisanship, is respectfully commended to the attention of the governments, the people and the press of the civilized world. To those who so generously participated in its preparation as members of the International Commission of Inquiry, the Trustees of the Carnegie Endowment for International Peace offer an expression of grateful thanks.

NICHOLAS MURRAY BUTLER,
Acting Director.

February 22, 1914.

MEMBERS OF THE BALKAN COMMISSION OF INQUIRY

Austria:

Dr. Josef Redlich, Professor of Public Law in the University of Vienna.

France:

Baron d'Estournelles de Constant, Senator.

M. Justin Godart, lawyer and Member of the Chamber of Deputies.

Germany:

Dr. Walther Schücking, Professor of Law at the University of Marburg.

Great Britain:

Francis W. Hirst, Esq., Editor of *The Economist.*

Dr. H. N. Brailsford, journalist.

Russia:

Professor Paul Milioukov, Member of the Douma.

United States:

Dr. Samuel T. Dutton, Professor in Teachers' College, Columbia University.

CONTENTS

Appendices

Maps

Illustrations

REPORT

OF THE

INTERNATIONAL COMMISSION

To Inquire into the Causes and Conduct

OF THE

BALKAN WARS

INTRODUCTION

Why This Inquiry?

Why this report, this inquiry? Is it necessary after so many other reports and investigations, after so many eloquent appeals made in vain,—appeals to pity, indignation and revolt, ringing at one and the same time from all countries, and from all parties, uttered by the voices of Gladstone, of Bryce, of Pressensé, of Jaurès, of Victor Bérard, of Pierre Quillard, of Anatole Leroy-Beaulieu, of Denys Cochin, and how many more great hearted men of world wide authority? It seems as if all this had gone for nothing. The facts that face us today are a tragic and derisive denial that any good has come of all this eloquence and feeling. Would it not be better for us to remain silent, and let things go?

We have been silent, we have let things go long enough. From the beginning of the first war, and in the terrible uncertainties of the following days, I denounced that one amongst the Balkan rulers, who took upon himself,—he being the only one who had nothing to lose by it,—except the lives of his subjects!—to precipitate the war. But that being done, we could only wish for the triumph of four young allied peoples in shaking off the domination of the Sultans of Constantinople, in the interest of the Turks and perhaps of Europe herself.

Let us repeat, for the benefit of those who accuse us of "bleating for peace at any price," what we have always maintained:

War rather than slavery;

Arbitration rather than war;

Conciliation rather than arbitration.

I hoped that this collective victory, heretofore considered impossible, of the allies over Turkey,—which had just concluded peace with Italy and which we still believed formidable,—would free Europe from the nightmare of the Eastern question and give her the unhoped for example of the union and co-ordination which she lacks.

We know how this first war, after having exhausted, as it seemed, all that the belligerents could lavish, in one way or another, of heroism and blood, was only the prelude to a second fratricidal war between the allies of the previous day, and how this second war was the more atrocious of the two.

Many of our friends urged us from that time to organize a mission, charged either to intervene or to become a witness in the tragedy. We refused to authorize any such premature manifestation, which could only be unavailing. As a matter of fact, none of the interested governments could admit, in the train of their armies, spectators who were independent judges. But peace at last accomplished, our caution had no further excuse. Our American friends understood this when they asked us to act, and we have not hesitated to respond to their insistence. The Americans, unlike Europe, do not approve of resignation, silence, withdrawal. They are young, and they can not endure an evil which is not proved to them to be absolutely incurable. Not the slightest doubt can be cast upon their impartiality in regard to the belligerents, the United States being the adopted country of important rival colonies, notably of an admirable Greek colony. For my part, I should not have accepted the responsibility of organizing a mission of whose disinterestedness and justice I had not been fully assured.

I love Greece. The breath of her war of independence inspired my youth, I am steeped in the heroic memories that live in the hearts of her children, in her folk songs, in her language, which I used to speak, in the divine air of her plains and mountains. Along her coasts every port, every olive wood or group of laurels, evokes the sacred origin of our civilization. Greece was the starting point of my active life and labor.[1] She is for the European and the American more than a cradle, a temple or a hearth, which each of us dreams of visiting one day in pilgrimage. I do not confine myself to respecting and cherishing her past. I believe in her future, in her eager, almost excessive, intelligence. But the more I love Greece, the more do I feel it my duty in the crisis of militarism which is menacing her now in her turn, to tell the truth and to serve her by this, as I serve my own country, while so many others injure her by flattery.

I presided over the famous Château d'Eau meeting on February 13, 1903, and came forward as a politician for Bulgaria and all the oppressed populations of the Balkan peninsula. That was a splendid year of agitation for great causes, for justice, liberty and peace; it was the unofficial but popular beginning of the Anglo-French *entente cordiale*. Generous year of 1903! My friends and I responded without any hesitation to the noble effort of growth and progress, of the material, intellectual and moral culture of Bulgaria.

As for Servia, whom we have never held responsible for the sufferings she has undergone, I count among her diplomats, more than colleagues, friends, men of the finest character who have impressed themselves upon the esteem of the political personnel (staff) of all Europe.

In Montenegro, where my duty as a Member of the International Commission appointed after the Berlin Treaty (1879–80), took me formerly to settle the boundaries of its rugged frontier, I knew some excellent men. I refrain from naming them, if they still live, for fear of compromising them, and I may say that I pitied them from the bottom of my heart, less for the heap of stones out of which fate made their country, than for the government that rules the stones. When European disagreements suspended our

---

[1]See footnote, page 3.

labors, I profited by them to travel in solitude through High Albania. I crossed the sad and fertile country from Scutari to Uskub, allaying the suspicions of Ypek, of Djyakoo and of Prisrend, then in full anarchy. I shall never forget the impression of sadness and astonishment that I carried away from this adventurous expedition. All these countries, not far from us, were then, and are still, unlike Europe, more widely separated from her than Europe from America; no one knew anything of them, no one said anything about them. I scarcely dared at this epoch, to publish, unsigned as a matter of professional discretion, a sketch of the ineffaceable impressions produced on me.[1] And nevertheless, all this horror will not cease to exist as long as Europe continues to ignore it. These peoples, mingled in an inextricable confusion of languages and religions, of antagonistic race and nationality, Turks, Bulgarians, Servians, Serbo-Croatians, Servians speaking Albanian, Koutzo-Valacks, Greeks, Albanians, Tziganes, Jews, Roumanians, Hungarians, Italians, are not less good or less gifted than other people in Europe and America. Those who seem the worst among them have simply lived longer in slavery or destitution. They are martyrs rather than culprits. The spectacle of destitute childhood in a civilized country is beginning to rouse the hardest hearts. What shall be said of the destitution of a whole people, of several nations, in Europe, in the Twentieth Century?

This is the state of things which the Americans wish to help in ending. Let them be thanked and honored for their generous initiative. I have been appealing to it for a long time, since my first visit to the United States in 1902. We are only too happy today to combine our strength, too willing to raise with them a cry of protestation against the contempt of the sceptics and ill-wishers who will try to suppress it.

The Objections

We have noted the objections that have been presented to us, and the principal ones are as follows:

How is the Carnegie Endowment for International Peace going to make an investigation into the atrocities committed in the Balkans? Why should a Commission interfere? If it discover that the atrocities were inevitable, inseparable from the condition of war, what an exposure of the powerlessness of civilization! If it find, as certain newspapers proclaim, that the evils are to be imputed to some and not to others, what hatred and bitterness will be

---

[1]Mach. Récit de mœurs de la Haute Albanie par P. H. Constant. Revue des Deux Mondes, 1 mars 1881. See in the same *Revue* several studies on *Provincial Life in Greece,* and under this same title a volume in 8º, Hachette 1878, id. Dionitza 1878; Galathée, Ernest Leroux, 1 vol. in 18 Paris 1878; Pygmalion, 1 vol. in 18; A. Lemerre, Paris, *Les Trois Sœurs,* text from a popular Greek tale, published in the Annual of the Association for Greek Studies; id. *L'Ile de Chypre; Lettres inédites de Coray; Superstitions of Modern Greece,* Nineteenth Century, 1880, London.

re-awakened between the scarcely pacified belligerents! We have heard this argument for thirty years. It has helped the evil to live and grow. We know what we must think about the results of European abstention. It is the fear of compromise, the fear of displeasing one or another of the nations, the terror, in short, of intervening reasonably and in time, which has brought about a crisis, the gravity of which is not only of yesterday and of today, but also of tomorrow. It is to the interest of all the governments, as well as of the peoples, that the light of truth should at last illuminate and regenerate these unhappy countries. The duty and the purpose of the Carnegie Endowment was to contribute in dissipating the shadows and dangers of a night indefinitely prolonged.

It has been further asked: What are you going to do in the Balkans, you French, you Americans, you English, you Russians, you Germans? Have you not enough to do with Morocco to look after, with Mexico, with South Africa, India, Persia? Yes, we have plenty to do at home, but let us give up all exterior action if we pretend to wait until everything in our own house or conduct is reformed, before we can attempt to help others. I do not consider the French State more perfect than any other human organization, but nevertheless my own imperfection need not prevent me from doing my utmost to be useful.

Other objections are of a less elevated order, but not less insistent. This for example: that everyone does not lose by war. Without speaking of the patriotism kept alive by war, the Great Powers lend their money to the belligerents and sell them the materials of war. This is good for trade and enriches both bankers and contractors. War is exhibited as an operation of twofold patriotism, of moral benefit, because it exalts heroism, and of material profit because it increases several important industries. A little more, and we shall be told that it nourishes the population!

We have replied to these sophisms over and over again. Once more we shall set aside the war that is defensive and in the cause of independence. Such a war is not to be confounded with any other, because it is the resistance to war, to conquest, to oppression. It is the supreme protest against violence, and generally the protest of the weak against the strong. Such was the first Balkan war,—and for this reason it was glorious and popular throughout the civilized world. We are only speaking of real war, such as a State undertakes in order to extend its possessions, or to assert its strength to the detriment of another country;—this was the case in the second Balkan war. Today no one gains in this sort of warfare. Both victor and vanquished lose morally and materially. It is false that peace encourages slothfulness. To speak only of France living under a rule of peace that has lasted for forty-three years, never has youth been more enterprising, more daring, more patriotic than in our day. In default of a war, courage applies itself to fertile invention, towards exploration, to dangerous scientific experiments, to aerial and submarine navigation. Is this a sign of decadence?

And as for trade, which certainly gains by selling a battleship at nearly a hundred million francs, is it possible not to foresee the terrible stoppage of work and the consequent crisis, that must ensue when the peoples, tired of the ruinous competition, will claim a juster balance between the expenditure really necessary for national defense, and that wanted for developing the resources of each country and its useful activity? Nobody will contest the fact that one or several industries do certainly profit by war. It will even be read in this report that a new and flourishing kind of business has been created since the two Balkan wars, that of artificial legs! But the main body of trade? The main body of the people? There is the whole question. On the one hand the increase of armaments leading inevitably to catastrophe, on the other emulation, economic competition leading to progress, always insufficient indeed, but better assured each day by general coöperation, and finally, to security.

Must we allow these two Balkan wars to pass, without at least trying to draw some lesson from them, without knowing whether they have been a benefit or an evil, if they should begin again tomorrow and go on for ever extending?

We have made up our mind. The objections that we have summarized are always the same, not one of them holds against the fact that the two Balkan wars, different as each was from the other, finally sacrificed treasures of riches, lives, and heroism. We can not authenticate these sacrifices without protesting, without denouncing their cost and their danger for the future. For this reason, I constituted our Commission, and today I am presenting the report which it has drawn up in truth, independence and complete disinterestedness.

Constitution and Character of the Commission

These words, truth, independence and disinterestedness, are not vain words. Men of great worth and of the sincerest good will, have been ready to suspend the occupations of their ordinary life, in order to respond to our appeal, and have made their investigations in exceptional conditions of impartiality and authority, and with untiring courage. They did not allow themselves to be baffled by fatigue or difficulties of any kind, numerous as these were; not even by cholera, nor were they led astray by the least illusion. Before leaving Paris, each one of them knew that owing obedience to no one, to no word of command, to no party or government, to no journal, to no representation, Balkan or European; expecting no decoration, no reward of any sort, neither thanks nor compliments; coming after the brilliant scouts of the great press of all the great countries, after the prejudiced or sensational information seekers; serving, in a word, no particular interest, but a very general interest; that they would give full satisfaction to none, and would displease everybody more or less. Each one of them deliberately placed himself above suspicion, above criticism, truly even above inevitable attack. It would be impossible to question the disinterestedness of the Commission, no member of it being remunerated, and the expenses of travel,—very modest indeed,—being publicly administered. But the Commission had to expect that objections would be made in refusing to acknowledge or in disqualifying some of its members. We knew all that. We took our precautions, not to avoid attacks, merely that they might be proved unjustifiable, and this is how I came to constitute our Commission. An ungrateful task, for which I have felt well rewarded, when I saw our work, in spite of troublesome presages and natural enough anxieties, coming none the less to a successful issue.

First, I consulted the men in Paris whom I consider to be masters of the question, Victor Bérard to begin with, whose experience and knowledge are equal to his devotion; and that is no small thing to say. I should have liked him to be one of us, and I have in any case to thank him for much advice of which we took advantage. I would also have liked to be able to add to our number our admirable and regretted F. de Pressensé and those of our valiant comrades of the struggle of 1903, of whom I have spoken. On his side, our friend President Nicholas Murray Butler is surrounded by men of generous sympathy, who form a phalanx, in the United States, of combatants always ready for the crusades of our own day, and he keeps us in constant touch with their views, aspirations and opinions. President Butler's collaborator, appointed to go to the Balkans, was Mr. Samuel T. Dutton, Professor at Columbia University, to whose impartiality and high moral integrity, I can pay no better tribute than by saying that he was not only a valiant fellow worker but an arbiter as well. I could say the same of Mr. Justin Godart, Deputy of Lyons, a politician of energy, accuracy and determination, whose rectitude can never be called in question even by his adversaries. The services rendered us by Mr. Godart were innumerable. Aside from the valuable part he took, like Mr. Dutton, in drawing up the report, he consented during the long journey through the Balkans to fulfil many other functions equivalent to those of president of the itinerary,—because the admirably united Commission over which I presided from Paris, had not thought it necessary to designate a vice president during its journey,—secretary general, treasurer, and reporter. Mr. Godart was all this and more, the trusted friend in whom every one could place reliance.

Two of our friends in Germany responded to our invitation, Professor Paszkowski of Berlin University, and Professor Schücking of Marburg, both proved and excellent men, as impartial as they are enlightened. The former, just at the moment of his departure, was unfortunately refused the necessary permission by the University authorities. The latter was stopped at Belgrade, and was, I am bound to say, totally misled, owing to circumstances of which I will add a word or two later.

Austria contributed in default of Professor H. Lammasch, our great and generous friend, whose health kept him at home, Professor Redlich, whose coöperation both in Vienna and Paris, has been invaluable.

Mr. Francis W. Hirst of England, editor of the *Economist,* well known for his noble campaigns for international conciliation, and the high integrity of his character, together with his distinguished colleague, Mr. H. N. Brailsford, was constantly present at our preparatory meetings in Paris. Mr. Brailsford was appointed with Messrs. Dutton, Schücking and Godart, to make one of the subcommittee which we decided to send to the scene of war.

From Russia, our friend Professor Maxime Kovalevsky and others were unsparing in their assistance. They were, in Europe, as Messrs. Root and Butler in the United States, the guarantors of the independence of the Commission. All our Russian friends were of the same opinion as ourselves in considering that the man best able to represent them, was Professor Paul Milioukov, member of the Douma, who gladly responded to their pressing invitation, as he did to ours. Professor Milioukov adds to his political authority, the distinction of being a scholar who not only knows the Balkan nations thoroughly, but their languages as well. He has been reproached for this, and so has Mr. Brailsford. Professor Milioukov was at once denounced as being violently hostile to the Servians, Brailsford as not less hostile to the Greeks. It is true that by way of balance I was represented as an impenitent Philhellene, Hirst as a Sectarian, and Kovalevsky as something still worse. Godart and Dutton alone escaped all criticism.

I am aware of course from experience that in the Balkans as in some other countries, that I know of, it is impossible to avoid the reproach of a party, if one does not take sides with it against the others, and conversely. Milioukov was perfectly just to the Bulgarians when we in Europe were all unanimous in praising and upholding them. Later on he blamed them, as we all did. He censured the fault of the Servians when censure was unanimous, as he denounced the offenses of the Turks and of the Greeks. But he also paid sincere tribute, to their merits, as he did to the merits of the Greeks and the Turks. His only sin, in the eyes of each, was his perfect impartiality. He was nobody's man, precisely what we were looking for. Brailsford, on the other hand, had been frankly partisan, but for whom? For the Greeks. He took up arms for them and fought in their ranks, the true disciple of Lord Byron and of Gladstone; and in spite of this fact, today Brailsford is held to be an enemy of Greece. Why? Because, passionately loving and admiring the Greeks, he has denounced the errors that bid fair to injure them, with all the heat and vigor of a friend and of a companion in arms. This did not seem to be a sufficient motive for demanding his resignation. As we could not condemn Brailsford for being at one and the same time, both the friend and the enemy of Greece, we kept him, and have been very fortunate in so doing.

At last our Commission was constituted, advised on all points, and ready to start on its journey. Before its departure, I notified the Turkish Ambassador of its existence and of its purpose, and also the three ministers in Paris of Bulgaria, Greece and Servia, formerly among my most distinguished colleagues. Only the Greek Minister for Foreign Affairs, at the beginning, made some reservations to which I replied, concerning the choice of Brailsford, accused of being a Bulgarophile.

Thus prepared, we were assured that our inquiry, even if it did not please everyone, could not be regarded with suspicion, nor, in any case, stopped by anyone. The instructions accepted both by the sedentary members of the Commission and those delegated to go to the Balkans, are summarized in the following extract of the letter I wrote August 21, to Mr. Justin Godart and his companions:

CREANS, *August 21, 1913.*

MY DEAR COLLEAGUES,
    * * * Sceptics will ask you what you expect to do? You can reply that you intend to obtain some light,—a little light,—and this will be much. A little light means appeasement and progress.

Your mission has as much economic as moral significance. When you return and publish your opinions, which I hope will be unanimous and which will certainly have the greater authority in that they are exceptionally disinterested, you will contribute to the better understanding in both hemispheres, of a very simple truth. That is, that these unhappy Balkan States have been up to the present, the victims of European division much more than of their own faults. If Europe had sincerely wished to help them in the past thirty years, she would have given them what makes the life in a country, that is, railways, tramways, roads, telegraphs and telephones, and in addition, schools. Once these fertile countries were linked to the rest of Europe, and connected like the rest of Europe, they would of themselves become peaceful by means of commerce and trade and industry, enriching themselves in spite of their inextricable divisions.

Europe has chosen to make them ruined belligerents, rather than young clients of civilization, but it is not yet too late to repair this long error. You are the precursors of a new economic order, exceedingly important for each one of the governments; you will be, because you claim no such distinction and because of your disinterestedness, the auxiliaries of their salvation. After having verified the evil which is only too evident, you will assist each government in repairing it, by making known by your report the real aims and resources of the country. And thus you will reassure the public which never likes to despond, and which will not admit that even a small part of Europe must lie fallow, when it can share the general progress which is going on feverishly everywhere else.

I hope that you will be able to suggest these views when you are conversing with such personages as you have occasion to meet. It is to the interest of each government that prejudicial legends should not be spread abroad. You will be able to confer a great benefit upon each of them.

Our Commission will upon its return, publish both in Europe and in America, a report which will be translated, widely circulated and commented upon. This report will contain, not the recital, but the confirmation and correction of facts already published. We are inclined to add to this a brief statement of the situation, drawn up by those specially interested, in regard to the past, the present, and the future.

The impartial juxtaposition of these diverse statements in the same international document, will be a powerful means of serving the truth and of disproving the accusation of injustice on our part.

Our conclusions will then follow, and these conclusions can not be anything but one more effort to reduce the disorders from which all the world suffers, and to establish confidence where at present there is only discouragement and anxiety.

DEPARTURE—INQUIRY—RETURN OF THE COMMISSION

The Commission left Paris on August 2, stopped at Vienna, where Professor Paszkowski of Berlin and Professor Redlich were waiting for them, and then continued on to Belgrade. There began difficulties which need not be exaggerated. The Servian government could have taken either of two extreme courses. The first, which it did not adopt, consisted in itself supplying the Commission, as we asked it to do, with its own version of the events, and at the same time with a statement of the economic resources of its country. It knew that these statements would be published fully and impartially in our report. It had an excellent opportunity by so doing, of confounding its enemies and of instructing its friends, and what is more, of making Servia known to the world at large. I must confess that I could not understand its rather ungracious refusal, which we may call diplomatic, in order to offend no one. I know very well the reproaches directed against Mr. Milioukov; but Mr. Milioukov was not the whole Commission. They had the right to decline his testimony. That of the other members of the Commission then became of more value; it constituted a recourse. To speak quite fairly, the Commission came at the wrong moment to Belgrade; but I wonder if, in analogous circumstances, the governments of the great countries would not be more summary and intolerant than the Servian government. The matter stood thus: The Commission arrived at Belgrade just at the moment of the triumphant return of the army, a triumph both sad and glorious, when the sight of the line of victors woke in the silent crowds as much sorrow as pride. Servia's great losses in the two wars must be taken into consideration, all the splendid youth and strength she sacrificed with unheard-of courage, the blood spilt not only to secure independence, but in a struggle of brother against brother, a struggle where victory itself means mourning. We must take into consideration too, there as elsewhere, the excitement of frenzied jingoist journals.

The second course consisted simply in stopping our Commission. There were both pretexts and means: transports requisitioned by the army, interminable delays, the uncertainty of communication, the bad state of sanitation, fear of cholera. * * * In the interests of the Commission itself, a government, without being entirely hostile or insincere, could have obliged it to retrace its steps. The ministry at Belgrade did nothing of the kind; it refused to communicate with the Commission and entirely ignored it, although its arrival had been announced both from Paris and upon reaching Belgrade, to the Minister of Foreign Affairs. An official communication of September 7, explains the government's attitude,[1] but as a matter of fact it did not prevent the Commission from remaining, in spite of a slight animosity provoked by some of the newspapers against Mr. Milioukov, nor of continuing on its way. The Commission was provided by the government with every facility for reaching the frontier and Salonica. This was a good deal and I will do it so much justice. I do not consider either that the Servian government was responsible for the attempts which were made to prevent our German colleague, Professor Schücking, from rejoining the Commission. In this connection, some strange maneuvers took place. Professor Paszkowski, being, as I said, detained at the last moment, Professor Schücking was named hurriedly to take his place. He was then at Ostend, from whence he set out with praiseworthy dispatch and devotion, but he could not reach Belgrade until some time after the Commission had already left for Salonica. What happened then? Who is to be blamed? One fact emerges: Professor Schücking was persuaded that there was nothing for him to do but go home; that the Commission had disbanded and had given up its work. Naturally enough Professor Schücking returned home, and only heard the truth from me when he was back in his own country.

The government of Greece was anxious above all things to base its attitude on that of its ally in Belgrade. The Commission was therefore welcomed under the strictest reservations. At first, Mr. Dragoumis, the Governor of Salonica, informed the Commission that, following the example of Servia, his government declined to acknowledge Mr. Milioukov, but that all the members of the Commission should have entire liberty of action. Then Mr. Brailsford in his turn and even more directly, was refused; his liberty was restricted to the point of twice trying to prevent him from going to Kilkich, which efforts of the authorities met with the congratulations of the press.

In the face of so many difficulties from the very beginning, the Commission

---

[1]The press is authorized to announce that the Servian government declares categorically that it has never been hostile to an investigation, but that, on the contrary, it desires the inquiry of an impartial commission into the Bulgarian cruelties from which the Servians and the Greeks have so greatly suffered. It is entirely to the interest of both Greece and Servia that the civilized world should know of the Bulgarian atrocities. If therefore, the work of the Commission has miscarried, the cause must be sought for in one of its members, the declared enemy not only of Servia but of Greece, well known for what he has said against her, not only in speech but in writing. Moreover, the Commission has never made itself known until it presented itself here. No country could tolerate as a member of a Commission a man whose partiality and animosity are only too well known.

asked itself if it should continue its work? It decided, strong in its independence and good faith, with the entire approbation of its President, not to discontinue, but to pursue its inquiry by all its means, where official aid failed it. The Commission has never ceased to protest, always with dignity, against the accusations of partisanship made against two of its members, and has never been divided for a single moment. The strength of its unity, so often and so roughly tested, will suffice to do away with any suspicion against its impartiality. Never for an instant were any of its members animated by the least desire to gather facts for prosecution against any particular people or State. On the contrary, they all desired to report nothing but the truth. They tried for instance, to get the replies of the Greeks and Servians to the accusations of the Bulgarians.

It must be recalled that the Greeks welcomed with courtesy and kindness, the member of the Commission who was sent to Athens, while the others remained in and about Salonica. Indeed all these things must be taken into serious consideration, when one thinks of the previous passions ruling in the unhappy country; of the daily violence exchanged morning and night between the papers; of the towns reduced to ruins; of the thousands of human beings wandering without refuge or aim; of the death, blood and crime crying everywhere for vengeance; of the *Te Deums* rising from churches whose very possession was disputed by rival fanaticisms.

THE REPORT

In spite of all, the Commission did not abandon its voluntary task, impeded or not. It was not stopped, and one by one accomplished the different steps of the journey, from Belgrade to Salonica, to Athens, to Constantinople, to Sofia, from Servia to Greece, to Macedonia, to Turkey, to Thrace, to Bulgaria. The investigation required five weeks. On September 28, it returned to Paris, where it was joined by the other members who had given their authorization, and here they planned together the broad lines of the report which has required nearly a year to draw up, translate and publish.

The preparation and publication of the report has cost more time and trouble than we expected, but happily what might have been a difficulty, complete harmony between all the members of the Commission proved to be a simple matter. The plan of the work once set on foot,—the historical chapter taking the place of a general introduction,—each of the members who had personally taken part in the journey, was entrusted according to his special ability with one or two chapters, under the collective responsibility of the Commission. This explains why no chapter is signed by its author, the Commission continuing up to the end to be animated by the same spirit of unity and the same ambition for truth. Each of the authors and the office of the Commission revised the proofs sent across continents at the cost of a good many complications. The

Commission meeting in Paris has acted as a reading committee, and chosen the pictures, few in number, to be published, avoiding as much as possible,—though it was no easy matter,—a vulgar collection of horrors. It was not desirable, however, to eliminate these completely, and they appear in the report as specimens, often incomplete, of the illustrations published wholesale by the newspapers. The report is followed by an appendix which the Commission would gladly have made more complete. There we had hoped to publish the official communications and protestations of the Greek and Servian governments, as well as their statistics giving the numbers of the killed, wounded and lost, and the estimate of material losses. It is not our fault, if these documents do not terminate our report, but in default of governmental information, veracious and verified information has not been wanting, as will be seen. The execution of the maps both in the text and apart from it, without which many pages of our report would be difficult to read, was carried out under the direction of the geographers, Messrs. Schrader and Aitoff. The editing of the index and the typographical correction of the proofs were entrusted to the personnel of our Paris office. The main divisions of the report forced themselves on our plan: first the causes of the two wars; then the theater of operation; the actors in the drama; the medley of nationalities engaged; the inevitable violation, or rather the non-existence of an international law in the anarchy of men and of things; finally the economic and moral consequences of the two wars, and the possible prospects for the future.

Nothing could be more necessary than the first chapter on the causes of the two wars. It was the prelude and the indispensable statement of affairs, not only for those who do not know but for those who know more or less but who forget. If our report contained nothing but this full and serious *exposé,* at once scholarly and equitable, its publication would be amply justified. We recommend those of our readers who assert that some of our members are actuated by pro-Bulgar sympathies, to read the pages in which is unfolded, from the conquest of the Turks and their taking of Constantinople, the fatality of the acts which led to the two last wars, among these acts, the outburst of folly, the unbridled militarism against the popular will. We draw attention to the aberration of the Commander-in-Chief of the Bulgar army, General Savov, who became the leader of a military party, and his monstrous outrage which calls everything into question, makes a holy war into a butchery, turns the heroes into brutes, who in short, by himself and in spite of Europe, precipitates the second war and its unknown tomorrows. This chapter seemed to me like a mirror faithfully reflecting a mass of complications, sometimes discouraging for the historian and still more so for the diplomat, but edifying for whoever attempts to protect his country from adventurers. One sees clearly in it the fundamental distinction which we never cease making, between the war of liberation and the war of conquest, between patriotism and crime.

The second chapter is both painful and absorbing. Here we shall be reproached for not taking sides. Here we ought to have said to each of the belligerents following the example of their press: "All the wrong is on the other side. The glory is entirely yours, the shame belongs only to the others."

There is to be seen what must be thought of these official classifications which pretend, in this horrible confusion where "God himself would not recognize his own," to assemble all the good under the same flag and all the bad under another. There is to be seen how the war kindled by intrigue, begins with the generosity of youth, to terminate without distinction of race, in the unloosing of the human beast. It is useless to dwell upon these massacres which we can not pass over in silence. I do not know whether an ideal war has ever existed, but it is time that the world should know what war really means. All the poet-laureates, the ephemeral glorifiers of these infamies whose authors we are commanded not only to absolve but to admire, and to hold up as examples to our children, all the crowd of officious writers are there to counterbalance our report, and to praise what we are determined to denounce in the interests of nations which require to be enlightened in regard to themselves.

Chapter III is not less lamentable, less harrowing, or less necessary, just because it will be more disagreeable to those who do not wish the truth to be known. Here the Greeks and the Bulgarians are no longer alone on the scene, the Turks and the Servians show what they can do. Here again, the Bulgarians are not spared more than the others; but the others have their share too. They will protest, they will reflect, and their reflections will do them more good than lying eulogy.

Chapter IV again holds up the mirror to an inextricable situation which must nevertheless be understood. Under the title "The War and the Nationalities," it discloses an excess of horrors that we can scarcely realize in our systematized countries, war carried on not only by armies but by mobilized gangs, and in reality by the medley of nations; local populations being "divided into as many fragments as there are nations fighting each other and wanting to substitute one for another. * * * This is the reason why so much blood was spilt in these wars. The worst atrocities were not due to the regular soldiers. * * * The populations themselves killed each other." Whoever wishes to judge of the evil and to look for more than the appearance of a remedy should meditate over this fourth chapter, and study the maps before forming too severe a judgment upon these competitions of horrors, and condemning as culprits peoples who turn and turn about, for centuries past have been crushed down.

Chapter V, "The War and International Law," is not less impartial than the preceding. Its conclusion is this: Every clause in international law relative to war on land and to the treatment of the wounded, has been violated by *all* the belligerents, including the Roumanian army, which was not properly speaking belligerent. Public opinion has made great progress on this question of late years. I confess that in my ardent participation in the two Hague Conferences, the conventions fixing the laws and customs of war, interested me infinitely less than those organizing arbitration, mediation and good will, which tended in fact to prevent war, and not to humanize it. To humanize war seemed to me then a hypocrisy and a satire, leading to its being too easily accepted, but since then I have recognized my error. War is not declared by those who carry it on. The armies are only instruments in the hands of the governments; and these armies are recruited among the youth of each country. We at least owe it to them to spare them sufferings which they have not brought upon themselves. To refuse to humanize war for fear of making it too frequent, is to let the weight of the governments' fault fall upon the soldier. In short, whatever amelioration diplomatic conferences can bring about in the horrors of war, it could never be enough. The torture of criminals is now suppressed. Should it exist—and what torture!—for soldiers and for hostile populations? The Commission has done its duty in contending that in spite of the Hague Conventions, the cruelty and ferocity and the worst outrages remained in the Balkans as the direct heritage of slavery and war.

Chapter V suggests as a subject worthy of the deliberations of the Third Hague Conference, the constitution of a permanent international commission, named in advance, and empowered in case of war to go and observe the application of its resolutions which the belligerents themselves have signed. This innovation, precisely because it would have too much reason for existence, will run a great risk of being considered indiscreet. It deserves more than to be passed over from prejudice.

We shall make a pause at Chapter VI. In an atmosphere of high and serene impartiality, the author contemplates the economic consequences of the war, and he concludes that in spite of appearances, it has been, apart from evil actions, because he does not desire to injure anyone, a bad and evil thing for every one, with the exception of course of the contractors who supplied the arms and ammunition, and the makers of wooden legs. Greece herself who is said to have made the maximum of possible gains, with the minimum of losses, because she was relatively far from the theater of war, even Greece has seen her national debt doubled. It is true that she will be able to retrieve her sacrifices by the new resources which she will draw from the islands and territories that are now part of her domain, but this is just where the question arises for her, as well as for all conquerors, even the happiest: Will the resources of which she assures herself, suffice to meet not only the expenses of the land improvement which her statesmen are unquestionably able to undertake, but also the military expenditure corresponding to her new ambitions? Here is Greece involved more deeply than she expected in the construction of armaments, competing with Italy, exposed in her turn to the temptation, to the fascination of dreadnoughts. For this hundreds of millions of capital will have to be borrowed, taxes imposed to pay the contributors, to say nothing of the always increasing cost of maintenance and consequent temptations, because a young nation whatever the wisdom of its rulers may be, will not easily resign itself to let its armaments, on land and sea become, as they do, old fashioned in a very few years, without having made use of them; it will not let its men of war lie at anchor and its soldiers remain idle in barracks. What will happen then? Greece, the beautiful, will in her turn, be torn between the militarists on the one side who proclaim their patriotism at every opportunity by means of their journals and the voices of their impatient orators, and, on the other side, by the party in favor of industry, of progress, seeing itself discredited while the sources of national riches are drained, and social revolt is engendered. * * * Greece is now going to discover how much it costs to abandon herself to the luxury of dreadnoughts. She is as yet only at the beginning. As to the other allies, and the Turks, we shall refrain from insisting upon their losses, which were very much greater than those of Greece, or upon the dangers that threaten their future. These are only too apparent.

The moral consequences of the Balkan wars are briefly indicated in the chapter which completes the report. In it may be found the long reverberation of the many crimes as disastrous for their authors as for their victims and their respective countries. We are shown millions of human beings systematically degraded by their own doing, corrupted by their own violence. It gives us a good example of the evil which elsewhere we strive to denounce and to combat, by showing us how the generations of tomorrow are corrupted by the heritage of their forefathers, and the young men taken from the necessary and urgent work of the farm and the workshop to be placed in the comparative idleness of barracks, to wait for the next war. All these apprehensions for the future are expressed without the slightest trace of animosity against one or other of these unhappy and misguided nations, but rather with a feeling of profound sympathy for them and for humanity. The conclusion of the chapter evolves itself definitely: violence carries its own punishment with it and something very different from armed force will be needed to establish order and peace in the Balkans.

THE LESSON OF THE TWO WARS

Never was a lesson clearer and more brutal. United, the peoples of the Balkan peninsula, oppressed for so long, worked miracles that a mighty but divided Europe could not even conceive. Crete, Salonica, Uskub, even Scutari and Adrianople they took, and after a few months they almost entered Constantinople. It was the end, the Gordian knot was cut. Disunited, they were forced to come to a standstill and to exhaust themselves further in their effort to begin again, an effort indefinitely prolonged. For, far from being a solution, the second war was only the beginning of other wars, or rather of a continuous war, the worst of all, a war of religion, of reprisals, of race, a war of one people against another, of man against man and brother against brother. It has become a competition, as to who can best dispossess and "denationalize" his neighbor. The Turks in any case remain in Europe. The hecatombs of the siege of Adrianople have been in vain; Macedonia, no longer a tomb, has become a hell. Thrace is torn in pieces. Albania erected into a principality, remains the most unhappy and the wildest object of the eager watching of Austria, Servia, Montenegro, Greece and Italy. The churches and the Christian schools are fighting among themselves, enjoying less liberty than under Ottoman rule. Constantinople, more than ever, will be the eternal apple of discord under the surveillance of the Russians, who are themselves under the surveillance of Germany, Austria Hungary and Roumania, in fact of all the Powers, friends, allies and enemies. Greater Greece, Greater Bulgaria, and Greater Servia, the children of contemporary megalomania, will in their turn keep a close watch over the Bosphorus. The islands bring on a contest between Turkey and Asia on one hand, and Italy, Greece, England and all the great European Powers on the other. The Mediterranean open to new rivalries, becomes again the battle-field which she had ceased to be.

A dark prospect, which however, might become brighter if Europe and the great military Powers so wished. They could, in spite of everything, solve the problem if they were not determined to remain blind.

The real struggle in the Balkans, as in Europe and America, is not between oppressors and oppressed. It is between two policies, the policy of armaments and that of progress. One day the force of progress triumphs, but the next the policy of rousing the passions and jealousies that lead to armaments and to war, gets the upper hand.

With the second Balkan war, the policy of armaments spreads more strongly than ever. After having been the resource of European governments, it is about to become their punishment.

A paradoxical situation! The competition of armaments could not go on indefinitely, at this time of open economic competition between all the peoples of the Old World and the New. Already by reason of the increase of our budgets, and in spite of desperate efforts, it is losing prestige in popular opinion. It is being questioned, and consequently condemned. The extravagance of armaments appears like the development of a monstrous business, incompatible with national work. In spite of all the workmen that it employs, the salaries it pays, the auxiliary activities it supports, the war trade only flourishes by universal insecurity, lives only upon the increase of public expense, by all of which the normal business of all countries suffers. Under this régime of armed peace, only the little countries or the new countries are favored, those which have no debts, no immense war budgets.

What finally succeeds in bringing armed peace into disrepute, is that today the Great Powers are manifestly unwilling to make war. Each one of them, Germany, England, France and the United States, to name a few, has discovered the obvious truth that the richest country has the most to lose by war, and each country wishes for peace above all things. This is so true that these two Balkan wars have wrought us a new miracle,—we must not forget it,—namely, the active and sincere agreement of the Great Powers who, changing their tactics, have done everything to localize the hostilities in the Balkans and have become the defenders of the peace that they themselves threatened thirty-five years ago, at the time of the Berlin Congress. We might be tempted to attribute this evolution of public opinion and that of the governments in part to the new education which we are striving to spread, but let us stick to facts: The exigencies of the universal competition, the increased means of communication, the protest of tax payers, and the dread of socialism and of the unknown, have been more efficacious in forcing the governments to think than any exhortations.

If this is so, why not end it? That is the dream, but how to realize it? Every one ignores it. A large body of persons, possessing immense capital, is engaged in the manufacture of armaments; more still, a formidable plant which must be sunk has been created and continues to be created every day. Is there anyone who will ignore this accumulation of strength and of riches? Who will be able to stop short this impulse? True, the home market is overstocked in every country with orders for armaments. Neither the jingo papers nor those in the hands of the federation of military contractors, who are so admirably organized into national and international syndicates, can urge indefinitely for a national consummation. There comes a time when public opinion refuses to submit any longer to this so-called patriotic régime; and the war trade, inspired with new ambition, turns its attention towards exportation. As the home market is not sufficient, a foreign market is created. The war trade believes that the foreign policy of a great nation is first and foremost the policy of armaments. The main duty of diplomacy according to it, is the struggle as to who shall carry off from a great rival nation, such and such a contract for guns, cannon or ironclads, and who shall subordinate political interventions or loans of money to army contracts.

The struggles become Homeric conflicts of influence and intrigue. Ambassadors can not disregard them without a kind of abdication. Has not even the Emperor of a great neighboring country made it a point of honor to militarize Turkey?—without any great success it is true. But what of Turkey or the colonies or the small states of few resources? An effort has been made to militarize North and South America, and Australia as well. Canada, whose future lies precisely in her exemption from all military burdens, has been forced to order a fleet from England, and to extract from a population still insufficient, the elements of a navy which they have done very well without for a hundred years! Australia has not hesitated. Brazil, the Argentine, Chile and the other republics of South America did resist, thus giving Europe an example of peaceful coöperation; but now their former good sense has been overcome by attempts of all sorts continually repeated. Commercial travelers in patriotism have hurried from every corner of Europe to demonstrate the necessity for ordering the biggest battleships possible. We may recall the extraordinary experience of Brazil, the first dupe of these campaigns, when her great "Armada" arrived from the English ship yards and she saw it make its first attempt to cannonade Rio de Janeiro! It was the beginning of disillusion, the mastodon killed by ridicule. Since then, the propaganda of armaments has declined, even in the United States, where, however, the yellow press, typical of its kind, has given its proofs and is agitating the matter again, thanks to the providential events in Mexico. In the last few years, the House of Representatives at Washington has refused to vote more than one ironclad against two. In Germany, the Krupp case, the Saverne events, and many other incidents, without speaking of the Berne Conference, have been the answer to the furious excitement of the pan-Germanic press. In Japan itself there has just burst the unprecedented scandal of the naval contracts.

Russia nevertheless, happily for the great war trade, forgets how much the disasters of her navy have cost, and once more has allowed herself to be imposed upon. Austria has capitulated too, even Spain asks nothing better than to be persuaded, inasmuch as she can afford it. But on the whole the enthusiasm was cooling when the practice of the new Balkan States came to renew it. The acclamations of the jingo press of all countries greeted these fortunate countries, new centers for imports.

Even the battleships with which Brazil and the Argentine are disgusted, are being handed over to Turkey and Greece. Constantinople will become a vast arsenal and a naval port, worthy of her name and her past. The Greek fleet will oblige Italy, whose ardor was declining, to increase her navy as well; and following this example, the great countries of Europe and America will not remain unaffected. The naval leagues will agitate, the embassies will report these imposing manifestations, by sending confidential despatches, communicated as soon as received to the leading papers. Patriotic speakers, in print and on the platform, will inveigh against the "lie of pacifism," and so the prediction of the Americans that "the next war will be declared by the press," will be realized.

Then the Greeks, the Turks, the Servians, the Bulgarians, the Montenegrins and the Albanians, armed to the teeth, provided with all the guns and all the dreadnoughts for which we have no further use, can kill each other once more, and even drag into their quarrel the European governments, who will be as they themselves are, victims of the press and commercial patriotism, or in other words, of the policy of armaments.

Confronted by these follies or these crimes,—the word matters little,—our sole resource while waiting for the day when we shall see the rise of an independent press, is our duty of speaking the truth which even the most sensible people hesitate to admit, for fear of compromising themselves.

In one of the speeches that I made in the Senate to free my conscience, before an audience sympathetic at heart, but fully determined not to support me, I calculated that France has imposed upon herself more than a hundred billion francs in unproductive expenditure during the last forty-three years, an average of more than two billion francs a year. This is the minimum price of armed peace for one country only. Several hundreds of billions in a half century for the Great Powers together!!

Think what United Europe might have done with these millions, had she consecrated even half to the service of progress! Imagine Europe herself, not to speak of Africa and Asia, penetrated and regenerated by the pure air, in its most distant parts, of free intercourse, of education and security. Can we picture what might have been the position today of these unfortunate Balkan peoples, if their patrons, the Great Powers of Europe, had competed with each other in aiding them, in giving them roads, and railways, and waterways, schools, laboratories, museums, hospitals and public works!

The most suitable title for this report would have been, "Europe Divided and her Demoralizing Action in the Balkans," but taking it all round this might have been unjust.

The real culprits in this long list of executions, assassinations, drownings, burnings, massacres and atrocities furnished by our report, are not, we repeat, the Balkan peoples. Here pity must conquer indignation. Do not let us condemn the victims. Nor are the European governments the real culprits. They at least tried to amend things and certainly they wished for peace without knowing how to establish it. The true culprits are those who mislead public opinion and take advantage of the people's ignorance to raise disquieting rumors and sound the alarm bell, inciting their country and consequently other countries into enmity. The real culprits are those who by interest or inclination, declaring constantly that war is inevitable, end by making it so, asserting that they are powerless to prevent it. The real culprits are those who sacrifice the general interest to their own personal interest which they so little understand, and who hold up to their country a sterile policy of conflict and reprisals. In reality there is no salvation, no way out either for small states or for great countries except by union and conciliation.

D'ESTOURNELLES DE CONSTANT.

CHAPTER I

The Origin of the Two Balkan Wars

1. THE ETHNOGRAPHY AND NATIONAL ASPIRATIONS OF THE BALKANS

It is not proposed in this chapter to enter exhaustively into a question on which there is a highly abundant literature already in existence, both in the various European and Balkan languages. The intention is simply to furnish the data indispensable to the reader who is interested in the work done by the Commission, though unfamiliar with the details of the questions at issue in the Balkan peninsula. Every page of the Report handles such a mass of ideas, facts and dates, which, though supposed to be generally known, are in fact not so, that it seemed impossible to plunge the reader at once *in medias res*. Those more familiar with things in the East may begin the Report at the next Chapter.

The actual course of events in the Balkans is a very close reproduction of the conditions existing previous to the arrival of the Turks in Europe. Then, as now, the Christian States were engaged in constant internecine strife for hegemony in the peninsula. Victory both in the tenth and again in the thirteenth century was with the Bulgarian State, which though still primitive in organization, owed its temporary ascendancy to the conquests of a military chief.

Then in the twelfth and fourteenth centuries came the turn of the conquering Servians. Intermittently, the Byzantine Emperors recovered their preponderance in the peninsula. The various peoples who had occupied the different regions from the third to the sixth century, A. D. (the indigenous population, Greek, Albanian, or Roumanian having been either driven out or assimilated) served only to swell the armies or figure in the imposing titles assumed by the autocrats of all these, Servians, Greeks, Bulgarians, Albanians, conjoined in a sort of Imperial organization, a "Great Servia" or "Great Bulgaria." The collapse of these ephemeral "Great" States produced no change in the ethnographic composition of the peninsula. Political structures fell and rose again without any attempt being made to fuse the populations into any sort of national whole. At that stage indeed the national idea was not as now closely connected with the State idea. The Bulgar, the Servian, the Wallachian, the Albanian remained Bulgarian, Servian, Wallachian or Albanian, throughout all the successive régimes; and thus the ancient ethnographic composition remained unaltered until the Turkish conquest came, leveling all the nationalities and preserving them all alike in a condition of torpor, in a manner comparable to the action of a vast refrigerator.

Even if the political constructions which followed one another and which were actually in conflict with one another at the advent of the Turks, had contained in them the germs of nationalities, the Turkish régime would have ruthlessly stamped them out.   The Turks unconsciously worked for their destruction in the most effective possible way.   They banished or assimilated the ruling class, that is to say the warrior class, in the conquered countries.   In the communes there remained no one but the village agriculturists, whose only ethical bond was that of religion.   Here again the Turkish régime did much to reduce the ethnic and national significance of the religious element to its lowest terms.   The religion of all the conquered nationalities being the same, *i. e.,* Oriental orthodoxy, the Turks ended by recognizing only one clergy as representative of the *rayas* (creeds), the one chosen being the Greek clergy, the most cultivated and in the capital (Constantinople) the most prominent.   The Phanar (the Greek quarter of Constantinople in which the Greek patriarchate is situated), finally became the sole orthodox church in Turkey; the last remains of the national autonomous churches which still existed at Okhrida (for the Bulgarians) and at Ipek (for the Servians) being abolished by the decrees of the Greek patriarchate of 1765 and 1767 respectively.   Consequently, a common race name was given to the orthodox populations in the official language of the Turkish bureaucracy: they were all *"Roum-mileti,"* from the name, *Romaios,* of the Greek people. (This is the name the modern Greeks gave themselves down to recent times.)

Nevertheless, although the people were thus merged and submerged, national consciousness was not completely obliterated.   There was always a certain discontent between the pastors and their flocks.   The latter could not forget that they had formerly heard mass celebrated in their national language by a priest whom they chose themselves and whose interests were not limited to taxes and state service.   The Greek priest, on his side, was expatriated in the midst of a Slav population; it was humiliating for a lover of the muses to dwell in a barbarian world, in the midst of "wearers of sheep skins."   The conditions being so, any favorable circumstance, any spark from outside, would be enough to re-light the flame of nationality.

It is impossible in this too brief sketch to follow in detail the course of the re-awakening of the national idea in the Balkans.   It goes back to the earliest days of the Turkish conquest.   The Servians and Roumanians, the last to be subdued by the Turks, were the first to claim their autonomy.   What especially favored the development of national consciousness among the Servians was the large proportion of their race which had remained outside the Ottoman conquest. Even apart from the Servians on the Adriatic, who had been open to the influences of Italian literature since the sixteenth century, those in Austria Hungary had tasted European civilization long before the Servians in Turkey.   Ragusa first, and afterwards Agram (in Slav *"Zagréb"*) were intellectual centers of the Servian nation before Belgrade.

In Servia proper the struggle for independence preceded the intellectual development of the nation.   While our Commission was in Belgrade a monument was erected, in honor of the first liberator of Servia, the founder of the present dynasty, Kara-Georges, who more than a century ago (1804) organized the first resistance offered by the people to its Turkish masters. In the year 1813 the first insurrection was defeated; Kara-Georges fled to Austria, and was killed in 1817. But a new leader had already appeared in the person of the founder of the second Servian dynasty,—recently extinguished with Alexander and Draga, namely Michel Obrénovits, the son of a peasant, like Kara-Georges. The second insurrection, with Michel at its head, was more successful than the first. The convention of Akkerman (1826) secured Servia a sort of autonomy under Russian protectorate, and the Hatticherif of 1829 confirmed and completed the act by making Servia a hereditary principality under the Sultan's suzerainty. A year later another Hatticherif gave the Servians the right to establish primary schools; and by 1836 there were seventy-two of these in the principality.

Greece, at the other extremity of the peninsula, had closely followed Servia's example. There, too, effort at national revival outside the country went on contemporaneously with the endeavors at revolt on which the wild mountaineers ventured from time to time. These mountaineers are known by the picturesque appellation of "thieves" (*Klephtai,* patriotic thieves, in distinction to *lestai,* brigands pure and simple).

The liberty of Greece proclaimed by the national assembly at Epidaurus was not recognized until the Act of February 3, 1830. Then the bases of national civilization asserted since 1814 by members of the Philiki Hétéria were formally laid down. We have already seen that thanks to the energy of the Phanar clergy, the Greek schools had maintained not existence merely but vitality, despite the Turkish rule, and sent out generations of educated Greeks.

This was not the fate of the countries in the interior—Bulgaria and Macedonia. It is true that the first indications of national consciousness appeared early, in the course of the eighteenth century. Down to 1840 they went on spreading in proportion to the increasing influence of foreign civilization (in the present case, of Russian civilization). It was not until 1852, however, that the first national Bulgarian school appeared, at Tirnovo. At the close of this period a movement in the direction of religious independence made itself felt. From 1860 on, a most bitter conflict broke out between the heads of the Bulgarian community at Constantinople and the Greek patriarchate, religion and nationality being identified on either side. Since Greek nationalism constituted a political danger for Turkey, while the Bulgarians had as yet formulated no political claim, their chiefs rather piquing themselves on their loyalty towards the Sultan, the Turkish authorities began to take sides against the Greeks in this national strife, and finally conceded to the Bulgarians the establishment of a national church subject to purely formal recognition of the patriarchal supremacy. This was the beginning of the Bulgarian *exarchy,* officially recognized by the Firman of 1870.

The Greeks, however, would not admit their defeat. The patriarch refused to accept the firman. The Bulgarians, supported by the Turks, retorted by electing their first exarch and making formal proclamation (May 11, 1872) of the independence of their church. Thereupon the patriarch, four months later, excommunicated the new church and declared it schismatic. This too hasty step served only to assist the Bulgarian cause. The Bulgarians having now secured what they desired, *i. e.*, a church wholly independent of the Greeks and thoroughly national, both in its head and its members, proceeded to fix the dioceses of the new church. Some of these dioceses were actually enumerated in the firman: the exarchies of Bulgaria today; others, which were also to form part of the national church, were in accordance with Article 10 of the firman to be fixed by a vote of the population.[1] Accordingly the exarchate took a plebiscite, as laid down in Article 11, beginning with the provinces of Uskub and Okhrida. Since a more than two-thirds majority there declared against the Patriarch the Porte gave its *berat* (investiture) to the Bulgarian Bishops of Uskub and Okhrida.

But Okhrida and Uskub are Macedonian. The question of Macedonia had thus definitely arisen. It is true that before 1873 the Greeks had already contended for this region with the Slavs. But it had not yet occurred to the Slavs (Servians and Bulgarians) to dispute about it among themselves. The young radicals in Servia and Bulgaria who between 1860 and 1870 disseminated the notion of a Southern Slav Federation, accepted the proposition that the populations of Thrace and Macedonia were as Bulgarian as those of Bulgaria, as a settled fact, traditionally established. The Bulgarian publicist, Lioubén Karavelov, wrote the following in 1869–70:

> The Greeks show no interest in knowing what kind of people live in such a country as Macedonia. It is true that they say that the country formerly belonged to the Greeks and therefore ought to belong to them again * * * But we are in the nineteenth century and historical and canonical rights have lost all significance. Every people, like every individual, ought to be free and every nation has the right to live for itself. Thrace and Macedonia ought then to be Bulgarian since the people who live there are Bulgarians.

And his friend the Servian Vladimir Yovanovits on his side, regarded Bosnia, Herzegovina and Metchia as the only Servian lands in Turkey, that is Old Servia in the most limited sense of the term, which shows that he accepted the view of Macedonia as Bulgarian.

Yet there existed in Servia at this epoch a section of nationalist opinion which declared that Old Servia included the whole of Macedonia and claimed it as having

---

[1]Article X of the Firman of March 11, 1870. * * * "If the whole orthodox population or at least two-thirds thereof, desire to establish an exarchy for the control of their spiritual affairs in localities other than those indicated above, and this desire be clearly established, they may be permitted to do as they wish. Such permission, however, may only be accorded with the consent or upon the request of the whole population, or at least two-thirds thereof.

formed part of the "Great" Servia of the time of Douchan the Strong. These Servian nationalists did not confine themselves to polemics in the press: they began to organize schools in Macedonia, where the Servian masters were instructed to teach in literary Servian and employ text books written in Belgrade. Mr. Miloyévits, one of the leaders of this movement, tells us that in 1865 there was only one school in Macedonia proper founded by the Servians; in 1866 there were already as many as six; in 1867, 32; in 1868, 42. From that time on the Servian government became interested in these schools and began subsidizing them. The Macedonian population on the other hand received the schools willingly. Were not the schoolmasters Slavs who had come to Macedonia to fight the Greek influence? Soon, however, it appeared that the Servian teachers were there to carry on propaganda for their nationality. The Bulgarian press was roused, and from 1869 on a lively dispute followed.

The partisans of the "Yougo–Slav Federation" consoled themselves with the reflection that this Servian nationalist doctrine only represented the views of a small group of journalists and *dilettante* historians and ethnographers. But as we have seen, it had already secured the support of the State. Two circumstances contributed to accentuate this tendency: one, the organization of the new national Bulgarian church,—the exarchy; the other, the diplomatic check to Servia's hopes of an outlet on the Adriatic.

Mention has already been made of an early success of the exarchist church in Macedonia—the two *berats* sanctioning the bishoprics of Okhrida and Uskub. Other victories were to follow. The Greeks, who had considered Macedonia as their patrimony, naturally viewed them with disfavor. It occurred to them, as a means of withdrawing the attention of the Bulgarians from Macedonia, to suggest the extension of the Bulgarian ecclesiastical organization to the Servian countries, Bosnia and Herzegovina. The suggestion pleased the Bulgarians, but although they accepted the Greek proposition, they did not renounce their Macedonian pretensions. The list of the exarchist dioceses to be created became a long one, embracing as it soon did the whole of Macedonia, Old Servia, Bosnia and Herzegovina.

The Servian government could not regard such claims with indifference, since it was fully aware of the inseparability of the ideas of nationality and a national church. The Servian Ministry therefore pointed out that while the ethnographic nature of the Macedonian dioceses formed subject of discussion, those of Old Servia were indisputably Servian. If the Bulgarian dioceses wished to form an exarchist church, the dioceses of the ancient Servian provinces must, in their turn, recognize the head of the church of the Servian principality as their spiritual head. Here was the whole Macedonian conflict in germ. Even the tactics employed foreshadow the course of recent events.

Servia joined Greece against the Bulgarian exarchy. The Servians, fighting against the national Bulgarian church, chose to remain subject to the Greek patriarch. He profited by this to impose Greek bishops upon them and persisted in giving a Greek denomination to their religious communities. Thus did the Servians in Turkey deprive themselves of their own free will of the most effective weapon in the national conflict. From this time on the "exarchist" was exclusively Bulgarian and the Macedonian population, called *Boulgari* from time immemorial, began to feel itself at once Bulgarian and Slav. Outside the national Bulgarian church, which thus remained the Slav church in Macedonia, there were only "patriarchists" of every kind—Greek, Wallachian or Servian united under one Greek ecclesiastical authority, that of Constantinople.

The second circumstance driving Servia to accentuate its Macedonian pretensions was the "occupation" of Bosnia and Herzegovina by Austria Hungary. It is now known that at the interview between Emperor Alexander II and Emperor Francis Joseph at Reichstadt on July 8, 1876, it was agreed that in the event of Servia or Montenegro winning independence, Austria Hungary should have the right to "occupy and administer" these provinces. The same terms were repeated in the Berlin treaty. At the same time Austria Hungary emphasized her assertion that she regarded Servia as within her sphere of influence.

At Reichstadt, Russia agreed not to make war on Servian territory, and when General Ignatiev suggested the annexation of Bosnia to the Austrian diplomats as the condition of recognition of the treaty of San Stefano, Count Andrassy replied by a counter proposition, that of leaving Russia full freedom of action in Bulgaria on condition of the proclamation of Macedonia's autonomy under Austro-Hungarian protection.

After the Berlin Congress, Austria Hungary entered into closer relations with King Milan of Servia. He signed the secret treaty of 1881, in which (§7) Austria Hungary formally declared that she "would not oppose, would even support Servia against other powers in the event of the latter's finding a way of extending its southern boundary, exception being made in the case of the Sandjak of Novi Bazar." In 1889, when this treaty was renewed, Austria Hungary promised in even clearer terms "to aid in the extension of Servia in the direction of the Vardar valley." Thus at the very moment when Austria Hungary was depriving Servia of any possibility of westward extension, by joining the section of the Servian population inhabiting Bosnia and Herzegovina to herself, Austrian diplomacy was holding out by way of compensation, the hope of an extension towards the south, in those territories whose population had, up to 1860–1870, been universally recognized as Bulgarian, even by the Servians.

From this time on nationalism distinctly gained ground in Servia. The whole of Macedonia was identified with "Old Servia" and "Young Servia," in its map, claimed the entire territory occupied under the rule of Stephen Douchan, in the fourteenth century. At this period the net work of Servian schools spread specially fast, thanks to the aid of the Turks, who here as elsewhere followed their habitual policy of playing off the Servian and Greek minorities against the stronger and more dangerous majority of the Bulgarian exarchists. In 1889 the Servian school manuals were for the first time published at Constantinople with ministerial sanction and the Servian school soon ceased to be secret and persecuted. In 1895–96 according to official Servian statistics there were 157 schools with 6,831 scholars and 238 male and female teachers. It is, however, noteworthy that eighty of these schools, comprising 3,958 scholars and 120 male and female teachers were situated in Old Servia properly so-called, that is to say, that more than half of them belonged to countries which were undoubtedly Servian.

Here are the statistics for the Bulgarian-exarchist schools for the same period: there were in Macedonia 1896–97, 843 such schools (against 77 Servian schools), 1,306 teachers (Servian, 118); 31,719 scholars (Servian, 2,873); children in the kindergarten, 14,713.

These figures show that at the close of the nineteenth century the overwhelming majority of the Slav population of Macedonia was sending its children to the exarchist Bulgarian school. The school became henceforth an auxiliary of the national movement, and independent of the church. The movement changed both its character and its object. Side by side with the ecclesiastical movement led by priests and assisted by the religious council of the community, there arose about 1895 a revolutionary movement, directed against the Turkish régime, whose object was political autonomy and whose leaders were recruited from the school teachers. On the other hand the resistance of the minorities, supported by the Turks, grew more pronounced. "Patriarchism" and "exarchism" became the rallying cries of the two conflicting nations. From this time on the ethnographic composition of Macedonia was only to be elucidated by an enumeration of "exarchist" and "patriarchist" households—a most uncertain and fluctuating method since the strife grew more complicated, so that one and the same family would sometimes be divided into "Bulgarians," "Greeks," "Wallachians" and "Servians," according to the church attended by this or that member.

The new generation in Servia therefor, now sought a more reliable and scientific means of determining nationality, and found it in language. Youthful scholars devoted themselves to the study of Macedonian dialects and sought for phonetic and morphological traces of Servian influence which might enable them to be classified among Servian dialects. Bulgarian linguists, on their side did the same, and insisted on an essentially Bulgarian basis in the Macedonian dialects.

The rival claims to Macedonia might be summed up under the following main heads:—

(1) "Historical rights" to the possession of Macedonia, acquired by Simeon the Bulgarian or Douchan the Servian. (Tenth or fourteenth century.)

(2) Resemblance in customs (above all those pertaining to the Fête of

New Year's Day—the *Slava,* claimed by the Servians as the sign of their nationality).

(3)   Religion—exarchist or patriarchist.

(4)   The spoken language.

Official Turkish statistics admitted only one principle of discrimination between the ethnic groups dwelling in Macedonia, namely religion. Thus all the Mahommedans formed a single group although there might be among them Turks, Albanians, Bulgarian "pomaks," etc.: all the patriarchists in the same way were grouped together as "Greeks," although there might be among them Servians, Wallachians, Bulgarians, etc. Only in the "exarchist" group, did religion coincide, more or less, with Bulgarian nationality. The Turkish official registers included men only; women were not mentioned, since the registers served only for the purposes of military service and taxation. Often nothing was set down but the number of "households." This explains the lack of anything approaching exact statistics of the Macedonian populations. Owing to the different principles and methods of calculation employed, national propagandists arrived at wholly discrepant results, generally exaggerated in the interest of their own nationality. The table subjoined shows how great is this divergence in estimate and calculation:

BULGARIAN STATISTICS   (Mr. Kantchev, 1900)

Turks	499,204
Bulgarians	1,181,336
Greeks	228,702
Albanians	128,711
Wallachians	80,767
Jews	67,840
Gypsies	54,557
Servians	700
Miscellaneous	16,407
Total	2,258,224

DIALECTS OF MACEDONIA
AFTER A. BÉLITS
FROM THE SERVIAN POINT OF VIEW

Timok Dialect.	Bulgarian Territory where Servian is spoken.
Prizrend Dialect.	Bulgaro-Macedonian Territory where Servian is spoken.
Serbo-Macedonian Dialect.	Non-Slavic Territory.

SERVIAN STATISTICS (Mr. Gopcevic, 1889)[1]

Turks	231,400
Bulgarians	57,600
Greeks	201,140
Albanians	165,620
Wallachians	69,665
Jews	64,645
Gypsies	28,730
Servians	2,048,320
Miscellaneous	3,500
Total	2,870,620

GREEK STATISTICS (Mr. Delyani, 1904)
(Kosovo vilayet omitted)

Turks	634,017
Bulgarians	332,162
Greeks	652,795
Albanians	
Wallachians	25,101
Jews	53,147
Gypsies	8,911
Servians	
Miscellaneous	18,685
Total	1,724,818

The Bulgarian statistics alone take into account the national consciousness of the people themselves. The Servian calculations are generally based on the results of the study of dialect and on the identity of customs: they are therefore largely theoretic and abstract in character. The Greek calculations are even more artificial, since their ethnic standard is the influence exercised by Greek civilization on the urban populations, and even the recollections and traces of classical antiquity.

The same difficulties meet us when we leave population statistics and turn to geographical distribution. From an ethnographical point of view the population of Macedonia is extremely mixed. The old maps, from that of Ami Boné (1847) down, follow tradition in regarding the Slav population of Macedonia as Bulgarian. Later local charts make the whole country either Servian, or Greek. Any attempt at more exact delineation, based on topical study, is of recent date. There are, for example, Mr. Kantchev's maps, representing Bulgarian opinion, and the better known one of Mr. Tsviyits representing Servian. But Mr. Tsviyits' ethnographic ideas vary also with the development of Servia's political pretensions. In 1909 he gave "Old Servia" a different outline from that he gave in 1911 (see his map published in the "Petermann" series); and in the hour of Servian victory on the eve of the second Balkan war, another professor at Belgrade University, Mr. Bélits, published his map, based on a study of dialects, a

---

[1]Recent Servian authorities avoid giving general figures or else, like Mr. Guersine, suggest a total for the Macedonian Slav population which approximates more closely to Mr. Kantchev's figures.

map which satisfied the most recent and immoderate pretensions. The Servo-Bulgarian frontier recognized by the treaty of March 13 is plainly inspired by the ideas of Mr. Tsviyits, while the line drawn by Mr. Bélits reveals and explains the causes of the breaking of the treaty and the war between the allies.

But we are anticipating. We must now return to the close of the nineteenth century to see two parallel and rival ideas ripening—the ideas of the autonomy and of the partition of Macedonia.

2. THE STRUGGLE FOR AUTONOMY

The part played by Russia in the liberation of Bulgaria is sufficiently well known. It is much less well known that this liberation was preceded in 1878 by a national movement on the spot. Of this we have spoken already in connection with the peaceful struggle carried on by the exarchate against the Phanariot Greeks. It was accompanied by a revolutionary movement whose aim was the independence of Bulgaria. As in Servia and in Greece at the beginning of the nineteenth century, the movement found allies among the semi-brigand, semi-revolutionary mountain chiefs, known as *haïdouks*. The principal leaders, the "apostles" of the movement, however, were revolutionaries of a more modern type, intellectuals whose education had frequently been acquired in foreign schools and universities. The generation of the "apostles" declared against the older methods of conflict, the ecclesiastical methods adopted by the *tchobadjis*, or nabobs of the Bulgarian colony at Constantinople. The people were with the apostles, and the era of insurrections began, bringing in its train the Turkish atrocities which Gladstone revealed to the civilized world. The Macedonian Bulgarians shared in this movement as well as the Bulgarians of Bulgaria proper. It was quite natural that the close of the Russo-Turkish war should see arising the idea of an "undivided Bulgaria," conceived within the limits of the treaty of San Stefano and including all the populations in Turkey regarded by themselves as Bulgarian. The protestations of Servian nationalism were stifled by the Servians themselves, for they, like Mr. Verkovits, had recognized all the countries enclosed within the boundaries of the Bulgaria of the future, imagined by Count Ignatiev, as traditionally Bulgarian.[1]

The fate of the treaty of San Stefano is familiar. The principality of Bulgaria was dismembered, and Macedonia remained in the hands of the Turks. This was the origin and cause of all subsequent conflicts. "Undivided Bulgaria," *tsiélo coupna Boulgaria,* became in future the goal and the ideal of Bulgarian na-

---

[1]It should be added that the ethnographic boundaries of Bulgaria, including therein Macedonia, were, previous to the treaty of San Stefano, indicated in the Minutes of the Conference at Constantinople in 1876. (See the debates of December 11/23.) The treaty of San Stefano as agreed upon between Russia and Turkey was, as is known, modified in essential respects and remade by the Berlin agreement, which divided this ethnographic Bulgaria in three parts: (i) The principality of Bulgaria; (ii) The vassal province of Eastern Roumelia; (iii) The Turkish province of Macedonia.

tional policy. Turkey replied by favoring minorities. An internal conflict followed by the use of means of which the late war has given an appalling example. From this time on there was no more security in Macedonia. Each of the rival nations,—Bulgarian, Greek, Servian, counted its heroes and its victims, its captains and its recruits, in this national guerrilla warfare and the result for each was a long martyrology. By the beginning of 1904 the number of political assassinations in Macedonia had, according to the English Blue Book, reached an average of one hundred per month. The Bulgarians naturally were the strongest, their bands the most numerous, their whole militant organization possessing the most extensive roots in the population of the country. The government of

the Bulgarian principality had presided at the origination of the Macedonian movement in the time of Stefane Stamboulov (about 1895). There was, however, always a divergence between the views of official Bulgaria which sought to use the movement as an instrument in its foreign policy, and those of the revolutionaries proper, most of them young people enamored of independence and filled with a kind of cosmopolitan idealism.

The revolutionary movement in Macedonia has frequently been represented as a product of Bulgarian ambition and the Bulgarian government held directly responsible for it. As a matter of fact, however, the hands of the government were always forced by the Macedonians, who relied on public opinion, violently excited by the press, and the direct propaganda of the leaders. There certainly was a "Central Committee" at Sofia, whose president was generally someone who enjoyed the confidence of the prince. This committee, however, served chiefly as the representative of the movement in the eyes of the foreigner; in the eyes of the real leaders it was always suspected of too great eagerness to serve the dynastic ambitions of King Ferdinand. It was in Macedonia that the real revolutionary organization, uncompromising and jealous of its independence, was to be found. For the origins of this internal organization we must go back to 1893, when, in the little village of Resna, a small group of young Bulgarian intellectuals founded a secret society with the clearly expressed intention of "preparing the Christian population for armed struggle against the Turkish régime in order to win personal security and guarantees for order and justice in the administration," which may be translated as the political autonomy of Macedonia. The "internal organization" did not aim at the annexation of Macedonia to Bulgaria; it called all nationalities dwelling in the three vilayets to join its ranks. No confidence was felt in Europe; hope was set on energetic action by the people. To procure arms, distribute them to the young people in the villages, and drill the latter in musketry and military evolutions—such were the first endeavors of the conspirators. All this was not long in coming to the notice of the Turks, who came by accident upon a depot of arms and bombs at Vinitsa. This discovery gave the signal for Turkish acts of repression and atrocities which counted more than two hundred victims. From that time on, there was no further halt in the struggle in Macedonia. The people, far from being discouraged by torture and massacre, became more and more keenly interested in the organization. In a few years the country was ready for the struggle. The whole country had been divided into military districts, each with its captain and militia staff. The central "organization," gathering force "everywhere and nowhere" had all the regular machinery of a revolutionary organization; an "executive police," a postal service and even an espionage service to meet the blows of the enemy and punish "traitors and spies." Throughout this period of full expansion, the people turned voluntarily to the leaders, even in the settlement of their private affairs, instead of going before the Ottoman officials and judges, and gladly paid their contributions to the revolutionary body. Self-confidence grew to such a point that offensive action began to be taken. The agricultural laborers tried striking against their Turkish masters for a rise in wages, to bring them up to the minimum laid down by the leaders of the "organization." They grew bolder in risking open skirmishes with the Turkish troops; and the official report of the "organization" records that as many as 132 conflicts (512 victims) took place in the period 1898–1902. At last European diplomacy stirs. The first scheme of reforms appeared, formulated by Russia and Austria in virtue of their *entente* of 1897. The Austro-Russian note of February, 1903, formulates demands too modest to be capable of solving the problem. The result was as usual; the Porte hastens to prevent European action by promising in January to inaugurate reforms. The Macedonian revolutionaries are in despair. A little group of extremists detaches itself from the Committee to attempt violent measures such as might stir Europe; in June bombs were thrown at Salonica. On July 20 (old style) the day of St. Elie (*Iline-den*) a formal insurrection breaks out: the *rayas* see that they are strong enough to measure themselves against their old oppressors.

It is the climax of the "internal organization" and that of its fall. The heroism of the rebels breaks itself against the superior force of the regular army. The fighting ratio is one to thirteen, 26,000 to 351,000; there are a thousand deaths and, in the final result, 200 villages ruined by Turkish vengeance, 12,000 houses burned, 3,000 women outraged, 4,700 inhabitants slain and 71,000 without a roof. [We quote throughout from the official report of the "organization."]

The decadence of the "internal organization" begins here, with the usual consequences—demoralization and Jacobinism. Traitors are searched out, and to an increasing extent discovered and executed; funds are extorted and employed on private purposes instead of on the national conflict; forced idleness condemns men to a life of disorder and coarse pleasure. The first period of the struggle is at an end (1897–1904).

Now, however, the whole of Europe begins to interest itself in the affairs of Macedonia. The second period opens; it is marked by attempts to organize European control over the Turkish régime (1905–1907). Macedonian autonomy becomes the distant goal of diplomatic efforts. Gradually an understanding begins to be reached, as questions are taken one by one, and the attempt is made to reform Turkish administration, police, finance and justice in Macedonia. We need not linger over the details of this portion of Balkan history, for it is but too familiar. Generally speaking, it is the repetition, on a larger scale, of what had been going on for half a century. First, unreal concessions, then, as soon as they begin to become onerous, general reform on paper which sweeps away and slurs over all practical details; and finally, the moment of tension once over, and the attention of Europe averted, the old order once again—with the single difference that the concessions agreed upon this time were more important. The loss of a whole province seemed threatened. So the reaction was all the greater. Instead of the Hamidian constitution of 1876, here was a new one, imposed this time on the sovereign by the Young Turk Revolution. Reforms were imposed [in the name of the people]. The Great Powers had nothing more to do in Macedonia. They departed amid the joyous cries of the multitude, while the leaders of the different nationalities, only yesterday on terms of irreconcilable hostility, embraced one another. The last attempt at the reconstruction of the Ottoman State was about to begin; the third and last period of our history (1908–12).

Its opening was of very happy augury. Proclaimed to the strains of the Marseillaise, the young Turkish revolution promised to solve all difficulties and pacify all hatreds by substituting justice for arbitrary rule, and freedom for despots. First and foremost it proclaimed complete equality as between the diverse nationalities inhabiting Turkey, in reliance on their Ottoman patriotism, their attachment to the *vatan,* to their fatherland one and indivisible. The partisans of Macedonian autonomy take up once more their hopes of reaching their end without alarming the susceptibilities of the dominant race. The revolutionaries and *comitadjis* of yesterday lay down their arms and go down from their mountains to the big towns; neither arms nor secret relations with the neighboring Balkan governments are any longer needed. Bulgarian Macedonians above all dream that they can now become good Ottoman patriots, while still faithful to their national ambitions.

It is a dream of but a moment's duration. The Young Turkish revolution proves itself from the very first narrow and nationalist. Far from satisfying the tendencies of re-awakening nationalism, it sets itself a task to which the absolutism of the Sultan had never ventured; to reconstruct the Turkey of the Caliphate and transform it into a modern state, beginning by the complete abolition of the rights and privileges of the different ethnic groups. These rights and privileges, confirmed by firmans and guaranteed by European diplomacy, were the sole means by which the Christian nationalities could safeguard their language, their beliefs, their ancient civilizations. These barriers once down, they felt themselves threatened by Ottoman assimilation in a way that had never been threatened before in the course of the ages since the capture of Constantinople by Mahomet II. This assimilation, this "Ottomanization," was the avowed aim of the victor, the committee of "Union and Progress."

Worse still: the assimilation of heterogeneous populations could only be effected slowly, however violent might be the measures threatening the future existence of the separate nationalities. The men of the Committee had not even confidence in the action of time. They wished to destroy their enemies forthwith, while they were still in power. Since national rivalries in Macedonia offered an ever-ready pretext for the intervention of the Powers, they decided to make an end of the question with all possible celerity. They were sure—and frequently stated their assurance in the Chamber—that the *ancien régime* was to blame for the powerlessness it had shown in Macedonia. They, on the other hand, with their new methods, would have made an end of it in a few months, or at most a few years.

Nevertheless it was the old methods that were employed. A beginning was made in 1909 by violating the article of the constitution which proclaimed the liberty of associations. The various ethnic groups, and especially the Bulgarians, had taken advantage of this article to found national clubs in Macedonia. As the pre-1908 revolutionary organizations had been dissolved by their heads, in their capacity of loyal Ottoman citizens, they had been replaced by clubs which had served as the nucleus of an open national organization. Their objective was now electoral instead of armed conflict; and while secretly arming there was neverthe-less a readiness to trust the Ottoman Parliament, to leave it to time to accomplish the task of regeneration and actual realization of constitutional principles. The Bulgarian revolutionaries had even concluded a formal agreement with the revolu-tionaries of the Committee of Union and Progress, according to which the return home of the insurgents was regarded as conditional only, and the internal organi-zation only to be disbanded on condition that the constitution was really put in force.

The Committee once in power saw the danger of these national political or-ganizations and entered on a systematic conflict with its allies of yesterday. From the spring of 1909 onwards, the partisans of the Committee caused the assassi-nation one after another of all those who had been at the head of revolutionary bands or committees under the previous régime. In the autumn of 1909 the final blow was aimed at the open organizations. (The Union of Bulgarian constitu-tional clubs included at that moment sixty-seven branches in Macedonia.) In November, the Chamber passed an Association law which forbade "any organi-zation based upon national denomination." An end was thus successfully put to the legal existence of the clubs, but not to the clubs themselves. Revolutionary activity began again from the moment when open legal conflict became impossible.

The Christian populations had good reasons for revolting against the new Turkish régime. Articles 11 and 16 of the revised constitution infringed the rights and privileges of the religious communities and national schools. The Ottoman State claimed to extend the limits of its action under the pretext of "protecting the exercise of all forms of worship" and "watching over all public schools." The principles might appear modern but in practice they were but new means for arriving at the same end—the "Ottomanization" of the Empire. This policy aimed at both Greeks and Bulgarians. For the Greeks, the violent enemies of the Young Turkish Movement from its beginning, it was the economic boycott declared by the Committee against all the Greeks of the Empire in retaliation for the attempts of the Cretans to reunite themselves with the mother country. It was forbidden for months that the good Ottomans should frequent shops or cafés kept by Greeks. Greek ships stopped coming into Ottoman ports, unable to find any laborers to handle their cargo.

Even more dangerous was the policy of Turkizing Macedonia by means of systematic colonization, carried out by the *mohadjirs*—emigrants, Moslems from Bosnia and Herzegovina. This measure caused discontent with the new régime to penetrate down to the agricultural classes. They were almost universally Bul-garian tenant farmers who had cultivated the *tchifliks* (farms) of the Turkish beys from time immemorial. In the course of the last few years they had begun to buy back the lands of their overlords, mainly with the money many of them brought home from America. All this was now at an end. Not only had the purchase of their holdings become impossible; the Turks began turning the tenants out of their farms. The government bought up all the land for sale to establish *mohadjirs* (Moslem refugees from Bosnia) upon it.

This was the final stroke. The leaders of the disarmed bands could now return to their mountains where they rejoined old companions in arms. The "internal organization" again took up the direction of the revolutionary movement. On October 31, 1911, it "declared publicly that it assumed responsibility for all the attacks on and encounters with the Turkish army by the insurgents in this and the previous year, and for all other revolutionary manifestations." The Young Turkish Government had not waited for this declaration to gain cognizance of revolutionary activity and take action upon it. So early as November, 1909, it had replied by an iniquitous "band" law, making the regular authorities of the villages, all the families where any member disappeared from his home, the whole population of any village harboring a *comitadji*, responsible for all the deeds and words of the voluntary, irregular associations. In the summer of 1910 a systematic perquisition was instituted in Macedonia with the object of discovering arms hidden in the villagers' houses. The vexations, the tortures to which peaceful populations were thus subjected can not possibly be enumerated here. In November, 1910, Mr. Pavlov, Bulgarian deputy, laid the facts before the Ottoman Parliament. He had counted as many as 1,853 persons individually subjected to assault and ill treatment in the three Macedonian vilayets, leaving out of account the cases of persons executed *en masse*, arrested and assaulted, among whom were dozens killed or mutilated. Adding them in, Mr. Pavlov, brought his total up to 4,913. To this number were still to be added 4,060 who had taken refuge in Bulgaria or fled among the mountains to escape from the Turkish authorities.

The year 1910 was decisive in the sense of affording definite proof that the régime established in 1908 was not tolerable. The régime had its chance of justifying itself in the eyes of Europe and strengthening its position in relation to its own subjects and to the neighboring Balkan States; it let the chance go. From that time the fate of Turkey in Europe was decided, beyond appeal.

This was also the end of the attempts at autonomy in Macedonia. To realize this autonomy two principal conditions were required: the indivisibility of Turkey and a sincere desire on the part of the Turkish government to introduce radical reforms based on decentralization. No idea was less acceptable to the "Committee of Union and Progress" than this of decentralization, since it was the watchword of the rival political organization. Thenceforward any hope of improving the condition of the Christian populations within the limits of the *status quo* became illusory. Those limits had to be transcended. Autonomy was no longer possible. Dismemberment and partition had to be faced.

3. THE ALLIANCE AND THE TREATIES

The most natural solution of the Balkan imbroglio appeared to be the creation in Macedonia of a new autonomy or independent unity, side by side with the other unities realized in Bulgaria, Greece, Servia and Montenegro, all of which countries had previously been liberated, thanks to Russian or European intervention. But this solution had become impossible, owing first to the incapacity of the Turkish government, and then to the rival pretensions of the three neighboring States to this or that part of the Macedonian inheritance. Mr. Dehn has tried to show on a map the result of this confusion of rival claims (see his sche-

-------- Boundaries of 1912	
⋈⋈⋈⋈ Servian Aspirations	
•••••• Bulgarian............".........	
×××××○ Rumanian..........."..........	
═══ Greek ....".......	

'After Dehn   Th. Weinreb del.

matic map).[1] There was hardly any part of the territory of Turkey in Europe which was not claimed by at least two competitors. These views on the inheritance of the "Sick Man" and for the realization of "great national ideas" in the shape of a "Great" Servia, a "Great" Greece, or a "Great" Bulgaria, made any united action on the part of these little States for their common ends impossible. In theory every one accepted the opinion that they must act together, that the Balkans ought to belong to the Balkan peoples, and that the great neighboring

[1]This schematic map is borrowed from the little book by Mr. Paul Dehn, *Die Völker Südeuropas und ihre politischen Probleme*. Halle, 1909; in the *Angewandte Geographie* Series.

Powers who might weaken or enslave the little Balkan States, must be kept off. In practice, however, the opposite course was adopted. Each courted Russia or Austria, in turn, sometimes even both at the same time, first one and then the other, with a view to opposing his neighbors and securing the prospect of his own country's hegemony.

Russia and Austria for their part naturally pursued their own interests in the Balkans,—interests that were by no means identical. Geography and ethnography have divided the Balkans into two spheres of influence, the Eastern and the Western, the Servian and the Bulgarian spheres. Diplomatic history has made them into the Austrian and the Russian spheres of influence, hence two opposing pulls—the "German pull" from North to South, and the "Slav pull" from East to West. The plain of the Vardar, which divides Macedonia into two parts, was destined to be the arena where the two influences met and battled. Russia traced the limits of its zone of influence in the treaty of San Stefano in 1878—the whole of Macedonia forming part of Bulgaria indivisible— the *tsiélo coupna Boulgaria*. Austrian policy has also had its treaties, concluded to countervail the Russian pull in the shape of the secret treaties of 1881 and 1889, made with King Milan—the Servian King—who for his part was promised the plain of the Vardar, and the Western half of Macedonia, on condition of Servia's renouncing its intentions upon the Adriatic, its "Pan-Servian" tendencies, that is, of consenting to the annexation of the Sandjak of Bosnia and Herzegovina, and finally all the Servian-speaking countries, as far as Zagréb.

Looked at from this general point of view, the idea of a Balkan alliance was contrary to the idea of partition, since alliance was the instrument of independence, the means to the realization of the idea of "the Balkans for the Balkan peoples," while partition subserved the ambitions of the great neighboring powers. As a matter of fact those who first conceived the idea of alliance were as far as possible remote from that of partition. They were the idealistic youth of 1870, of whom we have spoken above, and in their minds a "Yougo-Slav Federation" was a veritable union of the free and independent Slav democracies. Nor was the idea of partition clearly present to the mind of the first great politician who tried to realize a Yougo-Slav Federation under Servian hegemony, Prince Michel Obrénovits. On the eve of his violent death he was in treaty with Greece, Roumania, Montenegro and the revolutionary "apostles" of still subject Bulgaria, for the preparation of common strife against Turkey. What was the use of partition since there was the absolute property of each to be taken? It is true that with the Slav family itself there was by no means complete unanimity in the idea of alliance without partition. There were some Bulgarians, and those the most far sighted, who protested. Why ally against Turkey when whatever was taken from the Ottoman Empire was at the same time taken from the Bulgarian people as a whole? But for these latter the reply was taken from Turkey, which was trying the patience of the giaours even when they desired to be loyal; second from the young Bulgarian revolutionaries, crying, with the voice of their best representative, Lioubén Karavelov, the doyen of Bulgarian literature—"First of all we must have union, union, union—and when we are free each shall have what belongs to him."

A remarkable light is thrown by recent events upon these disputes at the end of the sixties. Neither the idea of alliance nor the conflicting claims which appeared at the same time disappeared in the fifty years that lie between us and Prince Michel's first attempts. He was slain in 1868 by assassins. "Thy thought shall not perish"—so it runs on his tombstone. It has, in truth, not perished; but it has become more complex. Mutual rivalries became more acute as the area to be partitioned became more confined while still leaving something to partition.

"England's responsibility" in these new complications and difficulties has been set forth by the Duke of Argyll:[1] we, therefore, need not linger over the blow struck at the idea of a federation of the Balkan nationalities when Bulgaria—one and indivisible—according to the treaty of San Stefano,—was divided into three by the Treaty of Berlin. The whole course of succeeding events was the result of this grave error. The most recent events lie there in germ.

The reunion to free Bulgaria of the still vassal Oriental Roumelia, and as the immediate consequence thereof, the Serbo-Bulgarian war of 1885, the growing rivalries between the nationalities in a still subject Macedonia, the new propaganda of the secondary nationalities, the isolation of Greece in its 1897 attempt, the fetishism of the *status quo*, mitigated and corrected as it was by the intrigues of the Powers, the miscarriage of the hypocritical plan of reforms in Macedonia in 1907–1908, the *intermezzo* of the Turkish revolution with its failure to solve an insoluble problem, then the greatness and decline of the Balkan "alliance"—all were the natural results of the mistake of Berlin,—a mistake which now everybody sees without the power to correct.

This same series of events has put obstacles in the way of the normal development of the highly national conception of an alliance between the Balkan peoples, has turned it aside from its true aim, that of preparing the way for federation; and by informing it with an alien egoism and mania have delayed its development and brought it prematurely to an end. Any judgment of men and events as they are today must take into account all this past, and not lay to the charge of the present the results of a negligence which goes back for decades.

The idea of Balkan alliance has come into life in our time with a significance quite different from that which it possessed thirty or forty years ago. It is no longer the young Slav enthusiasts' dream of a free federation of Balkan democracies. It is no longer the nationalists and Pan-Slav philosphers' notion of a Russian moral hegemony with Constantinople as its political center. The first

---

[1]See his book *Our Responsibility for Turkey.*

of these dreams was slain by the rivalry of the Balkan States; the second by their love of independence. The Balkan alliance in its later phase was but a tool employed by local policy encouraged by Russia, and directed, under the inspiration of Russian diplomacy, against Germanic pretensions, or in so far as advantage was taken of the device by Balkan statesmen against the invasions of Turkish "Ottomanism" and Athenian ambition towards autonomy. Alliance in this latest phase inevitably implied partition as an essential condition; the means being war with Turkey, the final end the conquest of Turkey in Europe.

The modern history of the alliance might start at the point where Mr. Bourchier[1] begins in his excellent articles on the Balkan League, that is to say, with the attempt of the Greek Minister, Mr. Tricoupis, in 1891, who openly proposed to Belgrade and Sofia the partition of Turkey in Europe on the basis of a treaty in which the future frontiers of the Balkan States were to be exactly determined in advance. To speak of such a plan to King Milan and to Stamboulov, was to communicate it to the Ballplatz at Vienna and to the Sublime Porte. The *pourparlers* did not get beyond a mere exchange of amiable courtesies. Austria Hungary had just renewed the treaty with King Milan which led to the fratricidal Serbo-Bulgarian war (1889 to 1895). Some years later she was to sign a secret convention with Roumania. In the event of a common war with Bulgaria, Roumania was to receive a portion of Bulgarian territory. It is the very territory, promised by Austria, which Roumania has just been given without war. In 1897, during the Græco-Turkish war, Mr. Deliannis renewed the proposals of Tricoupis. But his partition formula, repeated so often since, and not even now wholly renounced by the Greeks, was not to the Bulgarians' taste. They preferred negotiating with the Porte for new concessions for their churches and schools in Macedonia, to risking taking part in an ill-prepared and ill-conducted war. Soon after (1901) Austria Hungary brought about the Græco-Roumanian *rapprochement* which, together with the Austro-Servian treaty and the Austro-Roumanian convention, finally "enclosed" Bulgaria and threatened to paralyze its action in Macedonia. A Balkan alliance seemed as far remote as possible.

All the same the web spun with such pains was quickly to be broken. The revolution of 1904 in Macedonia made the question an international one. Wallachian propagandism and Greek "conversions" in Macedonia led to a diplomatic rupture between Greece and Roumania (1903). The murder of King Alexandre Obrénovits and the return of the Karageorgevits dynasty to Belgrade (1903) emancipated Servia from Austrian influence. The natural alternatives were either a *rapprochement* with Russia or the renaissance of the Yougo-Slav alliance. The young generation in Servia and Bulgaria went further and became once more enthusiastic for the federation idea. Writers, artists, students in Bel-

---

[1]The Balkan League—The *London Times,* June 4, 5, 6, 11, 13. Use has been made of these articles but the brief historical account which follows has been based on the Commission's own information.

grade and Sofia exchanged visits. Diplomatists followed suit. By 1904 people in Belgrade were discussing a scheme for an offensive and defensive alliance as a means of securing the autonomy of Old Servia and of Macedonia as far as possible by peaceful means, but in case of extremity, by force of arms. The names of those who took part in these *pourparlers* will reappear in 1911. They were Mr. Pachitch, at whose house secret conversations went on; Milovane Milovanovits, late minister of Foreign Affairs; Dimitri Risov, a Macedonian revolutionary who had become a diplomatist without losing his ardent devotion to the cause; Mr. Kessaptchiev at that time specially sent to discuss the alliance. But difficulties arose as soon as the frontiers began to be spoken of. The Servians gave their adhesion in principle only, to propose the very next day a geographical interpretation of the term "Old Servia," which extended it to cover the whole of the Sandjak. The Bulgarians regarded these claims as exorbitant; and finally after vain disputes lasting three days, the idea of an offensive alliance was given up. On April 12/25, 1904, a defensive alliance was however concluded. But this treaty, far too vague and general in its terms, had no practical result, thanks to the indiscretion of a Servian official who was also the correspondent of the *Neue Freie Presse*. The treaty was immediately divulged and seeds of distrust consequently implanted in the minds of the allies. The Servians regarded the treaty as annulled after the Bulgarian declaration of independence was made in 1908 without consulting Servia, and greatly to the detriment of Servian national policy, which was then passing through a critical phase, owing to the annexation of Bosnia and Herzegovina by Austria Hungary. The Servians accused the Bulgarians of profiting by their losses to improve their own international position instead of coming to their assistance. Old distrust was thus about to revive when Russian diplomacy took up the alliance idea again. The Russian diplomatists took the promises of a Young Turkish regeneration seriously, and proposed a universal Balkan alliance with a free and constitutionally governed Turkey as a member. They wanted an alliance facing towards the Danube rather than the Bosphorus. Balkan diplomacy knew well enough that the "Sick Man" was incurable; but the chance was seized. It is true that here again the old difficulties about partition rose. In 1909 Mr. Milovanovits vainly proposed the cession of Uskub and Koumanovo to Servia. In 1910 conferences were held at St. Petersburg with Mr. Milovanovits and Mr. Malinov, which, however, did not succeed in arriving at any result. Bulgaria was by no means disposed to sanction the Servian tendencies favored by Russian diplomacy, even in the highly general form of a possible extension of Old Servia, properly so-called, towards the south.

All the same in 1910, as we know, it became clear to all the world that the Young Turk policy of "Ottomanizing" the nationalities by assimilation was going to lead to catastrophe. Growing pressure on Bulgarians and Greeks in Turkey finally brought these enemies together. Mr. Venizelos, since 1910 head of the Athenian cabinet, as early as October proposed an agreement to

Sofia. Once more no agreement could be reached on the delimitation of spheres of influence. The Bulgarians were unwilling to hand over Kavala, Serres, Vodena, Castoria, Florina to the Greeks, in accordance with the old "Deliannis formula." But the condition of things in Macedonia made an understanding a matter of necessity. The only thing to do was to conclude an agreement. The heads of the Christian churches in Constantinople had to make similar representations to the Ottoman government, without waiting for any understanding. At Sofia discussions began as to how an understanding was to be arrived at, and a joint systematic protest was made in defence of the religious and educational privileges granted in common to the Christian communities by the ancient firmans of the sultans and by international treaties.

At Sofia the *pourparlers* dragged on throughout the Malinov administration. When Mr. Guéchov, in March, 1910, succeeded Mr. Malinov as head of the Cabinet, he stopped them. Then Mr. Venizelos proposed to Mr. Guéchov, under the seal of secrecy, in March, 1911, not merely an agreement to defend the privileges of the Christians in Turkey, but a defensive alliance, "envisaging the case of an attack" on one of the contracting parties. No reply was made to this proposition, which was kept strictly secret, since the Cretan difficulties might provoke a war in which Bulgaria had no desire to take part. The event which led Bulgaria to consider the necessity of a Balkan alliance in a yet more serious light was the beginning of the Turco-Italian war at the end of September, 1911. When the Italian ultimatum was issued, Bulgarian statesmen were on holiday; Czar Ferdinand and his first Minister were at Vichy. Milovanovits was watching at his post. B. Risov, Th. Théodorov and he discussed the project of an alliance at Belgrade, Vienna and Sofia. Mr. Guéchov hastened to return. Mr. Milovanovits met him at the station at Belgrade, got into his carriage and between Belgrade and the little station of Liapovo, the bases of an alliance were laid down in the course of a two hours' conversation. For the first time a Bulgarian minister recognized the necessity and possibility of territorial concession in Macedonia—Uskub and Koumanovo.

It might have been foreseen that public opinion in Bulgaria would, as invariably, be against any such transaction. Rather Macedonia autonomous as a whole under Turkish suzerainty than independent on condition of partition,—such had always been the Bulgarian point of view. Even in 1910, Mr. Malinov, as we have pointed out, prepared to wait rather than make concessions. So now Guéchov, once returned to Sofia, again decided to temporize. In December, Milovanovits renewed the alliance proposal; but after ten days without a reply he had to modify his proposition. Then and not until then did the Bulgarian government decide to treat. The *pourparlers* lasted all winter, and the treaty was concluded between February 29 and March 13, 1912.

In this treaty, which was kept secret, and of which the text was published later by *Le Matin*,[1] the fundamental point was the delimitation of the line of par-

---

[1]Monday, November 24, 1913.

tition "beyond which" Servia agreed "to formulate no territorial claim." A highly detailed map of this frontier was annexed to the treaty.[1] Bulgarian diplomatists still wished to keep an open door for themselves. That is why they left the responsibility for the concessions demanded to the Czar of Russia. "Bulgaria agrees to accept this frontier," they added, "if the Emperor of Russia, who shall be requested to act as final arbiter in this question, pronounces in favor of the line." Their idea was that the Emperor might still adjudge to them the "disputed zone" they were in the act of ceding, between the frontier marked on the map and Old Servia, properly so-called, "to the north and west of Char-Planina." "It goes without saying," the treaty added, "that the two contracting parties undertake to accept as definitive the frontier line which the Emperor of Russia may have found, *within the limits indicated below,* most consonant with the rights and interests of the two parties." Evidently "within the limits indicated below" meant between Char-Planina and the line marked on the map, "beyond which Servia agreed to formulate no territorial claim." That was the straightforward meaning of the treaty, afterwards contested by the Servians. The line of partition of which the treaty spoke corresponded fully with the ethnographic conclusions of the learned geographer, Mr. Tsviyits; conclusions which made a profound impression on the Czar Ferdinand at the time of his interview with Mr. Tsviyits. It was these conclusions probably which made the Czar decide to accept the compromise.[2] Mr. Tsviyits was also the first to communicate to the world, in his article of November, 1912, in the *Review of Reviews,* the frontier established by the treaty.[3] The reason why Bulgarian diplomatists decided on making a concession so little acceptable to public opinion is now clear. They did more. After deciding on eventual partition they reverted to the idea of autonomy and laid it down that partition was only to take place in case the organization of the conquered countries "as a distinct autonomous province," should be found "impossible" in the "established conviction" of both parties. Up to the "liquida-

---

[1] It is reproduced here from a reduced and simplified copy published in the *Echo de Bulgarie* of June 7/20, 1913.

[2] See Mr. Tsviyits' ethnographic map, published in his pamphlet *The Annexation of Bosnia and the Servian Question,* 1909. The map annexed to the treaty of Feb. 29 (March 13), 1912, differs from it to the advantage of Servia in the western region, but corresponds generally with it in the eastern part of the frontier agreed upon.

[3] Mr. Tsviyits' article has appeared in a Servian translation, but at that time Servian claims had already increased and the pamphlet was banned. In a second edition, adopted by the "Information Bureau," the passage describing the frontiers was simply omitted. The omitted passage runs as follows: "The Southern frontier of Old Servia, or the line dividing the Bulgarian and Servian spheres of interest (starts from the Bulgarian frontier, near Kustendil, by the line of partition between the rivers Ptchinia and Kriva-Réka, leaving Kriva-Palnika and Kratovo in the Bulgarian sphere and Uskub and Koumanovo in the Servian. The frontier then crosses the Ovtche-Polé, by the line of division between Bregalnitsa and Ptchinia, and passes the Vardar, to the north of Vélès. Thence it goes over the slopes of the Yagoupitsa mountains, and along the ulterior line of division, reaches the Baba mountain as far as Lake Okhrida, so that Prilepe, Krouchevo and the town of Okhrida are in the Bulgarian sphere and Strouga, Débar and Tétovo in the Servian.) Old Servia issues, through a narrow belt, on the Adriatic near Scutari, Alessio and (perhaps) Durazzo. [Passages within parentheses omitted.]

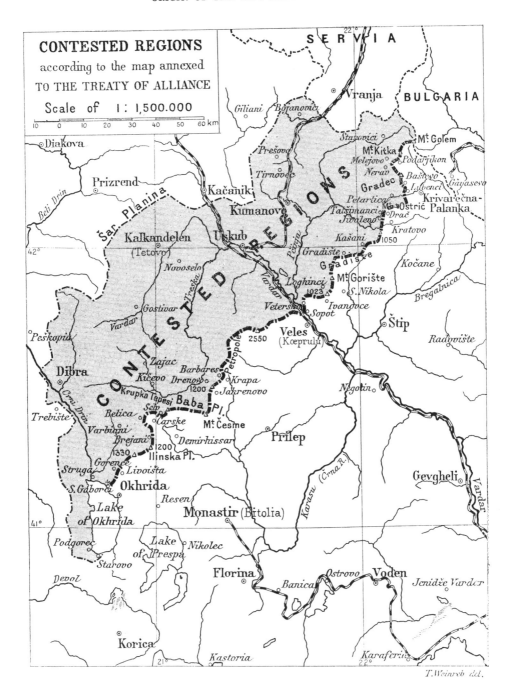

CONTESTED REGIONS
according to the map annexed
TO THE TREATY OF ALLIANCE
Scale of 1:1,500.000

T. Weinreb del.

tion," the occupied countries were to be regarded as "falling under common dominion—*condominium*." Finally the treaty was to remain defensive purely, until the two parties "find themselves in agreement" on "undertaking common military action." This "action" was to "be undertaken solely in the event of Russia's not opposing it," and the consent of Russia was to be obligatory. Turkey had been expressly designated as the objective of "action" in the cases forecast, but included was "any one among the Great Powers which should attempt to annex any portion whatsoever of the territories of the peninsula." Such were the precautions and provisions designed to guarantee Bulgarian diplomatists against abuse. All, however, were to fall away at the first breath of reality.

Sofia has been credited with a secondary interest in the Græco-Bulgarian agreement proffered by Venizelos in April, 1911. Since 1897 the Greek army had been considered almost a negligible quantity, and the advance made under French instruction was hardly known. But the Greek navy was needed to cut Turkey's communication with Anatolia via the Ægean Sea, and thus prevent the transport of troops to Macedonia. Thus as soon as the Serbo-Bulgarian alliance had been concluded in February, conferences with Greece were entered upon. The Greeks proposed to the Bulgarians to discuss the question of future frontiers. Since Greek aid was not rated high at Sofia, the Bulgarians were not inclined to make sacrifices, the more because of designs on Salonica. On this point previous negotiations had made it abundantly clear that the Greeks, so far from yielding would again propose their unacceptable frontier. It was therefore unhappily decided to leave the war to settle the question, with a secret intention of being the first to reach the desired spot. As for the alliance, it was concluded on a "purely defensive" basis with the promise "of lending the agreement no kind of aggressive tendency."[1] The principal object appeared to be the "peaceful co-existence of the different nationalities in Turkey, on the basis of real and actual political equality and respect of rights accruing from treaties or otherwise conceded to the Christian nationalities of the Empire." But it was foreseen that a "systematic attempt" on these rights on the part of Turkey might as readily be the *casus fœderis* as a direct attack on the territories of the contracting parties. It should be added that the expression "rights accruing from treaties" was inserted in the text on the insistence of the Bulgarian diplomats, who intended by this reference to treaties, Article 23 of the Treaty of Berlin, *i. e.,* Macedonian autonomy. Clearly in the hour of the conclusion of this treaty, May 16/29, 1912, complete vagueness prevailed as to eventual "action." The only thing which was clear was that Bulgaria was not going to make war on Turkey about Crete. To this end a declaration had been added to the treaty which merely bound Bulgaria to "benevolent neutrality" in the event of war breaking out "because of the admission of Cretan deputies to the Greek parliament."

---

[1]The text of the Græco-Bulgarian treaty was published by *Le Matin* November 26, 1913.

The Serbo-Bulgarian and Græco-Bulgarian treaties concluded, the King of Montenegro came on the scene in his turn. Nicholas was always ready to take part in any combination of the Balkan States against Turkey. He had spoken of it to Russia in 1888; he renewed his proposition at the Russian Embassy in Constantinople in July, 1911. When the Turco-Italian war began, in September, he was the first to propose common military action on the part of Servia, Bulgaria, Greece and Montenegro. An agreement was made with Bulgaria in April, 1912, and with Greece somewhat later. Belgrade remained. It was not on good terms with Cettigne, partly because of the patriotic rivalry between the two Servian States (each of which aspired to the rôle of "Piémont"); partly because of anti-dynastic intrigues supposed to be going on on either side and partly because of the reactionary régime of Nicholas, which drove all the educated youth of the country to emigration and conspiracy abroad. Bulgarian diplomats acted as intermediaries. Mr. Danev communicated to the Vienna *Zeit* an amusing account of the way in which the last stone of the Balkan alliance (which Russia wanted to build up against Austria Hungary) was placed at the end of May in the Hofburg at Vienna. None of these treaties however became effective until the end of September, after a series of events in Turkey which ended by seriously threatening the very existence of the nationalities in Macedonia. These events opened in the spring of 1912 with a revolt in Albania, a revolt which had been foreseen and taken into consideration by the enemies of Turkey. In summer the revolt bore fruit which exceeded all expectation. The cabinet resigned, the chamber was dissolved, the executive committee of the party of "Union and Progress," threatened with complete defeat, was compelled to grant the Albanians all they asked in order to stop the movement in Constantinople, a movement which the discontented army refused to prevent. This demonstration of Turkish weakness encouraged the new allies, the more so that the promises of Albanian autonomy, covering the four vilayets of Macedonia and Old Servia, directly threatened the Christian nationalities with extermination. The Servians hastened to oppose the plan of a "greater Albania" by their plan for the partition of Turkey in Europe among the Balkan States into four spheres of influence. Counting on the possibility of European intervention the organization of the autonomous provinces based on the ethnographic principle was undertaken with a minimum of success. But Europe did not "find itself."

The proposal made on August 14 by Mr. Berchtold, to assist Turkey in extending "decentralization" to the Christian nationalities was no more than a trial move, adroitly designed as a means of feeling the ground. Russia replied by an exhortation to the allies to abstain from aggressive action of any kind, and the endeavor to detach Bulgaria from Servia and Servia from Bulgaria. The reply of the allies, prepared with the utmost secrecy, was to conclude a series of military conventions, complementary to the alliances, which did this time anticipate and prepare for war.

The Bulgarian military convention, foreshadowed by the treaty, was signed as early as April 29/May 12. Bulgaria undertook in case of war to mobilize 200,000 men; Servia 150,000—minimum figures, since there could be no thought of conquering Turkey with an army of 350,000 men. Of these 200,000 men, Bulgaria was to dispatch half to Macedonia, and half to Thrace. At the same time the convention took into account the possibility of Austria Hungary's marching upon Servia. In that case Bulgaria undertook to send 200,000 men to Servia's assistance.

The basis of the Græco-Bulgarian military convention was different; it was concluded almost on the eve of general mobilization, September 13/26. Bulgaria promised, in case of war, an effective army 300,000 strong; Greece, 120,000. Bulgaria undertook to take the offensive "with an important part of its army" in the three Macedonian vilayets; but in case Servia should take part in the war with at least 120,000 men, "Bulgaria might employ the whole of its military forces in Thrace." Now that real war was about to begin and the main Turkish force was directed hither, it was high time to contemplate war in Thrace which had been left, in the hypothetical agreements, to Russia's charge, as Mr. Bourchier assumes. This made it necessary to change, define and complete the military agreement with Servia of April 29/May 12. The document was now more than once remodeled in consonance with new agreements arrived at between the heads of the General Staff of the two armies—such agreements having been foreshadowed in Articles 4 and 13. The special arrangement of June 19/July 2 provides that the necessary number of troops agreed upon might be transported from the Vardar to the Maritza and vice versa, "if the situation demands it." On August 23/September 5, the Bulgarians demand to have all their forces for disposition in Thrace, the Servians make objections and no agreement is reached. At last, three days after the Greek military convention (September 15/28), an understanding was arrived at. "The whole of the Bulgarian army will operate in the valley of the Maritza, leaving one division only in the first days on the Kustendil—Doupnitsa line." But if the Servian army repulsed the Turks on the Uskub—Vélès-Chtipe line—and advanced southward, the Bulgarians might recall their division to the theater of the Maritza to reinforce their armies, leaving only the battalions of the territorial army in Macedonia." Later, as is known, it was the Servians who sent two divisions with siege artillery to Adrianople. The Servians were later to declare the arrangements made by the two General Staffs forced and not binding, and to use this as an argument for treaty revision.

While making their final dispositions, the allies still awaited European intervention in Turkey. In vain. Friends only gave them counsels of prudence. Enemies were not sorry to see the allies given a drubbing by the Turks, whom everybody in Europe regarded as infinitely their superiors. During the two weeks in which final decisions were being made in Bulgaria, Mr. Sazonov traveled about in England and talked about Persia. When it appeared at the last moment that the Balkan States were going to act, thanks to Mr. Poincaré and with the conditional assent of Mr. Berchtold, it was thought advisable to issue, September 25/October 8, an Austro-Russian proclamation to the effect that if the Powers disapproved energetically of measures contrary to peace, they would take the execution of reforms in hand, subject to the suzerainty of the Sultan and the territorial integrity of Turkey; if war broke out, whatever were the issue, they would not permit any change in the territorial *status quo* of Turkey in Europe. Alas! while the reply to be sent to this note was under discussion, King Nicholas of Montenegro declared war on Turkey (October 9); on September 30/October 13 the allies formally demanded Turkey's consent to the autonomy of the European vilayets, redivided according to nationality. On October 4/17, Turkey declared war.

If it be now asked what were the causes of the first Balkan war, three principal ones may be found. First, the weakness and want of foresight of Turkey, on the verge of dissolution; second, the powerlessness of Europe to impose on a constitutional Turkey the reforms which she had succeeded in introducing into an absolute Turkey, and third, the consciousness of increased strength which alliance gave to the Balkan States, each with a national mission before it, namely, the protection of the men of its race and religion dwelling in Turkey, against the Ottomanization policy which threatened national existence. The first two reasons made the war possible and inevitable; the third guaranteed its success. In a few weeks the territories of Turkey in Europe were invaded by the allied armies and the whole country from the west of the fortified lines of Tchataldja and the Gallipoli peninsula, with the exception of Albania, in their hands as *condominium*. This was, at least, the principle acknowledged by the Serbo-Bulgarian treaty. This principle of the *condominium* had to be reconciled with the fact of the occupation and the new demands that rose up, the consequences of unexpected success. As might have been expected, partition was more difficult than conquest. Another war, the conflict for the "equilibrium," was to follow on the first, the conflict for freedom.

4. THE CONFLICT BETWEEN THE ALLIES

There had long existed germs of discord among the Balkan nationalities which could not be stifled by the treaties of alliance of which we know. Rather the texts of these treaties created fresh misunderstandings and afforded formal pretexts to cover the real reasons of conflict. There was but one means which could have effectually prevented the development of the germs—to maintain the territorial *status quo* of Turkey and grant autonomy to the nationalities without a change of sovereignty. This could not have been, it is true, a definitive solution; it could only be a delay, a stage, but a stage that would have bridged the transition. In default of an issue which Turkey rendered impossible by its errors, Europe by its too protracted patience and the allies by their success, the change was too abrupt. It produced the deplorable results we are to study under the aspect of the "excesses" committed by the different nationalities when reduced to an elementary struggle for existence carried out by the most primitive means.

We find this struggle in Macedonia from the first days of the Servian and Greek occupation onwards. At first there was general rejoicing and an outburst of popular gratitude towards the liberators. The Macedonian revolutionaries themselves had foreseen and encouraged this feeling. They said in their "proclamation to our brothers," published by the delegates of the twenty-five Macedonian confederacies on October 5/18, i. c., at the very beginning of the war: "Brothers:—your sufferings and your pains have touched the heart of your kindred. Moved by the sacred duty of fraternal compassion, they come to your aid to free you from the Turkish yoke. In return for their sacrifice they desire nothing but to reëstablish peace and order in the land of our birth. Come to meet these brave knights of freedom therefore with triumphal crowns. Cover the way before their feet with flowers and glory. And be magnanimous to those who yesterday were your masters. As true Christians, give them not evil for evil. Long live liberty! Long live the brave army of liberation!" In fact the Servian army entered the north and the Greek army the south of Macedonia, amid cries of joy from the population. But this enthusiasm for the liberators soon gave place to doubts, then to disenchantment, and finally was converted to hatred and despair. The Bulgarian journal published at Salonica, *Bulgarine,* first records some discouraging cases whose number was swollen by the presence of certain individuals, chauvinists of a peculiar turn, who gave offence to the national sentiment of the country by the risks they ran. "It is the imperative duty of the powers in occupation," said the journal, "to keep attentive watch over the behavior of irresponsible persons." Alas! five days later (November 20) the journal had to lay it down, as a general condition of the stability of the alliance, that the powers in occupation should show toleration to all nationalities and refrain from treating some of them as enemies. Four days later the journal, instead of attacking the persons responsible, was denouncing the powers who "in their blind chauvinism take no account of the national sentiments of the people temporarily subject to them." They still, however, cherished the hope that the local authorities were acting without the knowledge of Belgrade. The next day the editor wrote his leader under a question addressed to the Allied Governments: *"Is this a war of liberation or a war of conquest?"* He knew the reply well enough; the Greek authorities forbade the existence of this Bulgarian paper in *their* town of Salonica.

The illusion of the inhabitants likewise disappeared before the touch of reality. The Servian soldier, like the Greek, was firmly persuaded that in Macedonia he would find compatriots, men who could speak his language and address him with *jivio* or *zito*. He found men speaking a language different from his, who cried *hourrah!* He misunderstood or did not understand at all. The theory he had learned from youth of the existence of a Servian Macedonia and a Greek Macedonia naturally suffered; but his patriotic conviction that Macedonia must become Greek or Servian, if not so already, remained unaffected. Doubtless Macedonia had been what he wanted it to become in those times of Douchan the Strong or the Byzantine Emperors. It was only agitators and propagandist Bulgarians who instilled into the population the idea of being Bulgarian. The agitators must be driven out of the country, and it would again become what it had always been, Servian or Greek. Accordingly they acted on this basis.

Who were these agitators who had made the people forget the Greek and Servian tongues? First, they were the priests; then the schoolmasters; lastly the revolutionary elements who, under the ancient régime, had formed an "organization"; heads of bands and their members, peasants who had supplied them with money or food,—in a word the whole of the male population, in so far as it was educated and informed. It was much easier for a Servian or a Greek to discover all these criminal patriots than it had been for the Turkish authorities, under the absolutist régime, to do so. The means of awakening the national conscience were much better known to Greeks and Servians, for one thing, since they were accustomed to use them for their own cause. Priests, schoolmasters, bands existed among the Greeks and Servians, as well as among the Bulgarians. In Macedonia the difference, as we know, lay in the fact that the schoolmaster or priest, the Servian *voyévoda* or Greek *andarte,* addressed himself to the minority, and had to recruit his own following instead of finding them ready made. Isolated in the midst of a Bulgarian population, he made terms with Turkish power while the national Bulgarian "organizations" fought against it. Since the representative of the national minority lived side by side with his Bulgarian neighbors, and knew them far better than did the Turkish official or policeman, he could supply the latter with the exact information. He learned still more during the last few years of general truce between the Christian nationalities and growing alliance against the Turk. Almost admitted to the plot, many secrets were known to him. It was but natural he should use this knowledge for the advantage of the compatriots who had appeared in the guise of liberators. On the arrival of his army, he was no longer solitary, isolated and despised; he became useful and necessary, and was proud of serving the national cause. With his aid, denunciation became an all powerful weapon; it penetrated to the recesses of local life and revived events of the past unknown to the Turkish authorities. These men, regarded by the population as leaders and venerated as heroes, were arrested and punished like mere vagabonds and brigands, while the dregs were raised to greatness.

This progressive disintegration of social and national life began in Macedonia with the entry of the armies of occupation, and did not cease during the eight months which lie between the beginning of the first war and the beginning of the second. It could not fail to produce the most profound changes. The Bulgarian nation was decapitated. A beginning was made when it was easiest. The openly revolutionary elements were gotten rid of,—the *comitadjis* and all those who had been connected with the movement of insurrection against the Turkish rule or the conflict with the national minorities. This was the easier because in the chaos of Macedonian law there was no clearly drawn line of demarcation between political and ordinary crime.

To combat the Bulgarian schools was more difficult. The time was already long past when the schoolmaster was necessarily a member of the "interior organization." The purely professional element had steadily displaced the apostles and martyrs of preceding generations. But the conquerors saw things as they had been decades ago. For them the schoolmaster was always the conspirator, the dangerous man who must be gotten rid of, and the school, however strictly "professional," was a center from which Bulgarian civilization emanated. This is why the school became the object of systematic attack on the part of Servians and Greeks. Their first act on arriving in any place whatsoever was to close the schools and use them as quarters for the soldiery. Then the teachers of the village were collected together and told that their services were no longer required if they refused to teach in Greek or Servian. Those who continued to declare themselves Bulgarians were exposed to a persecution whose severity varied with the length of their resistance. Even the most intransigeant had to avow themselves beaten in the end; if not, they were sometimes allowed to depart for Bulgaria, but more usually sent to prison in Salonica or Uskub.

The most difficult people to subdue were the priests, and above all the bishops. They were first asked to change the language of divine service. Endeavors were made to subject them to the Servian or Greek ecclesiastical authorities, and they were compelled to mention their names in the liturgy. If the priest showed the smallest inclination to resist, his exarchist church was taken from him and handed over to the patriarchists; he was forbidden to hold any communication with his flock, and on the smallest disobedience was accused of political propagandism and treason. At first an open attack on the bishops was not ventured on. When Neophite, bishop of Vélès, refused to separate the name of King Peter from the names of the other kings of the allies in his prayers, and used colors in his services which were suspected of being the Bulgarian national colors, Mr. Pachitch advised the military powers at Uskub (January 4/17) to treat him as equal to the Servian bishop and with correctitude. This ministerial order, however, did not prevent the local administrator of Vélès, some weeks later (January 24/February 6 and February 4/17), from forbidding Neophite to hold services and assemblies in his bishopric, to see priests outside of the church or to hold communication with the villages. As the bishop refused to take the veiled hints given to him to depart for Bulgaria, an officer was finally sent to his house accompanied by soldiers, who took his abode for the army, after having beaten his secretary. In the same way Cosmas, bishop of Débra, was forced to abandon his seat and leave his town. It was even worse at Uskub, where the holder of the bishopric, the Archimandrite Methodius, was first driven out of his house, taken by force, shut up in a room and belabored by four soldiers until he lost consciousness (April 8/21). Cast out into the street, Methodius escaped into a neighboring house, in which a Frenchman dwelt who told the story to Mr. Carlier, French consul at Uskub. Under his protection, Methodius left for Salonica on April 13/26, whence he was sent to Sofia. The Commission has in its possession a deposition signed by the foreign doctors of Salonica who saw and examined Methodius on April 15/28, and found his story "entirely probable."[1]

The leaders, intellectual and religious, of the revolutionary movement, having been removed, the population of the villages were directly approached and urged to change their nationality and proclaim themselves Servian or Greek. The ecclesiastic Bulgarian reports written from every part of Macedonia are unanimous on this head. "You know," Bishop Neophite of Vélès said to his persecutor, "in your capacity as sub-prefect, what the Servian priests and schoolmasters are doing in the villages. They are visiting the Bulgarian villages with soldiers and forcing the people to write themselves down as Servians, drive out their Bulgarian priest and ask to have a Servian priest given them. Those who refuse to proclaim themselves Servians are beaten and tortured." We are in possession of the Servian formula of renunciation of Bulgarian nationality. This is the formula which the priests of these villages and their flocks had to address to Mr. Vincentius, the Servian metropolitan at Uskub:

> I and the flock confided to my charge by God were formerly Servian, but the terrors with which the Bulgarian *comitadjis* representing the revolutionary organization inspired us, and the violence they used towards us, compelled us and our fathers before us to turn from the patriarchate to the exarchate, thus making Bulgarians of the pure Servians we were. Thus we called ourselves Bulgars under fear of death until the arrival of our Servian army, until the moment of our liberation from the Turks. Now that we are no longer in fear of bombs, stones, and bullets, we beg your Holiness, on our own behalf and on behalf of our flocks, to deign to restore us to our Holy Church of Uskub, to restore us to the faith which we have for a time betrayed through fear of death. Kissing your holy right hand, we ask you to pray to God to pardon our sin. Signed at Sopot, March 28, 1913.

This formula was sent, in Servia, by a Servian official, Daniel Tsakits, secretary to the Malinska community at Koumanovo, to the Bulgarian priest, Nicolas Ivanov, with the following letter:

> Father Nicolas, thou shalt sign this letter that I send thee, and after thee all the villagers of Sopot are to sign likewise the Trsténitchani, the

---

[1]See the Appendix.

Piestchani, the Stanevchani, and the Alakintchani, who are thy parishioners. The whole to be ready by Saturday. Greeting from Daniel Tsakits, 27, III, 1913, Malino.

On the margin, Mr. Tsakits added that there must be twenty signatures per village and, to be the more sure of his man, gave him on the other side indications *ad oculos: e. g.:*

Priest Nicolas	Yané Troyine
Pétroche Kralo	Troyan Spasi
Ghélé Sparits	Pétrouche Yané

Trestenik.

Danil Naoumov	. . . .
. . . .	. . . .
. . . .	. . . .

Préote.

. . . .	. . . .
. . . .	. . . .
. . . .	. . . .

Stanevtsi.

. . . .	. . . .
. . . .	. . . .
. . . .	. . . .

Alakintsé.

. . . .	. . . .
. . . .	. . . .
. . . .	. . . .

"Take care that those who have signed do not make off."

The precaution was not superfluous, for priest Nicolas replied to this invitation by himself making off to Chtipe, to the protection of the Bulgarian authorities. This is what he wrote to the sub-prefect at Chtipe:

I did not desire to lead my parishioners to the Servian church. Since I could not renounce my Bulgarian nationality, I have emigrated. I should add that my family is exposed to the revenge of the Servian authorities and that my children, remaining in their birthplace, will be condemned to imprisonment at Belgrade if I do not immediately return.

The Servians have attempted to deny the authenticity of the secret Bulgarian documents cited above, and a small collection of secret Servian documents, likewise authentic, has actually been published to refute them. We shall return thereto; but upon the point that interests us it must be said that these documents only confirm what we have already said. "Anyone calling himself Bulgarian," writes a certain Peter Kotsov, a Macedonian Bulgar, in a letter of January 11/24, 1913, "risks being killed. The Servians have introduced their communal administration throughout the villages, and installed a Servian schoolmaster for every ten villages. We can not act and we are in a difficult position because the Servians have taken all the Bulgarians' arms. We do what we can, we call to the people; but we are all waiting for the Bulgarian army. Make it come as soon as possible, or we shall all be subjected by the Servians. Even the staunchest Bulgarians are ready to become Servians. The secret police has

REGIONS OCCUPÉES PAR LES BELLIGÉRANTS
FIN AVRIL 1913

numerous agents. Anyone who ventures to speak ill of the Servians exposes himself to much suffering.[1] In the South of Macedonia, in the Greek occupation zone[2] the same endeavors are being made to make the population Greek."

Here are some examples, from among thousands. A letter from the village of Dembesi (Castoria) on December 11/24, 1912, runs:

> The first care of the Greek officers and soldiers arriving here is to discover if the population of the said village and its environs is Bulgarian or Greek. If the population is pure Bulgarian, the officers order the peasants to "become Greeks again, that being the condition of a peaceful life."

Evidently here again the underlying assumption made is that the whole population was Greek in the past. "How long have you been Bulgarian?" the Greek officer asked at Khroupichta, for example. "For years," was the reply. "Return to old times then; become Greeks again," was the order thereupon. And he showed remarkable clemency. In the village of Gorno-Nestrame, when the population replied in Bulgarian to questions put in Greek, the Greek officer cried out angrily: *"Mi fonasété vourgarika"*—[Don't speak Bulgarian]: we are in Greece and anyone who speaks Bulgarian shall be off to Bulgaria. In some villages the question was put in this form: "Are you Christians or Bulgarians?" In several villages the inhabitants were made to sign petitions whose contents, unknown to them, were a demand for reunion with Greece. "What a shame," said the Greek gendarmes at Gorno-Koufalovo (March 12/25). "We have freed you. The voice of Alexander the Great calls to you from the tomb; do you not hear it? You sleep on and go on calling yourselves Bulgarians!"

Where then was the Bulgarian army for which people were crying in Macedonia and begging it to come soon, if Bulgarian Macedonia were to be saved? On the eve of the war, as we have seen, the Bulgarian General Staff insisted on having 100,000 men left free, according to the terms of the treaty, to fight back to back with the Servians in Macedonia, and thus effect a real *condominium* after the conquest. To defeat the Turks in the principal theater of war was first and foremost a matter of imperious strategic necessity. After the first

---

[1] The documents are published in an appendix to Balcanicus' book, *The Servians and Bulgarians in the Balkan War.* Our quotation is taken from the German translation *"Serbien und Bulgarien im Balkankriege, 1912–13, ins Deutsche übertragen von Dr. jur. L. Markowitsch, Wigand, Leipzig, 1913."* The French translation of the original perverts the meaning of the published documents. For example, in our quotation the first phrase (German *"Wer sich als Bulgare bekennt, dem droht die Lebensgefahr"*) is translated as "It is impossible for us to raise the people." The last phrase *"Wer was Schlechtes hier von Serben sagt, dem wird es nicht wohlergehen,"* is simply omitted.

[2] See the zones of occupation on the map (page 55) taken without alteration from Balcanicus' book to show the Servian point of view the more clearly. We have merely made the stippling rather more distinct and completed the Albanian frontier to the South, as projected at the London Conference (Balcanicus shows an Albania of which more than half is in Servian occupation), adding the line of the Serbo-Bulgarian frontier as agreed by the treaty of February 29/March 13, 1912. *Balcanicus* is the pseudonym of a well-known Servian statesman.

victories, however, and the repulsion of the Turks at Kirk Kilisse, Lulé Bourgas, Tchorlou, and Tchataldja, a new reason for continuing the war appeared. After the end of November the question might be put, as by the editor of the Bulgarian paper at Salonica, whether this was a war of liberation or of conquest. The war of liberation has in fact gained its end at Lulé Bourgas (October 31), Salonica (October 27), Monastir (October 28). Why go on pouring out the blood of hundreds of thousands of men and expending great sums of money down to the capture of Adrianople (March 13), of Yanina (February 24), Durazzo and Scutari (April 9)? The question was debated at length in all its details at Belgrade during the debates on the address at the beginning of November (new style), and at Sofia above all, in the three weeks of the election campaign (November 17–December 7). For divers reasons the two parties agreed to end the war in November, 1912, and the Servian opposition, as well as the Bulgarian opposition, tried to prove that statesmen and parties had committed a grave error in letting it drag on longer (down to May, 1913). In the first place, what had the Servians to gain by it? A discussion between the opposition orator, Mr. Drachkovits, and the deputies composing the majority in the Skupshtina (October 23/Nov. 5, 1913) will show:

> *Mr. Milorad Drachkovits:* For Bulgaria the breaking of the armistice and the new war spelt Adrianople, the most important fortress in the Balkans after Constantinople. For Bulgaria that meant the addition to the one sea she possessed of two others, and the permanent isolation of Constantinople. But what does that mean for us? What are we going to gain in compensation for the acquisition of Adrianople, of Thrace and of three seas, the desires of the Bulgarians?
>
> *A Voice from the Right:* We buy back Macedonia.
>
> *Mr. Drachkovits:* But gentlemen of the majority, we have already bought it back. We have acquired it.
>
> *Anastasius Petrovits:* And the treaty?
>
> *Mr. Drachkovits:* If you want Servia to put the treaty in force, first make Bulgaria do so. But you are freeing Bulgaria from an engagement which it contracted while making Servia responsible for an engagement into which it never entered.
>
> *Anastasius Petrovits:* It is that fact which, as the world recognizes, has given the government its most real rights over Macedonia.
>
> *Mr. Drachkovits:* We have not assisted all those who have recognized the fact; but we have assisted Bulgaria, which does not recognize it.

We shall see that it is in truth the eight months' delay which allows Servia to annul the treaty and keep the whole of Macedonia. But how do the Bulgarians come to allow the war to be thus prolonged? How did they, or rather how did their government fail to see that the occupation of Macedonia for eight months by the Servians and Greeks was going to prevent the attainment of the real end of the war,—the unification of Bulgarian nationality?

Here the case is more complex. The replies made to the attacks of Mr.

Ghénadiev by his predecessors, and especially by Mr. Theodore Théodorov, were plausible enough. Yet, it is true that Grand Vizier Kiamil asked for peace on October 29/Nov. 11, 1902. But the General Staff, among them General Savov, insisted that war should be recommenced without dragging on the *pourparlers*. You say that Turkey was ready at that time to hand over Adrianople? The case never arose. You cite as proof the mysterious mission to Constantinople of the Bulgarian banker, Mr. Kaltchev (December 10–13/23–26)? Without insisting on the fact that the government had no information about a mission that was entirely confidential (Mr. Guéchov's first act when hearing of it was to offer his resignation), Mr. Kaltchev himself and his interlocutor, Mr. Noradounghian, Foreign Minister in the Kiamil cabinet, made it known through the press that the questions at issue were the autonomy of Macedonia and Thrace and the *condominium* at Dedé-Agatch, and that there was no question of the *cession* of Adrianople.[1] Mr. Ghénadiev continued to talk of a third opportunity for negotiations: the interview between General Savov and Nazim Pasha and Noradounghian, at Tchataldja on December 26/January 8, at which the Turkish ministry resigned themselves to the abandonment of the beleaguered fortress in return for certain concessions in favor of Moslem religious establishments and subject to the undertaking that Greek pretensions to the islands were not upheld—but, Mr. Théodorov asserts, all that is false; if it were true the acceptance of conditions so equivocal would have been tantamount to a breach of alliance and would have stopped the regular negotiations going on in London.

In all these questions of fact, the last word has probably not yet been said. What is clear so far, is that in so far as Mr. Théodorov succeeded in exonerating himself, and the Danev Cabinet found excuses for missing all these happy opportunities for negotiations, it was only by means of casting the responsibility on others in higher places.

It will be seen from the preceding that by the end of 1912 there were two policies in Bulgaria: the policy of the cabinet and that of those in direct contact with the army. Ministers might be anxious to be faithful to the terms of the alliance; that consideration hardly troubled General Savov's *entourage*. The press has said a great deal about the romanticism of the latter, of Czar Ferdinand's desire to make a triumphal entry into Constantinople, of the white horses and precious Venetian saddle kept ready for the attack on Tchataldja. This followed immediately upon Kiamil's peace proposal of October 29/November 11, the prospects of which were notoriously weakened by its failure. After demanding Adrianople, a new frontier was proposed, Rodosto-Malatra, instead of Midia-Enos already adopted by international diplomacy. Such an extension of ambitions could not but hide from sight the principal object of the war. To desire to take Adrianople at whatever cost was to risk the loss of Macedonia.

---

[1]Kiamil asked that the garrison in Adrianople might be allowed to depart and passage be left free as far as Tchataldja.

To demand an outlet on the sea of Marmora was to have lost all feeling of the international position. Was it a pure chance that Macedonia was forgotten amid the secretive but remote ambitions which appeared thus unexpectedly on the horizon? A recollection of what was said in the second part of this chapter on the relations between the Bulgarian government and the revolutionary movement in Macedonia, will show that there was nothing accidental in this neglect. Distrust was ever active between the Bulgarian government and the Macedonian movement. The former was perpetually apprehensive that the *comitadjis* would involve them in internal or international complications. Now that Macedonia was on the point of being freed, everything was done to prevent the Macedonians themselves from having any direct share in the work of liberation. The reason may have lain partly in that notion of partition in Macedonia, admitted in the treaties, but unknown to the public at large, which had yet to become accustomed to it. In any case the 15,000 Macedonian volunteers who might have been left to fight in Macedonia itself, near their homes, were compelled to dwell throughout the war, far away from their villages, at Tchataldja and Boulaïr. The number of inconvenient witnesses of the work of denationalization in Macedonia was as far as possible reduced, and the taking possession of the conquered country by the Servian and Greek armies as far as possible facilitated. If the aim of these tactics was to facilitate partition, the result went beyond it. What was precipitated was the loss of Macedonia to the profit of the allies. Fear of a real liberation of the Macedonian nation brought about its conquest by the competitors. In January, the Macedonian legionaries of General Ghenev began accusing the Bulgarian government of having deceived the people in order to "sell Macedonia." In fact the government deceived only itself.

True, the Bulgarian government had no notion of making any sacrifice in turning its attention from Vélès, Monastir, Okhrida, Castoria and Florina, to which it should have been directed, to Salonica and Rodosto. They thought they could chew all they had bitten off. The members of the Russophil Guéchov-Danev cabinet believed it because they were sure of the sacredness of treaty obligations and believed that the existence of the arbitration was a sort of guarantee. The military party and public opinion were sure of the excellence of natural rights which they are ready to defend with the sword.

Were there not, nevertheless, certain premonitory signs which should have proved to the blindest the lack of prudence in combining such complete mistrust of others with such entire self confidence?

First there was the state of things in Macedonia above described. The denationalization process had gone much further there than diplomatists were willing to admit. The partition treaty had long been violated when Mr. Pachitch was still talking of introducing modifications into the treaty to save it from complete annihilation.

On September 15, 1912, that is to say, six and a half months after the conclusion of the treaty, and twenty days before the beginning of the war abroad,

Servia's representative received a secret circular demanding the incorporation in "Old Servia," beyond the agreed frontier, of the towns of Prilèpe, Kritchevo and Okhrida. With the victories of the Servian army, the list of concessions demanded rapidly lengthened. Mr. Pachitch was still only talking of Prilèpe, the town of the legendary hero, Marko Kralivits, when the army was asking for Monastir. When he asked for Monastir, the army insisted on a frontier coterminous with Greece. The government ended by accepting all the conditions laid down by the country, conditions that grew more and more exacting. The military party was powerful; it was led by the hereditary prince; and it invariably succeeded in overriding the first minister, always undecided, always temporizing and anxious to arrange everything pleasantly. The demands presented to the Bulgarians by Mr. Pachitch were as vague and indecisive as his home policy. He began in the autumn of 1912, by offering a revision of the treaty in the official organ. Then in December, in a private letter to his ambassador at Sofia, he informed Mr. Guéchov, the head of the Bulgarian cabinet, that revision was necessary. In January his ideas as to the limits within which the said revision should take place, were still undecided. In February he submitted written proposals to the Bulgarian government, and suggested that revision might be undertaken "without rousing public opinion or allowing the Great Powers to mix themselves up with the question of partition." At this moment Mr. Pachitch could still fancy that he had the solution of the conflict in his hand. He was to lose this illusion. His colleague was already writing his "Balcanicus" pamphlet in which he took his stand on the clause *pacta servanda sunt*, with the reservation *rebus sic stantibus*, and pointing to the changes in the disposition of the allied armies between the two theaters of war (see above), as infractions of the treaty which must lead to revision. In his speech of May 29, Mr. Pachitch ended by accepting this reasoning. At the same time the military authorities in Macedonia had decided to hold on. On February 27/ March 12, they told the population of Vélès that the town would remain in Servia. On April 3/16, Major Razsoukanov, Bulgarian attaché with the General Staff of the Servian army at Uskub, told his government that his demands were not even answered with conditional phrases. "This is provisional, until it has been decided to whom such and such a village belongs" (in the Chtip or Doïran areas). Major Razsoukanov learned that at the instance of the General Staff the Belgrade government had decided on the rivers Zletovska, Bregalnitsa and Lakavitsa, as the definite eastern limit of the occupation territory. The interesting correspondence published by Balcanicus in his pamphlet (see above) refers to the forced execution of this resolution in the disputed territories during the month of March. We have here, on the one hand, the Bulgarian *comitadjis* begging, according to the advice of the above letter, for the arrival of the Bulgarian force and trying, in its absence, to do its work, well or ill; on the other, the Servian army, setting up Servian administration in the villages, closing the Bulgarian schools, driving out the *comitadjis* and "reëstablishing order."

Between the two parties, contending in a time of peace, stood the population, forced to side with one or the other and naturally inclining to the stronger. Mr. Razsoukanov (who gives us confirmation of the methods employed by the Servian administration to "round off" the frontiers of the occupied territory) notes also the predominant state of mind of the army of occupation. According to him "the military party in Servia, with the heir apparent as its head," did not stop here. It "dreams of and works for a 'Great Servia' with the river Strouma at least as its frontier." "To insure possession of the occupied territories the Servians had to discover some compromise with the Greeks, and one was found." Mr. Razsoukanov was the first to make us acquainted with facts now confirmed by the Roumanian "Green Book." He states that—"I am inclined to believe that there was, over and above the treaty concluded between the 'military leagues' of the two countries, a similar agreement between the governments and the armies. That was why General Poutnik went, on March 9/22, to 'inspect' the garrison at Monastir, where there was barely a regiment, and the heir apparent had also gone on two occasions, likewise for 'inspection.' I rather think that in the special train, with which General Poutnik was provided by the Greeks, 'something' was decided between the two allies, to the disadvantage of the absent third; and that it was this special train, Salonica to Monastir, which the General went to 'inspect.' It is a fact that the Servian ambassador at Bucharest did on March 24/April 6, propose to Roumania a treaty of alliance against Bulgaria, and that on April 19/May 2, the Greek ambassador made the same proposition. Mr. Venizelos, on his part, confessed to the Chamber that Prince Nicholas—one of the interlocutors on board the 'special trains,'—as military governor of Salonica, largely contributed in the preparations of the Greek-Servian convention. This convention was concluded on May 16/29."

Evidently war was preparing. The Servian General Staff employed the time in fortifying the central position at Ovtché-Polé. The Greeks, after increasing their Macedonian army by the addition of the regiments released by the capture of Yanina, also tried to take up advanced positions in the area of Bulgarian occupation, at Pravishta and Nigrita. The *pourparlers* with Turkey, which had been resumed in London, were dragged on to give time to complete these preparations. On May 6, the Servian General Staff laid down the preliminary dispositions for concentrating to the east of Uskub. From May 15, a military convention and plan of concerted operations with Greece were under discussion. The Bulgarians, on the other hand, hastened to make peace with the Turks; this agreed, they diverted their armies from Adrianople and Tchataldja towards Macedonia and the Serbo-Bulgarian frontier. On either side preparations were made when a final diplomatic duel took place. Throughout, the opening of hostilities was never lost to sight. On May 12/25, Mr. Pachitch finally despatched to Sofia propositions relative to the revision of the treaty. He justified the new Servian demands by two classes of reasons. First, the clauses of the treaty had been modified in application; secondly, external circumstances not foreseen by the treaty had profoundly changed its tenor. The clauses of the treaty had been violated by the fact that the Bulgarians had not given the Servians military assistance, while the Servians for their part had aided the Bulgarians. The refusal to leave the Adriatic on the part of the Servians, and the occupations of Adrianople and Thrace by the Bulgarians, constituted two new violations of the treaty. Servia then was entitled to territorial compensation; first, because the Bulgarians had not rendered the promised aid; second, because Servia had assisted the Bulgarians; third, because Servia had lost the Adriatic littoral while Bulgaria had acquired Thrace. This time Mr. Pachitch was in accord with public opinion. This same public opinion had its influence on the Bulgarian government. Since the treaty of February 29/March 13 remained secret, the public could not follow the juridical casuistry based on a commentary on this or that ambiguous phrase in the text. The public renounced the treaty *en bloc* and would have nothing to do with the "contested zone." If the Servians transgressed the terms of the treaty in their demands Bulgarian diplomatists greatly inclined to act in the same way. If the Servians demanded an outlet on the Ægean as a necessary condition of existence after the loss of their outlet on the Adriatic, and insisted on a coterminous frontier with Greece to secure it, Mr. Danev left the allies and contravened the terms of the treaty when he laid before the Powers in London a demand for a frontier coterminous with Albania in the Débra region. At the same time Mr. Danev went against his ministerial colleagues and followed the military authorities in refusing to hand over Salonica. Austria appeared to have promised it him, after promising the Vardar plain to Servia. Thus on the one hand complications and broils were being introduced by the perversion to megalomania of the National Ideal: on the other (this was the standpoint of Guéchov and Théodorov), there was the endeavor to safeguard the alliance. With Servia drawing near to Greece, Bulgaria had to join hands with Roumania if it were not to find itself isolated in the peninsula. This was what Austria Hungary wanted, and it favored the policy. Roumania accepted, but on condition of receiving the recompense assured it by a secret convention with Austria in the event of war with Bulgaria: annexation of the Tourtoukai-Baltchik line. On these conditions Roumania would remain neutral; it even promised military assistance against Turkey! But Turkey was defeated and the Ministry pretended not to want to war with the allies. Why then sacrifice the richest bit of Bulgarian territory? Austria's effort broke against these hypocritical and formal—or too simple—arguments. At bottom war was believed to be inevitable and Russia, it was thought, would do the rest. Russia threatened Bulgaria with Roumanian invasion, if it came to war. By the end of May, Russian diplomacy made a final effort to avoid conflict. While agreeing to play the part of arbiter within the limits of the alliance, Russia gave counsels of prudence. Go beyond the Servian demands for compensation, they said: despite the implicit promise the Servians made you of demanding nothing beyond what the treaty gave them, agree to cede some towns outside the "contested zone," "beyond" the frontier which they had promised not to "violate."

This Russian solution, which could not satisfy the Servians, had not much chance of being accepted by the Bulgarians. The attitude taken by Russia filled the opposing parties with some doubts as to the impartiality of its arbitration. The Servians were sure that Russia had not forgotten the Bulgaria of San Stefano and the Bulgarians could not use Macedonia as a medium of exchange on the international market. On both sides the conviction was reached that the issue must be sought in armed conflict.

There was, however, one last attempt at avoiding open strife: the two initiators of the treaty of alliance, Pachitch and Guéchov, arranged a meeting at Tsaribrod on the frontier. They wanted to try to reach a friendly solution of the difficulties, without any "public" or "Powers." Alas, what was possible in the month of February was no longer so in May. In the first place the "public" of the political parties was there, in Belgrade, and they did not want to leave Pachitch *tête-à-tête* with the Bulgarian Premier. Before starting for Tsaribrod he had to read to the Skupshtina a summary of his reasons for a revision of the treaty; they were the same he had addressed to Sofia three days earlier (see above). But thus to divulge the secrets of diplomatic correspondence was to cut off the retreat. In such circumstances the speech of May 15/28 was the death-blow to the pacifist hopes of Mr. Guéchov on the eve of departure for Tsaribrod. The words attributed to Mr. Pachitch in an interview in an Agram paper are not at all improbable. "I was certain," he is reported to have said, "that the Bulgarians would reply by a declaration of war." Mr. Guéchov's situation was hardly more brilliant. He, too, had to fight at Sofia against a war party; but he was not going to make concessions. When he learned on May 17/30 that the Czar Ferdinand had received the leaders of the opposition on the previous evening and received their counsels of war with approval, Mr. Guéchov handed in his resignation. Mr. Pachitch did not know that on May 20/June 2, at Tsaribrod, he was speaking to an ex-Minister. Yet another issue or rather a means of delaying events was discovered: to hold a conference of the prime ministers of the allied States. On May 22/June 4, Mr. Guéchov's resignation was known to all. With him the last hope of escaping war disappeared.

At this moment the Czar of Russia made a final effort. On May 26/June 8, he sent a telegram to the Kings of Servia and Bulgaria in which, while noting the suggested meeting at Salonica and its eventual continuation at St. Petersburg, he reminded them that they were bound to submit their findings to his arbitrament. He stated solemnly that "the State which begins the war will answer for its conduct to Slavdom." He reserved to himself entire freedom to decide what attitude Russia would take up in view of the "possible consequences of this criminal strife." The secret diplomatic correspondence explains this threat. If Servia will not submit to Russian arbitration "it will risk its existence." If it is Bulgaria that resists, "it will be attacked, in the war with the allies, by Roumania and Turkey."

The threat was understood at Belgrade but merely created irritation. "Russia holds over us," it was said there, "the ever threatening danger of Austria's neighborhood, and because she knows that if she abandons us, our enemies across the Danube will hasten to exercise the severest pressure upon us, she thinks she can neglect us. * * * All favors go to the Bulgarians. We can not go any further in this direction. We have given way on the Albanian question, we can not give way in Macedonia. We can not condemn ourselves to national suicide because at St. Petersburg or at Tsarskoie-Sélo it has been so decided."[1]

In view of the tendencies of the militarist party, Mr. Pachitch sent in his resignation in his turn, on June 2/15. But the Russian Ambassador, Mr. Hartwig, was there to show the gravity of the situation and persuade the King, the members of the cabinet, the deputies, to yield to Russia's demands and unreservedly accept arbitration. Mr. Pachitch remained, and on June 8/21, Belgrade declared its willingness to accept arbitration; "without inwardly believing in it," as the Agram interviewer adds. And Mr. de Penennrun said "Mr. Pachitch had no more desire than Mr. Danev to betake himself to St. Petersburg. As a matter of fact although he endeavored to put himself in agreement with the critics and opponents in the Skupshtina, at the close of the eventful session of June 17/30, Mr. Pachitch declared that he in no way abandoned the point of view set out in his summary of May 15/28, and had accepted arbitration only because he had become convinced first, that it would proceed on an extended basis rather than within the limits laid down in Art. 4 of the secret annex to the treaty; and second, on condition that the "spheres of direction in Russia" agreed to consider the Greek-Bulgarian conflict *at the same time* as the Serbo-Bulgarian.

On this point the new allies had agreed; and Mr. Venizelos confirmed it in a paragraph communicated on the same day to the *Temps*. After Mr. Pachitch's explanations and the subsequent discussion in which the demand voiced was for the annexation of Macedonia rather than for arbitration (Mr. Ribaratz); and after it had been stated (Mr. Paul Marinkovits) that "the Servian people would rather trust to its victorious army than to the well known tactlessness of Mr. Pachitch," the Skupshtina reverted to the order of the day of a month previous. It renewed its decision "not to allow the vital interests of Servia to be abused." Mr. Drachkovits explained this condition which he laid down as follows: "The valley of the Vardar is a vital interest for Servia, and any arbitrament which leaves this vital need out of account *could not be accepted*." Some minutes before. Pachitch received in the chamber the telegram informing him of the

---

[1]These characteristic terms were recorded, some weeks later, at Belgrade by Mr. de Penennrun. See his book, *Quarante jours de guerre dans les Balkans*. Chapelot, Paris, 1914.

outbreak of hostilities. Turning pale, he withdrew. Arbitration then would not take place, and it would not be Servia's fault.

At Sofia, in fact, for military reasons to be explained, the final agony had been reached more quickly than at Belgrade. Here events were precipitated by conflict between the cabinet and the military party. As to the aim to be attained there was unanimity. The Servians must be forced to carry out the treaty and evacuate Macedonia to the south of the frontier agreed upon. But no agreement could be reached as to the means. Mr. Guéchov's favorite tactics were to temporize. We have seen how under the circumstances of debate precious time had been lost both by Guéchov and Pachitch. If concessions to Servia were to be made, they ought to have been made in January or at latest in February, when Mr. Pachitch proposed to act apart from the "public and the Powers," and while negotiations would still be undertaken under the most favorable conditions. If no concession was to be made, means should have been devised for resolving by force what it had been determined to regard as a question of force—"eine Macht-frage." It was then time to think of alliances and neutralities and pay for them with temporary concessions. It was necessary to know how not to yield to certain ambitions. Neither one nor the other was done. When Mr. Danev became Prime Minister, he took up with his portfolio an ambiguous position which Mr. Guéchov had rightly refused: that of working for war while remaining a partisan of peace. This internal contradiction was bound to act fatally and to paralyze those who believed in action and those who opposed it alike. Mr. Danev, and, to an even greater extent, his colleague, Mr. Théodorov, continued to the end convinced that they could keep all they had acquired. Mr. Danev even wanted to get more—without risking war. The militarists knew better.

A telegram of June 8/21 from General Savov to the commander of the fourth army, describes the state of things as follows:

> I. There is an alliance between the Servians and the Greeks whose object is to hold and divide the whole territory of Macedonia on the right bank of the Vardar with the addition of Uskub, Koumanova, Kratovo and Kriva Palonka for the Servians; Salonica and the regions of Pravishta and Nigrita for the Greeks. II. The Servians do not recognize the treaty and do not admit arbitration within the limits of the treaty. III. We insist that the arbitrators start from the basis laid down in the treaty, i. e., concern themselves solely with the contested zone. Since the non-contested territory belongs to us according to the treaty, we desire that it should be evacuated by the Servians or, at least, occupied by mixed armies for such time as the *pourparlers* are going on. We make the same proposition to the Greeks. IV. These questions must be settled within ten days and in our sense, or war is inevitable. Thus within ten days we shall have either war or demobilization, according as the government's demands are accepted or refused. V. If we demobilize now the territories mentioned will remain in the hands of the Greeks and the Servians, since it is difficult to suppose

that they will be peacefully handed over to us. VI. The discontent which
has recently manifested itself in certain parts of the army gives ground for
supposing that there is a serious agitation against war. The attention of
intelligent soldiers must be directed to the fact that should the army become
disorganized and incapable of action, the result will be as described in
paragraph v. Reply with the least possible delay whether the state of the
army is such that it can be counted on for successful operations.

The point of particular interest in this document is the indication afforded
of the state of mind of the Bulgarian army, which explains why the commander
was particularly anxious to have the question settled. Harvest time approached
and the Bulgarian soldier who, after what he had suffered and endured during
the long months of winter and spring at Tchataldja and Boulaïr, had then, instead
of returning home, been compelled to join the army on the western frontier,
had had enough. One thing or the other: it was war or demobilization: but in
any case there must be an immediate decision, for uncertainty had become intolerable. This state of mind was general and several officers told Mr. Bourchier what he repeated in the *Times,* "If the question is not decided in a week,
General Savov will no longer have an army."

It was under these circumstances that Mr. Danev summoned the Council of
Ministers on the morning of June 9/22. He told his colleagues that after a
sleepless night he had come to the conclusion that since, even after arbitration,
it was more than likely that Servia would make war on them, it was better to
carry it on now. Were the army once demobilized it would be difficult to bring
it together again in the autumn. In such conditions whatever was done must
be done at once. Clearly Mr. Danev was expressing the ideas of Savov. Mr.
Théodorov's reply was to the point. War between Christians would be shameful after the war of liberation. They ought to go to St. Petersburg: they would
get all they wanted there. If, afterwards, the Servians refused to conform to the
decision of the arbiter, all Europe would be on Bulgaria's side. All the other
ministers plead for peace with one exception,—Mr. Khritov, who represented
the war party in the Council and who was not allowed to speak by Mr. Danev,
who knew him. Mr. Danev then betook himself to the Czar's summer palace
at Vrana, near Sofia, to make his report. General Savov was also present. At
three o'clock in the afternoon Mr. Théodorov was summoned to explain the
reasons of the "populist" party *against* war. Mr. Théodorov emphasized the
reasons for going to St. Petersburg. Mr. Danev and General Savov gave their
consent thereto. They returned to Sofia; the Council was resumed; the Russian
Ambassador was summoned and the Council's decision communicated to him.
A demand was added, the significance of which is comprehensible enough after
what had been said, but which appeared to St. Petersburg in the guise of an
ultimatum. The demand was that the arbiter should publish his opinion within
eight days. It was added that Mr. Danev would start in three days. This was
nearly the "ten days" of Mr. Savov's telegram. Mr. Nécloudov then communi-

cated the agreeable news that Servia accepted arbitration unreservedly. The Russian government gave the Servian and Bulgarian governments four days in which to prepare their memoranda for the arbiter. On June 11/24, Mr. Théodorov received a fresh letter from the Bulgarian Embassy at St. Petersburg which strengthened his view and which he read to the Council of Ministers on the same day. It was stated there: "War will be our loss." "The Emperor and the Russian government have decided to arbitrate in conformity with and within the limits of the treaty. It was desirable to come at once since 'the absent are always in the wrong.' Otherwise Russia will not protect you in any way, France will give you no money, England and Germany will abandon you to your own resources. Since in this case Germany stands with the Triple Alliance no one can checkmate Russia's policy; Austria Hungary will not go beyond Platonic promises and Roumania finally will certainly occupy your territories while Russia can not defend you." (This letter referred to a report addressed to Mr. Danev a week previous.)

All this was opportunely said. These prognostics were later confirmed by facts. But those at Sofia who desired war drew one conclusion only,—Russia did not desire a strong Bulgaria; Bulgaria *fara da se*. The peace party was terrorized by the Macedonian patriots, who threatened to kill Danev at the station when he started for St. Petersburg, and to march the army on Sofia. Public opinion with few exceptions was for war. Under these circumstances the heads of the war party were ready for any risk. The timid and half initiated were told that half measures only were in contemplation, which would lead to skirmishings such as had frequently occurred with Servians and Greeks on the disputed frontiers. If anyone thought thus, he reckoned without his host.

On June 15/28, General Savov sent the following telegram to the commander of the fourth army:

> In order that our silence under Servian attacks may not produce a bad effect on the state of mind of the army, and on the other hand to avoid encouraging the enemy, I order you to attack the enemy all along the line as energetically as possible, without deploying all your forces or producing a prolonged engagement. Try to establish a firm footing on Krivolak on the right bank of the Bregalnitsa. It is preferable that you undertake a fusillade in the evening and make an impetuous attack on the whole line during the night and at daybreak. The operation to be undertaken tomorrow, 16th, in the evening.

The order to the second army is mentioned by General Savov in another telegram sent on the following day, the 16th, and even more interesting as it displays the motives which led the war party to risk action or supplied them with justifications. "In direction 24, I ordered the fourth army to pursue offensive operations and the second army as soon as it had completed its operations on Tchayasa, to begin immediately concentrating on the line marked out in order to attack Salonica. Messieurs the Generals are to bear in mind that our operations against the Servians and Greeks are undertaken without a formal declaration of war, mainly for the following reasons: (I) to bring the state of mind of the army up to a certain point and put them in a position (literal translation) to regard our allies up to today as enemies; (II) to accelerate the decisions of Russian policy by the fear of war between the allies; (III) to inflict heavy blows upon our adversaries in order to compel them to treat the more readily and make concessions; (IV) since our enemies are in occupation of territories which belong to us let us try by our arms to seize new territory until the European powers intervene to stop our military action. Since early intervention can be foreseen, it is necessary to act quickly and energetically. The fourth army must do all in its power to take Vélès at any cost, because of the great political significance of such a conquest. If the operations of the fourth army permit the second will receive the order to attack Salonica."

Re-reading this, the confused and childish reasoning of a general wishing to play the politician, it is now difficult to believe that the questions of war and peace were thus decided. General Savov said later that he merely followed an order—then he was silent. A story was told in his name that the order was given by King Ferdinand, and that he was threatened with a court-martial if he disobeyed it. During the election campaign at the end of 1913 public attention was almost exclusively occupied with the question of responsibility for June 16/29 and people were at great pains to discover the culprit. The investigation is not yet complete, and we need not linger over the more or less probable rumors current. To seek for a single culprit, however, is a mistaken method, inadequate to throw light on the deeper causes of the Bulgarian national catastrophe. Not one day in June alone, but the whole course of the two wars must be surveyed in the search for the culprit. As has been said a war of liberation became a war of conquest for the satisfaction of personal ambition: but its causes, too, lay in strategic necessities; in legitimate tendencies implicit in the traditional national policy; in the auto-hypnosis of a people which had never experienced a reverse and was intoxicated by successes, justly recognized by all the world for their military glory; in a misjudgment of their opponents based on well known facts in the past and ignorance of the present; in a word in that profound belief in their cause and their star which is a part of the national character.

The events which followed on the fatal 16 and 17/29 and 30 June, may be recalled in a few words. On the evening of the 17th the pacificist ministers learned with astonishment that while Mr. Danev was preparing to start for St. Petersburg and a Russian gunboat was waiting at Varna to convey him to Odessa, war had broken out on the frontier. On the morning of the 18th, the Council of Ministers met and after a very lively discussion in the course of which the cabinet threatened to resign, General Savov was forced to give an order stopping the offensive. The General himself was retired for having given the order. At the same time the Russian government tried to stop the movements of the Greek and Servian armies by the exercise of diplomatic pressure at Athens and Belgrade. There being no sanction behind the action, it was ineffectual. Two days before the outbreak of hostilities, Roumania, encouraged by Russia, declared to Bulgaria that she reserved for herself entire liberty of action in the event of war. Full advantage was taken of this, and it soon proved much more difficult to stop Roumania once in action, than to induce her to act. Next, Turkey showed itself more and more aggressive and intransigeant. A veritable avalanche of misfortunes indeed descended upon Bulgaria. A few more dates must be added. On July 1 the Greeks fell upon the Bulgarian garrison at Salonica, massacred several soldiers and took the rest prisoner. The Bulgarians could not hold the positions behind the rivers Zletovska, Bregalnitsa, Kriva Lakavitsa; they were stopped and driven back after several days' assault. On July 7 and 8, the Servian army took the offensive. On July 9, the Servians took Radovitch, the Greeks Strumnitsa. On July 11, the Roumanian army completed its mobilization and crossed the Bulgarian frontier without encountering any opposition. On July 12, the Turkish army of Tchataldja began re-conquering Thrace. On July 21, it was at Lulé Bourgas and Kirk Kilisse; on the 22d, it recaptured Adrianople, which had been hastily evacuated by the Bulgarians. On July 14, the Servians took Kriva Pahanka. On July 11, Bulgaria made its first appeal for help to Europe. On the 23d of July, Ferdinand appealed to the Czar to mediate. Without waiting for the results of this last proposal Mr. Danev resigned in despair. On the 15th during the five days of the crisis the enemies' armies continued their march and the Roumanians advanced on Sofia. A telegram from King Ferdinand to Francis Joseph demanded mediation for Roumania: on his advice, Ferdinand sent a telegram directly to King Carol. He demanded the cession of the triangle Danube-Tourtoukai-Baltchik as the condition of peace. His proposition was accepted on July 21, but the Bulgarians had still to fight the Greeks who had reached the frontiers of the Kingdom at Djouma-ya (25–30), while the Servians were besieging Vidine. Negotiations were at last opened at Bucharest on July 30, and a five days' armistice signed at mid-day on July 31. On August 4 it was extended for four days. The Peace of Bucharest was signed on August 10, and peace with Turkey concluded September 29, 1913. The reader may compare the boundaries established by these treaties (see the map) with the areas of occupation three months before the war. The extent of Bulgaria's losses is clear. Those who won claimed that "balance in the Balkans" had been secured, an end made of pretensions to hegemony, and peace thus secured for the future. Unhappily a nearer examination leads rather to the conclusion that the treaty of Bucharest has created a condition of things that is far from being durable. If the Bulgarian "conquest" is almost annulled by it, the Greek and Servian "conquests" are not well established. A later chapter (The War and the Nationalities) will afford abundant proof of this, and to it we refer the reader for conclusions.

TERRITORIAL MODIFICATIONS

IN THE BALKANS

1. CONFERENCE OF LONDON   2. TREATY OF BUKAREST

CHAPTER II

The War and the Noncombatant Population

1. THE PLIGHT OF THE MACEDONIAN MOSLEMS DURING THE FIRST WAR

The first of the Balkan campaigns was accepted by European opinion as a War of Liberation. It meant the downfall on one continent of the Turkish Empire; it was easy, as victory succeeded victory, to believe that it meant also the end of all the oppressions of race by race which for five centuries had made the history of the Balkans a record of rebellion, repression, and massacre. On a close view of what happened in Macedonia, as the Balkan armies marched southward, this War of Liberation assumes a more sordid and familiar aspect. It unleashed the accumulated hatreds, the inherited revenges of centuries. It made the oppressed Christians for several months the masters and judges of their Moslem overlords. It gave the opportunity of vengeance to every peasant who cherished a grudge against a harsh landlord or a brutal neighbor. Every Bulgarian village in northern Macedonia had its memory of sufferings and wrongs. For a generation the insurgent organization had been busy, and the normal condition of these villages had been one of intermittent revolt. The inevitable Turkish reprisals had fallen now on one village and now on another. Searches for arms, beatings, tortures, wholesale arrests, and occasional massacres, were the price which these peasants paid for their incessant struggle toward self-government. In all these incidents of repression, the local Moslems had played their part, marching behind the Turkish troops as *bashi-bazouks* and joining in the work of pillage and slaughter. Their record was not forgotten when the Bulgarian victories brought the chance of revenge. To the hatred of races there was added the resentment of the peasantry against the landlords (beys), who for generations had levied a heavy tribute on their labor and their harvests. The defeat of the Turkish armies meant something more than a political change. It reversed the relations of conqueror and serf; it promised a social revolution.

Only the utmost vigilance exercised by a disciplined army and a resolute police could have checked the natural impulse toward vengeance among the liberated Macedonians. In point of fact, the measures adopted by the Bulgarian government to protect the local Moslem population in northern and central Macedonia were inadequate and belated. The regular army was not numerous, and it marched rapidly southwards toward Salonica, leaving no sufficient garrisons behind it. No attempt had been made to embody the insurgent bands in regular corps, and they were left free over a broad and populous area to deal with the local Turks as their own instincts dictated.   Civil officials arrived to organize a regular administration in some cases a full six weeks after the Turkish authority had disappeared.   It is not surprising in these conditions, that the Moslem population endured during the early weeks of the war a period of lawless vengeance and unmeasured suffering.   In many districts the Moslem villages were systematically burned by their Christian neighbors.   Nor was it only the regions occupied by the Bulgarians which suffered.   In the province of Monastir, occupied by the Serbs and Greeks, the agents of the (British) Macedonian Relief Fund calculated that eighty per cent of Moslem villages were burned. Salonica, Monastir, and Uskub were thronged with thousands of homeless and starving Moslem refugees, many of whom emigrated to Asia.   The Moslem quarter of the town of Jenidje Vardar was almost totally burned down, in spite of the fact that this town was occupied by the main Greek army.   Even in the immediate neighborhood of Salonica, Moslem villages were burned by the Greek troops.   (See Appendix A, No. 12.)   The Greek population of the Drama district indulged in robbery, murder and violation at the expense of the Moslem inhabitants, until order was restored by an energetic Bulgarian prefect. (See Appendix B, No. 16.)

A curious document (Appendix A, No. 13a) drawn up by the officials of the Moslem community of Pravishta and sealed with its seal, gives a vivid impression of a kind of persecution which we believe to have been normal in the early months of the first war.   The district of Pravishta lies along the coast to the west of Kavala and is inhabited by about 20,000 Moslems and about 7,000 Greeks. It was occupied at first by Bulgarian bands under a *voyévoda* (chief) named Baptchev, and afterwards in part by Bulgarian and in part by Greek troops. Such civil administration as there was in the early stages of the conquest was conducted by the Greek Bishop, whom Baptchev obeyed, though with some measure of independence.   This document gives particulars, village by village, of the Moslems who were killed and robbed.   The lists are detailed, and give the names not only of the victims but of the assassins.   Some of the particulars of the robberies are also given in great detail, and in one village even the color of the stolen cows is stated.   Our experience shows that lists of this kind in the Balkans are usually accurate.   Exaggeration begins only when peasants attempt to give estimates in round numbers.   The number of Moslems killed in each village varied from one to twenty-five, and the damage done by robbery and looting from hundreds to thousands of pounds.

In the villages all these excesses seem to have been the work of local Greek bands.   The most active of these bands was led by a priest and a warlike grocer who was a member of the Bishop's council.   The Turks indeed accuse the Bishop of directing all these atrocities.   The total number of Moslems killed is 195.   Baptchev, in contrast to some other Bulgarian leaders of bands, appears to have behaved relatively well. His exactions or robberies amounted to about £T6,000, but he killed only in ten cases after the Bishop and his Council had passed sentence, and it is said of him and his men that they did no violence to women, and even rescued two from the Greeks. It is also said that Moslem women fled to escape violation from villages held by Greek troops to villages held by Bulgarian soldiers. While we think it probable that this document is accurate and truthful, it must be remembered that it is an *ex parte* statement. The Turks imply that the motive for the slaughter was simply a desire to intimidate their community by striking at its heads. But it is likely that the local Greeks had long standing grievances against many of these Turks. Vengeance and cupidity had probably as much to do with these excesses as policy. No villages appear to have been burned in this district, but enough was done to make the local Moslems feel that their lot was unendurable.

The burning of villages and the exodus of the defeated population is a normal and traditional incident of all Balkan wars and insurrections. It is the habit of all these peoples. What they have suffered themselves, they inflict in turn upon others. It could have been avoided only by imperative orders from Athens, Belgrade, and Sofia, and only then if the church and the insurgent organization had seconded the resolve of the governments. A general appeal for humanity was in fact published by the Macedonian insurgent "Internal Organization," but it appears to have produced little effect.

Devastation, unfortunately, was not the worst of the incidents which stained the War of Liberation. More particularly in northeastern Macedonia the victorious population undertook a systematic proscription of the Moslems. The Commission has before it full evidence of one of these campaigns of murder at Strumnitsa. It was probably the worst incident of its kind, but it is typical of much that happened elsewhere on a smaller scale. Our information comes (1) from the surviving Moslem notables of the town, who gave us their evidence personally (see Appendix A, Nos. 1 and 2); (2) from an American gentleman who visited the town shortly afterwards; and (3) from a Bulgarian official. Strumnitsa in the autumn of 1912 was under a mixed control; the garrison was Servian; there was a junior Bulgarian civil official; and Bulgarian insurgents were present in large numbers. A commission was formed under the presidency of the Servian commander, Major Grbits, and with him there sat two junior Servian officers, the Bulgarian sub-prefect Lieutenant Nicholas Voultchev, the leader of the Bulgarian bands, *voyévoda* Tchekov (or Jekov), and some of the leading inhabitants. The local Moslems of the town were disarmed by a house to house search. Some indiscriminate killing of Moslems took place in the streets, and thereafter an order was issued forbidding any Moslem to leave his house, under pain of death. A local *gendarmerie* was meanwhile organized, and while the Moslems passively awaited their fate, a *gendarme* and a Servian soldier went from house to house summoning them one by one before the commission. As each victim came before the judges, Major Grbits inquired, "Is he good, or is he bad?" There was no discussion and no defense. Each member had his personal enemies, and no one ventured to interfere with his neighbor's resentments. One voice sufficed to condemn. Hardly one in ten of those who were summoned escaped the death sentence. The victims were roughly stripped of their outer clothing and bound in the presence of the commission, while the money found on them was taken by Major Grbits. The condemned Moslems were bound in threes, taken to the slaughter house and there killed, in some cases after torture and mutilation. The fortunate minority received a certificate which permitted them to live, and in many cases there is reason to believe that as much as £T100 was paid for it. The motive behind these atrocities was clearly as much as cupidity as race hatred. The victims included not only the citizens of Strumnitsa, but also a large number of fugitives and prisoners from the surrounding villages. Our Turkish witnesses place the total of killed at the improbable figure of 3,000 to 4,000—a guesswork estimate. Our American and Bulgarian informants, who were both in a position to make a careful calculation, placed the total of those killed in this proscription at from seven to eight hundred. It is fair to add that steps were afterwards taken by the Bulgarian courts-martial to prosecute the guilty Bulgarian official, Voultchev, and the Bulgarian chief of bands, Tchekov, and a third person named Manov. All three have been sentenced to fifteen years' hard labor. The Servian government, on the other hand, has inflicted no punishment on Major Grbits, who was the senior officer and the person ultimately responsible for these atrocities.

The result of leaving Bulgarian bands at large with no adequate control was, if possible, still worse in the Kukush (Kilkish) region. Only a few Bulgarian regulars were left to garrison the town during the early weeks of the war, and the only authority which could make itself obeyed was that which the chief of bands, Toma of Istip, exercised with the aid of a commission of local Bulgarian notables. It drew up lists for the whole district, in which each of the Moslem inhabitants was rated at a certain figure, which might be represented as a poll-tax, but was in effect a ransom. To pay this ransom the Turks were often obliged to sell everything they possessed. Later, a band arrived under a certain Donchev, a notoriously cruel guerrilla chief, who acted on his own responsibility and has been disavowed and sentenced to death by the Macedonian revolutionary "internal organization." He is said to have burned 345 Turkish houses in one day in the villages of Raionovo, Planitsa, and Kukurtevo, shut up the men in the mosques and burned them alive or shot them down as they attempted to escape. It is said that Donchev's band massacred women and children; and this statement also is credited by Europeans who have ample local sources of information. An account of these events by Père Michel, the head of the French Catholic mission at Kukush, has been published. (See Appendix A, No. 6.) It was misused and distorted in some Greek and French newspapers, as though it referred to the doings of the Bulgarian regular army shortly before the second war. It was undoubtedly a truthful account of the excesses of the Bulgarian bands during the autumn of 1912.

A statement from a local Turk, who was recommended to us as an honest witness by a European resident, will be found in Appendix A (No. 7). Père Michel's statements, it should be added, were generally corroborated by the Protestant missionaries who worked in the same district. The Bulgarian bands in the Kukush region were left for some weeks unmolested in this work of extortion and extermination. There is ample proof that they slaughtered many hundreds of disarmed and disbanded Turkish soldiers, who had surrendered to the Greeks at Salonica, and were traveling through Kukush on their way to their homes in northern Macedonia.

The responsibility of the regular Bulgarian authorities is more directly indicated in the massacre of Turks which took place in the town of Serres shortly after its capture. Here there was an adequate Bulgarian garrison, and a regular administration. We have before us a full statement from the President of the Turkish community of Serres, which is confirmed by the Austrian vice-consul (a Greek), and other Greek residents. Their evidence is inevitably biased and exaggerated, but it was unfortunately confirmed in its main outlines by a confidential statement made to us by an American gentleman, who was active after the massacre in relieving the distress among the Moslems. The events which preceded the massacre are very obscure. Mysterious shots were fired, and a large number of Turkish soldiers were supposed (we do not know with what truth) to be in hiding in the town. On a charitable reading of the facts it is fair to suppose that the Bulgarian authorities feared a revolt. This may explain but can not excuse the slaughter which followed. The Turkish version of this affair will be found in Appendix A (No. 8). The estimates given by Turks and Greeks, which range from 600 to 5,000 killed, are certainly exaggerated. Our American informant, a cautious and fair-minded man, with a long and intimate experience of Macedonia, believed that the number of killed in the town was, at most two hundred. He insisted, however, that the massacre was deliberate and unprovoked, and that it was accompanied by pillage on a large scale and by the violation of many Turkish women and children. Similar excesses were perpetrated in the villages. The instruments of this atrocity were chiefly Macedonian insurgents (comitadjis), but they acted under the eyes of the Bulgarian military authorities, who had in Serres a regular force sufficient to control them.

These instances should suffice to give some idea of the sufferings of the Moslem population during the early weeks of the occupation. It would unfortunately be easy to multiply them. Details will be found in the Appendices of a minor massacre, much exaggerated in the press, carried out at Dedeagatch by the dregs of the local Christian population (Greeks and Armenians) with the aid of some Bulgarian privates of the Macedonian legion, who were accidentally left in the town without an officer (Appendix A, Nos. 9 and 10). A Bulgarian eye witness described to us the killing of a large number of local Turks at Uskub by Servians in the early days of the occupation (Appendix A, No. 11).

Incidents also occurred while Bulgarian regiments were on the march which led to savage reprisals. A volunteer of the Macedonian legion (*Opolchenie*), who was previously known to a member of the Commission as an honorable and truthful man, recounted the following incident as the one example of brutality which had come within his own experience. While marching through Gumurjina, the legion saw the dead bodies of about fifty murdered Bulgarian peasants. The dead body of a woman was hanging from a tree, and another with a young baby lay dead on the ground with their eyes gouged out. The men of the legion retaliated by shooting all the Turkish villagers or disbanded soldiers whom they met next day on their march, and killed in this way probably some fifty men and two or three women. The officers of the legion endeavored afterwards to discover the culprits, but were baffled by the solidarity of the men, who considered this butchery a legitimate reprisal. The Turks with whom we talked were on the whole agreed that the period of extreme brutality was confined to the early weeks of the first war. Many of them praised the justice of the regular Bulgarian administration which was afterwards established. From several of the Bulgarian officials who had to govern turbulent districts (*e. g.,* Istip and Drama) infested by bands with an inadequate military force to back them, we have heard in detail of the steps which they took to regain the confidence of the Moslems. Many of them were successful.

A real effort was undoubtedly made to check the lawlessness of the bands and to deal with marauding on the part of the troops. The records of the courts-martial which we have before us, show that it was in January, 1913, that the Bulgarian headquarters became alarmed at the frequency and gravity of the excesses reported from the occupied territories. A circular telegram (see Appendix A, No. 13) sent to commanders and governors in Macedonia and Thrace enjoined them to institute inquiries into all excesses committed against the inhabitants of the occupied territories, and reminded them that the honor of the army was at stake, and that an attitude of indifference on their part toward the crimes of individuals would lead the world to suppose that Bulgarian civilization was not superior to that of the enemy. In two later telegrams the courts-martial were instructed to deal promptly with such charges and to give precedence to such cases over all others, more especially where the complaints came from Turks. The tone of these instructions is all that could be desired. It is disappointing to learn that up to February 15, 1913, the courts-martial in Macedonia had passed sentence on only ten persons for murder, eight for robbery or pillage, and two for rape. A large number of cases was in the stage of inquiry ("instruction"), and these included seventy-eight cases of murder, sixty-nine of pillage, seven of rape, seven of robbery, disguised as taxation, fourteen of arson, and eighty-one of various kinds of robbery and dishonesty. Of the culprits thirty-seven were Macedonian insurgents, including six chiefs of bands (*voyévodas*). How many of these cases were completed and how many of the culprits were actually sentenced we do not precisely know, since the archives of the chief Macedonian court-martial were lost at the evacuation of Serres. But we are informed that more than 200 prisoners belonging to the Bulgarian army and to the irregular bands were in Serres gaol under sentence when the town was evacuated. There is reason to believe that they were then released, an unfortunate irregularity which may possibly have been unavoidable. These facts show that an effort was made upon a considerable scale in Macedonia to deal with the excesses committed against the Turkish population. It was somewhat tardy, and manifestly the prompt execution in the early weeks of the war of some of the more notable criminals would have produced a more salutary effect. Public opinion in the Balkans does not condemn excesses committed by Christians against Moslems as severely as neutral onlookers do. That is inevitable, given the historical conditions. But undoubtedly the chiefs of the Bulgarian army did make an attempt to clear its honor, and the attempt was successful in bringing about a great improvement in the conduct of the troops and their irregular allies. It is, moreover, creditable to the Bulgarian government that in order to check the spoliation of the Moslems, an edict was issued which made all transfers of land during the period of the war illegal and invalid.

It remains to mention the practice followed by the Bulgarians, over a wide area, of reconverting the pomaks by force to Christianity. The pomaks are Bulgarians by race and language, who at some period of the Turkish conquest were converted by force to Islam. They speak no Turkish, and retain some traditional memory of their Christian past; but circumstances have usually made them fanatical Mohammedans. They number in the newly conquered territories at least 80,000 persons, and are chiefly concentrated to the north and east of Nevrocop. The Bulgarian Holy Synod conceived the design of converting them *en masse,* and it was frequently able to reckon on the support of the military and civil authorities, not to mention the insurgent bands. It was not usually necessary to employ actual violence; threats, backed by the manifest power to enforce them, commonly sufficed to induce whole villages to submit to the ceremony of baptism. The policy was carried out systematically, and long before the outbreak of the second war, the pomaks in most districts conformed outwardly to the Bulgarian church, and listened with a show of docility to the ministrations of the priests and nuns sent by the Holy Synod to instruct them in the tenets of Christianity. This aberration, in sharp contrast to the toleration which the Bulgarian Kingdom has usually shown to the Moslems within its frontiers, must rank among the least excusable brutalities of the war. The Holy Synod argued that since force had been used to convert the pomaks to

Islam, force might fairly be used to reverse the process. The argument is one proof the more that races whose minds have been molded for centuries by the law of reprisal and the practice of vengeance, tend to a common level of degradation.

2. The Conduct of the Bulgarians in the Second War

The charges brought by the Greeks against the Bulgarians are already painfully familiar to every newspaper reader. Unlike the Bulgarians, the Greeks welcomed war correspondents, and every resource of publicity was at their disposal, while Bulgaria itself was isolated and its telegraphic communications cut. That some of these accusations were grossly exaggerated is now apparent. *Le Temps*, for example, reported the murder of the Greek Bishop of Doiran. We saw him vigorous and apparently alive two months afterwards. A requiem mass was sung for the Bishop of Kavala; his flock welcomed him back to them while we were in Salonica. The correspondent of the same newspaper stated that he personally assisted at the burial of the Archbishop of Serres, who was savagely mutilated before he was killed. (Letter, dated Livonovo, July 23.) This distressing experience in no way caused this prelate to interrupt his duties, which he still performs.

There none the less remains, when these manifest travesties of fact are brushed aside, a heavy indictment which rests upon uncontrovertible evidence. It is true that the little town of Doxato was burned and a massacre carried out there during and after a Bulgarian attack. It is true that the town of Serres was burned during a Bulgarian attack. It is also true that a large number of civilians, including the Bishop of Melnik and Demir-Hissar, were slaughtered or executed by the Bulgarians in the latter town. The task of the Commission has been to compare the evidence from both sides regarding these events, and to form a judgment on the circumstances which in some degree explain them. The Greek charges are in each case substantially true, but in no case do they state the whole truth.

In forming an opinion upon the series of excesses which marked the Bulgarian withdrawal from southeastern Macedonia, it is necessary to recall the fact that the Bulgarians were here occupying a country whose population is mainly Greek and Turkish. The Bulgarian garrisons were small, and they found themselves on the outbreak of the second war in a hostile country. The Greek population of these regions is wealthy and intensely patriotic. In several Greek centers insurgent organizations (*andartes*) existed. Arms had been collected, and some experienced guerrilla chiefs were believed to be in hiding, and ready to lead the local population. All of this in existing conditions was creditable to Greek patriotism; their race was at war with Bulgarians, and the more enterprising and courageous among them intended to take their share as auxiliaries of the Greek army in driving the Bulgarians from their country. From a nationalist standpoint, this was morally their right and some might even say their duty. But it is equally clear that the Bulgarians, wherever they found themselves opposed by the armed civil population, had also a right to take steps to protect themselves. The steps which they elected to take in some places grossly exceeded the limits of legitimate defense or allowable reprisal.

THE MASSACRE AT DOXATO

Doxato was a thriving country town, situated between Drama and Kavala in the center of a rich tobacco growing district. It had a large school, and counted several wealthy and educated families among its 2,700 Greek inhabitants. It was proud of its Hellenic character, and formed with two neighboring villages a compact Greek island in a rural population which was almost exclusively Turkish. A member of the Commission has visited its ruins. Only thirty homes are left intact among its 270 Greek houses. Enough remains of the walls to show that the little town was well built and prosperous, and to suggest that the conflagration must have caused grievous material loss to the inhabitants. The estimate of killed (at first said to number over 2,000) which is now generally accepted by the Greeks, is 600. We have had communicated to us an extract from an official Greek report in which 500 is given as an outside figure.

A large proportion, probably one-half, of this total consisted of civilians who had taken up arms. Women and children to the number of over a hundred were massacred in a single house, and the slaughter was carried out with every

FIG. 1.—RUINS OF DOXATO

FIG. 2.—FINDING THE BODIES OF VICTIMS AT DOXATO

conceivable circumstance of barbarity. We print in Appendix B (No. 14) a letter in which Commander Cardale, a British naval officer in the Greek service, describes the condition of the village when he visited it shortly after the massacre.

We print in Appendix B, Bulgarian accounts of the Doxato affair. Mr. Dobrev, who was the prefect of Drama and earned the good opinion of the Greeks by his conduct there (see the Greek pamphlet *Atrocités Bulgares,* p. 49), has told the whole story with evident frankness. (Appendix B, No. 16.) Captain Sofroniev of the Royal Guard, who commanded the two squadrons of cavalry which operated against Doxato, relates his own part in the affair clearly, and has shown us the reports of his scouts penciled on official paper. (See Appendix B, No. 15.) Lieutenant Milev in a communicated deposition describes his experiences with the infantry, and Lieutenant Colonel Barnev explains his military dispositions. (See Appendix B, Nos. 16a and 16b.) These four depositions leave no doubt in the mind of the Commission that the Greeks had organized a formidable military movement among the local population; that Doxato was one of its centers; and that several hundreds of armed men were concentrated there. Provocation had been given not only by the wanton and barbarous slaughter by Greeks of Moslem noncombatants, but also by a successful attack at Doxato upon a Bulgarian convoy. There was, therefore, justification for the order given from the Bulgarian headquarters to attack the Greek insurgents concentrated in Doxato.

It appears from Captain Sofroniev's report that his men met with an obstinate resistance from these Greek *andartes* and that one of his two squadrons lost seventeen killed and twenty-four wounded in the attack. In the charge by which he finally dispersed them, he believes that his men killed at least 150 Greeks, and perhaps double this number. These were, he assures us, all armed men and combatants.

We find it hard to believe that an irregular and inexperienced force can have resisted cavalry with an obstinacy that would justify so large a slaughter as this. A woman, moreover, was wounded in this charge. (See Appendix B, No. 16.) Captain Sofroniev states that his men took prisoners. He consigned these prisoners to the charge of the Turkish peasants who had come up from neighboring villages, full of resentment for Greek excesses against their neighbors. He allowed these Turks to arm themselves with the weapons of the defeated Greek insurgents. He might as well have ordered the massacre of his prisoners. These Turks had recent grievances against the Greeks, and they had come to Doxato in the rear of the Bulgarian force for pillage and revenge.

The cavalry operated outside the village. The force which entered it was an infantry detachment comprised in great part of Bulgarian Moslems (pomaks). According to Mr. Dobrev, who is clearly the franker witness, it became excited when a magazine of cartridges exploded in the village, and began to kill indiscriminately all the inhabitants whom it met in the streets, including some children. It remained, however, only a short while in Doxato.

FIG. 3.—GATHERING THE BODIES OF VICTIMS

FIG. 4.—BODIES OF SLAIN PEASANTS

Lieutenant Milev's account attributes this slaughter to the local Turks, and states that two of them were executed for their crimes. He represents the inhabitants whom his men killed as insurgents.

We can not explain this discrepancy. It is, however, clear that the systematic massacre was carried out by the local Turks who were left in possession of the place for the better part of two days. They pillaged, burned, and slaughtered at their leisure, nor did they spare even the women who had taken refuge in the houses of friendly Turks. So far there is little difference between Commander Cardale's version of events, based on local Greek sources, and the statements of our Bulgarian witnesses. What we heard ourselves in the village some weeks later agreed with what Commander Cardale has reported. The Bulgarian troops, after a sharp engagement, began the killing of the inhabitants, but presently desisted. "The greater part of the massacre," as Commander Cardale puts it, "was done by the Turks." He quotes, without endorsing it, the statement of the survivors that the Turks acted under the "direction" or "incitement" of Bulgarian officers. We gather that he heard no convincing evidence on this head, nor did we meet with anyone who had personally heard or seen Bulgarian officers giving directions to massacre. That charge may be dismissed as baseless. But some part of the responsibility for the slaughter falls, none the less, upon the Bulgarian officers. They armed the Turks and left them in control of the village. They must have known what would follow. The employment of Turkish *bashi-bazouks* as allies against defenseless Christian villagers was an offense of which Greeks, Servians, and Bulgarians were all guilty upon occasion. No officer in the Balkans could take this step without foreseeing that massacre must result from it.

It is fair none the less to note that the Bulgarians were in a difficult position. They could not occupy the village permanently, for they were threatened by Greek columns marching from several quarters. To leave the Turks unarmed was to expose them to Greek excesses. To arm the Turks was, on the other hand, to condemn the Greek inhabitants to massacre. A culpable error of judgment was committed in circumstances which admitted only of a choice of evils. While emphasizing the heavy responsibility which falls on the Bulgarian officers for this catastrophe, we do not hesitate to conclude that the massacre at Doxato was a Turkish and not a Bulgarian atrocity.

THE MASSACRE AND CONFLAGRATION OF SERRES

Serres is the largest town of the interior of eastern Macedonia. The tobacco trade had brought considerable wealth to its 30,000 inhabitants; and it possessed in its churches, schools and hospitals the outward signs of the public spirit of its Greek community. The villages around it are Bulgarian to the north and west, but a rural Greek population approaches it from the south and east. The town itself is predominantly Greek, with the usual Jewish and Turkish admixture. The Bulgarians formed but a small minority. From October to June the town was under a Bulgarian occupation, and as the second war drew near, the relations of the garrison and the citizens became increasingly hostile. The Bulgarian authorities believed that the Greeks were arming secretly, that *andartes* (Greek insurgents) were concealed in the town, and that a revolt was in preparation. Five notables of the town were arrested on July 1 with the idea of intimidating the population. On Friday, July 4, the defeat of the Bulgarian forces to the south of Serres rendered the position untenable, and arrangements were made for the evacuation of the town. General Voulkov, the Governor of Macedonia, and his staff left on the evening of Saturday, July 5. The retirement was hastily planned and ill executed. There is evidence from Greeks and Turks, and from one of the American residents, Mr. Moore, that some of the troops found time to pillage before withdrawing. On the other hand, stores of Bulgarian munitions, including rifles, were abandoned in the town, and some of the archives were also left behind. We gather that there was some conflict of authority among the superior Bulgarian officers. (See evidence of Commandant Moustakov, Appendix B, No. 26.)

The plain fact is that at this central point the organization and discipline of the Bulgarian troops broke down. Some excesses, as one would expect, undoubtedly occurred, but the Greek evidence on this matter is untrustworthy. Commandant Moustakov believes that the notables who had been arrested were released. We find, on the other hand, in the semiofficial Greek pamphlet *Atrocités*

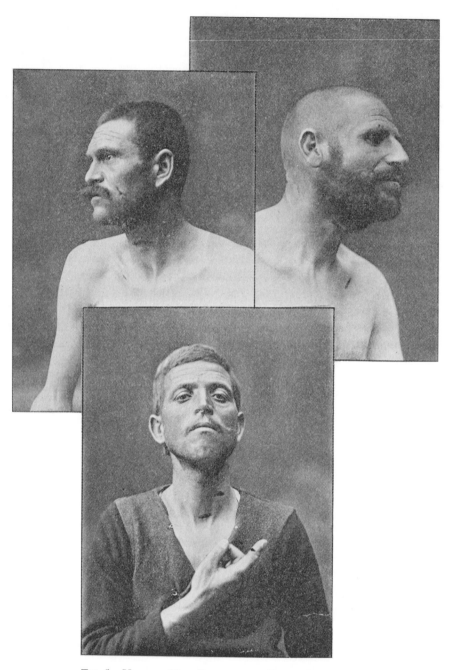

FIG. 5.—VICTIMS WHO ESCAPED THE SERRES SLAUGHTER

FIG. 6.—RUINS OF SERRES

Bulgares, the statement (p. 25) that the bodies of four Greek notables were found outside the town killed by bayonet thrusts; among them was the corpse of the director of the Orient bank. For this assertion the authority of the Italian and Austrian consuls general of Salonica is claimed. (See Appendix B, No. 17.) The member of our Commission who visited Serres had the pleasure of meeting this gentleman, Mr. Ghiné, alive, well, and unharmed, and enjoyed his hospitality. Such discoveries as this are a warning that even official statements regarding these events must be subjected to careful scrutiny. On the other hand, there is no doubt that some of the prisoners who were in gaol when the Bulgarians left the town, were slaughtered. This was done presumably by their gaolers without orders. The imprisoned Bulgarians, including many *comitadjis,* were probably released; it is conceivable that they had a hand in these excesses. The fact of a butchery in the prison is placed beyond doubt by the evidence of Mr. Arrington, the manager of the American Tobacco Company's branch. His porter (*cavass*), a Greek, had been arrested some days before, apparently because a rumor had got abroad that the famous Greek guerrilla chief, Captain Doukas, was in the town disguised as the *cavass* of a tobacco warehouse. Mr. Arrington demanded the release of his employe without result. After the departure of the last of the Bulgarian troops, Mr. Arrington visited the prison and found there a heap of thirteen corpses, among which was his man, severely wounded. He died shortly afterwards in hospital, but was able to tell his story. His Bulgarian gaoler had demanded a ransom of £10 for his release and would allow him

FIG. 8.—RUINS OF SERRES

FIG. 7.—RUINS OF SERRES

no facilities to procure it from outside. "We do things methodically here," said the gaoler. "You have four hours to live. Every half hour you will be beaten, and at the end you will be killed." He was in fact made to lie on his back and was pinned to the floor with a bayonet. Mr. Arrington stated that his arms and back, where he had been beaten, were "as black as his boots." The other twelve prisoners had evidently been treated with equal barbarity.

The main body of the Bulgarian garrison, with the headquarters, withdrew from Serres on Saturday, July 5. A panic followed, and a squadron of dismounted Bulgarian cavalry paraded the town to maintain order. The Greek irregulars and armed citizens were already under arms, and fired from some

FIG. 9.—RUINS OF SERRES

of the houses at this squadron. It camped that night outside the town, and entered it again on Sunday, but apparently without attempting to maintain complete control. On Monday, July 7 (if not on Sunday), the effective authority passed into the hands of the local Greeks. The Archbishop was recognized as governor of the town, and at his palace there sat in permanence a commission of the local inhabitants. Thirty armed Greeks wearing the *evzone* (highlander) uniform, who were, however, probably irregulars (*andartes*), had arrived in Serres, and one witness states that they were under the command of Captain Doukas. A Russian doctor in the Bulgarian sanitary service (Dr. Klugmann, see Appendix B, No. 22), who was left in the town, heard on Monday a Greek priest summoning the inhabitants to the Bishop's palace, where arms were

Fig. 10.—Ruins of Serres

distributed, first to the Greeks, and later to the Turks. From Monday morning
to Thursday evening these Greek irregulars and the citizen militia which they
organized were in possession of the town. Thrice they were threatened by small
Bulgarian detachments, which returned and skirmished on the hills outside the
town and at the distant railway station. But these Bulgarian scouts were not
in sufficient force to enter the town. A telegram dispatched on Thursday by
the Archbishop to King Constantine (see *Le Temps,* July 13), begs him to hasten
to occupy the town, which is, he says, defending itself successfully against the

Fig. 11.—Ruins of Serres

attacks of the Bulgarians. He mentions that he is governing the town, and states that it has been abandoned for a week by the Bulgarian authorities. He fears, however, that the citizens' power of resistance may soon be exhausted. These rather aimless Bulgarian attacks must have contributed to excite the local Greeks, and to inflame a spirit of vengeance.

The main concern of the Archbishop's Greek militia during this week was apparently to hunt down the Bulgarian population within the town and in some of the neighboring villages. It is conceivable that this measure may have been dictated in the first instance by the fear that the small Bulgarian minority inside Serres would coöperate with the enemy who attacked it from without. An armed Greek mob followed a few uniformed men from house to house, threatening the Bulgarians and all who should assist them to hide. Their houses were pillaged and their wives ill treated, while the men were arrested and taken singly or in batches to the Bishop's palace; there they were brought before a commission of laymen over whom a priest presided. Whatever money they possessed was taken from them by this priest, and the only question asked about them was, whether they were or were not Bulgarians. This process was witnessed by Dr. Klugmann, and the testimony of this Russian doctor entirely confirms that of our Bulgarian peasant witnesses. From the bishopric the prisoners were taken to the neighboring Greek girls' high school. In the school they were closely confined in several rooms by fifties and sixties. Fresh batches arrived continuously from the town and from the villages, until the total number of imprisoned Bulgarians reached 200 or 250. The gaolers were in part citizens of Serres, some of whom can be named, and in part uniformed irregulars. From the first they behaved with gross cruelty. The prisoners were tightly bound and beaten with the butt ends of rifles. The plan of the gaolers was apparently to slaughter their prisoners in batches, and they were led two by two to an upper room, where they were killed, usually by repeated wounds in the head and neck inflicted with a butcher's knife or a Martini bayonet. Each of the butchers aimed at accounting for fourteen men, which was apparently the number which each could bury during the night. The massacre went on in this leisurely way until Friday, the 11th. The prisoners included a few captured Bulgarian soldiers, a few peasants taken with arms in their hands (see evidence of the villager Lazarov, Appendix B, No. 20), and at least one local Bulgarian, Christo Dimitrov (Appendix B, No. 19), who was known to be an active associate of the Bulgarian bands. The immense majority were, however, inoffensive tradesmen or peasants whose only offense was that they were Bulgarians. Among them were four women, who were killed with the rest. The only mitigating circumstance is that five lads were released in pity for their youth, after seeing their fathers killed before their eyes. (See Blagoi Petrov, Appendix B, No. 21.) We are unwilling to dwell on the detailed barbarities of this butchery, of which more than enough is recorded in the appendices.

We must here anticipate a part of the narrative to explain that in the early morning of Friday, July 11, a Bulgarian regular force with cavalry and light artillery reached Serres, engaged the militia outside the town, defeated it, and began toward noon to penetrate into the town itself. There were still sixty or seventy of the Bulgarian prisoners alive, and their gaolers, alarmed by the sound of cannon in the distance, resolved to finish their work rapidly. Two at least of the prisoners (Angelov and Limonov) contrived to overpower the sentinels and escaped. Some of them, however, were bound and others were too enfeebled or too terrified to save themselves. They were led to the slaughter by fours and fives, but the killing this day was inefficient, and at least ten of the prisoners fell among the heaps of corpses, severely wounded indeed, but still alive. They recovered consciousness in the early afternoon, to realize that their gaolers had fled, that the town was on fire, and that the Bulgarian troops were not far distant. Ten of them struggled out of the school, and eight had strength enough to reach safety and their countrymen.

The Commission saw three of these fugitives from the Serres massacre, (Karanfilov, Dimitrov, and Lazarov, Appendix B, Nos. 18, 19, 20), who all bore the fresh scars of their wounds. These wounds, chiefly in the head and neck, could have been received only at close quarters. They were such wounds as a butcher would inflict, who was attempting to slaughter men as he would slaughter sheep. The evidence of these three, given separately, was mutually consistent. We questioned a fourth witness, the lad Blagoi Petrov, who was released. We were also supplied with the written depositions, backed by photographs showing their injuries, of three other wounded survivors of the massacre, who had found refuge in distant parts of Bulgaria which we were unable to visit. (See Appendix D, Nos. 56, 57, 58.) Among these was George Belev, a Protestant, to whose honesty and high character the American missionaries of Samakov paid a high tribute. The written depositions of the two men who escaped by rushing the sentinels, afforded another element of confirmation. Dr. Klugmann's evidence, given to us in person, is valuable as a description of the way in which the Bulgarian civilians of Serres were hunted down and arrested. The Commission finds this evidence irresistible, and is forced to conclude that a massacre of Bulgarians to the number of about two hundred, most of them inoffensive and noncombatant civilians, was carried out in Serres by the Greek militia with revolting cruelty. The victims were arrested and imprisoned under the authority of the Archbishop. It is possible that he may have been misled by his subordinates, and that they may have disobeyed his orders. But the fact that when he visited the prison on Thursday, he assured the survivors that their lives would be spared, suggests that he knew that they were in danger.

The last stage of the episode of Serres began on Friday, the 11th. Partly because they had left large stores of munitions in the town, partly because rumors of the schoolhouse massacre had reached them, the Bulgarians were anxious to reoccupy the town. Their small detachments had been repulsed, and it was with a battalion and a half of infantry, a squadron of horse and four guns, that Commandant Kirpikov marched against Serres from Zernovo, and at dawn approached the hills which command it. His clear account of his military dispositions will be found in Appendix B (No. 23). He overcame the resistance of the Greek militia posted to the number of about 1,000 men on the hills, without much difficulty. In attempting toward noon to penetrate into the town, his troops met with a heavy fire from several large houses held by the Greeks. Against these he finally used his guns. From noon onward the town was in flames at several points. The commandant does not admit that his shells caused the conflagration, but in this matter probability is against him. One witness, George Belev, states that the schoolhouse was set on fire by a shell. The commandant states further that the Greeks themselves, who were as reckless as the Bulgarians, fired certain houses which contained their own stores of munitions. It is probable that the Bulgarians also set on fire the buildings in which their own stores were housed. Both Greeks and Bulgarians state that a high wind was blowing during the afternoon. Serres was a crowded town, closely built in the oriental fashion, with houses constructed mainly of wood. The summer had been hot and dry. It is not surprising that the town blazed. We must give due weight to the belief universally held by the Greek inhabitants that the town was deliberately set on fire by the Bulgarian troops. The inhabitants for the most part had fled, and few of them saw what happened; but one eye witness states that the soldiers used petroleum and acted on a systematic plan. This witness (quoted in Appendix B, No. 17) is a local Turk who had taken service under the Bulgarians as a police officer while they were still at war with his country. That is not a record which inspires confidence. On the other hand, Dr. Yankov, a legal official who accompanied the Bulgarian troops, states that he personally made efforts to check the flames.

The general impression conveyed by all the evidence before us, and especially that of the Russian Dr. Laznev (see Appendix D, No. 57), is that the Bulgarian troops were hotly engaged throughout the afternoon, first with the Greek militia and then with the main Greek army. The Greek forces advanced in large numbers and with artillery from two directions to relieve the town, and compelled the Bulgarians to retreat before sundown. Their shells also fell in the town. The Bulgarians were not in undisturbed possession for so much as an hour, and it is difficult to believe that they can have had leisure for much systematic incendiarism. On the other hand, it is indisputable that some Bulgarian villagers who followed the troops did deliberately burn houses (see evidence of Lazar Tomov, Appendix B, No. 25), and that a mob comprised partly of Bulgarians and partly of Turks pillaged and burned while the troops were fighting. It is probable that some of the Bulgarian troops, who seem to have been, as at Doxato, a very mixed force which included some pomak (Moslem) levies, joined in this work.

The Bulgarians knew that the Greeks were burning their villages, and some of them had heard of the schoolhouse massacre. Any soldiers in the world would think of vengeance under these conditions. In two notorious instances leading residents were blackmailed. The experiences of Mr. Zlatkos, the Greek gentleman who acts as Austro-Hungarian consul, are related in Appendix B (No. 17a). His own account must be compared with the Bulgarian version, which suggests that some of his fears were baseless. The action of the Bulgarian commander in shelling the masses of armed peasants outside the town appears to us to have been questionable. Among them there must have been many noncombatant fugitives. His use of artillery against an unfortified town was a still graver abuse of the laws of civilized warfare.

To sum up, we must conclude that the Greek quarter of Serres was burned by the Bulgarians in the course of their attack on the town, but the evidence before us does not suffice to establish the Greek accusation, that the burning was a part of the plan conceived by the Bulgarian headquarters. But unquestionably the whole conduct both of the attack and of the defense contributed to bring about the conflagration, and some of the attacking force did undoubtedly burn houses. There is, in short, no trustworthy evidence of premeditated or official incendiarism, but the responsibility for the burning of Serres none the less falls mainly upon the Bulgarian army. The result was the destruction of 4,000 out of 6,000 houses, the impoverishment of a large population, and in all likelihood the painful death of many of the aged and infirm, who could not make good their escape. The episode of Serres is deeply discreditable alike to Greeks and Bulgarians.

EVENTS AT DEMIR-HISSAR

The events which took place at Demir-Hissar between the 5th and 10th of July possess a certain importance, because they were used as a pretext for the "reprisals" of the Greek army at the expense of the Bulgarian population. (See King Constantine's telegram, Appendix C, No. 29.) We shall have occasion to point out that the Greek excesses began in and around Kukush some days before the Bulgarian provocation at Demir-Hissar.

That Demir-Hissar was the center of excesses committed on both sides is indisputable. The facts are confused, and the evidence before us more than usually contradictory. This is not surprising in the circumstances. The Bulgarian army, beaten in the south, was fleeing in some disorder through Demir-Hissar to the narrow defile of the Struma above this little town. The Greeks of the town, seeing their confusion, determined to profit by it, took up arms and fell upon the Bulgarian wounded, the baggage trains, and the fugitive peasants. They rose too soon and exposed themselves to Bulgarian reprisals. When the Greek army at length marched in, it found a scene of carnage and horror. The Greek inhabitants had slaughtered defenseless Bulgarians, and the Bulgarian rear guard had exacted vengeance.

We print in Appendix B (Nos. 27, 27a, 28, 28a) both the Greek and the Bulgarian narratives of this affair. The Greeks as usual suppress all mention of the provocation which the inhabitants had given. The Bulgarian account is silent as to the manner in which their reprisals were carried out. Both narratives contain inaccuracies, and neither of them tells more than a part of the truth. Nor are we satisfied that the whole truth can be reached by the simple method of completing one story by means of the other. The Greek account is the more detailed and definite of the two for the simple reason that the Greeks remained in possession of the town, and were able to count and identify their dead. The Bulgarians believe that about 250 of their countrymen, wounded soldiers, military bakers, and peasant fugitives, were slaughtered there. It may be so, but the total is conjectural, and no list can possibly be furnished. The Greeks, on the other hand, have compiled a list of seventy-one inhabitants of Demir-Hissar who were killed by the Bulgarians. We do not question the accuracy of this list. But there is no means of ascertaining how many of these dead Greeks were killed during the fighting in the streets; how many were taken with arms in their hands and shot; and how many were summarily executed on suspicion of being the instigators of the rising. Two women and two babies are among the dead. If they were killed in cold blood an "atrocity" was perpetrated, but during a confused day of street fighting they may possibly have been killed by accident.

The case of the Bishop has naturally attracted attention. Of the four Greek Bishops who were said to have been killed in Macedonia, he alone was in fact killed. There is nothing improbable in the Bulgarian statement that he was the leader of the Greek insurgents, nor even in the further allegation that he fired the first shot. The Bishops of Macedonia, whether Greeks or Bulgarians, are always the recognized political heads of their community; they are often in close touch with the rebel bands, and a young and energetic man will sometimes place himself openly at their head. The Bulgarians allege that the Bishop, a man of forty years of age, fired from his window at their troops. The Greeks admit that he "resisted" arrest. If it is true that he was found with a revolver, from which some cartridges had been fired, there was technical justification for regarding him as a combatant. The hard law of war sanctions the execution of civilians taken with arms in their hands. There is no reason to reject the Greek statement that his body was mutilated, dead or alive. But the Greek assertion that this was done by a certain Captain Bostanov is adequately met by the Bulgarian denial that any such officer exists.

Some of the men in the Greek list of dead were presumably armed inhabitants who engaged in the street fighting. Nine are young men of twenty and thereabouts and some are manual laborers. Clearly these are not "notables" collected for a deliberate massacre. On the other hand, six are men of sixty years and upwards, who are not likely to have been combatants. These leaders of the Greek community were evidently arrested on suspicion of fomenting the outbreak and summarily "executed." It was a lawless proceeding without form of trial, and the killing was evidently done in the most brutal way. We are far from feeling any certainty regarding the course of events at Demir-Hissar. There was clearly not an unprovoked massacre as the Greeks allege. But there did follow on the cowardly excesses of the Greek inhabitants against the Bulgarian wounded and fugitives, indefensible acts of reprisal, and a lawless and brutal slaughter of men who may have deserved some more regular punishment.

The events at Doxato and Demir-Hissar, with the burning of Serres, form the chief counts in the Greek indictment of the Bulgarians. The other items refer mainly to single acts of violence charged against individuals in many places over a great range of territory. These minor charges we have not investigated, since they rarely involved an accusation against the army as a whole or its superior officers. We regret that we were unable to visit Nigrita, a large village, which was burned during the fighting which raged around it. Many of the inhabitants are said to have perished in the flames. We think it proper to place on record, without any expression of opinion, the Greek belief that this place was deliberately burned by the Bulgarians. We note also the statement made by a Greek soldier in a captured letter (see Appendix C, No. 51) that more than a thousand Bulgarian prisoners were slaughtered there by the Greek army. We have also before us the signed statement of a leading Moslem of the Nigrita district to the effect that after the second war the Greeks drove the Moslems from the surrounding villages with gross violence, because they had been neutral in the conflict, and took possession of their lands and houses.

It remains to mention the charge repeatedly made by some of the diplomatic representatives of Greece in European capitals, that the fingers and ears of women were found in the pockets of captured Bulgarian soldiers. We need hardly insist on the inherent improbability of this vague story. Such relics would soon become a nauseous possession, and a soldier about to surrender would, one supposes, endeavor to throw away such damning evidence of his guilt. The only authority quoted for this accusation is a correspondent of the *Times*. We saw the gentleman in question at Salonica, a Greek journalist, who was acting as deputy for the *Times* correspondent. He had the story from Greek soldiers, and did not himself see the fingers and ears. The headquarters of the Greek army, which lost no opportunity of publishing facts likely to damage the Bulgarians, would presumably have published this accusation also, with the necessary details, had it been capable of verification. Until it is backed by further evidence, the story is unworthy of belief.

The case against the Bulgarians which remains after a critical examination of the evidence relating to Doxato, Serres, and Demir-Hissar is sufficiently grave. In each case the Bulgarians acted under provocation, and in each case the accusation is grossly exaggerated, but their reprisals were none the less lawless and unmeasured. It is fair, however, to point out that these three cases, even on the worst view which may be taken of them, are far from supporting the general statements of some Greek writers, that the Bulgarians in their withdrawal from southern Macedonia and western Thrace, followed a general policy of devastation and massacre. They held five considerable Græco-Turkish towns in this area and many smaller places—Drama, Kavala, Xanthi, Gumurjina, and Dedeagatch. In none of these did the Bulgarians burn and massacre, though some acts of violence occurred. The wrong they did leaves a sinister blot upon their record, but it must be viewed in its just proportions.

3. The Bulgarian Peasant and the Greek Army

It required no artificial incitement to produce the race hatred which explains the excesses of the Christian Allies, and more especially of the Bulgarians toward the Turks. Race, language, history, and religion have made a barrier which only the more tolerant minds of either creed are able wholly to surmount. It is less easy to explain the excesses of which Greeks and Bulgarians were guilty toward each other. The two races are sharply distinguished by temperament. A traditional enmity has divided them from the dawn of history, and this is aggravated in Macedonia by a certain social cleavage. But for a year the two races had been allies, united against a common enemy. When policy dictated a breach, it was necessary to prepare public opinion; and the Greek press, as if by a common impulse, devoted itself to this work. To the rank and file of all three Balkan armies, the idea of a fratricidal war was at first repugnant and inexplicable. The passions of the Greek army were roused by a daily diet of violent articles. The Greek press had had little to say regarding the Bulgarian excesses against the Turks while the facts were still fresh, and indeed none of the allies had the right to be censorious, for none of their records were clean. Now everything was dragged into the light, and the record of the Bulgarian bands, deplorable in itself, lost nothing in the telling. Day after day the Bulgarians were represented as a race of monsters, and public feeling was roused to a pitch of chauvinism which made it inevitable that war, when it came, should be ruthless. In talk and in print one phrase summed up the general feeling of the Greeks toward the Bulgarians, *"Dhen einai anthropoi!"* (They are not human beings). In their excitement and indignation the Greeks came to think of themselves as the appointed avengers of civilization against a race which stood outside the pale of humanity.

When an excitable southern race, which has been schooled in Balkan conceptions of vengeance, begins to reason in this way, it is easy to predict the consequences. Deny that your enemies are men, and presently you will treat them as vermin. Only half realizing the full meaning of what he said, a Greek officer remarked to the writer, "When you have to deal with barbarians, you must behave like a barbarian yourself. It is the only thing they understand." The Greek army went into the war, its mind inflamed with anger and contempt. A

FIG. 12.—A POPULAR GREEK POSTER

gaudily colored print, which we saw in the streets of Salonica and the Pireaus, eagerly bought by the Greek soldiers returning to their homes, reveals the depth of the brutality to which this race hatred had sunk them. It shows a Greek *evzone* (highlander) holding a living Bulgarian soldier with both hands, while he gnaws the face of his victim with his teeth, like some beast of prey. It is entitled the *Bulgarophagos* (Bulgar-eater), and is adorned with the following verses:

> The sea of fire which boils in my breast
> And calls for vengeance with the savage waves of my soul,
> Will be quenched when the monsters of Sofia are still,
> And thy life blood extinguishes my hate.

Another popular battle picture shows a Greek soldier gouging out the eyes of a living Bulgarian. A third shows as an episode of a battle scene the exploit of the Bulgar-eater.

As an evidence of the feeling which animated the Greek army these things have their importance. They mean, in plain words, that Greek soldiers wished to believe that they and their comrades perpetrated bestial cruelties. A print seller who issued such pictures in a western country would be held guilty of a gross libel on its army.

The excesses of the Greek army began on July 4 with the first conflict at Kukush (Kilkish). A few days later the excesses of the Bulgarians at Doxato (July 13), Serres (July 11), and Demir-Hissar (July 7) were known and still further inflamed the anger of the Greeks. On July 12 King Constantine announced in a dispatch which reported the slaughter at Demir-Hissar that he "found himself obliged with profound regret to proceed to reprisals." A comparison of dates will show that the Greek "reprisals" had begun some days before the Bulgarian "provocation."

It was with the defeat of the little Bulgarian army at Kukush (Kilkish) after a stubborn three days' defense against a superior Greek force, that the Greek campaign assumed the character of a war of devastation. The Greek army entered the town of Kukush on July 4. We do not propose to lay stress on the evidence of Bulgarian witnesses regarding certain events which preceded their entry. Shells fell outside the town among groups of fugitive peasants from the villages, while within the town shells fell in the orphanage and hospital conducted by the French Catholic sisters under the protection of the French flag. (See Appendix C, Nos. 30 and 31.) It is possible and charitable to explain such incidents as the effect of an unlucky chance. The evidence of European eye witnesses confirms the statements of the Bulgarian refugees on one crucial point. These shells caused no general conflagration, and it is doubtful whether more than three or four houses were set on fire by them. When the Greek army entered Kukush it was still intact. It is today a heap of ruins—as a member of the Commission reports, after a visit to which the Greek authorities opposed several

Fig. 13.—A Popular Greek Poster

obstacles.   It was a prosperous town of 13,000 inhabitants, the center of a purely
Bulgarian district and the seat of several flourishing schools.   The bent standards of its electric lamps still testify to the efforts which it had made to attain a
level of material progress unusual in Turkey.   That its destruction was deliberate admits of no doubt.   The great majority of the inhabitants fled before the
arrival of the Greeks.   About four hundred, chiefly old people and children, had
found shelter in the Catholic orphanage, and were not molested.   European eye
witnesses describe the systematic entry of the Greek soldiers into house after
house.   Any of the inhabitants who were found inside were first evicted, pillage
followed, and then, usually after a slight explosion, the house burst into flames.
Fugitives continued to arrive in the orphanage while the town was burning, and
several women stated that they had been violated by Greek soldiers.   In one
case a soldier, more chivalrous than his comrades, brought a woman to the orphanage whom he had saved from violation.   Some civilians were killed by the
Greek cavalry as they rode in, and many lives were lost in the course of the
sacking and burning of Kukush.   We have received a detailed list from a Bulgarian source of seventy-four inhabitants who are believed to have been killed.
Most of them are old women, and eleven are babies.

The main fact on which we must insist is that the Greek army inaugurated
the second war by the deliberate burning of a Bulgarian town.   A singular fact
which has some bearing on Greek policy is that the refugees who took shelter
in the French orphanage were still, on September 6, long after the conclusion of
peace, closely confined as prisoners within it, though hardly a man among them
is capable of bearing arms.   A notice in Greek on its outer door states that they
are forbidden to leave its precincts.   Meanwhile, Greek (or rather "Grecoman")
refugees from Strumnitsa were being installed on the sites of the houses which
once belonged to Bulgarians, and in the few buildings (perhaps a dozen in number) which escaped the flames.   The inference is irresistible.   In conquering the
Kukush district, the Greeks were resolved to have no Bulgarian subjects.

The precedent of Kukush was only too faithfully followed in the villages.
In the Caza (county) of Kukush alone no less than forty Bulgarian villages were
burned by the Greek army in its northward march.   (See Appendix C, No. 52.)
Detachments of cavalry went from village to village, and the work of the regulars
was completed by *bashi-bazouks*.   It was a part of the Greek plan of campaign
to use the local Turkish population as an instrument in the work of devastation.
In some cases they were armed and even provided with uniforms.   (See Appendix C, No. 43.)   In no instance, however, of which we have a record were the
Turks solely responsible for the burning of a village.   They followed the Greek
troops and acted under their protection.   We have no means of ascertaining
whether any general order was given which regulated the burning of the Bulgarian villages.   A Greek sergeant among the prisoners of war in Sofia, stated in
reply to a question which a member of the Commission put to him, that he and
his comrades burned the villages around Kukush because the inhabitants had fled.

It is a fact that one mainly Catholic village (Todoraki) in which most of the inhabitants remained, was not burned, though it was thoroughly pillaged. (See Appendix C, No. 32.) But the fate of other villages, notably Akangeli, in which the inhabitants not only remained, but even welcomed the Greek troops, disposes of this explanation. Whatever may have been the terms of the orders under which the Greek troops acted, the effect was that the Bulgarian villages were burned with few exceptions.

Refugees have described how, on the night of the fall of Kukush, the whole sky seemed to be aflame. It was a signal which the peasants understood. Few of them hesitated, and the general flight began which ended in massing the Bulgarian population of the districts through which the Greeks marched within the former frontiers of Bulgaria. We need not insist on the hardships of the flight. Old and young, women and children, walked sometimes for two consecutive weeks by devious mountain paths. The weak fell by the wayside from hunger and exhaustion. Families were divided, and among the hundred thousand refugees scattered throughout Bulgaria, husbands are still looking for wives, and parents for children. Sometimes the stream of refugees crossed the path of the contending armies, and the clatter of cavalry behind them would produce a panic, and a *sauve qui peut* in which mothers lost their children, and even abandoned one in the hope of saving another. (See Appendix C, Nos. 33, 34, 35.) They arrived at the end of their flight with the knowledge that their flocks had been siezed, their crops abandoned, and their homes destroyed. In all this misery and loss there is more than the normal and inevitable wastage of war. The peasants abandoned everything and fled, because they would not trust the Greek army with their lives. It remains to inquire whether this was an unreasonable fear.

The immense majority of the Macedonian refugees in Bulgaria were never in contact with the Greek army and know nothing of it at first hand. They heard rumors of excesses in other villages; they knew that other villages had been burned; they fled because everyone was fleeing; at the worst they can say that from a distance they saw their own village in flames. It would be easy to ascribe their fears to prejudice or panic, were it not for the testimony of the few who were in direct touch with the Greek troops. In the appendices will be found a number of depositions which the Commission took from refugees. It was impossible to doubt that these peasants were telling the truth. Most of them were villagers, simple, uneducated, and stunned by their sufferings, and quite incapable of invention. They told their tales with a dull, literal directness. In two of the more striking stories, we obtained ample corroboration in circumstances which admitted of no collusion. Thus a refugee from Akangeli, who had fled to Salonica, told us there a story of butchery and outrage (see Appendix C, No. 39) which tallied in almost every detail with the story afterwards told by another fugitive from the same village who had fled to Sofia (Appendix C, No. 41). While passing through Dubnitsa we inquired from a group of refugees whether any one present came from Akangeli. A youth stepped forward, who once more told a story which agreed with the two others (Appendix C, No. 42). The story of the boy Mito Kolev (Appendix C, No. 36) told in Sofia, was similarly corroborated in an equally accidental way by two witnesses at Samakov (Appendix C, Nos. 37 and 38), who stepped out of a crowd of refugees in response to our inquiry whether anyone present came from the village in question (Gavaliantsi). We can feel no doubt about the truth of a story which reached us in this way from wholly independent eye witnesses. These two incidents are typical, and must be briefly summarized here.

Mito Kolev is an intelligent boy of fourteen, who comes from the Bulgarian village Gavaliantsi, in the Kukush district. He fled with most of his neighbors in the first alarm after the Bulgarian defeat at Kukush, but returned next day to fetch his mother, who had remained behind. Outside the village a Greek trooper fired at him but missed him. The lad had the wit to feign death. As he lay on the ground, his mother was shot and killed by the same cavalryman. He saw another lad killed, and the same trooper then went in pursuit of a crippled girl. Of her fate Mito, who clearly distinguished between what he saw and what he suspected, knew nothing, but another witness (Lazar Tomov) chanced to see the corpse of this girl (Appendix B, No. 25). Mito's subsequent adventures were told very clearly and in great detail. The essential points are (1) that he saw his village burned, and (2) that another Greek cavalryman whom he met later in the day all but killed him with a revolver shot and a saber cut at close quarters, while he spared a by-stander who was able by his command of the language to pass himself off as a Greek. The material corroboration of this story is, that Mito still bore the marks of his wounds. A shot wound may be accidental, but a saber wound can only be given deliberately and at close quarters. A trooper who wounds a boy with his sword can not plead error. He must have been engaged in indiscriminate butchery. Of this particular squad of Greek cavalry, it is not too much to say that they were slaughtering Bulgarian peasants at sight, and that they spared neither women nor children.

The evidence regarding Akangeli (Appendix C, Nos. 39–42, and Appendix D, No. 63, paragraph b) points to the same conclusion. In this Bulgarian village near the Lake of Doiran, refugees from many of the neighboring villages, who are said to have numbered 4,000 persons, had halted in their flight. A squadron of Greek cavalry, numbering about 300 men, with officers at its head, arrived between 3 and 4 p.m. on Sunday, July 6. The villagers with their priest went out to meet them with a white flag and the Greek colors. The officer, in conversation with the mayor, accepted their surrender and ordered them to give up any arms they possessed. The peasants brought bread and cheese, and thirty sheep were requisitioned and roasted for the troops. Some sixty of the men of the place were separated from the others and sent away to a wood. Of their fate nothing is known. The villagers believe that they were slaughtered, but we have reason to hope that they may have been sent as prisoners to Salonica. While the rifles were being collected the troopers began to demand money from both men and women. The women were searched with every circumstance of indignity and indecency. One witness, a well to do inhabitant of Kukush, was bound together with a refugee whose name he did not know. He gave up his watch and five piastres and his life was spared. His companion, who had no money, was killed at his side. While the arms were being collected, one which was loaded went off accidentally and wounded an officer, who was engaged in breaking the rifles. Two youths who were standing near were then killed by the soldiers, presumably to avenge the officer's mishap. Toward evening the soldiers forced their way into the houses and began to violate the women.

Another witness, the butcher who roasted the sheep for the troops, saw two young women, whom he named, violated by three soldiers beside his oven. Infantry arrived on Monday, and shortly afterwards the village was set on fire. During Sunday night and on Monday morning many of the villagers were slaughtered. It is impossible to form an estimate of the number, for our witnesses were in hiding and each saw only a small part of what occurred. One of them estimated the number at fifty, but this was clearly only a guess. We have before us a list from a Bulgarian source of 356 persons from seven villages who have disappeared and are believed to have been killed at Akangeli. Turks from neighboring villages joined in the pillage under the eyes of the Greek soldiers and their officers. The facts which emerge clearly from our depositions are (1) that the village submitted from the first; (2) that it was sacked and burned; (3) that the Greek troops gave themselves up openly and generally to a debauch of lust; (4) that many of the peasants were killed wantonly and without provocation.

It would serve no purpose to encumber this account of the Greek march with further narratives. Many further depositions will be found in the appendices. They all convey the same impression. Wherever the peasants ventured to await the arrival of the Greek troops in their villages, they had the same experience. The village was sacked and the women were violated before it was burned, and noncombatants were wantonly butchered, sometimes in twos or threes, sometimes in larger numbers. We would call attention particularly to two of these narratives—that of Anastasia Pavlova, an elderly women of the middle class, who told her painful and dramatic story with more intelligence and feeling than most of the peasant witnesses. (Appendix C, No. 43.) Like them, she suffered violation; she was robbed, and beaten, and witnessed the dishonor of other women and the slaughter of noncombatant men. Her evidence relates in part to the taking of the town of Ghevgheli. Ghevgheli, which is a mixed town, was not burned, but a reliable European, well acquainted with the town, and known to one member of the Commission as a man of honor and ability, stated that fully two hundred Bulgarian civilians were killed there on the entry of the Greek army.

Another deposition to which we would particularly call attention is that of Athanas Ivanov, who was an eye witness of the violation of six women and the murder of nine men in the village of Kirtchevo. (Appendix C, No. 44.) His story is interesting because he states that one Greek soldier who protested against the brutality of his comrades was overruled by his sergeant, and further that the order to kill the men was given by officers. It is probable that some hundreds of peasants were killed at Kirtchevo and German in a deliberate massacre, carried out with gross treachery and cruelty. (See also Appendix D, Nos. 59–62.) For these depositions the Commission assumes responsibility, in the sense that it believes that the witnesses told the truth; and, further, that it took every care to ascertain by questioning them whether any obvious excuse, such as a disorderly resistance by irregulars in the neighborhood, could be adduced. These depositions relate to the conduct of the Greek troops in ten villages. We should hesitate to generalize from this basis (save as to the fact that villages were almost everywhere burned), but we are able to add in the appendix a summary of a large number of depositions taken from refugees by Professor Milétits of Sofia University. (See Appendix D, No. 63.) While it can not assume personal responsibility for this evidence, the Commission has every confidence in the thoroughness with which Professor Milétits performed his task.

This great mass of evidence goes to show that there was nothing singular in the cases which the Commission itself investigated. In one instance a number of Europeans witnessed the brutal conduct of a detachment of Greek regulars under three officers. Fifteen wounded Bulgarian soldiers took refuge in the Catholic convent of Paliortsi, near Ghevgheli, and were nursed by the sisters. Father Alloati reported this fact to the Greek commandant, whereupon a detachment was sent to search the convent for a certain Bulgarian *voyévoda* (chief of bands) named Arghyr, who was not there. In the course of the search a Bulgarian Catholic priest, Father Treptché, and the Armenian doctor of the convent were severely flogged in the presence of the Greek officers. A Greek soldier attempted to violate a nun, and during the search a sum of £T300 was stolen. Five Bulgarian women and a young girl were put to the torture, and a large number of peasants carried off to prison for no good reason. The officer in command threatened to kill Father Alloati on the spot and to burn down the convent. If such things could be done to Europeans in a building under the protection of the French flag, it is not difficult to believe that Bulgarian peasants fared incomparably worse.

The Commission regrets that the attitude of the Greek government toward its work has prevented it from obtaining any official answer to the charges which emerge from this evidence. The broad fact that the whole of this Bulgarian region, for a distance of about one hundred miles, was devastated and nearly

every village burned, admits of no denial.   Nor do we think that military necessity could be pleaded with any plausibility.   The Greeks were numerically greatly
superior to their enemy, and so far as we are aware, their flanks were not har-
assed, nor their communications threatened by guerrillas, who might have found
shelter in the villages.   The Greeks did not wait for any provocation of this
kind, but everywhere burned the villages, step by step with their advance.
The slaughter of peasant men could be defended only if they had been taken
in the act of resistance with arms in their hands.   No such explanation will
fit the cases on which we have particularly laid stress, nor have any of the war
correspondents who followed the Greek army reported conflicts along the main
line of the Greek march with armed villagers.   The violation of women admits of
no excuse; it can only be denied.

Denial unfortunately is impossible.   No verdict which could be based on the
evidence collected by the Commission could be more severe than that which Greek
soldiers have pronounced upon themselves.   It happened that on the eve of the
armistice (July 27) the Bulgarians captured the baggage of the Nineteenth
Greek infantry regiment at Dobrinichte (Razlog).   It included its post-bags, together with the file of its telegraphic orders, and some of its accounts.   We
were permitted to examine these documents at our leisure in the Foreign Office
at Sofia.   The file of telegrams and accounts presented no feature of interest.
The soldiers' letters were written often in pencil on scraps of paper of every sort
and size.   Some were neatly folded without envelopes.   Some were written on
souvenir paper commemorating the war, and others on official sheets.   Most of
them bore the regimental postal stamp.   Four or five were on stamped business
paper belonging to a Turkish firm in Serres, which some Greek soldier had presumably taken while looting the shop.   The greater number of the letters were
of no public interest, and simply informed the family at home that the writer
was well, and that his friends were well or ill or wounded as the case might be.
Many of these letters still await examination.   We studied with particular care a
series of twenty-five letters, which contained definite avowals by these Greek
soldiers of the brutalities which they had practiced.   Two members of the Commission have some knowledge of modern Greek.   We satisfied ourselves (1)
that the letters (mostly illiterate and ill written) had been carefully deciphered
and honestly translated; (2) that the interesting portions of the letters were in
the same handwriting as the addresses on the envelopes (which bore the official
stamp) and the portions which related only personal news; (3) that no tamper-
ing with the manuscripts had been practiced.   Some minor errors and inaccuracies are interesting, as an evidence of authenticity.   Another letter is dated by
error July 15 (old style), though the post-bags were captured on the 14th (27th).
We noted, moreover, that more than one slip (including an error of grammar)
had been made by the Bulgarian secretary in transcribing the addresses of the
letters from Greek into Latin script —a proof that he did not know enough

Greek to invent them.   But it is unnecessary to dwell on these minor evidences of authenticity.   The letters have been published in *fac simile*.   The addresses and the signatures are those of real people.   If they had been wronged by some incredibly ingenious forger, the Greek government would long ago have brought these soldiers before some impartial tribunal to prove by specimens of their genuine handwriting that they did not write these letters.   The Commission, in short, is satisfied that the letters are genuine.

The letters require no commentary.   Some of the writers boast of the cruelties practiced by the Greek army.   Others deplore them.   The statements of fact (see Appendix C, No. 51) are simple, brutal, and direct, and always to the same effect.   These soldiers all state that they everywhere burned the Bulgarian villages.   Two boast of the massacre of prisoners of war.   One remarks that all the girls they met with were violated.   Most of the letters dwell on the slaughter of noncombatants, including women and children.   These few extracts, each from a separate letter, may suffice to convey their general tenor:

> By order of the King we are setting fire to all the Bulgarian villages, because the Bulgarians burned the beautiful town of Serres, Nigrita, and several Greek villages.   We have shown ourselves far more cruel than the Bulgarians.   *   *   *
>
> Here we are burning the villages and killing the Bulgarians, both women and children.   *   *   *
>
> We took only a few [prisoners], and these we killed, for such are the orders we have received.
>
> We have to burn the villages—such is the order—slaughter the young people and spare only the old people and the children.   *   *   *
>
> What is done to the Bulgarians is indescribable; also to the Bulgarian peasants.   It was a butchery.   There is not a Bulgarian town or village but is burned.
>
> We massacre all the Bulgarians who fall into our hands and burn the villages.
>
> Of the 1,200 prisoners we took at Nigrita, only forty-one remain in the prisons, and everywhere we have been we have not left a single root of this race.
>
> We picked out their eyes [five Bulgarian prisoners] while they were still alive.
>
> The Greek army sets fire to all the villages where there are Bulgarians and massacres all it meets.   *   *   *   God knows where this will end.

These letters relieve us of the task of summing up the evidence.   From Kukush to the Bulgarian frontier the Greek army devastated the villages, violated the women, and slaughtered the noncombatant men.   The order to carry out reprisals was evidently obeyed.   We repeat, however, that these reprisals began before the Bulgarian provocation.   A list of Bulgarian villages burned by the Greek army which will be found in Appendix C (No. 52) conveys some measure of this ruthless devastation.   At Serres the Bulgarians destroyed 4,000 houses in the conflagration which followed the fighting in the streets. The ruin of this considerable town has impressed the imagination of the civilized world. Systematically and in cold blood the Greeks burned one hundred and sixty Bulgarian villages and destroyed at least 16,000 Bulgarian homes. The figures need no commentary.

THE FINAL EXODUS

No account of the sufferings of the noncombatant population in Macedonia would be complete which failed to describe the final exodus of Moslems and Greeks from the territory assigned to Bulgaria. Vast numbers of Moslems arrived on the outskirts of Salonica during our stay there. We saw them camped to the number, it is said, of 8,000, in the fields and by the roadside. They had come with their bullock carts, and whole families found their only shelter in these primitive vehicles. They had left their villages and their fields, and to all of them the future was a blank. They did not wish to go to Asia, nor did they wish to settle, they knew not how nor where, in Greek territory. They regretted their homes, and spoke with a certain passive fatalism of the events which had made them wanderers. They were, when we visited them, without rations, but we heard that the Greek authorities afterwards made some effort to supply them with bread.

The history of this exodus is somewhat complicated. It was part of the Greek case to assert that no minority, whether Greek or Moslem, can safely live under Bulgarian rule. The fact is, that of all the Balkan countries, Bulgaria alone has retained a large proportion of the original Moslem inhabitants. Official Greek statements predicted, before peace was concluded, that the Moslem and Greek minorities would emigrate from the new Bulgarian territories in a body. The popular press went further, and announced that with their own hands they would burn down their own houses. When the time arrived, steps were taken to realize these prophecies, more particularly at Strumnitsa and in the neighboring villages.

We questioned several groups of these Moslem peasants on the roadside near Salonica. (Appendix A, No. 4.) We took the deposition of a leading Turkish notable of Strumnitsa, Hadji Suleiman Effendi. (See Appendix A, No. 3.) We questioned the Greek refugees from the same town who were at Kukush. We obtained Bulgarian evidence at Sofia. (See Appendix D, No. 65.) Finally, we have before us the confidential evidence of an authoritative witness, a subject of a neutral power, who visited the town before the exodus was complete. From all these sources we heard the same story. The Greek military authorities in Strumnitsa gave the explicit order that all the Moslem and Greek inhabitants of the town and villages must abandon their homes and emigrate to Greek territory. The order was backed by the warning that their houses would be burned. Persuasion was used and was, in the case of the Greeks, partially successful. They were told that the Bulgarians would massacre them if they remained. They were also assured that a new Strumnitsa would be built for them at Kukush on a splendid scale, and they were promised houses and lands. Some of the leaders of the Greek community eagerly embraced this policy and used their influence to enforce it. The Greek exodus was far from being spontaneous, but it was on the whole voluntary. Our conviction is that the Moslems yielded to force. It is true that they had had a terrible experience under the mixed Serbo-Bulgarian rule in the early weeks of the first war. But this they had survived, and most of them stated that Bulgarian rule, after this first excess, had been at least tolerable. Most of them departed in obedience to the order. Some vainly attempted to bribe the Greek soldiers. A few obstinately remained and were evicted by force. The same procedure was followed in the villages.

The emigration began about August 10. On the evening of Wednesday, August 21, parties of Greek soldiers began to burn the empty houses of the Moslem and Greek quarters on a systematic plan, and continued their work on the following nights up to August 23. The Greeks evacuated what was left of the town on August 27, and handed it over to the Bulgarian troops. The Bulgarian quarter was not burned, since the object of the Greeks was to circulate the legend that the non-Bulgarian inhabitants had themselves burned their own houses. To estimate the full significance of this extraordinary outrage, it must be remembered that it was perpetrated in time of peace, after the signature of the Peace of Bucharest.

A similar emigration of the Greek inhabitants of Melnik also took place under pressure. Their houses, however, were not burned, and there are indications that some of them will endeavor to return when the pressure is relaxed.

We found some hundreds of the Greek fugitives from Strumnitsa at Kukush. They are not, in point of fact, Greeks at all, but Slavs, bi-lingual for the most part, who belong to the Greek party and the Patriarchist Church. One woman had a husband still serving in the Bulgarian army; she at least was not a voluntary fugitive from Bulgarian rule. These people were camped amid the ruins of Kukush, some in the few houses which escaped the conflagration, and others in improvised shelters. They received rations, and hoped to see the "New Strumnitsa" arise on the ashes of what was once a Bulgarian town. From the windows of the Catholic orphanage the remnant of the genuine population of Kukush, closely imprisoned, watched the newcomers establishing themselves on sites which were once their own. The Greek authorities are apparently determined to dispose of the lands of the fugitive Bulgarian villagers as though conquest had wiped out all private rights of property. The fugitives from Strumnitsa are simple people. One man spoke rather naïvely of his first horror at the idea of leaving his native place. Later, he said, he had acquiesced; he supposed the authorities knew best. Another fugitive, a village priest, regretted his home, which had, he said, the best water in all Macedonia. But he was sure that flight was wise. He had reason to fear the Bulgarians. A *comitadji*, early in the first war, pointed a rifle at his breast, and said: "Become a Bulgarian, or I'll kill you." He forthwith became a Bulgarian for several months and conformed to the exarchist church. These "Greeks" will probably be well cared for, and may have a prosperous future. The Moslem fugitives furnish the tragic element of this enforced exodus. It creates three problems: What will become of these uprooted Turkish families? Who will acquire the lands they have left behind? By what right can the Greeks dispose of the Bulgarian lands in the Kukush region? The problem may solve itself by some rough exchange, but not without endless private misery and immense injustice.

In bringing this painful chapter to a conclusion, we desire to remind the reader that it presents only a partial and abstract picture of the war. It brings together in a continuous perspective the sufferings of the noncombatant populations of Macedonia and Thrace at the hands of armies flushed with victory or embittered by defeat. To base upon it any moral judgment would be to show an uncritical and unhistorical spirit. An estimate of the moral qualities of the Balkan peoples under the strain of war must also take account of their courage, endurance, and devotion. If a heightened national sentiment helps to explain these excesses, it also inspired the bravery that won victory and the steadiness that sustained defeat. The moralist who seeks to understand the brutality to which these pages bear witness, must reflect that all the Balkan races have grown up amid Turkish models of warfare. Folk-songs, history and oral tradition in the Balkans uniformly speak of war as a process which includes rape and pillage, devastation and massacre. In Macedonia all this was not a distant memory but a recent experience. The new and modern feature of these wars was that for the first time in Balkan annals an effort, however imperfect, was made by some of the combatants and by some of the civil officials, to respect an European ideal of humanity. The only moral which we should care to draw from these events is that war under exceptional conditions produced something worse than its normal results. The extreme barbarity of some episodes was a local circumstance which has its root in Balkan history. But the main fact is that war suspended the restraints of civil life, inflamed the passions that slumber in time of peace, destroyed the natural kindliness between neighbors, and set in its place the will to injure. That is everywhere the essence of war.

CHAPTER III

Bulgarians, Turks and Servians

1. ADRIANOPLE

The Commission was afforded a perfectly natural opportunity of investigating the atrocities attributed to the Bulgarians after they had taken Adrianople. On August 20, 1913, the *Daily Telegraph* published a very solid body of material sent to the paper by Mr. Ashmead Bartlett, and printed under the suggestive heading "Terrible Reports by a Russian Official." On August 26 and 27, this same report appeared in Constantinople in the official organ of the Committee of Union and Progress, *Le Jeune Turc.* Since, however, the latter contained details omitted by the *Daily Telegraph,* the information published in *Le Jeune Turc* was evidently first hand. On August 28 *Le Jeune Turc* revealed the source of its information as the result of an unofficial Russian contradiction inserted in *La Turquie* of August 27. "We are authorized," declared the unofficial organ of the Russian Embassy at Constantinople, "to give a categorical denial of the information of the *Daily Telegraph* reproduced in *Le Jeune Turc,* and attributed to a Russian official. No Russian official has been commissioned to make inquiries in Thrace and at Adrianople, or to obtain any kind of information: none is therefore in a position to supply such a report. Nor have the Russian consuls recorded the facts mentioned in the *Telegraph*." Replying to this denial, which certainly emanated from the Russian Embassy, *Le Jeune Turc* stated that "the document in question was not the work of a Russian official in active service, but of an ex-official, the Consul-General Machkov, who was in fact the correspondent of the *Novoie Vremya*." It should be added that Mr. Machkov's telegraphic "report" was rejected by his paper, and that, according to the statement of Mr. Machkov's colleagues of the Constantinople press, the expense of his telegram amounting to £T150, was repaid him by the Committee. *Le Jeune Turc* itself said: "Fearing, no doubt, lest the paper (the *Novoie Vremya*) being excessively Bulgarophil[1] might not publish the results of his eight days' inquiry in Adrianople, Mr. Machkov sent copies of it to the President of the Council of Ministers and the Foreign Minister."

The veracity of the document, which made a profound impression in Europe, is naturally in no way prejudiced by its origin and history, which do however assist an understanding of the spirit in which it is conceived. One of the members of the Balkan Commission came to Adrianople to follow up Mr. Machkov's information. He succeeded in getting in touch with the sources from

---

[1]This is not at all the case.

which it was largely derived, and had repeated to him verbally practically the whole of the facts and sayings contained in Mr. Machkov's account. The truth seems to be that while Mr. Machkov invented nothing and added practically nothing to the information he was able to collect in Adrianople, he did rely upon distinctly partisan sources, in so far as the medium through which his information came was Greek. The member of the Commission was at pains not to confine his inquiry to this medium. In addition to obtaining from the persons responsible for the administration of the city in occupation, a long series of official Bulgarian depositions (see Appendix G, 3), he succeeded in pushing his inquiries in Adrianople itself, in other than purely Greek areas, and in utilizing the depositions of Turkish prisoners at Sofia, collected by another member of the Commission (see Appendix G, 2). Thus without any intention of rehabilitating the Bulgarians, he succeeded in establishing the facts in a more impartial manner than could be done by Mr. Machkov, who had been known as a very pronounced Bulgarphobe since his tenure of the Russian consulate at Uskub, fifteen years previously.

The account of affairs in Adrianople falls into three sections: first, the capture of the town and the days immediately following,—March 26–30, 1913; secondly, the Bulgarian administration of the town during the occupation, and thirdly, the last days and the evacuation,—July 19–22, 1913.

THE CAPTURE OF THE TOWN

The particular charge made against the Bulgarians during this short period is that they were guilty of acts of cruelty against the Turkish prisoners and of pillaging the inhabitants of the town. Any clear establishment of their responsibility depends on a knowledge of the situation existing prior to the occupation. To throw light on this point we will refer to a document entitled *Journal of the Siege of Adrianople,* published in Adrianople itself over the initials "P. C.," belonging to a person well known in the locality and worthy of every confidence. So early as January 31 (new style), P. C. remarks that "the famine has become more atrocious: there is nothing to be heard in some of the poor quarters of the town but the cries of the little children asking for bread and the wailing of the mothers who have none to give them. From the Hildyrym quarter it is reported that a man has committed suicide after killing his wife and three children. A Turkish woman, a widow, is said to have cast her little ones into the Toundja. * * *" And so on. On February 12, P. C. speaks of the "famished soldiers," forbidden to receive alms, and who "beg you to cast your money on the ground, whence they may pick it up an instant after." On March 2, revolt broke out among the Hildyrym populace and the writer forecasts what was to follow in these words: "A day of vengeance and reprisals will come when the besiegers enter." The soldiery stole bread in broad daylight and refused to give it up when taken in the act. P. C. describes, two days after, how "groups of people pass you who can hardly hold each other up; most of their faces are emaciated, their skin looks earthy and corpse-like; others with swollen limbs and puffy countenances seem hardly able to stumble along. You see them chewing at lumps of snow to cheat their hunger." And nearly two weeks were still to pass before the surrender! On March 12 the following scene took place: "A soldier crossing the Maritza bridge suddenly stopped, beat the air two or three times with his hands and fell down dead." He was thought to be wounded but "it was only starvation." "Stretchers bearing dead or diseased persons pass in constant succession; the doctors predict an appalling mortality as soon as the mild weather comes." On March 19, "In the hospitals one death follows another; yesterday two new cases of cholera were reported." * * * "This morning a poor trooper was brought in, poisoned from browsing on grass. Since the spring the cases have been multiplied." On March 22, "We have had five deaths last night; at the moment the mortality is from 50 to 60 a day, the result not of any epidemic, but of pneumonia affections and physiological starvation. Many have eaten unwholesome or poisonous bodies." Finally, there is the extract referring to the "last day of Adrianople," *i. e.,* Wednesday, March 26, the day on which the town fell. It runs as follows:

> The streets and squares are gradually filling with emaciated and ragged soldiers, who march gloomily to the rendezvous or sit down with an air of resignation at the corners and along the walls. There is no disorder among them: on the contrary they present a picture of utter prostration and sadness. * * *   In contrast to the calm dignity of the Turks, the Greek mob showed an ever increasing meanness. They did not yet dare to insult their disarmed masters, but began to pillage like madmen, to an accompaniment of yells, blows and blasphemies. The Turks let them carry off everything without saying a word.[1]

It only remains now to place the picture thus given in juxtaposition with Mr. Machkov's report and the commentary by the Bulgarian authorities on the events at the moment of the entry of their troops, to see how the different accounts complete and confirm one another.

Take, to begin with, the truly awful fate of the prisoners incarcerated in the island of Toundja, Sarai Eski. A member of the Commission visited the island. He saw how the bark had been torn off the trees, as high as a man could reach, by the starving prisoners. He even met on the spot an aged Turk who had spent a week there, and said he had himself eaten the bark. A little Turkish boy who looked after the cattle on the island, said that from across the river he had seen the prisoners eating the grass and made a gesture to show the inquirer how they did it. General Vasov stated in his deposition (see Ap-

---

[1]These somewhat long quotations from P. C.'s book have been made because it is now a bibliographical rarity. P. C.'s impressions are confirmed by another *Journal of the Siege of Adrianople,* by Gustave Cirilli (Paris: Chapelot, 1913), see pp. 129-151, etc.

FIG. 14.—ISLE OF TOUNDJA
TREES STRIPPED OF BARK WHICH THE PRISONERS ATE

pendix G, 3) that he gave the prisoners permission to strip the bark off the trees for fuel, a fact confirmed by other trustworthy witnesses. The same general, from the second day on, ordered a quarter loaf to be distributed to the prisoners, which he took from the rations of the Bulgarian soldiery. This was confirmed by Major Mitov, who was entrusted with carrying out the order, which is moreover inscribed in the War Minister's archives (see Appendix G, 5). On the first day the victorious soldiery shared their bread with the prisoners and the starving populace. But touching incidents like this could not, any more than the general's order, supply the mass of the people with the food for lack of which they perished, and there are good grounds for believing that these poor wretches went on consuming the "unwholesome or poisonous" stuffs of which P. C. speaks. The mortality among the prisoners must have been severe, especially in the island, where cholera broke out again on the third or fourth day of the siege. There is evidence of a want of tents, which was indeed true of the whole army. The further fact that these unfortunate creatures passed the night exposed to all the rigors of rain and freezing mud, would in itself explain the increasing mortality. It is hardly possible to believe, after reading the descriptions published in the European press, for example Barzini's article in the *Corriere delle Sera,* that the isolation of the sick really had the good effects alleged by General Vasov.

The number of deaths has been variously estimated. Major Mitov speaks of thirty after the first morning. Major Choukri-bey, a captive officer, puts the number in a single day at a hundred; General Vasov estimated the total number of deaths at 100 or 200. The real figures must be higher. The Turk interrogated by the member of the Commission told him that the group in which he was, consisted of some 1,800 persons confined in a narrow space indicated by a gesture. On the night of March 15, 187 of them, he said, died of cold and hunger. The witnesses, it may be noted, put disease second or third among the causes of death. The main cause was still, as during the siege, weakness and exhaustion resulting from starvation, the agonizing effects of which lasted not only during the five days of the final struggle of which Mr. Vasov speaks, but for months. It must certainly not be forgotten that the explosion of the bridge over the Arda, and the destruction of the Turkish depots, made it difficult to provide food for 55,000 prisoners and inhabitants. But when all these admissions have been made, there remains as a fact not to be denied, the cruel indifference in general to the lot of the prisoners. This fact is fully confirmed by the depositions of the captive Turkish officers at Sofia. One is therefore bound to admit that the conduct of the victors towards their captive foes left much to be desired. Some of the rigorous measures reported by Turkish officers might be given as a reason against the attempts to escape made by certain prisoners. But that can not explain everything: what about the vanquished who were bayoneted at night and their corpses left exposed in the streets till noon? The case reported by Mr. Machkov, of the Turkish captive officer who, being too weak to march, was slain by the Bulgarian soldiers in charge, as well as a Jew who had tried to defend him, is fully confirmed by a reserve officer, Hadji Ali, himself a prisoner at Sofia. Mr. Machkov gives the name of the compassionate Jew, Salomon Behmi; and at Constantinople the very words uttered, in Turkish, by this Jew, "Yazyk, wourma" ("It is a sin: do not kill,") were reported to the member of the Commission. Hadji Ali knew the name of the slain Turk, Captain Ismail-Youzbachi, and saw him fall with his own eyes. The explanation given by General Vasov and the Baroness Yxcoull proves that the death of the thirteen Turks slain in the mosque at Miri-Miran can not be laid at the Bulgarians' door; but the depositions of the Turkish soldiers concerning the murder of the sick and diseased prisoners on the Mustapha Pasha route are more than probably true. We shall return to this question of the treatment of prisoners in the chapter dealing with international law.

A Greek version of the pillage of Adrianople reproduced by Mr. Machkov is unkind to a degree calculated to prejudice public opinion. Apart from Mr. Machkov and Mr. Pierre Loti, who merely repeats the Turkish version prevailing at the moment without verifying it, almost all the authorities agree in recognizing that the pillaging during the days that followed the fall of the town was due to the Greeks themselves—to some extent also to the Jews and Armenians, but mainly to the Greeks,—who simply fell upon the undefended property of the Turks. The quotations made above from P. C.'s journal foreshadow this truth, which is fully corroborated and removed from the region of doubt by the body of evidence collected by the Commission.

Pillage had begun in Adrianople before the Bulgarian troops entered the town, and continued until the occupation and the installation of the army was an accomplished fact. Innumerable scenes have been described by eye witnesses. A considerable number,—which could be indefinitely increased,—will be found in the Appendix.

Even during the entry by the Bulgarian soldiers the streets were occupied by the indigenous mob, which pillaged all the Turkish public buildings, beginning with the military clubs, and attacked private houses, beginning with the vacant abodes of the Turkish officers. Patrols were hastily sent out, who lost themselves in the labyrinth of streets, and the people were instructed to whistle for their aid. However, the mass of the Turks feared reprisals on the part of the Greeks. The patrols wandered hither and thither punishing a few malefactors to the cries of "Aferim" (Bravo!) from the Turks. But the Turks themselves told Mr. Mitov, who described the scenes to us, "you can not be everywhere at once." And so the pillaging went on.

An official (whose name we are not permitted to disclose) went through the streets on the second day of the occupation. Djouma-bey, the Secretary of the Vali, pointed out crowds of men and women on every side, carrying off the goods they had stolen. Going into the Hotel de Ville, he asked for a patrol and went out with Major Mitov. Everywhere the same sight met their eyes. A perpetual stream of women, making off with their plunder. He threatened them with his stick. Mr. Mitov pointed his revolver. The women made off, dropping their bundles; then, as the authorities passed on they saw the same women coming back and picking up their booty. They arrived at the mosque, where the populace had stored its household goods. Standing at the door the Bulgarian officer ordered the pillage to stop and the pillagers to go out one by one. As they passed out they were hit with the stick and the butt end of the revolver. The women, however, would not let go; in spite of the bastinado to which they were treated they stuck to their thefts. There were too many of them, both men and women, to be taken up and punished, and they took advantage of this accident of superior strength.

By the third day the patrols were regularly established; order began to be restored. Nevertheless pillage and robbery went on, though under new forms suited to the new conditions. Sometimes the thieves dressed themselves up as soldiers and having obtained entrance to a house in the guise of a patrol, plundered at their ease. It was at this point that the Bulgarian soldiers in their turn began to follow suit, or rather to coöperate with the rest in a new kind of division of labor. There is evidence to show that the patrols worked to protect— the thieves, on condition that they might share in their booty. Major Mitov himself admitted that the soldiers had, to his knowledge, often been induced by their Greek hosts to take part in pillage, every possible means of persuasion being tried as inducement.

Here again the authorities have simply had to admit their powerlessness. The member of the Commission responsible for the inquiry was told that a captive soldier "pomak" (*i. e.,* a Bulgarian Mussulman), well known in one of the consulates, was given a written permit to go about as a "free prisoner"; but on attempting to make use of his permit, he was robbed in the streets by the regulars, who stripped him of everything down to his boots. He returned to the consulate barefoot and a complaint was sent in to Commander Grantcharov. All he could do however was to renew the poor devil's permit and give him a medjide (4½ francs) out of his own pocket, to buy shoes.

Pillage even went on at the Bulgarian consulate in Adrianople. The consul, Mr. Kojoukharov, on returning thither from Kirk Kilisse, whence he had been transferred, found his trunks had been emptied. Mr. Chopov, chief of police in Adrianople, told us that he was unwilling to make inquiry into Mr. Kojoukharov's case, because he was a Bulgarian. On the other hand, Mr. Vasov told us that he refused to make domiciliary investigations, "to avoid disturbing the people," and perhaps also to avoid creating new opportunities for pillage. Such investigations were made, however,—and Mr. Vasov mentioned them himself,—in search of soldiers in hiding and disguise.

Moreover, complaints and requests for inquiries poured in from the pillaged people, especially from the Turks, to the number of two or three hundred a day, according to Mr. Mitov. Thereupon domiciliary investigations were instituted, with excellent results in many cases. A quantity of goods stolen from the Turks were discovered in the houses of the Greeks and handed back to their owners. The chief of police opened a depot in the Hotel de Ville for goods of doubtful origin and unknown ownership; and Mr. Chopov told the Commission that the stolen goods were brought in by the cart load. Certificates were then issued by the municipality stating that ownership of the goods had been acquired not by theft but by purchase. Mr. Mitov explained to the Commission that this became an ingenious and novel method of claiming ownership of certain goods which had in fact been bought, but at a very low price, by Jews and Greeks.

Domiciliary investigations of course furnished their own crop of abuses. Here again, however, Greek complaints can not always be taken as expressing the truth, and nothing but the truth, as is suggested by one case cited by Mr. Machkov. In his report he says: "Soldiers, armed with muskets, carried off a quantity of jewelry and precious antiques from two Greeks, the brothers Alexandre and Jean Thalassinos; they wrenched rings and bracelets from the hands of their sister."

A great deal has been said about the pillage of the carpets and library of the celebrated mosque of Sultan Selim. The evidence collected by the Commission enables us to settle this point. That the Bulgarian authorities, as soon as circumstances permitted, took every reasonable precaution for safeguarding the mosque is clear. It is however not true, nor did the interested parties ever try to spread the belief, that the mosque was not pillaged at all. In the first confusion the fine building served as a place of refuge and was filled by the wretched furniture of the poor Mussulman families who sought an asylum there. Mr. Mitov told us how these Mussulmen took their domestic utensils and their rags with them when they left. Mr. Chopov added that the carpets of the mosque were not injured and the representative of the military governor of Adrianople who was attached to the member of the Commission responsible for the inquiry certainly made no complaints on the score of this alleged vandalism.

FIG. 15.—MOSQUE OF SULTAN SELIM
A CUPOLA OF THE DOME RENT BY AN EXPLOSIVE SHELL

The case of the library is different. During an entire day it was at the mercy of the populace, thanks to the existence of a private entry overlooked by Mr. Mitov at his first visit. On returning to the mosque in the course of the next day he perceived clear traces of pillage. Books were lying on the floor; some had been torn from their bindings; everything believed to have been of value had evidently been removed. In Adrianople and in Sofia it is said that foreign orientalists, enlightened connoisseurs, were happily inspired to save precious manuscripts and rare volumes by buying them at their own expense. If the happy possessors, now that all danger of destruction is over, restore its property to the mosque, this action will have been admirable. The evidence of Baroness Yxcoull shows that order was restored in the mosque, as in the town of Adrianople, from the third day of the occupation.

THE BULGARIAN ADMINISTRATION

Let us now, leaving on one side other characteristic incidents, which could be multiplied *ad infinitum,* consider the general criticism passed on the Bulgarian administration, during the four months of the occupation,—March 13/26 to July 9/22. That the general impression on the part of the inhabitants of Adrianople today is decidedly unfavorable to the subjects of King Ferdinand is undeniable. Those representing Bulgarian authority have thus ample opportunity of estimating at their true value the official expressions of gratitude which were extended to them on behalf of the heterogeneous population of the town. The Turks are only too glad to pass once more under the sway of their national government. Both interest and patriotism have always made the Greeks hostile to the Bulgarians.

The testimony of foreigners is mixed. Mr. Klimenko, head of the Russian consulate during the siege, authorizes us to state in his name that up to his departure from Adrianople on April 7, he had no complaint to make of the Bulgarian régime. The judgment of the brothers of the Assumption, and to some extent of the Armenians, is equally favorable. The documents annexed to this volume contain a list, supplied by the authorities themselves, of the measures taken by the Bulgarian authorities to restore order and satisfy the various nationalities concerned. On the other hand, Mr. Gustave Cirilli, in his *Diary of the Siege,* speaks of the Bulgarian administration as creating "an irresistible tide of distrust or aversion"; due, according to him, "not so much to vexatious exactions which alienated the sympathies of the inhabitants," as to the extravagant nationalism of the Bulgarians, their efforts to impose their religious observances and language. At the same time Mr. Cirilli does justice to the administration of the last commander, Mr. Veltchev, of whom Mr. Machkov speaks so ill, describing his system as "the hand of iron in the velvet glove."

The Commission's competence was, of course, limited to a record of the externals of the régime. It is well known that the municipality retained its powers under the Bulgarian domination and that a majority on the council belonged to the nationalities (three Bulgarians, three Greeks, three Turks, two Jews, one Armenian). The Turks were better disposed than the other nationalities to a Bulgarian administration which saved them from pillage, and frequently passed official votes of approval upon it. The Greeks, on the other hand, did not conceal their hostility. Amusing stories are told of meetings between Mr. Polycarpe, the Greek Metropolitan, and representatives of the Bulgarian power, the former being visibly torn between deference due to constituted authority and inward revolt. The most exaggerated statements about the misconduct of the Bulgarians emanate from Greek sources. The measures taken by General Veltchev are the natural result of the temper of bold bravado which again took possession of the conquered or hostile peoples at the close of the occupation period. Mr. Bogoyev indeed told us (see Appendix G, 5) that Mr. Veltchev called the Turkish and Greek notables together and stated that he should hold the Greek Metropolitan specifically responsible in the event of any rebellion of the "Young" Greeks. The events described above on the Ægean coasts justified only too fully the Bulgarians' suspicions of the Bishop of Adrianople as the center of the patriotic Hellenic agitation directed to the recovery of Thracian autonomy.

In the irritation produced by national conflict, reinforced by the "vexatious exactions" to which the natives were subjected, lies the explanation of their verdict on the Bulgarian régime in Adrianople. Wholesale and retail merchants were thoroughly displeased with the new organization of the wagons employed for importing goods as well as with the maximum prices of commodities fixed by the Bulgarian authorities. The highly interesting explanations of Mr. Lambrev, *apropos* of Greek accusations on this head, will be found in the Appendix. They describe a most interesting social experiment whose aim was to harmonize middlemen's profits with the legitimate needs of the population.

Complaints also came from the owners of houses occupied by Bulgarian officers. Comparisons between Bulgarian and Servian officers are generally disadvantageous to the former. Even friends of the Bulgars admit that, as far as externals go, the Servians had "a more distinguished appearance" and that their bearing made a favorable impression, in contrast to Bulgarian "arrogance." Obviously, therefore, the Servian officer was, generally speaking, preferred as an inmate to his colleague. All the same it is also probable that, in the troublous days, many people were glad enough to have a Bulgarian officer in the house to keep off the blows of the mob and the dubious protection of the patrols. To this the Greek notables apparently afforded an exception, however; in certain cases they met the demands of the billeting committee with a blank refusal;[1] and it was sometimes necessary to use compulsion against them. For example, no suitable lodging being forthcoming for General Kessaptchiev, he was obliged, on his return from Salonica, to put up at the Hotel du Commerce.

It can hardly be denied that there were cases when departing officers,—and not only Bulgarian officers,—did take with them certain "souvenirs" of the houses in which they had dwelt. It is, however, a gross exaggeration to speak of "train loads of *pseudo* war *booty*" being sent to Sofia. Mr. Chopov himself has explained the "Chopov case" (see Appendix G, 6) and his explanation could be confirmed, if needful, by the evidence from Turkish merchants. There has been a certain amount of talk about the story of Rodrigues, an Austrian subject, and it is said that the Bulgarian authorities have promised the Inquiry Commission to assign responsibility, and refund the loss. Laces, ribbons and even ladies' dancing slippers are said to have been carried off from a house in Adrianople, the residence of Nissim-Ben-Sousam.

---

[1] The members of the Committee were Fouad-bey, the Mayor (a Greek doctor named Courtidis), an Armenian and a Jew.

A Sofia paper, the *Dnevnik,* reported the naive admissions of Mr. Nikov, a Bulgarian officer and another devotee of oriental knick-knacks. In the early days of the occupation, he saw an old Greek woman carrying a seat of exquisite workmanship, adorned with carvings in oriental taste. All the trouble and privation he had had to undergo in the long months of the siege, in the muddy trenches, came to his mind and strengthened his conviction that he had a right to the precious piece of furniture. So, instead of conveying it to the depot opened by Mr. Chopov, he took it from the old woman, whose right to it was the same as his own. These officers came and gave evidence before the Commission or made public confession. There must, however, be others who refrained from appearing or saying anything. The carpets of the mosque of Sultan Selim were not touched and Mr. Chopov bought his fairly and squarely. But a member of the Commission was told that there was a time when the price of carpets fell markedly low, and admirable "windfalls" were secured in Sofia.

Again, sums of money are said to have been extorted for the liberation of captured individuals. Mr. Chopov, for instance, speaks of the case of the Vali Habil, whose freedom is said to have been obtained by these means. The Greeks in Adrianople say that he paid the huge ransom of £T40,000. Such a scandalous transaction, had it really taken place, could not have passed unnoted; the story must be added to the legends circulated by the Greeks. At the same time the Commission would not venture to affirm that there were no abuses of this character, on a more modest scale. Tales are told in Adrianople of one Hadji-Selim, tobacco merchant and leader of a band, who was finally executed but whom, previous to his execution, they tried to compel to sign a cheque for £T1,000 to his credit as a deposit in the National Bank of Bulgaria. Hadji-Selim is said to have signed but to have repudiated his signature in prison on the eve of execution, in the presence of the public prosecutor, the director of the Ottoman Bank who had had the cheque presented to him, his assistant and some officers.

These incidents, of interest to the moralist in the tangle they present of human weakness and honest effort, conscientious performance of duty and the crimes that follow in the conqueror's train, may be left to the judgment of the reader: a judgment that must allow for the exceptional circumstances of a great city in a state of siege. There could be no question, at this stage, of the normal administration established later on when the Turks returned as a *"tertius gaudens,"* when war broke out again after the disagreement between the allies and the violation of the first conventions. We have only now to report the events of the last period of Bulgarian occupation.

THE LAST DAYS OF THE OCCUPATION

On July 6/19, the administrative officials in Adrianople received orders to return to Bulgaria. The telegram arrived at 11.30 at night; the public knew nothing of it. At midnight the Rechadie Gardens were still full of people, the inevitable cinematograph films passing before the idlers' eyes. The departure of the Bulgarians was sudden. That is why they left their cannon, their store of ammunition and their supplies behind them; why also the accusations of pillage and outrage made against them fall away, since the very conditions of their departure made them impossible. In their haste they even forgot to remove the sentinels stationed at the doors of some protected houses. Bulgarian merchants complained bitterly of the secrecy with which the move was carried out by the authorities. It did indeed take everybody by surprise.

The authorities left Adrianople on the night of July 6–7 (19–20). The Turks however did not arrive. In the city itself Major Morfov, with his seventy gendarmes, and Commandant Manov, represented law and order, but there were no regular authorities at the station or in the Karagatch quarter, and here deplorable incidents took place. On July 7, some eight military trains left the Karagatch station; by the time the last train but one departed the marauders were already at work and had to be fired at from the carriage roofs. A fire broke out in the depots, started, say the Greek witnesses, by a detachment of Bulgarian infantry on its way from the south towards Mustapha Pasha. Some of these same soldiers told the brothers of the Assumption that the depots had been fired by peasants, the Bulgarian army being beyond the station and the depots at that time. According to their statement the soldiers only set fire to the barracks, which was also used as an arsenal. Anyhow, there is no doubt that pillaging began under the eyes of the Bulgarians as they got on board the trains; that the pillagers were peasants from Karagatch and the adjoining districts, Tcheurek-Keuï and Dolou-djaros; that the soldiers tried to fire on them but the departure of the trains left them free to continue their pillaging. The peasants then armed the Turkish prisoners working on the railway—the same, evidently, of whom Mr. Bogoyev speaks. During the evening of July 7/20, the inhabitants of Karagatch laid in stores of petrol, meal, etc., taken from the depots.

Time went on and the Turks did not appear. The Bulgarians accordingly returned on the morning of Monday, July 8/21. They began by disarming the Turkish prisoners. The scene described by Mr. Bogoyev, when the Bulgarians fired on the prisoners and slew at least ten of them, must have occurred at this stage. According to the explanation given at the time by the Bulgarian officer holding the station, the prisoners tried to take flight in the belief that the Turkish army was already in Adrianople. When the Bulgarians asked where the Turkish prisoners could have got arms, they were informed that these were supplied by the population. From that time on the Bulgarians watched the inhabitants of Karagatch vigilantly. Their houses were visited and they were ordered to hand over whatever had been taken by anybody from the depots within a certain time (up to 3 o'clock in the afternoon), after which requisition would be made by force and punishment made.

Towards evening domiciliary visitations were in fact instituted. It is not quite clear how the forty-five persons arrested were selected. One of them, the sole survivor, Pandeli (Panteleimon), declared that it was his twelve-year-old son who had taken some meal from the depot; he, the father, had restored the booty, as was ordered, the original order having been that the goods restored should be deposited in the streets, but after that he and his comrades in misfortune had been detained to carry the sacks to the station. Pandeli described what followed in detail and his story, tested by the Commissioner making the report by comparison with two other witnesses, one grecophil, the other bulgarophil, is here reproduced. He said:

> In the evening (July 8/21) the wretched creatures were bound together in fours by their belts and conducted along the Marache road by an escort of sixty soldiers. Their money and watches were taken from them before they were bound. They were told that they were being taken to Bulgaria, but when the soldiers got near the bridge across the Arda, someone shouted, "Run quickly, the train is coming!" They crossed the bridge and reached the opposite bank. There they were placed in line, their faces to the river, and pushed into the water. A horrible scene followed. While the poor devils floundered about the soldiers fired on any whose heads appeared above the water. Pandeli owed his life to a desperate movement. As he fell into the water he broke with an effort the belt fastening him to his companions. In the water, alone and free, he began to swim, raising his head from time to time. The shots directed at him luckily did not hit him. He then pretended to be dead, and lying on his back, allowed the current to carry him along. For some time he lost consciousness, then found himself stopped by a tree. He crawled up the wooded bank on all fours. A coachman seeing him fled, terrified by his looks. During the night he made his way back to the Hildyrym quarter and went to the house of his apprentice. (Pandeli is a carpenter in the Karagatch steam mills.)

The photograph (p. 122) shows the corpses of some of the forty-four victims who were fished out of the river some days later. The miserable episode did not come under the cognizance of the responsible Bulgarian authorities, but there can be no doubt of its truth. The panic and excitement of the final moments of departure can not be held to exonerate those guilty of it. The member of the Commission who made inquiry on the spot, learned from the brothers of the Assumption that other persons were arrested for acts of pillage, but they were left as they arrived at the station, people shouting to the escorting soldiers from the carriages of the last train: "Hurry up, the train is going." This happened at three o'clock in the morning on July 9.

The departure of the Bulgarians was then a hurried one. It follows that it is false to urge that "the Bulgarians, knowing that the Turks were going to return, had made every preparation for the final massacre"; that "they were going to massacre the Mussulmen, while the Armenians, whom they had carefully armed, were to be compelled to exterminate the Greeks." The Bulgarians

Fig. 16. Victims Thrown Into the Arda and Drowned

made no preparations for their own departure, and the "nightmares" spoken of in the quotation from Mr. Pierre Loti's article in *L'Illustration,* never had any existence save in the lively imagination of the Greek population which had been heated by agitators. The dramatic picture of the "last night," as described by the eminent French author, thus betrays but too distinctly the sources from which it was drawn. Take one more detail in the same article. Mr. Loti speaks of a young Turkish officer, Rechid-bey, son of Fouad, "captured" by the Bulgarians in a final skirmish on the retreat. "They (the Bulgarians) tore out his two eyeballs," says our author, "cut off his two arms and then disappeared. This was their last crime." Assuredly Rechid's death did produce a profound impression in the Turkish army, where he had many friends. The Commission's investigator was shown the monument set up to his memory and recently consecrated on the Mustapha Pasha road. But as a matter of fact the Turks showed more equity than their admirer. When the investigator went to the office of the *Tanine* at Constantinople to verify the facts, he was told by the paper's special correspondent in Adrianople that in the affray Rechid had received a mortal wound from which death followed instantaneously. The mutilation was but too real; the torture, however, an absolute invention. Even at Adrianople people talked of Rechid's dismembered ears and hands—his hands being beautiful—but no one ever spoke of his eyes being put out.

The account given above of affairs in Adrianople is far from exhausting the evidence collected by the Commission. The curious reader may find fuller particulars in the Appendix, where he can read the documents in proof of what we say. Unfortunately the major portion of the depositions taken at Adrianople itself can not be published or reported in detail since they were given confidentially. But the reader will readily understand that it is those very depositions, collected on the spot, which corroborate and support those used by the Commission in this report.

2. THRACE

In order to gain a personal idea of events in Thrace in the course of the two wars, a member of the Commission went to see the villages situated to the east of Adrianople. He visited the villages of Havsa, Osmanly, Has-Keuï, Souyoutli and Iskender-Keuï. The first of these had been visited by Mr. Pierre Loti, who gave a description of it in *L'Illustration.* Unfortunately while describing the Bulgarian atrocities in this mixed village, Mr. Loti has not been informed that two steps off, at Osmanly, there was a Bulgarian village where the Turks had taken their revenge.

Havsa is composed of two quarters, the Mussulman and the Christian. The Christians here call themselves "Greeks" but they are Bulgarian patriarchists. Their quarter was not burned. The whole population remained there. The Turkish quarter, on the other hand, was almost entirely burned. The Turkish population fled the village on the Bulgarians' approach, that is to say at the beginning of the first war. These Turks took refuge in Constantinople and in Asia Minor. They are now beginning to come back; fifty or sixty families have arrived from Brousse, the Dardanelles and Akcheïr. One might have thought that everyone had gone; there could have been no one left to suffer atrocities. Unhappily there were some exceptions. Rachid, an aged inhabitant of the village, told what follows to a member of the Commission. Four Turkish families had been unwilling to take flight. They remained. The names of the heads of these families were Moustafa, Sadyk, Achmed Kodja, and a fourth whose name has escaped us. These families were slain by the Bulgarians, who also put to death Basile Papasoglou, Avdji, Christo, Lember-Oghlu and Anastasius. All the women were outraged, but it is not true, as Mr. Loti asserts, that they were killed. Only one woman, Aicha, was killed; and the wife of Sadyk, who was among the slain, went out of her mind.

In the village there were two mosques. One of the mosques was turned into an ammunition depot. Another, described by Mr. Loti, was really seriously damaged. The member of the Commission found traces of blood on the floor. The rubrics from the Koran in the interior were in part spoiled, the *Moaphil* place destroyed. the marble *member* half broken, the pillars smashed. The dung seen by Mr. Loti in the minaret had gone, but some traces of it remained. A hole made in the cupola enabled one to get above the higher portion of the ceiling; a hole had been made in the middle of the ceiling and Rachid stated to the member of the Commission that from here, too, dung was spread on the floor below. The sacrilegious intention was even more clearly visible in the way in which the cemetery was treated. "All" the headstones were not broken, as Mr. Loti states, but some of them were. It is likewise true that one of the graves is open. In the bottom of the trench the member of the Commission found the remains of a brandy bottle; relic of a joyous revel! Justice compels the further remark, that the authors of this infamous deed are unknown, and that there are grounds for attributing it to the people of the locality, rather than to the regulars. It was noted that the miscreants confined their attentions to recent headstones and graves, leaving the older ones.

As has already been said, at a short distance from Havsa is Osmanly, a Bulgarian village, and there the Turks took their revenge, when they returned after the retreat of the Bulgarians. There were 114 Christian Bulgarian houses in the village. Not a single one was spared. The churches in the villages were burned and razed to the ground. The member of the Commission could see nothing but the outline of the precincts and the remains of the walls. Research in the interior recovered nothing but the débris of two chandeliers. The member of the Commission, investigating among the cinders, discovered some bits of half burned paper; they were fragments of the Gospel and the Sunday office, in Greek characters (see p. 125). The population had fled to Adrianople and from the Bulgarian frontier, *i. e.,* towards Our Pasha. The whole of the cattle had been lost. Some dozen villagers were, however, working at the harvest in the village. They

explained to the member of the Commission that the oxen they were using belonged to Turks from other villages whose farmers they themselves were.

The next village is Has-Keuï, a repetition of Havsa. The Bulgarian quarter (here they are called "Greeks," and they sing in Greek at church) remained intact, but the cattle were carried off together with the produce of the harvest. Our traveling companion, a Turk, ventured the hypothesis that this might have been the work of *bashi-bazouks*. But a peasant who was present and spoke in Bulgarian to the member of the Commission, said distinctly that it was *"askers,"* the regulars who had pillaged and taken everything without payment. Going on to the Mussulman quarter, we found it still in a state of devastation. Of fifty-five houses only twenty-five remained. This portion of the village was empty, and it was explained to the Commission that the men of the village had gone to Adrianople in search of their families. The refugees who had returned (some twenty-five or thirty families) had gone to dwell in the Christian quarter.

Of the two mosques in the village, one had been entirely destroyed and razed level with the ground, and the school adjoining treated in the same way. The other mosque, which was converted into an ammunition depot, was also damaged, especially inside; several headstones in the cemetery have been broken down.

The two Mussulman villages situated between Has-Keuï and Adrianople,— Souyoutli-dere and Iskender-Keuï,—underwent the same fate as the preceding ones. Of the eighty-seven houses in Souyoutli only eight or ten, with forty or fifty inhabitants, remain. The population had gone to Anatolia. Those who return dwell among the ruins, which they arrange as best they can to shelter them from sun and rain. They call these wretched habitations *"colibi"* (huts).

Iskender-Keuï suffered even more severely. Out of eighty houses but four or five remain. The population fled to Adrianople; all have now returned. The few houses still standing owe their preservation to the fact that they were occupied by Bulgarians. The mosque and school of the village were razed level with the ground.

The conclusion to be drawn from this description is, that as a matter of fact, at the outbreak of the first war the Bulgarians destroyed the Mussulman villages, that the population fled almost to a man, and that the national Mussulman institutions, mosques and schools, suffered specially. Evidently these are not isolated or fortuitous events. They represent national tactics. Bulgarian officers have endeavored to explain this conduct to the Commission, pleading that the material of the houses was used to make winter cantonments for the army. Apart from the fact that such an explanation is equivalent to an avowal, it is inadequate to the extent of the devastation, and fails to meet the destruction of places of worship and schools.

Coming now to July, the Bulgarians began to retreat while the Turks assumed the offensive. Thrace again became the theater of war. Enver-bey is accused with considerable unanimity of having sent Arabian and Kurdish cavalry ahead of his regular troops. These "Arabs" are often indicated, in the victim's stories, as being the authors of crimes. The Commission has collected a body of evidence to the effect that Turkish officers themselves sometimes warned those whom they were protecting of the approach of the "Arabs," and told them to be on their guard. An "Arab" soldier, a Catholic, actually admitted to one of his friends that the *express orders* of their captains were first to burn and ravage, then to kill all the males, next the women (here again all took flight) ; and that he had personally carried out the orders given him. We should not mention this story were it not that it comes from an excellent source, the name of the soldier being known to us, though we naturally refrain from giving it here.

These remarks made and conclusions established, we may pass to another part of Thrace, in order to follow the advance of the Turkish offensive, in relation to alleged excesses.

The member of the Commission had opportunity of free conversation with the Bulgarian refugees in Constantinople itself. They passed through Constantinople in groups. The Commission's member did not encounter the group of ninety persons from the villages of Tchanaktche, Tarf, Yeni-Tchiflik, Seimen and Sinekeli; nor the group of 190 from Baba-Eski and Lulé-Bourgas. But the third group of sixty-two persons was still there. There were hardly any but old people, women and children. Most of them were refugees from the villages of Karagatch (130 houses), Koum-seid (twenty-eight houses), and Mesélim (ten houses), peopled by Bulgarians whom the Turks had brought from the village of Bourgas.

The following is the somewhat rambling story told to the Commission by an inhabitant of Koum-seid, who had reached Constantinople on the previous night, still haunted by recollected horrors:

It was Wednesday the 3d (16th). It was night and the village slept. All at once the Turks arrived. * * * The women and children were in a frenzy. * * * They asked for money. They killed many people. Nicolas the shopkeeper (*bakal*) was killed, Stoyan Kantchev was killed and also his son, fifteen years old. Next came the turn of Demetrius Stoyanov, Saranda Medeltchev, Demetrius Gheorgiev, Petro Stoyanov, Heli Athanasov and his brother, Cone Athanasov (these are his children); next Nicolas Gheorghiev, his wife and his twelve year old son; Demetrius Daoudjiski. Demetrius Christov, Christo Dimitrov—120 persons were gathered together in a single house; the Arabs arrived and asked them "Who are you?" and they replied "We are Greeks." Thereupon they were asked for money. Everything was taken. Their pockets were searched. On the cries of the victims the cavalry came up. They did not touch the people; it was the "Arabs" who attacked them. The attack on the village did not last more than fifteen minutes. Then the Turks went away in the direction of Lulé-Bourgas. * * * However, the next day more "Arabs" arrived. * * *

As the Commission left Constantinople, they met everywhere in Thrace the traces of this Arab cavalry, following on local reprisals and hatreds, and the excesses of the *bashi-bazouks* who took advantage of the anarchy inevitable in transition from one régime to another.

Unhappily time did not allow the Commission to visit the places which bore the first brunt of the rage of the Turkish army when it resumed the offensive; but the evidence collected by them at Constantinople and in Bulgaria, when collated with the reports of special Armenian delegations and some well authenticated documents emanating from a fresh official source, may supply the defect of personal observation. It seems that at the moment of crossing the frontier, which had appeared for some months so definitively established by the Bulgarian conquest, two sentiments ruled in the Turkish army and population. There was vengeance on those of their Christian subjects who had joined friendship with the Bulgarian invaders in the first instance, and then with the Armenians. The Greeks, although they too had suffered at the hands of the Turks, were rather on their side. They too profited by Turkey's recovery to wipe out the traces of Bulgarian domination and reëstablish their own national pretensions. They therefore hailed the Turks' return and often served them as guides and spies. The second feeling, natural enough in the Moslem population returning with the army to deserted villages, was to recover their goods and take them away from their new owners.

At Rodosto, retaken July 1/14, by 200 volunteers who arrived on board an Ottoman gunboat, the first act of the reëstablished Ottoman power was the following proclamation to the Christian and Jewish population of the Sandjak:

> Anyone in possession of goods or arms belonging to the government or cattle or goods belonging to emigrés in the local population, which have been appropriated during the Bulgarian occupation, is invited to come and restore them to the Special Commission sitting at Rodosto. Two days' delay are allowed, starting from today (July 5/18) for those who are in Rodosto, three days for those dwelling in the villages. After the lapse of this delay any one found with appropriated goods in his possession will be treated with all the rigor of the laws.

But the volunteers and emigrés returning home did not wait for the end of this nominal delay. The moment of their arrival they began pillaging and massacring the indigenous population. The volunteers had but just disembarked at Rodosto when they slew the Bulgarian commissary who handed the town over to them; they divided themselves into groups, with four or five *bashi-bazouks* at the head of each, and hastily organized pillage and massacre. They slew the Armenians whom they met in the market place, then the people being once shut up in their houses, ransacked the houses under pretext of searching for Bulgarian soldiers and officers there. The foreign consuls intervened; then the assailants turned their activities to the country outside the town, where no control could be exercised. The results were nineteen corpses buried in Rodosto and eighty-one victims disappeared and evidently slain in the fields. This last figure should be higher,—some put it at 300. The more well-to-do had to pay for their safety between twenty and sixty Turkish pounds a head. Money, jewels and watches disappeared. Even so they were well off, for at eight hours' distance from Rodosto, in Malgara, the catastrophe assumed much larger proportions. There the population was taken by surprise; there were no consuls. The heads of the Armenian community were arrested by the Governor at Rodosto. The Bulgarian police had just quitted the town, which for a day remained without any authorities or public force (July 1 and 2, old style). We can not here transcribe the eloquent story told by the Armenian delegation of what happened at Malgara in this state of anarchy. The reader will find it in the Appendix. But some points, common to the whole of this work of destruction, may be mentioned. Here again the motive is the same as at Rodosto and everywhere else; the military commander of the place addresses the Armenian notables summoned before him, in these terms:—"Armenian traitors, you have in your possession arms and other objects stolen from the Moslems." A sub-lieutenant uses the other argument referred to:—"You other Armenians, you have largely assisted the Bulgarians, but today you shall have your reward." Such terms encouraged the population not to wait until legal measures were taken. On the second and third days of the occupation public criers in the Armenian quarters order "those who have stolen goods belonging to Moslems or who are in possession of arms, to give them up." On the fourth day an opportunity for beginning the attack presents itself. Two terrified Armenians, on being called on by the soldiers to show them the Ouzoun-Keupru road, run away instead of answering. The signal is given; the soldiers, the crowd, put lighted torches soaked in petrol to the houses of the culprits; and the burning of the Armenian quarter begins. At the same time pillage and massacre are going on in the market. Some Armenian soldiers stop the fire, but it breaks out again in the market and thanks to the strong wind assumes terrifying proportions. Explosions of barrels of benzine, alcohol, etc., are heard; the crowd takes them for hidden bombs. Finally the Kaimakam, the representative of civil authority, arrives at Malgara, accompanied by the captain of police and a policeman. Even by standing surety for their lives, he hardly succeeds in persuading the frantic Armenians to come out of their hiding places and organize a little band of some fifty to sixty young people who get the fire under. Results, in the town itself, to say nothing of the environs: twelve Armenians killed, ten wounded, eight disappeared, seven imprisoned, eighty-seven houses and 218 shops burned; a material loss amounting to £T80,000.[1] This time there was also an epilogue.

---

[1] *Le Jeune Turc* of August 12 actually admits that 139 houses and 300 shops were burned at Malgara. It adds: "with the exception of two houses the entire village of Galliopa, consisting of 280 houses, was destroyed by fire; 299 houses were the prey of flames in eleven Christian villages, thirty-five persons were killed and nine wounded.

An Ottoman commission of inquiry tries to cast the responsibility of the pillage and assassinations * * * on the Armenians themselves.

The real massacre begins however when the Turkish army meets Bulgarians on its route, and the events described at Rodosto and Malgara fade before those which took place at Boulgar-Keuï, "a Bulgarian village," as its name shows. Boulgar-Keuï is, or rather was, a village of 420 houses some miles from the town of Kéchane and not far from another village of 400 houses, Pichman-Keuï, whose fate was similar. The information collected by the Commission as to these atrocious events comes from different sources and the evidence agrees in the smallest details. The refugees, women for the most part, scattered in all directions. They were found at Haskovo and Varna in Bulgaria, where two agents of the Balkan Relief Society questioned them and transmitted their depositions to a member of the Commission,—depositions that though coming from places very far distant from each other are identical in terms. Another member of the Commission was able to meet in Constantinople a male survivor of the horrors of Boulgar-Keuï and thus obtained possession of some unpublished Greek official documents which confirm and complete the oral depositions. From all these sources an absolute certainty emerges that the purpose was the complete extermination of the Bulgarian population by the military authorities in execution of a systematic plan.

These events recall those at Rodosto and Malgara, but the end is different. The Bulgarian peasants, like the populations of the towns referred to, had as a matter of fact appropriated the goods of the Turkish emigrés, their coats, domestic utensils, cash, etc. The Turkish soldiers in their turn lay hands on what they can find; they demand money, they carry off clothes, they lead off the big cattle over the frontier to the village of Mavro. Thus a whole week passes, July 2–7. Soon, however, everything changes. The order is given to collect the whole male population at the bottom of the village to receive instructions. The witness spoken of above believed the order to be a lie and preferred remaining at home, thereby saving his life. Nearly 300 men appeared. They were all killed on the spot by a fusillade. Only three men escaped, one of them being wounded (John K. Kazakov). The depositions of the women complete the picture. At Haskovo they told the agents of the English Relief Committee that the Turks went from house to house seeking for male inhabitants over sixteen years of age. Two shepherds, Dimtre Todorov and George Matov, added that the Greeks helped the Turks to tie the Bulgarians' hands with cords. A young woman refugee at Varna described how her husband, father and two of her brothers were shot in front of their house. Another stated that at Haskovo she had seen the Greeks sprinkle her husband and some other men with petrol and then burn them. Other women at Varna confirmed this horrible story and added that the number of victims who perished in this way was twenty-three. A shepherd saw the same scene, hidden in a neighboring place of refuge. The women put the total number of men killed at Boulgar-Keuï at 450 (out of 700). The Constantinople witness adds that all this was going on up to July 29 (old style) when he left the village. At the end of this period the Turks began sticking notices on the walls that there was to be no more killing. A portion of the population believed it and returned. But as the male population returned killing began again by twos, threes and fives. The people were led into a gorge and there shot down. The witness saw that at Pitch-Bonnar and at Sivri-Tépé: in the first place he saw as many as six corpses and recognized one of the six as the "deaf" Ghirdjik-Tliya.

The methods employed with the women were different. They were outraged, and Greeks, clad, according to the witnesses, in a sort of uniform, did the same as the Turks. In the villages of Pichman, Ouroun-Béglé and Mavro, the Greeks were indeed the sole culprits, and they outraged more than 400 women, going from one to another. Young men who tried to defend their betrothed were taken and shot. A woman of Haskovo described how her little child was thrown up into the air by a Turkish soldier who caught it on the point of his bayonet. Other women told how three young girls threw themselves into a well after their fiancés were shot. At Varna about twenty women living together confirmed this story, and added that the Turkish soldiers went down into the well and dragged the girls out. Two of them were dead; the third had a broken leg; despite her agony she was outraged by two Turks. Other women of Varna saw the soldier who had transfixed the baby on his bayonet carrying it in triumph across the village.

The outraged women felt shame at telling their misfortunes. But finally some of them gave evidence before the English agents. They said that the Greeks and Turks spared none from little girls of twelve up to an old woman of ninety. The young woman who saw her father, husband and brothers perish before their house was afterwards separated from her three children and outraged by three Greeks. She never saw her children again. Another, Marie Téodorova, also saw her husband killed before her eyes, and then, dragged by the hair to another house, she was outraged by thirty Turks. Two of her three children were seriously wounded and one of them died at Varna. Sultana Balacheva is the old woman of ninety with wrinkled face, from the village of Pichman, who was outraged by five Turks.

Here are some extracts from secret Greek reports not intended for publication which will serve to show that the same outrages repeated themselves in all the countries in which the Turks took the offensive: "Yesterday evening (July 4/17) from the first hour of the night (*i. e.*, sunset, *alla Turca*) to six o'clock, the Turkish population has invested the Greek village of Sildsi-Keuï (Souldja-Keuï to the northeast of Rodosto), set fire to it and massacred the whole village, women and children included, 200 families in all. The catastrophe was wit-

nessed by so and so[1] * * * No one escaped." Isolated massacres of shepherds and workers in the fields, during the same day, by Turkish soldiers and
inhabitants, are also mentioned in the villages of Simetli, Karasli (both southeast
of Rodosto), Titidjik, Karadje-Mourate, Kayadjik, Akhmetikli, Omourdje and
Mouratli. On the same day (July 4/17) Turkish soldiers killed at Kolibia near
Malgara the hegoumenos (abbot) of the Monastery of Ivéria, Eudocimus, the
priest Panayote and some other persons.

This was but the beginning. Since the population of the neighboring villages fled to Kolibia the Turks "after killing in the interior of the church, burned
all the families of the neighboring villages that had found refuge there" (report
on July 9). In Has-Keuï, another village near Malgara, the Turks burned "a
considerable number of families." In the same village (report of July 12) the
officer ordered the mouktar (head man of the village) to procure him three girls
for the night, "otherwise you know what will happen to you," the officer added,
showing his revolver. The mouktar refused and bade the officer kill him rather
* * * Then "the men were shut up in the church * * * all the women
were collected in a spacious barn and the soldiers banqueted for twenty-four
hours, outraging all the women from eight to seventy-five years of age." The
army took with it quantities of young girls from each village. At Kolibia a young
girl, pursued by a soldier, fell from a window. While her body was still breathing the soldier assaulted her.

The Greek report is at pains to add: "The *caïmacams* demand that a declaration be signed to the effect that all these infamies * * * were committed
by the Bulgarian army." The words explain why in the declarations published
in August, 1913, in *Le Jeune. Turc,* signed by Greeks and written in the name
of the population, the accusations against the Bulgarians are so numerous. The
object was in fact to clear the Ottoman troops of all the crimes committed.[2]

Let us add one more report of July 9 on the events at Ahir-Keuï (Aïor-Keuï
to the east of Visa) which proves that the same system was applied over the
whole area of the territories again occupied by the Turkish army: "Yesterday
evening, July 7, the police selected to guard the inhabitants of Ahir-Keuï sepa-

---

[1]Since all these places have remained in possession of the Turks the necessity of
concealing the names of the authors of the documents will be understood.

[2]For example, at Has-Keuï where according to the authority cited there were "a considerable number of families" killed or burned by the Turks. The following is the declaration of the village notables presented to the *caïmacam* of the Haïvebolou casa: "We deny
categorically the malicious insinuations made against the Ottoman army and in rebutting
them protest against crimes such as incendiarism and assassination perpetrated by the
Bulgarian army in our town at Has-Keuï and at Aktchilar-Zatar at the time of the Bulgarian retreat from these places." Signed Triandaphilou and Yovanaki, members of the
administrative council of the casa, Greek notables: Father Kiriaco, representing the metropolitan, Dimitri, vicar of Has-Keuï: Father Kiriaki, priest of Has-Keuï: Polioyos, Greek
commercial notability." See the *Union* July 24 which published in the same number a
supplement entitled *"Acts of Bulgarian Savagery in Thrace."* The member of the Commission who visited another village of the same name, Has-Keuï, near Adrianople, asked
to see Constantinos, the priest of the village, who also signed a list equally long, of Bulgarian misdeeds there. (See *Le Jeune Turc,* Sept. 2.) The priest did not appear.

rated men, women and children. All the men they beat pitilessly and wounded many with oxgoads; outraged the young girls and women, giving themselves up to libertinism throughout the night."

In this way this portion of Thrace was absolutely devastated. The Greek report of July 9 states that the Ottoman army "massacred, outraged and burned all the villages of the *casas* of Malgara and Airobol. Nine hundred and seventy families from the *casa* Malgara and 690 from the *casa* Airobol, *i. e.,* a population of 15,960 persons, have been either killed or burned in the houses or scattered among the mountains." If this be regarded as an example of the exaggeration not uncommon in Greek sources, confirmation may be adduced from a Catholic paper.[1] "A commissionaire who came from Malgara and arrived yesterday, August 23, at Adrianople, assures us that the whole number of villages burned or wholly destroyed round Malgara is not less than forty-five. He stated that he smelt the intolerable stench of many corpses as he crossed the fields in the neighborhood of Kéchane." A month after this deposition the member of the Commission who went to Constantinople heard there the story of a Greek, an English subject. About a thousand Bulgarians, men, women and children, were still wandering in the mountains, whither they had fled before the horrors described. But they were surrounded by Ottoman troops between Gallipoli and Kéchane and exposed to every imaginable kind of suffering. The witness saw numbers of terrible scenes and took some photographs. Under his very eyes a Turk opened the stomach of a child of seven years and cut it to pieces. The witness is known in Constantinople, and it is extremely important that his photographs should not be mislaid. We might still be ignorant of facts that have come to our knowledge; the whole of this persecuted population might have remained there, wandering among the mountains, awaiting the last stroke from the soldiers who surrounded them. Very luckily the Greeks made the mistake of taking these peasants for compatriots; they received permission from the authorities (who shared the error), to lead them to Lampsacus, at the other side of Gallipoli. Here the missions concerned themselves with their lot, and the Greeks sent a special steamer to bring them to Prinkipo. Only then did they discover that they were not Greeks but Bulgarians. They were thereupon driven out into the streets. Thanks to the intervention of the Russian Embassy and the aid of the Bulgarian exarchate they were reëmbarked and sent back to Bulgaria. Chief among them were women from Boulgar-Keuï, 412 of whom were seen by the English at Varna, as their fellow villager reported when questioned at Constantinople by a member of the Commission.

The space between the frontier ceded at London (Enos Midia), and the old Bulgarian frontier was traversed by the Turkish army in three weeks. The soldiers arrived with views deducible from the facts. An Arab Christian soldier of the Gallipoli army, of which we have spoken above, when asked why he had

---

[1] *La Croix,* August 24–25, 1913.

taken part in these atrocities, forbidden by his religion, replied confidentially in Adrianople, "I did as the others did. It was dangerous to do otherwise. *We had the order first to pillage and burn, then kill all the men."* * * *

Exceptions and distinctions were made however. There was a Bulgarian village, Derviche-Tépé, situated near two Turkish villages, one of which is called Khodjatli. When the Bulgarian army approached, during the first war, sixty Turks sought refuge with their Christian neighbors. They were given protection and did not suffer from the passage of the Bulgarian soldiers. Among others there was a rich cattle merchant who related the following story at Constantinople: "When the Turks returned they had the order not to touch the village. They said to the peasants: Be not afraid of us, since you saved our people; we have a letter from Constantinople to leave you in peace." But the exception confirms the rule. There were also exceptions in the contrary sense, as the history of the village of Zalouf proves. Zalouf was peopled by Albanians, Greek in religion. The next village, Pavlo-Keuï, was Bulgaro-Moslem (pomak). During the first war the Zaloufians pillaged Pavlo-Keuï, and then thought of baptizing the Pavlo-Keuïans. They called a Greek priest, Demetrius, and he converted the village. The Turks, on their return, not only killed Demetrius; they razed the village to the ground. At the same time Aslane, the neighboring Christian village, suffered comparatively little. At Zalouf, 560 persons were killed. On taking the offensive, the Turks transported their habits of pillage across the frontier. Among the villages destroyed in Bulgarian territory the Commission heard of Soudjak, Kroumovo, Vakouj, Lioubimits, etc. When according to the conditions of the treaty of peace, Mustapha Pasha had to be handed back to the Bulgarians, the Turks destroyed it completely, as is shown by the report of Mr. Alexander Kirov of October 19 (November 1), which is in the hands of the Commission. Mr. Kirov recounts that here too the return of the Turks during the second war was signalized by the massacre of the whole male population (eighteen persons). The old woman, who survived this appalling day, described how they killed them one by one amid the laughter and approving cries of the Moslem crowd. The headsman, a certain Karaghioze Ali, varied the mode of execution to amuse the mob. When a young man named Chopov asked to be killed more quickly, that he might not see such appalling scenes, Karaghioze Ali, smoking his cigarette, replied: "Be patient, my child; your turn is coming," and he killed him last. The old schoolmaster, Vaglarov, seventy years of age, was killed in the street, and throughout the day his head was carried by the beard from quarter to quarter. The mother of the writer of the report was killed on July 13/26, and thrown down a well. In the courtyard a portion of her hair, torn off with the skin, and her bloodstained garments, were found.

In Western Thrace traveling was impossible during the Commission's stay. Those places assigned to Bulgaria by the treaty of Bucharest, were inhabited equally by Greeks and Turks. After the departure of the Bulgarian army on

July 9 and 10 (July 22 and 23), the country was occupied by the Greek army and the population little disturbed, "probably thanks to the nomination of a European Commission of Inquiry" (*i. e.,* the Carnegie Commission), in the view of a Bulgarian journal, *Izgrève.* After its departure, however, September 6/19, up to the time of the definitive arrival of the Bulgarian army, the population was entirely in the power of the republican militia, *i. e.,* of the Greek *andartes* and Moslem *bashi-bazouks,* grouped by the priests, schoolmasters and secretaries of the Greek metropolitans (bishops). The Bulgarian population, expecting no good at the hands of this militia, was panic struck and threw themselves on all sides into Dedé-Agatch, where there were still some Greek regulars. But the military authorities did not permit them to enter the town, and the crowd of 15,000 refugees were stationed a quarter of an hour's distance off, in the Bulgarian quarter and barracks. On September 19, the last Greek troops left Dedé-Agatch with the steamer, and the Greek Metropolitan advised the Moslem volunteers of their departure. This is why the refugees, with the exception of about a hundred, had no time to seek shelter in the town. They were discovered by the *bashi-bazouks* "of the militia, and led to Teré and Ipsala like flocks of sheep." They passed the night at Ouroumdjik, where their money was taken from them and the schoolmaster from Kaïviakov, with his wife from Baly-Keuï, were massacred. On the morning of September 23, they met upon their way a company of Bulgarian volunteers, who delivered the larger part of the refugees from the *bashi-bazouks.* But during the retreat, the *bashi-bazouks* succeeded in massacring about one hundred women and children who had remained behind with the baggage, and they took away 100–150 women and children. The rest took the road for Bulgaria with their liberators. But on the morrow, September 24, there was another encounter with the *bashi-bazouks,* near the village of Pickman-Keuï. In this encounter 500 were slain and 200 women and children made prisoners. Newcomers had raised the total to 8,000. At the river Arda new slaughter awaited them. After the crossing they counted again and were but 7,200.

The lot of those who remained at Dedé-Agatch was no better. A public crier shouted on several successive days the orders for the Bulgarians to quit the town; recalcitrants and those harboring them, to be punished like dogs. The frightened Greeks filled several wagons with Bulgarians and sent them to Bulgaria. On their way they saw two wagons full of Bulgarian women and children at the station at Bitikili, and two other wagons at the station at Soffli. The number of Bulgarian villages burned in Western Thrace amounts to twenty-two and the massacred population to many thousands.

3. THE THEATER OF THE SERVIAN-BULGARIAN WAR

In the Appendix will be found a selection of the documents on which this part of the report is based. In Servia, of course the Commission was not accepted by the government and it was therefore compelled to rely on its own resources to prove the Servian thesis of the "Bulgarian atrocities." Nevertheless the documents contained in the English translation are official: the Commission obtained them by purchase from an intermediary.[1] If the conclusion were allowable that, enough having been done to satisfy public opinion, the Servian Government was not displeased in at least allowing information to reach us, the Committee would rejoice thereat while regretting the attitude which Mr. Pachitch found it necessary to adopt in regard to the Commission. In the documents, we have kept whatever seemed to be first-hand information, what seemed to us trustworthy and contained no glaring exaggeration. It will be seen that the documents become the more convincing in consequence. They are, for the most part, official reports sent by the head of the General Staff of the different armies to the General Staff at Uskub, in response to an order from the latter dated June 20/July 3, No. 7669. ("In accordance with the order of the General Staff No. 7669 of the 20th inst.," a phrase appearing at the head of many of the documents which we have omitted, in abridging them for publication.) Thus at the beginning of the war the Servian government took the steps necessary to secure that no single instance of "atrocities" committed by the Bulgarian soldiery should remain unknown to international public opinion. Unluckily for itself the Bulgarian government took no general step of an analogous kind, so that our data as to crimes of this order are necessarily incomplete.

By way of compensation we have, on the Bulgarian side, information of another kind presented spontaneously, so to speak, and recorded on his private initiative by Professor Milétits, in the depositions of eye witnesses of the destruction of Bulgarian villages during the Servian offensive. The refugees from the villages concerned were interrogated when they crossed the border, at Kustendil, on the state of things they had left behind them. We publish these among those depositions which refer to villages situated along the conventional boundary of the rivers Zletovska, Bregalnitsa and Lakavitsa, i. e., the boundary agreed upon by the two armies before the opening of hostilities. In the originals (transmitted to us in a French translation) the names of the witnesses,—eye witnesses in every case,—are given. Since the territories in question are actually Servian and the population has in part returned thither, we have thought it more prudent not to publish the names.

Concerning the regions round the old Serbo-Bulgarian frontier, the Commission has in its possession documents of two kinds. On the Servian side, since the Commission was unable to carry out their intention of going to Knjazevac

---

[1]We have not seen the book announced by the *Serbische Correspondent* of November 28/December 11, which appeared in Belgrade (publication of the *Servian Journalisten Verein*) in English on the "Bulgarian atrocities," but the summary of the contents does not speak of official documents, which constitute the most important and only authentic source; and some of the photographs mentioned also appeared in a recent book by Mr. de Penennrun, *"Quarante jours de guerre."*

they had to be content with the receipt of the documents here published. On the Bulgarian side, the Commission actually visited the neighborhood of Vidine, which had suffered Servian invasion.

Examining first the country which ultimately became the theater of the war, the regions situated near the ancient Serbo-Bulgarian frontier, the Commission admits that the two reports published on the ravages produced by the Bulgarian invasion at Knjazevac,—the Servian official report and the Russian report, are entirely convincing. In Mr. de Penennrun's book (p. 292) there is a photograph showing the room of a Servian doctor pillaged by the Bulgarians in the neighborhood of Knjazevac. Comparing this with the descriptions given by the prefect of the Timok department, Mr. Popovits (see Appendix H, 3), the accuracy of the latter is striking. Yet the first impression of the Russian witness, Mr. Kapoustine, on arriving at Knjazevac, was that of being in a town in its normal condition; and Mr. Popovits confirms this when he says that only isolated houses and shops were burned; twenty-six belonging to twenty owners. When however the houses and shops which appeared in a good state of preservation were entered, there is unanimous agreement (Mr. Popovits visited fifty and Mr. Kapoustine 100) in the sad admission of complete destruction. "It is not a case of mere pillage," says Mr. Kapoustine, "it is something worse; something stupefying." "One was absolutely dumbfounded," Mr. Popovits adds, "by the reflection that all that could have been done in so short a time, when there were, as the inhabitants assured me, only 10,000 soldiers." In fact, the pillagers were not content with carrying off the things of which they could make some use. What one might call a fury of gratuitous destruction seems to have led the destroyers on. They must have been drunk to behave as they did. Whatever could not be carried off was spoiled; the furniture was destroyed, jam thrown into the water-closets, petrol poured upon the floor, etc.

In the environs it was still worse. The peasants told Mr. Kapoustine that the Bulgarian soldiers went through the villages in groups of fifteen or twenty, pillaging houses, stealing money and outraging women. Mr. Kapoustine did not succeed in tracing the outraged women. But as the Commission knows from personal experience, the difficulty of conducting an inquiry of this nature, especially when the women go on living in the villages, they could not feel justified in rejecting the testimony of inhabitants who know that "in the village of Boulinovats seven women were outraged, two among them being sixteen years old; at Vina nine women, one of whom was pregnant; at Slatina, five, one of whom was only thirteen."

Turning from this to the impressions actually gained by the Commission in Bulgarian territory, it must be admitted that it is unfortunately true that the same methods were employed by the Servian invaders towards the Bulgarian population. Let us begin however by saying that we have seen homage rendered to the superiority of the Servian command in the Bulgarian press itself. A correspondent of the Bulgarian paper *Narodna Volia* felt constrained to admit that "to the honor of the Servian military authorities," there were in the village of Belogradtchik, occupied by the Servians on July 9/22, "few excesses or thefts committed by the army. Such as there were took place in the course of the first day and remained secret. The houses and the shops, where there was nobody, were ravaged. But on complaints being made by the citizens, the guilty soldiers were punished. The commandant, Mr. T. Stankovits, from Niché, a deputy in the Skupshtina, showed himself resolute in preserving order and stopping any attempts at crime." The same can not be said of the Bulgarian military authorities in the Knjazevac affair, on the admission of Bulgarians themselves, collected by the Commission.

But with this single exception the procedure in the one case was the same as in the other; another Servian socialist paper, the *Radnitchké Noviné,* admitted it frankly. It was in the villages that the population suffered most. "Quantities of people," the *Narodna Volia* continues, "were forced to hand over their money. In the villages of Kaloughère and Béla the gallows are still standing by which the Servian "committees" terrorized their victims. On the "committees" there was even a priest. Whole flocks of sheep, goats, pigs, oxen and horses were lifted. All the seeds that could be discerned were dug up. All the clothes and all the furniture were taken. The Bulgarian villages near the frontier naturally suffered most. Whole caravans came and went full of booty. The *Radnitchké Noviné* speaks of "heaps of merchandise and booty taken to Zayéchare and sold there. Also no small number of women were violated." The Commission can authenticate the truth of the statements in these papers by what was heard and seen at Vidia and in the neighborhood. Before leaving the Balkans a whole day was spent in visiting the village of Voïnitsa, and taking photographs there.

This village, in the Koula canton, comprised sixty-three houses; thirty-two were totally burned and the rest plundered and ruined. The Commission summoned some of the old men who had remained in the village after the arrival of the Servian troops. One of these old men, "Uncle" Nicholas, aged eighty, was killed in his house and his corpse covered with stones; the Commission photographed his tomb, where a simple wooden cross is to be seen. Another old man, "Uncle" Dragane, aged seventy, was also killed. A third, Peter Jouliov, aged seventy-three, had the idea of going up to the Servians with bread and *raki* (brandy) in his hands. For only reply one soldier ran him through with his bayonet and two others fired on him. "You have killed me, brothers," he cried as he fell. When the soldiers went, he crawled on his stomach some yards, to the nearest shelter. There for two days and two nights he lay in hiding in the forest without eating. His wounded foot was swollen and he had found no means of dressing it in the village of Boukovtsé. At last on the ninth day he reached the Servian ambulance. The doctor made a dressing for him and the old man thanked him and gave him six apples. "You do not belong to this place, I see," said the doctor, "since no one but you has given me anything. You are a man of God; thank you." Peter Jouliov himself told the Commission this simple and touching story.

At Voïnitsa there were also some old women who suffered. Three of them were killed: Yotova Mikova, aged seventy; Seba Chéorgova, seventy-five, and Kamenka Djonova. A witness, repeatedly beaten by the Servians who asked him why the population had fled, saw them set fire to the houses; only one was saved, and on it some one had scrawled in chalk the word *Magatsine*, to show that it was a food depot. Other witnesses saw the soldiers carrying off stolen furniture, carpets, woolen stuff prepared for carpet making, etc. Some peasants who thought that we were a government commission, sent to inventory their losses, brought us long lists of them. Here are some of the papers which we kept for information, after explaining to the villagers the mistake they made:

HOUSE OF TANO STAMENOV

1.	Woodwork 18 x 10 met. 19 windows, 14 doors............fr.	12,000
2.	Light woodwork 16 x 8	2,000
3.	A wine cask	200
4.	Miscellaneous (3 *badne*)	150
5.	Four barrels	50
6.	A German plow	75
7.	A caldron	400
8.	A machine, called *tarabi*	500
9.	A maize grinder	95
	Total	15,470

PROPERTY OF JOHN TANOV

1.	Maize 300 *crinas*[1] ....fr.	600
2.	Two oxen, with cart	1,000
3.	Grain, 30 *crinas*	80
4.	A vat of 600 *okas*[2]	80
5.	A barn 6 x 2 met..	50
6.	A plow	40
7.	Four big baskets (*kochla*)	50
8.	Wool (*45 okas*)	100
9.	Three stoves	100
10.	Two beds	40
11.	Six pigs and 3 porkers	200
12.	Eighty hens	80
13.	Haricots—10 *crinas*	60
14.	Wine, 20 k.	50
15.	Two hives	35
16.	A kitchen garden 1½ dec.................................	100
17.	Three tables	40
18.	Other indecipherable household goods	448
	Total	3,153

The property of another son, Alexander Tanov, fr. 900.

[1]About a bushel.
[2]Weight about 1,280 grams.

From the losses here sustained by a single family,—father and two sons, amounting to fr. 19,500 (and the prices are not overstated, so we were assured by the inhabitants of Vidine), some idea may be formed of the enormous figures of the estimated cost of the Balkan War to the inhabitants. The loss caused the Servian peasants by the Bulgarian invasions at Knjazevac is rated in the document we publish at fr. 25,000,000 or 30,000,000. No one, as far as we are aware, has tried to estimate the loss caused the Bulgarian peasants at Belogradtchik and Vidine by the Servian invasion.

In the principal area of military operations, in the canton of Kratovo, Kotchani, Tikveche, Radovitch, excesses are naturally to be expected of a different order from those due to military incursions on the Serbo-Bulgarian frontier. Here were two armies face to face for months at a short distance from one another. Each accused the other of provocation and acts of bad faith. The Bulgarians thought they were sure to defeat the old ally and new enemy at the first encounter. The Servians rejoiced in advance in the opportunity of restoring Servia's military reputation and revenging the defeats of 1885. Each side saw in the issue of the conflict the solution of difficulties that were, from the national standpoint, questions of life and death. The conflict over, the one side said, "We are not vanquished," and the other, after securing the price of victory, declared, "For the first time we have really fought; here are adversaries worthy of us." "Yes," Mr. de Penennrun agrees after seeing the two armies, "From the beginning this great war was savage, passionate. Both sides are rude men and knowing them as I know them I have the right to say that they are adversaries worthy of one another."[1]

The "savage war" opened in a way that was savage in the highest degree. The first shock was peculiarly cruel and sanguinary; it was to decide the fate of the campaign. The general staff of the *voyévoda* (Poutnik) (commander-in-chief), puts the losses of the two Servian armies during the one night attack (June 16/29 to 17/30) at 3,200 men: almost all the men who fell were slain by bayonet or musket blows, even after surrender. Mr. de Penennrun, who makes this statement, goes so far as to suppose that this Bulgarian fury was intentional and decreed by the commandant, who saw in it a means of striking terror and so of victory. According to him, the "atrocities were almost always enjoined by the officers on their men, who, despite their native harshness, hesitated to strike other Slavs, but yesterday their brothers in arms." The spirit of Mr. Savov's telegram already known to us seems to confirm this supposition, since it enjoins the commandant to "stir up the *morale* of the army," and teach it to "look upon the allies of yesterday as enemies." However that may be, the Servian documents we publish bearing almost exclusively on these first days of the war, June 17–19 to 25, do prove abundantly that this end was attained and much exceeded.

---

[1] *Quarante jours de guerre dans les Balkans.* Chapelot, Paris, 1913, pp. 39-40, 183.

The reader's attention is drawn in the first instance to documents 1, 3, 7, 10 (Appendix H). Here we have soldiers miraculously surviving from fights in which they were wounded, after enduring the same sufferings as their comrades who lie dead on the field of battle. They can recount the treatment inflicted by the Bulgarians on the wounded, and when they do so they speak as victims. The Bulgarian soldier's first movement was always the same,—to steal the money and valuables on the body which would soon be a corpse. After stripping the wounded man, the second movement,—the intoxication of combat being somewhat dissipated,—was not always the same. Should he be killed or no? Captain Gyurits (Appendix H, 2) tells us that he heard the Bulgarian soldiers discussing the question among themselves, and that massacre was decided on by the officer. Lieutenant Stoyanovits tells us that the men, after pillaging him, prepared to go off; but one of them reminded the others that there was still something to do, and then two of the soldiers ran him through with their bayonets, and the third struck him with the butt end, but without killing him. Lieutenant Markovits survived, after being pillaged, because the Bulgarian sanitary staff who had stripped him of his valuables did not want the trouble either of killing him or conveying him to hospital, as he asked them to do; instead they left him lying in the forest for three days until, on June 19, he was found there. Prisoners who were not wounded were pillaged likewise, and then kept with a view to extracting information from them (case of Lioubomir Spasits, Appendix H, 3) or let go and then fired on (Miloshevits, Appendix H, 4 (c)). There were cases however in which those who had money to offer were set free while those who had none had their throats cut. Cases were also quoted of whole bodies of prisoners being shot after capture. On the other hand a case is mentioned in which some wounded prisoners not only were taken to the Bulgarian hospital but made their escape, after they were restored to health, through the complicity of a Bulgarian sergeant (Appendix I, 4 (c)).

All this naturally refers only to cases in which the men were able to deliberate and choose. The horrors of battle itself, during which men were actuated and dominated solely by its fury, were appalling and almost incredible. The most ordinary case is that described in full detail in the two medical reports we publish. The profound impression produced by the death of Colonel Arandjelovits, who was killed during the retreat of July 8/21, and whose death is described in the first reports, is largely due to the personality of the victim, an officer known and loved by everyone, and decorated by King Ferdinand for his share in the siege of Adrianople. The scientific facts were that the colonel, grievously wounded but still alive, was finished by a discharge in the back of his neck and a bayonet thrust at his heart.[1] The nine soldiers killed during the engagement of July 9/22, perished in the same way, as the second report shows. They were wounded, more or less seriously, by bullets from a distance; then finished by

---

[1] See photograph of Mr. Arandjelovits in Mr. de Penennrun's book, p. 292.

violent blows on the head delivered close at hand with the butt end or bayonet, or by a discharge. There are quantities of instances of wounded Servian soldiers being stabbed to make an end of them.

Worse still, killing did not content them. They sought to outrage the dead or even to torture the living. Here we have the really savage and barbarous side of the second war. Some of the cases may have been exaggerated or inexactly reported. But they are so numerous that the agreement of the witnesses alone proves their authenticity. We will set them down in the order in which they appear in the documents, as indicated:

1. In the fight that took place near Trogartsi, Servian corpses were found with mutilated parts stuck in their mouths.

2. In the fight of June 17 and 18, Andjelko Yovits, still alive, had ears and nose cut (H, I, 2).

3. In the battle of Krivolak, June 21, a Servian volunteer had his eyes gouged out (H, I, 4 (b)).

4. On June 21 Zivoin Miloshevits and Bozidar Savits had their tongues cut out and chopped in pieces because they had no money to buy back their freedom with (H, I, 4 (c)).

5. On June 19 L. Milosavlevits saw the corpse of a Servian soldier with his eyes gouged out (H, I, 4 (c)).

6. Near the village of Dragovo a Servian corpse was fastened to a pillar with iron bands and roasted—seen by Corporal Zivadits Milits (H, I, 4 (c)).

7. On June 17 a Servian prisoner was thrown up in the air amid cries of hurrah! and caught on bayonets—seen by Arsenie Zivkovits (H, I, 4 (c)). The same case is described elsewhere, near the Garvantoi position.

8. On June 18 a Servian soldier was *put on a spit and grilled* (H, I, 4 (c)).

9. On June 25 Captain Spira Tchakovski saw the roasted corpse of a Servian soldier to the north of the village of Kara Hazani (H, I, 5).

10. Captain Dimitriye Tchemirikits saw two roasted corpses, one near the Shobe Blockhouse, another near the village of Krivolak (H, I, 5).

11. Mutilated corpses, with hands and legs cut, have been seen by the patrol in various places (H, I, 5).

12. On the battlefield mutilated corpses are found. One corpse had the skin of the face taken off, another the eyes gouged out, a third had been roasted (H, I, 6).

13. At the positions between Shobe and Toplika, June 24–25, mutilated corpses are found, some with the eyes gouged out, others with ears and noses cut; the mouth torn from ear to ear; disemboweled, etc. (H, I, 6).

14. At the Tcheska positions the corpse of a Servian soldier—a marine from Raduivatz—was burned (H, I, 8).

15. At Nirasli-Tépé, a soldier had his eyes gouged out (H, I, 9).

16. A Bulgarian lieutenant broke hands and crushed fingers under stones; evidence of Kosta Petchanats (H, I, 9).

17. At Kalimanska Tchouka the wounded left at the village of Doulitsa had their noses and ears cut, eyes gouged out and hands cut off (H, III, 7).

The Commission can find no words strong enough to denounce such outrages to humanity, and feels that the widest measure of publicity should be given to all similar cases, indicating the names of the culprits wherever possible, in order to curb barbaric instincts which the world is unanimous in blaming.

The Commission is not so well provided with documentary evidence as to the excesses which may have taken place on the side of the Servian army during the combat. Isolated cases, however, confirmed by documents and by evidence, show that the Servians were no exception to the general rule. In the Appendix will be found a *procès-verbal* taken by the Bulgarian military commission, which proves that five Bulgarian officers, Colonel Yanev (at the head of the Sixth Cavalry), Lieutenants Stefanov and Minkov, veterinary sub-lieutenant Contev and Quartermaster Vladev, were massacred. After having been taken prisoner at Bossilégrade on June 28/July 11, Colonel Yanev was ordered, on pain of being shot, to send the Bulgarian squadrons the order to give themselves up to the Servians. He obeyed, but his orders were not followed. The five officers were then taken outside and entrusted to an escort of ten Servian soldiers, who then shot them all, stripped off their boots and plundered them. The sixth, Doctor Koussev, had been wounded by a Servian soldier immediately after yielding, and this saved his life. A Servian doctor, Mr. Mitrovits, came to see him; expressed his astonishment and regret at seeing him wounded and conducted him to the Servian ambulance, whence he was conveyed to the Mairie. The precipitate retreat of the Servians, who had to abandon their own wounded, saved him. We have seen his deposition, which confirms the *procès-verbal*.

The conduct of the Servians on the battlefield is characterized further by the deposition of a Bulgarian officer in the 26th, Mr. Demetrius Gheorghiev, wounded near the Zletovska river during these same days at the beginning of the war (June 21/July 4). His story is as follows:

> Our people had beaten a retreat. I crawled into the thicket. Near-by, in a clearing, a petty officer of the 31st was lying groaning. I advised him not to groan for fear of being discovered. I should have been discovered likewise. I was right. A Servian patrol passed, saw him and killed him. I was not seen, however; I was hidden in a hollow. A little further away from me, at a distance of three or four hundred paces, a petty officer of the 13th lay, Georges Poroujanov. I saw the patrol discover and assassinate him also. Finally, on June 22, the Servian ambulances appeared. I saw and called to them. They asked me, "Have you any money?" I had 900 francs. I replied "Yes." Then the ambulance men came up to me. One of them took the money. They thereupon put me on a stretcher and carried me to the village of Lepopelti.

The rest of Mr. Gheorghiev's story is omitted. After many difficulties, upon the refusal of the Belgrade doctor, Mr. Vasits, to attend to him because

FIG. 18.—BODIES OF FIVE MURDERED BULGARIAN OFFICERS [SEE P. 143]

he regarded him "as an enemy," Mr. Gheorghiev was taken to the Russian mission and there attended.[1]

If the information as to the conduct of the Servian soldier on the field of battle does not amount to much, our Bulgarian documents call up a sad enough picture of the treatment they meted out to the population in the conquered territory.

Here again the accusations are mutual. We publish a Servian document (Appendix H, III) which gives a general description of the ravages produced in the theater of war, along the left bank of the River Zletovska and the right bank of the Lakavitsa. The document attributes the ruin of these villages, the destruction of property and the violence endured by the population, to the Bulgarians. This may be admitted so far as it concerns the Moslem population, who, according to the document, fled before the Bulgarians and returned later with the Servian army. But the other portion of the population was Bulgarian and it evidently can not have suffered at the hands of the Bulgarian army, except in so far as the population inhabiting the theater of war must inevitably suffer. We know from the Bulgarian document we publish that the opposite is the case, at least in case of the villages whose names reappear in the Servian and in the Bulgarian list, and in that of quantities of others not mentioned by the Servians. What we see is the Bulgarian population fleeing before the Servian army to escape violence and vengeance at the hands of the returning Turks, or awaiting their hour on the spot. The evidence of the refugees is formal and decisive. They were perhaps not sufficiently removed from the events to judge them fairly; but their intimate and profound knowledge of local conditions compensates for this.

Let us stop and consider these depositions from peasants, priests and schoolmasters. whose names are known to the Commission. We see everywhere the reappearance of the Servian army, giving the signal for exodus. It is true that the Servians sometimes declare that they are bringing with them "order and security," and threaten the population with burning and pillage, only in cases where those who have taken flight will not return. Some of the more credulous do return. What awaits them?

It must be recalled that the Servian soldiers do not arrive alone. They are accompanied by people who know the village and their inhabitants better. And there is Rankovits, a Servian *comitadji* turned officer, who had been carrying on propaganda in favor of King Peter in these same villages since March. Then there are the *vlachs* (Wallachians, Aroumanians) put in charge of the administration, because they are ready to call themselves "brothers of the Servians," on condition of being allowed to enrich themselves at the expense of the population. Their formula for the Bulgarian population, the most numerous, is as follows: "Up to now you have been our masters and pil-

---

[1]For the treatment of the wounded by the Servians, see also Chapter V.

laged our goods; it is now our turn to pillage yours" (Appendix H, IV). But the most important point to notice is that the Turks appeared with the Servian army, called by them to their aid and free to pursue them when their turn should come (see Chapter IV). The Turks had vengeance to enact for probable spoliation committed by the Bulgarian army; and in addition for forced conversions (Chapter IV). This is what happens. Take the village of Vinitsa (given in the Servian document as having been burned and ravaged by the Bulgarians, "during their retreat"). The Servian soldiers, as soon as they entered, began asking the villagers, "one after another, are they Servians or Bulgarians?" Anyone replying "Bulgarian" is forcibly struck. Then the Commander of the troops chose seventy peasants and ordered them to be shot. In other villages, as we shall see, the order was executed; here it was recalled and the peasants taken to Kotchani. Three days after the Servian entry, the Bulgarian army returns (June 27) and then leaves the village again. It is only then, after having tried Servian "order and security," that the population "mad with terror at the prospect of new tortures," leaves the village. The old people, however, remain. They are witnesses of the pillage of all the shops and all the houses of the Servians. In the Appendix will be found the names of the persons killed and tortured for the sake of their money, and women outraged at Vinitsa.

At Blatets, the same story. The Turks denounce Bulgarian "suspects." Another witness says, they point them out "as being rich." Some twenty are imprisoned; a boy's eyes gouged out to make him say where there is money. Another is thrown into the fire for the same reason; whole quarters are pillaged and burned. Then the suspects are led away from the village. The officer cries "Escape who can!" The soldiers fire on the fugitives and bring them all down. At Bezikovo some twenty dead are noted, a child a year and a half old burned alive, three women outraged, two of them dying. Sixty houses are burned and the harvest also, and the stock carried off. In the village of Gradets, where the Servian cavalry promises "order and security," only a few old men are left and go to meet the soldiery. On hearing the promises, fifty to sixty peasants, who believe in them, return. Then by express order the Turks throw themselves on the houses; between sixty and seventy men are seized, led outside the village and there stabbed amid the despairing cries of the women who followed their husbands. The Turks want their share; they take three picked young girls and carry them off to their village with songs and cries. The next day the village is in flames. A day later the chase of the fugitives begins.

Some 300 went forth; only nine families reach Kustendil. The others are killed or dispersed. "The Servian bullets rained down like hail;" men, women, children fell dead. In the village of Loubnitsa the Servian soldiers asked the wife of a certain Todor Kamtchev for money. As she had none, they stabbed a child of four years old in her arms.

At Radovitch, a town, pillage is the rule. Under pretext of gifts for the

Red Cross the peasants paid fifteen, thirty, forty-five Napoleons, to escape the tortures awaiting them.   The guide who points out the "rich men" here is Captain Yaa, an Albanian, a former servant in the Servian agency at Vélès, now head of a band protected by the military government.   Our witness concludes: "At Radovitch the Servian officers collected a lot of money."   In the surrounding villages too "a great deal of money was extorted."   The Servians undressed and searched a woman for money; then outraged her at Chipkovitsa.   At Novo-Sélo the women fled into the forest; but the men who remained were plundered. At Orahovitsa, a Turkish local magnate from Radovitch wants to have his share. He arrives, accompanied by Servian soldiers, and once more money is extorted from the women by burning their fingers; and arms are carried off.

These are fragments of the dismal annals of these days at the end of June (old style) in a small territory which afterwards became the property of the invading state.   "Order" of a kind is restored, the conquest once accomplished, and some of the refugees have returned to their villages.   We shall have further opportunity of returning to the "order" similarly established in the annexed territories.   For the moment we add one observation.   The things we have described, horrible as they are, show in their very horror abnormal conditions which can not last.   Fortunately for humanity, nature herself revolts against "excesses" such as we have observed in the conflict of two adversaries.   In blackening the face of the other each has tarred his own.   After judging them on their own evidence, we have to remember that in ordinary times they are better than the judgment each is inclined to pass on the other and to impose upon us.

CHAPTER IV

The War and the Nationalities

1. EXTERMINATION, EMIGRATION, ASSIMILATION

The reader who has perused the preceding pages and followed the endless chain of deplorable events studied and described by the Commission, has doubtless discovered the common feature which unites the Balkan nations, though it is necessary to discover that war is waged not only by the armies but by the nations themselves. The local population is divided into as many fragmentary parts as it contains nationalities, and these fight together, each being desirous to substitute itself for the others. This is why these wars are so sanguinary, why they produce so great a loss in men, and end in the annihilation of the population and the ruin of whole regions. We have repeatedly been able to show that the worst atrocities were not due to the excesses of the regular soldiery, nor can they always be laid to the charge of the volunteers, the *bashi-bazouk*.[1] The populations mutually slaughtered and pursued with a ferocity heightened by mutual knowledge and the old hatreds and resentments they cherished.

The first consequence of this fact is, that the object of these armed conflicts, overt or covert, clearly conceived or vaguely felt, but always and everywhere the same, was the complete extermination of an alien population. In some cases this object expressed itself in the form of an implacable and categorical "order"— to kill the whole male population of the occupied regions. We are in possession of some letters from Greek soldiers, of unimpeachable authenticity. These documents, though written in our own day, throw back to the time of the Assyrian conquest. "We have taken a small number of prisoners and them we have killed, such being the orders received * * * in order that the dirty Bulgarian race may not spring up again" * * * "We are,"—such is the order,— "to burn the villages, massacre the young, and spare none but the old people, children and minors." Here the intention is clearly to spare none but those no longer capable of carrying on the race and those still young enough to lose their nationality by receiving a Greek education.

It was the same in Turkey, as we have seen in describing the events which took place in the environments of Malgara and in Thrace generally. Men, women and children were separated, and all killed without exception. Here the testimony of the Christian Arab soldier shows that, at least in certain por-

---

[1]This term of dismal memory has taken on an altogether fresh significance during the latest wars. A *bashi-bazouk* is no longer necessarily a Turk. He is the volunteer, the *Freischarler* of all the belligerent nations without distinction; the Bulgarian *comitadji*, the Greek *andarte;* generally speaking he is any combatant not wearing the uniform of the regular.

tions of the Turkish army, when the offensive was taken, the "order" was given to proceed systematically. It would be too much to assume that the outrages committed on women were the realization of an "order."

The orders given to the Slav armies were perhaps a trifle less barbarous. It does not, however, follow that there was no intention of conquering the territory without maintaining an alien population there. "Orders of extermination" were not given, orders to the contrary were indeed given [see below]. But in private conversations the same idea is constantly met. What proves that it was not a mere mode of speaking, is the fact that the Turkish population suffered at the hands of the Bulgarians, and the Albanian population at the hands of the Servians as well. As regards the Bulgarians, this is proved by the villages in which all the Turkish quarters were burned, and which were visited by the member of the Commission in Thrace. As to the Servians, we possess authentic evidence in the shape of a letter from a member of the Servian army, published in the Servian Socialist paper *Radnitchké Noviné,* of October 9/22. The contents of this letter resemble only too closely the letters of the Greek soldiers. True, the reference here is to an expedition made to repress a revolt. "My dear Friend," writes the soldier, "I have no time to write to you at length, but I can tell you that appalling things are going on here. I am terrified by them, and constantly ask myself how men can be so barbarous as to commit such cruelties. It is horrible. I dare not (even if I had time, which I have not) tell you more, but I may say that Liouma (an Albanian region along the river of the same name), no longer exists. There is nothing but corpses, dust and ashes. There are villages of 100, 150, 200 houses, where there is no longer a single man, literally *not one.* We collect them in bodies of forty to fifty, and then we pierce them with our bayonets to the last man. Pillage is going on everywhere. The officers told the soldiers to go to Prisrend and sell the things they had stolen." The paper which published this letter adds: "Our friend tells us of things even more appalling than this (!) ; but they are so horrible and so heartrending that we prefer not to publish them."

The object of the Albanian expedition, referred to by the correspondent of the *Radnitchké Noviné,* is known to have been the repression of the plans of the Albanians who had at this period revolted against the Servians. The Albanian revolt was represented by the Servians as the result of the activities of the Albanians in autonomous Albania, and at the same time of Bulgarian conspiracies. These two reasons are probable enough, but they do not exclude a third,— the state of mind of the Albanian population in subjection to Servia. This population had its own reasons for complaining of the Servian administration. The event is explained in a letter from Elbassan, published by a Bulgarian paper, (*L'Écho de Bulgarie,* September 28/October 11), and alleged to come "from a very reliable source." The Commission was not able to verify these statements, but there are no reasons for doubting them, in view of all that has been seen and heard:

On September 20 last (new style), the Servian army carried off all the cattle of the Malesia of Dibra. The herdsmen were compelled to defend themselves, and to struggle, but they were all killed. The Servians also killed the two chieftains of the Liouma clan, Mehmed Edem and Djafer Eleuz, and then began pillaging and burning all the villages on their way: Pechkapia, Pletza and Dochichti, in lower Dibra; Alai, Beg, Machi, Para, Oboku, Klobotchichta, and Solokitzi, in upper Dibra. In all these villages the Servians committed acts of horrible massacre and outrage on women, children and old people. In the town of Dibra itself the authorities published an order to the effect that the bazaar was not to be opened on Sunday or the inhabitants to come out of their houses on that day. Forty-eight notables were arrested. When the Servians saw that the inhabitants of the pillaged villages, of which a list has been given above, had come to reclaim their cattle and were surrounding the town, they had the notables brought out of prison and killed them in the most shameless way. Henceforth terror and despair reigned among the Albanians of Dibra and the neighborhood, and they rose in revolt. They attacked the Servians with arms, or with hatchets, stones and sticks; they killed some of them and drove the rest out of the town. Nearly all of the men who were killed were Servian officials; the soldiers who remained alive fled to the other side of the Radika river.

After this story, the truth of the general description published by the same paper on October 3/16 need not be doubted:[1]

The following villages, with a mixed Albanian and Bulgarian population, were pillaged and burnt—Lochnani, Lissitchani, Gitoche, Dibrichta, Harlichte, Dessovo, Gradechnitsa, Ptchélopek. Many Moslem families from these villages, including women and children, were pitilessly massacred. On entering the village of Portchassie, the regular Servian army led all the husbands outside the village, and then brought the wives thither to exact money from them in the shape of ransom, if they wanted their husbands set at liberty. After the ransom had been paid, however, the wretched men were shut up in the mosque, which was then blown up with four shells. In the village of Sulp, seventy-three Albanians suffered a horrible death, and forty-seven others from the village of Ptchélopek were basely assassinated. Was it not the Prefect of Krouchévo, when the Servian army returned from the Albanian frontier, who openly told them to burn all the villages situated between Krouchévo and Okhrida?

Thus the Albanian petitioners, who on September 21 addressed themselves to the Great Powers in the name of the populations of Djakova, Ipek, Plava, Goussinie and the ex-vilayet of Kossovo, did not exaggerate when they stated, as regards this other theater of the revolt, that "the Servian and Montenegrin regular troops undertook and did everything, from the first day on which they

---

[1]See also the *Reichspost* of September 29, and the enumeration of massacres committed in the first fortnight of September, 1913, as set forth in the petition of the meeting of Albanian representatives at Scutari on September 21, quoted above.

invaded the Albanian territory, either to compel the inhabitants to lose their nationality, or brutally to suppress the Shkiptar race."

Houses and whole villages reduced to ashes, unarmed and innocent populations massacred *en masse,* incredible acts of violence, pillage and brutality of every kind—such were the means which were employed and are still being employed by the Serbo-Montenegrin soldiery, with a view to the entire transformation of the ethnic character of regions inhabited exclusively by Albanians.

We thus arrive at the second characteristic feature of the Balkan wars, a feature which is a necessary correlative of the first. Since the population of the countries about to be occupied knew, by tradition, instinct and experience, what they had to expect from the armies of the enemy and from the neighboring countries to which these armies belonged, they did not await their arrival, but fled. Thus, generally speaking, the army of the enemy found on its way nothing but villages which were either half deserted or entirely abandoned. To execute the orders for extermination, it was only necessary to set fire to them. The population, warned by the glow from these fires, fled in all haste. There followed a veritable migration of peoples, for in Macedonia, as in Thrace, there was hardly a spot which was not, at a given moment, on the line of march of some army or other. The Commission everywhere encountered this second fact. All along the railways interminable trains of carts drawn by oxen followed one another; behind them came emigrant families and, in the neighborhood of the big towns, bodies of refugees were found encamped.

At Salonica the Commission visited one of these camps, and made inquiries of the Islamic Committee, whose business it was to transport the refugees to Anatolia. They were Turkish emigrants. Some of them had left their villages several weeks ago; they came from all parts of Macedonia, from Soundja, Djoumaya-Bala, Nevrocope, Pétritche, Razlogue, Tchakova, Démir-Hissar, Osmanié, Bérovo, Radovitch. At the beginning of September, when the Commission made its inquiry, about 135,000 emigrants had passed through Salonica since the beginning of the second war. Each steamer starting for Anatolia carried some 2,500 bound for Mersina, Adalia or Iskendéroum. Why were they quitting their villages? The Commission wished to learn the reason from their own lips. Some of its members went to the camp, without taking the official guide, and entered into conversation with isolated groups of emigrants:—"Who are you, whence do you come, wherefore have you departed?"—"We have come"—the old man waved his hand to indicate the plain dotted with carts—"from twenty-six different villages. It has taken us twenty-five days to get here, and we have been here for ten. We were afraid of the Bulgarians."—"Why?" Thereupon we heard the story which the reader knows from the chapter on Thrace. "But this happened during the first war, and now?"—"Now * * * the Greeks have given us the order to go." "Whither are you going? Who is feeding you?" Silence. Nobody knows.

Figs. 19, 20, 21.—Refugees Encamped Outside Salonica

FIG. 22.—THE COMMISSION LISTENING TO REFUGEES IN THE SAMAKOV SQUARE

At the Islamic Committee one thing only was known, namely that 50 Turkish pounds a day was spent on buying bread. In the last four days, 3,000 men had had their voyage to Anatolia paid for them, and the Committee's resources were at an end. The Greek government, in spite of the promises of money and land lavished to secure the departure of all these people, was doing nothing.

In Bulgaria things were very much the same. The Commission visited various places where refugees were temporarily gathered—Djoumaya, Samakov. The government estimated that as many as 111,560 emigrants fled to Bulgaria. These refugees were divided into 38 cantons. About 50,000 of them came from the parts of Macedonia now belonging to Servia or to Greece; of these only 2,400 were repatriated. Thirty thousand came from parts of Thrace which have remained under Turkish rule. These figures were published on September 12/25 (*Écho de Bulgarie*). On December 22/January 4, 1914, another Bulgarian paper, the *Mir*, published more detailed statistics of the refugees under this latter head. Unfortunately, in the course of the events of the last two months, the number of these emigrants from Turkey rose from 30,000 to 51,427 men, women and children. This was the population of 108 abandoned villages and of 10,934 houses. Winter, which was beginning when the Commission was in Bulgaria, has since come on. We learn in the letter from Haskovo, dated October 24/November 6, that those among the emigrants who possessed carts, oxen or camels were sent after the Bulgarian army to Gumurjina, and 6,209 others had to be sent by railway. Were these all the others? The same correspondent describes them to us as being insufficiently clad and ill-sheltered, exposed to the cold and threatened with pneumonia and with typhus, sometimes lacking bread throughout whole weeks.

While the 80,000 Bulgarian refugees are addressing their supplications to Sir Edward Grey, the telegraphic agency at Athens informs us that 100,000 others, Greeks by nationality, are fleeing from Bulgarian administration.[1] Exact statistics are not available, and we are aware that reliance can not be placed on figures given by popular meetings, or by official agencies. Nevertheless, it may be believed that we are not dealing here with isolated cases, but with a real exodus; a portion of the picture to be seen throughout the Balkans. The Turks are fleeing before the Christians, the Bulgarians before the Greeks and the Turks, the Greeks and the Turks before the Bulgarians, the Albanians before the Servians; and if emigration is not so general as between the Servians and the Bulgarians, the reason is that these two nations have not, so to speak, en-

---

[1] The Athenian correspondent of the *Times* gives these figures on August 21; they record the numbers passing the frontier. He himself has them from an "individual coming from Macedonia" who "gave him details on the emigration movement going on in the districts of Upper Macedonia, which the Greek troops are clearing all the time." This agrees with the information received by the Commission from the refugees themselves, at Salonica and Sofia, as to the specific character of this exodus, which was prepared and encouraged by the Greek authorities who offered carts and even motors to those who agreed to emigrate. (See below.)

countered on their own soil, while that soil coveted by each, namely Macedonia, they regarded as already peopled by men of their own race.[1] That is why we have to deal here with a mitigated form of the same principle of the conflict of nationalities. The means employed by the Greek against the Bulgarian, by the Turk against the Slav, by the Servian against the Albanian, is no longer extermination or emigration; it is an indirect method which must, however, lead to the same end, that of conversion and assimilation.

One example of these forced conversions during the Balkan wars has become classic—that of the pomaks by the Bulgarians. The pomaks are a people of Bulgarian mountaineers, converted to Islamism by the Turks centuries ago. To the number of some 400,000 they inhabit the high plateaus of Northern Macedonia. The male population of the nearest villages spoke Turkish and had become entirely Mahometan; the women on the other hand continued to speak Bulgarian and remained faithful to certain Slav customs. In the more remote centers, however, among the mountains of Rhodope, or Tikvéche, the pomaks remain faithful to monogamy, and to their national songs; the Slav type was even purer there since they only intermarried among themselves. Unlike the Slav aristocracy in the Balkans, they had not become subject to Islam in order to safeguard their social position. It was a peasant population, although throughout two centuries the young men had served in the Turkish army, and they still preserved its warlike and fanatical spirit. Traces of forced conversion to Islam may sometimes be perceived in certain proper names of places, such as Méhrilote or Hibili (in Eastern Rhodope). There, too, the places pointed out called in Bulgarian "Délen" or "Sétchen," that is to say, the place where those were "separated," who agreed to pass over to Islam, and those massacred who refused. Unhappily the modern conqueror has revived these remote historical recollections.

To revive a consciousness of lost nationality in the minds of their kinsmen, the Bulgarians employed force and persuasion, persuasion of a type as brutal as force. The Commission is unable to cite any individual instance, but there is no reason for doubting those recorded in accounts emanating from Greek or Servian sources. The story of a witness returned from Macedonia is quoted in a despatch of August 21, transmitted by the Athenian correspondent of the *Times:*

> The Moslems were ranged in groups. Each group was given some baptismal name, generally a name honored in the Bulgarian church or in Bulgarian history. An exarchist pope then passed from group to group and took aside each of his catechumens *sui generis;* and while sprinkling his forehead with holy water with one hand, with the other he compelled him to bite a sausage. The holy water represented baptism, the piece of

---

[1] As this chapter is going to press, Queen Eleonora of Bulgaria speaks in the *Neue Freie Presse* of 60,000 refugees in Bulgaria, destitute of shelter or clothing.

sausage renunciation of the Moslem faith, since the Koran forbids the eating of pork. The conversion was completed by the issue of a certificate adorned with a picture of the baptism of Jesus, the price of which varied between one and three francs. A friend who arrived today from Thrace told me that what is happening in Macedonia is also happening there. He showed me two baptismal certificates. He added that the converted were obliged to give up their fez, and the converted women to walk in the streets with their faces uncovered.

In an official report to the Sub-Prefect of Kavadar, on March 2, 1913, a petty Servian official, Mr. Drakalovits, says:

At Pechtchévo (Malèche plateau) a special committee has been formed, with the Bulgarian Sub-Prefect, Chatoyev, as its President, and among its members John Ingilisov, the director of Bulgarian schools, and the priest, Chatoyev, the brother of the Sub-Prefect. This committee was instituted to convert all the Turks of Malèche to Christianity. By order of the committee, 400 peasants of the place were armed with muskets and sticks; they attacked Turks of the neighboring villages and forcibly led them into the church at Verovo, where they were all baptized. Finally on February 17, baptism was carried out at Béloro, where there were ten Turkish families and ten Bosnian (Servian) Mahometan families. Pechtchévo alone was spared, the reason being (so we were told) that the Sub-Prefect would not allow violence in the town. A Turk from Pechtchévo told us that every Turkish house had to pay two pounds for its protection. Four Turks who could not pay such a sum hanged themselves in despair in their houses. In the other Turkish villages conversions were not exacted, because the population was too poor, whereas the Turks at Pechtchévo were known to be rich.

The Commission more than once had opportunity to discuss these conversions with the Bulgarian civil and ecclesiastical authorities. They were not denied by either, although they unanimously regarded them as an outrage on humanity and a grave political error in the case of people who were to be Bulgarian subjects. The following judgment, which is no less severe than anything written even by the enemies of Bulgaria, is commended to the attention of the reader. It is that of an intellectual, the Bulgarian writer, A. Strachimirov:

Those who stand for the thought and the honor of our country ought to know that our authorities have, in the countries on the frontier inhabited by the pomaks and recently liberated, acted in a way which is a disgrace to their country and to humanity. One aim alone was kept in sight—that of personal enrichment. Conversion was only a pretext. It did not save the poor pomaks from atrocious treatment except where the priests with whom they had to deal were conscientious men. Such cases, however, were rare. The ecclesiastical mission was beneath criticism. High rewards were paid, but the priests sent to carry out this task in the pomak villages were drunkards and criminals who could not be kept in Bulgaria. The behavior of the police was monstrous. In Bulgaria no one has and no one can have any idea of the atrocities committed by prefects, heads of police, and priests. Yet at first these pomaks showed the most absolute submission to our army. In the last two decades they had conceived a hatred for Turkism. Their principal grievance was the defective condition of their mountain roads and the burden of annual duties. They knew that this state of things had been largely remedied in Bulgaria, and they held to the idea that the Bulgarian government would at least give them roads. At Dary-deri a pomak, an officer in the reserve of the Turkish army, came before the authorities and had himself baptized because he was fired by the idea that the Bulgarians brought nothing but good with them. He was at last disillusioned, and he and his children were massacred by their neighbors.

Nevertheless the Bulgarian government is not ignorant as to the steps which should be taken to satisfy the population of the annexed region and secure their gratitude. It has itself declared in a manifesto addressed "to the inhabitants of the newly liberated region, published the day after the conclusion of the Treaty with Turkey, September 16/29, 1913,"—most formal orders are given to the Bulgarian civil and military authorities to display the greatest kindness to the inhabitants of the annexed territories, to *respect their faith and their nationality,* to refrain from any attack on their personal liberty, and to maintain the inviolability of their houses and their property. The citizens of new Bulgaria are to enjoy, *without distinction of religion or nationality,* the same rights which are secured by the constitution of the kingdom to all its citizens. Respect for religious freedom and for education is enjoined, and also respect for the religious beliefs and usages, the mosques, cemeteries and other holy places of all citizens alike.

If only these maxims could be applied today and "the tragic recollection of bloody events which have involved the contending nations and their subjects in misfortune could forever disappear in the triumph of peace, love and concord!"

As a matter of fact, an understanding between Bulgaria and Turkey, based on these fair promises, is by no means impossible. Many Turks have been under the Bulgarian régime since the origin of the kingdom; they seldom had to complain of their new masters. They were always on the side of the government. On the other hand, the principle of religious and educational liberty, although rejected by the Young Turk government, is an ancient Turkish principle, to which there would be prudence in reverting, after so many trials and defeats. The fact that very few Bulgarians are left in Turkey would facilitate such a reversion. There is thus reason for hoping that the treaty of Constantinople may bring together two governments who have no longer any ground for dispute and who might find themselves in agreement, as regards the rights of their kinsmen. A happy beginning has been made in Thrace. It is now necessary to create an efficient administrative apparatus—it is far from being in existence as yet, unfortunately—to put these excellent principles in practice.

One can not say as much, unfortunately, of the work of the treaty of

Bucharest. The lines of demarcation therein laid down are far from being natural or consonant with the national tendencies of the peoples. The third treaty of Bucharest has sown a new seed of discord in its violation of the sentiment of nationality: it divides the Balkan territories on the principle on which the treaty of Vienna divided the national regions of Europe in 1815. This historical example suggests that here, too, national reaction will follow on the work of diplomatic and political reaction.

It only remains to set out the facts, or rather to complete the outline sketched in Chapter I, to afford convincing proof of this. What has become of Macedonia, so often the apple of discord, now that the work of concord appears to be completed? It displays nothing but violence, and suggests no hope of ultimate harmony.

2. SERVIAN MACEDONIA

A comparison of the ethnographic and linguistic maps drawn up by Messers Kantchev, Tsviyits (Cviyic) and Bélits, with the new frontiers of the treaty of Bucharest reveals the gravity of the task undertaken by the Servians. They have not merely resumed possession of their ancient domain, the Sandjak of Novi-Bazar and Old Servia proper (Kosovo Polé and Métchia), despite the fact that this historic domain was strongly Albanian; they have not merely added thereto the tract described by patriotic Servian ethnographers as "Enlarged Old Servia" (an ancient geographical term which we have seen twice enlarged, once by Mr. Tsviyits and again by Mr. Bélits);[1] over and above all this, their facile generosity impelled them to share with the Greeks the population described on their maps as "Slav-Macedonian"—a euphemism designed to conceal the existence of Bulgarians in Macedonia. And their acquisitions under the treaty of Bucharest went beyond their most extravagant pretensions. They took advantage of the Bulgarians' need to conclude peace at any price to deprive them of territories to the east of the Vardar, for example, Chtipe and Radoviche, where Bulgarian patriotism glowed most vividly and where the sacrifices accepted by Bulgarian patriots for the sake of freeing Macedonia, had always been exceptionally great. This was adding insult to injury.

Mr. Skérlits, a Servian deputy and member of the opposition, closed his speech in the Skupshtina on October 18/31, 1913, with these memorable words: "We do not regard territorial results as everything. Enlarged Servia does not spell, for us, a country in which the number of policemen, tax collectors and controllers has been doubled. New Servia, greater Servia must be a land of greater liberty, greater justice, greater general well being. May Servia, twice as great as she was, be not twice as weak but twice as strong."

Unfortunately these generous words are but *pia desideria*. For some time the government hesitated. Nevertheless, Mr. Pachitch must have understood

---

[1]See chapter I, p. 29.

that the question whether Servia's acquisitions were to make her twice as weak or twice as strong depended on the policy pursued in Macedonia. During the days spent by the Commission at Belgrade the question was debated. There were two antagonistic views. One, represented by Mr. Pachitch himself, wanted a "liberal" régime in Macedonia and the avoidance, at any price, of a "military dictatorship." The population of the new territories was to be left to express its loyalty spontaneously; to wait "until it realized that its new lot was sweeter than the old." Military circles, however, did not share this view. They were for a military administration, since a civil administration in their view, "must be incapable of repressing the propagandism sure to be carried on by the Bulgarians."[1] True, the "liberal" régime as projected by Mr. Pachitch was not so liberal as the Bulgarian manifesto to the inhabitants of the annexed countries had hoped. The new citizens were not to possess the franchise for fear lest a new "Macedonian" party should thus be brought into the Skupshtina to upset all the relations between the contending parties in the kingdom and form the mark of common jealousy. Some sort of local franchise or self-government was considered. A kind of compromise was suggested in the shape of military administration with a civil annex and representatives of the departments at Belgrade, on the familiar plan employed in Bosnia and Herzegovina before the 1908 annexation. In any case, the question of the administration to be erected in Macedonia displayed so wide a divergence between the views of Mr. Pachitch and his colleagues, apart from the military group, that Mr. Pachitch's resignation was talked of.

Mr. Pachitch neither resigned nor insisted on his own standpoint. Silence fell on such isolated voices as that of the President of the Skupshtina, Mr. André Nicolits, who protested in the foreign press against the exceptional régime in Macedonia and asked for constitutional guarantees. The *Piemont,* the organ of the military party, declared that such notions were "opposed to the interests of the State," and assured the Servian public that "the population of Macedonia had never for a moment thought of elections, or communal self-government," etc.; that "nothing save a military régime could be entirely just, humanely severe and sufficiently firm to break the will of individuals or groups hostile to the State."

Macedonia had thus to be viewed as a dependency, a sort of conquered colony, which these conquerors might administer at their good pleasure. In the course of the debates on the address in the Skupshtina (November) this attitude found highly definite expression in a reply of Mr. Protits, a member of the cabinet, interrupted by a member of the opposition. "The question," said Mr. Protits, "is—are we to apply to Old Servia the constitution created by the Servian Kingdom and which has had happy results?" Mr. Paul Marinkovits—

---

[1]See the *Stampa,* August 13/26. The contents of these communications came to our knowledge at Belgrade itself, from reliable, first-hand Servian sources.

"But Old Servia *is* the Servian Kingdom."—"*No, it is not the Servian Kingdom.*"

Such was the spirit in which the Servian government on September 21/ October 4, issued a decree on "public security" in the recently acquired territories, which amounted to the establishment of a military dictatorship, and called forth cries of horror in the foreign press. The document is so characteristic and so important that, despite its length, we quote it *in extenso:*

Article 1. The police authorities are authorized, in case of a deficiency in the regular organization for securing the liberty and security of persons and property, to ask the military commander for the troops necessary for the maintenance of order and tranquillity. The military commander is bound to comply immediately with these demands, and the police is bound to inform the Minister of the Interior of them.

Article 2. *Any attempt at rebellion against the public powers is punishable by five years' penal servitude.*

The decision of the police authorities, published in the respective communes, is sufficient proof of the commission of crime.

If the rebel refuses to give himself up as prisoner within ten days from such publication, he may be put to death by any public or military officer.

Article 3. Any person accused of rebellion in terms of the police decision and who commits any crime shall be punished with death.

If the accused person himself gives himself up as a prisoner into the hands of the authorities, the death penalty shall be commuted to penal servitude for ten or twenty years, always provided that the commutation is approved by the tribunal.

Article 4. Where several cases of rebellion occur in a commune and the rebels do not return to their homes within ten days from the police notice, *the authorities have the right of deporting their families whithersoever they may find convenient.*

Likewise the inhabitants of the houses in which armed persons or criminals in general are found concealed, shall be deported.

The heads of the police shall transmit to the Prefecture a report on the deportation procedure, which is to be put in force immediately.

The Minister of the Interior shall, if he think desirable, rescind deportation measures.

Article 5. Any person deported by an order of the Prefecture who shall return to his original domicile without the authorization of the Minister of the Interior shall be punished by three years' imprisonment.

Article 6. If in any commune or any canton the maintenance of security demands *the sending of troops, the maintenance of the latter shall be charged to the commune or the canton.* In such a case the Prefect is to be notified.

If order is restored after a brief interval and the culprits taken, the Minister of the Interior may refund such expenses to the canton or the commune.

The Minister may act in this way as often as he may think desirable.

Article 7. Any person found carrying arms who has not in his possession a permit from the police or from the Prefect, or who shall hide arms in his house or elsewhere, shall be condemned to a penalty varying from three months' imprisonment to five years' penal servitude.

Anyone selling arms or ammunition without a police permit shall be liable to the same penalty.

Article 8. Any person using any kind of explosives, knowing that such use is dangerous to the life and goods of others, shall be punished with twenty years' penal servitude.

Article 9. Anyone who shall prepare explosives or direct their preparation or who knows of the existence of explosives intended for the commission of a crime shall, subject to Article 8, be punished by ten years' penal servitude.

Article 10. Any person receiving, keeping or transporting explosives intended for a criminal purpose shall be punished by five years' penal servitude, except where he does so with the intention of preventing the commission of a crime.

Article 11. Any person who uses an explosive *without any evil intention,* shall be punished by five years' penal servitude.

Article 12. (1) Anyone deliberately harming the roads, streets or squares in such a way as to endanger life or public health, shall be punished by fifteen years' penal servitude.

If the delinquency be *unintentional* the penalty shall be five years.

(2) If the author of the crime cited above causes danger to the life or health of numerous persons, or if his action results in the death of several individuals (and this could be foreseen), he shall be punished by death or twenty years' penal servitude. If the crime be unpremeditated the punishment shall be ten years.

Article 13. Any attempt at damaging the railway lines or navigation, shall be punished by twenty years' penal servitude. If the attempt is not premeditated the punishment shall be for ten years.

If the author of such attempt has endangered the life of several individuals, or if his action results in death or wounds to several persons, he shall be punished by death or twenty years' penal servitude.

Article 14. Any person injuring the means of telegraphic or telephonic communication shall be punished by fifteen years' penal servitude. If the act is not premeditated the penalty shall be five years.

Article 15. Generally speaking the concealment of armed or guilty persons shall be punished by ten years' penal servitude.

Article 16. *Anyone who knows a malefactor and does not denounce him to the authorities shall be punished by five years' penal servitude.*

Article 17. Those instigating to disobedience against the established powers, the laws and the regulations with the force of law; rebels against the authorities or public or communal officers; shall be punished by twenty-one months' imprisonment up to ten years' penal servitude.

If such acts produce no effects, the penalty may be reduced to three months.

Article 18. Any act of aggression and any resistance either *by word* or force, offered to a public or communal officer charged with putting in force a decision of the tribunal, or an order of the communal or police public authority, during the exercise of his duties, may be punished by *ten years' penal servitude* or at least six months' imprisonment, *however insignificant be the magnitude of the crime.*

Any aggression against those helping the public officer, or experts specially called in, may be punished by the same penalty.

If the aggression offered to the public officer takes place outside the exercise of his official duties the penalty shall be two years' imprisonment.

Article 19. Where the crimes here enumerated are perpetrated by an associated group of persons, the penalty shall be fifteen years' penal servitude. The accomplices of those who committed the above mentioned misdeeds against public officials shall be punished by the maximum penalty, and, if this is thought insufficient, they may be condemned to penal servitude for a period amounting to twenty years.

Article 20. Those who recruit bands against the State, or with a view to offering resistance to public authorities shall be liable to a penalty of twenty years' penal servitude.

Article 21. Accomplices of rebels or of bands offering armed resistance to Servian troops or the public or communal officers, shall be punished by death or by at least ten years' penal servitude.

Article 22. Persons taking part in seditious meetings which do not disperse when ordered to do so by the administrative or communal authorities are liable to terms of imprisonment up to two years.

Article 23. In the case of the construction of roads, or, generally speaking, of public works of all kinds, agitators who incite workmen to strike or who are unwilling to work or who seek to work elsewhere or in another manner, from that in which they are told and who persist in such insubordination, after notification by the authorities shall be punished by imprisonment from three months up to two years.

Article 24. Any soldier or citizen called to the colors who does not follow the call, or who refuses in the army to obey his superiors, shall be condemned to a penalty varying from three months' imprisonment to five years' penal servitude.

Soldiers who assist any one to desert from the army or who desert themselves, and those who make endeavors to attract Servian subjects to serve with foreign troops, shall be punished by ten years' penal servitude.

In time of mobilization or war the penalty for this delinquency is death.

Article 25. Anybody releasing an individual under surveillance or under the guard of officials or public employes for surveillance, guard or escort, or setting such person at liberty, shall be condemned to penal servitude for a maximum period of five years.

Where such delinquency is the work of an organized group of individuals, each accomplice shall be liable to a penalty of between three and five years' penal servitude.

Article 26. The Prefects have the right to prescribe in their name police measures to safeguard the life and property of those subject to their administration. They shall fix penalties applicable to those who refuse to submit to such measures.

The penalty shall consist of a maximum period of three years' imprisonment or of a pecuniary fine up to a thousand *dinars*.

The edicts of the Prefects shall come into force immediately, but the Prefects are bound to communicate them at once to the Minister of the Interior.

Article 27. The crimes set forth in the present regulations are to have precedence of all other suits before the judicial tribunals and judgment upon them is to be executed with the briefest possible delay.

Persons indicted for such offences shall be subject to preventive detention until final judgment is passed on their cases. Within a three days' delay the tribunal shall send its findings to the High Court, and the latter shall proceed immediately to the examination of this decision.

Article 28. The law of July 12, 1895, as to the pursuit and destruction of brigands, which came into force on August 18, 1913, is applicable to the annexed territories, in so far as it is not modified by the present regulations.

Article 29. Paragraphs 92, 93, 95, 96, 97, 98, 302 b, 302 c, 302 d, (so far as concerns paragraphs b and c) 304, 306, and 360, and Section III of the penal code which do not agree with the present regulation, are null and void.

Article 30. The present regulation does not abolish the provisions of paragraph 34 of the penal military code, in connection with paragraph 4 of the same code, paragraphs 52 and 69 of the penal military code and paragraph 4 of the same, which are not applicable to civil persons.

Article 31. The present regulation is in force from the day of its signature by the King and its publication in the Servian press.

We order our Council of Ministers to make the present regulation public and to see that it is carried into effect: we order the public authorities to act in conformity with it, and we order each and all to submit to it.

Executed at Belgrade, September 21, 1913.

PETER."

In the words of the Socialist Servian paper, *Radnitchké Noviné,* "If the liberation of these territories is a fact, why then is this exceptional régime established there? If the inhabitants are Servians why are they not made the equals of all the Servians; why is the constitutional rule not put in operation according to which 'all Servians are equal before the law'? If the object of the wars was *unification,* why is not this unification effectively recognized, and why are these exceptional ordinances created, such as can only be imposed upon conquered countries by conquerors? Moreover, our constitution does not admit of rules of this nature!"

As a matter of fact, if one did not know what Macedonia is, one might guess it from the publication of these ordinances. Clearly Macedonia was not "Old Servia" unified, since the population is treated as "rebels in a perpetual state of revolt." What the ordinances had in view were not isolated criminals,— they had accomplices and people who would hide them everywhere. To punish the culprit? That was not enough while his family remained; his family must be deported and the friends who were unwilling to "denounce" the culprit, his "associates," who seized the opportunity of "setting him at liberty" when he was "under surveillance, guard or escort" by officials or public employes—they must be deported too. In short, a whole population was "recalcitrant," and to resist it there were only these "public or communal officers" invested with extraordinary powers. What were they to do, when the population, not content with offering passive resistance, became "aggressive." This population, called to the colors, refused "to obey the call." When asked to "work" on the "construction of roads" or on any communal works, they struck, they preferred to work "elsewhere or in some other manner." Finally, each one "refused to give himself up as a prisoner," always holding himself ready to attack the public officers, "to resist them if not by force at least by word!" This last crime is punished by the ordinances by "ten years penal servitude, or at least six months imprisonment *however insignificant be the words or the deeds.*" The hope openly expressed to the members of the Commission from the first half of August onwards, was that thanks to these measures an end will be made of the resistance of the alien population in Macedonia in five or six years!

The military party knew what it was about when it insisted on the publication of this Draconian edict, which was but a quasi legal sanction given to the actual activities of the powers in occupation in Macedonia. But such a formal admission on paper (in a document immediately published in the foreign press) frightened more than the members of the Servian Opposition. Thus, on October 15/28, the Servian government, after three weeks' reflection, published certain changes in the ordinances of September 21. The obligation laid upon the troops for coming to the assistance of the civil power became less general. It was now only in the case of "grave and serious trouble" that they were to do so. But the right possessed by the Minister of the Interior not to charge the population "if order was reëstablished quickly" (see Article 6) was limited by the control of the Council of Ministers.

The scandalous Article 26, giving legislative power to the Prefects, was amended by the addition of the following clause:—"On condition that the ordinances of the Prefects accord with existing ordinances and the laws." The extent of the sanction contemplated in Article 26 (imprisonment up to three years and a fine up to fr. 1,000) was reduced to one month and fr. 300. But these amendments merely *confirm the rest of the edict, and they were clearly insufficient.* The opposition press continued to attack the government and to demand the reign of law for the population of the annexed territories and the extension to these territories of the constitution of the kingdom. "If deputies for the annexed territories had seats in the Skupshtina," said the *Pravda* of November 13/26, "the foreign press, which is at present ill-disposed towards Servia, would no longer be able to retain the credence which its malicious inventions have won in Europe as regards the Servian atrocities." "A nation can not be conciliated," it added a few days later, "by giving it an inferior position under the law." Another paper, the *Novosti,* tried to harmonize these objections with the official theory of a Servian Macedonia. "A military régime," it said, "is perfectly adapted to a conquered country whose population speaks a different language, but this is not the case with a country whose population is entirely Servian. That is why," the *Novosti* concluded, "the introduction of a constitutional régime in the new territories is absolutely justified."

The government could not admit that it was precisely this condition of identity of nationality which was lacking in Macedonia. The ministerial organs were reduced to saying "that the level of culture" was not sufficiently high among the Macedonians, and that their "State consciousness" was not sufficiently developed to permit the immediate grant of full political rights. Finally on November 23/December 6, the government decided to announce the draft of an abridged constitution for Macedonia, which was to be put in force for a period of ten years. This constitution did not sanction the liberty of the press nor of meetings; it conferred the right neither to elect nor to be elected. Rights of self-government were not given to the electoral assemblies of the prefectures, sub-prefectures or communes; the magistrates were not irremovable and the courts of criminal justice did not include juries. The death penalty, abolished by Article 13 of the Servian constitution, was reëstablished by the simple omission of this article in a simplified "constitution." In a word, it could be said that the Turkish "law of vilayets," in combination with the ancient rights and privileges of the Christian communities, granted to the different nationalities by treaties and firmans, gave far better assurance of mutual toleration, and even a more effective rein on the arbitrary power of the administration, than was afforded by this new draft constitution, which, from the administrative point of view, did nothing to abolish the measures laid down in the ordinances of September 21.

The opposition press did not fail to point this out. On November 28/December 11, the *Pravda* asked, "Are the people of the annexed territories to have fewer rights now than they possessed under Turkish régime?" The *Novosti* said:—"The population has no rights, only duties." The *Pravda* pointed out that it is better to follow Cavour than Bismarck, and suggested (December 1/14), that these "dictatorial paragraphs" were on the high road to Zabern. Finally, despite the assurances of the official organ, the *Sammouprava,* to the effect that the new constitution guaranteed the personal property of the individual in every case, as well as the moral and economic development of the country, the world refused to believe it—and rightly, as we shall see.

As a matter of fact, if it was desired to make "Servian" Macedonia a reality instead of allowing it to remain what it was,—a national illusion in which aspirations were translated into accomplished facts,—it was necessary to understand, however little one might approve, the tactics of the government. If the opposition were to be logical they must renounce their national view. If they insisted upon that, they must admit that for the real attainment of their object of an ethnic "unification," everything remained to be done. To admit the end was to sanction the means, *i. e.*, the extermination, or at least the elimination of alien elements, and above all of the Bulgarian element. It was the existence and the permeation of these elements which throughout decades constituted the essence and, so to speak, the Gordian knot of the Macedonian problem. To endeavor to escape from the problem by pretending not to know its essential elements, was to elude difficulties instead of solving them.

The Servian government and the military party to which the task of making an end of the difficulty was entrusted, marched direct to the attainment of their end. They made, on a truly imposing scale, a sociological experiment *in anima vili,* which governments and nations far better equipped than the Servian kingdom could not have carried through with success.

We have seen the beginning of this work of assimilation through terror. It was not until the beginning of the second Balkan war gave the signal for putting everything which still bore the Bulgarian name into the melting pot, that means were employed to carry out this object which surpassed anything seen hitherto. Let us look first at the steps taken by the Servian government against the heads of the National church in Macedonia.

The members of the Commission were profoundly moved by the depositions which the six dignitaries of the Bulgarian church were good enough to make before them during their visit to the Holy Synod at Sofia. These dignitaries were the Archbishops Auxentious of Pelagonia (Monastir-Bitolia), Cosmas of Dibra (Débar), Méletius of Vélès, Néophyte of Uskub (Skopié), Boris of Okhrida, and the Archbishop of Dibra's Vicar, Ilarion Bishop of Nichava. All the prelates came to enter a formal protest before the Russian Ambassador at Sofia against the declaration made by the Servian embassy at St. Petersburg, to the effect that the Bulgarian Archbishops of Macedonia had themselves asked to leave their dioceses. "If the Servian government," they said in their written protest, "really never intended to drive us forth we are ready to return as soon as it may be possible to guard the flocks whose legitimate pastors we are."[1]

We have seen that the Servian and Greek governments had taken all possible steps to isolate these pastors from their flocks. When the second war was about to break out, the Bulgarian Archbishops regarded themselves as prisoners within their Metropolis. Their visitors were watched, questioned, loaded with blows and put to the torture. The priests were not even allowed to see their superiors except at church, and divine service was the only opportunity which these Archbishops had of showing themselves to such persons as were still bold enough to enter a Bulgarian church. June 17/30, the day on which the outbreak of hostilities became known, was the term of their residence in Macedonia. Each in turn, they eagerly told us of their last impressions. Mr. Néophyte of Uskub had, on the evening of the 17/30, been shut up in his own house, and throughout two days his cook alone was allowed to go out of the Metropolis to purchase food. A most thorough investigation then took place, after which the cook herself was kept prisoner for two days. The Archbishop had no food save bread passed in to him through the window by his neighbors, at great

---

[1]The Servian declaration was published on August 12/25, in the St. Petersburg paper the *Novoyé Vremia.* The reply of the Archbishop S. E. M. Nekloudov was signed on August 29/September 11, at Sofia.

personal risk to themselves. The cries of the cook drew the attention of the police, and she was once more allowed to go out, this time under escort. On June 24/July 7, the head of the police came and suggested to the Archbishop that he should go to Salonica, his personal security and respect for his inviolability being guaranteed (this, as we shall see, was not superfluous). Mr. Néophyte refused; he was there by the will of the people and there he intended to remain. "To what end, since you can not exercise your functions?"—"For example, in my private capacity, to purchase Turkish houses, if you please," he replied. An hour later they returned to the charge. The prefect regretted that he had not been obeyed, for he could no longer answer for the Archbishop's safety. Finally, in the evening the comedy came to an end; the Archbishop was made to read an indictment under twelve heads. He had said prayers for four monarchs, instead of for King Peter alone; he had not said prayers for the Servian Archbishop; he had busied himself with civil matters, ordering a priest from the village to come and see him in the Metropolis, etc. When Mr. Néophyte refused to sign, he was given two hours in which to prepare himself for departure, and then sent through Niché to Smederévo, on the Danube, whence he departed for Bulgaria.

At Vélès the officials of the Archbishopric were arrested and the archives were ransacked so early as January 24/February 6. The Suffragan Bishop was obliged to leave Vélès after another attack on the Metropolis on February 4/17, in which an official of the Metropolis, Mr. Mikhilov, was beaten and maltreated to such an extent that he lost consciousness. On March 28/April 10, Archbishop Melétius returned to Vélès. He was closely watched by the police, and during his whole sojourn at Vélès he was only allowed to see three priests and one instructor. On June 17/30, he, like Mr. Néophyte, was made a prisoner in his own house. On June 24/July 7, he was told in his turn to leave the town. Thinking that this was a temporary measure, he agreed on condition of remaining at Uskub until the end of the war. He signed a document to this effect. On the 25th he was told that Mr. Néophyte had left Uskub and that he had an hour in which to follow him. Mr. Melétius then asked for a written order. "The order will be sent to you at the frontier" (this was a lie). We will say nothing of the incidents of the voyage. Mr. Melétius rejoined Mr. Néophyte at Smederévo, and they were both sent through Raduivatz to Roustchouk.

The other three Archbishops, from Monastir, Okhrida and Dibra, did not get off so easily. They were sent via Salonica to Constantinople. On June 17/30, the police arrived, accompanied by officers and soldiers, to arrest the staff of the Archbishopric of Monastir. In the course of the perquisition which took place, rough drafts of reports of acts of violence committed by the Servians on the Bulgarian population were discovered, addressed to the Metropolis at Salonica and the Minister of Foreign Affairs at Sofia. Here the sequestration lasted up to the 24 h, on which date the authorities proceeded to a sort of inquiry.

Stress was laid "on relations entered into with a foreign government," and the article of the criminal code relative to this form of crime, prescribing a penalty of twenty years imprisonment, was read out. After having thus prepared the ground, the authorities returned in the afternoon. "You will start tomorrow for Bulgaria." "Impossible, it is too soon." "Papers found upon you have annoyed the military authorities; we are ordered to bring you before a court-martial. A court-martial, as you are well aware, does not at this moment always observe the laws; it often judges as seems fit to it and the sentences passed are executed on the spot; well, to save you from such a fate, the prefect is being so kind as to make himself responsible for the Archbishop's departure tomorrow in the morning." "Agreed." "First of all, a little formality has to be gone through. Here is the draft of a letter. Be so good as to transcribe it in Bulgarian, and state over your own name that, 'owing to the hostilities between Servia and Bulgaria, it is unpleasing to you to remain at Monastir.' What? You refuse? Then there is the court-martial. Let us see." Mr. Auxentius signed, though his conscience protested. On the next day he was sent to Salonica, and thence made his way to Bulgaria via Constantinople and Odessa.

The case of Mr. Boris of Okhrida is similar. The papers found in the Metropolis of Monastir also included reports from the Archbishop of Okhrida to the Ministry at Sofia. The chief commander at Uskub was immediately informed of this and telegraphed the order for the Archbishop's arrest. On June 25/July 8, he was roused at three o'clock in the morning and given ten minutes in which to prepare himself to depart for Monastir. He had hardly time to take a shirt and an overcoat with him. At Monastir the same prefect, Mr. Douchane Alimpits, played the same little scene. The books of the law were brought, Mr. Boris was questioned, a protocol was read to him in which the existence of a revolutionary committee, preparing a rebellion against the Servian authorities, was inferred, and of which Mr. Auxentius was accused of being the president and Mr. Boris his assistant. Its members were the deacons and inspectors of the Archbishopric, the secretaries, priests, schoolmasters and notables. In vain did Mr. Boris endeavor to prove that this accusation was simply the fruit of an overheated imagination. Mr. Alimpits went on repeating accusations of "treason," deserving the penalty of death by shooting, etc. He then displayed a most active desire to see Mr. Boris saved from the death which threatened him, and out of his pocket he drew a paper written in Servian. Thereupon, Mr. Boris read the sketch of a declaration somewhat as follows: On the outbreak of the fratricidal war he regarded his mission as fulfilled, he renounced of his own free will the dignity of exarchist Metropolitan of the diocese of Okhrida, and asked for a permit to Salonica and an escort to accompany him thither. Mr. Boris replied that the whole Bulgarian population of the diocese had chosen him as their spiritual chief; he could not renounce his charge on any pretext; he regarded such a demand as an outrage, while the declaration could not be valid even for the end they had in view. The prefect, with some annoyance, repeated the order, adding that it was the desire of a higher commander, and that in case of refusal all preparations were made for bringing the Archbishop before a court-martial and destroying him as a traitor in the interests of the State.

"As for me," so Mr. Boris stated to the Commission, "I recalled the fate of victims who had been slain and of whom no traces had been left; the death of the schoolmaster Luteviev, slain by the soldiers at Prilèpe, after the banquet at which he had ventured to sing the praises of the Bulgarian army and propose the health of King Ferdinand; of Stamboldgiev, a citizen of Monastir, who was sacrificed with his whole family. Further, I recalled the inhumanity of these wretches, who compelled their own Archbishop Michael to leave his diocese. I recalled likewise that these were men not given to joking, men who tore their princes and their kings to pieces, and * * * with profound bitterness, and in the depths of my soul something of shame, I obeyed the order of this brute of a captain, an order which I could not recall." * * * On the 26th Mr. Boris left for Salonica and rejoined Mr. Auxentius there. Two days later the regent of the Archbishopric of Dibra, Bishop Ilarion of Nichava, arrived there likewise. He was less fortunate than the others, for at Salonica he was imprisoned and remained there in confinement for twenty-seven days. The reason was that the Greeks, having no Bulgarian bishops among their prisoners, were already sorry that they had let Messrs. Auxentius and Boris go. They therefore kept Mr. Ilarion as a hostage, and did not set him at liberty until two days after the conclusion of peace.

The departure of the bishops was the end of the exarchist church in Macedonia, the end of the official and recognized existence of Bulgarian nationality. The powers in occupation were not slow in drawing conclusions thus harmonious with their desires. We know in fact that they did not even wait for their departure to set to work on the complete destruction of "Bulgarism" in Macedonia. During the first months of occupation, September, October, and even November, it was still possible to explain what happened as the result of misunderstanding, and as the abuse of power by irresponsible elements or by local authorities; later, however, this explanation became untenable. From the commencement of 1913 we have to deal with a systematic persecution of the Bulgarian nationality, more particularly in the regions assigned by the treaty of February 29, 1912, to Servia. After March, at which date it became clear that Servia was not going to secure an outlet on the Adriatic littoral, and after the Bulgarians, on the other hand, had succeeded in taking Adrianople (March 13/26), there was no longer any concealment of the preparations which were being made for the complete annexation of all the occupied territories in Macedonia. The conclusion of peace with Turkey (May 17/30), and the speech delivered by Mr. Pachitch in the Skupshtina, were the signal for beginning preparations for conflict between the allies, the search for arms held by suspects, the call to the colors of all those on whom it was thought reliance could be placed. Two weeks later, every one in Macedonia was saying war with Bulgaria was imminent, and acting on that belief. On July 17/30 the decisive moment arrived.

For six months, while waiting for the allied armies to take up arms, the Servians had been carrying on guerrilla warfare in Macedonia, side by side with the regular army. They armed their old bands, whose captains and soldiers wore military uniform. At Uskub, a central committee of "national defense," with branches in other Macedonian towns, was formed side by side with the higher command, upon the arrival of the troops. The population of Uskub called their station behind the house of Weiss, near the Russian consulate, "the black house," from the name of the league itself, "the black hand."[1] The worst crimes were committed by this secret organization, known to all the world and under powerful protection. It was of distinct advantage for the regular government to have under its hand an irresponsible power which, like this, soon became all powerful, and which could always be disowned if necessary. There were so many things which were not crimes, but which, from the point of view of Servian assimilation, were worse than crimes. Such, for example, as being too influential a citizen, wise enough, while remaining an ardent Bulgarian patriot, not to contravene the orders of the authority, and whose past called for vengeance; the Bulgarian flag, a business house, a library, a chemist shop kept by a Bulgarian, or a café, not amenable to the prohibition of public meetings, etc. The man was taken, one evening he was led into the "black house" and there beaten; then for whole months he lay ill, if indeed he did not disappear completely. Our records are full of depositions which throw light on the sinister activities of these legalized brigands. Unhappily *all* the names can not be cited. * * * Each town had its captain who soon acquired fame. At Koumanovo there was a certain Major Voulovits and his assistant Captain Rankovits; at Vélès one Voino Popovits, a Vassa, a Vanguel, etc. Where complaints were made to the regular authorities, they pretended to know nothing of the matter, or if the person complaining was obscure they punished him. If he were a personage, as for example in the case of the Archbishop of Vélès, his complaint was met by sending the bands from the town of Vélès down to the villages * * * only to replace them immediately afterwards by bands from Uskub.

---

[1]The Belgrade *Tribune* published ("Serb. Cor." November 18/December 1) revelations by an anonymous officer who had been a member of the secret organization of "the black hand." The object of this organization, formed on the principle of the Carbonari, was, according to him, the liberation of the Servians from the Turkish yoke. Later on, the comrade by whom he had been initiated, told him that owing to the incapacity of the radical government it was necessary to replace this organization by another which was to be *composed of members of other political parties.* He clearly regarded the "black hand" as being formed of government partisans.

It was in the villages that the activity of these bands assumed its most fatal form. In the towns the regular authorities kept up appearances and did not concern themselves with the bandits; but lower in the administrative scale, in the village, the responsible and the irresponsible mingled and were lost in one another. This was the easier that from the end of 1912 on the administrative posts in the villages were filled by men of the type already described in Chapter I—paid representatives of national minorities, Serbo-manes, or Græco-manes, who very often had served as spies with the Turks. * * * These people, while possessing a highly intimate knowledge of affairs, had their own scores to wipe off * * * they had only to utter the name of one of their enemies, and the bands arrest him, leave him to find a ransom, beat him or even kill him with impunity. This is the régime of anarchy summed up in a letter published in the *Manchester Guardian* and given below.[1]

What were the results secured by this implacable system at the time of the beginning of the Serbo-Bulgarian war? A Bulgarian schoolmaster has described them as follows: "Even if one were an European one would declare oneself Servian, if one were alone, without support, in that state of unrestrained brigandage, fostered by the legal power." The end, however, was not yet attained, and, on the outbreak of the second war, the powers in occupation seized the opportunity to undertake new measures of repression which made an end of the open existence of Bulgarian nationality. Progress of this repression in different parts of Macedonia can be traced in the depositions taken by

---

[1]After citing the Servian ordinances of which we have spoken above the English paper goes on: "This is the theory of Servian coercion. The practice is worse. Servia is not a country with a large educated population. It has indeed some 80 per cent of illiterates. It has to supply rulers for a conquered territory which almost equals it in extent, and the abler men regard life in rural Macedonia as exile. Unworthy agents are invested with sovereign powers. The consequences are vividly, if briefly, described in a personal letter which arrived recently, and is translated below. The writer is a man of high character and a minister of religion—it is safer not to indicate his church. He is a native of the country, but has had a European education, and is not himself a member of the persecuted Bulgarian community:

The situation grows more and more unbearable for the Bulgarians—a perfect hell. I had opportunities of talking with peasants from the interior. What they tell us makes one shudder. Every group of four or five villages has an official placed over it who, with six or seven underlings, men of disreputable antecedents, carries out perquisitions, and on the pretext of searching for arms steals everything that is worth taking. They indulge in flogging and robbery and violate many of the women and girls. Tributes under the form of military contributions are arbitrarily imposed. One village of 110 families had already been fined 6,000 dinars (£240) and now it has to pay another 2,000 (£80). The priest of the village, to avoid being sent into exile, has had to pay a ransom of £T.50. Poor emigrants returning from America have had to pay from ten to twenty Napoleons for permission to go to their homes. The officials and officers carry out wholesale robberies through the customs and the army contracts. The police is all powerful, especially the secret service. Bands of Servian terrorists (*comitadjis*) recruited by the government, swarm all over the country. They go from village to village, and woe to anyone who dares to refuse them anything. These bands have a free hand to do as they please, in order to Serbize the population. Shepherds are forbidden to drive their flocks to pasture lest (such is the excuse) they should supply the Bulgarian bands with food. In a word it is an absolute anarchy. We shall soon have a famine for the Serbs have taken everything, and under present conditions no one can earn a living. Everyone would like to emigrate, but it is impossible to get permission even to visit a neighboring village."

the Commission at Sofia from Bulgarian intellectuals, refugees from Macedonia, and completed by the reports of the Bulgarian ecclesiastical authorities.

It was to be expected that those territories in Macedonia which were, according to the treaty, to remain Servian, should receive the most serious attention. Uskub, Koumanovo, Tétovo, Gostivar, in a word the whole northeast corner of Macedonia, was to feel the first brunt of Serbization. At Koumanovo, the priest Yanev, the Archbishop's vicar, was driven out on March 11/24, after a violent scene with one of those Servian chieftains who became officers, one Liouba Voulvits. He pulled the priest by the beard, beat him and finally said to him that "he would not kill him, because the Servians were a civilized nation, not savages like the Bulgarians." "I give you up to this evening to clear out of Servian territory, otherwise, dog, you shall be killed." The violence used by this same Voulvits in the villages whose population he was persuading to become Servian, not to read Bulgarian books, etc., may be passed over in silence. This same Voulvits employed the same tactics for the vicars of Kratovo and Palanka, and for the population of the villages. As a result, the towns of Koumanovo, Palanka, Kratovo, Gostivar and the surrounding villages, the *nehié* of St. Nicolas, and the villages of Uskub and Tétovo, were formally proclaimed Servian at the moment of the outbreak of the war. Schoolmasters and priests who were unwilling to submit fled and took refuge in Bulgaria. The only places left to resist were the towns of Uskub and Tétovo.

To terrorize the population of Tétovo was easy. Tétovo had been in a state of panic since May 23/June 5. The municipal authorities, followed by bands and a crowd of Turkish children, harangued the inhabitants, inviting them to become "volunteers" against the "worst enemy" of the Servian state. These processions took place daily for three days, but the end not being secured, they were followed by repression, domiciliary visitation and the persecution of suspected citizens. A certain Pano Grantcharov, or Ghérov, tried to commit suicide to escape being entered as a Servian volunteer. Greater success was gained in the villages, after beating the inhabitants, as was done at Stentché, Volkovia, Jiltché, Raotintsi, Léchok. On May 29/June 11 the priest Anguélov, the Archbishop's vicar, was incarcerated and the prefect told him that all those calling themselves Bulgarians were regarded as rebels against the authority. They were evidently in a hurry to make an end of Bulgarism, and on June 6/19, all the presidents of communes and all village priests were summoned together in a Serbized monastery. The representatives of Servian temporal and ecclesiastical power were present, and after a long discourse in honor of the historic glories of Servia, it was proposed to the assembled priests and heads of communes, "that they should become Servian and send a telegram to King Peter." A single priest saved himself by flight and two village priests were absent.

At Uskub, under the eyes of the foreign consuls and in the presence of "the higher commander," difficulties were met with in the execution of official

Serbization. But "the black hand" supplied what was wanting in official activity, and several of its exploits are known to the Commission.[1] The state of mind of the soldiers quartered at Uskub may be illustrated by a little story.

On March 7/20, towards 6 o'clock in the evening, a Bulgarian, Demetrius Gheorghiev, was standing at the door of his house on the Vardar bridge. A little distance off, at the door of another house, there was a Servian officer, Major Boutchits. At this moment the Bulgarian General Pitrikov entered the town, and his orderly, one Igno, passing along the road, greeted Dimtché. Mr. Boutchits at once makes a sign to him to draw near, pushes him into the corridor of his house, kicks him with his feet, turns him twice over on the ground, cracks his skull and finally is trying to suffocate him, when his father coming up with soldiers saved his life. All the time Mr. Boutchits accompanied his blows with cynical oaths upon his "mortal enemies," the Bulgarians.

In January the Uskub government made a first attempt at patriotic statistics. The sub-prefect, Boro Milanovits, ordered the heads of the communes to enter the Bulgarian population as Servian on pain of fine and imprisonment. This time the schoolmasters and priests were also invited to proclaim themselves Servian. But the matter did not go off smoothly. On March 16 the peasants of the village of Nerézi complained to Archbishop Néophyte. When he spoke to Tserovits, the prefect, the latter pretended that the thing was being done by "stupid officials" for whom he excused himself before the Archbishop. He then summoned the village priest and forbade him to visit his parishioners until he had obtained the permission of the Servian Archbishop. The villagers of Nerézi were arrested as they came out of the Bulgarian Metropolis and were cast into prison. From this time on the peasants from the villages were afraid to go to their Archbishop. Next, the same thing was tried with the inhabitants of the town; terrorization went on throughout Passion week, and it was hoped that the result would be that they would be too much frightened to come to the Bulgarian church on Easter day. The Archbishop again complained at the Russian consulate and at the prefecture, and the Bulgarian population, that is to say the great majority of the Christian population at Uskub, took advantage of the last opportunity which it was to have of going to its own church and taking part in the religious procession of the second Sunday. Resistance on the part of priests and schoolmasters in the town went on despite every kind of persecution up to the end of May. On May 11/24, the national festival of St. Cyril and St. Methodius, the population disregarded the order forbidding shops to be closed. A number of domiciliary perquisitions took place on the morrow, with the object of discovering a new revolutionary organization.

At the end of May opportunity for a new demonstration of independence was afforded by the enrolling of volunteers. As at Tétovo, the enrolment took

---

[1] It was this band which beat Methodius. See Chapter I.

place by force and on May 26/June 8, all those enrolled were gathered together at Uskub. Almost all the "volunteers" told the military authorities that they had been brought there by force. Their relations came with them and made statements before the consuls. Some people were fined and imprisoned, but the government was obliged to abandon the use of force and from the whole prefecture at Uskub there remained but fifteen or sixteen genuine "volunteers." In the course of the following days there arrived at Uskub volunteers from Tétovo, Gostivar, Kirtchevo, Dibra and Okhrida, and Albanians from Katchanik, in all some 500. All these new comers heard what had happened and thereupon declared that they too were unwilling to serve. They were all sent back except some Bulgarians, who being accused of having stirred the volunteers to resist, were shot.

On the heels of these events there followed the fatal day of June 17/30. The arrests began at midday and continued until the evening. On the 18th some 200 schoolmasters, officials of the Metropolis, priests, notables and other suspected citizens were imprisoned. Ninety-nine selected from among them were incarcerated in the Mitrovitza prison, the most remote spot possible from the theater of the war. At Uskub arrests went on continually. There were three hundred selected prisoners, some of whom came from the villages. Some were beaten, others paid their guards to escape beating. At Tétovo, at the same time, as many as 200 persons were arrested; at Koumanovo—a pacified town—there were 150 arrests, while some hundred of those arrested at Palanka were sent to the prison of Préchovo. Three villagers from Palanka, unable to march, were killed by the soldiers on the Koumanovo road, like true prisoners of war,— Balkan war.

Now at last it seemed that victory might be celebrated. On June 25/July 8, after the departure of Archbishop Neophyte, several priests and notables were called upon to proclaim themselves Servians, and when they gave an evasive reply, they were "permitted" to hold a meeting in the court of the Church of St. Demetrius. It was a trap. Fifty or sixty persons arrived, but instead of being allowed freedom to discuss together, they were addressed by the chaplain attached to the "higher command," who ended by inviting them to sign a declaration which he brought out of his pocket. With full hearts and tears in their eyes they signed. The authorities summoned the public criers, who proclaimed in the streets that a reconciliation had taken place, that the exarchists had recognized Servian nationality and the Servian church. On the morrow the Cathedral church of the Holy Virgin was thrown open and the Servian and Bulgarian priests thanked God together for reuniting them in a single nation and a single church. The Belgrade papers published congratulations and the official agency communicated the news to the foreign press.

By way of completing the victory thus gained, an emissary was sent, under pretext of taking clothes to his relations, to Mitrovitza to persuade the notables under arrest there also to proclaim themselves Servians. They were given Servian papers to read, full of glorifications over the event. Many hesitated and they grew to be a majority. The soil thus prepared, a clerk attached to the military command appeared before the prisoners. In his hand he had a list of the "Uskub Bulgarizers," but he said he was not sure of it and wanted to verify it. Clearly there was some mistake, for the whole body had been noted down as "Bulgarizers," according to the declaration of the first to whom the question had been put. As a matter of fact, it was only the schoolmasters, the officials and a few town dwellers who were "Bulgarians." The others were ready to declare themselves Servians. They were given another week for reflection. Then the same clerk brought them a declaration to sign, in which they made formal renunciation of the exarchy and asked to be set at liberty. Most of them signed; those who entered themselves as Bulgarians were declared rebels and convicted agitators. Nevertheless, both classes were kept in prison until the conclusion of the treaty of Bucharest, July 29/August 11. On their return to Uskub, the schoolmasters were invited to remain in the Servian service, or in the event of refusal to go to Bulgaria. Forty-two signed a declaration to the effect that they preferred to be sent back, and by August 6/19 they had arrived at Sofia, coming by way of Niché and Pirotus. A few days later they were followed by two other bodies of schoolmasters from Uskub. The Serbization of the Uskub prefecture was an accomplished fact.

At Vélès—the first object of Servian pretensions "beyond the frontier" agreed upon by the treaty—we find the same methods employed and the same stages in the process of Serbization. The name of the captain of the legalized band who chased the successor of Archbishop Melétius from Vélès on February 4/17 after the usual savage scene, was Voino Popovits, and that of his assistant, Douchane Dimitrievits. An *interim,* lasting down to the turn of Melétius on March 28/April 10, was employed in seizing the Bulgarian monasteries and churches in the town. At the end of February the schoolmasters were invited to become Servian officials, and when they refused, they were threatened with persecution. The local "black hand" made one or two examples, and the schoolmasters were compelled to stay at home or at least to refrain from exchanging greetings in the streets, on pain of being maltreated. Here on the eve of Easter the local bands sent into the villages were replaced by bands from Uskub, which the consuls had asked to have sent back. In order to spoil the national festival of St. Cyril and St. Methodius (May 11/24), the administrative authorities ordered the population to repair the streets. The inhabitants of Vélès did not obey; disregarding the wishes of the authorities they shut their shops to celebrate the festival.[1]

On June 17/30 a particularly large number of arrests took place at Vélès. All the schoolmasters of the town and villages were arrested, as well as all

---

[1]This is perhaps the origin of Article 23 of the Ordinances of September 21.

the priests and officials of the Metropolis, and between 150 and 200 inhabitants of the village. This was a form of recognition of the strength of national feeling in this little town, which had been one of the most active centers of the Bulgarian national movement, ever since its beginning. Martyrs too were not lacking. On June 18, in the evening, a priest, John Avramov, was dragged out of prison and taken with five young men from the Koinik quarter into the "black house." The priest's throat was cut and his body thrown over the bridge into the Vardar. The current carried his corpse down and threw it up by the side of the stream, where near the shore, the water is almost stagnant. His beard had been plucked out. Nobody dared to take up or bury the body. On the morrow it had disappeared. The five young men were killed together and their relations failed to find their bodies.

These measures may serve as typical. On the 28th two priests, D. Antonov and G. Mikhilov, were set at liberty with a number of notables. The intention here was quite plain. They were assembled in a sort of gathering which passed a resolution renouncing the exarchy, recognizing the Servian church, and declaring themselves Servians. This declaration was followed by a solemn service. A month later, on July 25/August 7, all the inhabitants and schoolmasters remaining in prison were likewise set free, after declaring themselves Servians. On August 5/18, a proposal was made at the prefecture to all the schoolmasters and mistresses, that they should either become Servian teachers or leave the town. With a single exception (Mr. Brachnarov) they all consented.

At Monastir (Bitolia), the chief place of the vilayet, and likewise coveted by the Servians "beyond" the frontier, the counting of the population was begun by the middle of December. Special commissions were sent into the villages with the object of persuading the population to declare itself Servian, by forcing the churches and the schools to become Servian. After that the disarmament of the population followed.

From the second half of February on the situation grew worse. Bronislav Nouchits, the well known Servian dramatist, who was the prefect, was regarded as too moderate, and replaced by someone more sympathetic with the views of the military party and of "the black hand." Acts of violence against individuals and the arbitrary imposition of fines became of more frequent occurrence. The Metropolis felt its isolation growing. A panic was created in the population by the case of the Stambouldjiev family, which was massacred within doors without the discovery of any traces of the criminals.[1] The persecution of Bulgarians became more violent after the declaration made by Mr. Pachitch. Individual priests and schoolmasters were compelled to yield and to declare themselves Servians. Those who were recalcitrant were dealt with by the method of "disarmament," accompanied by domiciliary perquisitions and torture.

In the course of the days June 17 to 19 (June 30 to July 2) more than

---

[1] See above Mr. Boris' reference to this case.

600 persons were arrested at Monastir. They were kept in strict confinement until July 13/26, when the Bulgarian defeat had become perfectly well known. Then the less turbulent among the peasants and artizans began to be set free, on condition of taking no part in national agitation. At the same time the less prominent inhabitants were invited, according to the quarters in which they lived, to sign the declaration, the text of which was afterwards published in an official Servian paper in Bitolia, *Opchtinské Noviné*. The text, which may serve as a specimen of what was asked of the Bulgarian population and of what it was endeavored to make them believe, is as follows:

> In order that, once for all, the question of our national feelings may be firmly established, and that a serious error may, at the same time, be wholly refuted, we, Slavs from Bitolia, hitherto attached to the exarchy, do today, being assembled in the orthodox church of St. Nedelia, state as follows: (1) That we are familiar from history that we have been Servians since ancient times, and that the Turks conquered the countries which we now inhabit from the Servians five and a half centuries ago. (2) That there is no difference either in nationality or in faith, or in language, or in customs between us and the Servians, as is proved by many remembrances and by the Servian schools, which were the only ones in existence in these lands up to the time of the Turco-Servian war of 1876–78. (3) That our ancestors were, and that we are, called Servians, but that under the recent influence of Bulgarian propaganda, and above all under the terror caused by the *comitadjis*, we have, in quite recent times, begun to turn our eyes to the Bulgarians, in the hope that, thanks to their preponderance in what was once the Turkish kingdom, they would be better able than the Servians to free us from our servitude. (4) That in the last war with the Turks, the Bulgarians instead of assisting and freeing us, appropriated Thrace and liberated non-Slav populations. (5) That the Servians have, by superhuman efforts and enormous sacrifices, taken these lands unassisted and so put an end to our servitude. (6) That both before and after the war the Servians treated us really as their brothers, while on the contrary the Bulgarians were at pains to separate us from our liberators. (7) That on the 17th of last month the Bulgarians attacked the Servian army, which shed its blood for them before Adrianople; an attack for which the whole civilized world condemns them. (8) That the Bulgarians desired to expose the people of these countries to new misfortunes and to destruction by their attempt at sending hither bands of brigands to burn the villages and pillage the people. Wherefore, we declare our entire solidarity with our Servian brothers and liberators: with them we will work in the future, shoulder to shoulder, to strengthen our country—Greater Servia.

When the signatures even of the most obscure and timid of the inhabitants had thus been collected, with the assistance of the police, the commander summoned a meeting of notables. An old merchant, Piperkov by name, when invited to sign, replied: "I am an old man, sixty years of age. My father always told me that my grandfather was Bulgarian. Therefore we do not consent to sign, and nothing but force can compel us to do so." The commander then gave him twenty-four hours for reflection. They met to the number of eleven in a private house; two of the number were inclined to submit to the Servian power. The other nine remained inflexible and were arrested. Their wives went to the Russian and Austrian consulates, whereupon they were again set at liberty and given a new period of twenty-four hours in which to sign. They then did sign (using their Bulgarian names, ending in *ov*, not in *itz*, which was in itself an act of defiance) a declaration drawn up by themselves, in which they described themselves as "Ottoman subjects free from Turkish rule by the victorious Servian army who would, in the future, remain faithful to their liberators, whose subjects they regarded themselves." The individual who told us this story at Salonica, added that these unfortunate men could not at this moment admit the possibility that Monastir might become Servian: they were as yet entirely ignorant of the issue of the war.

On July 10/23, the schoolmasters were called before the commander, and by order of the general staff the proposition was made to them with which we are already familiar, namely, to renounce the exarchy and become Servian officials by at once signing individual requests to this effect. They were promised higher salaries and assured that the years they had already served would be taken into account in estimating their pension. The schoolmasters declared that they were unwilling to go against their consciences; they asked to be allowed to live as private individuals and Servian subjects until the political situation of the country was decided. They were told that in that case a circular from the general staff would order their expatriation on the next day. Their statements that they were natives of the country, that most of them were married and had children, that they had property and other local ties, and that the question of the expatriation was one for their own private judgment, were entirely disregarded. Here as elsewhere the irrevocable decision had gone forth,—whosoever calls himself a Bulgarian must betake himself to Bulgaria. The final argument produced by the authorities was as follows: "The exarchy pays you, that is to say Bulgaria pays you; we are enemies of Bulgaria and that is why we treat you as agents *provocateurs* of an enemy power." No attention was paid to the protest that the salaries of most of the schoolmasters had been paid by religious communities. On July 13/26 they were escorted, to the number of thirty, through Prilèpe and Vélès, and thence through Uskub, where they were joined by the other protesting teachers from Prilèpe (seventeen) and from Kesen (six), to Smédérévo. On July 28/August 10 an Austrian Danube steamer landed them at Lom (Bulgaria). It is unnecessary to lay stress on their sufferings upon the way.

At Monastir the end was gained. On July 7/20, divine service was held for the solemn celebration of "unity, concord and love," in which service the Bulgarian priests who had just renounced their exarchy officiated jointly with the Servian clergy. After the service a meeting took place at which Mr. Tavet-kovits, the moving spirit of Servian administration in Monastir, made a speech on the reconciliation of the people and their return to the bosom of Servia. After his speech the declaration with which we are familiar was read out, and the meeting terminated amid cries of "Long live Servia! Long live the Servian army! Long live King Peter! Long live Prince Alexander, the liberator of Monastir!"

There is little to add about the other towns in the Monastir prefecture. We have in our possession an interesting document about Prilèpe, "the town of Mark Kralievits," the legendary Servian hero, in the shape of a proclamation issued by the commander of the place, Mr. Michael Menadovits, dated March 6/19. This shows that Mr. Menadovits had lost any illusion as to the "love and concord," of the liberated population. Prilèpe, it should be said, was, like Vélès, one of the strongholds of Bulgarism in Macedonia, and so Mr. Menadovits learned to his cost. "I can no longer recognize," he writes, "the people of Prilèpe of whom I was so proud! Agitators and enemies of the Servian people (who are well known to me) have stirred up such a ferment among the peaceable and honorable citizens of this town, that I no longer know my old Prilèpeans. What! Do you repay my love for you by plots against my life? Is this your gratitude for my kindness that you conspire in your houses to cut my head from my shoulders? My patience is at an end. The Bulgarian army whose arrival you await so impatiently from day to day, is not coming. You will be sorry to hear that it is never coming; do you understand? That I can assure you of, with all the weight of my name and my position! Even to wish for it is a disgrace. If you want to know to whom Prilèpe belongs, go up on to the heights of Monastir, to the mountain of Babonna, *Bakarno Goumno,* and ask your question of the graves of the sons of Servia which are there. * * * I address myself for the last time to the honorable men of Prilèpe: Remember that the secret society called *Nodnykra* is a more dangerous enemy to you than to me. To you, cowardly agitators, I cry, 'do not play with the lives of peaceful citizens! * * * Massacre Servian soldiers and officers if you like, but remember that the payment for their deaths is a far more terrible death!' "

The Servian commander of Resen (Resna) was equally dissatisfied with the state of feeling in that town, which was a republican center, and the birth-place of the Turkish Major Niazi-bey, who started the revolution in 1908 there. On December 9/22, 1912, he had called the notables of Resen before him to accuse them of being disloyal subjects, and of fomenting discord between rival nationalities. He added that it was in his power to have them all killed and hanged without distinction, great and small, and even old men with white beards (by which he meant the Archbishop's vicar) if they did not improve and hand over to him the Bulgarian propagandist leaflets. (The leaflets in question were the declaration of war by King Ferdinand and the proclamation by the Bulgarian

Red Cross which had been left with the vicar by some travelers from Bulgaria.)

On December 14/27, all the schoolmasters of the towns and villages were summoned, and told by the commander that "everything taken by the Servian army would be kept by Servia," and that in future their salaries would be paid them from the Public Instruction office at Belgrade. In reply to the question, "Were there no private schools in the Servian kingdom?" the commander at first said nothing. Then, *"Pardieu,"* said he, "I do not know, but you may be quite at ease about what I told you, since Turkey no longer exists." On March 15/28, they began taking the census, in which there was no heading "Bulgarian." Special commissioners went from house to house, meeting resistance everywhere. In the lists the Bulgarian designation ending in *ov* was successfully preserved and only five households entered themselves as Servian. Since, however, the official list included no heading but "Servian," the papers published the figures as being the totals of the Servian population. "Disarmament" began in July, accompanied by the usual violence. The numerous examples of such violence found in our documents may be passed over in silence.

On June 17/30 between forty and fifty citizens and 250 and 300 villagers were arrested at Resen, and kept in confinement for a month. A village priest was offered his liberty, on condition of praying in the church that God might give victory to the Servians. After a few moments' hesitation, the priest replied to his interlocutor, "I can not pray to God except for the end of the war." On July 10/23, the schoolmasters were brought out of prison and offered the usual alternative—"Sign a request to be nominated as Servian officials, or you shall be expatriated as Bulgarian agitators and spies." Some signed, the others first hesitated and then withdrew their request, after a categorical protest against expatriation had been made by a professor. He declared that it was illegal, as applied to native persons who had committed no criminal act and possessed a perfect right to live at home as private individuals. He with five others was, as we have seen, dispatched to Uskub. On July 11/24, the priests of the town and the villages were compelled to renounce the exarchy and recognize the Archbishop of Belgrade as their spiritual head. On July 26/August 18 some notables were summoned, to whom the declaration signed at Monastir was read out. They protested against it. "The exarchy," they said, "is not a form of propaganda; the exarchy is the work of the people, who constituted their church at a representative assembly of all the towns in Macedonia. The Bulgarian *comitadjis* did not teach us to be Bulgarians, but the Servian and Greek *comitadjis* do claim to teach us to change our nationality." A new form of declaration was then proposed: "Seeing that the exarchy and the orthodox church are one and the same, we declare ourselves Servians." When the notables again refused their approval they were all sent to prison and dispatched to Salonica, "in order," so they were told, "that the Greeks may massacre you." There they spent eighteen days under arrest, in a little room with eighty other Bulgarians. They were then sent to Bulgaria via Constantinople and Bourgas.

Krouchévo (the third town of the Monastir prefecture) shows the same extortions, under color of requisitions, and the same acts of violence and domiciliary perquisitions under pretext of a search for arms. On the 17/30, the Servian soldiery left the town and their place was taken by a band with one Vanguel of Uskub at its head. Since the reputation of the acts of violence committed by the band had gone before it, five former Bulgarian *comitadjis,* living in the town, formed a band of their own and took to the hills. On June 19/July 2 all the notables were arrested. The prison was in the basement of the government building, and through the bars of their windows the captives overheard the sub-prefect, Evto Bekrits, delivering a harangue from the balcony to a newly formed band of *vlach* (Roumanian) and Grecizing (*Romanize*) inhabitants, on June 22. "In the absence of the army you are authorized to act. Since Bulgaria has declared war, you are authorized to do as you please with anyone calling himself a Bulgarian." On the next day, Vantcho Iogov, one of these recruits, beat a Bulgarian merchant, Demetrius Krestev, in the open market because the latter had a Bulgarian sign. On the merchant's complaint the sub-prefect issued a notice ordering the removal within twenty-four hours of all signs in the Bulgarian language: they were ordered, on pain of court-martial, to be replaced by Servian signs. (The same facts are repeated everywhere, at Uskub, Vélès, Prilèpe, etc.) We need not mention the other acts of violence committed under pretext of domiciliary perquisition. Even women were beaten and imprisoned for calling themselves Bulgarian. On June 29/July 12, the birthday of King Peter, all the prisoners were brought into the government hall. The sub-prefect promised them an amnesty if they would agree to admit that they were Servians. Two of them replied in the name of all the others that it was solely as Bulgarians that they could be loyal subjects of Servia and useful to the State. They were immediately taken back to prison where they remained for another month. On July 17, Vantcho Belouvtchéto, chieftain of the Bulgarian band, was killed by the soldiers of the Servian band, after two hours of real fighting. His head was cut off and carried in triumph all round Krouchévo. Towards evening it was put on the threshold of the prison, the door having been thrown open for the purpose. "So shall heads of all those who call themselves Bulgarian be treated," said the sub-prefect. On the next day he summoned the Archbishop's vicar, and ordered him to sign the written declaration. The vicar, terror stricken, signed without reading, and so did the other priests. Two schoolmasters followed their example, but two others refused. An hour later, they were sent under escort via Prilèpe to Uskub, where they remained for two more weeks imprisoned, until peace was concluded. On August 4/17, they were expatriated; their families meanwhile remaining in Macedonia.

Even greater resistance was met with in the assimilation of the places on the western frontier of Macedonia, at Okhrida and Dibra (Débar) on the borders of Albania. We find here, as everywhere else, the ordinary measures of "Serbization"—the closing of schools, disarmament, invitations to schoolmasters to become Servian officials, nomination of "Serbomanes," "Grecomanes," and *vlachs,* as village headmen, orders to the clergy of obedience to the Servian Archbishop, acts of violence against influential individuals, prohibition of transit, multiplication of requisitions, forged signatures to declarations and patriotic telegrams, the organization of special bands, military executions in the villages and so forth. The numerous arrests effected on June 17/30, extended impartially to all classes. At Okhrida, too, the threat of expatriation was successfully used to compel priests and professors collectively to renounce the exarchy. The imprisoned professors were compelled to accept their salary from the Servian Ministry of Public Instruction and to sign its receipts. Yet, up to the middle of September, the spirit of the people was not altogether broken. At Débar, external submission hardly concealed feelings of revolt. The exarchist clergy (forty priests) in the month of May formally renounced the exarchy by a solemn process of retractation, followed by an oath upon the Testament. As at Resen, the schoolmasters proved more recalcitrant. They were arrested on June 17/29 and kept in prison until the middle of July. Their ultimate fate is unknown to us. We do, however, know that during the months of August and September, the idea of resistance remained alive in the population. There was a great deal of talk of a scheme of "union" with the Holy See, as a means of preserving nationality after the abolition of the exarchist church. This idea appears to have originated spontaneously in the minds of the population of Monastir. Preparations were also being made for armed resistance, with the definite design for claiming Macedonian autonomy. The Servian government laid great stress on the fact that the Bulgarian *comitadjis,* under the direction of the *voyévodas,* Milan Matov, Stephen Khodjo, Peter Tchaoumev and Kristo Traitchev, had taken no part in the Albanian insurrection. In fact we know from an interesting story told by one of the initiated, and published in a Bulgarian paper,[1] that Mr. Matov had organized a band at El Bassan and prepared an appeal to the Bulgarians and the Moslems in conjunction with the Albanians. Owing to the refusal of the Albanian government this appeal failed, but Matov had behind him private assistance and support. He was in communication with the chieftain Tchaoumev at Okhrida, and with the Albanian and Bulgarian population in the villages. The little Servian garrisons, taken by surprise, had to beat a retreat, and for several days Okhrida, Struga and Débar were in the insurgents' hands. There was even talk of organizing a provisional Macedonian government at Okhrida.

These events were bound to react on the state of feeling of the populations of Western Macedonia. But at Prisrend and Diakovo, as well as at Débar and

---

[1] See *Izgrève* of October 24/November 6—"The truth about the Albano-Macedonian insurrection."

at Okhrida, the Servians soon made an end of the Albanian insurrection. The Albanian population to the number of some 25,000 souls took flight after defeat. Those who remained underwent the familiar treatment at the hands of the Servians. The Bulgarians also suffered severely. All the notables were imprisoned or shot. A number of mixed Albanian and Bulgarian villages were burned in the regions of Dolna-Réka, Gorna-Réka and Golo Urdo. After this the official "classification" of Macedonia might be regarded as completed.

In August, when the Commission went through Belgrade (August 10/23, to 12/25) the struggle was still going on as we see. In the occupied territories the Bulgarian population was still contending, and at Belgrade Mr. Pachitch was still unwilling to yield to the military party on the question of Macedonian administration. Since the crisis was not settled, the Commission might prove an inconvenient witness. This was probably one of the reasons why it was not desired at Belgrade that the Commission should move about freely. This apprehension was betrayed when a Belgrade paper accused a member of the Commission of seeking to distract the Commission from its principal object by arranging for them to visit Uskub, Vélès, Mitrovitsa, Prisrend, Monastir, Tétovo, etc.[1]

True, it was stated that there was no general objection to visits from strangers. Only they must be controlled. In our manuscript chronicle of events in Macedonia, we find under the date of February 10, a remark by the Vicar of Koumanovo: "Yesterday evening three Europeans, Englishmen, arrived in our town. According to the Servians they were sent to study the condition of the population. They were put up by the vicar of the Servian Archbishop. Today they made a tour of the town and went to see the authorities. A number of Bulgarians (among them the wife and brothers of Ordé Yovtchev, who has disappeared) endeavored to interview them, but the government admitted nobody. Only a body of Turks were received and questioned as to the actual conditions of their life. Having been terrorized in advance, they stated that they 'lived well.' " Sufficient honor has been done the Commission to admit that it was not so easily satisfied as these simple tourists.

Is the work of false pacification, as revealed by our documents, definitive

---

[1]*Balkan*, August 13/26. The Commission had not had any such intention, because the time at its disposal and the itinerary drawn up before its departure from Paris did not allow of it. As regards Mr. Pachitch, it should be noted that the most substantial reason given, by him, for his refusal to the Commission, was that "the army would resent" the presence of one member in the interior. The campaign directed against the presence of this member of the Commission is still going on in the Servian press. The Paris correspondent of the *Politika,* of Belgrade, reports in the issue of November 11/24, that this member had offered a sum of fr. 40,000 to the Russian photographer, Tchernov, in the name of the Carnegie Endowment, for the purchase of photographs in his possession of "Bulgarian atrocities," in order to withdraw the said photographs from publicity. This offer Mr. Tchernov was alleged to have refused. The truth is that two members of the Commission went to see the photographs which Mr. Tchernov exhibited in the Grand hotel of Paris, as evidence not of Bulgarian "atrocities," but of "war atrocities" in general. They found the photographs very interesting and quite authentic, and ordered some of them for the Commission, which Mr. Tchernov agreed to print at a stipulated price. Such is the manner in which falsehoods are spread.

or lasting? A doubt is suggested by the ordinances of September 21. All that the Commission has since learned confirms such doubts.

True, the Servians are optimistic, to judge from the articles which have appeared in their press. This optimism, however, is *sui generis,* and satisfied with very little. Take the patriotic and militarist paper *Piemont,* which rejoices over the condition of affairs in Chtipe at the end of October:

> In Chtipe things are like old Servia. People are getting busier and go about and work freely, there is no longer anyone who calls himself a Bulgarian, and if you happen to say the word Bulgarian before the citizens you are seized and sworn at. Everywhere in the streets people sing only Servian songs and dance Servian dances. Vicentius, Archbishop of Uskub, who arrived on the 5th/18th, was received at the Bregalnitsa bridge by the population of all creeds, Turks and Jews. In the last few days the first betrothals have taken place according to our custom; our photographer, Kritcharevits, has got married; the orchestra of the Fourteenth Regiment played at the wedding amid indescribable rejoicings. The young women of Chtipe are pretty; they are a trifle prudish, but that fault will mend.

Here is another correspondence sent from Monastir to Vienna via Salonica on October 14:

> The town of Monastir is almost surrounded by a military cordon. The measures taken by the Servians in apprehension of any movement among the Bulgarians grow more and more Draconian * * * The authorities desire to compel the Bulgarians to send their children to the Servian schools (the Bulgarian schools are closed). To this end policemen go from house to house warning people that those who do not send their children to the Servian schools will be fined—the fines being, fr. 100 for those who do not send their children to school at all, fr. 200 for those who send them to non-Servian schools (there are some *vlach* (Roumanian) schools), fr. 600 for those sending them abroad without the knowledge of the authorities. Young people between nineteen and thirty are not allowed to leave the country.

Here is another correspondence from Monastir, published in the Bulgarian paper *Mir,* of November 29/December 12:

> On November 12/25, fifty-one Bulgarian peasants were killed in the Boumba quarter, and another at Tchenguel-Karakolé, by the authorities themselves. The policemen make a practice of pillaging the peasants as they return from making their sales and purchases at market. A number of peasants from the villages of Ostriltsi, Ivanovtsi, Rouvtsi, Bala-Arkava, Vochéni, Borandi, have disappeared. At the village of Krouchévo five persons (whose names are given) were beaten; at Ostriltsi nine; at Ivanovtsi, eight; at Berantsi, nine; at Sredi, seven; at Obrachani, four; at Padilo, three, etc.

At Okhrida, after the retreat of the *comitadjis* at the beginning of October (see above) a panic seized the whole population. There was no village without its victims, chief among them being priests and schoolmasters. In the beginning of October alone three priests, five teachers and some 150 villagers, Bulgarian citizens, were killed, without counting 500 Turks and Albanians. Whole quarters were destroyed on the plea that they belonged to rebels; the houses of the families of the chieftains Tchaoulev, and Matov, were among those destroyed. All the young men of any intelligence, to the number of fifty, were imprisoned. They were tortured at least once a day, and often left without food for three days. All the priests were arrested because on December 14 and 15, they had prayed in the churches for King Ferdinand and Archbishop Boris; when interrogated they replied that such was Tchaoulev's order.[1]

At last the Servians themselves are beginning to admit that things are not going as they should. Here, as in Bulgaria, the organs of the opposition press lay the blame and the responsibility on the personnel of the administration. The *Balkan* declares that this personnel is in no way different from that of the Turkish régime. The government press makes excuses but can not deny the fact: "There are not enough trained officials. The conditions of life in the conquered countries are too difficult to call forth a sufficient supply of competent candidates."[2] The real difficulty, however, the state of feeling of a population subjugated but not subdued—was not remedied. Measures were taken to combat such opposition as was left. They were not quite sure of the clergy, still less of the teachers who had taken the oath. In Belgrade itself the Commission heard the question discussed whether it would not be better to send the Bulgarian officials, although they had submitted, into really Servian regions, such as Metohia and Kosovo Pole. The favorable impression to be produced outside by these quasi-voluntary acts of submission, which also were useful in assisting to hide the complete lack of candidates for administrative posts, led at the moment to the simple registration of Bulgarian officials among the Servian staff. Later, conditions changed. On October 19/November 1, a Bulgarian paper speaks of eighty-eight schoolmasters who had come from old Servia (Kosovo and Metohia) and were nominated to former Bulgarian schools (twenty-one to Uskub, nineteen to Monastir, seven to Prilèpe, ten to Koumanovo, six to Okhrida and twenty-five to Vélès). On November 11/24, the *Serbische Correspondenz* speaks of 200 professorial candidates from Croatia and Hungary, ready to take their places in "new Servia." If reliance can be placed on the correspondence published in the Bulgarian press, the attendance at the new schools is not great, despite the fines for absence. Nevertheless, the number of Servian schools increased, although they were inferior to the Bulgarian

---

[1]Correspondence of October 16/29 in the *Politika*, and that of December 19/January 2 in the *Vozrajdanie*.

[2]See the controversy between the *Balkan*, the *Pravda*, the *Novosti*, the *Odjek* and even the *Piémont*, on the one hand, and, on the other, the *Sammouprava* in December.

schools, both in number and in quality.[1]   According to official Servian statistics (*Serbe Corr.* November 29/December 12), there are now 395 schools where there were 193, with 350 teachers, where there were 240.   What is being taken over is the Bulgarian inheritance.   At Uskub a training school for teachers has even been opened.   But among the 380 students, 260 come from Old Servia and only 120 from the conquered territory, according to the Servian authority.

The most serious difficulty which remains to be overcome, is the state of mind of the population.   The latest reports in our possession do not show any improvement.   The same steps continue to be taken for dealing with discontent, which is general, by means of terrorism, which is not growing less.   The *Mir* of December 23/January 5, contains an *Albanian correspondence,* from which we quote:

> At Kritchovo, 150 peasants were beaten in the presence of the authorities; seventeen persons killed by blows and the corpses burned.   The others too were seriously wounded and thrown into the stable without any sort of medical aid.   At Novo-Sélo five peasants were beaten by the Servian gendarmes.   At Plasnitsa we found six peasants killed by a Servian patrol, forty peasants killed in October, five houses burned.   Gvayace was attacked by a Servian band, forty peasants were killed and their corpses thrown into the wells.   In October, in the same village, 200 peasants were killed and 800 Turkish books carried off.   Toukhine was pillaged by a Servian band.   At the same time a Servian theater was being opened at Uskub, and the Minister of Public Instruction intrusted Professor Ilits to collect popular songs in the annexed territories; and it was cited by the Minister for the Interior as proving that "the fullest liberty of conscience was granted to all confessions in the practice of their religious observances," that the Moslems were permitted to hunt on their feast days (*Serbische Correspondenz*).

The most elementary condition to be fulfilled before toleration towards a conquered country can be claimed, is clearly that formulated by the Greek delegates at the peace conference at Bucharest, and extended to all belligerents by the Bulgarian delegates, but rejected because of the refusal of the Servian delegate: "Whereas war against the Ottoman Empire has been undertaken by Bulgaria, Greece, Montenegro and Servia, in order to guarantee to all the nationalities the conditions of free development; whereas it is impossible that this noble inspiration should not have survived the events that have since separated the former allies * * * Bulgaria, Greece, Montenegro and Servia recognize with the newly annexed territories autonomy for the religious communities and freedom for the schools."[2]   Had this condition been accepted, we might indeed have be-

---

[1] See the interesting report by a Servian professor Mr. T. M. Yakovlevits, on "The condition of Bulgarian schools at Macedonia in comparison with Servian schools," published October 16/29 in the *Serbska Zastava.*

[2] See the *Procès-verbal* No. 10 of the Bucharest Conference session July 26/August 8, 1913.   Likewise rejected was the proposal of the representative of the United States at

lieved in "the establishment of friendly relations between the four States," and the possibility of "insuring to the populations called upon to dwell together an era of justice and wide toleration." The Servian delegate, however, replied that "the question, in so far as it concerns new Servian subjects, is regulated by the constitution of the Servian kingdom"—a statement which, as we have seen, was not true. The results of this refusal have been seen. It has been easier to conquer than it will be to keep the fruits of conquest. The Servian press is full of apprehension as to the true sentiments of the conquered population, and is constantly envisaging some rising danger from outside. Today it is Albania preparing new disorders for the spring; yesterday the Bulgarian *comitadjis* were crossing the Roumanian frontier with false passports to get somewhere in Macedonia. (*Serbische Correspondenz,* November 26/December 11). Another day America is allowing Macedonian conspirators from Tétovo or Doiran to organize committees for the recovery of the autonomy of their enslaved country (*Tregovinski Glasnik*) in New York, Chicago, Portland or St. Louis. A new emigration is at hand with its army of between 15,000 and 20,000 Macedonian workmen, who can not be brought under any ordinances. The *Pravda* is evidently right in thinking that it will not be necessary to wait twenty-five years for a Zabern. But, we repeat, the condition is "autonomy for the religious communities and freedom for the schools,"—a return, that is to say, to the minimum of liberalism which did up to the last few years exist in fact, guaranteed by international treaties, even in old absolutist Turkey.

3. GREEK MACEDONIA

The documents in the possession of the Commission are less complete for Greek than for Servian Macedonia. But the data at its disposal are sufficient to establish the conclusion that here too the same situation is repeated, down to the smallest detail, of the assimilation of the Bulgarian population in Southern Macedonia (Vodéna, Castoria, Florina). The procedure is quite analogous to that employed to assimilate the same population in the north. As to the alternative system, which consists in the extermination of the Moslem population, it was repeated on the eastern frontier of Macedonia, on the confines of Thrace, like the analogous Servian system on the western frontier on the confines of Albania. The only difference is that the two methods of assimilation and extermination are here pursued with even more system and even less humanitarian sentiment. Is it indeed a "human" race, this "dirty" (*sale*) Slav? They are not *anthropi.* They are *arkoudi*—bears. The word recurs frequently in our depositions, and corresponds perfectly to the *Bulgarophage,* sentiment that was

Bucharest, Mr. Jackson, to insert into the peace treaty a provision according full civil and religious liberty to the inhabitants of any territory subjected to the suzerainty of any one of the five Powers or which might be transferred from the jurisdiction of one Power to that of another, "with the same recourse to 'the public law of the Constitutional States represented' which would have afforded the consecration of long usage."

consciously being developed in the army and among the populace by means of patriotic verse and popular pictures, of which specimens will be found in the Appendix.

We begin with Salonica, the natural center of Greek Macedonia. The Commission received no great facilities on the part of the Greek government for inquiry into the facts that interested them at Salonica. All the same, the members took advantage of the fact that they were free to come and go in the town, to investigate the available sources of information. True, the indigenous population with some few exceptions hid away, the Greeks out of hostility towards the Commission (as their articles in the local press well show); the Jews from fear of responsibility. The foreigners remained and although the very name of Bulgaria had been proscribed, there were still some belated Bulgarians. From Bulgarian governesses about to embark the next day, a member of the Commission learned the details of the days, June 30, July 1 (June 17, 18), of the Bulgarian downfall, which took place soon after the beginning of the second Balkan war. Later the Commission was able to test their evidence by that of others; on its return the highly important written evidence of the Bulgarian prisoners liberated at the end of the year 1913, was added to the oral testimonies and confirmed and corroborated it. The most important place among the later testimonies belongs to the recollections of the commander of the Bulgarian garrison at Salonica, Major Velisar Lazarov, which appeared in the Bulgarian paper *Politica* in November.

Without lingering over the numerous incidents that took place between the actual masters of the town and those who aspired to take their place, we may draw the general conclusion that relations between the Greek and Bulgarian military living side by side in Salonica, were extremely strained during the whole time of common occupation. After April, 1913, there were but three companies of the Fourteenth Macedonian regiment whose status was regulated in May by a special convention between the two governments. This little garrison was quartered in some dozen houses situated in the different quarters of the town, Hamidie street, Midhat-pasha street, Feisli street, etc. Every day as many as sixteen pickets were set to guard the official institutions and the lodgings of the high military, civil and ecclesiastical Bulgarian officials. The Bulgarian military force was thus distributed in the eastern portion of the town.

On June 17/30, General Kessaptchiev, representing the Bulgarian government at the Greek quarter general, left Salonica because of the opening of hostilities. Some army officers who accompanied him to the station were persuaded that the Greeks were preparing an attack. Mr. Lazarov then went in all haste from the station to the Bulgarian General Staff, opposite St. Sofia, to warn his officers and men. Thence he went to Feisli street, to the Turkish schoolhouse, where most of the Bulgarian soldiers were quartered. A letter from the Greek commander, General Calaris, followed him thither. The general informed him that hostilities had been opened by the Bulgarian army and proposed to him to leave Salonica with his garrison within an hour, after giving up his arms. At the expiration of this delay, the Bulgarian army in Salonica would be regarded as hostile and treated accordingly.

General Kessaptchiev's train started at one o'clock. Mr. Lazarov received Calaris's letter before three. Half an hour before, at 2.30, the Greek soldiers had begun the attack on the Bulgarian pickets. Mr. Lazarov wrote his reply amid shots. In it he asked permission to communicate with his superiors by telegraph. At five o'clock, after two hours of steady firing, the Greeks gave the order to cease. There had been a misunderstanding. Then the French consul, Mr. Jocelin, arrives and wishes to speak with Mr. Lazarov. "Very good," is the reply of Mr. Calaris. After five minutes waiting this is the reply that came: "The conditions are refused." Mr. Jocelin departed. The fusillade began again on both sides. The French consul had been told that Mr. Lazarov would not see him. The last hope of preventing the catastrophe disappeared. Towards evening cannon and shell began to speak. Night came on; an hour after midnight the Greeks again ordered, "Give up arms!" Mr. Lazarov's reply was the same. He asked permission to communicate with his superiors. Fighting began again, with redoubled fury. Many houses were in flames, some were destroyed by cannon, about eighty peaceable citizens and nearly a hundred Bulgarian soldiers were killed. The night ended and Mr. Lazarov himself this time offered to surrender on condition of keeping arms (without bayonets), baggage and money. The conditions were accepted; then on the pretext that the Bulgarian soldiers might have tried to keep the bayonets, refused. The Bulgarian soldiery were arrested unconditionally.

On the morning of June 18/July 1, two merchant steamers, poetically named *Mariette Ralli* and *Catherine,* were ready to convey the prisoners to Greek fortresses. There were no arrangements for the comfort of the prisoners on these boats, and no intention of making them. The soldiers were shut up in the hold of the boats, near the engines and the coal, in an insupportably thick atmosphere. The officers, to the number of twenty, were lodged in a cabin with two beds. Neither officers nor soldiers were allowed on the bridge. The only drink they were given was stale water mixed with brine, and on the second day, some mouldy biscuit as their only food. Yet the officers were soon to see that their lot was not the worst. After the soldiery, persecution of the Bulgarian civil population at Salonica began, under pretext that they were all *comitadjis.*

The members of the Commission of Inquiry heard horrible stories of what happened at Salonica in the streets and in the Bulgarian houses on July 18. But there again it is not always convenient to cite the names of those who suffered, still less of those who gave evidence. We shall begin with a foreigner, at once victim and witness, who was taken for a Bulgarian and consequently for a *comitadji.* His story, which we shall cite *in extenso,* will serve as an example.

John (Jovane) Rachkovits, Austrian subject, born in Dalmatia, was a merchant in Salonica. On June 17/30, he came out of his shop to go to the Austrian post office, where he had an order for fr. 300 to cash. He had the sum of ninety francs in his pocket. A spy pointed him out to the police as a Bulgarian *comitadji*. This was enough to cause him to be arrested, brought before the police, interrogated, and his reply being doubted, put on board the steamer and shut up in the coal bunker. There he spent three days and three nights, in company with seventy-two Bulgarian prisoners. All that he had was stolen from him, and when he tried to protest, in his quality of Austrian subject, his Austrian passport was snatched from him and torn in pieces. Some soldiers were shot during the crossing, and he "suspected" that some one had been thrown into the sea. [We shall see that this suspicion was well founded.] No bread was given out. only biscuits. The drinking water was brackish. When they arrived at Trikeri (the prison at the opening of the Gulf of Volo), they were given bread, olives and onions. There was no doctor at Trikeri, and the prisoners died at the rate of five to seven a day. After protests from the Austrian consul, Mr. Rachkovits was sent back to Salonica, but he suffered even more on the return voyage. His hands were tied so tightly behind his back that his chest was strained. Afterwards water was poured on the cords to make them tighter still. Ten days after his arrival at Salonica a member of the Commission saw his swollen and diseased hands; part of the skin had been taken off and the marks of the cords could still be clearly seen.

Here is the fate of another civil prisoner, this time a real Bulgarian, Spiro Souroudjiev, a notable known in Salonica. He had already been arrested, questioned and set at liberty. A week later he was arrested again and sent to Trikeri. He was a rich man, and his wife succeeded in seeing her husband again by paying the sum of £T500 (the figure was given to a member of the Commission by people who knew). But in what a state did she see him! The poor man was half dead, and could not speak. At his second interview with his wife, he could only just pronounce the words "We have been horribly beaten." His clothes smelled of excrement. For seven nights he had not slept, having been fastened back to back with another prisoner. On his wife's insistence he was transported to the French hospital of the Catholic sisters, but the next day he was transferred to the cholera barracks, where, after two injections, he died.

Here is a third case, and one of a kind that will not be forgotten. The victim is the vicar of the Bulgarian Archbishopric at Salonica, the Archimandrite Eulogius, who by duty and conviction alike represented the national Bulgarian cause throughout the whole vilayet. This time we have a declared enemy of Macedonian Hellenism. A member of the Commission made his acquaintance during his journey to the Balkans in January, 1913. He was a highly educated man, having studied at an ecclesiastical high school in Austria Hungary, and then in Paris; an enlightened and ardent patriot of noble and elevated views. He was subjected to persecution by the Greek authorities even at this time, and took great pains in the use of the Bulgarian language in the teaching of the Episcopal See, which the Greeks frequently tried to prevent. The Bulgarian soldiers lodged just in front of the Episcopal house; and it was thanks to the protection of the temporal power that the spiritual maintained its existence. But with the extinction of this last dream of Bulgarian sovereignty, the Archbishopric was at an end. The Archimandrite Eulogius lived his last on June 18/July 1. During the night attack he escaped by hiding under the staircase; in the morning he was taken and put on board the steamer *Mariette Ralli,* where Commander Lazarov and Dr. Lazarov, a doctor at the hospital, joined him and conversed with him. Their two depositions have now been published,[1] and it is important to compare them with the assertion of the agency at Athens, that "It appears from the public inquiry that Eulogius was at the head of Bulgarian *comitadjis* at Salonica, who fired on the Greek troops *which were trying to reëstablish order.* Eulogius was killed at the moment he fired on the Greeks."

Unfortunately it is not true that Eulogius died in defending himself against the Greek soldiers who were "reëstablishing order" by sacking the Bulgarian Episcopal palace. About midday on the 18th the two brothers Lazarov saw him on board the *Mariette Ralli.* Towards evening on the same day he was transferred on board the *Catherine.* On the 19th at half past two the *Catherine* took to sea. Three hours later, Eulogius was no more. Here again eye witnesses confirm what the Commission heard said in Salonica. F. Doukov, a Bulgarian prisoner, just returned to Varna from Greece, says for example:

> He was arrested on June 17 about midday, and incarcerated in the post office at Top-hane. At seven o'clock, four soldiers from the bank picket were brought to the post office also, and with them the cashier of the bank, Helias Nabouliev, and Jankov, the accountant. On the next morning all the Bulgarians who had been taken were gathered together, Nabouliev was called, stripped and deprived of fr. 850. The others were also pillaged. Before noon all the prisoners were put on board the steamer, Nabouliev and Jankov a little later. On the same day towards evening, the vicar of the Salonica Archbishopric, the Archimandrite Eulogius, was brought with his deacon, Basil Constantinov, and George Dermendjiev, the Metropolitan archvicar, his secretary, Christian Batandjiev, being put on another steamer. Before noon on the 19th several Greeks from Salonica came on board the boat and jeered at and beat the prisoners. The Archimandrite was maltreated in the most shameful way. In the afternoon at half past two the steamer started. When it passed the big promontory of Kara-Bournon, the Archimandrite was thrown into the sea. Three shots were fired at him and he

---

[1]The story of Commander Lazarov in the *Politica* of November 14/27, 1913 (in Bulgarian) and that of Dr. Lazarov as an appendix to the *Reply to pamphlet by the Professors of the University of Athens—Bulgarian Atrocities in Macedonia,* by the professors at the University at Sofia, p. 115.

drowned. J. Nabouliev, Jankov and Nicolas Iliev were put to death in the same way.[1]

Another witness is Basil Lazarov, the forester of Kazanlik, who says:

On June 19, at half past three in the afternoon, 223 soldiers, eight men employed on the railway, Ghnev and Vatchkov, officials at the station, Tordanov, the physician of the Fifth Hospital, Mr. Nabouliev, cashier of the Bulgarian National bank, Mr. Jankov, the accountant of the same bank, Eulogius, vicar of the Bulgarian Archbishopric of Salonica, and many other Bulgarians and a large number of peaceable citizens of the Macedonian countries occupied by the Greeks, were conveyed on board the steamer *Catherine* to the Island of Itakon. After a voyage of three hours, near Cape Kara-Bournon, we saw a man being put to death; the Greek soldiers threw the Archimandrite Eulogius into the sea, and fired three shots at him for fear he might escape drowning. On June 21, about seven in the evening, Jankov the accountant, Nicolas Iliev the courier, and Nabouliev the cashier were called up to the bridge. When they went up the exits of our prison were shut by means of planks, and we were told not to try to get out. At this moment the three persons whose names I have just given had already been cast into the sea.

Another eye witness, the soldier, G. Ivantchev, described the scene of the murder of Rev. Father Eulogius in the following words:

We were a number of soldiers on board the steamer. I happened to stand a little apart. The Greek soldiers ordered our people to go down into the hold. When I found myself alone I was afraid of being thrown out of the ship and held my breath. At this moment the Vicar of our Archbishopric, the Rev. Father Eulogius, was brought up and two Greek soldiers having hastily robbed him transfixed him with their bayonets and threw him into the sea. I saw his long black hair floating for some time on the water, and then everything disappeared.

The Bulgarian Telegraphic Agency actually gives the names of the Greeks at Salonica who came on board the steamer on June 19/July 2 to see Eulogius maltreated. "The President of the Greek revolutionary committee, a fanatic called Cherefa and Dr. Mizo Poulos" were the people "who came on board the *Catherine* where the *andarte* hit the Bulgarian prelate twice and even kicked him in the shins.

After such scenes of refined barbarism, it is hardly necessary to record the numerous stories of domiciliary perquisitions and arbitrary arrests which took place at Salonica during the days between the 17th and the 19th, which have come to the knowledge of the Commission. The picture may be completed by mentioning that avarice as well as cruelty played its part in all this. The victims were systematically robbed before they were put to death, and frequently

---

[1]*Politica.* October 20, 1913 (old style).

money was taken as a ransom for life and liberty. Money was taken from the soldiers who were sent to Trikeri, but most of them kept something back. The device employed by the Greek guards to compel their prisoners to give up what they had kept back was as follows:[1]

> Twenty-eight prisoners were transferred from the ship to the shore in a little boat. When they got near land, the Greeks made holes in the bottom of the boat and it began to fill with water. The prisoners were then asked to give up their money on pain of being drowned. Our witnesses say that the threat was not vain; two prisoners who had no money were drowned. All the others gave what they possessed.

Even at Salonica people who did not want to be sent to prison or shut up paid the police agents who took them. When in the first instance the arrest was made by officials of a lower grade, the business was easier and cheaper. Thus at Salonica names are given of people arrested and set free the same day at the police station. Once the prisoner was transported to the central prison, it became more difficult and troublesome; but all was not yet lost. Thus the Dermendjievs, father and son, paid £T100, Mr. Piperkov, fifty pounds, and Mr. Kazandjiev an amount not known. The case of Mr. Karabelev, a Stamboulist deputy from Plevna, and proprietor of the Grand Hotel, is more complicated. Being arrested eleven days before the catastrophe of June 30, he handed over the key of his strong box to the Russian consul. A proposal to set him at liberty at the price of twenty-five Napoleons was made. The police then appeared to make a legal perquisition in his strong box. It was too late; the police found the strong box broken and the whole contents, diamonds, bonds and some thousands of Turkish pounds disappeared!

But a simple plan open to any Greek soldier was to appear in a Bulgarian house and say: "Your money or your life." A story is told by a Bulgarian in the documents of Mr. Milétits.[2] "On June 20/July 3, two soldiers came into our house and threatened to kill G——, as they had already killed many other Bulgarians. You can imagine the fear and horror which filled the house. The soldiers then said that they would not touch him if he gave them fr. 500. G—— had a hundred francs which he offered them, but the soldiers refused it. G—— then told them to wait while M—— went to get some money from Yosko M—— found two Cretan policeman who suddenly appeared, told them what was going on and brought them to the house. The soldiers made off and the incident was thus at an end."

To the knowledge of the Commission these brave Cretans more than once turned what might easily have become a tragedy into a farce. The Cretan

---

[1] This story was heard by the Commission at Sofia, and they are acquainted with the names of the Bulgarian prisoners who witnessed it.

[2] Documents on the Greek atrocities extracted from the book by Professor L. Milétits, *Greek Atrocities in Macedonia*, p. 65.

police often had to defend the Bulgarian population at Salonica against the tacit complicity of the *evzones* and the Greek soldiers with the Greek population. Here is another scene in the Commission's documents: After June 18 one of the two houses occupied by the Bulgarian girls' school remained unhurt. The schoolmistress, Ivanova, came to lock the house up. She found Greek soldiers feasting before the door. Seeing Miss Ivanova shutting the doors, the Greek inhabitants suggested to the soldiers getting in by the windows. Soldiers and inhabitants climbed up to the window and pillaged the property of Miss Ivanova: they then asked for her keys to make legal perquisition. The schoolmistress complained to the Cretans. They asked her to show them the Greek houses in which the stolen goods were to be found. She went from house to house with the police, finding here her cushion, there her clothes, and in another house her wardrobe, which a Greek soldier had sold for five francs.

The abuses committed in such an atmosphere may readily be imagined. Worse, however, than these abuses was the use of legal force. The notion of having to deal always with *comitadjis* became a kind of obsession. The prisons of Salonica were overflowing with Bulgarians, arrested in the town itself and in the vilayet, for having dared to proclaim themselves Bulgarians. It was reckoned that between 4,000 and 5,000 had been sent to Greece while as many as a thousand were shut up in the prisons at Salonica (at Yedikoule, at Konak, and in the "new" prison). We shall have another opportunity to return to the condition of these prisons and their inmates and to the violations of the Red Cross conventions during the memorable days of the 17th, 18th and 19th of June. We may, however, quote here the case of a witness who was heard by the Commission, to show the way in which people who had committed no crime but that of being Bulgarians were being treated at this time. This was a scholar of the Salonica *Realschuli*, Demitrius Risov, a youth of seventeen. On June 17, he was walking in the street when he was arrested and led "before a captain." The latter asked him, "Who are you?" He replied, "I am Bulgarian." He was searched and a photograph of his father, a Bulgarian officer, found upon him. "What is that?" Without waiting for a reply, the officer hit him and sent him to prison under the guard of a soldier. There there were seventeen policemen and soldiers who beat him for five or ten minutes, until he lost consciousness. He was thrown down from the top of a step-ladder, and since the ladder had no steps he fell against the wall and lay there for some time in the mud and wet. In the evening as many as thirty other civil prisoners were brought in, and since there was very little room below the ladder, Risov had to stand on it. In this position he heard a Cretan policeman boasting of the massacres of civilians. By way of proof one of the policemen produced a paper in which there was a severed human ear, which Risov said that he saw less than a yard off. Everybody laughed at this proof of courage. At the end of about an hour and a half, they saw Risov sleeping as he stood. Somebody pushed him and he fell down.

A soldier came down after him and said, "Only wait two or three hours and we will send you all to sleep for good." Some peasants among the prisoners began saying their prayers and making the sign of the Cross, when they heard these words. Forty-eight hours passed thus, during which no food was given them, despite their complaints; then the door opened again and Risov was pointed out and again interrogated. To frighten them, he said that when he was arrested he had been to the American consulate before starting for America. He was set at liberty. But the way was long and Risov knew that Bulgarians found in the streets were being killed every day. He asked for a written passport, or a soldier to take him home. The officer refused; Risov went out alone and taking precautions returned to his family. Alas, he found his mother in tears, for his father, an old man of sixty-five, was in prison. Thence he was sent to Greece. His younger brother, who had been severely beaten, was very ill; his elder brother, a deaf mute, had also been beaten, for they had taken his infirmity as a device. A week later the Cretans visited the house again. They looked for somebody or something. They took hold of the deaf mute and pulled his tongue to make him speak. They found nothing, and left the house, threatening, "If you do not become Greeks in three days, we will water your deaf mute with petrol and burn him with the house." The mother, in despair, threatened to go out of her mind. Risov then remembered that the mother of one of his friends was a Frenchwoman. He asked her to get the consulate to intervene. Salvation thus came at last from France. After a new perquisition the Risov family was left in peace.

The Commission could quote other witnesses of the same kind, but it seems that what has been said is sufficient to enable the reader to draw his own conclusions.

The country behind Salonica is inhabited by a yet more mixed population, from the nationalist point of view, than that of Northern Macedonia (see the ethnographic map). Apart from the Hellenic population, which occupies a narrow strip to the south of Macedonia, the Tchataldjic peninsula, and the coasts, which constitutes a more or less important part of the town population, you meet Bulgarians, Turks, Wallachians (*Vlachs* or Roumanians), Albanians, Jews, Gypsies. At the end of the two wars and the oppressive measures of which we shall speak, the ethnographic map of Southern Macedonia had undergone profound changes. But we have a recent picture of the state of things before the war in the ethnographic map just published by Mr. J. Ivanov, of the University of Sofia—in 1913.[1] The total numbers belonging to the various nation-

---

[1]Ethnographic map of Southern Macedonia, representing the ethnic distribution on the eve of the 1912 Balkan war, by J. Ivanov, lecturer at the University of Sofia. Scale 1: 200,000. Explanatory notes. Sofia, 1913, p. 8. The author employed the Turkish electoral lists and the *Salnamés*, Greek statistics made in 1913 by Mr. Kalixiopoulos; the unpublished returns of the detailed statistics undertaken by the 1912 Exarchate, and the new Roumanian statistics of A. Rubin & Co. Noe, etc., and "verified all information at his disposal on the spot." The map shows all the towns and villages in proportion to their size, and marks the proportions of the various nationalities in color.

alities in a territory a little larger than the portion in the same region ceded to the Greeks by the Turks was as follows:

Bulgarians	329,371
Turks	314,854
Greeks	236,755
Wallachians	44,414
Albanians	15,108
Gypsies	25,302
Jews	68,206
Miscellaneous	8,019
Total	1,042,029

The statistics accepted by the Greeks differ considerably from these. To give some idea of the difference, the figures of Mr. Amadori Virgili are reproduced (in brackets) with those of the *Messager d'Athènes* of February 2/15, 1913, quoted in a recent work by Mr. Charles Bellay, *L'irrédentisme hellénique* (Perrin, 1913), as representative of the Greek point of view:

SANDJAKS (*Divisions of vilayets*)

	Servia		Salonica		Serres		Drama		Total	
Orthodox Greeks	111,000	(119,466)	224,000	(233,508)	92,000	(96,513)	46,000	(47,852)	473,000	(497,339)
Exarchist Bulgarians	1,500	··	75,000	(70,096)	121,000	(98,586)	2,000	(2,120)	199,500	(170,802)
Moslems	59,000	(80,702)	200,000	(189 600)	118,000	(122.303)	105,000	(124,100)	482.500	(516,705)
Wallachians	760	(1,460)	6.000	(3,928)	1,350	(980)			8,110	(6,368)
Jews		(43)	61,800	(65,730)	1,400	(3,005)			63,200	(68,778)
Gypsies			900		7,500		250		8,650	
Servians			1,400						1,400	
Miscellaneous		(3)		(2,314)						(2,317)
	172,260	(201,674)	569,100	(565,176)	341,250	(321,387)	153,250	(174,072)	1,236,360	(1,262,309)

Clearly, in the Greek statistics, the Moslem total is swollen by the addition of the pomaks (Bulgarian Moslems), from whom, in the Bulgarian statistics, the Turks are separated. In the Greek figures the "orthodox" Greeks include the patriarchist Bulgarians and Wallachians, whom they call "Bulgarophone Greeks" or "Wallachophones" (Roumanianizers). With these exceptions, the difference is not considerable, when it is remembered that the territory is not quite the same; and it may be admitted that if language rather than the religion is used to determine nationality, Mr. Ivanov's figures are or were nearer the truth. The polemics of the Servian press put the number of "Slavs" annexed by Greece at 260,000; a figure which the Greek press reduced to 120,000. The secret Greek-Bulgarian treaty, as we know, contained no indication as to the frontiers on which the two parties had agreed. This was one more incitement to "Hellenic irridentism." In Greece, as in Servia, two opposing tendencies were at work after the first successes of the Hellenic army. Like Mr. Pachitch, of Belgrade, and Mr. Guéchov, of Servia, Mr. Venizelos was for moderation, seeing therein the sole means of safeguarding their common creation, namely, the Balkan alliance. The discontent of the military party grew more and more outspoken, and as in Servia so in Greece, found a leader and interpreter in the person of the heir to the throne. The Greek *diaspora* was a much stronger and older organization than the scattered colonies gathered round the Servian school-masters and band leaders. Here the patriotic organization was based on a considerable settlement of really Greek population, and was accustomed to obey the word of command from Athens. From the months of January and February onwards, a regular campaign was organized, with addresses, memoranda, telegrams, congress resolutions, etc., despatched to the Ambassadorial Conference in London and to the Hellenic government, all demanding annexation by Greece. On March 1/14, one of these memorials was presented to the Hellenic chamber in the name of the "Hellenes of Thrace and of Eastern Macedonia, who constitute almost the whole of the Christian population of these regions." The petitioners "proudly proclaim that Hellenism alone has, in the present war, made more moral and material sacrifices than any other of the allies or than all the allies together"; and demand their national regeneration through union with their mother country, Greece.[1] Mr. Venizelos entered an interpolation here, and his reply afforded a remarkable example of a political wisdom, soon to find itself swept away by the chauvinistic passion of the dominant party: "Necessarily," said the initiator of the alliance, "Greek populations and groups composed of these populations will pass under the domination of our allies. And the reason is not that these countries have been conquered by our allies, or that our allies demand it, but the force of geographical considerations. This is so true that even were our allies disposed to allow us to extend our frontiers towards their regions, and encompass the Greek populations, I at least, in my capacity of responsible Minister, would never accept a line of demarcation which for us is full of peril. If we are to go on extending in unbroken continuity along the sea, to encompass all the Greek population of Thrace, Greece thus extended and without any vertebral column, would be weaker than if its frontiers were rounded off differently. * * * I hope that no one from these benches will encourage resistance on the part of these disturbed and troubled populations." When he was violently attacked for these words, Mr. Venizelos added: "A similar declaration was made three or four weeks after the declaration of the war of liberation. * * * From that time on I have stated that I was making the sacrifice of a large part of Hellenic Thrace. * * * I felt it my duty to communicate this statement to the Chamber because * * * I knew that a movement was being worked up among their Greek populations which are destined to remain inside of Greater Greece. * * * Those who are urging such an attitude upon them are the true enemies of their country."

Nevertheless, while speaking against the procedure of the patriotic Hellenic

---

[1] See this and the sixty-two other memorials published in the appendices to the interesting and instructive work of Mr. Charles Bellay, *L'irrédentisme hellénique,* cited above.

organizations in Thrace, Mr. Venizelos said nothing about Eastern Macedonia, which came within the scope of the "Deliannis formula," nor about Southwestern Slav Macedonia, at whose expense it was evidently hoped to accomplish the "rounding" of the Greek frontiers. As a matter of fact, the common Greek-Servian frontier had been already discussed in the "Salonica-Monastir train," and it is clearly in this sense that Mr. Venizelos understood the division among the allies of which he spoke in the chamber. This idea of a "division" of the territories in *condominium* among all the allies has already been substituted for the idea of Serbo-Bulgarian "arbitration." Some days after Mr. Venizelos's declaration, the heir, Prince Constantine, became King of Greece (March 6/19).

The effects of this change made themselves felt on the relations between the Greeks in occupation and the indigenous population. We may begin our examination of these relations with Castoria. From the beginning of the occupation, the authorities there pretended to ignore the very existence of the Bulgarian population. It is true that Prince Constantine's proclamation on November 14/27 announced that in the occupation regions the Greeks would respect the language and religious customs of the nationalities. That however did not affect the Bulgarians, who evidently were no more than "Bulgarophone Greeks" in the eyes of authority. Announcements and appeals to the population were published in Greek, Turkish and Yiddish, exactly as though the Bulgarian language did not exist, and Bulgarian remonstrances remained unheeded. To make the reality harmonize with this theory, the occupation army had recourse to the acts of violence which we know. After a sufficient demonstration had been made by the population, of the fate awaiting those who persisted in calling themselves Bulgarians, formal retractations began to be demanded. These declarations, which the villagers were forced to sign, conformed in the Castoria region to two types. According to one of the two declarations, the people were made to say that they had been Greeks from the most ancient times, but had called themselves Bulgarians under the influence of Bulgarian propaganda. According to the other, they were made to say that up to 1903 the population had been Hellenic, but that between 1903 and 1906, they had been forced to call themselves Bulgarians by the threats of the Bulgarian bands and *comitadjis*. The two models ended with the same declaration, namely, that immediately on the army's arrival the population felt its Hellenism and asked to be received into the bosom of the "Great Church of Jesus Christ." The Bulgarians were not "Christians" in "our sense." The Greek bishop of Castoria received the deputations sent to him from all the villages, and was in fact the center of this active assimilation. The *evzones* played the part of apostles in this conversion at the bayonet's point. As examples we may cite the villages of Gabrèche, Drénovéni, Tchernovitsa, Tourié, Ragoritchani, Dembéni, etc. In the villages of Bréznitsa, Gorno and Dolno Nestrame, all the inhabitants were thrown into prison and driven thereby to call themselves Greeks. The reply given to a man who said he was a Bulgarian was: "Wast thou born at Sofia; there are no Bulgarians in

Macedonia; the whole population is Greek." To maintain this principle, a passport was given to those few natives who had to be admitted to be Bulgarians, declaring them to have been born in Bulgaria. The Commission knew of a passport of this kind given to the incumbent of the Bulgarian diocese of Castoria, although the man was born at Résen (in Macedonia) the Greek passport stated that the place of his birth was in Bulgaria. He was in fact permitted:

νὰ μειαθῇ εἰς θεσσαλονίκγυ καὶ ἐκειθιν εἰς ιηὺ βουλγαρίαν ἐξ σς καταγέται·

and this was not an isolated case. The Mahometan pomaks of the village of Gervéni were also entered as Greeks by the enumeration commission; from the moment at which they spoke Bulgarian and not Turkish, they were revealed as Greeks.

Victory secured in the villages which were disarmed, then came the turn of the intellectuals, the Bulgarian clergy, schoolmasters and officials. A number of persons whose names and cases are cited in the documents in the possession of the Commission, were arrested, beaten, put in prison and even killed. The Bulgarian Metropolis of Castoria was, at first, ignored by the authorities so far as its legal institution went; then cut off from the population under severe penalties for any communication; and finally, about the beginning of June, formally blockaded by twenty or thirty soldiers and searched by the police. Afterwards, by order of the government, all the officials and schoolmasters were shut up in their own houses until further orders. At this moment the Greek papers were already talking of the war as imminent. The *Embros,* in a letter from Salonica, said on June 14/27, "the great struggle for the existence of Hellenism *will begin in a few days.*" On June 14/27, *Proodos* said, "We are on the eve of war. * * * On his departure for Salonica the king took his field uniforms with him. * * * The war proclamation * * * is ready." War began on the 17/30, and the Greek citizens of Castoria were singing before the Metropolis verses inviting "A draught of Bulgarian blood." On July 31, after the conclusion of the treaty of Bucharest, the *frourarque* of Castoria summoned the head of the diocese, the officials of the Metropolis, and the schoolmasters, and told them "By order of the new government I give you forty-eight hours delay, in which to quit Greek territory." The expatriated, all natives of Macedonia, were given certificates to the effect that "they were returning to Bulgaria, where they were born." "He who goes to live in Bulgaria," was the reply to the protests, "is Bulgarian. No more Bulgarians in Greek Macedonia."

We have also sufficiently complete data on events at Vodéna (now called Edessa). Our informant there, as at Castoria, remembers how the Hellenic army entered in triumph on October 18/31, amid cries of joy from the population. Each house harbored ten to twenty soldiers, freely and without asking pay, and the town distributed gratuitously 6,000 *okas* of bread per day. The time had not come of forced requisitions, without receipt, demanding everything without allowing any merit to the giver, who had to obey. Ten days later, the Greeks were beginning to say, "We shall cut your tongues to teach you to speak Greek." They began confiscating private property, and sending things they liked to Greece; furniture, cattle, etc. The churches and schools were immediately taken, the Slav inscriptions destroyed, the offices burned, the priests beaten and driven out. Then began the arrest of influential persons in the different villages, such as Vestchitsa, Tsarmarinovi, Piskopia, Arsène, St. Elvas, Vettécope. The soldiers said to the notables in prison in Vestchitsa, "If you want to be free, be Greeks."

War once declared—June 20, 21/July 3, 4, as many as 200 Bulgarians, the vicar, priest, notables, schoolmasters, inhabitants of the town and of the villages, were arrested. They were beaten and sent in fours to Salonica. On June 30 the last Bulgarian church was confiscated; the Slav national images of St. Cyril and St. Methodius were burned and their ashes covered with dung. (The Greeks and Servians regarded these images, symbols of the independence of the Slav church, with special detestation.) At the beginning of July the population was asked to sign the following declaration: "Under compulsion from the ex-archist propaganda, and terrified by the *comitadjis,* we became Bulgarian. We now confess the true orthodox faith and our Hellenic nationality." Emissaries were then sent to Salonica to offer liberty to the prisoners from Vodéna if they would declare themselves to be Greeks. "We remained pure," Mr. Atanasov, one of these prisoners, records, "our consciences immaculate, and we were all thirty-three freed without making any engagement on August 7/20.[1] But a Bulgarian schoolmaster from the village of Palati, who became a Greek, wrote in a Greek paper, *Iméra,* that the prisoners had not suffered in any way and that "not a hair of their heads had been touched." He only forgot one thing, according to Mr. Atanasov: that had they remained in prison a month after this, not one would have come out alive. Mr. Atanasov gives a picture of the Salonica prisoners, which is known to be unhappily too correct. "There were 130 of us in a single room," he said, "and often we had to stand throughout a whole night, waiting our turns to lie down. For fifty days we remained in this same room without crossing the threshold. The air we breathed can be imagined. There were others who had been there 100 days and more without having been interrogated. Their shirts were indistinguishable from their coats. In addition to this filth and to the infection of the air, our food was ill-cooked bread, full of impurities. We were as though buried alive, waiting for death to set us free. I intentionally omit the moral suffering caused by the soldiers who were let in for the purpose. Among us there were wretched prisoners from Gumundjé, Yénidje-Vardar, Florina, Castoria and Salonica. After a delay of five to six days at Salonica, they were sent into exile. Some were sent directly from the

---

[1]See the story of Mr. G. Atanasov, published in the *Mir,* September 30/October 13.

station to the steamer; on embarkation their money and watches were taken from them; they were ill-treated; sometimes they were thrown from the top of the ladder into the hold. A man from Gumundjé had his ear cut open, another his head broken; some had bayonet wounds, and all had been struck with the butt end of musket or stick."

We have before us also depositions of witnesses as to what happened at the Kaïlaré sub-prefecture. Situated between Vodéna and Castoria, it was naturally treated in the same way. There, too, Bulgarians were forced to become Greeks, and the peasants made to sign a declaration testifying that they had become Bulgarians only fifteen years ago and under compulsion from the *comitadjis.* The Slav offices were destroyed; the Bulgarian clergy were not allowed to administer the sacrament until they had been ordered to do so by the Greek bishops; the schoolmasters were driven out and the scholars forced to attend Greek schools under threats of punishment for the parents. Soldiers were billetted on the Bulgarians, and requisitions made without either payment or receipt; *andartes,* placed in control of the administration, persecuted the Bulgarian population in every way, killing the men, outraging the women and burning the houses with impunity. We could give names of the persons and villages which suffered. The villages most often mentioned are Emboré, Rakita, Biriatsi, Kontsi, Débrétsé, etc.

Despite all these persecutions, it may be said that in Greek Macedonia the simple fact that the ethnic difference between conquerors and oppressed is greater than in Servian Macedonia did serve to protect the Bulgarian population against assimilation. Although the victors were satisfied with having changed names and statistics and teaching the peasants to say "Good morning" and "Good evening" in Greek instead of in Bulgarian, there was no real change in national consciousness.

There was indeed one thing which hampered the assimilation by the Greeks of the Slav element, namely, the presence of that same element in the immediate neighborhood. True, in Servian Macedonia the elements which outside still call themselves Bulgarian, are forced to give themselves out as *pravisrbi,—* true Servians. But that does not prevent the conservation of the sentiment of Slav affinity. In the allied Servian government, this sentiment found expression in a tendency to desire the conservation and protection of the Slav element in Greek Macedonia. It is interesting that the first news received from Salonica by the Commission of the Greek drownings, was given by a citizen of the allied nation which had just taken precautions against the importunate curiosity of the Commission as to its own relations with the "Macedonian Slavs." The oppressed Slavs in Greek Macedonia in their turn seemed to look more favorably on the oppressors of their brothers in Monastir and Okhrida. If they may not have Bulgarian schools, some of them are ready to ask for Servian ones,—so long as they may keep their Slav school. The only objection of the Greek ally to the

Servian ally is that the latter does not reciprocate by tolerating Greek schools in Servian Macedonia, or, if he allows them to be opened, forbids school children to attend them. Tit for tat. The Greek papers only disagree as to the number of Slavs with a moral right to protection by the Slav ally. Recognition of the very existence of the Slav element, although reduced to 120,000, is thus implied beyond dispute.

This is not the case with the Moslem element, though equally numerous in Greek Macedonia. True, our documents prove that at the beginning of the occupation, when it was a question of ferreting out the Bulgarian committees, the help given by the Turkish element was highly appreciated by the *andartes*. Their end once accomplished, however, and especially after the treaty of Bucharest, the tactics adopted towards the Moslems were entirely changed. The *Jeune Turc* seems justified in its complaints of the lot of its co-religionists in Macedonia. "Mass arrests of Turks and Jews," it states towards the middle of October, "take place daily in Salonica on the most ridiculous grounds. Espionage is widely developed and persecution is attaining revolting dimensions." Unhappily the truth is worse. Another Turkish paper, *Tasfiri Efkiar,*[1] adds that persecution extends from town dwellers to simple villagers. "The Moslems of the neighborhood of Poroï (between Doiran and Demir-Hissar), were shut up in forty wagons and conveyed to Salonica. The Greek authorities also persecuted the Moslems of Langadina (northeast of Salonica); on pretext of disarmament all the young people were conveyed to Salonica and ill treated. At Saryghiol (near Koukouche), all the men were conveyed to Salonica and the Greek soldiers then outraged the women and young girls. At Sakhna, at Serrès and Pravishta, conversion was carried on with such success that in the case of Sakhna not one Moslem is left." "The number of Turkish prisoners in the Salonica area amounts to the enormous total of 5,000," adds the *Echo de Bulgarie* (December 20/January 2). Some months later, Mr. Ivanov remarks in his "Explanatory Notes" that "the Turkish groups of Saryghiol (south of Kaïlaré), Kaïlaré and Ostrovo, strong in numbers and prosperity, were particularly severely tried after the Greek invasion. All the towns and the villages of the region were laid waste and the population sought safety in flight. Flight, too, was the resource of the Moslem population of the towns in the Yénidjé valley, especially Voden, Négouche (Niansta), Karaféria (Véria), Yénidjé-Vardar. This last town suffered most of all; the whole market and the Moslem quarters were laid in ruins."

We must now glance at Eastern Macedonia, of which we spoke in chapter II, and whence the Bulgarian population fled *en masse* to Bulgaria, the Turks and Greeks taking the road to Salonica. Documents not hitherto mentioned complete the picture of what is almost a total extermination. As the most authoritative document for the violence with which the Turkish population was treated

---

[1] These two quotations are from the *Mir,* of October 24 and November 2 (old style).

by the Greeks, we publish in Appendix A, 13 *a,* a complete list of persons killed and pillages effected in one casa in Pravishta (O. de Kavala). The original document was given to the Commission in Turkish; it is an official *procès-verbal,* drawn up and sealed by the Moslem community of Pravishta. It contains names and facts solely; but these names and facts have a dreary eloquence. "Of the 20,000 Turks of this casa only 13,000 remain." "Among the persons killed there are unhappily many *imams,* Turkish notables and men of education. This shows that the Greeks were pursuing a definite object." Here is the picture of the central city of Pravishta, taken by the Bulgarian *comitadji, Voyévoda* Baptchev, but where the Greek Bishop, presiding at the improvised tribunal, pronounces the sentences of death executed by Baptchev, while protecting the young Turkish girls and the mosques against the fanatical chauvinism of the Archbishop."

As to atrocities committed by the Greeks in the northern part of eastern Macedonia (principally populated by Bulgarians), the Commission collected at Sofia a portion of the depositions afterwards published by Professor Milétits.[1]

Out of all our documents we select as a specimen the story of a merchant, Nicolas Témélkov, which gives a general picture of the state of the country after the retreat of the Greek army, which as regards the whole region traversed between Strumnitsa and Djoumaya, was picturesquely characterized by another witness in the phrase "There was not a cock left to crow." Mr. Témélkov, whose evidence is not included in Professor Milétits's document, allows us to give his name. Towards the end of August (old style) he was returning from Bulgaria with some refugees. He crossed the Krésna Valley, in the upper Strouma. In the village of St. Vratche there were only some men feeding on the corn which had fallen on the road from the military convoy. The women did not dare to appear; they remained hiding in the mountains. The priest of the village, Constantine, and five notables, had been killed, and no one knew where their bodies were. Passing through the village of Lechnitsa you met nobody. The village of Sclara had been burned, but twelve or thirteen families were left. The other families were still in the mountains, in fear of another Greek invasion. All the women of the village between the ages of ten and fifty had been collected by the Greeks in the house of Mito Konstantinov, and divided among the soldiery one woman to every thirty soldiers. A girl of eighteen years old, Matsa Andone Pantchéva, who had finished her school time, would not give herself up. She offered them money to give to the women of the streets if they would leave her in peace. The soldiers got sixty Turkish pounds. When, after that, they still tried to outrage her, she resisted, crying, "I had rather die honest." She was killed by bayonet thrusts.

---

[1] See his *Greek Atrocities in Macedonia during the Greek Bulgarian war,* Sofia, 1913, and *Documents,* extracts from this book, published with certain changes in style, Sofia, 1913.

Mr. Témélkov and his companions then passed through the villages of Khotovo and Spatovo. There was nobody there; the population still kept to the hills. The villages had been burned to the ground. They passed through Mandjovo and Tchiflitsi, which the Greek press stated had been burned by the Greek population, who would no longer live there under the Bulgarian régime. Mr. Témélkov, like the other witnesses, states that the town had not been burned; only the military casino, hotel and post office (in the same building as the casino), had been burned. The Greek houses were empty; the Greeks had taken their furniture with them. Mr. Témélkov was told that the Greeks emigrated by the express orders of the Greek government; the order being given when it was known that Melnik was to remain Bulgarian. Automobiles and carts were supplied to enable the Greeks to take all their goods with them to Démir-Hissar. The men were beaten to make them take the carts and go. The same order was given and executed at Névrocope, where force had to be employed to make the Greek inhabitants depart. By order of the officers, all the contents of the big Bulgarian shops in Melnik belonging to Témélkov Nadjiyanev (the father of Témélkov), and Constantine Pope-Tachev, were seized. The little Bulgarian shops and private houses were left to be pillaged by the population.

Mr. Témélkov had news from his father and mother, who remained in Melnik, while he fled to Bulgaria. The military authorities sent for his father and said to him, "What are you going to do now? We want men here, not bears. Become a Greek, if you want to live here." Mr. Témélkov's father, an old man of sixty, replied, "I was born in this country and I shall remain here without changing my nationality." He was summoned a second time and asked, "Where are your sons?" "They are in Bulgaria." "You must give up their property." "They have none." Then some officers ransacked the house and found the dowry of Mr. Témélkov's wife, which amounted to £T250. This money was seized. Then Témélkov, the father, a rich merchant, was asked for 400 pairs of empty sacks for aniseed, and 100 for cotton, which had cost him eighty Napoleons. Then Mr. Nadjiyanev was taken to Ormane-Tchflik and to Livounovo, under pretext of taking him before the commander. When they arrived at Ormane, he was threatened with death and asked for money. He promised to give it and the same Greek officers took him back to Melnik. He paid them £T180. He however possessed another property at Scalvé. All his corn, wheat and barley were seized (30,000 and 40,000 *okas*) and his sixteen bullocks. For all that £T200 was paid him. Finally on the Greeks' departure, it was decided to kill him and his wife. But a Greek friend, Nicolas the *bazardji,*[1] warned him, and advised him to flee with the Greeks without delay, since within a few hours they would come to look for him. He agreed, took flight and hid in the Bulgarian village of Kaïkovtsi. While he was being searched for at Démir-Hissar, he escaped on horseback across the Pirine mountains. But he did not return to Melnik. Worn out, he stopped at Scalvé, and died there of exhaustion.

---

[1] Coppersmith.

Counting the Bulgarian villages whose burning he remembers, Mr. Témélkov names: Marikostinovo, Morino Polé, Koula, Kapatovo, Kroumidovo, Dzigvélia, Mandjovo, Tchiflitsi, Khotovo, Ladarévo, Laskarévo, Sclavé, Spatovo, half of Livounovo (after the departure of the general staff), Ormane Tchiflik, St. Vratche, Polévitsa, Khrsovo, half of Vrana, Katountsi, Spantchévo, the upper and the lower town. He told us that only the mountain villages are left. The whole of the furniture, cattle and grain was taken by the Greeks. But the last stroke certainly was the destruction of the town of Strumnitsa, almost under the eyes of the Commission. An Austrian officer, Mr. Br—, tells us that he was taken by the population of Strumnitsa for a member of the Commission, when, after the end of the war he was making his way on horseback between Sofia and Salonica in company with a German officer, Mr. de R. T. Mr. Br— published his story in the Vienna *Reichspost,* and sent a report to the Austrian consulate at Sofia. This is his story, which thus falls within the scope of the Commission's inquiry:

> On July 28 (old style), peace was concluded. On August 8 [the day before he started on his journey], that is to say, ten days after the conclusion of peace, the Greek military element began burning and pillaging the town. The method of incendiarism was as follows: benzine was poured on the different buildings, they were then set on fire and blown up with pyroxiline bombs. I have never been able to discover the chemical composition of these bombs. They did not explode until thrown upon the fire. I sent a piece to the Austrian Legation at Sofia. At the same time the Greek soldiers compelled the inhabitants to hide in their houses, and cut off all the water pipes and fountains, so that there were no means of putting out the fire. Throughout the whole time, between August 8 and 15, motors came and went three times a day to carry off the stolen property. Everything was carried off that the people had not succeeded in hiding, even chairs, boxes, frames, portraits, beds, etc. Anything that could not be taken was destroyed. All the cattle of one of the biggest proprietors in the region, the Moslem Nasif-effendi was stolen, and his house burned after his wife had been so outraged that she died of it. His child was taken from him and not found again. All the goods of the Jew Novak Kozé were taken from him, and his wife outraged. A rich merchant, Bandésev, had all his goods taken, and motors came and went for two days to take everything out of his house. His wife, too, was outraged, "and so on."

Mr. Br— left Strumnitsa on August 24 (old style). But the Commission has highly trustworthy evidence from a person who was at Strumnitsa August 15/28—*i. e.,* who saw the end of the fire. The evidence of another witness, a Strumnitsa governess, Miss Itcheva, who remained in the town throughout this time, has been published by Mr. Milétits.[1] From all these sources we know

---

[1] *Documents,* pp. 166-168. We have also the evidence of a Bulgarian schoolmaster, who reached Strumnitsa on August 19.

that the destruction of Strumnitsa was but the execution of part of a plan drawn up at the conclusion of peace by the Greek authorities. "From July 27 on," says Miss Itcheva, "the Greeks began a propaganda among the Greek population, and invited them to leave the country. They put into their minds the fear of being tortured or even killed by the Bulgarians. They promised the people to build them a 'new Strumnitsa' in the town of Koukouche.[1] The Greek king himself was going to look after the population. As a matter of fact it was known beforehand that after the forced expatriation of the Greeks, Jews and Turks, the town itself was dedicated to destruction like Xanthi, Gumuldjina, and 'the other places in Thrace.' The foreign consuls at Strumnitsa thus informed, consulted together and telegraphed to their representatives to make representations at Athens. The Greek government agreed to keep all these places until the arrival of the Bulgarian army. But this news was received at Salonica on August 8/21, the very day on which the fire began in Strumnitsa. During the ten previous days the Greek inhabitants had come and gone in the town at their leisure, carrying off their goods in motors put at their disposal by the government. The Turks and Jews had been compelled to follow them. This operation completed, the Greeks set fire to the markets in the southwest portion of the town, near the house of the Greek doctor, Rixopoulo. The idea was that the news being spread in Salonica *before the catastrophe*, international opinion might be made to think that the population had set fire to their own houses, out of fear of remaining under the Bulgarian yoke. The population of the Bulgarian quarters (but a quarter of the whole), seeing the market on fire, came out into the empty streets, and during the night of the 8th and 9th they succeeded in putting out the fire. They thought then that the Greek army was gone; in reality it was only hidden. On the morning of the 9th, the Greek soldiers appeared and threatened to kill the Bulgarians. From that time the Bulgarian population retired to its houses and did not dare to come forth and put out the fire. It was then that the Greeks cut the water pipes and broke the fire engines. In the evening the fire was relighted, and during the night the Greek and Turkish quarters began to burn. The Greek soldiers no longer hid—a great number of witnesses saw them at work. They had bombs in their hands, which they put under the buildings, and in a few minutes the houses were in flames. Six or eight soldiers were seen setting fire to the barracks three times before they got it going." A *vlach* told our witness that a uniformed Greek policeman had awakened him and his family and told him to come out at once, as his house was going to be burned, and would be as soon as they had cleared out. This lasted a whole week, until by the 15th the entire town, with the exception of the two Bulgarian quarters, lay in ashes. Three days later the Bulgarian army arrived. One of our informants told us that

---

[1]Vladevo, a village near Vodéna, has actually been called "New Strumnitsa."

an attempt was made to get the Bulgarian Lieutenant Colonel sign an official declaration to the effect that the *houses had been burned by their owners*. The Bulgarian officer refused.

The Strumnitsa affair throws a vivid light on a number of similar events where the intention and preliminary organization are not so easily discernible. If it seems to transcend all the instances hitherto given, this is simply due to the fact that we have been better able to follow it up. In concluding this part of our report with this act of unqualified horror, we have only to set down the moral conclusion.

The events described above serve to afford one more confirmation of an ancient truth, which it is useful to recall. That legitimate national sentiment which inspires acts of heroism, and the perverted and chauvinistic nationalism which leads to crime are but two closely related states of the collective mind. Perhaps indeed the state of mind is the same, its social value varying with the object to which it is directed. We regard as just and legitimate, we even admire the deeds, the manifestations by which nationality defends its existence. We speak constantly of the "good cause" of oppressed nationalities, or nationalities struggling against difficulties to find themselves. But when these same nationalities pass from the defensive to the offensive, and instead of securing their own existence, begin to impinge on the existence of another national individuality, they are doing something illicit, even criminal. In such a case, as we have seen, the theory of State interests and the State feeling or instinct, is invoked. But the State itself must learn to conform to the principle of the moral freedom of modern nationalities, as it has learned to accept that of individual freedom. It is not nationality which should sacrifice its existence to any erroneous or out-worn idea of the State. In applying this sound maxim to the facts of the second Balkan war, the conclusion is forced upon one, that in so far as the treaty of Bucharest has sanctioned the illegitimate claims of victorious nationalities, it is a work of injustice which in all probability will fail to resist the action of time. Would it not be more in consonance with the real feeling of solidarity of peoples to re-cast the treaty, than to wait for the development and ripening of its evil fruit? The question of the moment is not a new territorial division, such as would probably provoke that new conflict which the whole world wishes to avoid. Mutual tolerance is all that is required; and it is justified by the fact that the offence is mutual. The confused tangle of Balkan nationalism can not be straightened out, either by attempts to assimilate at any price, or by a new migration. But in the question of the Macedonian Slavs in Greek Macedonia, each national group needs the protection of some neighboring State,—the Roumanians, the Bulgarians, the Turks, the Greeks, even the Servians. The way to arrive at such mutual protection is simple enough—a return to the Greek-Bulgarian proposals so wrongly rejected at the Bucharest Conference. All that is needed is an effective mutual guarantee of religious and educational autonomy. If there be any utility in the grave lesson of the events we have described, it must be to lead the allies of the day before yesterday, the impassioned foes of yesterday, the jealous and frigid neighbors of today to solidarity tomorrow in their work for the welfare of the Balkans. The treaty of Bucharest needs to be revised and completed in this sense, if it is not to be broken down by some new caprice of history.

CHAPTER V

The War and International Law

Our whole report is an answer to the question put in this chapter. That answer may be summed up in a simple statement that there is no clause in international law applicable to land war and to the treatment of the wounded, which was not violated, to a greater or less extent, by all the belligerents.

This chapter is not, however, a mere recapitulation of what has been already said. We have reserved for this stage some questions touching more nearly on the domain of international law in time of war. As for the questions already considered we shall use the opportunity of adding supplementary notes and quoting certain documents not referred to in previous chapters.

1. Before speaking of the war, let us look first at the question of treaties. We have seen that the Balkan war was the result of the violation (an extraordinary violation, be it said) of a treaty which was itself the basis of common action crowned with success, and a treaty which assumed the continuance of common action for eight years. We have seen, it is true, that Servian politicians plead not circumstances which did not extenuate (since they did not recognize what they did as a misdeed), but which would have authorized their violation of the treaty of February 29/March 13, 1913, with the Bulgarians. They recalled a clause of which much has been said in international law to the effect that treaties are to be observed—*pacta sunt servanda*—only if there is not change in the condition of things—*rebus sic stantibus*. After the statesmen[1] came the professors to prove, on scientific data, the sound foundations of these patriotic claims. Dr. Mileta, Dr. Novakovits and Dr. Lazar Markovits (who translated Balcanicus' book into German,) published in the Belgrade *Diebo* two articles in which they had recourse to Keffler, as authority Bluntschli, Jellinek, Martens, and above all a recent study by Mr. Erich Kauffmann, professor at Kiel University, *Das Wesen des Völkerrechts und die claudula rebus sic stantibus* (Tübingen Mohr, 1911, p. 231) to prove that Servia had a right to demand revision of the treaty and, in case of refusal, to regard it as abrogated.[2] On the authority of Professor Kauffmann, the Servian professors cited as precedents, the Russian declarations of October 29–31, 1870, on 'the Black Sea, and of June 13, 1886, on Batoum; the refusal of Prussia and Austria Hungary in 1864 to conform

---

[1]In Chapter I, reference was made to a book by Balcanicus (pseudonym of one of the Members of the Cabinet) which opened the campaign for treaty revision in the government journal *Sammouprava* in April, 1913. His book consists of the collected articles that appeared in the paper.

[2]See the reprint of the articles by Novakovits and Markovits (in Servian) *Srpsko-bourgarski ongovove so glediehta medjunarodnog prava.* (The Serbo-Bulgarian treaty from the standpoint of international law.) Belgrade, 1913.

to the London Protocol of 1852; the annexation of Bosnia and Herzegovina in 1908. The authors of the articles add the revision, in 1912, of the Franco-Spanish treaty of 1904 on Morocco.

This report is not a legal study, and we may leave to specialists the task of deciding whether the clause *rebus sic stantibus* can be applied to the question of revision and to the breach of the treaty. The Commission expressed its opinion (Chapter I) when they showed that the allegations of a change in the circumstances was but a *pis aller,* to which recourse was had upon the failure of the attempts at giving a forced interpretation to the terms of the treaty and thereby proving that the Bulgarians had been the first to violate it. What makes the violation particularly odious, is that a condition vital, nay essential, to one of the contracting parties, indispensable to the conclusion of the treaty, was violated by another party as soon as the common end had been attained. The Servians did not show what the English call "fair play." It is true that on both sides the question was regarded as one of "force"—(*eine Macht-frage*). If formal right was entirely on the side of the Bulgarians, they lost their moral right in so far as they transformed the war from one of liberation to one of conquest (see Chapter X). But even so the moral right of Macedonia remained, guaranteed by the treaty, violated by the war, and abolished by the treaty of Bucharest. If the clause *rebus sic stantibus* could be applied to the loss of the Adriatic and the acquisition of Adrianople, why could it not also be applied to the Roumanian occupation? If the Serbo-Bulgarian treaty ceased to be in force from the moment when there was no longer any real force to defend it, why should the treaty of Bucharest stand after the occupation ceased? Such are the dangerous conclusions that could be drawn from the Servian application of the clause,—and above all from its method of application. It may be said, with Jellinek, that there is not only no international treaty, but even no general law to which the clause *rebus sic stantibus* may not be applied. There could be no progress were there no means of adapting legislation to changing circumstances. But it does not follow that the series of necessary adaptations can be understood as a series of breaches of the law (*Rechtsbrüche*). One law is changed by another law. A treaty must be changed by another treaty. This principle is formally recognized in one of the cases cited as "precedents" by the Servian professors, that of Russia's refusal in 1870 to regard herself as bound by Articles XI and XIV of the treaty of Paris of 1856. In a note of November, 1870, Lord Granville protested categorically against such a violation of the principle of the obligatory force of treaties. Italy and Austria Hungary supported the English protest. A new conference was summoned in London on January 17, 1871, and on Lord Granville's motion it began its sitting with this unanimous resolution: "The plenipotentiaries of North Germany, Austria Hungary, Great Britain, Italy, Russia and Turkey, this day joined in conference, recognize that it is an essential principle of the law of nations that no Power can release itself from its treaty obligations, or modify their provisions, without the consent of the contracting parties reached by friendly understanding." This is a principle which can not be abrogated by any precedent or sophistry, if international law is to be a reality at all.

2. The question of the *opening of hostilities* is regulated by the Convention of the Second Hague Conference, the first article of which lays it down that "hostilities between the contracting Powers can not commence without preliminary notice, of no equivocal kind, which must take the form either of a reasoned declaration of war or of an ultimatum with a conditional declaration of war." The Conference however rejected, on the ground of "the exigencies of modern war," the Netherlands' amendment which tried to insist on twenty-four hours' delay after the declaration.[1]

Much was not asked therefore, and the little that was asked did not rule out surprises or the use of military ruse. But the case of course was not foreseen of a State's opening hostilities without itself knowing clearly whether it wished to begin war. It is true that there could be no surprise, since the Servians and Greeks had regarded war as inevitable from the beginning of time. They were in fact in a much better state of preparation, from a military point of view, than the Bulgarians. The latter in beginning war were "without being aware of it, playing the Servians' game," as Mr. de Penennrun well observes.[2] As for the Greeks, we have seen that King Constantine left Athens for Salonica on June 14/27, with the war manifesto in his pocket and "grounds for supposing that war would that week begin all along the line from Pirot to Elevtéra."[3] Were General Savov's telegrams haply known to the Greeks? Anyhow the element of the unexpected in the opening of hostilities was evidently taken thoroughly into consideration by the adversaries. But this does not prevent the judgment that the steps taken by the Bulgarians did formally contravene international endeavor to make appeal to mediation or arbitration, which in this case was provided for in the treaty. The undertaking to this effect in the Serbo-Bulgarian treaty was formal. A mutual undertaking was made in Article 4 of the secret annex, in terms that admitted of no tergiversation or misunderstanding: "Any difference that may arise as regards the interpretation or execution of any one of the clauses of the treaty, of this secret annex and of the military convention, shall be submitted for definitive decision to Russia as soon as one of the two parties shall have declared that they regard it as impossible to reach an understanding by direct negotiation." The Servians had consented to the execution of this clause and their reservations were in no sense obligatory on the

---

[1] See the discussion on this subject at the Second Hague Conference. *Lemonon,* 344-345.

[2] Cf. up. cit., p. 72. Mr. de Penennrun published a fac-simile (pp. 32 and 48) of an order taken on a Bulgarian officer and dated June 16/29, with dispositions for the commencement of hostilities on the morning of the 17/30. The Bulgarians on their part have published a fac-simile of the war proclamation prepared in advance by the Servians with the date June 18 inserted in writing in the printed text (see the *Mir* of June 28). The printed proclamation ran—"Our Greek allies" and "our Montenegrin brothers march with us against the Bulgarians."

[3] See Chapter IV, the article by *Proodos* of June 14/27.

arbiter. Had the Bulgarians, after this, violated the clause while continuing to invoke it, they would have sanctioned the violations which the Servians had allowed themselves in Macedonia, and dealt a final blow at the legal existence of the treaty. This is why, while recognizing that Servia's violation made conflict inevitable, the responsibility of formal breach must lie with the Bulgarians.

The element of ruse was not lacking either. The Servian papers have published stories of a banquet given by Bulgarian officers to Servian officers, at which they were photographed together a few hours before the battle; and told how, as they took their visitors home, the Bulgarians measured the distances and observed the dispositions of the advance guard. The Servians also accused the Bulgarians of having tried to prejudice international opinion by instructing their Ambassador at Belgrade, Mr. Tochev, to enter a protest against an alleged act of Servian aggression eight hours after the nocturnal attack of June 16/29–17/30. If as there is reason to suppose, although Mr. Tochev denied it in the press, he was one of those who pressed on the war and was *au courant* with the events that were to take place, this action is all the more blameworthy. But to accuse Mr. Tochev of not having been in a position to know what was happening on the Bregalnitsa at the moment when he was making his remonstrance at the Ministry at Belgrade, is excessive. The telephone was there; thanks to it, Mr. Hartvig could accuse Mr. Danev, on June 9, of "protesting" against Servian agreement to Russian arbitration; and it must have been in equally good working order a week later.[1]

3. We are on much firmer ground when we pass to the law and custom of land warfare, violated by all the belligerents despite the existence of an international convention signed by them all: namely, the "Convention concerning the laws and customs of land warfare," and the annex accompanying it, elaborated at the Second Hague Conference in 1907, which have replaced the Convention of July 29, 1899, signed by the Powers after the first Hague Conference. Bulgaria, it is true, made certain reserves on the question of an amendment changing the 1899 Convention. This amendment forbade any belligerent to force the members belonging to the nation of his opponents dwelling in his territory, to take part in operations of war against their own country, and provided further that if the said belligerent invaded the enemy's country he might not compel the inhabitants to give information about the opposing army and its means of defence. But with this exception, Bulgaria, like the other representatives of the Balkan States, signed the Convention.

In its first article the Convention lays it down that "the contracting powers shall give their armed land forces instructions in conformity with the regulations * * * annexed to the present Convention." Since by Article 3 the belligerent party was made "responsible for all acts committed by persons forming part of its armed forces" (and under "armed forces" the regulations com-

---

[1]Mr. Tochev has denied these revelations which Mr. Hartvig himself said were incorrectly reported by his interviewer, Mr. Gantchev. See the *Mir*, November 13/30, 1913.

prised, over and above the regular army, the "militia" and "volunteer corps"),
it might have been expected that the governments signing the Convention would
feel a particular interest in seeing that their army knew their obligations. Was
this done in the Balkans? In particular, were any such notions introduced into
the military instruction of soldiers and officers? The Commission's information
on this important head is incomplete, owing to the lack of aid from the Greek
and Servian governments in their inquiry into the war. Indirectly, however, the
conclusion may be reached that the 1907 Convention (and likewise that of 1899),
remained unknown to the Balkan armies generally, with the possible exception
of one or two isolated officers. All that was known was the Geneva Convention,
more or less. Today, as in 1900, "the conscientious exercise of the Hague Convention by the governments signing it, is still to come. They must give their
armies instruction in conformity with the Convention. It is desirable that such
instruction should form part of the compulsory teaching in military training
establishments and in the instruction of the soldier. *Only on this condition can
the application of the Hague Convention be seriously guaranteed.*"[1] In the
Balkans these words of Mr. Marten's are at this day a *puim desiderium* as they
were ten years ago. As far as the Commission is aware, exception can only be
made, and that to a limited extent, in the case of Bulgaria. The Commission
learned that the Convention of Geneva, at any rate, was taught to the officers
in training, not to the soldiers. Only in Bulgaria was the Commission able,
after repeated attempts and through a private source, to procure documents
showing that during the last war at least some efforts were made by the heads
of the different army corps to stop crimes against the laws and customs of war.
These documents possess such interest in view of the Commission's object, that
they are here translated verbatim, with regret that they are the only ones we
can quote:

I

*Order to the Twenty-second Infantry Thracian Regiment of his Royal Majesty Charles
Edward Saxe Coburg Gotha N. 93. October 14, 1912, Pekhtchevo Camp*

I have noticed that certain soldiers of the regiment, after crossing the frontier, commit arbitrary acts which become serious crimes in time of war. I see with great regret that
the heads of companies consider these acts lightly as of no weight, and permit them to be
done under their eyes. Thus in the camp at Tsarévo-Sélo, I saw some soldiers leave the
camp and go into the neighboring village, which had been abandoned by its inhabitants, to
pillage, each for himself, forgetful of his duty of remaining at his post. I have also seen,
in camp, soldiers taking from somewhere unknown goods and cattle in order to make
themselves a meal different from the company's. Thus a large number scattered. This
shows either that the soldiers are too greedy or that their superiors do not look after their
food. I have also seen some soldiers either through negligence or by intention, destroying
the telegraph lines, doing damage to houses left vacant by the people and even going into
Bulgarian houses. [Here there is a small *lacuna* in the MSS.] Some of them behaved ill
to the wounded and captive enemy soldiers. It might seem superfluous, but it is necessary
to recall to the captains of companies that it is their duty to explain to the soldiers the
provisions of the laws and the responsibility of anyone offending against them. I order
that the following instructions as to foraging and the penal laws be conveyed to all the
soldiery:

[1]See preface to a book by Mr. F. de Martens, *La Paix et la Guerre.* Paris, 1901.

1. All factories, furnaces, workshops, military depots, transports, provisions, State and communal banks within the sphere of our army are military booty. The property and provisions of individuals are not to be touched. If the population has left the town or village, but the authorities remain, their property also is inviolable. Even in cases where there are no public powers, private property is regarded as belonging to the State or the commune. Military booty is State property. This is why the appropriation of objects of military booty is regarded and punished as a theft of State property.

When a regimental detachment enters an inhabited place where there are goods forming military booty, the head of the detachment must take steps to preserve these objects and if possible remove them after making a report to the general staff of the regiment; but he must not take anything without express orders. The head of a detachment may not take goods he needs except in case of extreme necessity, or when permission has not arrived in time.

When a detachment gets no supplies of food, the head may make requisition himself of what is necessary to feed his men and fill up his reserve, if broken into. In such a case he must send in a report. Receipts must be given for goods requisitioned.

Soldiers are absolutely forbidden to prepare their food themselves. The ration allowed is more than sufficient. It should be remembered that it is one of the most important of the captain's duties to know how to make good use of local food supplies.

2. The soldiers must be made to understand that the Turkish telegraph lines are necessary for our communications, and they must not destroy them.

3. It must be remembered that military honor, the laws and customs of war and international conventions oblige us to treat the peaceful population of the enemy's country well and prisoners of war the same. It is not becoming in a soldier to show courage against a disarmed enemy, incapable of defending himself. Prisoners are in the power of our government, not of the individuals and corps who have captured them. Ill treatment of prisoners is forbidden; to assassinate an enemy soldier who has given himself up or been taken, is to commit a murder. To pillage dead or wounded soldiers and prisoners is also a crime according to our laws.

4. The following articles of the military penal code are to be read to the soldiers:

Article 241. Those guilty of pillaging the dead on the battlefield are committed to a disciplinary company for six months to one and one-half years, with confinement in cells and transference to the second conduct grade.

Article 242. Those guilty of pillaging the wounded or prisoners are committed to a disciplinary company for two to three years with confinement in the cells and transference to the second conduct grade. If the pillage has been accompanied with violence the punishment is death.

Article 243. Anyone guilty of having intentionally burned or otherwise destroyed munitions of war or other objects of defence and commissariat, in places being defended against the enemy, or of destroying or damaging the telegraphs, water pipes, railways, bridges, dykes and other means of communication, shall be punished with death.

Article 246. Those guilty of premeditated murder, of outrage, pillage, brigandage and premeditated arson, shall be punished with death.

Seal of the Regiment.

Commander of the Regiment, COLONEL SAVOV.
Adjutant Major, CAPTAIN GHIGEV.

II

Army Order No. 69, Lozengrad (Kirk Kilisse), December 13/26, 1912

Information has reached the general staff which, to our great regret, causes us to suspect that certain individuals and corps allowed themselves to commit with impunity various acts of pillage and violence against the peaceable population of the conquered countries. Since actions of this kind, highly blameable and inhuman, compromise the Bulgarian name and the Bulgarian nation in a high degree, and on the other hand sap the confidence of our future subjects (especially the peaceful Moslem population) in our power to guarantee their honor, property and life, I order:

1. That the commanders of the armies and the military governors take severe and prompt measures to open an inquiry on actions of this kind committed in the zone of occupation of the army under their charge, and to bring the culprits immediately before a tribunal in accordance with the law, without distinction of rank or class. * * * The

members of the Military Hierarchy are notified that they must be severe and show no clemency in suppressing actions of this kind; they must not forget the weight of responsibility resting on them if they do not observe this conduct.

2. That the most stringent measures be taken to introduce order and discipline in the rear guard of the army. The persons not belonging to the army, and those who while belonging to the army, do not behave worthily, are to be sent immediately into the Kingdom.

3. That the military as a whole be warned that the peaceful population of the country occupied is placed without distinction of creed or nationality under the protection of our military laws, and that in conformity with these laws any unjustifiable severity, any violence and any injustice will be punished. I invite the military and civil authorities to devote themselves to the attainment of the end proposed.

4. In conclusion, let it not be forgotten we have undertaken the war in the name of an elevated human ideal—the liberation of this population from a régime made insupportable by its severity and its injustice. May God help the valiant sons of Bulgaria to realize this noble ideal, may they assist in restraining one another from compromising this great and glorious work in the eyes of the civilized world, and of their dear native land!

The Aide-de-Camp of the Commander in Chief.

GENERAL LIEUTENANT OF THE GENERAL STAFF SAVOV.

It is with the sense of moral well being that one pauses, in the midst of the horrors which we have been compelled to describe, to read these lines, so different in their spirit from the august threats which speak in the well known telegram of King Constantine: "To my profound regret I find myself involved in the necessity of making reprisals in order to inspire their authors (the authors of the 'Bulgarian monstrosities'), with salutary fear and to cause them to reflect before committing similar atrocities." To compare the conscientious spirit which animates these men, full of desire to preserve the high character of their mission, with the boastfulness based on hatred and reproach for "barbarian hordes" who "have no longer the right to be classed in the number of civilized peoples," is to be prepared to see a change in the standard of values.

Alas, in the actual practice of the "laws and customs of war," the contrast grows less. The sublime and the hateful, heroism and barbarism, come near together. Nevertheless, the desire to remain just and noble is a merit which we desire to note. It is a tendency we have only found among Bulgarian officers and intellectuals. It will certainly cause us satisfaction if, after the publication of this report, the information lacking to us shall be produced in the shape of similar documents, which not satisfied to make a candid avowal were equally anxious to apply a remedy. Unhappily, other indications prove that even the consciousness of having committed faults and crimes is wanting.

Faults and crimes are found in profusion everywhere. We will recapitulate them, comparing the sad reality with the fine resolutions taken in the Hague Convention of 1907, which were signed by the belligerents. In our classification, we will follow the order of the articles in the Convention. We begin with the important question "Prisoners of War."

Article 4. Prisoners of war are in the power of the enemy government, but not of the individuals and corps who have captured them. They are to be treated with *humanity*. All their personal possessions, except arms, horses and military papers, *remain their property*.

Article 5. Prisoners of war may be subjected to imprisonment in any town, fortress, camp or place, with the obligation of not going outside certain fixed limits; but *they may not be imprisoned* unless the security of the State urgently demands it, and then only during the continuance of the circumstances necessitating this step.

Article 6. The State may employ prisoners * * * with the exception of officers, on works. These works *shall not be excessive,* and must have nothing to do with the operations of war * * * Work done for the State shall be *paid for* according to the military rates in force * * * The Government * * * is charged with their *maintenance.* As regards food, *sleeping accommodation and clothing* prisoners shall be treated *on the same footing* as the government troops * * * Prisoners *escaping* may be subjected to *disciplinary penalties.*

Article 23. *To kill or wound an enemy* who having laid down his arms, or having no means of defence, has yielded at discretion, is forbidden.

What a gulf between these generous maxims of an enlightened age and the realities of the Balkan war! Inspiration in the one case is drawn from the principle of Montesquieu: "The whole right which war can give over captives is to secure their person so that they can no longer do any harm."

In the other case we go back almost to the maxims of Germanicus and of antiquity as a whole: "Make no prisoners." Their fate here is decided by revenge and cupidity, the sole difference being that instead of being carried into slavery, people are pillaged and killed, or else killed and pillaged. Prisoners are still made, but very few on the battlefield, and those taken are often not left to live. The overheated mind of the soldier can not understand that the disarmed and wounded enemy whom he finds lying on the ground is a *prisoner of war,* whom he ought neither to kill nor to wound in accordance with Article 23 of the Convention quoted, and Article 2, of the revised Convention of Geneva (1906).[1] In the Balkans they kill their man. If he is made prisoner, disapprobation from very high quarters is sometimes incurred. "What is the use of dragging this rubbish about?" Such was the phrase reported to the Commission by a Bulgarian prisoner who said he had heard it spoken by a high Servian official, when the ambulances were carrying the Bulgarian wounded.

As to the Bulgarians, numerous cases are quoted in our Chapter III, on the assertion of documents collected by the Servian general staff. For the Greeks we have, in the first place, the admissions made in the famous letters and reports of their soldiers. "We only took (during an attack) a few (prisoners) *whom we killed, for such were our orders.*"

It is still more horrible that when the battle is over, any prisoners that are made are not kept: it is preferred to make an end of them. Here are some more terrible admissions from Greek letters. "Out of the twelve hundred prisoners made at Nigrita, only forty-one are left in the prison." * * * "We took fifty (Bulgarian *comitadjis*) whom we divided among us. For my part I had six and I did 'clean them up.' I was given sixteen prisoners to return to the division, but I only brought two back. The others were eaten in the darkness, massacred by me." We can not quote any admission on the part of the other belligerents equal to these. But, acts of this sort, fewer in number perhaps, must

---

[1]See for previous changes *Armand du Payrat: The Prisoner of War in Continental Warfare.* Paris, A. Rousseau, 1910, pp. 133–135.

be imputed to all. The following is a Servian story published by the Servian Socialist paper *Radnitchké Noviné* (No. 162, August 12/25):

> We imprisoned 300 Bulgarian soldiers. We were ordered to put up a machine gun in a valley. I guessed the object of these preparations. The Bulgarian prisoners watched us at work and seemed to guess what was awaiting them. We put them in a line: then our machine began to work along it from one end to another. * * * When we buried them we found in the pocket of a non-commissioned officer *Le Messager Ouvrier* and a detailed journal of the war. Probably he was a socialist democrat.

Assassination of prisoners on the march is also found among the Bulgarians. But the motives are different. Those who can not march or who tried to escape are killed (contrary to the provisions of Article 6 of the Convention, which imposes "disciplinary penalties"). The mass massacre of Turkish prisoners by the Bulgarians at Stara Zagora is explained (but naturally not justified) by a panic produced by rumors announcing the arrival of the Turkish army.

A Turkish prisoner at Sofia, Mr. Haki-Kiamil, of the fifth regiment of sharpshooters, told us of an episode whose detestable character admits of no doubt, although here again it was a question of panic. He gave himself up to the Bulgarians in the neighborhood of Adrianople. Soon afterwards a panic arose and the Bulgarian officers ordered all prisoners to be killed. They were put at the bottom of a wall and all shot. He himself received eleven wounds but was saved by the ambulance. Captain Noureddine and Lieutenant Nadji were also killed at Adrianople on the day of the capture of the town, after having given themselves up. They were escorted by non-commissioned officers. The soldiers said to them, "You have done us a lot of harm with your machine guns; now you are going to pay for it." And they began to kill the prisoners—twenty soldiers and two officers. Before the end of the slaughter, a Bulgarian officer arrived and saved the life of the witness, of one Medmed Begtchete, and another soldier. The third prisoner told us that a body of 157 prisoners was taken from Erikler. The soldiers beat these prisoners and pushed them with their sticks. Three prisoners wounded in the feet could not march fast enough; they were bayoneted.

The few among the wounded who did not die under such horrible treatment were, once they reached the hospital, on the whole well treated by the sanitary staff. It is true that sick enemy soldiers occupying the same room often behaved in a most unworthy manner towards them, especially in the earlier days. Later, an improvement almost always took place; thanks to the hospital staff (mostly foreigners), the rights of humanity were restored. The members of the Commission found this to be the case wherever they have happened to visit the hospital.

As regards the next stage, the treatment of healthy prisoners incarcerated in various spots, the divergence from the prescriptions of the Convention, was not

FIG. 23.—A BULGARIAN RED CROSS CONVOY

FIG. 24.—ROUMANIAN RAVAGES AT PETROHAN

wide in Bulgaria or in Servia. Generally speaking, despite mutual recrimina-
tions in the press, prisoners did not suffer severely either at Sofia or at Belgrade.
A Bulgarian officer, Mr. Kissditzy, told us at Sofia that the quarters for officers
and particularly for soldiers were bad at Belgrade; for example, there were as
many as a hundred persons in a room which only held thirty. The medical
treatment was insufficient; the Servian doctor, our friend, Mr. Vasits, came
rarely. The other doctor, a Greek from Gumurjina teased the prisoners so
that they themselves asked not to be attended by him. The Turkish prisoners
we saw at Sofia looked tolerably well, but they complained of the bad quality
of the food. The Greek prisoners did not criticize the food, which they said
was mediocre. A Servian prisoner in flight from Bulgaria, a farmer, said: "There
was enough bread; they (the Bulgars) gave us what they had themselves." As
to prisoners' work (allowed by the Convention) the Bulgarian government states
that those employed on State works were remunerated at the same rate as the
Bulgarian soldiers, that is to say, they got no money but were lodged, fed and
clothed. Those working in connection with private enterprise, "ought" to receive
a stated daily wage. The Minister admits that malversion was possible, but
knows no case of it. The Turkish soldiers explained to the Commission that
they were *forced* to work on the fortifications against Knjazevac (contrary to
the Convention) and that they received no pay.

All this, however, is nothing in comparison with what the prisoners of war
endured in Greece. Contrary to the Convention they were *shut up* in prisons,
not temporarily but permanently. These Greek prisons ("the Bastilles of the
twentieth century" as the *Patris* called that at Athens, May 29) were horrible. Bulgarian prisoners returning in October from Priekes, from Ithaca,
and from Nauplion, told appalling stories. We select one which is very well
substantiated as a specimen.[1] The author, Mr. Lazarov, was captured on board
the steamer *Catherine*, on which the horrible scenes of drowning which are
described in Chapter IV took place.

On June 24/July 7, we arrived at the Island of Ithaca. The soldiers
were the first to disembark. They were all searched and shut up in the
prison. Then the civil prisoners were taken off and beaten one after
the other, before being shut up. We heard agonizing sobs from children
and old people of seventy. The prison is constructed in the middle of the
sea,[2] on a plateau of 3,100 m. c. of which 2,000 are occupied by the
building. The prison is damp and gloomy. There we spent a month locked
up, during which time we only had three hours a day to breathe the open

---

[1]Mr. Lazarov's story was published by the *Mir*, October 24/November 6.

[2]In the official Greek denials a great deal of fuss is made because the stories of the
Bulgarian prisoners allude to the "uninhabited islands" of Ithaca and Trikeri, whereas
Ithaca is inhabited by 20,000 inhabitants, and Trikeri is not an island but a big town at
the extremity of the Volo peninsula. As regards Ithaca, Mr. Lazarov replies that the
prison is clearly situated near the channel of the island. Trikeri was taken by the
prisoners for an island, probably because they could not see behind the mountain, the
lower portion of which unites it to the continent.

air in the courtyard. At the end of the month we were let out, but for this fifty centimes were taken from each of us. Nevertheless the civilians continued shut up until October 22/November 4. The only people who saw the country were those who were led into the town to work as street porters. Before going into the prison, the 223 soldiers had taken from them 108 pairs of boots, ten belts, a pair of trousers, eight razors, five watches, four purses, thirty francs, and a cross which had been given as a reward for courage. We sent a written protest to the Commander of the Island of Ithaca. He returned it to us saying that he could do nothing since he did not know the culprits, although we had named them in our report. From the civilians there were taken fr. 3,882 (a thousand francs being taken from Nabouliev alone, the man who was drowned), without counting coats and shoes. Their protest was equally unavailing. Although there was spring water in the town, well water was brought to us in barrels: it was stony and tasted detestable, indeed it was hardly drinkable, and we could not use it for cooking our soup which consisted exclusively of beans. We were fed mainly on chick-peas, lentils, haricots, rice, potatoes, stinking and rotten olives, bad fish, poor cheese and raisins. Out of 226 dishes only twenty-two were meat dishes. And this meat was goat, which even dogs will not touch with us. For three days, June 18, 24 and 25, we had no food at all and ten times we were only given one meal in the twenty-four hours. There was absolutely no medical attention. Men who were grievously ill were left without attention. The dampest room in the prison was assigned for a hospital, and the sick were left there without medicine, food or medical attention, that they might die, not that they might recover. We had, in fact, to look after ourselves. Those among us who belonged to the ambulance service, secretly visited the hospital to see the sick people and make out prescriptions, which we sent into the town in wine bottles. We had to pay ten times too dear for our medicine and our pockets were empty. Collections had to be made to buy milk, eggs, etc., for the sick. Those who had toothache had to put up with the services of the town barber, who made extractions at two francs a tooth. Our ambulance people had even to look after the Greek sanitary staff, who complained that their doctor understood nothing, and refused to look after them; that they could not get medicine and that the chemists would not give the State credit. Throughout the time of our imprisonment we had fifteen soldiers sick, without counting civilians. The principal diseases were fever, diarrhea, stomatitis, angina, erysipelas, etc. A typhoid patient in a delirious state came out of his room, which was two yards from the sea, and drowned himself. I myself suffered from rheumatism for two months and a half; not only was I never attended by a doctor, I was not even given a mattress, but had to lie on the damp boards. After enduring great sufferings on September 13/26, we sent a request to the commander asking him to remove us from the damp prison and place us in houses suitable for prisoners of war, to treat us as prisoners of war and not as convicts; to give us blankets as many of us had no cloaks; to allow us to write to our relations, and to go out into the town to buy necessaries; to provide us with water fit for washing instead of dirty water. Only this last request was granted. Our allowances were paid us regularly, one franc, fifty centimes per month for a soldier, three francs for a corporal, nine francs for a non-commissioned officer of low grade, fifteen francs for a higher grade non-commissioned officer and for a sergeant major. Two days after our departure we were asked to sign a declaration in Greek to the effect that we had been well treated, and took away with us all that we had brought. Not to sign was impossible. We signed making, however, a reservation by adding two letters upon which we had agreed: O. M., private opinion, which they did not see (*ossobayé mneniyé*).

The captive officers were no better treated, as may be seen from the story of Major Lazarov, commander of the Bulgarian garrison at Salonica. Mr. Lazarov describes their sufferings on the steamer, their four days stay at Piraeus, in a damp and dirty prison, where they slept on boards in an unwholesome atmosphere, were ill fed, not allowed to go out except to be photographed, and then were exposed to the insolence of the crowd and the curiosity of journalists. After their departure, these journalists stated in the press that the Bulgarian officers had been received in the best families, had mixed in high society, visited theatres and cinemas, but that since they had abused their hospitality they had finally been sent to Nauplia, because one young officer had been incorrect in his behavior to some ladies of the high society of Piraeus. Mr. Lazarov, after his return to Bulgaria, sent the following telegram to Mr. Venizelos:—

> The captive Bulgarian officers of the Salonica garrison protest energetically against the way in which they were treated during their captivity in Greece. They were robbed of their baggage and most of them of their money, thrown into a medieval prison, where they were buried alive in a dungeon in the fortress of Nauplia, deprived of air and light, deprived also of any communication with their families. The doctors not excepted, they endured every humiliation and every form of suffering that the most refined cruelty could invent.

Here we do not speak of the "civilians," although their sufferings, especially in the dungeons in Salonica, were even greater. In their case the point of view taken was that they were rebel Greek subjects. It may be noted that generally speaking the term, "prisoner of war," was interpreted too widely in the Balkans. At Sofia, the Commission was greatly astonished to see old men of eighty years and children pass before it in the guise of "prisoners" returned from Servia. We questioned these good people, who were dressed as peasants, and discovered that they belonged to the population of villages in remote regions, and had endured a form of temporary servitude in the middle of the twentieth century. The 1907 Convention demands that there should be "a fixed distinctive mark recognizable at a distance," to show who is "belligerent." At a distance it is easy to see the age of these old people and to see therefore that they could not be called "prisoners of war." (The photographs in the possession of the Commission of a "review of prisoners" at Sofia, prove clearly enough that one could see from a long way off the sort of people with whom one had to deal.)

By Article 23 of the 1907 Convention, "It is forbidden * * * to use arms, projectiles or other material likely to cause needless suffering."

With regard to the "needless suffering," we already know that there were a thousand ways of causing it. The fundamental principle of the introductory Article (22) of the chapter on the "methods of injuring" was interpreted in the Balkans in an inverse sense, and the maxim there employed ran—"Belligerents have an unbounded liberty of choice of means of injuring the enemy." As regards forbidden arms and projectiles, the rules of the Convention remained a dead letter. It is known that during the first Balkan war expanding or "dum-dum" bullets were used by the Turkish soldiers. It will be seen that the same projectiles were used by Christian soldiers.

As regards the Bulgarian army, the Commission is in possession of official Servian reports to the general staff of Uskub, from Tsrny Vrah on July 13, and from Bela-Voda on July 21, 22. General Boyovits wrote from Tsrny Vrah (No. 2446) that "the enemy is using 'dum-dum' bullets, a fact confirmed by the doctor." Eight days later, Colonel Marinkovits (Choumadia division, second reserve, No. 2070) sends specimens of these bullets and of dynamite projectiles to the general staff, with some observations communicated to him by the commander of the Tenth Regiment, Second Reserve. The commander's remarks are as follows:

> During the fighting with the Bulgars it was observed that in each combat they employed a quantity of "dum-dum" bullets. Herewith are sent five bullets and a portion of one. In addition, it was noticed that they used ammunition with dynamitic contents; this was specially remarked during the engagement at Bosil-Grad, where the majority of the wounded, even though slightly wounded, died very soon. As an example, there may be cited Milovan Milovanovits, fourth company, third battalion of this regiment, who comes from Bresnitsa, district of Liubits, department of Rudnik. He was wounded in the leg and although immediately attended by the army doctor, he died within an hour. I shall receive accounts of the use of these bullets from the commanders of the Tenth Regiment, first reserve and the third surplus regiment, first reserve. I know of a case in the Tenth Regiment, first reserve, where a sergeant was wounded by a bullet of this kind and had his whole face destroyed.

The testimony of the doctor was sent by Colonel Marinkovits on the same day, July 21 (No. 2079), to the general staff: "In connection with the report, No. 2070, today's date, I beg to submit the report of the commander of the Third (Auxiliary) Regiment, first reserve. On perceiving in the course of the engagement with the Bulgars on July 15 and 17, that the enemy's bullets had a totally different effect from hitherto, I consulted the army doctor, whose statement is as follows:

> I have not much experience of dum-dum bullets, but according to the accounts of the wounded and of all the participators in the combats of Preslata, with the Albanians, I beg to state my opinion to the commanders

that the Bulgars have a certain amount of these bullets at hand, and especially used them at night. The action of these bullets consists in their expansion when striking a body; thus the wounds are deformed and heal with greater difficulty. I beg that this be verified on the patients, and that attention be drawn to the fact in appropriate quarters."

On the following day, July 22 (No. 2085), the statement of the army doctor, Mr. Mihilovits, was sent to the general staff. It was countersigned by Colonel Marinkovits:

> In connection with the reports, 2070 and 2079 of yesterday's date, I have the honor to send you the following report of the army doctor of the Tenth Regiment, first reserve.

In reply to the commander's question whether the Bulgars employed dumdum bullets, or bullets of a dynamitic nature, in the combats along the Vlasina frontier, the doctor made the following statement:

> I beg to state that I found eight cases among the wounded of our first battalion, who fell in the combat of the 7th inst., where the injuries had been caused by firearms of small caliber. In each case the flesh looked as though it had been dragged and torn with a pair of tweezers. There were two openings in each case, where the bullet had penetrated and emerged, *i. e.*, it passed right through. These holes were both disproportionately large. One of these eight cases of injuries caused by dum-dum bullets is very characteristic, namely, that of Sergeant Krasits, of the first battalion. He has the right side of his upper lip cut and the whole of his face and throat are covered with burns about the size of a five para piece [this is about the size of an English penny]. Sergeant Krasits was brought to the hospital three hours after he had been wounded. His head was much swollen, especially his face and eyes. His lids were swollen to such an extent that he could not see. His eyeballs were uninjured. In my opinion, Sergeant Krasits's injuries were caused by a rifle bullet of dynamitical or other explosive contents. It is quite obvious in his case. In several other cases of injury, it may be stated with certainty that they were caused by dum-dum bullets. Many of the wounded whom I attended that day told me that the Bulgarian bullets explode a second time when they enter the body.

As for the Greek army, the Commission received a *procès-verbal* signed on July 21/August 3, at Sofia, by Dr. Toramiti (head of the Austrian Red Cross mission), Dr. Kohl (head of the Princess Elizabeth of Reuss' mission), and Dr. Mihilowsky (head of the Clementina hospital at Sofia). On the request of General Savov, these officers formed a special commission to determine whether or no dum-dum bullets had been used in the Servian army. Their conclusions are as follows:

A packet was put before them composed of four samples, the ends of which had obviously been artificially filed with a view to assisting the action of the bullets, contrary to the provisions of the Geneva Convention. The samples do not appear to represent something *specially manufactured, but rather something improvised;* they are something half way between an ordinary bullet and an explosive bullet. The wounded men examined by the Commission, Peter Khristov, of the sixty-second infantry regiment, and Michael Minovski, of the second regiment, showed more serious wounds than are produced by normal bullets in steel cases, wounds that may be attributed to explosive bullets. Similar wounds, however, might be produced by a bullet meeting a rigid object on its way, and so entering the body out of shape.

The following is a copy of the verbal note sent by the Bulgarian Minister of Foreign Affairs to the embassies of the six great Powers at Sofia, July 24/ August 6 (No. 2492), on the employment of the dum-dum bullets by the Greek army:

In the course of recent actions, the Greek troops used bullets against the Bulgarian soldiers which have the ends cut and carry incisions of two millimeters in diameter and 4-5 millimeters in depth, in the middle of the grooved portion: the *ravages produced by these bullets in the human body* are ten times worse than those made by ordinary bullets. While the wounds made by the ordinary Greek bullet passing through the human body show a diameter of 6.5 millimeters—equal to the caliber of the Greek rifle,—those produced by the bullets with their ends cut are as much as *seven centimeters in diameter,* that is to say, the wounds are ten times as bad. The doctors attached to the army operating against the Greeks bear witness to the existence of hundreds of cases of this kind. Three doctors, two being foreigners, in fact drew up a statement *ad hoc.*

The effect of bullets cut in this manner and incised in the middle of the grooved portion, may be explained as follows: As a result of its impact on the human body the cut bullet alters its shape while continuing its movement, while the air in the cavity formed in the middle of the grooved portion is compressed and, tending to recover its normal density, acts as an explosive, at the moment of the deformation of the bullet in the human body. The result is terrible wounds.

The use of bullets of this kind having been prohibited by Article 23 of the Regulations of the Laws and Customs of Land Warfare, drawn up by the Second Peace Conference at The Hague in 1907, the Royal Ministry of Foreign Affairs protests against the infraction of this provision committed by the Greek troops, and begs the Royal Imperial Embassy of * * * to be so good as to bring the above facts to the knowledge of their government.

The military authorities are in possession of three cartridges containing the bullets in question.

Photographs of these Greek cartridges were shown to the Commission; on them Greek letters can be seen—HEΣ 1910 and ΕΠΚΕΛΛΑΣ. The filed

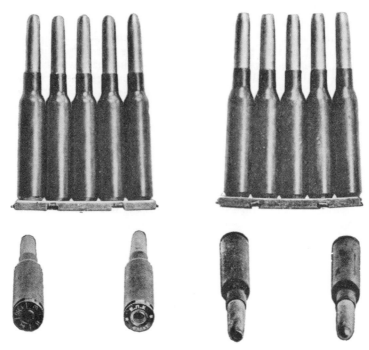

FIG. 25.—SHORTENED GREEK CARTRIDGES

ends can also be seen very distinctly. Before judging the facts alleged in the document cited, the reserves made by the doctors consulted at Sofia must be remembered. The bullets in question are "improvised," and not officially manufactured; moreover, a certain number of the wounds explained by the action of dum-dum bullets are capable of another explanation. This certainly does not change the nature of the offence, but it may change its degree, and leave in suspense the question of guilt. The governments concerned ought to make it their interest to make inquiry among themselves with a view to discovering the explanation of the facts established, instead of merely denying them, which would lead to a suspicion of their guilt.

4. *Article 23 f.*

The undue use of the white flag is forbidden.

Article 32. It (the white flag) enjoys inviolability, as do the trumpet, the bugle and the drum, the standard bearer and the interpreter who accompany it. A captain to whom a white flag is sent is not compelled to receive it in all circumstances. He may take all the necessary steps to prevent the white flag from taking advantage of the opportunity to reconnoitre. In case of abuse he has the right to retain the white flag temporarily.

Generally speaking proper respect for the white flag was lacking in the atmosphere of mutual distrust, a distrust perhaps justified in part by the contempt for moral obligations and formal rights to which this report bears witness. The parties accused each other mutually of attempts at "undue use." This, however, can not justify the direct attacks on bearers of the white flag, which indubitably took place. A telegram from Uskub, published in the Servian press,[1] records the following fact. The commander of the Servian troops besieging Vidine at 11:30 in the morning of July 18/31, sent an officer and three horsemen to inform the commander of the garrison at Vidine of the conclusion of an armistice, and to begin *pourparlers* on a line of demarcation. The bearer of the flag of truce was on the road, the trumpet was played and a soldier carried the white flag. When the flag was thirty paces from the village of Novo Seltsi, the Bulgarians opened fire. The envoy was not wounded, but his two companions were hit. The telegram does not state what followed, but the Bulgarians evidently ceased to fire and the bearer of the flag of truce completed his task.

The Servians were guilty of even more serious violation of the Conventions regulating the use of the flag of truce. On June 18/July 1, an order was given to the Bulgarian army to cease the offensive. For forty minutes the Bulgarians ceased and some officers were sent as bearers of the flag of truce. This, as we know, was the last opportunity on which it was still possible to avoid war, since the government at Sofia had disavowed the orders given by General Savov, and he had been obliged to beat a retreat. We possess the stories of those who bore the flag of truce, which show the reception given by the Servians to this attempt to stop the hostilities which had hardly begun. Lieutenant Bochkov was arrested; his eyes were bandaged, and he was led first before the commander of the regiment, and then before the commander of a division. Contrary to the Convention, he was told that he was taken prisoner. He refused to remove his bandage himself, and was thereupon told that he was regarded as a spy. The affair was reported to Prince Alexander, the heir to the throne, who replied that he refused to negotiate with the Bulgarians, or to receive envoys from them. Here he was, of course, within his rights, but he had transgressed them for the two following reasons, in declaring the man Bochkov prisoner: (1) the Bulgarians had not declared war; (2) he had not got full power. Nevertheless, Mr. Bochkov had been sent with a flag of truce by the commander; and when the heir-apparent accused him of being a spy, he replied that it was not usual for spies to appear with their eyes bandaged. Alexander's sole reply was to push him brutally with his hand. His photograph was taken and published in the Servian papers as that of a Bulgarian spy. With his own eyes he saw a Bulgarian peasant shot by the order of the heir to the throne, who accused him of being a spy. He himself was led off on foot behind a horseman who was charged to take him to Uskub; he had to sleep on the street while his escort lay under a roof. Throughout the journey to Belgrade,

---

[1] See the *Odyeke* of July 22/August 4.

he was insulted and mocked at.   Another bearer of a flag of truce, Reserve Lieutenant Kiselitsky—of whose imprisonment we have already spoken,—reports the same fact. "We had two white flags (with Mr. Bochkov). The Servians took us prisoners and again began firing on our lines." Mr. Kiselitsky saw a Bulgarian soldier thrown out of his litter to make room for a Servian soldier, on the order of the heir to the throne. He saw Bulgarian prisoners being pillaged all along the way. He himself was insulted and made the mark of dubious jokes. The Commission heard a third witness, Mr. Maguenev, an officer of the 31st Regiment of Reserve. He was one of the bearers of a flag of truce, who was asked to give his full authority. He replied that he was ordered not to enter upon *pourparlers,* but to inform the Servians that the Bulgarians had received orders to stop firing. The Servian Lieutenant-Colonel Solovits then took his revolver, cartridges, etc., but stopped when Mr. Maguenev said that if he did so he would blow his brains out. He was then sent to the general staff and the firing began again. They tried to pass him off as a *comitadji.* The prefect of Niché swore that he knew him, that he was one Stephen Yovanovits, born at Vélès. Although this attempt failed, the Servian policeman who took him to Belgrade shouted to the crowd which assembled at every stop: "Behold the Bulgarian spy." He was insulted like the others.

An even more serious case is that of Captain Minkov, of the general staff, who was also sent to the Servians as the bearer of a flag of truce. When he reached the Servian line, Minkov asked to be led before the commander. The commander, an old man, interrupted him and without leaving him time to explain himself said, "We are no longer in 1885. You may have an order to stop hostilities but we have an order to go straight on to Kotchani." With these words, he struck Mr. Minkov with his riding whip, and said, "You are my prisoner." Four soldiers siezed Mr. Minkov, and as they moved the commander shouted the order again. The witness of this scene, Petko Ivanov, a Bulgarian non-commissioned officer, who accompanied the captain and told us the story, could not understand the words spoken at this point, but he gathered their general sense, the more that at that moment the soldiers fired and he saw Captain Minkov fall. He saw the captain stretched on the ground, struggling for a few minutes in convulsive agony; then he was led off himself. The tragedy of this scene was enhanced by the fact that at the moment of its occurrence the Bulgarian army had received the order to cease the offensive.

5. *Article 27.* During sieges and bombardments, all necessary measures shall be taken to spare as far as possible sacred edifices, hospitals and places in which sick and wounded persons are collected, so long as they are not at the same time being employed for directly military purposes. It is the duty of the besieged to indicate such edifices and places by special visible marks, to be notifed in advance, to the besieger.

Article 21. The obligations of belligerents as regards the service of the sick and wounded are regulated by the Convention of Geneva.

We have here two of the Articles in the legislation agreed upon between belligerent nations with which compliance was clearly very easy, and most important for the belligerents themselves. Nevertheless, even this Article was violated. The places and circumstances are precisely indicated in a report by a Russian doctor at the Bulgarian hospital at Serres, Mr. P. G. Laznev.[1] Mr. Laznev took over the direction of the hospital after the departure of the Bulgarian troops on June 23/July 6. Side by side with the Red Cross flag which already floated there, he caused the Russian national flag to be hoisted. Mr. Laznev's story is as follows:—

> On the next and following days, the members of the Greek revolutionary committee repeatedly presented themselves. They took away arms belonging to the sick, which had been placed in the cellars of the hospital. They did not indulge in any other acts of violence; on the contrary, they offered their services. The women of the town stole some of the goods belonging to the cholera patients. After the arrival of the Greek troops, as before, Apostol, the Greek Bishop of the town of Serres, was at the head of the municipal administration. He told us that the stolen goods would be restored to the soldiers, and the women thieves executed; their names were known. The stolen goods were not restored, and not one of the thieves was punished.
>
> On June 28, the Bulgarian infantry and mountain artillery appeared on the heights above the hospital. A combat took place between the Bulgarians and the *Comites* who were hidden behind the hospital. The *Comites* were compelled to retire, and the Bulgarians were in possession of the hospital. This, however, lasted but for half an hour, since more powerful detachments of Greek infantry and cavalry came up. An uninterrupted fusillade and cannonade took place between the enemies and lasted from three to six o'clock in the evening. As before, the hospital was the center of the fray, since it served to cover the Greeks, as it had but now covered the Bulgarians. Many windows in our hospital were broken and we were obliged to place the sick on the ground near the wall, to protect them against stray bullets; as it was, one of our patients was wounded in the ear by a ricochetting bullet. I tried in vain to show the Greeks, as before the Bulgarians, that the hospital should not be chosen to cover the enemy's troops. They would not listen.

Evidently the inviolability of the hospital was abused by both sides, with the effect that the sole condition under which the hospital was inviolable, was annulled. No account at all, in fact, was taken of war legislation. The combat over, violence followed. Let us quote further from Mr. Laznev:

> The victors then arrived worn out and exasperated by the battle. They could not be said to enter; they forced the doors of the hospital. They then threw themselves on the soldier belonging to the ambulance service who barred the way; he was clad in his white hospital apron and carried the

---

[1] Dr. Laznev's report is published by Professor Milétits in his collection "Documents, etc.," pages 107–140. The passages quoted are taken from a copy of it in our possession.

red cross on his left arm. This did him no good for he was cruelly beaten. They then forced the doors of the rooms reserved for the wounded, their rifles in their hands. They threatened them all with death, because "the Bulgarians had burnt the towns."[1] I and my assistant, Kamarov, tried to defend the wounded to the best of our power, by means of course of persuasion, not of arms. Kamarov received several blows on the chest and the shoulders from the butt ends of muskets. The nozzles of the muskets were turned towards me. Raising my voice, I told them, through my interpreter, that I was neither a Bulgarian nor a Greek, and that they had no sort of right to do any acts of violence where the red flag and the Russian flag were floating. I succeeded in persuading them, and they went off. The patients got off with a serious fright. At this moment, I heard a noise in the upper story in which were the kitchen, the dining room and my room. I went up to see what was going on. I found some Greek soldiers busy pillaging, under pretext of searching for arms. Each was taking what he could lay his hands on, glasses, towels, sugar—nothing escaped. I found my room in a state of frightful disorder. Some dozen soldiers were busy, forcing the locks of my boxes and trunks, and rifling them. All the things had been thrown out and were lying about everywhere. Each was taking what pleased him—cigarettes, tobacco, sugar, my watch and chain, my linen, my pocket book, my pencils—nothing was beneath their notice. I was very much afraid, because in my hand bag there was both my money and that of the hospital; luckily, however, the Greeks did not see it. An officer appeared and seeing the Russian national flag and that of the red cross affixed to the balcony, had them torn down, despite our protestations, and hoisted the flag of the Greek navy. Until nightfall the Greek soldiers went on coming in groups, each of which had to be appealed to not to maltreat the patients. This day, June 28, was the worst for the Serres hospital. From June 29 onwards, they began sending us Greek cholera patients, and little by little looked upon us with more favorable eyes.

The Commission was informed of a case in which the sick found in hospitals by the Greeks were even more cruelly treated. Dr. Tauk was a Turkish doctor, attached to the hospital in the town of Drama. When the Greeks took Drama, they found five sick Bulgarian soldiers in the hospital. They ordered the doctor to give them up. The doctor refused. The Greek authorities thereupon had the wounded taken out of the hospital, and these five were conveyed to a barracks outside the town. Our witness, whose name we are not able to give, states that these wounded men were massacred.

At Vidine, the Commission had the opportunity of finding that the Servian army could not be altogether exonerated from behavior of this kind. The Bulgarian hospital in this town seems to have served as a mark for the Servian artillery during the siege. The proof is a *procès-verbal* signed by the director of a hospital, by the priest of Vidine, Mr. Nojarov, by the departmental doctor, Boyadjiev, and two other members of the medical corps. The Commission visited the spot and was able to verify these statements in the *procès-verbal*.

---

[1]For this alleged "fire" see the evidence of Dr. Laznev himself and his colleague, Mr. Klugmann, in Milétits and in our Chapter II.

This day, July 17/30, about four o'clock in the afternoon, the Servian artillery directed a violent fire against the walls of the Vidine hospital. Round the hospital there fell more than twenty shells, in the court and in the street. One shell struck the infectious ward, in which wounded soldiers and other patients were being treated; it destroyed two walls and exploded in a room, wounding the patient, George Trouika, from Iassen, in the Vidine canton. The red cross flag was hoisted near the demolished part of the building. Another shell struck the main ward, piercing the cornice under the roof below the red cross flag without exploding. But the fall of the projectile created a panic among the wounded, and even those in a serious condition and those who had lost limbs, threw themselves on to the staircase. The above mentioned facts are confirmed by photographs taken by Mr. Kenelrigie, an English engineer, and Mrs. Kenelrigie.

The firing on the hospital by the Servians was intentional; they knew that many wounded people were being treated there. The flags served as targets. The hospital is situated outside the town, and is visible from ten miles off, especially from the position occupied by the Servian artillery. Moreover, two white red cross flags, one two meters square, the other one meter, eighty, were floating from the walls of the hospital.

6. *Article 25.* It is forbidden to attack or bombard, in any way whatsoever, houses, villages, dwellings or buildings which are not defended.

Article 28. It is forbidden to hand over a town or place, even when taken by assault, to pillage.

The most important instance of violation of Article 28 would, if the accusations made against the Bulgarians were true, be that of Adrianople. But we have seen that the commander did all that was in his power to put a stop to pillage (begun by the population itself), as soon as the town was taken. This can not be stated with equal certainty as regards individual soldiers, who attempted to take part in the pillage. Unfortunately, the case was different at Kniajévats, where it is evident that the military authorities connived at pillage, which assumed extraordinary proportions. The Commission will not refer to the treatment of Salonica by the Greeks, because that episode belongs to a period previous to the Commission's inquiry, and has not formed the subject of any special study.

The cases where villages were pillaged are so numerous that we can not go into them at this point. It may, however, be stated, that it was almost normal in the case of certain localities referred to in this report.

Cases of bombardment of undefended places, in violation of Article 25, are also known to the Commission. An Englishman named R. Wadham Fisher, who at first watched the progress of the war and afterwards took part in it as a lieutenant in the fifth battalion of the Bulgarian militia, stated to us that the Turkish fleet had bombarded places situated on the shores of the sea of Marmora, namely, the little town of Char-Keuï (Peristeri), and the village of Miréftchi (Myriophyto), although they were not fortified and had no artillery. At Char-Keuï, it is true, there had been some Bulgarian militia, which was driven off by the Turkish attack on January 26, 1913. According to Mr. Fisher, the Bulgarians left seventeen wounded there.   Three days later, January 29/February 11, when they returned, they found that they had all been killed by the Turks.   "I saw," said Mr. Fisher, "the dead body of a child of fifteen years, stretched out on the ground near the fountain whither he had come to draw water, with a jug in his hand.   A girl of twelve years old, who bore the marks of twelve bayonet wounds, had been outraged by four Turks.   She soon died.   Six old women of about seventy-five years old had also been killed.   Two young girls, the daughters of the priest, had been carried off by the Turks on their steamers.   So much for 'pillage.' "   *   *   *

7. Let us now to another order of facts: the relations of the conquerors and powers in occupation, to the inhabitants of the occupied territories.   Here the mass of facts is so enormous that to recapitulate them, after what has already been described, would be superfluous.   We may, however, pause a moment to touch upon a class of misdemeanors which may be said to have been of daily occurrence, in order to make the picture of the violations of the laws of warfare complete, and once again confront the text of the law with the tragic reality.

Let us begin with the contributions and requisitions to which all the inhabitants were subjected, and which were foreseen and regulated by the terms of the Convention of 1907:

Article 48.   If the power in occupation, within the occupied territory, raises taxes, duties and tolls for the advantage of the State, it is to do so as far as possible in accordance with the scale and distribution in force in the country.   *   *   *

Article 49.   If   *   *   *   the power in occupation raises other taxes in money in the occupied territory, this is only to be done to meet the needs of the army or of the administration of the said territory.

Article 51.   Contributions are only to be collected by the authority of a written order *   *   *.   A receipt shall be given to the contributors.

Article 52.   Payments in kind and services requisitioned   *   *   *   shall be proportionate to the resources of the country.   As far as possible they shall be paid for in ready money, if not, receipts shall be given.

The Commission has in its possession a number of proofs which show that the regulations were not carried out by the Powers in occupation, Servians and Greeks; especially not by the latter.   Among the documents in the Commission's possession there is occasionally mention of a number of receipts for goods requisitioned, but the documents are generally valueless.   The Commission heard of cases in which, instead of writing the value of the goods taken upon the receipt, oaths or jokes were written upon it; for example, so much "rubbish" was taken; or there were simply illegible words.   Corn, hay and cattle, to the value of fr. 30,000, was taken from an old man of seventy years of age, Mitskov by name, of Krouchévo, in return for which a receipt for fr. 100 was offered him.   As he was courageous enough to protest, he was shut up in the dampest cell of the dungeon at Krouchévo.   Next day his son was summoned, compelled to accept the hundred francs and sign the receipt.   More often, however, no receipt was given the villagers.   Sometimes some excuse was made, but this was comparatively rare. The excuse generally given was, that "Turkish" property was being taken, not that of the Slav inhabitants. One particularly interesting instance may be quoted in full:

A Servian soldier, Milan Michevits, arrived in the village of Barbarevo (canton of Kratovo), with several men belonging to his company. He made requisitions in every house, and arrested a man called Guitcho Ivanov, to compel him to declare that his corn is Turkish corn. Another individual, Arso Yanev by name, is beaten and tortured during the whole night, to compel him to say that his sheep are Turkish sheep. With the same object he arrested, beat and tortured Guiro Yanev; he beat Ordane Petrov to make him call his cow Turkish property; he tortured Moné Satiovsky, an old man of eighty years of age, by stripping him to the skin and making him stand the whole night on a hill, to force him to state that the fifteen goats taken from him are Turkish; etc.

We frequently find that goods thus taken were sent to Servia or Greece. We know of cases in which Servian officers obtained "subscriptions" for the red cross; and others in which the resources of the area were absolutely exhausted by the repeated levy of contributions, etc. In fact, it goes without saying that where pillage is organized in this way and left thus unpunished, no respect for established rules regarding requisition and contribution can be expected.

8. *Article 47.* Pillage is formally forbidden.
Article 45. To compel the population of an occupied territory to take the oath to the enemy power is forbidden.
Article 46. Family honor and family rights, the life of individuals and private property, religious convictions and the practice of worship, are to be respected.

The reader need only recall Chapters II to IV of this Report, to reach the conclusion that in the Balkan war pillage was universally admitted and practiced. So far as we know, the orders above, published by the Bulgarian military authorities, represent the sole attempt made to recall to the soldiers the opposing principle of international law as applied to warfare. And even this order proves that the principle was violated and that subalterns enjoyed an indulgence which encouraged rather than prevented crime. Nevertheless the operations of the Bulgarian army were carried on in regions where the mass of the population was composed of kinsmen. The time was insufficient to allow of "reëstablishing and securing order," in accordance with Article 43, of the Convention of 1907. The forces "in occupation" were the Greek and Servian armies; it was into their hands that "the authority of legal power" passed for the most part in the regions conquered from the Turks. We know that their first act, in their capacity as "Power in occupation" was, as soon as the cession had taken place, to compel the population to "take the oath" and to recognize themselves as Servians or Greeks. According to the treaties the occupied territory ought to have been regarded as possessed in *"condominium"* by all the allies. But we have seen that all the relations between the population and the occupying army were, from the very beginning, perverted by this tendency to appropriate the occupied territory and to prepare for its annexation; this created a relation as between conquerors and conquered. Thus the solemn words of Article 46 have all the effect of sarcasm.

"*Family honor and family rights, the life of individuals and private property* * * * *are to be respected.*" In reality, no one is astonished by outrage; they forget even to look upon it as a crime. In this connection, the Bulgarians are probably less guilty than the others. More patriarchal or more primitive in their ideas, they preserve the feeling of the soil, and are more disciplined than the others. The mocking Greek women call them "girls in great-coats." This certainly could not have been said of the Greeks.

"Individual life" was certainly rated cheap during these months of war, and "private property" at nothing. Theft was as common as outrage, and both represented infringements of the law of warfare. This was the so-called "peaceful occupation," as carried on most notably by the Roumanian army. Some acts of destruction carried out by the Roumanians at Petro-hane, the highest point on the road between Sofia and Vidine, are fresh in the memory of the Commission. The little villa in which the late Prince of Battenberg used to spend the night when he came there for hunting, was destroyed, and the meteorological station ruined, the splendid instruments broken and the observation records, the work of many years, torn up and burned. In comparison with this the unfortunate scientists of the observatory thought nothing of the young women outraged in the neighboring village, or the food and cattle taken and not paid for; they sank into insignificance in comparison with this irreparable loss. This was "peaceful" occupation. Previous chapters have shown what occupation by force was like.

Was any tenderness shown for "religious convictions" and "the forms of worship"? Unhappily not. We have described the destruction of mosques and churches, the ruin of sepulchral monuments, the profanation of tombs. One party began: the other came to take revenge; it was a form of tit for tat. We have verified and partly confirmed Mr. Pierre Loti's description of what happened at Havsa, while drawing his attention to the events of a neighboring Christian village. For Mr. Loti's edification, another example of Turkish sacrilege may be given. We read in a Greek report of July 9/22 as follows:

> Yesterday about three o'clock in the afternoon, the sailors of the Turkish warship, which has been anchored at Silivri for the last four days, went to the cemetery of the orthodox Greek community and overthrew all the crosses on the graves there.

Against this there may be set a Turkish complaint, sent by Colonel Dr. Ismail Mail to the commander of the garrison at Stara Zagora, where he and a great number of Turkish soldiers were held captive. "Several days ago," writes

Dr. Ismail Mail, on April 3/16, "a captive soldier came here and told us that various means, advice, promises, threats, had been employed to compel him and his compatriots, 'Moslem pomaks,' to conversion. * * * I replied by telling the soldier not to be worried, since such a thing seemed to be impossible. Today, however, I learn that some 400 prisoners, all Moslem pomaks, have been led away into an unknown place." * * * Dr. Ismail Mail protests because of the risks of "contagion." As to the result of his complaint we are ignorant, but we have already had occasion to say that the Bulgarians themselves admit that, in their relations with the pomaks of the occupied countries, the principle of Article 46 was not observed. Moreover, the mere fact cited above affords an instance of the violation, or of the intention to violate, Article 18: "Every latitude is left to prisoners of war in the exercise of their religion."

To sum up, there was, as we said at the beginning of this chapter, no single article in the Convention of 1907 which was not violated, to a greater or lesser degree, by all the belligerents. International law as governing war exists, and its existence, if not always known, is at least guessed at by all the world. Yet, although all the belligerent States had signed the Conventions in question, they did not regard themselves as bound to conform to them.

It should, however, be added that the mere fact of the presence of the Commission in the Balkans has already done something to recall the nature of their obligations to the belligerents. Where, as in Eastern Thrace, the Commission was expected, a Bulgarian paper observes that "the atrocities have diminished." On the Albanian frontier, on the other hand, where atrocities were beginning again, the journey of the Commission was opposed. In this connection a question was raised by a Servian paper which deserves notice, whatever be the motive for their action. On the very day of the forced departure of the Commission (August 13/26), the *Trgovinski Glasnik* tried to justify the action of the Servian government by stating that an international inquiry, claiming juridical powers, was going to be undertaken in the Balkans, whereas such powers belonged exclusively, in an independent and sovereign country, to the government. The establishment of such an inquiry was, according to the paper, a limitation of sovereignty and an interference with the rights of the State. In so far as the State does not consent and grant special permission for inquiry to be made, the mere nomination of such a Commission constituted by itself "an act of international arbitration."

The organ of "the mercantile youth of Belgrade" indubitably went rather far. The function of the Commission was in no sense "juridical," and its conclusions (to some extent foreseen by the paper referred to), are in no way analogous to intervention by international diplomacy. The Commission only represented pacificist public opinion, although in the course of its work it frequently received assistance from the States concerned. This was the case in Bulgaria, where it had the opportunity of interrogating official personages on the facts which interested it; where it received information not only from private persons but from the government itself; and where it was permitted to search the archives (the Greek letters) and to communicate with State institutions (the government departments, the Holy Synod). This was also the case in Greece to some extent.

Nevertheless the question raised by the *Trgovinski Glasnik* is not superfluous, and the Commission deals with it here. Were it possible for there to be a commission of inquiry with the belligerent armies, during war, not in the shape of an enterprise organized by private initiative, but as an international institution, dependent on the great international organization of governments, which is already in existence, and acts intermittently through Hague Conferences, and permanently through the Hague Tribunal,—the work of such a body would possess an importance and an utility such as can not attach to a mere private commission. Nevertheless, the Commission has succeeded in collecting a substantial body of documents, now presented to the reader. It has, however, met with obstacles, in the course of its work, which have cast suspicion on its members. A commission which was a permanent institution, enjoying the sanction of the governments which signed the convention, could exercise some control in the application of these conventions. It could foresee offences, instead of condemning them after they had taken place. If it is stated, correctly enough, that conventions can not be carried out so long as they do not form an integral part of the system of military instruction, it may be stated with even more force, that they can not be carried out without a severe and constant control in the theater of war. Diplomatic agents and military attachés are given a special place with the army in action. Military writers have already mooted the idea of establishing a special institution for the correspondents who follow the army. Attention ought, therefore, to be given to the control which could be exercised by an international commission, not there to divulge military secrets, but as the guardian of the army's good name, while pursuing a humanitarian object.

If the work we have done in the Balkans could lead to the creation of such an institution as this, the Commission would feel its efforts and its trouble richly rewarded, and would find there a recompense for the ungrateful task undertaken at the risk of reawakening animosity and drawing down upon itself reproaches and attacks. May their task then be the prelude to a work destined to grow!

CHAPTER VI

Economic Results of the Balkan Wars

From the economic point of view war is a destruction of wealth.

Even before war is declared the prospect of conflict between the countries, in which serious difficulties have arisen, affects the financial situation. Anxiety is aroused and failures caused on the market by the fluctuations of government and other securities of the States concerned. Credit facilities are restricted; monetary circulation disturbed; production slackened; orders falling off to a marked degree; and an uncertainty prevails which reacts harmfully on trade.

Then comes the declaration of war and mobilization. The able bodied men are called to the standards; between one day and the next work stops in factories and in the fields. With the cessation of the breadwinners' wage, the basis of the family budget, the wife and children are quickly reduced to starvation, and forced to seek the succor of their parishes and the State.

The whole of the nation's activities are turned to war. Goods and passenger traffic on the railways come to an end; rolling stock and rails are requisitioned for the rapid concentration of men, artillery, ammunition and provisions at strategic points.

Not only does the country cease to produce, but it consumes with great expense in the hurry of operations. Its reserves are soon exhausted; the taxes are not paid. If it can not appeal for loans or purchases from abroad, it suffers profoundly.

Then the fighting begins, and with it the hecatombs of the battlefields, the earth heaped with dead, the hospitals overflowing with wounded. Thousands of human lives are sacrificed; the young, the strongest, who were yesterday the strength of their country, who were its future of fruitful labor, are laid low by shot and shell. Those who do not die in the dust or mud, will survive, after countless sufferings, mutilated, invalided, no longer to be counted on for the prosperity of the land. And it is not only the population, that essential wealth, that is thus annihilated. In a few hours armies use up, for mutual destruction, great quantities of ammunition; while highly expensive supplies of cannon, gun carriages and arms are ruined. There is destructive bombardment of towns, villages in flames, the harvests stamped down or burned, bridges, the most costly items of a railway, blown up.

The regions traversed by the armies are ravaged. The noncombatants have to suffer the fortune of war; invasion, excesses and it may be flight, with the loss of their goods. Thousands of wretched families thus seek security at the price of cruel fatigue and the loss of everything, their land and their traditions, acquired by the efforts of many generations.

The Commission arrived in the Balkans after the fighting was over, and was able to study the results of the war, at the very moment when, the period of conflict closed, each nation was beginning to make its inventory.

The armies were returning to their homes after demobilization. The soldier again became peasant, workman, merchant; the hour of the settling of accounts, individual and collective, had struck.

The government, which had been in the hands of the military during the war, was restored to the civil authorities and the period of regular financial settlement began.

Nevertheless, the traces of the war were still fresh. The Commission noted them. If the corpses of the victims were not visible their countless graves were everywhere, the mounds not yet invaded by the grass that next summer will hide them away. Visible too were the wounded in the hospitals and the mutilated men in the streets and on the roads; the black flags, hanging outside the doors of the hovels, a dismal sign of the mourning caused by the war and its sad accompaniment, cholera.

The members of the Commission saw towns and villages laid in ashes, their walls calcined, the house fronts torn open by shell or stripped of their plaster by riddling shot. They went through the camps at the city gates where streams of families fleeing before the enemy made a halt. All along the roads they came upon their wretched caravans.

The Commission has endeavored to make an estimate of the cost of the double war. Instruction on this head is needful. Public opinion needs to be directed and held to this point. It is too easily carried away by admiration for feats of arms, exalted by historians and poets; it needs to be made to know all the butchery and destruction that go to make a victory; to learn the absurdity of the notion, especially at the present time, that war can enrich a country; to understand how, even from far off, war reacts on all nations to their discomfort and even to their serious injury. As Mr. Léon Bourgeois put it at a conference recently held at Ghent:

> The smallest, imperceptible movements of the keel of every barque that sinks or rises in the tiniest port on the coast of France, Belgium or England, are determined by the vast ebb and flow of all the tides and currents that together make up the breathing of the ocean. In the same way the profit and loss of every little tradesman in the corner of his shop, the wages of every workman toiling in a factory are influenced incessantly by the tremendous pulsation of the universal movement of international exchange.

Every war upsets this universal movement, especially today when the solidarity of international interests is so marked. Let us see how far the Balkan war was a cause of national and international economic disturbance.

FIG. 27.—THE DEAD SHARP-SHOOTER

FIG. 26.—IN THE TRENCHES

FIG. 29.—A FUNERAL SCENE

FIG. 31.—SCENE FROM THE KOUMANOVO BATTLE

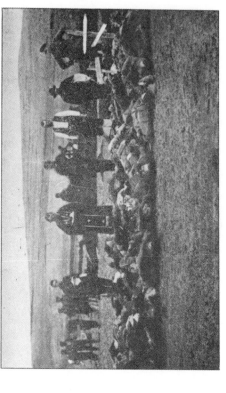

FIG. 28.—THE ASSAULT UPON AÏVAS-BABA

FIG. 30.—IN THE BARB-WIRE DEFENCES OF ADRIANOPLE

Fig. 32.—Service Burial

Fig. 33.—A Battlefield

Fig. 34.—Forgotten in the Depths of a Ravine

FIG. 35.—PIECE OF ORDNANCE AND GUNNERS

The balance sheet of the war must bear at its beginning, in order to characterize it properly, the list of the dead and wounded. Human lives brutally destroyed by arms, existences broken off in suffering after wounds and sickness, healthy organizations mutilated for ever; this is the result of the war, these its consequences of blood and pain.

Below is the sinister inventory.

Bulgaria had 579 officers and 44,313 soldiers killed. Seventy-one officers, 7,753 soldiers are reported missing,—how many of these are dead? One thousand, seven hundred and thirty-one officers, 102,853 soldiers were more or less seriously wounded. A great number of these will remain invalids, reduced greatly in strength or deprived of a limb. An idea of the extent of the ravage caused upon the surviving men who were struck by projectiles, may be gathered from the following telegram published by the agencies, October 20, 1913. The telegram comes from Vienna:

> Queen Eleonora of Bulgaria, who distinguished herself during the war by her humanitarian efforts, has just ordered a large number of artificial legs to be supplied to the soldiers who underwent amputation.
> The Queen has had workmen experienced in this line sent to Sofia to open a factory for artificial legs in the town.

This is an economic result of war to be noted,—the creation of the artificial leg industry.

Servia published first of all the following losses: about 22,000 dead and 25,000 wounded. These figures were given to us, dated September 30, 1913, by the secretary of the Minister for Foreign Affairs.

Information coming from another source gives a smaller number of dead, 16,500, but a greater number of wounded, 48,000. Sickness is said to have attacked 45,000 men of the Servian army. On February 27, 1914, the official figures were given to the Skupshtina by the Minister of War. They are 12,000 to 13,000 killed; 17,800 to 18,800 dead as the result of wounds, cholera, or sickness; 48,000 wounded.

Servians and Bulgarians bore their wounds with a physical endurance that all the doctors and surgeons remarked upon. The wounds healed rapidly. This shows that these people are sober and their organs are not poisoned and enfeebled by alcohol.

It was impossible for us to find out the figures of the Greek, Montenegrin or Turkish losses. In spite of our persistence in asking the Greek Minister of Foreign Affairs for this information, we have not yet been able to get it; reports on this matter not yet having been centralized. The losses of the Greeks must have been a good deal less than those of the Bulgarians or Servians. The Montenegrins are said to have had a great many killed in proportion to their number on account of their attitude under fire. Their pride made them expose themselves to the bullets, refusing to lie down or shelter, fighting as in the old times when weapons were of short range and less murderous.

From Turkey we have no official information, in spite of our reiterated requests. It is probable, too, that Turkey possesses no means of establishing even approximate statistics. All that the war correspondents have related enables us to say that Turkey must have paid heavy toll to death, as much from the blows of their enemies as from the epidemics following their want of care and lack of provisions in the panic of confusion and defeat.

This is not all. Arms were not only taken up against the belligerents, but massacres took place in Macedonia and Albania. Old people, villagers, farmers, women and children, fell victims to the war. What must their number be?

It is not possible to compute, chapter by chapter, the extent of the material losses by destruction of property. The Balkan States in their claims before the Financial Commission of Paris, did not detail them, except Greece, which certainly underwent the smallest loss in the first war. In the war of the allies, the part of Macedonia which was given to Greece was, on the contrary, widely devastated, and the vast fires of Serres, Doxato, Kilkish, were real, material disasters.

Greece has made the following claims for destruction of property due to the first war:

> In the course of hostilities, the Ottoman armies fleeing before the Hellenic armies, left behind them a country absolutely devastated by pillage, massacre and fire. Nearly 170 villages were the prey of fire, several thousand old people, women and children escaping from death, ruined, starving, exhausted, sought and found refuge in the neighboring provinces of Greece. For several months they lived at the expense of the Hellenic government, which when the campaign was over, had to supply them with means to enable them to go back to their native country.
>
> The Hellenic government has met 414 claims for these unfortunate victims.
>
> Among the claims, ninety came from burnt villages where the losses, duly certified by competent Metropolites, amount to fr. 7,737,100.
> The total of the 414 claims is fr. 10,966,370.

The preceding chapters have given the reader some means of forming for himself an idea of the devastation committed in the Balkans. The photographs which we reproduce spare us from describing it. The havoc committed was of two kinds: one lawful and the other directed against private property.

The first was that which strategy or the security of the troops necessitated. Bridges blown up by dynamite, railway tracks destroyed, fortifications razed, the bombarding of the cities that offered resistance, burning the hiding places of the enemy, destroying, in retreat, provisions and ammunition, in order to leave nothing for the enemy; all these are lawful acts in time of warfare.

Then there are the reprisals; made as they are in the ardor of the struggle,

FIG. 36.—RUINS OF VOINITSA

in the heat of victory and in a moment of anger, they are often an excuse for odious vengeance, for unpardonable violence against things and people.

And once started, how is it possible to hold back the soldiers? They set fire to everything, pillage and destroy for destruction's sake. In the Balkans there was, in this way, ruin of every kind amounting to millions.

The Balkan wars were not, however, in point of view of their economic consequences, wars such as may occur between great industrial states. They exhibit special characteristics which we must throw into relief.

General mobilization would be a real disaster in any industrial country. Every factory, except those which provide the necessaries of existence or armaments, must be shut down in the absence of their hands. Even those which might contrive to keep running by using the labor of women and those old men

FIG. 37.—RUINS OF VOINITSA

exempted from military service, could not do so long in the stoppage of the necessary supplies of raw material which follows the requisitioning of the permanent way and rolling stock of the railways for the transport of troops.

Furnaces shut down, machinery silent, huge factories deserted,—such is the immediate result of mobilization. It is a dangerous time for capital investments, and, if prolonged, leads to heavy failures.

Workmen's families subsisting on weekly or fortnightly wages are soon reduced to starvation when the husband and grown-up sons have gone to the front. Small economies can not keep the wife and children left behind going for long. Millions of persons are thrown on the resources of the parishes and of the State, and in spite of the heavy charge thus created, the people endure severe privations.

At a time of mobilization payment of debts is suspended by the moratorium. This causes great inconvenience to trade which is further deprived of a great body of consumers. Provisions become dear, communication with the exterior is cut off, and with the interior monopolized by the military administration, production is at a standstill. Those who draw their income from investments or pensions find the sources of their daily expenditure dried up; this is the case with landlords whose rents do not come in and bondholders whose interest is reduced or delayed by the State, which is giving all it has to the war.

The point need not be labored; it is easy to imagine the immediate distress which is produced in any highly developed industrial State by mobilization.

These consequences were found by the Commission to have been produced in the Balkans to some extent, remarkably lessened, however, by the fact that Servia and Bulgaria are almost exclusively agricultural countries, and that Greece, too, although more developed industrially, is predominantly agricultural.

From the appearance of the countryside in Servia and Bulgaria one would hardly have guessed that war had deprived the fields of their normal laborers. In the husband's absence the wife worked in the field, taking a kind of pride in producing a good harvest. Thus when foreign trade restarted there were considerable quantities of oats and maize from the fields to export and current coin came in to pay for these exports. The Bulgarian Minister of Commerce put the receipts that would come into the country from the sale of cereals as soon as trade restarted at fifty-five or sixty million francs' worth (two million, two hundred thousand, to two million, four hundred thousand pounds).

Thus in the Balkan States war has not produced the depths of individual misery which it would cause in a country with an industrial proletariat dependent on a daily wage. Over a large part of Bulgaria, Servia and Greece the circumstances under which the family lives and develops are those of peasant proprietorship. When the head of the family went to join the army he left his dependents in a homestead, in which there was always a certain supply of provisions on the soil from which food of some sort was always to be gotten.

Though there was less comfort, there was no such distress requiring the succor of the State as would arise where the workers live in large agglomerations.

In the fields the women and children continued to subsist on their own resources, and to produce. The calls upon the savings banks came from the towns, and from the soldiers, who did not wish to join the army without some pocket money. In Bulgaria, down to July, 1912, the rate of deposits and withdrawals from the savings bank was normal. In July marked variations began. The number of deposits fell from 22,834 in July to 19,914 in August, and their value from fr. 3,167,645 to fr. 2,889,400. This tendency grew more marked; in September there were 10,516 deposits worth fr. 2,020,723; in October 3,637 worth fr. 1,193,656. The effect on withdrawals was naturally still more marked. In February, 1912, their total exceeded three millions, higher than at any time in 1911. In August the figure was the same. September, when mobilization took place, saw a perfect rush of depositors; on the same day on which the mobilization order was issued, all those presenting themselves received in full the sums demanded. Seven paying desks were opened. On the 18th payments were limited to fr. 500; on the 29th to fr. 200, the rest of the sum demanded being paid five days later. Exception was made in the case of soldiers; they were paid in full without delay. This limitation of payment lasted for twenty-five days. In September fr. 4,210,244 were withdrawn. It was the only month in 1912 in which withdrawals exceeded deposits. Throughout the war the total of the latter remained at a pretty high level.

In 1913 business became regular; in May deposits rose to over three millions. July, the month in which demobilization took place, was a repetition of August of the previous year. Withdrawals exceeded deposits, being fr. 1,573,196 against fr. 1,209,522.

The figures supplied us by the savings bank acting in connection with the Athenian banks show that there was no panic among savings bank depositors in Greece either. The total amount of deposits was fr. 40,257,000 on June 30, 1912; it had risen to fr. 59,365,000 on June 30, 1913.

Those who suffered most from the war in Bulgaria and Servia were the artisans, small traders and small manufacturers. Their position will not be able to be gauged till after the expiry of the moratorium. In Bulgaria it was proclaimed on September 17, 1912, to last a year. The Commission was in Sofia when it terminated; representatives of the banking houses having agreed to prolong it in fact. They decided simply to take steps to protect themselves against suspected debtors without going so far as to act against them.

The Servian moratorium was prolonged by law to January 3, 1914.

In Servia and Bulgaria the war put a stop to all productive transport by rail; in Greece to most of the sea transport. Greece had eighty-seven ships held up at Constantinople, and twenty-three cargo boats in the Black Sea. The receipts of the Bulgarian railways, which amounted to fr. 29,602,355 from September,

Fig. 38.—Ravages of the War.

Fig. 39.—Ravages of the War

FIG. 40.—RAVAGES OF THE WAR

FIG. 41.—RAVAGES OF THE WAR

1911, to September, 1912, were nonexistent for the corresponding period 1912–13. The rails and stock were mobilized and used exclusively for the army, which owed the State a sum of fr. 7,637,418 on account of transport. On the other hand, mobilization involved considerable wear and tear of material and special accommodation works; war brought with it the destruction of bridges; at Dedé-Agatch, Greece seized some engines and carriages which had just been disembarked on their way to Bulgaria. Bulgaria's expenses from these sources are put at fr. 22,984,680.

Thus for Bulgaria the railways' account works out at: loss of receipts, nearly fr. 30,000,000; expenditure on repairs and purchases, fr. 23,000,000. On the other hand, the State is in its own debt on account of army transports to the extent of nearly fr. 8,000,000. Figures under this head for Servia are not available. In 1911 the receipts from its railways amounted to fifteen to sixteen million francs, a sum which must have failed entirely during the war.

Greece estimates the cost of railway transport of her troops at fr. 6,000,000, and sea transport at fr. 30,000,000.

Just as the war did not prevent the harvest in Bulgaria and Servia from being collected, Greece, at the top of a wave of economic prosperity, was able to support it too without a crisis. Its economic activity was impeded but not brought to a standstill since the army was thrown at once across the frontiers invading Turkish territory; the soil of Greece itself was spared the movements of troops and battles.

The absence of the men on active service did, of course, cause a stoppage of industrial productivity. For example, the central office of the National Bank of Athens was 120 employes short, a third of its staff. Grave losses were sustained by the mercantile marine, which is one of the principal Greek industries. But there was no financial panic. The moratorium was used exclusively by the Bank of Athens, and for a very short time, because of its branch establishments, in Turkey. Government stock fell at the beginning of the war, but the fall was brief; business soon revived and rising prices followed.

The balances of the savings banks instituted by the banks increased, as has already been pointed out. There was a slow increase in loans on securities; a falling off in loans on goods.

The war showed Greece that she had resources to some extent scattered all over the world. Effective aid in men and money came from those of her sons who had emigrated. The exodus of the Greek population is so considerable that Mr. Repoulis, Minister of the Interior, found it necessary to pass a law for its regulation. From 1885 down to the end of 1911, 188,245 Greeks left their native land, most of them going to the United States. In 1911 the total, 37,021, was composed of 34,105 men and 2,916 women. The age distribution was as follows: between fourteen and forty-five, 35,485; under fourteen, 1,006;

over forty-five, 430. Thus, those who leave are the flower of the population. Emigration takes 9.5 in every thousand a year; in Italy only 5.8 per thousand.

It is true that the Greek abroad guards his nationality and his traditions jealously; and when his country is in danger he returns, no matter how remote he be, to defend it. In the late war between 25,000 and 30,000 men came back to Greece and helped to carry the national arms to victory.

At all times Greek emigrants bear their share in the national prosperity by sending home their capital. In 1910 fr. 20,427,062.65 were received from America in postal orders; in 1911, fr. 19,579,887.65. From the same source there stood in the banks deposits amounting in 1910 to fr. 55,471,460; in 1911 to fr. 47,323,059. The influx of wealth, resulting from emigration, will certainly end in arresting the tide of departures. The Greek, indeed, leaves his country because the supply is in excess of the demand of labor; also to some extent under the stimulus of the love of adventure, because of a character more inclined to commercial than productive activity, and because of the attractions held out by emigration offices.

The capital thus acquired abroad will enrich the country. There are plenty of places, admirably watered, which are not used for market gardening. Greece imports fr. 210,000 worth of eggs; honey, a national product, is also imported. According to Mr. Repoulis, the ignorance of the cultivators is something incredible, with the result that the soil produces but half the average yield in wheat of more advanced countries. Very high prices for land are now being gotten in some provinces, thanks to the emigrants' money. When they have made their fortune, the Greeks come back more and more to settle in their native country, bringing with them new methods and a spirit of initiative, thus keeping on the land, by giving them work and instruction, the peasants who would otherwise have gone abroad in their turn.

The maintenance of a monetary currency by Greece during the last war is due in part to the fact that the emigrants who returned to take their places in the ranks brought considerable sums of money with them which they deposited specially in the national bank. Between September 30, 1912, the month in which war was declared, and July 31, 1913, the amount of deposits in the national bank grew steadily. From fr. 197,785,000 at the former date it rose to fr. 249,046,000 on the latter. The same is true of all the branches of the Bank of Athens. The total, which was fr. 352,762,000 on June 30, 1912, rose to fr. 441,681,000 on June 30, 1913.

Thus, thanks to the preponderance of agriculture, to the system of small estates, and, in Greece, to emigration, Bulgaria, Greece and Servia were able to bear a long war, which was sometimes painful and cruel, without any pause in their production, and without any deep upheaval; this is due to the economic resistance shown by each family firmly established on its own land.

Nevertheless, there were antagonistic tides of feeling, due to national jealousy and enmity, which threw numerous families into exile.

One of the saddest spectacles presented to the Commission was the case of the refugees. Their presence caused grave financial difficulties to the States which took them in and their reëstablishment presented an important economic problem. The refugees seen by the Commission in Greece and in Bulgaria were fugitives from countries which conquest and treaties had transformed into alien territories. In Greece there were Moslems from parts of Macedonia and Thrace, now Bulgarian, who followed the Greek army, encouraged thereto, according to the evidence we have collected, by the Greeks, who promised them protection, subsistence, lands. In Bulgaria there were again Moslems and in larger number Bulgarians who had fled before the Serbs and Greeks, the new and jealous masters of the parts of Macedonia in which they had been established.

A sort of classification thus took the place of the tangle of nationalities in Macedonia and for a time the population of the country, newly divided between Servia, Greece and Bulgaria, was willy nilly divided according to nationality within the new frontiers. This did not last, for the emigrants, weary of wandering and of the pain of starvation and drawn to their abandoned fields, gradually returned home.

At the gates of Salonica the Commission saw a countless herd of more than ten thousand persons stationed in the plain. The families were installed under the high wagons with heavy wooden frames and wooden wheels, without iron hoops, which had brought them there with their worldly goods in the shape of a rug or two and a few domestic utensils. The cattle were straying in the field. As need drove them the refugees sold their animals for ludicrous prices, a cow for two pounds, an ox for three. The men hung about ready for long idle talks with strangers. In Salonica all the unoccupied houses were filled with refugees.

At Sofia the schools and public buildings sheltered thousands of these wretches. Everywhere the Commission came upon them, waiting in crowds for the free food distribution, drawn up in long lines of caravans on the roads, collected in groups under any sort of shelter, suffering from famine, decimated by disease. In the market place of Samokov a woman told us her story, which was that of most: "When they cried out that the Greek horse were coming, my husband took two children and I took two. We ran. In the scrimmage I dropped the smallest one, whom I was carrying. I couldn't pick him up again. I don't know where my husband and the other two are. I want him, I want him," she cried again and again, as she told us of the poor little one, trampled under foot. In her arms she held the one she had saved. In the night he died.

It is impossible to think without emotion of what this exodus of peoples caused by war represents in terms of suffering and tears.

FIG. 42.—REFUGEES

FIG. 43.—REFUGEES

Fig. 44.—Refugees

Fig. 45.—Refugees

FIG. 46.—REFUGEES

FIG. 47.—REFUGEES

Fig. 48.—Refugees

Fig. 49.—Refugees

For the State the refugees were a heavy burden. Greece had close on 157,000 refugees on her hands, all of which cases were investigated and assisted. The maximum number was reached on August 11, when there were 156,659 refugees. The necessary means of transport were provided for the Moslems who desired to go to Turkey-in-Asia, by national committees constituted for the purpose. The Commission saw two great transport loads of these emigrants leave Salonica. For the others Greece had to provide food, and meat, bread and biscuits were distributed among them. Philanthropic societies collected clothes and blankets for them. The State estimated the cost per refugee at fifteen centimes, which shows that only the necessaries of bare subsistence were, provided.

Committees were appointed to consider the best means of settling the remaining refugees, whose number was put at about 90,000. Landowners and manufacturers came forward with offers of employment for larger and larger numbers every day, as agricultural and day laborers and farmers. The villages abandoned by the Bulgar population and the vast Turkish public domain afforded lodging and land.

Greece, who has already established thousands of refugees, under identical conditions, in Thessaly, hopes to derive much profit from the living wealth of this influx of population. The period of disorder once over, the people, well directed and well distributed, will be an element of prosperity to the nation. But, before this day comes, great expenditure will have been required on maintenance, buildings, agricultural implements and the small capital sum to enable each family to take root. To put the expenditure at twenty-five or thirty million francs is not an excessive estimate. The experience gained in Thessaly in 1906 may afford a basis for calculation. After the Roumelian incidents, there were 27,000 Greek refugees. After the first shock was over a certain number of families returned; 3,200 remained, representing between 17,000 and 18,000 persons. Greece undertook to establish them as peasant proprietors. For two and a half years they were maintained at an expense of nearly twelve million francs. Then land was bought, villages created, houses built for their establishment, at the cost of an additional thirteen million. Greece had no intention of making them a present of all that, but the advances have been repaid on so small a scale, that the loan has become a bad debt.

This experience should serve also to show the error of making the State the creditor of poor refugees. The declared intention of Mr. Diomedes, the Finance Minister, is to make the refugees of 1913 peasant proprietors through the medium of an agricultural bank, which will advance them the necessary money.

Bulgaria harbored 104,360 persons. There, as in Greece, they had to be supported so far as resources permitted. At Sofia the Commission could see that real attention was given to the refugees, with important help, it is true, from charitable societies. The cost of their daily maintenance was estimated at forty centimes per head.

Of these refugees some 30,000 came from parts of Thrace recovered by Turkey, and 50,000 from Macedonian districts assigned to Servia or Greece. According to returns made by the Bulgarian government, 40,000 persons, or 10,000 families, left their homes without hope of returning. Homes will have to be found for them then on the banks of the Maritza or the Arda or on the Ægean littoral; the expense of such settlement will be heavy and may be put at eighteen or twenty millions. It is not only the unhappy refugees, however, who present a problem of nationality and of settlement to the countries which have harbored them.

Foreign concessionaires and heads of industrial concerns are established in the conquered territories; their status must be defined in relation to the conquering countries, allowance being made for rights already acquired. The task is a delicate one, and was handed to the Financial Commission in Paris, which arrived at a solution in June–July, 1913. The Balkan States have succeeded to the rights and charges of the Ottoman Empire with regard to those enjoying concessions and contracts in the ceded territories. No one has contested the principle of this succession, and it is probable that had any difficulty been raised about it the Great Powers would have upheld the material interests of their subjects.

On the question of the nationality of these companies, the Financial Commission on Balkan matters sitting in Paris, unanimously agreed that a non-Ottoman company should, under whatever circumstances, retain its nationality, despite the annexation of the territory in which its field of operations lay. Turkish companies having their headquarters and their entire works in the same annexed territory, should adopt as their right, the nationality of the annexing State.

Companies with headquarters in Turkey, while the whole of their workings lay within a single one of the annexing countries, might elect to adopt the nationality of the annexing country, and in that case to transfer their headquarters thither or state that they intended to retain Ottoman nationality.

The position of mining concessions was determined as follows:

Succession will take place by right without any further formalities than a conventional deposit and the registration of the terms of the agreement, the whole free of stamps or any expense. The mining regulations of the annexing State apply to the concessionaires only in so far as they involve no infringement of acquired rights, that is to say, in so far as they are not contrary to the clauses in the concession, agreement or contract. At the same time such clauses can not be made use of to appeal against the application of police supervision and inspection designed to secure safety in working or against forfeiture of the concession where work is not done. The annexing governments succeed the Ottoman government in the obligation to hand over, free of charge, a warrant with the same judicial force as the Imperial firman, and issued by a competent authority, to mining concessionaires whose concessions were signed before the outbreak of hostilities but not confirmed by firman until after the declaration of war. This same succession by right applies to forest and port concessions.

There are still a number of important problems to be solved. They concern:

1. The position of companies whose workings will in future lie within two or more territories, such as the lighthouse company, road and railway construction companies, etc.

2. The determination of the distribution of mileage securities, the calculation of receipts, and the share thereof accruing to the different governments, and the charges on the said share.

Probably a permanent Liquidation Committee will be instituted in succession to the Financial Committee to ensure detailed application of the principles it has laid down; while an Arbitration Tribunal, international in character, will be set up for the final adjudication of matters in dispute.

In the territories ceded to the Balkan States the Imperial Ottoman government had conceded the construction and working of eleven lines of railway, of five ports (Salonica, Dedé-Agatch, Kavala, St. Jean de Medua, Goumenitza), of high roads, hydraulic works (Maritza, Boyana, Okhrida). Sixty-three mines had been conceded. The nationality of the concessionaires was as follows:

```
Ottoman  ......................................................  37
British  ......................................................  10
French  .......................................................   1
French  and  Austrian  ........................................   3
Ottoman  and  Hellenic  .......................................   2
Italian  ......................................................   6
German  .......................................................   1
Ottoman,  French,  Italian  ...................................   1
Ottoman  and  Austrian  .......................................   2
```

The Ottoman State had passed sixteen contracts for the lease of forests to nine *entrepreneurs*.

There were, moreover, a certain number of tramway, lighting, motive power, hydraulic power, and mineral water concessions outstanding, permits for mining and quarry exploitation, and a large number of contracts for the construction of roads, public buildings and other works of public utility and for forest workings which had been made either by the central government or by local authorities.

The Balkan wars simply emptied the factories and fields of their male workers. Out of 2,632,000 inhabitants, Greece mobilized 210,000 men; Bulgaria 620,567 out of its 4,329,108 inhabitants; and Servia 467,630 men out of 2,945,950 inhabitants. The result was a considerable deficit in the taxes collected, a falling off in the state receipts. We will quote the example of only one country, Servia, the same phenomenon having occurred to the same extent in the other belligerent countries. Servia experienced the following variations in its monetary resources. Taxation produced 2,879,577 dinars in the month of October, 1913, against 591,315 in the corresponding period of 1912, and 5,817,493 in 1911; that is, an increase in 1913, of 2,188,251 dinars on the results for 1912.

In the first ten months of the year 1913, taxation, which had brought in 33,911,817 dinars in 1911, and 24,443,984 dinars in 1912, only brought in 10,623,800 dinars. The decrease of 13,820,184 dinars between the figures for 1913, and those for the year before, is explained by the peculiar circumstances. In 1912, the taxes were in fact regularly paid for the first nine months, whereas during the greater part of the corresponding period of 1913, Servia was in a state of war.

Then, too, war, besides depriving States of their ordinary receipts, causes heavy expenditure on armaments, ammunition and equipment; the Balkan States estimated this expenditure as follows:

Bulgaria

Expenditure on the army	fr.	824,782,012
Pensions and Maintenance of prisoners of war		487,863,436
Total	fr.	1,312,645,448

Greece

Expenditure on the army	fr.	317,816,101
Expenditure on the navy		75,341,913
Pensions		54,000,000
Maintenance of prisoners of war		20,000,000
Total	fr.	467,158,014

Montenegro

Expenditure on the army	fr.	100,631,100
Maintenance of prisoners of war		2,500,000
Total	fr.	103,131,100

Servia

Expenditure on the army	fr.	574,815,500
Maintenance of prisoners		16,000,000
Total	fr.	590,815,500

Are these figures to be regarded as exact? They are evidently open to the suspicion of being exaggerated. They were supplied by the belligerent States to the Financial Commission as a basis of the claims to be formulated and indemnity or compensation awarded against the defeated Turk. As one of the ministers whom we saw told us, the States "pleaded" before the Commission. The case is not yet decided. But there is already more moderation about the corrected figures furnished by some States. Thus in a document sent us by the secretary general to the Servian Foreign Minister (Appendix I) the total of the various heads under which war expenditure is classified amounts to but fr. 445,880,858, a reduction of fr. 128,934,642 on the total sent in to the Finance Commission.

In the absence of documents it is to be presumed that Montenegro can not have spent fr. 103,000,000, even if its reserves were exhausted, its allies and friends called in and everything possible in the country requisitioned.

After this comment we may ask how the hundreds of millions consumed by the war have been or are to be paid? The belligerents have depleted their treasuries. They will seek to get what is necessary by means of loans. At home they will convert the requisition bonds into government stock. In Bulgaria three hundred millions of those bonds are in circulation; a third will be paid up and the rest consolidated. But for the greater part of the bill appeal will be made to European financiers. The result will be a considerable increase in the public debt of the Balkan States.

On June 1, 1913, the Hellenic government made an attempt to justify the sums at which its expenditure on army and navy had been valued; i. e., fr. 393,158,014, and estimated that of this total fr. 119,598,213 was outstanding debt, which would make its real cash expenditure fr. 273,559,801.

What were the resources available to meet such a heavy expenditure? On the eve of the war the treasury contained fr. 122,856,768 of gold drawn from the following sources:

Available balance from the 1910 loan........	fr. 73,537,941
Budget surplus from 1910 and 1911.........	19,318,827
Postponed expenditure on the 1912 and 1913 budgets and funds used provisionally, about	30,000,000
Total	fr. 122,856,768

After the declaration of war Greece acquired resources as follows:

Treasury bonds discounted by the Greek National Bank	fr. 10,000,000
Advance arranged in Paris, December, 1912..	40,000,000
Advance arranged with the Greek National Bank, April, 1913.....................	50,000,000
Advance arranged with the same, May, 1913..	40,000,000
Total	fr. 140,000,000

The grand total then of the sums contained in the treasury and obtained by a series of financial operations, amounts to fr. 262,856,768.

The treasury possessed on June, 1913, some fr. 12,000,000. It spent fr. 250,856,768, a sum which with the addition of the debt outstanding, practically corresponds to the total returned expenditure. There thus remain fr. 119,398,213 of expenditure not yet settled, and the pensions and repairs of armaments, etc. There is also the organization of new territories to be provided for, and which for a considerable time will bring in nothing in the way of receipts. Finally, the receipts for 1912 and 1913 being markedly diminished by the war, there is sure to be a deficit from these two sources.

Thus one may conclude, from figures furnished by Greece herself, that the State debt, amounting to fr. 994,000,000 on January 1, 1913, will be augmented, as the result of the increased expenditure and diminished budget receipts due to the war, by some fr. 500,000,000, which will produce by way of interest and sinking fund an annual charge on the budget of fr. 35,000,000 to pay for the expenses of the war. That is to say the sum, fr. 37,650,712, actually required for debt, according to the 1913 budget, will be almost doubled.

The effect of war expenses on public finance in Bulgaria was put as follows by the delegates before the Finance Commission on July 2:

Part of the expense incurred by the Bulgarian treasury during the war has already affected the public debt. On September 1 last the consolidated debt, consisting of the 6 per cent loan of 1892, 5 per cent of 1902 and 1904, 4½ per cent of 1907 and 1909, 4¾ per cent of 1909, amounted to fr. 627,782,962. The floating debt amounted to close upon fr. 60,000,000, i. e., fr. 32,875,775 to the National Bank of Bulgaria, fr. 2,040,398 to the Banque Agricole, and fr. 25,000,000 of treasury bonds. The total Bulgarian debt consequently amounted to fr. 687,699,135 before the war. It has since risen by about fr. 395,000,000. The situation on May 1, 1913, was as follows:

Consolidated debt	fr. 623,635,206
Floating debt to the National Bank	60,625,398
Debt to the Banque Agricole	313,583
Treasury bonds	125,829,000
Treasury bonds (requisition bonds)	249,815,300
Excess over from previous statements	23,071,304
Total	fr. 1,083,289,791

The consolidated debt has been reduced by the normal operation of the sinking fund, by a little over four millions. The advances made by the National Bank of Bulgaria have almost doubled. Treasury bonds to the value of 125 millions have been issued abroad. Finally, the major part of the expenses of the war have been met by the issue of requisition bonds.

From the beginning of the war down to May 1, Bulgaria spent rather over fr. 400,000,000 and increased its debt by fr. 395,590,737. Let us hasten to add that this sum is far from representing the real cost of the war. Sums incurred and not yet met are not included. The indirect expenses, above all, of recreating matériel and commissariat, paying pensions to the wounded and to the families of the dead soldiers, which would more than double the total 400,000,000, are not included.

The total, further, does not include the losses to the Bulgarian treasury involved in the diminution of receipts and economic and other losses.

The Servian public debt, which was 659 million francs, has also been heavily swollen,—by about 500 millions.

Territorial conquest imposes obligations on the conquerors which must aggravate their financial position. Moreover, Servia's new territories must be organized, equipped with administrative machinery and officials, reforms must be introduced, industrial arrangements improved, railways laid, and the army increased. The Turkish debt which weighs on them must be cleared off.

The Financial Commission made an estimate of the share of the Ottoman debt accruing to the Balkan States in return for their annexations.

Three systems of distribution were suggested. Only those figures need be given which show that the share of nominal capital in the loans and advances of the Ottoman government in circulation at the end of the war, transferred to the Balkan States, will amount to between twenty-three and twenty-four million Turkish pounds, or 575 to 600 million francs.

It is not easy to foretell what economic alterations will be effected in the country by the new distribution of territory, which regions will benefit and which suffer by the change. Greece, which has been isolated, as its railways did not form part of the European system, is thinking of changing this state of things, which is harmful to its development.

The breaking up of Macedonia will alter the position of the trade centers, which each government will place in the middle of its own territory. This will certainly be to the detriment of Salonica, whose commercial hinterland is intersected by the new frontiers. In November, 1913, the receipts of the custom house of Ghevgheli on the Servian-Greek frontier amounted to 600,000 dinars. When Servia has organized its new territory, the Ghevgheli custom house will in all probability be an obstacle to trade with Salonica.

The events of the Balkan war reacted upon Austria Hungary and Russia. Before and during the period of crisis these two States held themselves in readiness for any eventuality and remained partially mobilized for several months. These preparations must have cost Austria Hungary alone some thousand million crowns.

Roumania also mobilized and invaded Bulgaria at the moment when Bulgaria stood opposed to the Greek, Servian and Turkish armies. But as the price of this intervention, which was absolutely without danger, Roumania received a rich territory equal to a twelfth of the whole area of Bulgaria, and paying in thirty to thirty-two million francs worth in taxation annually to the Bulgarian Exchequer. So she was amply repaid.

As soon as peace was concluded, the belligerent States set in search of money. Servia first took steps to obtain the millions needed to repair its losses and realize its conquest, from the international finance market. The Skupshtina voted a projected loan of 250 million dinars, half to cover the cost of the war, the other half to go in subventions to agriculture, especially in the provinces of New Servia.

Bulgaria and Greece are also looking for the necessary millions. Turkey the same. A thousand millions of francs (£40,000,000) is an inside estimate of what the Balkan States want from the savings of Europe. The capital will be supplied them by loan establishments, controlled, however, clearly, by the governments of the countries where the shares are issued and taken up.

It is right and proper that government should make the pecuniary aid thus afforded to the Balkan nations subject to certain considerations of general interest. It is the duty of governments which allow millions to be borrowed from the savings of their people to see that conditions are imposed salutary to borrowers and lenders. The wealth lent must go to increase industrial and agricultural values above their present level; unproductive and dangerous trade must be limited. In a word, governmental intervention should take the form of refusing to authorize a loan unless the borrowing nations guarantee to restrict their armaments within definite limits. European governments which really care for peace, ought to use this powerful argument.

Finally, the Balkan States, immediately after the war, took up the position of conquerors; in Belgrade, in Athens and in Sofia, the sovereign and the troops made triumphal entries.

Today, the Balkan States are acting as beggars. They are seeking to borrow money to pay their debts and build up again their military and productive forces.

Such is the result of the war. Hundreds of thousands of deaths, soldiers crippled, ruin, suffering, hatred and, to crown all, misery and poverty after victory. War results in destruction and poverty in every direction.

CHAPTER VII

The Moral and Social Consequences of the Wars and the Outlook for the Future of Macedonia

In the first war there was much of that cheerful response to the call to arms, that fearlessness and that heroism which have been sung by poets in all time, and which the world has ever approved. Centuries of oppression and suffering at the hands of the Turks, the unpromising outlook for good government in Macedonia because of hostile factions in the Turkish government, and the possibility of the alliance of Greece, Servia, and Bulgaria in what seemed a just and holy cause, were felt to fully justify the concerted movement against the Turks. The peasants who cheerfully left their homes and their families, while the government took their animals and their carts for purposes of transportation, went forth in a glow of national feeling and patriotism not unmixed with the thought of liberating their brothers in Macedonia. Though the instincts and motives which inspired them were primitive, they were nevertheless real and genuine and belonged to that class of better human traits which war is believed by many to call forth.

From first to last, in both wars, the fighting was as desperate as though extermination were the end sought. However glorious the public accounts appeared, the Turkish war and the war of the Allies constituted a ghastly chapter of horrors. Both among the regular troops as well as the irregular bands which accompanied the armies, there were many of low, criminal, and even bestial type, with no human feeling and no care for civilized standards, who were ready at all times to do atrocious deeds; and the history of the first war, however lofty in purpose it may have been, is tarnished by many burnings, slayings, and violations for which no possible excuse can be given. There is evidence to show that in some cases these acts were committed by soldiers acting under orders. It is to be feared that many a young man learned for the first time to commit acts of violence and crime not permitted in civilized warfare.

We have to do with the second war chiefly, and it is here that moral results and consequences are the most terrible. The nations which had been in alliance and had invoked the aid of Heaven in a war of deliverance suddenly awoke to fierce hatred of each other. National jealousy and bitterness, greed for territorial expansion, and mutual distrust, were sufficient to initiate and push forward the most uncalled for and brutal war of modern times. Those who fought side by side at Tchataldja and Adrianople were now ready to kill, mutilate, and to torture each other.

To the man who sits at home, or to the casual observer, war assumes a certain glamor. It seems to be the open door to glory and renown. The Commission witnessed at Belgrade, at the close of the second war, the return of some of the crack Servian regiments and the celebration of the victories, with processions of soldiers, triumphal arches, banners, flowers, and music. The King, Crown Prince, distinguished officers and the populace all entered into the spirit of a grand holiday. Similar scenes were enacted at Sofia, Salonica, Athens, and Bucharest. It would be difficult to say which caused the greater joy,—the victories over the Turks or those over their former allies, the Bulgarians. In the speeches made on these occasions there was, we venture to say, little mention made of the fact that nearly one hundred thousand young men, more or less, were lost to the nation, either through death, wounds, sickness, or massacres. The mothers and sisters of the lost soldiers who, in mourning dress, were scattered numerously through the crowds, received, we venture to say, little public notice. Each of the three nations which fought, and Roumania, who seized an auspicious moment to steal a choice piece of her neighbor's territory and force her to sign a treaty at the point of the bayonet, posed before the world as those that had defended a righteous cause.

We also saw the demobilization of the Servian troops, for we met in our slow journey of two days from Belgrade to Uskub more than thirty military trains loaded with men, horses, oxen, carts, cannon, equipage, and, I fear, much property unlawfully taken from the homes and shops of noncombatants. Often the railway carriages were decorated with flowers or branches of trees. Now and then one could hear patriotic songs. Thus the going and returning of the soldiers was attended with patriotic ardor and joy. This is the brighter side of the picture; but it is the reverse side, so dark and sinister, which we are compelled to examine. Upon this picture only one ray of light seems to fall.

We visited the great military hospitals at Belgrade and Sofia and the smaller Greek hospital at Drama. In the midst of maimed, sore, and suffering humanity devoted women, some of them from other lands, some persons of high station—for example, the wives of the Servian minister in London and the Greek minister at Athens, both of American birth, and Queen Eleonora of Bulgaria— were ministering patiently and sympathetically, not only to those who were recovering, but to the dying as well, and in all cases there were a few, a very few, of the enemy receiving apparently the same care as the others. We heard also of instances of self denial and magnanimity on the battle field, and we wished that there had been more of them.

In considering the moral effects of the atrocities which have already been so fully described, we must take account of the sufferers as well as those guilty of committing them. When a band of soldiers or *comitadjis*, either under orders or, as was many times the case, under the impulse of hatred, greed, and lust, surrounded and attacked a village, the very doors of Hell seemed to be opened. No language can describe the tortures and griefs which followed. Repeated instances of death by fright of girls and young children attest the horror of the orgy of crime which was enacted. In one house in Doxato, to which fifty persons had fled for safety, all but one little girl, Chrisanthe Andom, were slaughtered like beasts in the shambles. In the same town a well to do family of thirteen owned and occupied one of the best houses. After extorting £3,000 from the head of the family on the promise that they would be spared, the Bulgarians and Turks proceeded to kill them all. These are typical instances of the many which are found in the depositions contained in the appendices. Can we estimate the moral effects of such atrocities upon the survivors? They are often stunned by the enormity of their losses. Despair is written on their faces. This was true of a Bulgarian and his wife in the village of Voinitsa. They stood beside a wretched shack in which they were trying to live, while a few meters away were the ruins of their once attractive home, which contained the savings of a lifetime, and which the Servians had destroyed. Widespread and almost universal maltreatment of women and girls by the soldiers of the three nations has left behind moral consequences which can not be estimated.

But what shall we say of the reflex influence upon the perpetrators? When before, in modern times, have troops been commanded by their officers to commit atrocities? That this was done is shown by letters of Greek soldiers captured by the Bulgarians and copies of which are to be seen in Appendix C. Greek officers on the other hand claim to have captured evidence that Bulgarian commanders were guilty of permitting and directing atrocities in Greek towns. The moral effect upon hundreds and thousands of young men, who either participated in or were cognizant of these crimes officially sanctioned, can not easily be effaced. Acting upon a people who have not obtained the stability of character found in older civilizations, the moral loss is irretrievable.

To this list of primary consequences must be added the long series of reports and instances of torturing, mutilating, and slaying of wounded soldiers collected by the Foreign Office at Belgrade, each report containing the names of the victims, the name of the person making the report, and properly attested by the commanding officer. Then there are instances of ill treatment of prisoners, especially of Turks by Bulgarians and of Bulgarians by the Servians and Greeks. No less serious were the sufferings of Turkish refugees, more than 200,000 in number, who were either driven out by the Greeks or who, from fear of the Bulgars, fled from the territories about to be occupied by them. We saw thousands of those refugees in and near Salonica, and thousands more at Drama and Kavala. They were always a pitiful sight, camping as they were on the open ground, without shelter, the children often being nearly naked, with winter approaching, and not knowing where they would find a home and safety.

They had left their farms and their crops, taking with them only some animals, which were often stolen from them, or which they were compelled to sell for a mere pittance. We saw some of them embarking on steamers for Asia Minor, where it is to be feared that many will die from hunger and exposure the coming winter. More than 135,000 Bulgarians were fugitives from territory newly occupied by the Greeks. This list includes priests, schoolmasters, and leading citizens whose interests and sympathies are known to be Bulgarian.

It is sufficient to refer to what has already been said about nationalities. There could be no more appealing picture of moral and social confusion than that of metropolitan bishops, schoolmasters, and notables who have been arrested, maltreated, and imprisoned without due process of law. If permitted to live, they were driven from their homes and compelled to leave behind the churches and schools which they had cherished, as well as the property belonging thereto or to them personally. Often they were prevented from communicating with their families before they were driven away. These supreme acts of intolerance on the part of Greece and Servia toward educational institutions, which had long been a saving grace in Macedonia, may find some defense in the militant nature of the national propaganda which priests and schoolmasters carried on; but such coercion and ill treatment employed by one set of Christians against another, all adherents of the same orthodox church, can not hope to escape the censure of the civilized world. They were fiendish, both in their conception and in their execution, and were appropriate only to the times of the Spanish Inquisition.

Statistics showing the number of Bulgarian, Servian, and Greek schools and teachers in Macedonia before the new alignment of territory are impressive, as showing Bulgarian enterprise in education, and in suggesting the vast moral and social harm which is wrought in their destruction. Here again the moral consequences are far reaching, for they affect 60,000 pupils and 1,600 teachers and strike a blow at the educational and social advancement of the communities involved. They also convict the Greeks and Servians of mal-administration and intolerance at the very beginning of their avowed work of reconstruction. Recalling that under the Turks there had been a high degree of liberty in education and worship, is it strange that large populations are now wishing that the Turks were again in control? In some respects, at least, war for the deliverance of Macedonia has brought to the people of that country a new set of sufferings and trials. The vice-rector of a *Real Gymnasium* in Salonica, attended and supported by Bulgarians, told one of the Commission of his own experience. After twenty years of service as director of science in that institution, during which time he had organized physical, chemical, and zoölogical laboratories equal, if not superior, to any others in that region, he had been compelled to see his work utterly destroyed. Standing in the street a few days before, he had witnessed the systematic looting of the entire building by soldiers and others, and the destruction of whatever was not carried away.

A daily journal called *The Independent,* published in Salonica, in its issue of September 4, publishes an interview with Mr. Tsirimocos, the Greek Minister of Public Instruction and Culture, in which he sets forth elaborate plans for primary and secondary education in Macedonia. No mention, however, is made of the schools which have been destroyed and of the hundreds of teachers who have been driven away or of his plans for filling their places.

Reference has already been made to the reflex psychological effect of these crimes against justice and humanity. The matter becomes serious when we think of it as something which the nations have absorbed into their very life,—a sort of virus which, through the ordinary channels of circulation, has infected the entire body politic. Here we can focus the whole matter,—the fearful economic waste, the untimely death of no small part of the population, a volume of terror and pain which can be only partially, at least, conceived and estimated, and the collective national consciousness of greater crimes than history has recorded. This is a fearful legacy to be left to future generations. If we look for palliating causes of these gross lapses from humanity and law, we must find them in the extreme youth of these nations, the immaturity of national and civic character, as well as in the conditions which have beset them during their long period of vassalage. Life was cheap; nothing was absolutely safe or sure; deeds of injustice and violence were common facts in their daily lives; and danger of some kind or other was generally imminent. Events, however revolting, are soon forgotten by the outside world and it is in the inner consciousness of moral deterioration and in the loss of self respect that the nations will chiefly suffer.

There is one other fact, partly economic but distinctly social, which should not be overlooked. Including Turks, upward of a million and a half of men have been under arms during the past year. For those who have been demobilized and have returned to their homes and vocations there is little to be said in this connection, but to the large contingents which are kept in the service, composed mostly of young men, there is a probability of permanent harm. To be withdrawn from useful productive labor is bad enough; but life in the barracks, with much idleness in the streets of cities and large towns, is sure to be demoralizing and harmful. The Commission in its wanderings seemed everywhere to be enveloped by soldiers, who went to increase the number, already large, of those who thronged the cafés and places of amusement. War causes many kinds of human waste and this is one of them. The life of the recruits who are kept in service under present conditions in the Balkan States is unnatural and not favorable to moral growth.

The next portion of our inquiry relates to present social conditions in these countries and the future prospects for Macedonia. To what extent have Greece, Servia, and Bulgaria shown themselves competent to administer their new domains? What are the guaranties of their future growth in good government and the arts of civilized life? Each nation is working out its destiny under a constitutional government in which the people are duly represented. While there is a certain instability caused by the number of political parties, there is the free play of popular will and opinion. Undoubtedly the most promising safeguards and the most important means of progress are found in the systems of education which the several nations have established. Each has its university, technical, secondary and primary schools, and all have taken steps to organize all of these forms of special education which are considered essential in modern times. Greece, by reason of her longer period of independence, has been able to extend and broaden her system and to connect it somewhat with the economic interests of the people. For example, she has a good number of agricultural schools distributed in her several provinces. Servia has also shown worthy attempts to make her schools of social importance through the study of agriculture and domestic economy. The fact that not more than seventeen per cent of the people of Servia can read and write indicates, however, that the system has not been efficiently applied so far as the elements of education are concerned. As one friend of the nation has expressed it, "Education in Servia is strong at the top and weak at the bottom."

Bulgaria, in her thirty-four years of independent existence, has made rapid progress in organizing an efficient school system. The reduction of illiteracy in Bulgaria has proceeded so rapidly during the last ten years that it is possible to predict that before many years the people will all substantially be able to read and write. Similar results may properly be expected in Greece. Bulgaria is considerably in advance of her neighbors in the relative number of schools and teachers provided, in the literacy of both males and females in the entire population, in the number of recruits who can read and write, and in the provision for secondary education. But the efficiency of school systems can not be judged by statistics alone; it is necessary to inquire concerning the results of education as seen in the social and economic life of the people. We may properly ask whether education has been effective in improving healthfulness, thrift and good taste as seen in the homes; in modernizing commercial and industrial methods; and in raising standards of public health and sanitation.

In the capital cities, especially in Sofia, Athens, and to some extent Belgrade, we see well paved streets, a system of public water, partially constructed sewers, and many indications of civic enterprise. The beginnings in these directions are found also in some of the large towns; but in the villages, in which dwell the majority of the people, there is still a large amount of squalor, dirt, and confusion, which have been transmitted through the centuries with little change. There is too much complacency on the part of officials, too low a standard of human comfort and welfare among the masses. This conservatism and backwardness whereby the people cling to the methods of their ancestors, can only be overcome by more vigorous methods of social education than have yet been applied. Every schoolmaster and every schoolmistress should become a working agent for social regeneration, not only in the old sections of these States, but especially in the new. They should not only train the children in habits of cleanliness, health, and neatness, for which the studies in the official program make provision, but they should try to reach sympathetically and helpfully the parents as well. They should tactfully suggest better plans for making the homes convenient and comfortable, by the use of proper floors, simple but useful furniture, better provisions for health and decency, and the planting of grass, shrubbery, and trees. They should also encourage a healthy rivalry in these and other directions, so that the whole village may become interested in the idea of freeing itself from all obnoxious sights and smells, and in keeping its streets smooth and clean, so that every citizen may be proud of his home and its surroundings.

The relatively low place held by women in the Balkan States, as shown by the high rate of illiteracy of females, is emphasized when so large a proportion of the peasants are under arms and the hard labor in the fields must be performed by women, frequently without the aid of animals. Examples of loyalty and devotion thus afforded do not compensate for the physical and social loss. A people can not rise high in the social scale while women are permitted to bear the heaviest burdens and perform the hardest labor. The greatest social need in the Balkan States today is the raising of the standard of home life among the peasants and the elevation of women by education which is both cultural and practical.

The conditions in Macedonia make it necessary that broad, considerate, and helpful administrative methods be applied. Those forms of coercion, intolerance, and anti-social management, to which reference has been made already, give to Greece and Servia a bad name before the world. Nothing short of complete, generous provision for education undertaken along social and vocational lines will make amends for the evil done. The situation is serious and far from hopeful; something more than military force is needed. The Commission has met several governors, civil and military, in new Greece who, possessed of real sympathy, are endeavoring to help a distressed and long defrauded people to repair their losses and to enter hopefully upon a new era of security and peace. Any attempt to revert to former methods of national propaganda through bands of more or less irresponsible adventurers should be discountenanced and vigorously opposed. Such brigandage is worse than war, for it promotes incessant fear and insecurity and renders civilized life impossible.

In the older civilizations there is a synthesis of moral and social forces embodied in laws and institutions giving stability of character, forming public sentiment, and making for security. In some notable cases there is the re-enforcement of the Church in its teaching of righteousness and charity and in its practice of social service. This is largely wanting in the Balkan States. The Church does not systematically teach either morals or religion; its bishops and priests are the employes of the State and they are the propagandists of nationality. Conversion with them means a change from one nationality to another, whether accomplished by persuasion or force. Religious conviction or faith have nothing to do with it. As typical of the methods of conversion employed, a Bulgarian teacher from Macedonia reported that one Sunday the Servian soldiers surrounded a Bulgarian church. When the worshipers came out at the close of the service, a table stood before the door upon which were a paper and a revolver. They were to choose between these; either they were to sign the paper, signifying that they thus became Servians, or were to suffer death. They all signed. But what a travesty upon the true mission of a church and what a perversion of the idea of human government!

The Commission, from what they have seen and heard, indulge in no optimism regarding the immediate political future of Macedonia. Servia is now at war with Albania, Bulgaria is brooding over what she regards as her unjust treatment, and Greece is not yet sure of her tenure in some parts of the new territory. None of these nations can reduce their armies to a peace footing, for their neighbors are as ready to break treaties as they are to make them. Doubtless the greatest menace to the moral and social welfare of the Balkan States is the increasing tendency to militarism, whereby they become a prey to the agents of the makers of guns and other war material, involving enormous expenses and leading to national impoverishment. Where the economic interests of a people are mainly along agricultural lines and where scientific farming is not largely developed and where most of the people are relatively poor, there can be only a moderate annual surplus. If this is required to pay interest on the national debt, as well as to provide for the abnormal cost of occasional wars, national progress will be retarded and enterprise will be throttled. What the Balkan States need today more than anything else is a long period of assured peace so that industry and education may have a broader and richer development.

This suggests a final inquiry concerning the relations of the Balkan States to the new world movement for international coöperation and justice. The bearing of international law upon the conduct of war and the treatment of people and of private property by belligerents has already been discussed. It is the larger moral question which is here raised, for upon it depends the future destiny of the Balkan peoples. If the treaty of Bucharest had been in accord with fair play and justice, or if the question of boundaries could have been referred to mediation, there would have been stronger hopes that the interrelation of the Balkan nations could be improved and strengthened, that through cultural exchange, trade, and friendly intercourse these peoples would begin to learn what other nations have discovered, viz., that their interests are mutual, that in a high human sense they are one, that they injure themselves by trying to injure one another. Under present conditions, which this report has fully disclosed, the case seems well nigh hopeless; and yet, in each country, were found men and women of rank and education who expressed the most fervent wish that hatreds and jealousies might be removed and that good will and co-operation might take their place. What then is the duty of the civilized world in the Balkans, especially of those nations who, by their location and history, are free from international entanglements? It is clear in the first place that they should cease to exploit these nations for gain. They should encourage them to make arbitration treaties and insist upon their keeping them. They should set a good example by seeking a judicial settlement of all international disputes. The consequences of the recent war, economic, moral, and social, are dreadful enough to justify any honest effort by any person or by any nation to alleviate the really distressing situation.

The recently dedicated Peace Palace at The Hague stands as a witness to the new and larger patriotism. As in the long past individuals have brought precious gifts to their favorite shrines, so have the nations of the earth from the East and West brought to this temple their offerings in varied and beautiful forms, thus pledging their belief that through justice peace is to reign upon the earth. The Commission has performed as well as it could a serious and trying duty. In reporting to the world its findings it has felt obliged to use plain words, to make revelations which are at once startling and painful; but its members feel like appealing to the world for sympathy and aid on behalf of nations which have heavy burdens to carry and hard lessons to learn, among which is the supreme value of peace and good will.

APPENDICES

Documents Relating to Chapters II, III, and VI

APPENDIX A[1]

Documents Relating to Chapter II

THE PLIGHT OF THE MACEDONIAN MOSLEMS DURING THE FIRST WAR

No. 1. EVIDENCE OF RAHNI EFFENDI, *of Strumnitsa.*

The Bulgarian army arrived on Monday, November 4, 1912. With the two Bishops and two other notables I went out to negotiate the surrender of our town with the commandant. On entering the town, the Bulgarians disarmed the Moslem inhabitants, but behaved well and did not loot. Next day, a Bulgarian civil authority was established, but the Servians had the military control. The Bulgarian army marched on to Doiran; on its departure looting and slaughter began. I saw an old man of eighty lying in the street with his head split open, and the dead body of a boy of thirteen. About thirty Moslems were killed that day in the streets,—I believe by the Bulgarian bands. On Wednesday evening, an order was issued that no Moslem might leave his house day or night until further notice. A commission was then formed from the Bulgarian notables of the town; the Servian military commander presided, and the Bulgarian Civil Governor also sat upon it. A local gendarmerie was appointed and a gendarme and a soldier were told off to go round from house to house, summoning the Moslems, one by one, to attend the commission. I was summoned myself with the rest.

The procedure was as follows: The Servian commandant would inquire, "What kind of a man is this?" The answer was simply either "good" or "bad." No inquiry was made into our characters; there was no defense and no discussion; if one member of the commission said "bad," that sufficed to condemn the prisoner. Each member of the commission had his own enemies whom he wished to destroy, and therefore did not oppose the wishes of his fellow members. When sentence was pronounced the prisoner was stripped of his outer clothes and bound, and his money was taken by the Servian commander. I was pronounced "good," and so perhaps were one-tenth of the prisoners. Those sentenced were bound together by threes, and taken to the slaughter house; their ears and noses were often cut off before they were killed. This slaughter went on for a month; I believe that from three to four thousand Moslems were killed in the town and the neighboring villages.

NOTE.—At this point the conversation became general and the four notables from Strumnitsa each related how he had lost a son, a grandson, or a brother in this massacre.

No. 2. ABDUL KERIN AGA, *of Strumnitsa,* confirmed the statements of the previous witness. His own son was brought bound to the gate at his house; he then went to Toma, the chief of the Bulgarian bands, and tried to bargain with him for his son's life. Toma demanded a hundred pounds; he had previously paid on two different occasions £50

NOTE.—[1]The reader will note here and there in the appendices faulty phraseology, which has not been translated into good English. These documents reproduce testimony given by soldiers, peasants and uneducated people, and the Commission has endeavored to preserve the original wording in all such cases.

and £70 to save this same son. He told Toma that he had not the money ready, but would try to sell a shop if the Bulgarians would wait until evening. Toma refused to wait and his son was shot.

No. 3. HADJI SULEIMAN EFFENDI, *of Strumnitsa,* agreed with the account which Rahni Effendi had given of the doings of the commission. The Servian troops left the town and Bulgarians replaced them, and remained up to the outbreak of the second war. On the whole they behaved fairly well. There was, however, some looting when they evacuated the town after their defeats in the second war; and about thirty people were then killed, including the Greek priest. The Greek army then occupied the town. They subsequently gave the order that the Moslems must abandon the town; and added that they, the Greeks, would burn the houses if the Moslems would not. I myself offered £3 to the Greek patrol which came to burn down my house. The sergeant refused to take it, and said that if he did not burn the house another patrol would. The buildings were all systematically burnt, and the same thing was done in about thirty-two neighboring villages. "We [pointing to the others who were present] were all large farmers, employing, each of us, nearly 300 laborers and tenants; now we have nothing." (See also No. 65.)

No. 4. The Carnegie Commission visited the camp of the Moslem refugees outside Salonica and talked with two groups of them who came from villages near Strumnitsa. The Greeks told them that the Bulgarians would certainly massacre them if they stayed in the town; they urged, and pressed and persuaded. Most left under pressure. A few remained, and these were forced to leave. They heard that other villages had been burnt after they left, and some of them actually saw their villages in flames. They had received no rations from the Greeks for four days; they had no plans for the future, did not wish to go to Asia, nor yet to settle in Greek territory. They saw "no good in front of them at all."

A group of these refugees from the village Yedna-Kuk, near Strumnitsa, gave their experiences during the first war. The Bulgarian bands arrived before the regular army, and ordered the whole male population to assemble in the mosque. They were shut in and robbed of £300 in all. Eighteen of the wealthier villagers were bound and taken to Bossilovo, where they were killed and buried. The villagers were able to remember nine of their names.

No. 5. The officials of the *Comité Islamique,* of Salonica, informed us on September 1 that there were 135,000 Mohammedan refugees in and around the town, most of whom had arrived since the second war. Of these, six or eight thousand had already gone to Asia Minor, chiefly to Mersina, Adalia, and Skenderoun. The Greek government had promised to supply five steamers, and in the last few days 3,000 had received tickets. The committee reminded the Greek government that it was responsible for the refugees now in Salonica, since it had obliged them to quit their homes. It has requested the government to supply these refugees with bread. The committee was then spending £50 daily on bread. In reply to questions, the committee did not believe that any considerable number of the Moslem refugees would be given lands in Greek Macedonia. Some perhaps might be given at Kukush, but not more than one or two thousand people could be absorbed as farm laborers.

No. 6. EARLY EVENTS AT KUKUSH, *in the autumn of 1912.*

The Catholic priest Gustave Michel, superior of the mission at Kukush, gave the following information to the correspondent of *Le Temps* (July 10). He could testify to certain massacres perpetrated by the Bulgarian bands at Kurkut. A Bulgarian band led by Donchev shut all the men of the place in the mosque, and gathered the women round it, in order to oblige them to witness the spectacle. The *comitadjis* then threw three bombs at the mosque but it was not blown up; they then set fire to it, and all who were shut up in it, to the number of about 700 men, were burnt alive. Those who attempted to flee were shot down by *comitadjis* posted round the mosque, and Père Michel found human heads, arms, and legs lying about half burned in the streets. At Planitsa, Donchev's band committed still worse atrocities. It first drove all the men to the mosque and burnt them alive; it then gathered the women and burnt them in their turn in the public square. At Rayonovo a number of men and women were massacred; the Bulgarians filled a well with their corpses. At Kukush the Moslems were massacred by the Bulgarian population of the town and their mosque destroyed. All the Turkish soldiers who fled without arms and arrived in groups from Salonica were massacred.

NOTE.—The Commission failed to meet Father Michel, and must leave to the correspondent of *Le Temps* the responsibility for his statement.

No. 7. ALI RIZA EFFENDI, *of Kukush,* states that the Bulgarian bands entered Kukush on October 30, after the Turks had left. Toma of Istip, their leader, installed himself as governor, and told the people to have no fear. Both Servian and Bulgarian detachments passed through the town, but only a very few soldiers were left there while the main army went on to Salonica. After the occupation of Salonica, disarmed Turkish soldiers in groups of two to three hundred at a time marched through Kukush on their way to their homes. They were captured by the Bulgarian bands and slaughtered, to the number of perhaps 2,000. A commission of thirty to forty Christians was established, which drew up lists of all the Moslem inhabitants throughout the district. Everyone was summoned to the mosque and there informed that he had been rated to pay a certain sum. Whole villages were made responsible for the total amount; most of the men were imprisoned and were obliged to sell everything they possessed, including their wives' ornaments, in order to pay the ransom. They were often killed in spite of the payment of the money in full; he, himself, actually saw a Bulgarian *comitadji* cut off two fingers of a man's hand and force him to drink his own blood mixed with raki. From the whole county (Caza) of Kukush £T1,500 were taken. The chief of bands, Donchev, arrived and matters were still worse. He burnt three Turkish villages in one day, Raianovo, Planitsa and Kukurtovo— 345 houses in all. He shut up the men in the mosques and burnt them alive; the women were shut up in barns and ill used; children were actually flung against the walls and killed. This the witness did not see, but heard from his Christian neighbors. Only twenty-two Moslem families out of 300 remained in Kukush; the rest fled to Salonica. Twelve small Moslem villages were wiped out in the first war, the men killed and the women taken away. He was in Kukush when the Greeks entered it. The Bulgarians in leaving the town burnt nothing but the bakers' ovens. The Greeks systematically and deliberately plundered and burnt the town. He believes that many aged Bulgarian inhabitants were burnt alive in their houses. He himself found refuge in the Catholic orphanage.

No. 8. REPORT SIGNED BY YOUSSOUF EFFENDI, *President of the Moslem Community of Serres, and sealed with its seal.*

On November 6, 1912, the inhabitants of Serres, sent a deputation to meet the Bulgarian army and surrender the town. Next day Zancov, a Bulgarian Chief of bands, appeared in the town with sixteen men, and began to disarm the population. A day later the Bulgarian army entered Serres and received a warm welcome. That evening the Bulgarian soldiers, on the pretext that arms were still hidden in the houses of the Moslems, entered them and began to steal money and other valuables. Next day the Moslem refugees from the district north of Serres were invited to appear at the prefecture; they obeyed the summons; but on their arrival a trumpet sounded and the Bulgarian soldiers seized their arms and began to massacre these inoffensive people; the massacre lasted three hours and resulted in the death of 600 Moslems. The number of the victims would have been incalculable had it not been for the energetic intervention of the Greek bishop, and of the director of the Orient bank.

The Moslems of the town were then arrested in the cafés, houses and streets, and imprisoned, some at the prefecture and others in the mosques; many of the former were slaughtered with bayonets. Bulgarian soldiers in the meantime entered Turkish houses, violated the women and girls and stole everything they could lay their hands on. The Moslems imprisoned in the overcrowded mosques were left without food for two days and nights and then released. For six days rifle shots were heard on all sides; the Moslems were afraid to leave their houses; and of this the Bulgarian soldiers took advantage to pillage their shops. Moslem corpses lay about in the streets and were buried only when they began to putrify. For several days the Bulgarian soldiers destroyed houses and mosques in order to obtain firewood. The corn and animals of the Moslems were seized by the Bulgarian authorities without any receipt or note of requisition. Complaints made on this subject were ignored. The furniture and antiquities belonging to the schools, mosques and hospitals were taken and sent to Sofia. The Bulgarians subjected several Moslem notables to all sorts of humiliations; they were driven with whips to sweep the streets and stables; and many a blow was given to those who dared to wear a fez. In a word, during the Bulgarian occupation the Moslems were robbed and maltreated both in the streets and at the prefecture, unless they had happened to give board and lodging to some Bulgarian officer. The Bulgarian officers and gendarmes before leaving Serres took everything that was left in the shops of Moslems, Jews and Greeks, and pitilessly burnt a large number of houses, shops, cafés, and mills.

September 5, 1913.

No. 9. Lieutenant R. Wadham Fisher [*an English Volunteer in the Fifth Battalion of the Macedonian Legion*].

Lieutenant Fisher explained the circumstances of the massacre which occurred at Dedé-Agatch. "A sharp fight took place outside the town between the legion and the army of Javer Pacha; wherever the Turkish villages showed the white flag, our troops were forbidden to march through them. Our men had been much inflamed by reports of outrages committed by Turks on Bulgarians near Gumurjina. We entered Dedé-Agatch under fire towards 9 p.m. after marching and fighting all day. Javer Pacha insisted on withdrawing into the town and we were obliged to pursue him. Bullets were still whistling through the streets, but the local Greeks came out to show us where the Turkish soldiers were posted. The Greeks feared a massacre and regarded our coming as their salvation. I saw something of the search for arms; no one was harmed. At 11 p.m. we received an order to withdraw from the town, and to march to a village twenty-five kilometers away. Some 150 men were left in the town, either because the order did not reach them or because they were too exhausted to obey it. No officer was among them, and they were organized by a private soldier, Stefan Boichev, a contractor of Widin. The Greek bishop afterwards stated that Stefan Boichev had done good service in reëstablishing order. On November 19 the lower class Greeks and the soldiers began to pillage the town together. A certain number of the local Turks were undoubtedly killed. These excesses must be explained by the absence of any officers.

No. 10. Boris Monchev, *Bulgarian Mayor of Dedé-Agatch.*

This witness confirmed Lieutenant Fisher's account, believed that not more than twenty Turks were killed in the massacre, and insisted that the local Armenian porters (*hamals*) had taken the chief part in the disturbances. There were in the town fully 8,000 Turkish refugees, of whom all the men were armed and had taken part in the fight outside the town, from 7 to 9 p.m. After the first disastrous night, everything was done to maintain order by a commission which included the Greek bishop and himself. The 142 Macedonian volunteers obeyed their orders. The Bulgarian army returned to the town six days later, November 25, and order was fully restored.

The notorious incident of the killing of Riza-bey, the Imperial Turkish Commissioner of the Junction railway line, is to be explained by the fact that as he was being taken under arrest to the school he attempted to snatch a rifle from a Macedonian volunteer, and was killed by the volunteers on the spot.

In the course of a search on the eve of the second war twenty-seven Gras rifles and letters used for signalling were found in Greek houses; also a store of rifles at the bishop's palace. In consequence of this, fifty leading Greeks were arrested as hostages for the good behavior of the town, and sent to Bulgaria. It is probable that some of these were liberated after paying bribes. The town was without a regular government from July 22, and much robbery took place; but he had previously taken the precaution of sending the Armenian *hamals,* who were always a troublesome element, out of the town.

No. 11. Vasil Smilev, *a Bulgarian Teacher at Uskub.*

He stated that on the entry of the Servian army into Uskub, efforts were made by the Servian authorities to persuade all the Bulgarian teachers to join the bands which they were forming in order to pursue the Turkish bands. He served for twenty or thirty days, but left the band because it was continually engaged in burning, torturing and killing. He witnessed the slaughter of eighteen Turks who had been collected in the Bulgarian school of the Tchair quarter of the town. They were killed in the open and their bodies thrown into a well near the brickworks. This happened about 9 p.m., four days after the festival of Saint Paraskeva. He named four of them. Later he witnessed the Servian chief of police, Lazar Ilyts, who had been responsible for this massacre, superintending the pillage of the village Butel. Near this village he met a number of Albanian villagers fleeing from their village. A Servian major unveiled and kissed a young girl among them. Her father killed him on the spot. Thereupon the Servian band massacred the whole body of fugitives, men and women, to the number of sixty. This he witnessed personally and reported it at the time to the Russian consulate. After this he refused to have anything further to do with the Servian bands. He was expelled afterwards from Uskub with the other Bulgarian teachers.

No. 12. A Moslem Notable *of Yailadjik* (name suppressed), a village one and a half hours' distant from Salonica, states—On Nov. 7, 1912, most of us fled to Salonica, leaving about twenty-five men in the village. On the 8th the Bulgarian soldiers came and did no harm, except to take the food and forage they required. They passed on after spending a day and a night, and two days later the Greek soldiers came, together with people from the neighboring Greek villages. They killed fifteen Moslems, and took all the furniture, 9,500 sheep and goats, 1,500 cattle, and all the grain which they could find, and then burned the 250 houses of the village.

No. 13. Bulgarian Courts-Martial.

On January 10, 1913, the headquarters of the Bulgarian army issued the following telegraphic order (No. 2360) to the commanders and military governors of Thrace and Macedonia:

> Following on the secret order of December 13, I order and hold you personally responsible for the execution of my order that inquiries be instituted into all excesses,

robberies, and violations, which may have been committed against the inhabitants of the enemy's country occupied by the troops under your orders. We came to liberate these countries in the name of freedom and order, and the commander-in-chief can not remain indifferent towards the criminal acts of individuals, since otherwise we should lead the world to suppose that our civilization is in no respect superior to that of our adversaries, and the honor of the Bulgarian army would thereby be compromised. This would result in causing unforeseen difficulties to our country. The Bulgarian army must prove to the eyes of the whole world that now, as always, justice and legality are supreme within its ranks and that criminals do not go unpunished. Report immediately on the subject of the crimes which you have ascertained to have taken place and the measures you have adopted.

On February 15, 1913, the Supreme Military Tribunal transmitted to the President of the courts-martial the following order:

(No. 989). Report immediately the number of persons condemned up to the present moment for various crimes, and especially murders, violations, and pillage committed against the local population, whatever its nationality, and particularly the Turkish population. * * * The essential interests of this State demand that cases of this kind should be dealt with with the utmost despatch and should be given preference over all others. The military courts must enable the government to show the civilized world that the crimes committed in the course of the war of liberation have not gone unpunished.

No. 13a. A report drawn up by the Moslem community of Pravishta, on the atrocities committed in that town and the neighboring villages since the withdrawal of the Turkish authorities on October 24, 1913.

[NOTE.—The names of all of the killed (195 in all) and of some of those robbed, and also those of the aggressors, are fully given in the original Turkish document, but are omitted in the following summarized translation].

Village of Giran.—Twenty-one Moslems killed by the Greeks of the village of Nikchan, and a sum of about £T3,000 stolen. Six hundred goats were also stolen for the benefit of the Greek church at Nikchan and 2,400 goats taken by the Greeks of Djerbelan.

Village of Palihor.—Six Moslems killed by the band commanded by Demosthenes, headmaster of the Greek school of Palihor, pillage to the extent of about £T3,000. One woman (named) was violated by Demosthenes and another.

Village of Micheli.—Demosthenes and other Greeks pillaged the village, carried off many oxen and much corn and stole credit notes for a sum of £T3,000.

Village of Drama.—Two Moslems killed by Greeks of Pravishta.

Village of Osmanli.—Six Moslems killed by Greeks of Holo; about £T1,500 stolen.

Village of Samalcol.—Twenty-one Moslems of this village were taken by Miltiades Machopoulos of the band of Myriacos Mihail to the ravine of Casroub, where they were massacred by the Greek bandit Leonidas and others. Over £T1,500 were stolen from them; a shop looted of stock worth £T1,500, and about £T7,000 stolen in the village generally.

Village of Tchanahli.—Two Moslems killed by Greeks of Holo; 200 sheep and a mule stolen.

Village of Mouchtian.—Twenty-five Moslems killed by Myriacos Mihail, his band and some local Greeks in the ravine of Casroub. "In the twentieth century of progress, the skeletons which may still be seen in this ravine, present to the eyes of Justice a monument capable of enlightening her regarding Hellenic civilization." About £T3,000 stolen.

Village of Dranich.—£T2,000 in money, seven goats and 1,000 sheep stolen by the Greeks of Palihor and Nikchan.

Village of Ahadler.—Nine Moslems killed by Greeks of Casroub, and sums amounting to £T258 stolen.

Village of Tchiflik.—Ten Moslems killed by the same Greeks of Casroub, and about £T1,000 stolen.

Village of Pethor.—Fourteen Moslems killed by the grocer Myriacos Mihail, member of the bishop's council, Panahi, priest of Boblan, and Miltiades Machopoulos. [The band led by these three men is frequently mentioned.] Local Greeks stole about £T1,500.

Village of Rehemli.—Three Moslems killed by Greeks of Holo.

Village of Sarili.—Five Moslems killed by Greeks of Pethor, and about 1,000 sheep and goats stolen.

Village of Dedebal.—Eight Moslems killed by Myriacos Mihail and his band; about £T1,000 stolen.

Village of Deranli.—Three Moslems killed by Myriacos Mihail and his band; about £T3,000 stolen.

Village of Orphano.—Three Moslems killed by the Greeks. One of these was seized by the priest Panahi on a telephonic order from the Greek bishop of Pravishta and killed at Essirli. The bishop had had the telephone removed from the Turkish governor's office to his own house, and by this means he gave orders to the whole district.

Village of Boblan.—Eight Moslems killed by Myriacos Mihail and his band, specially sent for the purpose by the bishop; about £T800 stolen.

Village of Carpan.—Four Moslems killed by the band of Myriacos Mihail sent by the bishop. The Greeks of Carpan stole all the goods and corn belonging to the local Moslems, and did not leave them even the grain which they had in their household jars. The Greek bravoes brutally robbed the women of their ear-rings. Later Greek soldiers joined the villagers and began to violate the young women, until they were obliged to take refuge in the towns and villages held by Bulgarian troops. About £T500 was stolen in this village.

Village of Leftera.—Four Moslems killed by Greeks. The wife of Arnaut Agouchagha, who voluntarily embraced Islam fifty years ago, was taken to Pravishta to be reconverted to Christianity. She told the Bulgarian chief, Baptchev, that she did not consent to this conversion. Baptchev had her released, but on her return to the village she was "odiously lynched by Greek savages." Baptchev took £T500 from a Turk at the instigation of the Greek priests of the monastery of Nozlé, who also robbed the villagers of about 2,000 sheep.

Village of Kochkar.—Two Moslems killed by Greeks of Drazeni and about £T1,000 stolen.

Village of Kale Tchiflik.—Five Moslems killed, and all the cattle seized by the priests of Nozlé.

Village of Devekeran.—Four Moslems killed by Greeks of Pravishta; about £T500 stolen.

Village of Essirli.—Nineteen Moslems killed in the ravine of Casroub by Greeks of that village. About £T1,500 stolen.

Village of Kotchan.—One Moslem killed to satisfy the vengeance of the bishop and of the priest Nicholas. "It is worthy of remark that many Imams figure among the list of victims in the district of Pravishta * * * further that the victims are almost always men known for their enlightenment. * * * The reason why the assassins killed Imams and the most enlightened notables for choice is obvious when one reflects that there are 13,000 Moslems in this district out of a total population of 20,000."

Town of Pravishta.—Ten Moslems were killed, including one woman, while the town was held by Bulgarian bands, under the command of a chief named Baptchev, who established himself in the governor's palace and acted as governor and commandant. They were killed by three Greeks (named) and the Bulgarians. On the evening when an assassination was to take place, the students of the Greek school assembled in the courtyard of the government house and sang the Greek national anthem.

The Greek bishop formed a municipal council composed of the priest Nicholas, the grocer Myriacos Mihail, and others (named). The sentence of death was passed by this council, approved by the archbishop, and communicated to Baptchev to be carried out. Similar councils were formed in the villages which took their orders from that of Pravishta. The Bulgarian chief Baptchev served as the tool of the Greek bishop and notables. In this town the Moslem population has incurred a loss of about £T3,000, stolen by the Bulgarian bands, guided by the Greeks.

The daughter of the commander of the gendarmeries, Suleiman Effendi, who is now in Constantinople, was summoned one night to the bishopric to be converted to Christianity. The bishop threatened her, in order to convert her, but the Bulgarian chief Baptchev, when he heard of this, went to the bishopric, saved the girl, restored her to her family, and thus prevented her conversion. Some days later he gave her a passport to go to Constantinople.

Thanks to the orders issued by Baptchev the mosques of the town and the villages were preserved intact, and no one was molested on account of his religion.

Neither the Bulgarian officers, nor their soldiers nor even the members of the bands committed any violence against women, but Baptchev took money to the value of about £T6,000.

The priest Panahi of the village of Nikchan and the Greek antiquarian Apostol, of the village of Palihor, who disapproved of the unworthy conduct of the bishop, were killed by his orders. The Bulgarian authorities after a careful inquiry were convinced of the bishop's guilt. The bodies of the victims of the town of Pravishta are still in the ravine of Cainardja, at the place called Kavala Bachi.

We certify that this report is in complete agreement with the registers of the Moslem community of Pravishta and true in all its details.

[Seal.]   Moslem Community of the Caza of Pravishta, 1331.

APPENDIX B

Documents Relating to Chapter II

THE CONDUCT OF THE BULGARIANS IN THE SECOND WAR

A. THE DOXATO AFFAIR

No. 14. EVIDENCE OF COMMANDER CARDALE, R. N. (Reprinted from the *Nation* of August 23, 1913).

MY DEAR CASSAVETTI,—I received your wire yesterday, and have taken twenty-four hours to consider my reply. You see my reports of what I saw at Doxato have been so garbled by reporters and others that I am naturally rather chary of saying anything: not that this applies in your case, of course. Also, as you may well imagine, the horrors of that place of blood have so got on my nerves that I hate to speak of them. Still, as you ask me, I will tell you all I saw, and you have my full permission to make use of all, or any portion, of this letter you may think fit for the purpose of publication.

I went to Kavala immediately after the Bulgarians vacated the place; my duties there I need not go into. I was acting under the orders of the Greek government, which, as you know, I am serving at present. On my arrival there I heard many stories of the horrible occurrences at Doxato, and it was alleged that practically all the inhabitants had been massacred by the Bulgarian troops passing through on their retreat. You will probably understand that having had a surfeit of these yarns, and knowing that war is not fought in kid gloves, I did not believe all I heard, and at first believed that it was purely a question of the burning of the town by retreating Bulgarians enraged by their reverses, and perhaps a few regrettable incidents where noncombatants had been killed in the excitement of a retreat. However, after seeing wounded and mutilated persons being brought into Kavala from Doxato day by day, and hearing detailed accounts from disinterested persons in Kavala of all nationalities, I determined to go to Doxato to see for myself what had occurred. I accordingly took a carriage and drove there, accompanied by a Greek naval officer, a Greek gentleman of Kavala, and my Greek *angeliophores*. The distance is about seventeen miles. I have not measured it on the map, as I have none with me at present, but I estimate it at that. It took us about three and one-half hours to drive. The Bulgarians must have left Kavala in a hurry, as they did not even strike their tents, which we found standing some miles outside on the Phillipi road.

At each village we passed through on our way to Doxato we found some of the wretched survivors of the Doxato massacre, who were homeless, but did not wish to return to their ruined homes there after all they had suffered. Arriving at Doxato we found it like a town of the dead, everything burned and devastated, and such an odor of blood and decomposed bodies as I never hope to encounter again. Indeed, five minutes before we entered the town, while driving through the plain, the stench was insupportable. In this plain were heaps of corpses thinly covered with sand, where the survivors had tried, for sanitary reasons, to cover up their dead, but they were all too few to do so thoroughly, and for all practical purposes the bodies were unburied. On entering Doxato we found a few persons who were still living among the ruins of their former homes, and from them we endeavored to get an account of what had occurred. Practically all the Greek portion of the town was burned, and one saw everywhere in the streets charred remains of what had been human bodies. Burial in the town had been impossible, so they had covered the bodies with petroleum and disposed of them in that way.

In some of the gardens and courtyards we saw children's graves, each with a few wild flowers on them, but they do not appear to have buried any except the children. Poor souls! after the horror of it all, one wonders how they buried anyone. The Turkish quarter was, with a few exceptions, unburned. According to the accounts of the survivors, it was there that the greater part of the massacres took place. I saw many rooms where the floors were soaked with blood, and rugs, mats, and cushions were covered with blood and human remains. The very stones in the courtyards of these houses were stained with blood; it is said that most of those who were killed in these yards were stoned to death. The survivors showed us one house surrounded by a high wall enclosing a courtyard and vineyard where a number of Greeks were put to death, and certainly the place was marked with blood-stains everywhere in the yard and garden; hoes and other agricultural implements stained with blood we found there also, and the steps leading into an outhouse were covered with blood, where the survivors state children were overtaken and killed. I was informed, apropos of this courtyard, that the house and environs were the property of a Turk, who, on hearing of the possibility of a massacre, had sent round to the Greeks of Doxato to offer a sanctuary to their women and children, and that after upwards of 120 were assembled there, he and several of his compatriots, under the direction of a Bulgarian officer, had butchered them all! This, of course, is simply what I was told by the survivors. I can only say from my own personal observation that the place was like a shambles, and, whoever did the deed, there must have been a very considerable number killed in this place. In fact, the vineyard, courtyard, and the house leading out of them reminded me forcibly of the stories one has read of the Cawnpore massacres. One hears of places reeking with blood; without wishing to be sensational, this little town did literally do so. They told us that Bulgarian cavalry riding into the place cut down some of the inhabitants, and that the infantry, following soon after, killed all they found in the streets, but that after that the greater part of the massacres were carried out by the Turkish inhabitants incited by the Bulgarian officers. How far this is true I can not say, not having been there at the time to see for myself, but certainly it is significant that the Turkish quarter was not burned, that very few Turks seem to have been killed, and that all the original Turkish inhabitants have fled, while their houses are intact but bloodstained, and bearing the evidence of unspeakable atrocities. I might, perhaps, give you more details of the evidence of atrocities which took place, but there are some things one can not bring oneself to speak about. I have been asked to estimate the number who were killed at Doxato. It is quite impossible to do so, as many who are supposed to have been killed have, I understand, since been found, having escaped at the time the massacres took place. By counting the bodies I saw, and the heaps of charred remains and the evidences of massacres in the gardens and court-yards, I estimated that the number killed was not less than 600, and that the greater number of these were women and children: how many more than this number there may have been it is impossible to say.—With kindest regards, believe me, yours very sincerely,

HUBERT CARDALE.

Hotel Impérial, Athens,
August 4, 1913.

No. 15. EVIDENCE OF CAPTAIN SOFRONIEV, of the King's Guard.

"I commanded two squadrons of the Macedonian cavalry, a regular body of troops, consisting largely of reservists. On July 10, while stationed at Otoligos, about 20 kilometres from Doxato, I sent out scouts. They reported that the last detachment of our troops retiring from Kavala had been fired upon by the villagers of Doxato, some of whom wore the Greek uniform. They killed many of our men and looted the convoy. The horse-cars escaped, but those drawn by oxen were captured. I sent Sub-Lieutenant Pissarov with thirty troopers to report on what was happening at Doxato and to reëstablish order. My first scout then returned from a second expedition, and reported that he had encountered a large force of Greek insurgents marching from Kavala, and that he had learnt from Turks that they were under Greek officers. They had killed all the Bulgarian and Turkish villagers whom they captured on the way. He saw beheaded children and women whose bodies had been ripped open. There was a general panic among all the population of the country side. (We saw the original penciled note of this scout's report). Lieutenant Pissarov reported that Greek troops were quartered near the ruins of the bridge at Alexandra. The Greeks were killing without pity men, women and children. Doxato was strongly occupied and two Greek battalions with mountain guns were marching up from Valtchista. He had assisted the local Bulgarian and Turkish population to flee. [We saw the original text of this report.] I then reported to the commander of my division, General Delov; he ordered me to go at once to Doxato to make those responsible prisoners, and to restore order. I started on the night of July 13, but lost my way in the dark and found myself at dawn between Doiran and Doxato. I had with me two mounted squadrons of about 250 men. The enemy opened fire at once and three scouts whom I sent to reconnoitre their position were killed. The heaviest fire came from the edge of the village Doxato. The plain was black with people looking for cover. I sent one squadron towards Doxato, and the other, under my own command, advanced toward Doiràn. Firing continued for about two hours, seventeen of my squadron were killed and twenty-four wounded. We eventually charged with the sabre. The enemy, who were all armed, kept their ranks and awaited our onset. At least 150 of them were killed in the charge, possibly as many as 300. Many surrendered. I then heard that the Greek column from Valtchista was marching to Alistrati. I therefore decided to withdraw and hurried to join the column of Lieutenant Colonel Barnev. I left the Turks, who had hurried up from neighboring villages, to guard my prisoners, and told them to disarm the people of Doxato, and to keep order. They armed themselves with rifles and cartridges, chiefly Martinis and Gras, taken from the Greek dead. We had had no earlier dealings with these Turks, but they always helped our scouts with news. Next day, July 14, we fought a battle to allow the peasant fugitives to reach the mountains. The fleeing Turks from Doxato told us that the Greeks had killed all the Bulgarians and Turks whom they found in Doxato. I asked them why they did not flee in time. They replied, "Because we were giving ourselves up to rapine and vengeance." My scouts reported this day that a terrible thing had happened in Doxato. The Turks began to massacre and then the Greeks came and massacred the Turks; the fields were covered with bodies. Next day, July 15, the Greeks destroyed the purely Bulgarian village of Guredjik. The villagers were unable to flee, and were massacred almost to a man; three or four escaped and gave me the news."

In reply to questions the Captain stated, that he was not himself actually inside the town of Doxato. Probably some of the infantry may have gone there, but of this he can not speak with certainty; he can give his word of honor as an officer that the men of his two squadrons killed no peaceful citizens.

From a written deposition by Captain Sofroniev, we take the following passage:

> On returning to the neighborhood of Doxato [from attacking the distant body of insurgents] towards 2.30 p.m. we saw the Turks who had previously fled, and were now returning to the village in a state of savage excitement. [*Exaltation forouche.*] As we had no time to spare, we told them to gather the rifles scattered about. At the same moment we saw the village take fire. I do not know who caused that.

No. 16. EVIDENCE OF MR. GIVKO DOBREV, *Civil Governor of the Drama District.*

The population of the Drama district totaled 18,000, of whom 13,000 were Moslems, and of these latter 3,000 were pomaks and the remainder Turks. Doxato, with two neighboring villages formed a Greek oasis in a compact mass of Turks, with whom it was always in conflict. It thus naturally became the center of the Greek insurgent movement. During the first war, in the latter half of October, the Greeks, acting as allies under the shelter of our troops, began to take their private revenge upon the Turks, killing, looting and violating. The administration had been organized from among the local notables, chiefly Greeks, more especially the Bishop, who knew of all these atrocities. The appetite for robbery grew, and the Greeks began to enforce declarations from the Turks assigning their lands. The Bulgarian government accordingly, with a view of protecting the Turks, published a general edict declaring all contracts regarding land made during the period of the war invalid. I reached Drama on December 3, though the place had been taken on November 5. I was too late to prevent much injustice to the Turks, but I returned their mosques to them in spite of the protests of the Greeks, and helped them to get back some part of their stolen goods.

On July 8, the Bulgarian officials left Kavala, and the place remained for a week without regular government. A reconnaissance was sent on July 10, to learn what was happening in Kavala; and in the course of it one trooper was killed and one wounded at Doxato. A larger party was sent out on the 11th, numbering about thirty men, and this also was fired upon from Doxato. On the night of July 11, a larger party, composed of two squadrons of cavalry, two companies of infantry, and four guns. [NOTE.—There is here a discrepancy of one day in the dates given by Captain Sofroniev and Mr. Dobrev; the dates of the former are accurate]. There was now a regular insurrection in Doxato, which aimed at cutting off Drama from the shore. The cavalry surrounded Doxato. The infantry were received with a volley, whereupon the commander threatened to use artillery and thrice demanded the surrender of the town. When the artillery began to fire, five to six hundred armed men, and all the local population took to flight. Our cavalry pursued them. The village was set on fire by our shells, and an enormous explosion took place, as if a depot of ammunition had been set on fire. The explosion continued intermittently for quite an hour. The Bulgarian infantry was composed largely of Moslems, from the Bulgarian kingdom. It became excited during the explosion of the magazine and began killing indiscriminately. It is possible that children were killed. I arrived on the afternoon of July 12 [13?] and found that the local Turks were going about from house to house, robbing. I saw one house with its door half open, and a woman killed inside. The house was pillaged. I saw a Turk standing on a ladder in the act of pouring petroleum from a tin over the house in order to set it on fire. I ordered him to stop, but others began to do the same thing in other parts of the town. I again visited Doxato at 2 p.m. next day, July 13 [14?]. The houses were still burning and most of the people had fled to the neighboring village of Tchataldja. The rest ran to meet me. There were women among them, of whom one had been wounded by a trooper's saber. I took her to Mr. Lavalette's farm to be cured. Everything was quiet in Tchataldja. Its mayor and notables had asked me on the previous day to send soldiers to their village, since the insurgents of Doxato were trying to induce them to join in their rising, and were threatening them. I sent sixty men. Later, I sent police, on July 14 [15?] to bury the corpses at Doxato. They counted 300 killed. While this was going on the Greek army arrived, marching not from Kavala but from Ziliahovo. Some of my policemen were killed by the Greek population.

No. 16a. DEPOSITION (COMMUNICATED) OF MR. MILEV, *Sub-Lieutenant of Reserves, formerly Mayor of Philippopolis and Prefect of Stara-Zagora, who Commanded a Detachment of Infantry at Doxato.*

On the morning of July 13, a detachment comprised of cavalry, infantry and artillery marched from Drama toward Kavala in order to watch the movements of the *andartes*. At a distance of one kilometer from Doxato, we were received with rifle shots. This fusillade became hotter as we approached the village. Parliamentaries were sent in advance, but the Greeks refused to receive them and went on firing. Then the infantry formed in line of battle and continued its march, but without firing. At 500 paces from the village the order was given to answer the Greek fire, and to aim specially at the school, which was the headquarters of the *andartes*, and over which the Greek flag was flying. The firing continued for two hours, after which the *andartes* left the school, set fire to it, and fled towards Kavala. When the infantry entered Doxato, it realized that not all the *andartes* had left the village, for several of them continued to fire on our troops from the Greek houses. Then the fighting began in the village and lasted till midday, when the resistance of the inhabitants of Doxato was broken. Only twenty-seven *andaries* were killed in the village; the rest succeeded in escaping toward Kavala and the neighboring hills.

The people of Doxato had succeeded in effecting the escape of most of their women and children, who left on July 11 for Kavala. After the battle, the Bulgarian infantry found only about a hundred women and children in the village, and these were by order placed in several houses and courtyards, and protected by the Bulgarian soldiers against the local Turkish and gypsy population, who from the beginning of the fight were burning, pillaging and violating women and girls. Two Turks were caught in the act, and were executed on the spot by Bulgarian soldiers. The Bulgarian army has therefore no crime on its conscience. If women and children were killed in some isolated parts of the village (it was one long street, a kilometer in length) that was the work of local Turks and gypsies.

It was afterwards proved that the *andartes* under the instigation of Greek soldiers and officers deliberately set fire to the school, in order to burn some Bulgarians alive, who were shut up in it, to the number of about twenty. These were laborers arrested in the fields, and were found bound hand and foot by the Bulgarian soldiers who delivered them, after being kept four days without food.

The army left Doxato at 2 p.m., leaving twenty soldiers behind to keep order.

No. 16b. COLONEL BARNEV, *who directed the operations against the evzones and andartes round Doxato, has made the following deposition* [*communicated*]:

On the morning of July 13 the two squadrons of cavalry which I commanded reached the neighborhood of Doxato, and there I found other Bulgarian detachments sent for the same purpose. At about 800 paces from Doxato, I met an orderly with dispatches. As I was engaged with the orderly, I directed Captain Sofroniev to continue the forward march in the direction of Doxato-Kavala, after which I would rejoin the troops. I noticed that all the country round the village was occupied by armed men, who lost no time in opening fire. The company under Sub-Lieutenant Milev, which was advancing to the south in a line parallel to ours, changed front towards Doxato, in the presence of this unexpected attack, formed in order of battle and advanced on the village; for the fire was directed against it, and threatened it seriously. The situation demanded first defence, and then the energetic pursuit of the *andartes*. The appearance of the squadrons of cavalry put the *andartes* to flight, and they were forced to leave their positions and seek refuge on the heights to the northeast of Doxato, where they entrenched themselves. Meanwhile other troops and *andartes* were reported coming from Kavala. In presence of these insurgents, who in their turn opened a heavy fire upon us, we were obliged to attack them, for we were exposed to a murderous fire. Part of them retired to the same heights, from whence they kept up their fire. The cavalry charged then. After the pursuit I gave the order to attend to the wounded, to carry them into shelter, and to send them away by the road Dadem-Tchiflik. We had hardly passed the village of Doiran when Sub-Lieutenant Tanev sent me an orderly to inform me that *andartes* coming from Kavala were advancing; that they had already occupied the heights near the ruins of Alexandros; and that the road to Dadem-

Tchiflik was also cut. I sent Captain Sofroniev in haste in the direction in question; the insurgents fled to Kavala. At this moment I received word from my scouts that a Greek column was reported marching from Valtchista in the direction of the station Anghista-Alistrati. Seeing our retreat threatened, I gave orders to return and occupy our original positions (the pass of Prossetchen).

From information received, the local Moslems, moved by vengeance against the Greeks, gave themselves up to excesses till midnight. It is these excesses which have been attributed by the Greek press to Bulgarian soldiers.

All the descriptions of the alleged misconduct of my troops at Doxato are false. I deny these accusations, and affirm that the Bulgarian soldier has given every proof of tolerance and discipline.

B. Events at Serres

No. 17. [*Note.* In the semi-official Greek pamphlet *Atrocités Bulgares,* published by the director of the university at Athens, the narrative published by Signor Magrini in the *Secolo* is adopted as an authoritative statement of the Greek case. Signor Magrini states that he was present at the inquiry conducted at Serres by the consuls general of Austria and Italy, who had come from Salonica to hear witnesses on the spot.]

We were able to reconstitute the eventful week through which the Macedonian town passed. On Friday, July 4, the Bulgarian advocate adviser attached to the Italian consul, informed him that the following order had arrived:[1]

"If it appears that Serres is lost to the Bulgarians, destroy the town."

On the evening of the same day General Ivanov, beaten at Lahana, passed through Serres station on his way to Demir-Hissar. On Saturday, July 5, the shops and houses were pillaged; seventeen notables were massacred;[2] four other notables, among them the head master of the gymnasium, the director of the hospital, and the manager of the Orient bank, were led outside the town and killed with bayonet thrusts.[3]

Thereafter General Voulkov, Governor of Macedonia, and all the Bulgarian officials, soldiers, and gendarmes left hurriedly. On Sunday and Monday the town was tranquil in expectation of the arrival of the Greek army; the inhabitants armed in order to repel a probable attack by the *comitadjis.* On Tuesday and Wednesday skirmishes took place between the inhabitants and groups of soldiers who attempted to enter the town and to set it on fire. On Thursday the inhabitants, foreseeing the catastrophe, sent a deputation to Nigrita to demand help, but it was too late.[4]

With the Austrian consul general, I questioned the Moslem Ahmed-Hafiz, formerly attached to the Bulgarian police; he made the following declarations:

On Thursday evening the Bulgarian officer Monev appeared at my house and told me, that the Bulgarians were going to burn Serres next day. He invited me to join in the pillage and the burning with a band of Moslems. I refused. Then Monev asked me for petroleum; I replied that I had none. On Thursday, during the night, four guns were posted on the hill Dutli, which commands Serres, and next morning about eight o'clock the bombardment began and created an enormous panic. Soon more than 500 infantry, several groups of cavalry, numbering ten each, and fifty

---

[1]We can discover no confirmation of this statement.

[2]This may refer to the thirteen persons murdered in the prison. Clearly not all of them were notables.

[3]The manager of the Orient bank is alive and well, and was never wounded.

[4]Observe that all mention of the schoolhouse massacre is suppressed.

comitadjis entered the town, armed with bombs, and the atrocities began. Among the soldiers several officers were recognized, including Dr. Yankov, secretary of General Voulkov and councilor of the government, and the late chief of police Karagiosov and Orfaniev, chief of the gendarmerie of Serres. Clearly there was a well-arranged plan. The doors of the houses and shops were opened with sticks tipped with iron, with which the soldiers were provided. The buildings were entered and pillaged; the booty was loaded on some hundred wagons, specially got together for this purpose. Then the houses, emptied one by one, were sprinkled with petroleum and other inflammable substances and fire put to them. By an application of the law of the economy of effort, in each group of three houses, only the middle one was set on fire, clearly in the belief that the wind, which was blowing with violence, would complete the work of destruction. The soldiers fired on the inhabitants who attempted to save the burning houses, consulates, and foreign buildings.

In the quarter Kamenilia twenty-eight persons, among them Albert Biro, a Hungarian, were massacred. The Austrian vice consul with the people who had sought refuge in the consulate was carried off to the mountain, his magnificent house was pillaged and then burned. All the buildings protected by foreign flags were treated in the same fashion. At the Orient bank an attempt was made to open the safe by means of a bomb, but it failed, and the assailants had to content themselves with burning the building. The Italian consular agency, a well-built house, surrounded by a vast garden, was saved almost miraculously from destruction; it is the only house saved in a whole quarter which was burnt down, and the Italian consular agent Menahem Simantov explained to us, that at noon on Friday several infantry soldiers ordered him to open his house, in which 600 people had taken refuge, mainly women and children. He showed himself at a window, the soldiers demanded £T400. His knowledge of Bulgarian enabled him to save them. He persuaded the soldiers to be content with £54 and to withdraw. The presence of the young Bulgarian Mavrodiev, says Simantov, saved the agency from catastrophe. None the less in the course of the day it was necessary to buy off other soldiers with a fresh ransom. The agency, filled with refugees, was surrounded on all sides by flames; we were barely able to protect it.

No. 17a. STATEMENT OF MR. ZLATKOS, *Vice Consul of Austria Hungary at Serres:* (*Atrocités Bulgares,* p. 23.)

On Friday toward noon soldiers of the regular [Bulgarian] army attacked my house, forcing me to go out into the street with my family and a large number of persons, who had fled from the massacre and the fire and had taken refuge with me. Immediately thereafter we were led up to the mountain. All the children and women who accompanied me were threatened with death, and it is only by paying large ransoms that we were released. I am safe and well, but as my house fell a prey to the flames I am, with my family, without shelter or clothing. All our subjects who live here are in the same situation as myself.

No. 18. THE SCHOOLHOUSE MASSACRE (*see also Nos. 56, 57, 58*). *Evidence of Demetri Karanfilov, formerly a dairyman and afterwards a Bulgarian gendarme at Serres.*

On Saturday, July 5, the Bulgarian army left the town. I was unable to go with it since my wife was ill. Everything was quiet until Monday. There then arrived Greek *andartes* (Insurgents) with villagers and some soldiers. I hid and saw very little of what went on. On Tuesday, shots were fired at my house and I heard voices say, "Bulgarians live here." They came in and searched for arms. There were one or two soldiers among about twelve men. I was then taken to the Archbishop's palace and brought before a civil commission, which included the Archbishop of Serres (an old man) and a young bishop, who presided. The soldiers said to me on the way, "We've come to exterminate the Bulgarians." The bishop asked me who and what I was. I replied, "A Bulgarian gendarme." I was searched and five francs were taken from me. I was then taken to a room of the girls' high school, and was kept there for four days, guarded by both soldiers and civilians, who came both from Serres and from the villages. Many other Bulgarians were with me. We received bread once a day, and were not at first maltreated. Ten people were taken up to a room above and never came back. We heard cries, and believe they were killed. I was ordered with three other men to carry out two corpses. They were covered with blood, and I believe that they were Bulgarians of Serres. On Friday morning, a soldier came in and said: "Don't fear, our army is coming, but do all that we tell you." So we were rather relieved. Then those in our room were bound two by two, taken upstairs and were never seen again. When my turn came; I was bound with another man taken up to a room which was full of corpses. There were quite fifty of them; you couldn't see the floor, some were lying in heaps, and there was blood all over the place. I was then struck with a Martini bayonet on the back of the head and through the neck and on the shoulder. [We saw these wounds and also a hole in the man's coat.] The blow on my shoulder was dealt me by Christo, a neighbor of mine. I do not know who the others were. When I fell, another fell on top of me; I fainted and came to some time afterwards. I noticed that somebody else was moving, and soon five or six were stirring. The Greeks had all gone and we heard a fusillade outside. The town was already in flames and soon the school would be burnt also. We went out of this room and saw another room heaped with corpses. Some were still alive and groaning. The doors were open and we made up our minds to go out, crossed the street, went up the hill, and met the Bulgarian soldiers, who tended our wounds. I have had no news of my wife to this day.

No. 19. EVIDENCE OF CHRISTO DIMITROV, *Miller of Serres.*

On July 5 I left my mill on the advice of a Bulgarian soldier, and went to my house to fetch my wife and children. There were shouts of *Zeto!* (the Greek cry) all round, and neighbors shouted "the Greek army is coming." My neighbors bade me have no fear and undertook to save me. I slept that night at home, and saw next morning a crowd of Greeks and Turks in the street, who shouted that they would destroy everything Bulgarian. I saw them arrest two men from Dibra, Marko and Christo. Three Greeks returned to Christo's house and came out with his wife half an hour later; she was crying "Is there no one to save me!" The crowd in the street was shouting, "Show us the Bulgarian houses." On the 6th, I went to a Turk's house for hiding. On the 8th the crowd came again shouting, "There are still Bulgarians here." My neighbors tried to save me, but in the end when the crowd threatened them, they advised me to go quietly to the Archbishop's palace, as I had done no harm. The neighbors came with me to give evidence before the Archbishop in my favor. But I was taken straight to the school and robbed on arrival of my money (5 Napoleons) while soldiers stood around. I spent the day there with about twenty other Bulgarians. That evening I was bound and taken up to a room where eleven dead bodies were lying on the floor. I was ordered to lie down; my hands and feet were bound behind me; I was heavily struck and left. I talked with two other men in the room who were still alive, including my neighbor Christo of Debra, and each asked the other "What crime have we committed?" I recognized two Greeks among our jailers, a certain Janmaki, brother of the Greek Consul Cavass, and one Taki, son of the innkeeper Peter. They said to an *evzone*, "We must not leave one alive." They then beat Petro, Christo, and Procop to death with a big stick. Another Greek civilian then came in and, pointing to me, said: "Fourteen are enough; we can't bury them all. Let us leave this one till tomorrow." They evidently reckoned that they could only bury fourteen in a night. The others were then taken out, and Petro, who was not quite dead, was forced to walk. "We'll kill him down there," they said. I was left alone, bound. On Thursday morning, July 19, I was taken down to another room, where were some men from Strumnitsa; I asked and received some bread and water. Eight men were then brought in from the villages. The Greeks all the time kept shouting, "Long live King Constantine!" On Friday morning, July 11, my wife arrived, and brought me some bread, some tobacco and three francs. Women looking out of the neighboring houses threatened me, "You Bulgarian dogs, we'll kill you all, to the last man." Then four Bulgarian soldiers were brought in as prisoners, three Bulgarian *comitadjis* and the secretary of the mayor of the village of Topoleni. About eleven o'clock I heard the Greek women of the quarter calling out to the men, "Flee! for the Bulgarians are coming, and they will kill you." About sixty surviving prisoners were brought together; about fifty other Greeks came in, including some *evzones,* who bound the prisoners and took them out two by two. Mine was the sixth turn. I was led to an upper room, ordered to lie down, and received four wounds. I then groaned and feigned death. [We saw the scars of his wounds and the holes in his coat.] Others were then brought in and killed. I heard a sort of gurgling, like the sound which sheep make when they are being killed, in the room next door. Presently I heard firing outside, and the Greeks went down to fight, and left us alone. I saw that all was clear. Ten of us were alive and rose to go out, but two, Ilia Penev and Simon, fell at once and could not proceed. Eight of us got safely out to the hills and reached the Bulgarian soldiers. I have heard no news of my wife since that day.

No. 20. EVIDENCE OF DIMITRI LAZAROV, *of Moklen, near Serres.*

Seven men were sent from our village by the mayor to see if the Bulgarians were still in possession of Serres. Three gendarmes were among us, and all of us had our rifles. [He gave the names of all seven.] We were arrested near the village of Soubashkoi by about one hundred armed Greek villagers. They kept us for five days in the village schoolhouse; ropes were arranged from the rafters to hang us. Then firing was heard in the neighborhood and the Greeks, in fear lest Bulgarian troops should arrive, took the ropes down. There were five Bulgarian soldiers prisoners in the same place. I saw four of these shot in the garden of the school in daylight; the fifth begged hard for his life and was saved. We were now bound with this soldier in groups of four and were taken to the Bishop's palace. I had one hundred piastres in money, and of the others, one had £T2 and another £T14. We were taken before a priest, who was alone in a room. I think he was a bishop; the *evzones* took our money, and put it on the table before the priest, who put it in a drawer. We asked for water. They gave it us, but the *evzones* struck us in the face before the bishop. He asked us no questions, and we were taken to the school. The *evzones* beat us and mocked us with shouts of "hourrah!" (the Bulgarian cry). The gendarmes were taken to a room apart. In our room there were ten dead bodies; these were afterwards removed by Turkish porters. One of the gendarmes died this day from beating. We were stripped perfectly naked. Next day, Friday, July 11, forty-four new Bulgarian prisoners were brought in. [The witness, like all Balkan peasants, reckoned the dates from the nearest church festival.] About midday we heard cannon—perhaps twenty shots. Then we could see from the window that the town was in flames. Three soldiers wearing the Greek uniform came into our room, but one of them wore *vlach* trousers. They took four prisoners out to another room. We heard cries. The same three then came back with their hands and bayonets covered with blood; we tried but failed to get out by breaking the windows. I was taken out almost the last to a room full of dead bodies. The *vlach* struck me two blows on the head and two on the neck, and I fell. [We saw his wounds, the skull was deeply indented.] Another man fell on top of me and I lost consciousness. When I came to I heard rifle firing. Four men rose with me. Angel Dimov of Carlukavo is the only one I knew. We found water, which the butchers had used to wash their hands. We heard the Bulgarian cry "hourrah," went out, and found a Bulgarian soldier who got a mule for me. The whole town was on fire.

No. 21. EVIDENCE OF BLAGOI PETROV, *of Serres, mason, aged eighteen years.*

On July 10 four citizens of Serres, whom I knew, dressed in Greek uniform, took me to the schoolhouse prison. About one hundred others were there. We were beaten with the butts of their rifles and most of us had our hands tied to something, such as the pillars. An armed Greek civilian came in and said, "We must not kill these young lads, but we'll give them a beating." They insisted that I should stay to see my father killed; they even promised to give me my liberty at once if I would kill my father with my own hand. About one o'clock I saw him killed with five blows from the butt of a rifle; many others were killed at the same time. Five youths were released. The names of my father's murderers are, Teochar, a mechanic, and Athanasios Petrov, a tobacco worker.

No. 22. EVIDENCE OF DR. KLUGMANN, Russian civil doctor, employed at Serres in the special service organized by the Bulgarians to deal with the epidemic of cholera.

On going out to my work as usual at eight o'clock on Sunday morning July 6, I found all the houses shut and the people beginning to flee. A Bulgarian officer with two or three soldiers was in the street, with rifles presented, but they did not fire. Towards midday firing began and went on all day, but I can not say who was responsible. Monday was quiet. I went out on my balcony and saw a priest announcing to the people in the street, "Let any one who wants a gun go to the bishopric and get it." I saw them coming out armed, an hour later. Rifles were given out to Turks. Firing began soon afterwards and went on all day and night. On Tuesday morning some Greek *andartes* came to my house and arrested me. It was useless to explain that I was in the town to fight the cholera for the benefit of the whole population; I was taken to the bishop who, fortunately, spoke Russian, and eventually released me. I was again arrested on Thursday and taken by the bishop's orders to the Greek hospital. During all this time the Bulgarians up and down the town were being arrested. Another Bulgarian who was arrested at the same time as myself was beaten by the soldiers in my presence. On Thursday, while I was at the bishop's palace, about twenty-five Bulgarian prisoners were brought in before a commission composed of priests and civilians. As far as I could understand the proceedings they were condemned to death [the doctor knows little or no Greek, but thought he could guess the meaning of what went on]. I was removed with the bishop's consent to the Bulgarian hospital, where there was another Russian doctor, Laznev, and an assistant named Comarov. On Friday morning we saw the whole population fleeing in the direction of Nigrita. About eleven o'clock shots were fired from the hill behind our hospital, fourteen or fifteen in all. The firing went on for an hour. Toward midday everything was quiet. I then saw that the town was burning. In the afternoon many Greek soldiers entered the hospital and threatened to kill me. They stole everything in the hospital, including Dr. Laznev's watch. [NOTE.—Dr. Klugmann went on to give many details of the difficulties which he and his colleagues in the Bulgarian hospital met with from the Greek authorities.] I wish in conclusion to affirm my strong conviction that the Bulgarians can not have burnt Serres. I am unable to say how it was set on fire.

No. 23. EVIDENCE OF COMMANDANT IVAN KIRPIKOV.

On Thursday, July 10, while at Zurnovo, I received orders to march on Serres with my column, to look after the munitions which had been left in the town, to resume the administration, and to restore order. I understood this to mean that I was to stay in the town, if possible, unless driven out by superior force. I had a battalion and a half of infantry, one squadron of cavalry, and one battery of artillery. We marched throughout the night, and by six o'clock on Friday morning were within five or six kilometers of Serres. I met on the way two companies of the dismounted cavalry, who had been driven back from the town the day before by the insurgent population. I ascertained that the Greeks held three positions on the hills surrounding the town, and estimated from their fire that they must number at least 1,000 rifles. I used my artillery against each of their positions in succession, and our infantry was able eventually to capture all three positions. From the last hill above the town I saw the population fleeing from the town in all directions over the plain. The enemy's fire meanwhile continued from several houses, from an old tower, and from a little hill which was practically in the town. I sent a detachment to march down the principal street with orders to shout as they went that the people should keep calm and fear nothing. My men were fired upon from every house as they marched, and balls fell even where I was standing with the artillery. I then directed one of my guns against two big houses, from which the fire chiefly came. This had the effect of checking it. I then sent three patrols of ten men each to report if our depots were intact. They were fired upon.

I now noticed groups of people in three large masses in the plain, near the railway line. I could see with my glasses that they were all armed and were wearing the Greek peasant costume peculiar to certain villages which we regarded as the center of the Greek propaganda. I sent a squadron to the railway station, but it was stopped by hot fire from the station. I now realized that a counter attack was being prepared and decided to march through the town and give battle to the groups of men near the station. Meanwhile a big building exploded, presumably a magazine. I sent my patrol to see what it was, but they were again repulsed from the same big building. I ordered my patrol to localize the conflagration which had now begun in various places. The groups of peasants had now begun to advance on the town. We never reached the house that was blown up and my infantry were never able to penetrate far into the town because of the continual fire from the houses. As they marched, Moslems and Bulgarians began to join our men and to embrace them.

I now realized that the force opposed to me was much superior to my own, and my object now was to clear the plain and isolate the town. I ordered my guns to fire on the groups in the plain. The fire was now spreading all over the town. With my binoculars I could see large columns of the Greek regular army approaching from Orlov. I continued to use my guns in order to keep the groups dispersed. I then heard of another column of the regular army which was approaching from another direction. Realizing that I should be unable to face these, I sent patrols to our depots, which were in front of the governor's palace, with orders to blow them up if they found them intact. I then arranged to cover my retreat. Shells had begun to fall in the town from the Greek guns, and some of these fell on the hospital. The Greek vanguard with the townsmen attacked our rear guard. They shelled us steadily as we retreated, and some of their shells fell among refugees from the town who had fled to us.

In reply to a question whether he knew anything regarding the Austrian vice consul, the commander replied, that his patrols reported to him as follows:

> We met a person who said he was the Austrian vice consul; we took him and his family with us for his own protection, to ensure that neither the population nor the troops should molest him. We asked him if he preferred to come with us, or to stay in the town? He said he preferred to come with us. Later, when he saw that the Greek army was arriving he changed his mind and wished to go back to the town. This we allowed him to do.

Before leaving the town [continued the Commander] some Bulgarian civilians came to me and told me that about 250 Bulgarians had been imprisoned and massacred in the school house. The refugees who fled with us, told me that the explosion which we had heard, came from a Greek magazine of cartridges, which the Greeks themselves set on fire. The wind was blowing violently from east to west, and this house, which was in the east of the town, seems to have started the conflagration. I can not believe that our shells caused the fire. We have often tested this; they do not have the effect of setting houses on fire.

No. 24. EVIDENCE OF DOCTOR YANKOV, *Advocate and Counselor to the Governor of Serres.*

I left Serres on July 5, and heard later that a detachment was returning. I accompanied it on Friday morning, July 11. Our detachment fired two cannon shots against the enemy, who was outside the town towards the north. On entering the town it pursued the Greeks, who were not regulars but *andartes*. Towards half past eleven I saw flames in the town. I notified the commandant that we were causing loss to the state. He replied that our shells could not possibly be the cause of the conflagration. The cavalry then entered the town and I went with it, accompanied by Karagiosov and Orfaniev. On the invitation of a leading Mohammedan I entered his house and found there about one hundred Turks including many notables. We spoke of the conflagration, which was increasing, and went out with several Turks to attempt to check it. In the town I learnt that one of the two Bulgarian depots of rifles was already burning. The Greeks had set it on fire. The houses in Serres are closely packed together, the streets are very narrow, and the wind was violent, so that the fire spread rapidly. I looked for fire engines at the municipality, but failed to find them. I went to look elsewhere and then heard that the Bulgarian army was already in retreat. I met the vice consul of Austria, Mr. Zlatkos, a Greek, and with him about a hundred Greek refugees. He demanded my protection. I accompanied him back to the town, a distance of perhaps one hundred metres. Karagiosov disappeared and we have had no further news of him.

No. 25. EVIDENCE OF LAZAR TOMOV, a Bulgarian Teacher at Uskub.

Mr. Tomov was driven out of Uskub, and traveled to Serres during the early days of the second war. He passed through Doiran, saw that all the Bulgarian villages were burned, and near the village of Gavaliantsi saw the corpse of a little cripple girl, wounded and mutilated. She was about fourteen years of age. On July 11, he entered Serres with the Bulgarian army, but did not actually penetrate into the town. He saw heaps of corpses in the girls' school, and met four of the survivors of the massacre. One of them was the man Lazarov. The Bulgarian troops were moved to intense indignation, but there was no outbreak. He saw both Turks and Bulgarian villagers setting houses on fire. Turks were carrying sacks through the streets, from which he inferred that they were looting.

No. 26. EVIDENCE OF COMMANDANT MOUSTAKOV, Secretary to General Voulkov, Governor of Serres and Macedonia.

Referring to the documents published in the Greek pamphlet *Atrocités Bulgares*, p. 54, in which he is represented as proposing the arrest of a number of Greek notables, the commandant explained, that neither of the orders therein attributed to him is genuine. There was no reason why he, working in the same office as General Voulkov, should have addressed a written communication to him. The commandant produced the official register in which his orders were copied.

(1) The first order attributed to him bears an authentic number (No. 8265). An order with this number does exist and is entered in the register; but its contents are quite different from those of the document published in the pamphlet. (2) No order bearing the number 8391 exists.

[We examined the register, which fully bore out the commandant's statement. The numbers in the register were not consecutive, and no entry had been made corresponding to the number in the pamphlet].

Further, in reply to the statement made on p. 30 of this pamphlet that disguises and other compromising articles had been found by the Greeks in the governor's house, the Commandant stated (1) that no such articles had ever been in his possession and (2) that in any event they can not have been found, since the house, which belonged to Nechid-bey, had been burned before the entry of the Greeks.

In explanation of the circumstances which attended the evacuation of Serres, the Commandant stated that on Saturday, July 5, there was in the early morning a panic in the town, due to a rumor that the Greek army was approaching. The town was almost entirely deserted. The Bulgarian troops went out to reconnoitre; he himself went about calming the people. By his orders a squadron of dismounted cavalry marched through the town singing. It was fired on from the houses, and one soldier was killed and another wounded. This occurred about 5.30 p.m. Two men were arrested and probably killed. At 9 p.m. he left the town with General Voulkov. A detachment of about 200 men of the territorial army was left behind under Commandant Toplov; but in view of the danger of surprise attacks it passed the night outside the town and entered it again the next day, again retiring at nightfall. The Commandant returned on July 8, towards midday on a locomotive, with ten soldiers. He found Serres station surrounded by Greek *andartes* and skirmished with them till evening. He had asked for cannon, which arrived late; he remained in the neighborhood of Serres on the hills on July 9, but neither used his cannon nor entered the town. On July 11 took place the attack in force under Commandant Kirpikov. He himself had intended, if he had been able to enter the town, to burn the Bulgarian stores and depots of munitions which had been left behind. The larger force had no doubt the same orders.

With reference to the statement that prisoners were killed by the Bulgarians on leaving the town, the Commandant explained that headquarters were aware of a revolutionary movement among the Greeks of Serres; the Greeks had large quantities of arms. He had inquired of the commandant *de place* what measures had been taken to prevent an outbreak. The reply was that "this in no way concerned him." On July 1 there were five Greek notables under arrest at the prefecture. He failed to obtain any explanation as to what would be done to them. The idea was that by arresting these notables a revolution might be prevented. This was an absurdity, but he believes these men were in the end liberated.

On July 3 Mr. Arrington asked him to procure the release of his imprisoned porter (*cavass*). He explained that this was a matter which concerned the Commandant and not the Governor. He ascertained that two or three *cavass* belonging to the tobacco warehouses had been arrested because the rumor was in circulation that the famous Greek insurgent chief, Captain Doukas, was in the town disguised as the *cavass* of a tobacco warehouse. He gave orders before leaving Serres, that prisoners of all races including some thirty or forty Bulgarian *comitadjis* accused of crimes committed during the war should be released. The prisoners numbered about 105 men. The Greeks and Turks among them were persons of no importance. No soldiers were left at the prison, and its governor had fled. It is conceivable that the Bulgarian prisoners may have killed the Greek prisoners.

C. Events at Demir-Hissar

No. 27. Report of the General Commanding the Sixth Division of the Greek Army, *dated July 12.*

I have the honor to inform your Majesty that an officer of my staff sent to Demir-Hissar, reports as follows:

The Bulgarian captain of gendarmerie, Meligov (Velikov?) arrested the bishop, Mgr. Constantine, the priest Papastavrou, the notable Sapazacharizanou, and over one hundred other Greeks, who were imprisoned in the confines of the Bulgarian school. On July 7 and 8 the Bulgarian soldiers and gendarmes massacred them, and requisitioned Turkish peasants to bury them in the precincts of the school, outside the wall on the east side. An officer of my staff ordered the exhumation of the bodies in order to verify the facts. He found the heaped bodies of the victims at a depth of over two meters.

Further, officers and soldiers violated several girls; they even killed one, named Agatha Thomas, the daughter of a gardener, because she resisted them.

The shops of the town have been sacked and destroyed, with all the furniture of the houses of our countrymen, of whom some were saved by the Turks who sheltered them in their houses. The town in general presents a lamentable spectacle of destruction.

No. 27a. The report of the commission of Greek deputies which visited Demir-Hissar, contains the following additional details:

> The number of notables arrested was 104; eighty were at once killed by bayonet thrusts. Twenty-four others, by feigning death, survived, though seriously wounded. Among the victims are two women and two babies aged two and three years. * * * The bishop and three priests were killed by Captain Anghel Dimitriev Bostanov with his own hand. He first gouged out their eyes and cut off their hands. * * * All these atrocities were committed by the soldiers and noncommissioned officers of the Bulgarian regular army belonging to the Twelfth and Twenty-first regiments. * * *"

There follows an account of the search for arms at the bishop's palace, in which this statement occurs: "The soldiers knocked at the door, and as the bishop resisted, they broke it down." In describing the exhumation of the bodies, it is stated that only eight were actually exhumed. The corpse of the bishop was lying face downwards. The Commission have before it an official list of seventy-one persons killed and five wounded, and of others who have disappeared, making a total of 104. It includes one priest (not three), and is comprised largely of working men who can not have been "notable."

No. 28. In its issue of July 13/26, the official *Echo de Bulgarie* published the following statement:

As regards the acts of repression at Demir-Hissar, it is necessary to explain that the Greek population of this town, roused by agitators, revolted on July 8, when the Bulgarian troops withdrew. It pillaged the military magazines, the public buildings, and the Bulgarian houses, and massacred a number of soldiers who fell into its hands, as well as the sick and wounded of an ambulance train which arrived that day from Serres. The bodies of sixteen soldiers were found in the immediate neighborhood of the town; the exact number of those massacred in the town itself has never been exactly ascertained.

The rebels took up positions all around the town, whence on the following day a Bulgarian detachment coming from Serres in ignorance of what was going on, was obliged to dislodge them by force. On its entry into the town, it was met with a fusillade from other rebels concealed in the houses. Order was none the less promptly restored. Some individuals taken with arms in their hands were shot. An inquiry was held into the events of the previous day. The murderers and the instigators of the movement were arrested, and some of them were executed. It was established that the Greek prelate was the chief leader, and that he had set the example to the rebels by himself firing the first shots from his window against soldiers who were passing his house. Further, a revolver was found in his pocket, with several of its cartridges used.

To explain the severities employed in restoring order at Demir-Hissar, it must be added that on the same day, July 9, Greek troops burned the Bulgarian villages in the neighborhood of Demir-Hissar, notably Gorni-Poroi, Dolni-Porio, Starochevo and Kechislik.

28a. The following supplementary narrative from Bulgarian official sources has been communicated to us:

On July 5, as our troops were withdrawing towards the defile of Rupel, a panic occurred in Demir-Hissar, and some shots were fired in the Greek quarter. There were, however, no casualties, and order was speedily restored by the civil administration, which remained in the town (see No. 46). From July 5 to July 9 the town was relatively calm.

Troops retreating on Djumaia were continually passing through it, and the bakeries were working to supply our troops at Rupel. During these days Major Stephanov of the general staff of the second army passed twice through the town; he states that no one in the town complained of ill treatment by our troops or officials. Meanwhile, the Greek army advancing along the Salonica-Serres road toward the bridge over the Struma, at Orliak, was driving the fugitive population before it (see Nos. 33 and 35). On July 7, the Greek artillery on the right bank near the burned bridge of Orliak, fired on the fugitives and on the villages in the plain of the Struma (see Greek soldiers' letters, No. 51), and this increased the stream of fugitives, some of whom passed through the town itself. The panic in Demir-Hissar now became irresistible, and the administration abandoned it. The Greek population thus became the master of the town, and rushed through the streets with the Greek flag, firing on our wounded soldiers, our baggage and ambulance trains, and on the fugitive population. A body of from 120 to 150 *andartes* under the command of a Greek officer arrived in the town, from the direction of the plain. At this moment the Greek bishop went into the streets at the head of about twenty armed Greeks, and gave the order to fall upon all Bulgarians. Fighting followed in the town. Two Bulgarian gendarmes who were guarding our military stores were killed; all the bakers were slaughtered at their ovens; many of our wounded were killed, and a large number of the peasant fugitives, including women and children. The street fighting, the massacres and general disorder continued all day, and many were killed on both sides. The Greek bishop was probably killed during this fighting. The Greek army entered Demir-Hissar in the evening of this day. What was left of the Bulgarian population in the town fled to the mountains, pursued by the Greek troops and armed civilians, who massacred it whenever they overtook it.

There was no Bulgarian officer at Demir-Hissar after the evening of July 10, when the administration left the town.

The Ministry of War states that Lieutenant Velikov was not there. No such name as Captain Anghel Dimitriev Bostanov is to be found in the registers of the active or reserve army. It is not for the first time that this has happened. More than once in the telegrams of General Dousmanis, Generals Kovatchev and Voulkov are mentioned as being in the neighborhood of Demir-Hissar or Serres, when in fact they were either opposing the Serbs or were at Dubnitsa.

More than 250 wounded Bulgarian soldiers and peasants fleeing from Kukush, Doiran and Lagadina were killed at Demir-Hissar.

APPENDIX C

Documents Relating to Chapter II

THE BULGARIAN PEASANT AND THE GREEK ARMY

No. 29. King Constantine's Telegram. *July 12, 1913.*

The general commanding the Sixth Division informs me that Bulgarian soldiers under the command of a captain of gendarmes gathered in the yard of the school house at Demir-Hissar over one hundred notables of the town, the archbishop and two priests, and massacred them all. The headquarters staff ordered the exhumation of the bodies, with the result that the crime has been established. Further, Bulgarian soldiers violated young girls and massacred those who resisted them. Protest in my name to the representatives of the powers and to the whole civilized world against these abominations, and declare that to my great regret I shall find myself obliged to proceed to reprisals, in order to inspire their authors with a salutary fear, and to cause them to reflect before committing similar atrocities. The Bulgarians have surpassed all the horrors perpetrated by their barbarous hordes in the past, thus proving that they have not the right to be classed among civilized peoples.

(Signed)   Constantine, *King.*

The above telegram was sent to the representatives of Greece in the European capitals.

No. 30. Evidence of Father Joseph Radanov, *of Kukush.*

On July 2 he could distinctly see from Kukush that the surrounding villages were on fire, Salamanli among others. Fields of corn and stacks of reaped corn had been set on fire even behind the Greek positions. The Greeks moreover had fired upon the reapers who had gone to work in the early morning in their fields. The refugees from the neighboring villages began to arrive upon the heights called Kara-Bunar about a mile away, and were there bombarded by artillery.

Next day (July 3) the battle approached the town, but the Bulgarians retained their position. About midday the Greeks began to bombard Kukush, but when I left no house had taken fire.

No. 31. Father Jean Chikitchev.

I took refuge after midday on July 3 with Father Michel and meant to stay with him. I saw the shells falling upon the sisters' orphanage. I saw the hospital struck by a shell. There were at this time no Bulgarian troops in the town, although they were in their positions in front of it. The town was unfortified. The bombardment seemed to be systematic. It could not be explained as a mistake incidental to the finding of the range. Quite forty shells fell not far from the orphanage and three or possibly four houses were set on fire. At this point I left the town and fled with the refugees. Next night it looked as if the whole plain were burning.

Note.—Both the above witnesses are priests of the Catholic Uniate Church. (See also 63a.)

No. 32. Mr. C. [*the name may not be published*] a Catholic resident in the village of Todoraki near Kukush, states than on July 6 the Greek commandant of Kukush arrived accompanied by thirty infantrymen and eighty armed Turks. He was bound and left exposed to the full sun without food or water from 7 a.m. until 3 p.m. His house was pillaged, and 200 francs taken with all his personal property. On being released he learnt from the villagers that they had lost in all £T300 during the pillage. Two men were beaten and twelve were bound and sent down to prison in Salonica. The women were not maltreated.

No. 33. Peter Shapov, *of Zarovo near Langaza, a shepherd.*
He was taking his sheep and goats on the road to Demir-Hissar when Greek cavalry overtook the refugees on the edge of the town and began to slash out with their sabres to left and right. They took 600 goats belonging to himself and his two brothers. One of his brothers was wounded by a cavalryman and died afterwards at the Bulgarian frontier. The Bulgarian army was quite half an hour's walk away. There were no Bulgarian troops near them.

No. 34. Mate, *Wife of Petro of Bogoroditsa, near Langaza.*
I saw the Greek cavalrymen when they entered our village. I fled and in my haste was obliged to leave a baby of eighteen months behind in the village in order to flee with this one which I have with me, a child of three. I saw our village in flames. I want my child.

No. 35. Elisava, *Wife of Georghi of Zarovo, near Langaza.*
We all fled when the shells began to fall in our village and got safely to Demir-Hissar. Then I heard people saying the Greek cavalry are coming. There was a panic; children fell on the ground and horsemen rode over them. I lost my children, save one whom I was able to carry. My husband had two others with him. I do not know what has become of him, and have not seen him since that day.

No. 36. Mito Kolev, *a boy of fourteen from the village of Gavaliantsi, near Kukush.*
On Wednesday, July 2, after the fighting at Kukush, the peasants fled from our village except a few old people. I fled with the rest and reached Kilindir. On Thursday I went back three hours' walk to our village to collect our beasts and find my mother. I found her and was going along the road back to Kilindir with others. As we were leaving our village I saw a Greek cavalryman in uniform on horseback. He fired his rifle at me and missed. I threw myself on the road, pretending to be dead. He then shot my mother in the breast and I heard her say as she fell beside me, "Mito, are you alive?" and that was the last word she spoke. Another boy came up and ran away, when he saw what had happened. The soldier pursued him, shot him, and then killed him with his sword without dismounting. Then I saw a little cripple girl named Kata Gosheva, who was in front of us hiding in a ravine. The soldier went after her, but I do not know whether he killed her. He then came back, passed us and met other cavalrymen. A certain miller of the village named Kaliu, who could speak both Greek and Bulgarian, then came up and lifted me up. The miller had a Mauser rifle. He hid in the ravine when he saw that the two troopers were hurrying back and I hid in some hay. I heard the horses' hoofs going towards the miller. They talked, and I suppose he must have surrendered. He then came back to where I was and the miller said, "Mito, Mito, come out or the cavalry will kill you." So I came out. We both then went to the school house where we found other Greek troopers. I was quite sure they were Greeks because I recognized the uniform.

They used to come to our village sometimes before the war broke out. They questioned the miller in Greek and wrote something and gave it to him. The miller then said, "Let's go to the mill. It is about fifteen minutes from the village." We stayed there for an hour. In the meantime, three other Greek troopers came up from another direction. The miller went to meet them and showed them his piece of paper. The miller told me to gather straw, and he did the same. The troopers set fire to it so as to burn down the mill. [In reply to a question, Mito explained that the mill was not the miller's personal property. It belonged to the village community, which employed him.] The miller took away his mattress on his horse, which was at the mill. The troopers then left us and went to the village. We followed and the miller said to me, "We had better ask them for another bit of paper so that they will let us go to Salonica." Then some cartridges which had been left behind began to explode in the mill. This brought up other troopers at a gallop. They fired on us. The miller said something to them in Greek, showed them the paper and they chatted. [Mito only speaks Bulgarian.] I saw them looking at me. Then one of them drew his revolver and fired. The ball went through my clothes without wounding me. I fell down, pretending to be dead. He fired again and this time the ball went in at my back and came out at my breast. Then, still on horseback, he struck me on the shoulder with his sabre and the same blow wounded my finger. [Mito lay down and showed exactly how it happened. He still had the scars of all these wounds. The position was perfectly possible.] Blood was flowing from my mouth. I hid in the corn all the rest of the day and saw the village take fire in three places. The cavalry then gathered together and then rode off. I was in pain, but managed to walk away. I met two Bulgarian neighbors on my way and one of them took me in his cart to Doiran. There I met my father and had my wounds dressed in the military hospital. We fled through the mountains, and I was taken to the hospital in Sofia.

No. 37. Vladimir Georghiev, of Dragomirtsi, near Kukush.

I left the village when the war began and afterwards went back to find some of my property. I saw the Greek cavalry, perhaps a whole regiment of them. There were ten in our village with officers. I managed to hide in some reeds near the village. I saw Gavaliantsi burning. About 2 o'clock eight cavalrymen passed and burned the mill. They then went into the village to finish the burning. I also saw our own village Dragomirtsi burning, and heard two or three shots fired. Toward 6 o'clock I fled and on my way met Mito Kolev, who was wounded and could hardly walk. Mito said he could not ride, so it was no use to offer him my beast. I left him and went on. (See also 63d.)

No. 38. Christo Andonov, of Gavaliantsi.

He was beaten by the Greek soldiers. He saw the mother of Mito Kolev near the Greek cavalrymen and supposes she must have been killed. He did not see what happened very distinctly as he was at considerable distance. He saw the boy named Georghi Tassev killed with a sabre thrust by a trooper who was one of five. Some way off Kata Gosheva, the lame girl, was killed with a sword. This he saw quite distinctly. He was hidden in the ravine at the time.

Note.—These two witnesses were in a crowd of refugees at Samakov. In passing through the market place we inquired whether anyone present came from the village of Gavaliantsi. They stepped forward and told the above stories when asked to explain what happened to them after the battle of Kukush. See also the evidence of Lazar Tomov, No. 25.

The Affair of Akangeli

No. 39. Mr. G., a Catholic inhabitant of Kukush, interviewed at Salonica, made the following statement:

"After fleeing from Kukush, I arrived at Akangeli with some thousands of refugees from all the surrounding villages. It is close to the station of Doiran. Between two and three p.m. on Sunday afternoon (July 6) the Greek cavalry arrived, possibly 300 of them, with officers. The inhabitants went out to meet them with white flags and the priest at their head. About 120 people of the village were told off to look after the cavalry horses. These people disappeared and no trace could be found of them next day. That evening the women, both natives and refugees, were all violated, often repeatedly. The soldiers pillaged and killed, but would spare a man's life for five piastres or so. Probably fifty inhabitants of Akangeli were killed. I and another man were bound together by the cavalry. Six piastres and a watch were taken from me and my life was spared, but my companion was killed at my side. Women and girls were stripped and searched to find money. I saw many cases of violation myself. It was done more or less publicly, sometimes in the houses but sometimes in the fields and on the roads. I saw the village burnt and witnessed another case of the murder of a peasant."

In reply to questions he stated that he saw the corpses of the fifty inhabitants after they had been killed. Some were shot and some were bayoneted. Again in reply to a question he was certain there was no conflict in the neighborhood and no shots were fired, but the villagers were told to collect their rifles and surrender them. They did so and one went off accidentally in the hands of an officer who was breaking it. He was wounded, and the soldiers at once killed a boy who was standing near. Turks joined with Greeks in the pillage and so did the infantry, which arrived next day.

No. 40. GEORGHI CHARISANOV, of Selo-Surlevo.

He took refuge in Akangeli. A squadron of Greek cavalry arrived on Sunday afternoon, gathered the refugees together and demanded arms, telling them not to fear. They then began to beat and rob. The Turks who followed them assisted in the pillage. On Monday, Greek infantry came and joined in sacking the village. Anyone who resisted was killed. There was a general panic and everyone fled who could. There were refugees from quite fifteen villages in the place. The soldiers violated women all the time, even little children. The soldiers went round from house to house on Sunday night and ordered the people to open the doors. They had a native of the village with them in order to give confidence to the people. Women were searched for money. About one hundred men were taken to look after the horses of the cavalry and these disappeared. On Monday the village was burned. We had given ourselves up quite voluntarily to the cavalry and welcomed them, and had surrendered about one hundred rifles. There was no excuse for what the soldiers did.

No. 41. MITO ILIEV, a butcher of Akangeli.

I was there when the Greek army arrived on Sunday afternoon towards four o'clock. Reckoning from St. Peter's day it must have been July 6. The village was filled with refugees from Kukush district, perhaps 4,000 altogether. The people went out to meet the cavalry by each of three roads. There were about 400 of them. We made a white flag and showed the Greek colors. Everything went quietly at first. The commandant asked for the mayor, and inquired in Turkish whether he would surrender and give up the arms of the village. We fetched our rifles (generally old Martinis) and piled them on a cart. The soldiers called for bread and cheese which were brought out. They then said, "Who is the butcher here, that he may kill sheep for us." I was chosen and troopers went with me to fetch and kill thirty sheep. Meanwhile the soldiers began to demand money from everybody. I saw a young man, a refugee from another village, whose name I do not know, killed with a sword because he had nothing. I was told that a boy of fifteen was killed about this time, but did not see it. The people were now gathered together in the square of the village and told to sit down. This I witnessed. The Greek commandant then came and asked, "Where do all these people come from?" Then he separated the men of Akangeli from the rest to the number of about sixty and sent them to a wood called Chaluk. Nothing more was ever heard of them. I went on cooking the sheep. Then the soldiers began to violate all the women. I heard cries going on all night, especially about 11 o'clock. The soldiers were not drunk, and they had officers with them. I stayed all night at my oven, and saw the two daughters-in-law of Stovan Popovali violated in front of me, a few paces away by three soldiers. Next morning, when we talked together in the village, I heard of many other violations. On Monday the Greek infantry arrived, seized me and told me to lead them to Dourbali. I led them there, and as I went off Akangeli began to blaze. I heard cries and rifle shots on all hands. When I got to Dourbali I fled to Atli, half an hour away, and hid in the house of my partner Saduk, a Turk. I sent Saduk to see what had become of my wife and family. He came back and said that everyone was being killed in the village, that he had seen many corpses, that my house was not burnt, but that there were three dead bodies in front of it. Saduk advised me to flee, and I did so. The Turks in our own village (Akangeli) behaved well, but strangers from other Turkish villages came and joined in the pillage.

In reply to questions the witness stated that an officer was accidentally wounded in the arm while examining one of the revolvers which had been given up. This he saw personally, but denied that it explains the killing of the young man who was the first to be killed with a sword. That happened some distance away.

No. 42. Stoyan Stoyev, aged 18, of Akangeli.

This witness, at Dubnitsa, in reply to a question addressed to the group of refugees, whether any of those present came from this village or had passed through it in their flight, related in outline almost exactly the same story as the last witness, including the details about the conversation between the commandant and the mayor. The pillage, he said, began while the arms were being gathered. A rifle went off accidentally, and an officer was wounded, while the Greek soldier was emptying it. This he saw from a distance of about forty meters. Then the cavalry drew their swords and some people were killed, certainly two youths. At this point he hid and saw little more. He heard from a friend of his, a youth who came running out of the house of Dine Popov, that his wife was being violated. He then fled to a Turkish village. (See also 63b.)

No. 43. Anastasia Pavlova, a widow of Ghevgheli.

Shortly before the outbreak of the second war I was staying with my daughter, a Bulgarian school teacher in the village of Boinitsa. A Greek lady came from Salonica, and distributed money and uniforms to the Turks of the place some six or eight days before the outbreak of the second war. She also called the Bulgarians of the village together, and told them that they must not imagine that this village would belong to Bulgaria. She summoned the Bulgarian priest, and asked him if he would become a Greek. He replied, "We are all Bulgarians and Bulgarians we will remain." There were some Greek officers with this lady who caught the priest by the beard. Then the men who were standing by, to the number of about fifty, had their hands bound behind their backs, and were beaten by the soldiers. They were told that they must sign a written statement that they would become Greeks. When they refused to do this they were all taken to Salonica. When the men were gone, the soldiers began to violate the women of the place, three soldiers usually to one girl. [She named several cases which she witnessed.] The soldiers came in due course to my house and asked where my daughter was. I said she was ill and had gone to Ghevgheli. They insisted that I should bring her to them. The Greek teacher of the village, Christo Poparov, who was with the soldiers, was the most offensive of them all.

They threatened to kill me if I would not produce her. The soldiers then came into the room and beat me with the butts of their rifles and I fell. "Now," they said, "you belong to the Greeks, your house and everything in it," and they sacked the house. Then sixteen soldiers came and again called for my daughter, and since they could not find her they used me instead. I was imprisoned in my own house and never left alone. Four days before the war I was allowed to go to Ghevgheli by rail with two soldiers to fetch my daughter. She was really in the village of Djavato. At Ghevgheli, the soldiers gave me permission to go alone to the village to fetch her. Outside the village I met five Greek soldiers, who greeted me civilly and asked for the news. Suddenly they fired a rifle and called out, "Stop, old woman." They then fired six shots to frighten me. I hurried on and got into the village just before the soldiers. They bound my hands, began to beat me, undressed me, and flung me down on the ground. Some Servian soldiers were in the village and interfered with the Greeks and saved my life. My daughter was hidden in the village and she saw what was happening to me and came running out to give herself up, in order to save her mother. She made a speech to the soldiers and said, "Brothers, when we have worked so long together as allies, why do you kill my mother?" The soldiers only answered, that they would kill her too. I then showed them the passport which had been given to me at Boinitsa. I can not read Greek and did not know what was on it. It seems that what was written there was "This is a mother who is to go and find her daughter and bring her back to us." The Greek soldiers then saw that it was my daughter, and not I, who was wanted and my daughter cried, "Now I am lost." The soldiers offered me the choice of staying in the village or going with my daughter to Ghevgheli. I begged that they would leave us alone together where we were until the morning, and to this they agreed. In the night I fled with my daughter, who disguised herself in boy's clothes, to a place two hours away which was occupied by Bulgarian soldiers. I then went myself to Ghevgheli and immediately afterwards, the second war broke out. The Bulgarians took the town and then retired from it, and the Greeks entered it. The moment they came in they began killing people indiscriminately in the street. One man named Anton Bakharji was killed before my eyes. I also saw a Greek woman named Helena kill a rich Bulgarian named Hadji Tano, with her revolver. Another, whose name I do not know, was wounded by a soldier. A panic followed in the town and a general flight. Outside the town I met a number of Greek soldiers who had with them sixteen Bulgarian girls as their prisoners. All of them were crying, several of them were undressed, and some were covered with blood. The soldiers were so much occupied with these girls that they did not interfere with us, and allowed us to flee past them. As we crossed the bridge over the Vardar, we saw little children who had been abandoned and one girl lying as if dead on the ground. The cavalry were coming up behind us. There was no time to help. A long way off a battle was going on and we could hear the cannon, but nobody fired upon us. For eight days we fled to Bulgaria and many died on the way. The Bulgarian soldiers gave us bread. I found my daughter at Samakov. My one consolation is that I saved her honor.

No. 44. ATHANAS IVANOV, *of Kirtchevo, near Demir-Hissar.*
Our village is purely Bulgarian and consists of 190 houses. I am a shepherd and look after the sheep of the village. When the Greek army approached, most of the other villagers fled, but I was late in going and remained behind to see that my family had all got safely away. On July 16, while my wife was gathering her belongings, the Greek soldiers arrived. Some of them told a young woman, a relative of ours, who was in front of the house, to go and find bread for them. Her husband had already been seized. I went to look for her. I found a sentinel with a fixed bayonet in front of her house. I rushed past him, and found that she had just been violated by a soldier, while another stood over her with his bayonet, and then the second soldier also violated her. She had had a baby only

three days before. I then met Peniu Penev, who said to me, "You can speak Greek. All our wives are being violated; come and talk to the soldiers." I entered the courtyard of a house and saw three women on the ground who were being violated. One was wounded in the leg and another in the arm. [We took the names, but see no object in publishing them.] This was about three p.m. Many other women were there, crying. I then went out in fear, and when I had gone some distance, saw that the village was burning. I met a woman trying to put out the fire with water. The soldiers came up and violated her. I saw six soldiers trying to violate a young girl. Another soldier protested, but they threatened him with their bayonets. A sergeant then told this man to stop interfering and ordered him to arrest me and take me to the officers, who were at a place some half an hour's distance from the village. [In reply to questions, the witness stated that two cavalry officers were in the village, but were not in the courtyard, where most of the violations were going on. There were, however, non-commissioned officers among the infantry in the village.] When I got to the camp and was brought before the officers, the officers said, "Take him away and fling him into the flames." On my way back to the village, I met nine other villagers and saw them all killed with the bayonet. Their names were Ivan Michailov, Angel Dourov, Pavlo Zivantikov, Ilio Piliouv, Peniu Penev, Peniu Christev, Athanas Belcov, Thodor Kandjilov, Gafio Demetrev. I escaped at the moment by saying I was a Greek, when the soldiers asked, "What kind of creatures are these?" I can speak a little Greek. At dusk I managed to run away. They fired but missed me. I know nothing of what happened to my wife, but my children are saved. (See also Nos. 59–62.)

No. 45. A Woman from Ijilar, near Kukush, seen at Salonica. Name suppressed.

Everything in our village was plundered and burnt including the school and the church. All this was done by Greek soldiers of the regular army. The inhabitants mostly disappeared. Soldiers kept sending for peasants to supply them with sheep. Four would go and never return, and so on at short intervals until hardly anyone was left. "What am I to do now? I have nothing left but the clothes I wear."

No. 46. Anton Michailov and Demetri Gheorghiev, of German, near Demir-Hissar. (See also Nos. 59–62.)

On July 5 (Saturday), we went to the market at Demir-Hissar. A panic presently took place. Everybody said that the Greek cavalry was coming. We went up to a height from which the plain was visible. We could see no cavalry, but a lot of refugees coming from the other direction, from Barakli Djumaia. The Greeks of German, when the town was cleared, began to pillage the Bulgarian shops. They armed themselves and distributed arms to the Turks. We found the corpses of two Bulgarian soldiers in the garden of Doctor Christoteles. The refugees whom we met from the country all said that the Greeks were everywhere killing and burning; so we returned to our village which was still intact, gathered our things together and fled.

Some of the villagers, however, remained in German. Some days after we had left, Greeks and Turks arrived together and began to pillage, burn and kill. We believe that 180 men, women and children were killed. German had 100 houses, and about half the population remained. We heard of the fate of the others from a young man named Demitri Gheorghiev [not to be confused with our witness of the same name], who told us that the people were gathered together by the Greeks and Turks, the men in the church and the women in the house of Papa Georghi. Some of the men tried to escape from the church, but were all shot at once. This was a signal for the massacre. The men were first searched and robbed, and then killed. Young Demetri jumped from the window of the church and had the good sense to lie down as if he were dead when he was shot at. He told us that some insurgents (*andartes*) had arrived from Athens and organized everything. There is only one other survivor of the massacre, namely, Papa Georghi.

NOTE. We made a uniform rule of refusing to allow witnesses to give us any information at second hand, but in this instance (and also in No. 50) since the alleged massacre had been so complete the circumstances seemed exceptional.

No. 47. ANTON SOTIROV, *a Priest from the village of Kalendra near Serres,* stated that Greek regulars and Turks came and burnt the Bulgarian houses at their village and killed an old man, the only one of the inhabitants who remained behind. This he saw from some little distance.

No. 48. GEORGHI DIMITRIEV, *of Drenovo near Serres,* stated that his village was burnt by Greek infantry on a Tuesday about noon. He saw an old women named Helena Temelcova, aged about 80, shot and then beheaded by a Greek soldier. He was hidden behind some stones on rising ground and shortly afterward managed to flee. He saw the village burnt by the Greeks.

No. 49. MR. V. *Seen at Salonica. Name suppressed.* Was made prisoner by the Greeks at Pancherovo. He speaks Greek well and pretended to be a Greek and was released. He saw three men of the village killed, apparently for motives of robbery. Their names were Angel Michail, Athanas Bateto, and the latter's son. Athanas had £T21. The peasants of this village had gone out to meet the troops with a white flag. This occurred on July 23. Eleven prisoners, who were taken at the same time as himself, were all killed on the hillside in the Kresna pass. These were armed men.

No. 50. NICOLA TEMELCOV, *of Melnik, formerly a teacher, now a merchant.*
Between July 11 and July 16, last, all the Bulgarian inhabitants of the Melnik district fled to Old Bulgaria, and he went with them, but had recently visited Melnik. In the village of Sklava, as he passed through it, all the women were gathered by the Greek soldiers in the house of Mito Constantinov, and the women were distributed among thirty soldiers. One girl of eighteen named Matsa Anton Mancheva resisted stoutly and offered money to the amount of £T60. The Greeks took her money and still attempted to violate her. She resisted and was killed. Melnik has not been burnt, with the exception of the officers' club, the hotel and the post office. The Greek houses are empty and the furniture gone. His father and mother remained in the town and told him their story. The Greeks said to them, "We do not wish to have bears living in our country. We want men." By "bears" they meant the Bulgarians. The officers took everything belonging to the witness on the pretense that he had fled. They demanded produce belonging to his father to the amount of 18 napoleons. They then took him out to his farm at Orman-Tchiflik and threatened him with death. He paid £T180 for his life and was taken back to Melnik. All this was done by officers. They took quantities of wheat, rice and barley from his father's farm and also the buffaloes. The order was given that everything and everybody must be cleared out of Melnik and go to Demir-Hissar, and the government put both automobiles and wagons at the disposal of the Greek inhabitants for this journey. Those who were unwilling to go were beaten. This his father related to him. His father, an old man, has since died from exhaustion and mental worry.

No. 51. EXTRACTS FROM LETTERS OF GREEK SOLDIERS *found in the mail of the nineteenth regiment of the Greek seventh division, captured by the Bulgarians in the region of Razlog.*

(*1*)   RHODOPE, 11th July, 1913.
This war has been very painful. We have burnt all the villages abandoned by the Bulgarians. They burn the Greek villages and we the Bulgarian. They massacre, we massacre,

and against all those of that dishonest nation, who fell into our hands, the Mannlicher rifle has done its work. Of the 1,200 prisoners we took at Nigrita, only forty-one remain in the prisons, and everywhere we have been, we have not left a single root of this race.

> I embrace you tenderly, also
> your brother and your wife
> SPILIOTOPOULOS PHILIPPOS.

(2) Mr. Panaghi Leventi,
Doctor
Aliverion
Eubœa.

I also enclose herewith, the letter of congratulation from my commandant, Mr. Contoghiri in which he praises my squadron, which on the occasion of the short stay of a few days of our division, received the order at five o'clock, to march to the north of Serres. During the march, we engaged in a fight with the Bulgarian *comitadjis,* whom we dispersed, after having killed the greater part. We burnt the two villages of Doutlii and Banitza, the homes of the formidable *comitadjis,* and passed everything through the fire, sparing only the women, the children, the old people, and the churches. All this was done without pity or mercy, executed with a cruel heart, and with a condemnation still more cruel.

Merocostenitza, 12th July, 1913.
The outposts of the Army.

> Love to you and also the others.
> (signature unreadable)
> sergeant.

(3) Mr. Sotir Panaïoannou,
in the village of Vitziano, parish Ithicou
Tricala de Thessalie.
River Nesto, 12th July, 1913.

Here at Vrondou (Brodi) I took five Bulgarians and a girl from Serres. We shut them up in a prison and kept them there. The girl was killed and the Bulgarians also suffered. We picked out their eyes while they were still alive.

> Yours affectionately: COSTI.

(4) Bulgarian Frontier, 11th July, 1913.
DEAR BROTHER JOANI:

Here is where the *archicomitadjis* live. We have massacred them all. And the places we have passed will remain in my memory forever.

> SER. CLÉTANIS.

(5) RHODOPE, Bulgarian Frontier,
11th July, 1913.
BROTHER MITZO:

And from Serres to the frontier, we have burnt all the Bulgarian villages.   .   .   .

My address remains the same: 7th Division, 19th Regt.; 12 Battalion at Rhodope.

> JOAN CHRISTO TSIGARIDIS.

(6) NESTOS, 13th July, 1913.
Village Bansta,

If you want to know about the parts where we are marching, all are Bulgarian villages, and everyone has fled. Those who remain are "eaten" by the Mannlicher rifle and we have also burnt a few villages. The Bulgarians suffered the same fate at the hands of the Servians.

S. Nakis.

(7) In the desert, 12th July, 1913.
. . . in Bulgarian territory, we are beating the Bulgarians who are continually retreating, and we are on the point of going to Sofia. We enraged them by burning the villages, and now and again when we found one or two, we killed them like sparrows

Your brother George (name unreadable)
I am writing you in haste.

(8) Zissis Coutoumas to Nicolas Coutoumas.
With the present I give you some news about the war that we have made against the Bulgarians. We have beaten them and have reached the Turkish-Bulgarian frontier. They fled into Bulgaria and we massacred those who remained. Further, we have burnt the villages. Not a single Bulgarian has been left. God only knows what will come of it. I have nothing more to write you. I remain, your Son Zissis Coutoumas. Many compliments from Thimios. He is well as also the other young men here.
12th July, 1913.

(9) M. Zaharia Kalivanis,
Erfos—Milipotamos,
Rethimo, Crete.
Rhodope, 13th July, 1913.

Seal
of the Commandant of
Public Safety, Salonica
We burn all the Bulgarian villages that we occupy, and kill all the Bulgarians that fall into our hands. We have taken Nevrocop and were well received by the Turks, many of whom came to our ranks to fight against the Bulgarians. Our army is in touch with the Servian and Roumanian armies, who are 32 kilometers from Sofia. With regard to ourselves we are near the ancient frontier.

S. Z. Kaliyanis.

(10) July 15th, 1913.
My Brother Sotir:
Thanks to God, I am well at the moment of writing you. We are at present on the Bulgarian-Thracian frontier. As far as the war is concerned, I can not tell you anything about the situation and what takes place. The things that happen are such that have never occurred since the days of Jesus Christ. The Greek army sets fire to all the villages where there are Bulgarians and massacres all it meets. It is impossible to describe what happens. God knows where this will end. The time of . . . has come for us to start eating one another.

Love from your brother Panaghis Beglikis.
I am writing you in haste.

(11) Bulgarian Frontier,
12/VII/1913.

Everywhere we pass, not even the cats escape. We have burnt all the Bulgarian villages that we have traversed. I can not describe it to you any better.
Your loving brother
Georges (corporal).

My address is as follows:
    To Corporal
    Sterghiou George,
12th Squadron, 3d Battalion, 19th Regt.
    7th Division—if away, send on.

(*12*)   RHODOPE, 13th July, 1913.
MY DEAR LEONIDAS:

Keep well, as I am. That is what I wish you. I received your letter, which gave me great pleasure. I also received one from Aristides, who is well, and writes that he has also been enrolled, which pains me, because my sufferings are such that could not be consoled by tears, because everything is lost, because you can not imagine what takes place in a war. Villages are burnt, and also men, and we ourselves set fire and do worse than the Bulgarians.

                        Your affectionate brother,
                                            THOMAS ZAPANTIOTIS.

(*13*)   Mr. Démetrios Chr. Tsigarida
    For the Greek Army,   at Mexiata
    as souvenir of the   Hypati—Phtiotis.
    Turco-Bulgarian war.   COPRIVA (?), 11th July, 1913.

            —
        Seal
    of the Commandant
    of the 19th' Regt.

            —

I was given 16 prisoners to take to the division and I only arrived with 2. The others were killed in the darkness, massacred by me.

                        NICO THÉOPHILATOS.

(*14*)   IN BULGARIA, 13th July, 1913.

What a cruel war is taking place with the Bulgarians. We have burnt everything belonging to them, villages and men. That is to say, we massacre the Bulgarians. How cruel! The country is inundated with Bulgarians. If you ask how many young Greeks have perished, the number exceeds 10,000 men.

                        Your Son, TSANTILAS NICOLAOS.

P. S. Write me about the enrolments that are taking place. They are surely on the point of enlisting old men. Curses on Venizelos.

(*15*)   To Georgi D. Karka (Soldier)
            First Section of the Sanitary Corps, 9th Division.
                                        Arghirocastro,
                                            Epirus.
The River Nestor,
    12th July, 1913.
DEAR BROTHER GEORGI:

Thank God I am quite well after coming through these five engagements. Let me tell you that our division has reached the river Nestor, that is to say, the old Bulgarian Frontier, and the Royal Army has passed this frontier. By the King's orders we are setting fire to all the Bulgarian villages, because the Bulgarians burned the beautiful town

Serres, also Nigrita and a lot of Greek villages. We have turned out much crueller than the Bulgars—we violated every girl we met. Our division took 18 pieces of artillery in good condition and two worn out pieces, altogether 20 cannon and 4 machine guns. It is impossible to describe how the Bulgars went to pieces and ran away. We are all well, except that K. Kalourioti was wounded at Nigrita and Evang the Macedonian got a bayonet wound while on outpost duty, but both are slight cases. Remember me to our countrymen and friends, although after coming through so much, thank God I am not afraid of the Bulgars. I have taken what I had a right to after all they did to us at Panghaion.

My greeting to you,

N. ZERVAS.

(Some illegible words follow.)

(*16*)

M. Aristidi Thanassia,
Kamniati.
Commune of Athanamow,
Trikala,
Thessaly.

14 July, 1913.

DEAR COUSIN:

I have received your letter of the 1st and I am very glad that you are well, as, after all, so are we up to now. Let me tell you, Aristidi, all we are going through during this Bulgarian War. Night and day we press on right into Bulgarian territory and at any moment we engage in a fight; but the man who gets through will be a hero for his country. My dear cousin, here we are burning villages and killing Bulgarians, women and children. Let me tell you, too, that cousin G. Kiritzis has a slight wound in his foot and that all the rest of us, friends and relations are very well including our son-in-law Yani. Give my greeting to your father and mother and your whole household, as well as my cousin Olga.

That is all I have to say,

With a hearty hug. Your brother,

ANASTASE ATH. PATROS.

(*17*)

M. George P. Soumbli,
Megali Anastassova,
Alagonia, Calamas.

Rhodope, 12th July, 1913.

DEAR PARENTS:

* * * We got to Nevrokop, where again we were expected, for again we fought the entire day, and we chased them (the enemy) to a place where we set on them with our bayonets and took eighteen cannon and six machine guns. They managed to get away and we were not able to take prisoners. We only took a few, whom we killed, for those are our orders. Wherever there was a Bulgarian village, we set fire to it and burned it, so that this dirty race of Bulgars couldn't spring up again. Now we are at the Bulgarian frontier, and if they don't mend their manners, we shall go to Sofia.

With an embrace,

Your son,

PERICLI SOUMBLIS

7th Division, 19th Regiment, 12th Company,
Salonica.

(*18*)

M. Christopher Kranea,
Rue Aristotle et de l'Epire 48.

Athens.

Rhodope, 14th July, 1913.

DEAR BROTHER CHRISTOPHER:

I am writing from Rhodope, a Bulgarian position, two hours away from the old Bulgarian frontier. If God spares me I shall write again. I don't know how much further we shall go into Bulgarian territory or if we are to have any more fights, as I don't know what further resistance we shall have to meet. If this war is to be the end of me, I pray the Almighty to comfort you greatly; and above all my mother and the relatives; but I hope that God will preserve my life. The money you speak of has not come yet. I have sent a few "bear-leaders" into a better world. A few days back my god-father Vassil Christon, tried his hand at shooting eight *comitadjis*. We had taken fifty whom we shared among us. For my share I had six of them and I did polish them off.

That is all I have to say.

Greeting from your brother,

DIM. KRANEAS.

(*19*)

M. Georges N. Yrikaki,
Vari-Petro, Cydonia,
Canea, Crete.

Macedonia, July 12, 1913.

DEAR GEORGE:

* * * After that we went forward and occupied the bridge over the Strouma. A lot of Bulgars were hidden in different spots. After we had occupied the bridge we found numbers of them every day, and killed them. The Bulgars have burned the bridge to stop our advance towards Serres.

With greetings,

F. VALANTINAKI.

This is my address—
STILIAN VALANTINO,
    19th Regiment, 3d Battalion, 9th Company, 7th Division.
    Macedonia.

(*20*)

To A. M. Nicolas Hartaloupa,
Ksilokastro,
Tricala, Corinth.

Rhodopian Mountains, 18/7/1913.

DEAR BROTHER NICOLAS:

I am very well and I hope you are as well as I am. We have turned up close to the Bulgarian frontier. We are constantly pressing on and putting the enemy to flight. . . . When we pass Bulgarian villages we set fire to them all and lay them waste.

With an embrace,

Your brother,
A. V. THODOROPOULOS.

(Same address.)

(*21*)   To Mme. Angheliki K. Lihouidi,
                                                      Manastiraki,
                                                              Acarnania,
                                                      Ksiromera—Vonitza.

Rhodope, July 13, 1913.
DEAR MOTHER:
    I send you my greetings. I am in good health. * * * We have to—such is the order
—burn the villages, massacre the young, only sparing the aged and children. But we are
hungry. * * *
    With greeting,
                                          Your son,
                                                      JEAN LIHOUIDIS.

(*22*)   To M. Christo Tchiopra,
                                                      Petrilo, Arghitea,
                                                              Karditza,
                                                                  Thessaly.

The River Nestor,
    July 13, 1913.
DEAR KINSFOLK:
    My greeting to you. I am well and hope you are in good health. * * *
This is something like real war, not like that with the Turks. We fight day and night and
we have burned all the villages.
                                          With greetings,
                                                      KAMBAS NICOLAOS.

(*23*)   Independant Cretan Regiment,
                                                      12th Company,
                                                              To
                                          Corporal Em. N. Loghiadi.
                                          Leaskoviki, Epirus.

Dobrisnitza, 12th July, 1913.
    * * * today I am answering your letters of the 22nd of May and the 21st of
June. * * * We have had a little engagement near the Strouma with the refugees from
Koukouch and Lahna. The guns mowed them down on the road. We did not succeed in
occupying the bridge, which they burned in their retreat toward Serres.
    This letter is being sent from Méhomia.
                                          Greeting from,
                                                      E. N. LOGHIADIS.

(*24*)   To M. Dimitri Koskinaki,
                                                      Skardelo, Milopotamo,
                                                              Retimo,
                                                                  Crete.

Nevrokop,
    July 12, 1913.
DEAR COUSIN:
    I am well and I hope you are, too. * * * We burned all the Bulgarian villages on
our route and we have almost reached the old frontiers of Bulgaria.
    With an embrace,
                                          Your cousin,
                                                      S. KALIGHÉPSIS.

(*25*)   11 July, 1913.

I have not time to write much; you will probably find these things in the papers. * * *
It is impossible to describe how the Bulgarians are being treated. Even the villagers—
it is butchery—not a town or village may hope to escape being burned. I am well and so is
cousin S. Kolovelonis.

With a loving embrace,

Your brother,

N. Brinia.

(*26*)   The Bulgarian Frontier,
                                                              11th July, 1913.

Dear Brother Anastase:

I hope you are well. Don't worry, I am all right. We have had a lot of engagements, but God has spared my life. We had a fight at Nevrokop and took 22 cannon and
a lot of booty. They can't stand up to us anywhere, they are running everywhere. We
massacre all the Bulgarians that fall into our clutches and burn the villages. Our hardships are beyond words.

Your brother,

Nicolas Anghelis.

I embrace you and kiss my father's hand.

(*27*)   Dobrountzi,
                                                              13th July, 1913.

Dear Brother:

All the villages here are Bulgarian, and the inhabitants have taken to flight as they
did not wish to surrender. We set fire to all the villages and smash them up,—an inhuman
business; and I must tell you, brother, that we shoot all the Bulgarians we take, and there
are a good number of them.

With an embrace,

Your brother,

Al. D——geas.

(Illegible.)

(*28*)   Banitza,
                                                              11th July, 1913.

My Dear Leonidas:

I can't find paper to write to you, for all the villages here are burnt and all the inhabitants have run away. We burn all their villages, and now we don't meet a living soul.
I must tell you that we are close upon the old frontiers of Bulgaria. We have occupied
the whole of Macedonia except Thrace. * * *

I want an immediate answer.

This is my address,

Corporal George Korkotzi,

19th Regiment, 3d Battalion, 11th Company, 7th Division—wherever we may be.

No. 52.—A. Burned Villages in Bulgarian Territory, District of Strumnitsa

The list of burned villages which follows will be found to be accurate, in the sense
that it includes no villages which have not been burned. But it is far from complete, save
as regards the Kukush and Strumnitsa regions. Many other Bulgarian villages were burned,

particularly in the Serres and Drama districts. In many cases we have not been able to discover the exact number of houses in a village. It will be noted that the list includes a few Turkish villages in Bulgarian territory burned by the Greeks, and a few villages burned by the Servians. The immense majority of the villages are, however, Bulgarian villages burned by the Greek army in its northward march.

The number of burned villages included in this list is 161, and the number of houses burned is approximately 14,480.

We estimate that the number of houses burned by the Greeks in the second war can not fall short of 16,000.

The figures which follow the names indicate the number of houses in each village.

Eleven Bulgarian villages burned by the Greeks, with number of houses in each: Dabilia (50), Novo-selo (160), Veliussa, Monastira, Svrabite, Popchevo (43), Kostourino (130). Rabortsi (15), Cham-Tchiflik (20), Baldevtsi (2), Zoubovo (30).

Nine Turkish villages burned by the Greeks: Amzali (150), Guetcherli (5), Tchanakli (2), Novo-Mahala (2), Ednokoukovo (80), Sekirnik (30), Souchitsa (10), Svidovitsa (10), Borissovo (15).

Two Patriarchist villages, Mokreni (16), and Makrievo (10), with three-fourths of the town of Strumnitsa, about 1,000 houses and shops.

In all over 1,620 houses.

District of Petrits.—Fourteen villages burned by the Greeks: Charbanovo, Breznitsa, Mouraski, Mitinovo, Ormanli, Michnevo, Starochevo, Klutch, Koniarené, Kalarevo, Mikrevo, Gabrené, Skrit and Smolaré (the two last partially).

District of Razlog.—Dobrinishta (298).

District of Gorna.—Djoumaia, Simitli, Dolno-Souchitsa and Srbinovo (200)—the last burned by the Greeks after the peace of Bucharest.

District of Melnik.—Sixteen Bulgarian villages burned by the Greeks: Spatovo, Makriko-stenovo, Sklavé (30), Sveti-Vratch (200), Livounovo (60), Dolni-Orman (90), Tchiflitsite, Prepetcheno (20), Kapotovo, Kromidovo, Harsovo (100), Dolna-Oumitsa, Hotovo, Spatovo (16), Spanchevo (30), Otovo (60).

District of Nevrokop.—Seven Bulgarian villages burned by the Greeks: Dolna-Brodi (300), Libiachovo (400), Kara-Keuï (40), Godlevo, Tarlis (10), Obidin, Tcham-Tchiflik, and ten houses in the town of Nevrokop; also the Turkish village of Koprivnik (100).

B. Burned Villages of Bulgarian Nationality in Greek Territory

District of Salonica.—Bulgarian villages burned by the Greeks: Negovan, Ravna, Bogorod.

District of Ziliahovo.—Bulgarian villages burned by the Greeks: Skrijevo, Libechovo, Kalapot (partially), Alistratik (partially), and Guredjik.

District of Kukush.—Forty Bulgarian villages burned by the Greeks: Kukush town 1,846 houses, 612 shops, 5 mills. Idjilar (70), Aliodjalar (50), Goliabache (40), Salamanli (15), Ambar-Keuï (35), Karaja-Kadar (25), Alchaklish (13), Seslovo (30), Stresovo (20), Chikirlia (15), Irikli (20), Gramadna (100), Alexovo (100), Morartsi (350), Roschlevo (40), Motolevo (250), Planitsa in part (180), Nimantsi (40), Postolar (38), Yensko (45), Koujoumarli (30), Bigliria (18), Kazanovo (20), Dramomirtsi (115) in part, Gavalantsi (45), Kretsovo (45), Michailovo (15), Kalinovo (35), Tsigountsi (35), Harsovo (50), Novoseleni in part (20), Malovtsi (20), Vrighitourtsi (15), Garbachel (30), Haidarli (10), Daoutli (18). Tchtemnitsa (40), Rayahovo (150) in part. Gola (15).

In all 4,725 buildings.

District of Doiran.—Eleven Bulgarian villages burned by the Greeks: Akanjeli (150), Dourbali, Nicolits, Pataros, Sourlevo, Popovo, Hassanli, Brest, Vladaia, Dimontsi, Ratartsi.

District of Demir-Hissar.—Five Bulgarian villages burned by the Greeks: Kruchevo (800), Kirchevo (180), Tchervishta (170), German (80), and Djouta-Mahala.

District of Serres.—Six Bulgarian villages burned by the Greeks: Doutli (100), Orehovatz (130), Drenovo, Moklen, Frouchtani, Banitsa (120).

District of Gevgheli.—Fifteen Bulgarian and three Vlach villages burned, mainly by the Greeks, but in two cases by the Servians: Sehovo, Schlopentsi, Matchoukovo, Smol, Baialtsi, Marventsi, Orehovitsa, Smokvitsa, Balentsi, Braikovtsi, Kostourino, Mouïne, Stoyacovo, Fourca, and Ohani, Houma and Longountsa (*vlach*).

C. Burned Villages of Bulgarian Nationality in Servian Territory

District of Tikvesh.—Five Bulgarian villages burned by the Servians: Negotin (800), Kamendol, Gorna-Dissol, Haskovo, Cavadartsi (in part) (15), etc.

District of Kotchana.—Three Bulgarian villages burned by the Servians: Sletovo, Besikovo, Priseka, etc.

APPENDIX D

Documents Relating to Chapter II

THE SERVIANS IN THE SECOND WAR

No. 53.—EVIDENCE OF GEOGHI VARNALIEV, *Headmaster of the Bulgarian School at Kavadartsi, near Tikvesh.*

On July 1, when the battle of Krivolak began, he was arrested with seven other Bulgarian notables and informed by the prefect that a state of siege existed, and that they would be kept as hostages till the end of the war. They were three days in prison, but were released after the Servian defeat. The secretary of the Servian prefect did everything possible to ensure their safety. Some drunken gendarmes were, however, left behind in the Servian retreat, and these killed the servant of the mayor and wounded a woman. The Macedonian volunteers of the Bulgarian army then occupied the town and behaved well, but left on July 7. There then began a systematic burning of all the Bulgarian villages in the neighborhood. This was carried out by Turks, accompanied by Servian soldiers and officers. Among the villages burned were Negotin (800 houses), Kamendol, Gornodissal, Haskovo, etc. The peasants from these places came to their town and told their stories of massacre and pillage. On July 8, the Servians arrived in Kavadartsi and killed twenty-five Bulgarians, mostly refugees from neighboring villages, among them were the mayor and five notables of their own town. The mayor was accused of tearing up a Servian flag and helping the Macedonians. Two lads aged thirteen and fifteen, named Dorev, were killed because a bomb had exploded near their house, and they were absurdly suspected. He saw the bodies, which were all buried, still bound, just outside the town. He witnessed the pillage of about thirty shops and the burning of fifteen houses. Four women went mad from fear in their flight from Kavadartsi and two of them are said to have killed their own children, lest they should fall into the hands of the Servians.

No. 54.—EVIDENCE OF TWO OLD VILLAGERS, *natives of Istip, who walked to Sofia, a journey of three days and three nights, in order to give their testimony to the Commission; their names must be suppressed since they live in Servian territory.*

They stated that they left Istip with the Bulgarian troops and sought refuge in the neighboring villages. Bands of Turks arrived and went round from village to village, burning the houses and violating the women. In the village Liubotrn, which was burned, eleven men and three women were killed and most of the women were violated. The leader of the Turkish band was a certain Yaha, of Vélès, who had always led the *bashi-bazouks* under the Turks. He had under him about 300 men, and laid waste all the country around Istip, Radovishta and Kochana. Many women were carried off by the Turks to their own villages. Later on the pomaks of Tikvesh arrived with wagons and did much plundering. The district was now relatively calm and the Servians were disarming the Turks, but they believed that the arms taken from some Turks were secretly given back to others.

[NOTE.—The above evidence, general in its character, relates to much that the witnesses saw and to much which they learned from others. It does not all rank as first-hand evidence, but appeared to be too serious to be disregarded.]

No. 55.—Evidence of Lieutenant R. Wadham Fisher (see also No. 9).

After the conclusion of peace Lieutenant Fisher visited the district overrun by the Servian army in the second war. He found the village of Sletovo near Kotchana, which he knew well, burnt down. He also visited the village Besikovo. Here the Montenegrins had killed twenty-eight of the villagers, a child had been burned alive in a house, and four women had died as the result of violation. In the next village, Priseka, five or six men had been killed and four women had died as the result of violation. In these villages everything had been taken, crops, clothes and money, and the people were starving, without shelter, on the mountain side. The Servians had used their corn in the trenches as bedding, and the peasants were reduced to picking out the grains from it. The Servians were levying a house-tax of five francs, even on burned houses.

Extracts from the Evidence Collected by Professor Milétits

No. 56.—The Schoolhouse Massacre at Serres.   *Deposition of George T. Belev, of Strumnitsa, a Protestant, aged 32.* (See also Nos. 18-26.)

Mr. Belev was serving as a bearer in the medical corps attached to the Seventieth Bulgarian regiment. He had transported two wounded soldiers from Nigrita to Serres. In Serres, on Friday, June 21, he entered the bakery of an acquaintance, a man from his native town. He was there arrested by Greeks and confined for two days, together with four other Bulgarian soldiers.

The deposition continues thus:

On Tuesday, June 25, we were taken to the bishop's palace to appear before a commission. In the hall there were several men sitting at a table in a corner, among them an ecclesiastic. They looked at us and said, "Take them away." From there we were taken to the girls' school, near the bishopric. The door was shut, and we were given the word of command in Bulgarian, "March. Form ranks." The following eight persons had been brought from the bakery [the names follow]. We found there four soldiers from Old Bulgaria. When we had formed our ranks, an *evzone* came up to us, and with him a certain Captain Doukas, and many Greeks of the town. They took from us one by one our coats and belts and all the money we had. From Theodore Inegilisov they took eight Napoleons and a watch, and from me a silver watch worth thirty francs, and ten francs which were in my purse. Then they placed us beside the staircase, drew their Turkish sabres, and ordered us to mount. Two of them with drawn sabres took up position on either side of the stairs, and as we went up they rained blows upon us. I received a blow on the left hand. Pando Abrachev had his right hand broken and his head cut open, and the others were also struck. We were then driven into a room about twenty-five meters square, where we were kept during Tuesday and Wednesday.

On Tuesday, we had nothing to eat and were not allowed to go to the lavatory * * * [He explains how he dressed Abrachev's wound.] * * * On Wednesday, we each received half a loaf and were allowed to go to the lavatory under escort. On Thursday, the Greek bishop arrived and went over all the rooms. He made a sort of speech to the prisoners. "We are Christians. Our Holy Gospel forbids us to massacre. We are not like the Bulgarians, we shall allow you all to return to your homes. Fear nothing, we shall do you no harm." He added, "Give them bread and water," and went away. We felt more at ease, believing that a bishop would not lie, and passed the rest of the day in hope. But in the evening, men were chosen from all the rooms and taken away, to the number of fourteen. They selected the Bulgarian *gendarmes* who had been arrested and the militant *comitadjis,* including Christo Dimitrov, who had a mill in which he used to shelter revolutionaries. * * * Thirteen of these were slaughtered on the second story, and we heard their cries. We still hoped that a selection would be made, and that we should not all be killed. * * *

Next day (Friday, June 28) Dimitrov was brought back alive to our room. After him came a Greek priest. He opened the door of our room, and said in mockery, "Good day, lads." We did not answer. He repeated it, and still we were silent. Then he said, "Why don't you answer? 'Good day' is a civil word. Aren't you Bulgarians?" We did not answer. Then he asked us, "Would you like to see your glorious Tsar Ferdinand? Would you like to enter Salonica. So you shall, quite soon." Then the priest went away.

Two hours later we heard firing. Our troops were entering the town. We were sure that it was our army, for the Greek guns could not have been heard from that particular quarter. As soon as the Bulgarian guns came into action, the Greeks ran all over the building to gather us together in one room. We were seventy persons, pressed like herrings in a little room and there we remained for half an hour. Meanwhile they ran to see whether the Bulgarians were coming in. When they had ascertained this, they made us come out two by two, to bind our hands. Then those who were bound were led up to the upper story and killed. The first to be taken up was a little Greek of the village of Kolechino, near Strumnitsa, who had lived in Serres for seven years. He had been imprisoned by mistake. He begged for his liberty, explaining that everyone knew he was a Greek, that he was married and was a rich merchant. But no heed was paid to him, and he was killed. There was time to massacre all the seventy persons; it did not take more than an hour. There were plenty of executioners, and they worked quickly. Thirty men were bound, and then when they saw that this took too long, they stopped binding us.

Among the executioners was Charalambi Popov, a Grecized Bulgarian, the same baker in whose house I was arrested. The others were inhabitants of Serres, and two *vlachs* belonging to the Greek party from Poroi. One named Christo often came to Strumnitsa, and many a time I have gone surety for him. The other who is lame is named Tzeru, and knows no Greek. He killed with a yataghan, with which he severed the head from the body. The others used Martini bayonets, but some had Bulgarian Mannlicher bayonets. * * * I was taken with three others, two of them men from Dibra, and none of us were bound. We mounted the stairs, crossed a large hall and entered a big room. I went first and the executioner followed with his bayonet in his hand. * * * We were half dead with fear, and could hardly walk. Through the door of the room I could see slaughtered men, and some who were still alive and groaning. One was decapitated. The room was full, and the bodies lay two or three on top of each other. There was no room for me. Then the executioner made me go to another little room which was empty. It was my acquaintance the *vlach*, Christo. I took one step into the room, and at the next step he struck me in the neck. The force of the blow was broken by my collar, but I fell on my face. He then put his foot on my back, and struck me six blows with the bayonet, on my back, behind my ear, under the right jaw, and in the throat. When the sisters of charity afterwards gave me milk, it flowed through this last wound. I don't remember crying, and did not feel it when the index finger of my right hand was cut off, nor did I lose consciousness * * * In the big room three or four people were killed at once, but in this little room the other victims had to look on while I was dealt with. I heard one of the men of Dibra struggling at the door of the room and trying to snatch the bayonet, until another executioner came up to help, and then they beat him pitilessly. He cried out, "What harm have I done to you. Leave me alone." Then they caught his hands, and flung him on top of me. I felt a heavy weight. They cut his throat and finished him by thrusts in his back. His blood flowed all over me and soaked my coat until I felt the warm stream wetting my body. He died on the spot and never stirred. Two others were then brought in and killed on top of us. They did not struggle; they were already half dead from fear. Then came more.

Some time afterwards there was a dead silence. I heard nothing but the firing of rifles and cannon. When I realized that there was none left in the building I decided to get out from under the heap of bodies which had been weighing on me and drenching me with blood for about an hour. I rose with difficulty, sat down in a corner, and dressed my wounds, knotting a handkerchief round my neck from which the blood was flowing. It hurt a good deal, but I drew the handkerchief tight. I got up, found that I could walk, and went into the next room. There I found Christo Dimitrov sitting among forty dead bodies. He got up and began to walk, and others also stirred. * * * From the window no one was to be seen, and shells and balls were flying. A shell fell near our building and set it on fire, and we saw that we should be burned alive unless we went out * * * Eight men gathered at the door. There were about twenty wounded men who might have been saved, if there had been anyone to help. One, the ninth, Ilia, a tilemaker of Gevgheli, came down the stairs, but fell near the door. * * * [He goes on to relate how he found the Bulgarian troops and was placed in a vehicle, and ultimately, after much suffering, reached Mehomia and eventually was nursed at Tatar-Bazardjik.]

No. 57.—Extracts from a Deposition by Dr. P. G. Laznev, *a Russian physician in charge of the Bulgarian Hospital at Serres.*

After complaining that the Greek women of Serres pillaged the hospital, and stating that the Greek *andartes* behaved well in their dealings with it after the Bulgarian evacuation Dr. Laznev continues:

"On July 11, the Bulgarian infantry with mountain guns appeared on the heights which command the hospital, and a fight ensued between them and the Greek insurgents who were sheltered behind the hospital. The insurgents were driven back, and the hospital was in the possession of the Bulgarians. That lasted only for a half an hour, for stronger detachments of Greek infantry and cavalry arrived, and a continuous exchange of rifle and gun fire went on from three to six p.m. As before, the hospital was the center of the fighting. Our windows were broken and I was obliged to lay the sick on the floor in order to shelter them. One of them was wounded. Neither Greeks nor Bulgarians would listen to my remonstrances. At the end of the fight the Bulgarians withdrew. About an hour before their withdrawal the town was set on fire. Then came the victors, fatigued and excited by the fighting. They burst in, knocked our orderly down and beat him cruelly, threatened to kill the sick 'because the Bulgarians had burned the town'; struck my assistant Komarov on the chest and shoulders with the butts of their rifles, and pointed the barrels of their rifles at my breast. Finally I induced them to go away. Others meanwhile pillaged the upper story of the hospital, and stole everything, including my personal property. [Details follow of the difficulties which the doctor experienced in dealing with the Greek authorities.] As to the burning of Serres, I am obliged to declare that I do not know its causes. I can only make guesses. It may have been caused by the Bulgarian shells. As a strong wind was blowing, a fire started in one place would spread easily to the neighboring buildings. I can not accept the theory of the Bishop of Serres (that the Bulgarians first sprinkled the houses with petroleum and then two days later set them on fire). In that case the conflagration would have started simultaneously in the several quarters of the town."

No. 58.—Deposition of Ilia Petrov Limonev, *a fisherman of Doiran, serving in the 70th Bulgarian Regiment* (Fourth Battalion, Fifteenth Company), was imprisoned in the School at Serres, and succeeded in breaking out and disarming the sentries. His narrative contains two interesting details. His detachment, reduced to thirty-two men, was separated from its battalion, and retreated through Demir-Hissar to the village of Kavakli. On July 6, it was surrounded by a Greek company numbering 200 men, and surrendered. "After disarming the Bulgarian soldiers, the Greeks bound them and massacred them. In this fashion twenty-four Bulgarian soldiers were slaughtered in the most barbarous fashion, when at length a Greek officer arrived, and said that that was enough. The eight men who survived, including Limonev himself, were brought to Serres on the 8th, cruelly beaten and shut up in the girls' school." Among the sixty Bulgarian civilians imprisoned with them in an upper room, were four women, one of them very old. Describing what he saw after his escape, Limonev states that the Greek artillery mistook the Greek refugees near the station for Bulgarians, turned their machine-guns upon them, and killed an immense number.

No. 58a.—DIMITRI AUGUELOV, *wine merchant of Serres,* arrested on July 7, was shut up in the school, escaped with a Jewish prisoner on Friday, and was concealed by Jews of the town.

No. 58b. STRATI GEORGHIEV, *of the Dibra district,* was arrested on July 10 by ten armed Greeks and five Turks. A Turk told him that all who wore the costume of Dibra would be put to death, because they were Bulgarians. Among the corpses on Friday he saw an old woman with her head cut open, and three young women, all killed. There were fifty corpses in the room. He escaped with Belev and the others, severely wounded.

No. 59.—EVENTS AROUND DEMIR-HISSAR.

A group of Bulgarian villages in the neighborhood of Demir-Hissar was the scene of a systematic massacre. Most of the inhabitants of these villages, German, Kruchevo, Kirtchevo, and Tchervishta, had fled early in the second war. Letters were then sent out over the signature of Dr. Christoteles, an influential Greek doctor of Demir-Hissar, which invited them to return and assured them of safety. (See No. 44.) Marko Bourakchiev, of Kirtchevo (180 houses) had returned to his village with about eighty other families. On the arrival of the Greek troops on July 15 (he states), the villagers made them welcome and brought all they called for. Suddenly he heard the roll of a drum and an indescribable tumult followed, amid which he heard the cries and groans of the dying. He left his house and saw his neighbor Stoiana Tchalikova in a pool of blood, dead of bayonet wounds, and the corpse of little Anghel Paskov. He went back to his own house and saw two or three soldiers searching his grandmother for money. She had none and they cut her throat and plunged their bayonets into her breast. They then seized him and took him into another house, where were other soldiers and *andartes.* They began to discuss something which seemed important. He was forgotten and a soldier made him pour out water for him to wash his blood stained hands. Then the soldier made a sign to him, and pointed to the door. He fled as fast as he could, and those who pursued failed to overtake him. From a hill he saw the village in flames.

Dimitri Guidichov and Ivan Radev, who also escaped from the village, relate that the men were shut up in two houses and burned alive. Forty women were shut up in the house of Anghel Douriov and there beaten, undressed, and violated. Four women (named) were killed, and four (named) were carried off by the soldiers. Twenty peasants of Tchervishta and Kruchevo were also massacred at Kirtchevo, together with two priests.

Paul Chavkov adds that he saw the soldiers taking seven or eight women naked to Gorno-Brodi. (See also No. 44.)

No. 60.—At German the same procedure was followed. Thirty families returned as the result of Dr. Christoteles' letter and welcomed the Greek troops. The men were shut up in the church and the women in the priests' house. One of the men, Dimitri Georg-hiev, escaped from the church and afterwards met Apostol Kostov of German, to whom he told his story. One woman also escaped, Stoianka Konstantinova, aged twenty. It is not known where she is at present. Some distance outside the village, as she was fleeing, she met her uncle, Thorma Ivanov, who was returning to it. She could hardly speak in her terror, and her uncle quotes these words: "I can't, I can't tell you anything. There's no describing what I've seen. God! how they tortured us, undressed us naked, while we cried and wept. * * * I am saved, but the others. * * * The village is burning. They were killing in the streets. Cries and the sound of shots were coming from the church. All the men were massacred there." The uncle and the niece fled together. He reached Bulgaria, but she remained behind on the way with some other peasants of German. (See also No. 46.)

*No. 61.—*Ilia Konstantinov, *of Tchervishta,* relates that when the peasants of his village returned in response to the doctor's letters, twenty of their notables, himself among them, were taken to Kirtchevo. He saw them all massacred, the women led away, and the village burned, but managed himself to escape.

*No. 62.—*The same thing happened at Kruchevo. Nearly all the inhabitants returned and welcomed the Greek troops. The officer made them a speech, in which he told them that they were all Greeks and not Bulgarians. That same evening, the soldiers forced their way into all the houses (800 houses), pillaged everything and violated all the women and car-ried off the prettiest girls.

Ivan Bojov and Haralampi Jankoulov relate some incidents which they witnessed in the sack of Kruchevo. The soldiers (1) robbed George Tochev of £T250; (2) robbed Ivan Kakidine and killed him and his wife; (3) killed the widow, Ransa Hadjieva, because she had less money than they demanded; (4) killed Soultana Xalianova because she locked her house to protect her two daughters and daughter-in-law; (5) violated and then killed Vela Harmanova and Ransa Souchova; (6) took the daughter of the priest, Theodore Staev, gouged out his eyes, and two days later took him to Kirtchevo, where he was killed with the other notables.

*No. 63.—*Summary of Evidence Collected by Professor Milétits.

(a) Athanase Ivanov of Kukush who fled from the town on July 4, saw from his brother's house at a distance of three or four hundred paces the slaughter of two old men, three women and a little girl, by the Greek cavalry. The Greeks were then driven back by Bulgarian cavalry and the witness fled with the latter.

(b) Kolio Delikirov and Ivan Milev, of Akangeli, state that the Greek officer (see Nos. 39-43) ordered the villagers to bring their arms and all the money they possessed. The arms were given to the Turks, and the money kept by the Greeks. Four peasants (named) brought each of them from £T100 to £T150. While the arms were being given up, a rifle went off by accident, and the Greek soldiers fell upon the peasants, who fled in every direc-tion. But they were soon surrounded and bound. Fifteen only were released, in order to fetch food for the soldiers; some of these fled and hid. Those who remained in the hands of the Greeks were massacred. * * * The young women were taken to a place called Karakol and violated. Two girls from Pataros, who were in the house of the teacher, Dimo Christov, were violated until they died.

(c) Vanghel Kazanski, of Kazanovo, saw the Greek cavalry between Gavalantsi and Dragomirtsi riding down old men and women who were fleeing. They shot Mitza Kou-schinov, and then dismounted, but he could not see what followed.

(d) Mito P. Stoyanov, of Moritolovo, states that Greek cavalry killed the mayor and gendarme of the village with their sabres.

(e) Mito Nicolov and his brother, Petro, of Doiran, in their flight, saw three Bulgarian villagers fleeing from Kodjamatli overtaken by Greek cavalry and killed.

(f) Thomas Pop Stoyanov, son of the priest of Dolna Djoumaia, states that his father and twenty-five notables of the village were killed by the Greek troops, and that four women were beaten or violated until they died [gives names].

(g) Gotze Ivanov, of Popovo, who left his village on July 6, states that the Greeks gathered the arms of the peasants and pillaged. The men were separated from the women and on the first day thirty disappeared. The women and girls were gathered in the house of Colio Theodorov and violated. Slava Coleva was violated and then killed in the street. Only three men escaped alive. The village was burned.

(h) Eftim Mitev, of Moklen, states that fifteen shepherds of his village, whom he names, were caught by the Greeks near Kalapot and massacred.

(i) Nicholas Anastasov, of Alistratik, states that Greek troops killed nine Bulgarian villagers, after first imprisoning them, also two young women and four children.

(j) Ivan Christodorov, of Guredjik, states that he saw Greek soldiers enter the houses of the village and begin to violate all the women. He fled.

(k) G. Markov, of Pleva, states that forty men of his village were taken outside it by the Greeks and slaughtered.

(l) Blagoi Ikonomov, of Mehomia, names four men killed and two women violated in his town. There were others.

(m) Dinka Ivanov, of Marikostenovo, states that all the women in his village were violated. He fled, was fired on, but escaped.

(n) Ivan Stoitchev, of Sveti-Vratch, says that the same thing happened there, and also at Polenitsa.

(o) At Pancherevo, the people awaited the Greeks and welcomed them, and were rewarded by the killing of six, and the carrying off of ten, of whom three escaped.

(p) At Grada, all the women were violated. At Matchevo, four villagers were killed.

(q) At Roussinovo, a woman died as the result of violation, three men were killed, and two women and a girl were carried off by the Greeks. The village was burned.

(r) At Smoimirtsi, the priest and people went out to meet the Greeks. The priest was tortured and died. A man was killed.

(s) From Vladimirovo, fourteen girls and an old woman were carried off by the Greeks.

(t) The people of Oumlena met the Greek troops. All the women were violated. Two were carried off, and kept for six days by the officers. One old woman died of ill-treatment, two men killed and five houses were burned.

No. 64.—From the official reports of some of the Bulgarian prefects in the new territories, we extract the following statements:

(a) The losses due to the systematic pillage by the Greek army in the following places is estimated thus in francs:

MEHOMIA. Grain, 356,850 fr.; cattle, 164 fr.; household goods, 402,200 fr.; merchandise, 160.24 fr.; total, 759,374.24 fr.

BANSKO. Grain, 350,000 fr.; cattle, 200,000 fr.; household goods, 340,000 fr.; merchandise, 200,000 fr.; total, 1,090,000 fr.

NANIA. Grain, 30,000 fr.; cattle, 35,000 fr.; household goods, 41,000 fr.; merchandise, 5,000 fr.; total, 111,000 fr.

DOBRINISHTA. Loss by burning, 1,145,000 fr.; by pillage of grain, 200,000 fr.; cattle, 40,000 fr.; total, 1,385,000 fr.

Further, in Mehomia, seven old men were killed, two women beaten to death, and eleven old women violated. At Bansko five men were killed and four old women violated.

(b) At Petrits, twenty of the Bulgarian citizens were tortured by the Greeks to extort money. The method was to bind their arms behind their backs and then to twist the ropes with an iron instrument, one specimen of which was left behind. Twenty names are given, with the sums extorted, which range from £T3 to £T25. Four were killed. There were many violations, but the victims conceal their names.

(c) In the Strumnitsa district, occupied partly by Greeks and partly by Servians, £T90 in money was taken by soldiers from seven men [named] in the village of Rablich, £T160 at Smiliantsi, £T100 at Inevo, £T200 at Yargorilitsa, £T70 at Radovitsa, etc. Six men, three women, and several children [named] were killed at Loubnitsa, five men and a woman [named] at Radovitch, two women [named] at Oraovitsa, and seven inhabitants [no names] at Pideresch.

No. 65.—EXTRACTS FROM AN OFFICIAL REPORT (*communicated*) by OFFICER CANDIDATE PENEV, *Aide-de-Camp of the first battalion of the 26th Infantry.*

On the road leading to Strumnitsa, between the villages Ormanovo and Novo Selo, in the defile on the right bank of the river, I found a soldier of the Tenth (Rhodope) Infantry crucified on a poplar tree by means of telegraph wires. His face had been sprinkled with petroleum and burned. I recognized that he was a soldier from the epaulettes which had been torn off and flung down near him. The body was already in a state of decomposition. Further to the west I found another soldier of the Thirtieth Infantry. His body was buried in the sand, and nothing was visible but the head, which had been sprinkled with petroleum and burned. The eyes, nose and ears had disappeared. A soldier of the First (Prince Alexander's) Infantry was hanging head downwards, with his feet bound with telegraph wire. The epaulettes lying in the mud showed that the unhappy man was a mechanician. His ears and hands had been cut off, and his eyes torn out. Further along the same road I found many other unburied bodies mutilated, belonging to soldiers of the Second, Sixth and Eighth divisions.

(NOTE.—It is proper to note that the authors of these disgusting outrages may possibly have been Turks.)

On the way the peasants told us with tears in their eyes of the inhuman treatment which they had met with from Greek officers and soldiers. At Ormanovo, the commandant of Petrits had all the men imprisoned in the police office, where they were kept without food for three days, and ill-treated by the Greek soldiers. They were made to pay £T1 (23 fr.) for a drink of water. All the women and all the girls over eight years of age, were shut up in a house and violated. The same thing happened in Bossilovo, Dabine and Robovo. In this last village the Greek soldiers bound the priest and violated first his daughter and then the other women before his eyes. They then shot the priest and his daughter and burned the village.

Two-thirds of the town of Strumnitsa has been burned, notably the "Grecoman" and Turkish quarters, and some Greek houses in the Bulgarian quarter, together with the public buildings and the barracks. At the moment when the Greeks were about to set fire to the Bulgarian quarter, where several houses were already in flames, Mr. Cooper, the American Protestant missionary, arrived from Salonica. Mr. Cooper went to the Greek commandant and begged him to stop the burning, declaring that he would appeal to the

British consul at Salonica. The fire was stopped by order of the commandant. I have this statement from Mr. Cooper himself, who sent photographs of the town burned by the Greeks to the British consul. The new Bulgarian church, a solid stone building, is half destroyed by three bombs which the Greeks placed in it to blow it up. The Bulgarian hospitals are also in ashes, and the Bulgarian wounded who had remained there were left without care or food. The Greek sentinels appropriated all the bread, milk, etc., which the good women of the town brought to the soldiers. Finally the wounded soldiers were shut up in the Turkish tower, which was set on fire. Their charred bodies were still lying there on September 16, when the Greeks evacuated the town. * * * A school teacher informed me that on the night of August 23, she was taken to the barracks, where she was first outraged by the Greek commander and then by twenty-four soldiers, one after the other. She is now in a pitiful condition.

Documents Relating to Chapter III

THE ACCUSATION

REPORT BY A RUSSIAN OFFICER

(From *Le Jeune-Turc*, August 26 and 27, 1913)

On August 20 the London *Daily Telegraph* published an interesting report on the Bulgarian atrocities in Thrace, and particularly at Adrianople.

This report, of which the text is given below, came from a Russian official and was transmitted to St. Petersburg.

I had occasion to visit Adrianople and its environs in company with ten or more foreign correspondents representing the largest newspapers and telegraphic agencies. The eager readiness with which the Turkish government gave us the necessary permits and afforded us facilities for making our inquiries, prove that the Turks felt sure that we could make no discoveries that would harm them; that on the contrary, publication of the truth could only be to their interest; *a most thorough and detailed inquiry proved that in this the Turks were right.* I shall say nothing of the atrocious manner in which 15,000 Turkish prisoners and some 5,000 Turkish civilians were treated in the first four days during which they were mewed up like cattle in the island of Sarai, where, in the rain, they perished of cold and hunger, with no food but the bark of trees and the soles of their old shoes. They died in hundreds every day, so that when the time for departure to Bulgaria came, there were but some 10,000 of them left. That is well known.

I shall confine myself to facts not hitherto published. The diplomatic corps and the inhabitants, whether Turkish, Greek or Israelite, are unanimous in the indignation with which they describe the excesses of the Bulgarian occupation.

In most of the better Mussulman houses the windows and doors were battered in, the furniture taken away; even the houses of the generals were plundered, as for example that of Abouk Pasha, who commanded the Fourth Army Corps.

Not a single valuable carpet was left in any of the mosques, including the celebrated mosque of Sultan Selim.

The library belonging to the latter, a collection in its kind unique, was also very severely handled. Burglary was not confined to the houses of the Turks. *Those belonging to Greeks and Israelites suffered in the same way.* Train loads of so-called war booty were sent to Sofia. These are concrete facts. Soldiers armed with rifles carried off a quantity of jewels and precious antiques from the house of two Greeks, the brothers Alexandre and Jean Thalassinos. These soldiers also tore rings and bracelets from the hands of the sister of the Thalassinos. A patrol appearing in the house of the merchant Avramidi on the usual pretext of searching for arms, carried off £T70 in a trunk.

Colonel Zlatanov, head of the gendarmerie, put the brothers Athanasius and Chritodoulos Stavridis in prison, and only set them free on payment of forty pounds.

A rich Austrian-Israelite, Rodrigues, left his house in the charge of three Bulgarian officers on his departure for Constantinople; on his return he found his house empty. Everything, even the piano, had disappeared and been sent to Sofia. In the same way the houses of two rich Israelites, Moses Behmoiras and Benaroya, were plundered. Rich property owners, particularly Moslems, were forced by threats of death to consent to fictitious sales or long lease of their holdings. A case of this kind is that of Ibrahim-bey, a man of large independent means, living in Abdula-Hamam Street. Chopov, the head of police, himself sent three cases of stolen carpets to Sofia, using a Russian subject as his intermediary.

Every morning the dead bodies of numerous Moslems killed in the night, were found. Even now the corpses of Turkish prisoners covered with wounds are pulled out of the public wells. The authorities never troubled about trifles of this kind.

Among the most revolting and best known cases is that of the murder of a captive Turkish officer by a Bulgarian soldier in the middle of the open street on the first day of the Bulgarian occupation. He was an old man, so worn by the privations and fatigue of the siege that he had not the strength to walk. The soldier forced him on by hitting him with the butt end of his musket. An Israelite, Salomon Behmi, implored the soldier to have pity and let the old man rest. Enraged by this intervention, the soldier killed both men with his bayonet. On the same day eight soldiers plundered the house of three Turkish brothers, clockmakers, and carried off more than 500 watches. One of them, Aziz Ahmed, they killed with their bayonets and went on striking him even after he was dead. The others escaped by flight.

On the third day of the occupation some twenty Bulgarian soldiers first plundered and then hideously butchered thirteen Turks, three being Mollahs, and Aziz Youssouv, the Muezzin, in the Miri-Miran mosque. I saw the traces of blood there myself and my colleagues photographed them.

An even more revolting story is that of ten Turkish soldiers who are at this moment undergoing treatment in the Egyptian Red Cross hospital.

On evacuating Adrianople, the Bulgarians sent 200 Turkish prisoners, under escort, to Mustapha Pasha; *all the sick and wounded who had not sufficient strength to march were killed on the way.*

The column was then divided into three; the body containing the ten soldiers referred to above, was composed of sixty prisoners. At a given moment the Bulgarians told them that they were free and could go where they would. The wretches were not given time to take a dozen steps before the Bulgarians opened fire on them by their officers' orders. They were all killed with the exception of ten, who were severely wounded and pretended to be dead. For four whole days they lay hidden in the forest, without any food. Among them were Camber Ouglou Camber, Hassan Ouglou Hay, Emis Ouglou Emin, belonging to the first and second battalions of the Kirk Kilisse *redifs*. [The other names follow.] Almost all of them suffered from gangrene, from which two have already died. The fate of the other two bodies is unknown. The Greek Metropolitan describes how two priests sent out with gendarmes in search of mishandled Greeks, discovered dozens of corpses of captives, riddled with bullets and bayonet wounds, on the banks of the Maritza. Hassiz Effendi, schoolmaster in the village of Koumarli, reports officially that the retreating Bulgarians collected some fifty Moslems in the mosque under pretext of searching them for arms, and massacred them there; further that in the village of Amour, the Bulgarians carried off two Mussulman girls, the eldest being twelve years old. Their fate is unknown.

Hassiz Effendi further notes with satisfaction that in many villages numbers of Moslems were rescued by the Greek women.

In bringing this martyrology to a close, I should like to mention a fact of incredible atrocity. On the first news of the approach of the Turks—Sunday, July 7—the Bulgarians set fire to the provision depot at the Karagatch station.

Some starving Greeks saved several sacks of meal. On the following Monday the Bulgarians returned, arrested forty-five of these wretches and binding them together in fours, cast them so into the Maritza, while they fired on any who attempted to escape. Only a single individual, Panteleimon, succeeded in effecting an escape by sinking under water and pretending to be dead. Some days later the corpses were drawn up. I will send photographs of the drowned men.

What the women of Adrianople have had to endure is beyond imagination.

Outrages were committed against Greek, Jewish and even Armenian women, despite the Armenians' devotion to the Bulgarian cause. Naturally the worst violence was directed against the Turkish women. Respect was shown neither for rank nor age. Among the women violated there were as many girls of tender years as aged women. Many of these girls are now actually with child. And those who could afford to do so have gone away to hide their shame in remote regions. Many have lost their reason. Most keep silent about their misfortune, for reasons easy to understand.

Stories by Witnesses

Here are some examples: Hamid Nouri, mufti of Adrianople, told me the following story with tears in his eyes: "Some days before the departure of the Bulgarians many persons passed the night under his roof because of the threats they had uttered of destroying the town and exterminating the population. Opposite to him there dwelt the wife of a Turkish Major, held prisoner in Bulgaria, with her two young daughters. An hour after sunset piercing cries were heard coming from this house: 'Take whatever you will but do not touch my daughters. Are there no Moslems to defend our honor?' The mufti sent the Bulgarian soldiers, assigned him by the authorities to protect his many-times pillaged abode, to succor the women. A moment later a soldier came back and told him indignantly that all the Bulgarian soldiers were violating the three women but that he could do nothing for they threatened to kill them with their muskets. For three hours the despairing cries and groans of the women went on. When the soldiers departed the mother and daughters lay senseless. All the persons who had sought asylum with the mufti on this night declare that they are ready to bear witness to the truth of this story."

Another example. On the same day four Bulgarian officers entered the house of a rich Israelite, Salomon ben Bassat. The women and young girls made their escape by clambering over a wall into the neighboring houses: but the children were left on the first story. A female servant, aged eighteen, who came back for them, was violated twice by each of the officers; at last she escaped by saying that they would find the lovely daughter of the owner of the house in the upper story. The officers went up and the girl fled, leaving bloody tracks behind her. She is still in hospital.

The mufti referred to above and all the inhabitants without distinction of religion say that a few days after the entry the Bulgarians closed all the mosques which had previously been dishonored and used as latrines. Bulgarian soldiers relieved themselves publicly from the minarets in order to insult the Moslems. They imitated the Muezzin's call and uttered vulgar indecencies about Mahomet, religion, the Sultan and Choukri Pasha, the former governor of the fortress.

On receiving a complaint from the mufti, General Veltchev, the Bulgarian commander, demanded to have the culprits pointed out. When the mufti showed him, from a window, a Bulgarian soldier in the act of satisfying a natural need from the summit of the minaret, General Veltchev replied sarcastically that "one can not, after all, deprive a poor soldier of inoffensive distractions."

General Veltchev

At this stage it may be observed that the unanimous declarations of the consuls, the Metropolitan, the mufti and all those who had opportunity of speaking with General Veltchev, go to show that he was always excessively cruel and brutally arrogant. He said openly—and the remark appears to harmonize with the serious views of his government—that Bulgaria had no need either of Greeks or Moslems, and that they would take advantage of the first opportunity to wipe out the whole Greek and Mussulman population. He expressed the intention of replacing them with 28,000 Armenians from Rodosto and Malgara.

That this was no vain threat was proved by the atrocious treatment to which the Turkish prisoners and male population were subjected during the first days of the Bulgarian occupation. To this day the cannon of the Keyi fort are leveled at the town.

I may mention here a characteristic incident in which the Greek Metropolitan of Adrianople played a part, by way of giving a clearer picture of this Bulgarian general, who appears unfortunately to have been a pupil at our military academy. On June 25, His Eminence Polycarp went to the government to ask to be permitted to put up for the night Athanasius, Bishop of Kavala, who had been brought hither, with twenty notables belonging to the town, under escort, all of them having been kept standing throughout the whole day in the court in the midst of every kind of prisoner. Veltchev brutally told Monsignor Polycarp that he was going to hang and shoot all the Greek notables of Adrianople, beginning with the Metropolitan, because instead of remaining quiet they showed themselves hostile to the Bulgarians. On the Metropolitan's attempting to justify himself, Veltchev cried out savagely in Turkish: *"Sous!"* (Be silent!) The savage reproof of the general lasted for an hour, during which the orthodox prelate stood. Veltchev addressed him as "thou" throughout and continually threatened him and all the Greeks with death. Finally losing patience, the Metropolitan could bear no more. "Massacre," he cried, using the familiar form. "Don't be afraid, I shall massacre" replied the brave general, "but I shall not, naturally, ask your permission to do so."

It is necessary for an understanding of the general's mind to remember that the Bulgarians, from the Commander-in-Chief down to the last soldier, never ceased repeating "Adrianople has been taken by our arms at the cost of the blood and lives of thousands of Bulgarians. Therefore the place and even the lives of the inhabitants belong to us; we have the right to do whatever we please." This threatening attitude of the Bulgarians distressed the population and caused the consuls great anxiety. They telegraphed to Sofia, where energetic representations were made by the legations.

Consular Intervention

According to instructions received, Mr. Machkov, the Russian consul, and Mr. Cuinet, the French consul, presented themselves before Mr. Veltchev on the following day, and warned him, in the names of their respective governments, that the Bulgarian troops must not touch the Greek or Turkish inhabitants.

"With what right do you interfere in our discords?" Veltchev rudely replied, losing his small measure of self-control. "Are the Greeks and Turks subject to your jurisdiction?"

"No," replied Mr. Cuinet, "they are not subject to our jurisdiction; they are still Turkish subjects." Mr. Machkov remarked coldly that in making his communication he was acting under orders from his government; any further discussion seemed to him useless.

The consuls at once departed, leaving the high and mighty Bulgarian commander in a state of complete consternation. The consuls do not admit that the conversation was exactly as I have reported; but I have good authority for what I say.

That the Russian consulate, which is at this time markedly Bulgarophil and whose very *raison d'être* lay in its protection of the Christians and particularly of the Bulgarians, should have been treated by the Bulgarian authorities with such unconcealed and arrogant hostility, is a fact which I could not pass by in silence. The Bulgarian military authorities in their public utterances treated Russia with contempt, saying that Bulgaria owed Russia no gratitude because her object in freeing it had not been the liberation of the Bulgarian peoples, but the creation of new Russian provinces, which Europe would not allow. On every occasion, whether propitious or no, the Bulgarians declared that they would absolutely ignore our consulate.

The Russian consulate had the greatest difficulty in saving from Bulgarian excesses the families of the old Mussulman *cavasses* (armed porters) who had devotedly served the Bulgarian cause for nearly thirty years. The grateful recognition of the people towards the Russian consulate grew in proportion to the inflexible hostility of the Bulgarians to it; they knew that they owed the salvation of their lives and property to Russian intervention. The Moslems recall with pathetic gratitude that during the Russian occupations their religious feelings were respected, the soldiers called the old Turkish women "mother," and the young girls "sister," and shared their food with the poor. Even the Servian soldiery left pleasant memories behind them. While the Bulgarians broke down the doors to enter the houses, rudely demanded the best rooms and good food such as the owner was often in no position to give; ill-treated men and women and carried off carpets, clothing and furniture, the Servian officers politely asked leave to spend the night in some corner, made no noise, gave thanks and a tip to the servant when they went away, and begged their hosts to visit them should they ever pass through Servia. Truly a striking contrast.

The Return of the Turks

What precedes explains why the Turkish troops were received with open arms by the whole population on their return to Adrianople. People remembered that during the siege, Choukri Pasha, the commander in Adrianople, and Ismail Pasha, governor of the fortress, displayed a fatherly solicitude for all without distinction. The Turks fully justified the enthusiasm of their reception by their extraordinary moderation. From the time of their arrival perfect order reigned in the city; there was not a single case of aggression. Some excesses were committed by the Kurdish irregular cavalry in a village in the environs, but all those concerned were arrested, court-martialed and shot.

At Mustapha Pasha some soldiers who tried to set fire to a house were killed on the spot by an officer. Contrary to Bulgarian precedent the Turkish authorities declared that they would tolerate no disorder. In view of what has been said it need cause no astonishment to find the Turkish, Greek and Jewish population ready to depart if they heard that Europe insisted on the cession of Adrianople to the Bulgars. The Greek Metropolitan and the mufti appeal through me to Russian public opinion to secure that should the Bulgarians return, a month of delay may be accorded in which the inhabitants of Thrace may peaceably effect their expatriation.

Such without more words, is the terrible result of my eight days' inquiry.

APPENDIX F

Documents Relating to Chapter III

THE DEFENSE

REPORT ADDRESSED TO THE COMMANDER OF THE KEHLIBAROV RESERVE ON THE CHARGES MADE
BY THE LONDON DAILY TELEGRAPH

To the Commander Kehlibarov Reserve,
    Military Magistrate at Adrianople.
Sir,
    The staff office of the army sends you herewith a copy of an article which appeared in an English newspaper, the *Daily Telegraph,* and requests you to prepare a documentary report on the matter in order to make the truth public.

For the Chief of Staff,
(Signed)   Staff-Colonel Nérézov,
Chief of the Intelligence Department.
(S) Commanding-Staff-Officer Topladjicov.

To the Chief of Staff of the Army (in the City).
    In obedience to the above order, I submit the following report upon the questions at issue.
    I. I entered Adrianople with the first detachments of the infantry, the twenty-third and the fifty-third, on the day that the fortress was captured, and I was immediately nominated military magistrate. I held this position until the recapture of the city by the Turks. I was therefore enabled to judge of the situation, and to know of nearly all the important events that occurred in the city and the environs, as well as the affairs that came under my personal and official notice.
    II. The Turkish prisoners were taken to the island of Sarai because there were no barracks, some having been burned by the Turks, and others being infected with cholera. The Turkish officers were quartered in the one or two available ones that remained.
    During the first two days the proper quantity of bread could not be given to the prisoners because even our own soldiers were on short rations. In spite of this a quarter of the portion of bread served to each Bulgarian soldier was deducted and distributed to the Turkish prisoners. Two days later a sufficient quantity of bread arrived, and thereafter equal portions were served to our soldiers and to the prisoners. The latter were never subjected to any cruelty.
    III. It is true that a certain number of Turkish and Jewish houses were pillaged, but not by our soldiers. The local Greek population alone are to be blamed for these crimes. I was able to see this and to verify it personally many times from the moment of my arrival in the city. Later on, when order was reëstablished in the city, numerous complaints of offences committed by the Greeks, such as the looting of houses, incendiarism, pillage and so on, were addressed to me in my official capacity by the Turkish population.

I took out more than twenty actions on such complaints. These facts may be verified by examining the papers in the office of the public prosecutor or those on my own shelves.

There is also the sacking of the mosques. For this the Greeks, who had a frenzy for looting, must again be blamed. It was the Greeks who murdered thirteen Turks in one of the mosques of the city. A number of Greeks attempted to pillage the aforesaid mosque and the neighboring Turkish house. The Turks wished to prevent them, and seeing that they were threatened fired upon the assailants, killing one Greek and wounding others. The rest of the Greeks took flight and informed a patrol that the Turks were barricaded within the mosque; that they were firing upon the passers-by; and that they intended to blow up the whole quarter with dynamite. The Bulgarian soldiers urged the Turks to open the door and to give themselves up, and upon their refusal, fired upon them. Several Turks fell and several soldiers were wounded. But the Greeks, greedy for plunder, were the sole cause of the incident. Thanks to their falsehoods, they caused the death of one of their own number.

The carpets and the books of the mosque of the Sultan Selim were never scattered. They were guarded by a sentinel and everything was replaced as it had been originally.

IV. In regard to the Turkish officer who was killed, the truth has been equally distorted. This officer was neither wounded nor sick nor escorted by a soldier. He was hiding in a house and was discovered, and when he was being taken to the guard house he tried to escape and hide in the crowd. He was captured by another soldier, upon whom he drew his revolver, but had not time to shoot before he was himself shot by his captor and fell dead. No Jew interceded for him. The officer had resisted with force. The proof is the revolver drawn from his pocket.

As to the pillage of the jeweler's shop, it is an invention pure and simple. There is no such shop in Adrianople. All the shops which sell more or less precious articles are in the Marché d'Ali-Pacha, which was guarded by sentinels from the moment the city was captured. Nor is it true that other shops were pillaged by our soldiers. The truth is, that the Greek population, knowing of the rich Turkish houses, misled our patrols by telling them that suspect persons were hiding in such and such houses, where they also were concealing fire arms, and when our soldiers went to investigate, the Greeks thrust themselves in too, and either looted whatever they could lay their hands upon then and there, or else waited till the soldiers had gone and then stole at their leisure. The Turks themselves will, if need be, confirm all that I assert. As to the commander of the garrison, I must admit that he was most attentive to everybody and particularly, even a little too much so, to the Turks. None of the assertions made by the newspaper are true. I never left the garrison, and I was aware of everything that happened.

The account of the incident with the Greek Metropolitan of Adrianople is a shameful lie. It was not the commander of the garrison who was arrogant and insolent, but the bishop himself. I was in the office of the *aide de camp* when the Greek bishop came to make the application for the See of Kavala. He entered and without waiting to be asked, seated himself in an easy chair. He crossed his legs, and without making known the object of his visit began to smoke. He would only speak on general topics, where he went every day and how polite and amiable all the people were to him. He was none the less the leading spirit of the association that had for its object the buying of arms and the inciting of the Greek population to rebellion. But let the facts speak: First, arms were found hidden in a Greek church. The vicar of the church declared that rifles were being procured with which to arm the local Greek population, and that the bishop knew of it. Second, a manifesto coming from the above named association, an incitement of the Greek population to rebellion against the Bulgarian authorities was signed. Third, the Greek head schoolmaster, Gilo, was arrested, in the midst of inciting the Greeks and above all the Turkish prisoners at Bosnakony, to rise against the Bulgarians, assuring them that they had a sufficient number of rifles and even guns. Fourth, the same Gilo, the Metropolitan, and Dr. Courtidis, formed a committee of which we know all the members, the place of meeting and the decisions taken. No steps were taken by us in this matter, first, because the commander of the garrison and the deputy of the governor opposed it, and second, because it was on the eve of the recapture of Adrianople by the Turks, and there was not sufficient time.

This committee organized a plot against the commander of the garrison, and the authors of the attempt were arrested with revolvers in their hands. I took a public action on this account. For details of this, also, public documents may be consulted.

All of these facts, and many others of which the *Daily Telegraph* does not speak, may be corroborated by public documents, and by various other proofs.

I hand in my report a little late, because I only received the order on October 23, in the evening.

TOPALDJICOV.

Former Military Magistrate at Lozengrad and at Adrianople.
(S) Commandant of Kehlibarov Reserve.

Sofia, October 25/November 7, 1913.

———

Order No. 3 to the garrison at Adrianople.

Adrianople, March 15, 1913.

That one quarter of the rations of bread allotted to each soldier of the companies within the garrison and of the eastern section, be deducted, today and on March 16 and 17, and sent each day at ten a.m. to the office of the commandant in the north of the city, between the bridge of Toundja and the military depots, and allotted to the prisoners.

Chief of Garrison: Gen. Major Vasov.
Chief of Staff: Major of States General Volkov.

General Vasov explained to the Commission that this order was given to the Commandant on the 14th, and was obeyed at once, although being an oral command it had to be authenticated in writing. From the 17th, the General added, each prisoner was given a whole loaf of bread.

THE MILÉTITS PAPERS

1. On the Treatment of the Turkish Prisoners During the First Months Subsequent to the Taking of the Town of Adrianople

The whole of what has been said up to now, by persons whose impartiality is more than dubious, about the bad treatment to which the Turkish prisoners were subjected after the taking of Adrianople, is a tissue of revolting calumnies. The documents appended afford proof of the care taken by the military authorities for the maintenance of the prisoners both in the way of food and sanitary provision, and this despite the deplorable conditions, both as regards administration and sanitation, in which our troops found themselves on their entry into Adrianople, thanks to the fact that the Turkish authorities had destroyed all means of subsistence and primary necessaries in the town. As Appendix I shows, the vanguard of the garrison in Adrianople immediately on the entry into the town gave orders that a quarter of the bread rations of every Bulgarian trooper should be deducted for the benefit of the prisoners. It is true that the prisoners suffered from hunger during the two days immediately following the fall of the town. But the Bulgarian soldiery were in the same case, most of them having got rid of their bread at the moment of the final assault. Those who had kept it shared it fraternally on their entry with the famishing population. Everybody was, in fact, in the same position, a position which could not immediately be remedied because they, the Turks, had destroyed the railway bridge over the Arda, which made the work of the commissariat infinitely more difficult.

The behavior of our soldiers to their Turkish fellows was beyond reproach. The very fact of victory filled the Bulgarian soldiery with generosity towards the adversary of overnight. From the day of the capture the Bulgarian soldiers mingled with the prisoners, fraternized with them and held friendly converse.

To avoid the spread of cholera and other epidemics, it was decided to bivouac the Bulgarian troops as well as the prisoners outside of the town. A sufficient number of tents could not be furnished either for the prisoners or the troops. Nevertheless, twelve sanitary tents were put up in the island of Sarai, and reserved strictly for the prisoners. All the captive Turkish doctors were retained exclusively for attendance on the prisoners. Moreover, the necessary precautions were taken for disinfection, to prevent the spread of the disease which carried off numerous victims every day among the prisoners, who were already enfeebled by the privations they had endured during the siege. An edict of March 29, issued by the head of the garrison, enumerated measures to be taken to prevent the spread of cholera among the prisoners, who were thereby ordered to receive a daily ration of 1 loaf, 100 grammes of rice and 200 grammes of meat, the same as that of the Bulgarian soldiers.

2. Housebreaking, Robbery and Pillage, Attributed to the Bulgarian Soldiery in the Town of Adrianople

It is a fact that a number of thefts by way of housebreaking and pillage did take place in the days immediately preceding and following the capture of the town, but all of these, almost without exception, are attributable to the Jewish and above all, to the Greek population. They set to work from the night of March 12, when it was obvious to everyone that the fall of the town was imminent. Pillage on the part of Greeks and Jews went on all over the town, even while our troops were effecting entry and they had to intervene to drive off the marauders with blows of the whip and flat of their swords. The Turks who had had to look on despairingly while their goods were pillaged hailed the assistance of the Bulgarian soldiers. The pillagers did not only plunder private houses; they sacked public buildings as well. Cherif-bey, director of public property, describes how the Greeks broke the doors of his house and carried off the furniture. The government offices, he says, were treated in the same way; part of their furniture being discovered later in the warehouses of the following business firms:—Moses Levi Patchavradji, the German bank, the Bank of Salonica, Avram Baruch, Toledo, Toledo-Rodrigue, Gustav Tschinare, Moses Ovaliche, and others. The firms in question stated that all the objects thus found had been purchased by them from Greeks and from some Armenians. A quantity of stolen goods were bought from a certain Djavid Ousta, son of one of the Russian consul's domestics, by the firm of Salomon Menahem. The whole of the furniture of the Turkish military club and the goods of several Turkish notables were afterwards discovered in the hands of Greeks in the vicinity. During the earliest days of the occupation hundreds of complaints were lodged by Turks, who knew the Greeks by whom they had been pillaged. Many dared not give names for fear of reprisals. The Bulgarian troops touched nothing in the mosques. The library of the Sultan Selim mosque was found to have been ransacked. This again was the work of the population, which knew its value and the desirable specimens existing there. There was a persistent rumor current to the effect that the "Selimie"

Koran, an object of great price, both on account of its antiquity and the richness of its gold binding, was in the possession of the Russian consul.

However that may be, order was restored with praiseworthy celerity on the entry of the Bulgarian troops, despite the fighting that was still going on in the southern and north-western sections. A series of orders was issued from time to time, which aimed at establishing the fullest measure of public security and ameliorating the prisoners' lot. An order from headquarters permitted nearly half the prisoners at Adrianople to return to their homes as new citizens of the Bulgarian crown, without distinction of nationality.

An order of March 17, o. s., No. 6, issued by the head of the garrison for the amelioration of the lot of the remaining prisoners, ordered that 3,000 prisoners should be dispatched to the interior daily. Another order of March 21, o. s., enjoined the officer in charge of the prisoners to distribute a certain number of them in the villages immediately adjacent to Adrianople, Bosna-Keuï, Anir-Keuï, Emirli and Tatar-Keuï. Other orders issued from headquarters on March 17, o. s., No. 65, and on March 20, No. 121, and that issued by the head of the Adrianople garrison on March 29, o. s., show the consideration devoted to the case of the Turkish prisoners.

At the entry of the Bulgarian troops there were in Adrianople, over and above the prisoners, more than 25,000 Turkish peasants who had taken refuge there before the investment began. Throughout the whole period they were provided with food. A special commission was set up under the presidency of a superior officer and composed of two officials, an officer and two Turkish notables, one being the mufti of Adrianople, to restore the Turkish refugees to their villages, reëstablish them in their houses, and supply the most necessitous with means to start work again on their fields. Since the Greeks used to attack Turkish refugees on their return to their homes in order to plunder them and theirs, guards of three or four soldiers were posted in every village to protect the Turks against Greek aggression. These steps were carried out and the mufti more than once expressed to our authorities the gratitude for their care felt by the Mussulman population. And yet, when the Turkish troops crossed the frontier and advanced on Adrianople and Mustapha Pasha, the first act of Turks and Greeks was to massacre most of the guards set for their protection who had not succeeded in beating a retreat. Most of the Turkish officials found in Adrianople at the taking of the town were removed with their families and those of the officers by land and sea to Constantinople. As they got on board they thanked the representatives of the Bulgarian authorities, with tears in their eyes, for the attentions they had received. These people are living and could, if needed, confirm what has been said above.

3. *Alleged Excesses Committed by the Bulgarian Troops at the Evacuation of Adrianople*

The allegations made by certain interested persons as to the cruelty exercised towards prisoners and population by the Bulgarian troops on evacuating Adrianople are so many revolting inventions. When the Turkish army from Tchataldja and Boulaïr advanced towards Adrianople, the prisoners were divided into bodies of 1,000–2,000 strong, and dispatched to the interior of Bulgaria, each body being under the convoy of twenty or thirty veterans of the territorial army. To say that the prisoners were ill-treated, or still worse, massacred *en masse* on the way, is absolutely false. The very size of the escort would make such a statement hardly admissible.

4. *Alleged Execution of Forty-five Greeks Who Are Said to Have Carried off Sacks of Flour from the Depot Because They Were "Dying of Starvation"*

The truth about this incident, which has been grossly exaggerated by unscrupulous persons, is as follows:

On July 7, o. s., when it appeared that the Turkish troops must be near at hand, the Greeks of Karagatch, aided by those of the village of Bosna-Keuï, armed themselves and took to pillage, thereby causing a fearful panic among the population. They butchered five soldiers belonging to the Territorials and some twenty Turkish prisoners working at the station. These men, who are described as "dying of starvation," profiting by the panic they had aroused, next threw themselves on the provision and clothes depots and regularly pillaged them. The sentinels on guard at the depots did no more than their duty in firing here and there on the insatiable robbers.

As to the corpses of these same Greeks, said to have been drawn up from the Maritza, the truth is as follows: The prison in Adrianople was filled with more than 262 criminals, most of whom were Greeks, 100 having been incarcerated for acts of murder against Turks and some fifty for robbery, incendiarism and outrages. On the night of July 7–8, o. s., the prisoners confined in one of the cells in an upper story, facing east upon the main street, succeeded in sawing through the bars of one of the windows, whence thirty-two made their escape by means of a belt. But when they reached the Yanak-Kichla bridge and found it guarded, the prisoners, to the number of twelve, seeing themselves threatened by a patrol coming up from behind, threw themselves into the Toundja in the hopes of swimming across. The soldiers opened fire on the fugitives and succeeded in killing them. These are the bodies seen in the Toundja.

5. Alleged Ill-Treatment Endured by the Greek Bishop of Adrianople at the Hands of the Head of the Garrison

According to information prior to the outbreak of hostilities, a committee really existed in Adrianople, in the time of the Turks, whose object was to use every available means to secure the closing of Bulgarian schools and churches in Thrace and to Hellenize the inhabitants. The Greek bishop of Adrianople, the chairman of this committee, was in constant touch with the Greek patriarchate and the Athenian government, which supplied him with the necessary resources for pursuing the end in view. The committee's activity continued after Thrace had been conquered by our troops. It began to agitate for the autonomy of Thrace and the expulsion of the Bulgarians. Arms were distributed to the Greek population through its instrumentality and attacks made on the representatives of constituted authority. An emissary of the Athenian government, George Pouridi, was at this time at Adrianople, where he coöperated with the bishop to stir the committee to activity. On May 21, o. s., when General Savov happened to be in the Greek bishopric making a speech on the birthday of King George, Pouridi succeeded in getting out of prison and making his way to the bishopric and the room where Savov was with the intention of assassinating him. He was arrested by the chief of the guard and sent back to prison. Three attempts, of the same kind, on the life of the head of the garrison were made by Greeks, who were in each case arrested in the act of putting their design into execution. In spite of repeated demands, the Greeks never willingly handed over the arms in their possession. In the course of domiciliary visitations to houses and churches, considerable quantities of arms were discovered, abandoned by the Turks and gathered up by the Greeks. At times of most serious crisis, the telegraphic lines between Adrianople and the front were cut. The culprits—again Greeks—were arrested and delivered over to justice.

It was in view of facts like this that the head of the garrison at Adrianople was ordered to entreat the Greek bishop of the town to use his influence with his flock to induce them to behave as citizens and respect the established order, failing which the bishop himself should be held responsible for any infringement of public order which might be imputed to the Greek community. The order was carried out simply and fully as it was given. The whole story of a violent scene between the bishop and the commandant is a piece of pure fantasy, as is that of the assassination of a Turkish officer and an Israelite by a soldier in the main street.

Finally what has been said above of the orders issued by the chief of the garrison of Adrianople alone gives some idea of the pains taken to insure order and security in the town and its environs. On the other hand, the papers of the examining magistrates and military procurators permit one to state that an inquiry was opened on every crime committed; in every case the guilty persons were arrested and condemned, irrespective of nationality, by regularly constituted tribunals, whose sentences were strictly in accordance with established law. The result of all this could but be excellent. Exemplary order was established without delay, and all the citizens without distinction of nationality enjoyed full liberty. Confirmation of this fact is afforded by a number of foreigners of distinction who came to Adrianople, among them an Englishman, Brigadier General R. G. Broadwood, who visited the town shortly after it was taken, and whose statements are not open to doubt. The recognition by impartial persons of a state of affairs so praiseworthy could not but excite the animosity of our adversaries who left no stone unturned in the endeavor to deceive public opinion, and traduce the name of Bulgaria. It may moreover not be superfluous to remark that the secretaries of most of the foreign consulates at Adrianople, including the Russian, are Greeks, who had always been used by the Greek bishop to prejudice the Bulgarian cause in the eyes of their respective governments, and defend the criminal activities of their Greek compatriots. This fact casts a curious light upon reports issued by the secretaries of certain foreign consulates at Adrianople, who carefully refrained from avowing their real nationality, hidden beneath the cloak of their representation of foreign Powers.

Documents Relating to Chapter III

DEPOSITIONS

1. LETTER OF BARONESS VARVARA YXCOULL TO MR. MAXIME KOVALEVSKY

Salsomaggiore, August 29, 1913.

My dear friend:

· I have spoken so much to you of Bulgaria, and you have always shown such interest in the topic, that I do not hesitate to write to you where truth makes my doing so an actual obligation, à propos of an article which appeared in a recent issue of the *Daily Telegraph,* emanating ostensibly from a Russian diplomatist, commissioned by his government to make an inquiry into the "Bulgarian atrocities" at Adrianople. I say "ostensibly," for fortunately the position of the person responsible for the "information" which was collected *in two days,* has been officially repudiated. The story is the work of a newspaper correspondent (his name is not given) who, *propio motu,* undertook an "inquiry," if such a word can be used, to describe highly difficult investigations requiring far more time, if they were to be serious or more or less truthful. I say more or less truthful, for it seems to me that, *post factum,* considering the state of mind of the ex-belligerents, the national characteristics and mutual passions, it is almost impossible to arrive *at the whole truth.* Certainly I make no claim to do so; but I should like to prove from facts that happened under my eyes that the best intentions—and no doubt the correspondent was animated by such,—often arrive at results far enough removed from reality. He states among other things, that the town of Adrianople was sacked, pillaged and half destroyed by the Bulgarians when they entered it. I went to Adrianople on the third day of the Bulgarian occupation, and my first impression on getting well into the town was one of profound astonishment at the order reigning, despite the fact that the police force at that time mustered but thirty men; at the sight of streets literally overflowing with troops going hither and thither, obviously rejoicing in that victory but without anything that could give or was meant to give offense to the vanquished.

There was a great crowd by the Sultan Selim mosque, trying to effect an entrance, but the doors were closed and the sentinels refused all admittance. When they saw me in the dress of a sister of charity and accompanied by a slightly wounded Bulgarian officer, they let us in by one of the little side doors where there was no press. When I asked why the public was not admitted without special permit, the sentry replied that some damage had been done by the soldiery on the first day, whereupon measures had been immediately taken. I looked about me anxiously, *fearing for what I might see* and expected to notice signs of irreparable damage, *but, with the exception of a hole in the roof made by a shell* during the siege, in the angle of one of the small staircases, I saw nothing but perfect order; the sumptuous carpet, of incalculable value, had been carefully rolled up, the flags covered with matting, the wrought iron chandeliers which adorn the interior of the mosque all in good condition, with the exception of a dozen which may have been long wanting, everywhere irreproachable cleanliness. Assuredly the Sultan Selim mosque did not at that time present the appearance of a building which had been "sacked and soiled."

Thence I went to a consulate, where I was given a thrilling account of the ravages committed in the mosque of which sinister details had been reported. Great was the surprise of the people there when I described what I had just seen. If such stories were possible at that moment, in the town itself, what legends might grow up in the course of months!

The *Daily Telegraph's* correspondent is equally remote from reality in his description of the murder of a Greek by the Bulgarian troops. The incident took place while I was in Adrianople; I saw the dead body, which was left covered up but exposed to the public on the spot where it fell. The Greek, an Ottoman subject, discovered a certain number of Turkish soldiers hidden in a little mosque; he pointed out their hiding place with his finger to the Bulgarian officer passing by with his half company. The Turks evidently saw the gesture, for a volley of musketry immediately came through the half closed windows and the Greek fell, mortally wounded. The Bulgarian officer then gave the order to fire on the hidden men; and if my memory does not deceive me, thirty were killed. I think that the officer acted rightly.

In the early days there were frequent cases, especially at night, when persons in hiding, Turkish soldiers or others, took advantage of the absolute darkness in which the town was plunged, to fire on the passers-by. The governor general accordingly issued an order, which was posted everywhere, stating that all the inhabitants of the houses whence these shots came should be bayoneted. This order was indispensable, for the victims of these attacks from behind door and window amounted to a considerable number. Whatever its severity, it saved many lives.

I can state that although I was in Adrianople four times during the fifteen days subsequent to the capture of the town, I never heard that the Bulgarian soldiers committed acts of violation, of pillage, or any kind of excess. There were some cases of robbery on the first day; but they were immediately and severely punished and not repeated. I should certainly have known of any instance, however trifling, of this kind, and I do know that although certain foreigners, collectors of antiques, did offer large sums for carpets and other valuables, no one found anything for sale twenty-four hours after the entry of the Bulgarians.

The destruction caused during the siege, by the shells of the besiegers, was very small in proportion to the quantity of shot used. I think I am correct in stating that in almost every street, not in all, there were at most one or two houses *demolished*. A most incorrect interpretation has again been given to "atrocities" committed on the Turkish prisoners suffering from cholera. The régime to which they were subjected was undoubtedly severe,—exposed as they were to the rain and the still cold nights, and altogether deprived of attention. But how could it be otherwise when the hospitals of Adrianople were already overflowing with Turkish wounded and in such a deplorable state that I could only get twenty places (under abominable conditions) for Bulgarian officers (almost on the point of death) who could not be carried further, and who had absolutely to be moved from Karajousouff. This was the name of the little Greek village, seven miles from the town, in which was situated the Russian mission of the Kaufmann brotherhood, of which I had been at the head for five months (two months during the siege of Adrianople being spent at Karajousouff). We had fifty-eight tents for the wounded, more than 5,000 of whom passed through our hands on the days of the attack. With the best arrangement, it was impossible for us to keep all the seriously wounded cases. Room had to be made at any cost, and it was to provide for that that I betook myself, on the third day, to Adrianople.

Despite all my efforts, despite the desire of the Bulgarian authorities to provide me with what was so indispensable, I only succeeded in getting these twenty beds. The rest of the wounded had to be moved first to Kirk Kilisse (Lozengrad, fifty-five miles from Karajousouff), and then owing to want of room at Lozengrad, to Mustapha Pasha (seventy miles off), by carts drawn by oxen over very bad roads. If the Bulgarians were unable to provide any sort of accommodation at Adrianople for their own wounded, was it to be expected that they should succeed in lodging thousands of Turks suffering from cholera who had to be isolated from the other prisoners and wounded?

From the humanitarian point of view the lot of those poor fellows is obviously to be deeply commiserated, and the Bulgarians ought to have treated them otherwise. I merely state the facts as they were, and point out that in the given circumstances actions which at first sight appear appalling do become explicable. In any case the accusation should be directed not against the Bulgarian army but against the abominable medical administration which has escaped criticism altogether. If one is to talk at all about cruelty and inhumanity personified during war, which is itself the negation of all humanity, the terms must be applied to the unheard of sufferings and the absolute want of attention endured by the brave Bulgarian soldiers. These heroic men sacrificed their lives for the country in a spirit of joyous exaltation, worthy of the ancient stoics. They perished hideously, mainly because of the carelessness, the ineptitude, the incapacity, the abominable indifference of the military medical authorities, who, with but rare exceptions, showed a complete contempt for the science and profession which they had the undeserved honor to exercise. It is at their door that the guilt will lie; they should be judged and punished so that they may not in the future perpetuate the harm they did during the war.

The European press has been full of "Bulgarian atrocities" against Turks, Greeks, Serbs, etc. It is strange to see so impassioned a unanimity in making accusations that are difficult, almost impossible, to verify. During the course of what was called the "second war,"—that is to say, from the resumption of hostilities to the capture of Adrianople, not a single foreign correspondent was allowed with the Bulgarian army. Our mission alone was with the advance guard; and I can certify that during the two months I spent at Karajousouff, not only did I never see a case of mutilation of wounded or dead; I never heard one spoken of. After the siege, I saw Turkish corpses lying by the hundreds on the roads and in the fields. They were hideous because decomposition had begun; they lay unburied for several days because there were not enough people to collect all the dead, Bulgarians and others, and the heat of the sun was already great. But *I never saw* one that was mutilated. We saw dozens of Turkish wounded. They complained bitterly of the horrible way in which they had been treated by their officers, but no one of them said anything of "Bulgarian atrocities."

When I left Adrianople, I saw the members of the English Red Cross mission, who had come to nurse the Turkish cholera patients. They complained of the want of proper accommodation, of the lack of attendance and care, but no one spoke to me of cruelties practiced by the Bulgarians on the Turkish prisoners. Here and there such cases of course occurred, but I shall never believe that the Bulgarian soldiers at fault acted with the knowledge, or as is sometimes stated, under the instigation of their officers.

To sum up, my impression is, from a stay of five months and a half in the midst of the soldiery at Philippoli, Kirk Kilisse, Mustapha Pasha and Karajousouff, that the war was a crusade of ascetics inspired by a fanatical patriotism. The orgies, the debauches, the "women" who play so big a part in war, were altogether absent. Neither during the long months of the siege nor in the joy of victory did I ever see a drunken soldier or officer.

I could go on with this letter forever, for as I think of the past, still so near and already so terribly obliterated, thousands of incidents recur to my memory, lit up, all of them, by the flame of a patriotism ready for any renunciation; but I fear to trespass too far on your patience. All I want to do is to give you the testimony of an eye witness to the inaccuracy of certain accusations.

Europe is guilty of profound injustice in covering with a cloud of hideous crime men who fought under exceptionally trying conditions, fought with a stoical heroism, making no murmur, dying like martyrs without a complaint, their hearts full of faith in the greatness and force of their country.

I think I know the Bulgarians, good and evil; and I can not but bow before them with the most profound respect and the most ardent admiration.

If you think that what I have told you can be of any utility, make what use of this information you think good.

Yours very sincerely,

V. YXCOULL.

2. EVIDENCE OF TURKISH OFFICERS CAPTURED AT ADRIANOPLE COLLECTED BY THE COMMISSION AT SOFIA

The two following depositions were drawn up by Major Choukri, of the Engineers, and Captain Jummi, third battalion.

Oral Depositions

No. 1. CHOUKRI-BEY, *Major, Governor of Adrianople.* He was seated in his office when the Bulgarians entered the town. His subordinates reported to him that four Turkish officers had been killed in the town and that the Bulgarians had searched their pockets and rifled them. Similar practices took place even in the barracks in which his office was situated. It was at this moment that Lieutenant Nikov made his appearance to take over the governorship. Mr. Choukri complained of what had occurred to Mr. Nikov, but the latter was unwilling to take his complaints seriously. Choukri discovered among other things, that Lieutenant Adil had been robbed in a similar way at the same barracks, and it was through Choukri's protection that Lieutenant Adil was spared such things in the future. Choukri told Mr. Nikov of the existence of a store of meal in a certain mosque, only to discover later that the Bulgarian officer had sold the meal for his own profit.

Two days later Mr. Choukri was imprisoned on the island of Sarai. It is impossible to describe all that was endured by those imprisoned on that island. The Bulgarian soldiers actually killed the Turkish prisoners simply to get their water bottles. "With my own eyes," said the witness, "I have seen seven prisoners massacred on the pretext that they were trying to escape, although they were really only going to draw water from the river." The officers were left for three days and four nights without nourishment. Soldiers and even officers were reduced to eating the bark of the trees, and gnawing their shoe leather to assuage the pangs of hunger. Some hundred perished in a single day of starvation and sickness. According to Mr. Choukri the deaths totaled 3,000.

No. 2. EYOUB, *Captain of Artillery,* was sent with Refik and Ali-Nousrat as bearer of a flag of truce to announce the surrender of the northern district. He and his companions were greeted by combined fire from artillery and infantry, despite the white flag. When they reached the area occupied by the seventh regiment of artillery, the soldiers disarmed the plenipotentiaries, relieved them of watches and purses and refused to bring them before the governor. A soldier struck Eyoub with the butt of his musket and threatened to kill them all three. The first soldier was joined by a second who plundered the two lieutenants. But a third protested against the behavior of his comrades and led

Choukri and his companions before Mr. Nikov, the Bulgarian lieutenant, who in turn brought them before the colonel of the twenty-third regiment, commanding the northern district. He dictated the terms of surrender to them. Nikov promised Choukri that he would discover the guilty soldiers and compel them to restore what they had stolen. On the next day, however, Eyoub saw Nikov mounted on his horse. * * * He tried to impress a better point of view upon him, but Mr. Nikov forbade him to say any more about it.

No. 3. Tahsine, *Captain of the Corps of Sharpshooters.* (*Nichandje.*)

The Turkish soldiers in the Marache section surrendered to the Servians, who disarmed them without any molestation, and held them for three days after which they led them away, under guard, to be handed over to the Bulgarians. On the way loud reports were heard. The Servians composing the escort concluded that some trickery was preparing. Nevertheless they continued their march. Crossing the bridge of Arda, they advanced along the Karagatch road, near to the railway station, at which point a Bulgarian officer met them to take over the prisoners. Again a report was heard, followed by a salvo; the result of the drama was that sixty Turkish soldiers and four Servian soldiers lay dead, and a Servian sergeant was wounded.

On the most natural explanation the Bulgarian soldiers were responsible for the shots. The Servians refused to hand over their prisoners, and an animated dispute broke out between the Bulgarian and Servian officers. The colonel of the Twentieth Bulgarian Regiment, who arrived while the dispute was going on, ordered the Bulgarian sentinels to surround the first group of Turkish officers and put them under arrest. Some of us who knew Bulgarian understood him to say that we were all to be shot. Drawing his sword, he commanded all the captives, officers and soldiers alike, to lie down on the ground. He asserted that they still had revolvers in their possession for which he wished to have them searched. Thereupon the Servian officers remarked that he would not find so much as a knife on the unfortunate Turkish prisoners. At that moment a bomb exploded. The Bulgarian officers immediately declared that it was the Turks who had thrown it and that they should all be executed. Another bomb went off, but it fell in such a way that it was impossible to accuse the Turks. Thereupon to the great astonishment of the prisoners, the Bulgarian officer declared that their lives were spared. "We have already discovered the Turkish officers who were to blame," he said, "and they have paid their debt."

No. 4. Hamdi-bey, *in command of an artillery battery.* Coming from Marache, he was marching in the midst of a body of seven officers, three mounted, the other four on foot. Some Bulgarians fired upon them; the frightened horses made off at a gallop. It was then that the three mounted officers, Major Fouad-bey, Major Rifaat-bey (both attached to the fourth regiment of artillery) and Captain Iffan, were slain. The four officers on foot took refuge in a café. The Bulgarians followed them thither, but some Servian officers, appearing on the spot saved their lives. Nevertheless, the Bulgarians plundered them of everything down to their pocket handkerchiefs. A Bulgarian captain, Mr. Popovtchev, of the first company of the first battalion of Pioneers, witnessed the whole scene without a single word of protest. A Turkish artillery captain was robbed of ninety pounds Turkish money and a ring. Mr. Popovtchev tried to recover the stolen money but his inquiries only resulted in the recovery of one Napoleon and five *medjids* (a twenty piastre coin, worth about 3s. 8d.). Having nothing to eat the Turkish officers had to pay as much as three francs for a bit of bread.

No. 5. Ismail Mail, *staff doctor* (see also a report by him on the forced conversion of the pomaks), actually saw some Bulgarian soldiers bayonet two Turkish soldiers at the time of the surrender of Adrianople, and throw their corpses into the river. Later, at Stara Zagora, he saw the Bulgarian sentinel slaughter a Turkish soldier, Halil-Ali-el Sultanieh, without any provocation. The soldier's name was entered on the rolls as having died of disease. He also saw his orderly Ahmed-Omer, one of the eleventh medical company of Conia, killed at Stara Zagora by a Bulgarian soldier without any good cause.

No. 6. HADJI-ALI, *officer in the reserve,* serving in the police at Adrianople, deposes that the wife and sister of a Turkish paymaster living next door to him were outraged and then butchered by the Bulgarian soldiery. He saw with his own eyes Ismail-Yousbachı (Captain) killed in the street by Bulgarian soldiers on the day of the surrender of the town. A Jew protested against the murder, only to pay for his protest with his life. Further he saw 400–500 inhabitants of Adrianople kept prisoners in the Konak courtyard of the commandant's headquarters. The Bulgarian soldiers stood on guard outside the entry, four Bulgarian *comitadjis* inside. While the soldiers pushed the inhabitants into the yard, the *comitadjis* struck them with the butt ends of their guns. In the yard he saw four or five dead bodies. He suspects that all these Konak prisoners were killed, but is not absolutely certain on the point.

Deposition of Captain Jummi

After the fall of Adrianople, Mr. Minev came to dress my wounds; he took our field glasses and pocket pistols, saying he would keep them in remembrance of us. We were taken to Tatar-Keuï. General Savov treated us well and ordered us to be taken to Sofia. This night,—the night of the 13–14,—we spent there, some twenty of us officers. On March 14 we were dispatched on foot towards Simenli, in the direction of Sofia. At Simenli we were conducted to a Mussulman house, only inhabited by some women and old men between sixty and seventy; the other men, among them one old man, had been assassinated by the Bulgarians; the women had been violated. Two hours later the order was given for us to be taken to Kadi-Keuï, to take train there. Lieutenant Boris opposed the order and set us on the march again. We spent four nights thus. One night several of us officers happened to be in the yard of a little Mussulman house. The people tried to ill-treat us, but Major Stefanov of the thirtieth regiment gave us some bread and brought us to the tents, where 13,000 prisoners were. During that day 500 grammes of bread were given out to us; the Bulgarian soldiers took their money and watches from the prisoners. (The next sentence is unintelligible; the witness appears to state that the reply made to prisoners who asked for bread was to strike them with bayonets.) I saw a Bulgarian soldier about to strike a Turkish soldier with the butt of his musket and Lieutenant Boris authorizing him by a gesture and the words "Do so!" Four days later, thanks to Stefanov, we were taken to Adrianople. On the road I saw the corpses of nine Turkish soldiers and a wounded man, his face so bathed in blood that it was an indistinguishable mass. The wounded man was lying alone in the fields. My comrade saw four dead bodies arranged in the form of a cross.

CAPTAIN JUMMI,
Fourth Regiment, Third Battalion.

Deposition of Choukri, Major in the Engineers

I commanded the Engineers on the south front of Adrianople. Under my orders there were two captains, Ata-bey and Atif-bey. After the surrender, at the moment when the Bulgarian soldiers had effected entry on the south side in the Greek quarter Keuï, they began, under the guidance of the Greeks in Adrianople, to enter the houses and to seize whatever they found there. Everything we had was given over to pillage except the trunks we had deposited with an Armenian, a Russian subject and brother to the dragoman of the Russian consul. This same Armenian gave shelter to the wife, child and female servant of engineer Captain Atif-bey. The Bulgarian soldiers, led by some Greek natives, forcibly entered the house of the said Armenian during the night. They seized the trunks which belonged to us, and Captain Atif-bey's horse; they asked for two hundred Turkish pounds as a ransom for the captain's wife and kept repeating their demand, leaving them no peace till they paid over nine Turkish pounds on the first day and three more on the second.

CHOUKRI,
Major of the Engineers.

3. DEPOSITIONS OF BULGARIAN OFFICIALS

GENERAL VASOV, *Military Governor of Kirk Kilisse (Lozengrad)*, from November, 1912, *Commander of the army of the eastern section of Adrianople*, and from March 13, 1913, *Commander of the garrison*, from April onwards *Governor of Thrace*. His army took Adrianople by assault on March 13/26 at eight o'clock in the morning.

I reached Ghébéler, twelve miles from Adrianople, and rejoined my troops at ten o'clock in the morning. The army passed through the town amid the plaudits and hurrahs of the population. The Turkish inhabitants were in the streets in great numbers. Orders were given to the troops to bivouac in the quarters between the Toundja and the Maritza. I soon perceived that there were too many soldiers in the town and accordingly telephoned from the house of the commander of the Turkish cavalry to the commander of the army not to let the troops of the other sections enter.

The Turkish soldiery made prisoner within the town (they had cast their arms into the Toundja) who belonged to the eastern section, were collected in the island of Sarai. They numbered about 12,000 or 15,000. There were moreover on the island some civilians, or more precisely, persons attired in civil garb. Since these were many of them soldiers in disguise, I found it necessary to issue an order stating that any persons found hiding soldiers should be shot. I then ordered the prisoners shut up on the island to be counted and divided according to regiments. About ten days were allowed for this enumeration, in view of clearing them away from the island. The prisoners of the Servian section, who had made submission to the Servians, were under guard in the Hildyrym quarter. The prisoners of the southern section were in cantonments at Tcheurex-Keuï. The total number of prisoners amounted to 50,000 to 55,000 men.

As I had to hand Choukri Pasha over to General Ivanov at five o'clock in the afternoon, I immediately sought him out. Choukri and the officers of the general staff asked us to allow them to keep all that they had with them. Choukri wanted to keep his former house at Kadyrlyx. All this was granted. About March 15, they were allowed to depart for Bulgaria, the subordinate officers, from the rank of colonel downwards, being detained in Adrianople. As they were departing, I told Choukri that his orders for the destruction of the food depots had displeased me. I pointed out to him that the people who would suffer thereby were the unfortunate prisoners from his army who had, as I informed him, told me (on March 14, the day after the surrender, I had visited them,) that they had not eaten for five whole days, which meant that they had fed insufficiently or not at all during the last three days of the siege. I explained to Choukri the inconvenience caused us by the destruction of the Arda bridge, the annihilation of the provision depots, and the difficulty and delay of communication with Mustapha Pasha. Choukri's reply was that he had not ordered the depots to be burned; it was the work of *tachapkaris* (hooligans). I told him that I had ordered a levy of a quarter of the bread rations distributed to our soldiers to save the Turkish prisoners from dying of hunger, and he thanked me for it. This measure was intended as a temporary expedient until the goods expected from Baba-Eski and Mustapha Pasha could arrive. From the second day

(March 14) onwards, these quarter portions were given out to the enemy soldiery. Some days after—perhaps as early as the 15th—I divided the grain among the regiments forming my troops, in order that so far as commissariat went, they might be on an equal footing with the Bulgarian army.

The prisoners asked permission to take bark off the trees to light fires with, as it rained and was cold. Even our soldiers had no tents. Permission was given and they cut off the bark with knives and pickaxes.

One of the reasons for isolating the prisoners on the island of Sarai was the presence of infectious cases after the third or fourth day of the capture of the town. Choukri told me that cholera had appeared ten days before March 13, but that, at the time of the entry of the Bulgarian troops, it had disappeared. In effect, however, the disease did not spare the island, and we had to send Turkish doctors to isolate the infectious cases, nurse them, and bury those who died. I should estimate that the epidemic did not cause more than 100 to 200 deaths among the population of the island.

The story of the prisoners being reduced to eating the bark of the trees I dismiss as purely legendary. It is true that we could not do much for them, for our own men were very ill provided for. We did not distribute hot food, but they were given bread enough to keep off starvation. When the prisoners of war were rejoined by the famished inhabitants of the town, we decided to spread them out along the railway line that passed through the suburbs for greater ease of provisioning. In this way we only had to feed the poor population of the town proper, say some 15,000 to 20,000. In this matter we were greatly assisted by the English section of the Balkan committee. When the bridge was reconstructed, the prisoners were regularly provisioned; certain officers were specially told off to superintend it and provisional dwellings were put up. The English consul, Major Samson, can testify to these facts. General Broadwood actually wrote a letter which appeared in the *Times,* about the middle of April or towards the end of the month (old style,) to defend the Bulgarians from the accusations made against them.

The incident of the murdered Jew is possible. The soldiers were exasperated. In general, however, there was very little violence. At the same time it is not impossible that prisoners may have been killed during the night, but the facts have not come to my knowledge. There certainly was not wholesale assassination of prisoners. The incident of the Miri-Miran mosque is known to me from the story of Colonel Zlatanov. It is as follows: Certain Turks, fearing to be attacked, shut themselves up in the mosque with their wives and children. While the troops were passing through there some were shot, no one knew whence. A young Greek appeared and told the soldiers that people were firing on them from inside the mosque. A fairly big patrol moved in that direction, led by the Greek. Shots were fired from the mosque; the guide fell, and I saw his dead body myself. At that point our soldiers attacked the mosque with drawn bayonets and killed the men, sparing the lives of the women and children. This was the first regrettable incident to occur. I went to the spot in person, accompanied by Zlatanov and witnessed what follows. The Greek youth was slain fifteen or twenty paces from the mosque. Inside there were some ten Turks slain. Two among them, a mollah of some fifty-five years old and a young man of twenty, were still breathing. I ordered them to be taken to the hospital and a *procès verbal* to be drawn up. This is the solitary incident of bloodshed within my knowledge at Adrianople. While I held command, not a single man was shot. I was replaced by General Veltchev about April 1 (old style). The mufti repeatedly expressed his gratitude to the Bulgarians. On the second or third day, I called him before me in order to calm his previous terror, and he told me that he had not expected such humane behavior towards the Turkish population in a town taken by assault. I saved Mr. Behaeddine, who had insulted a Bulgarian officer, from court-martial. As to my general system, I described it in the paper *Mir,* while an article by me appeared several days ago, previous to this deposition, for which I had then no anticipation of being called upon. [The translation of the article follows.]

As to pillage on the entry of the Bulgarian troops, this is what I saw of it. It was the Christians who pillaged the Turks. I had to send three regiments, one of cavalry, two of infantry, to watch over the town. Nevertheless, all the Turkish stores (of clothes, provisions, etc.) were pillaged in the course of the first day. I ought immediately to have set about making domiciliary investigations, but throughout the period of my governorship (down to July 1, old style,) I refused to sanction such inquiries, in order not to disturb the people. Some house visits did take place by order of the officer commanding the town, but *only* in response to private requests. I gave permission to the officer commanding the town (Mr. Chopov, and his successor, Markov,) to open a depot for goods whose ownership was disputed and their origin dubious. As for depredations committed in houses inhabited by Bulgarians, the Austrian and Belgian consuls came before me with demands for damages in cases of which they gave names and particulars. I did not comply with the demand, since the allegations were incapable of proof. I have not heard of Mr. Chopov's carpets. I myself lived in the house of Akhmed-bey, opposite the Sultan Selim mosque. The house was full of furniture. The proprietor can be asked whether the least thing was found missing.

In an article which appeared in the *Mir* of Sofia, dated June 19, 1913, and entitled *The Negotiations at Constantinople,* Lieutenant General of the Reserve Vasov added, over his signature, the following remarks:

I am no enemy to the Turks; on the contrary, I am on terms of intimate friendship with them for we have many common interests, and I think I have given irrefragable proofs of these sentiments. The Mussulman population and the holy places of its worship at Adrianople owe their preservation to me. After the town was taken, I allowed no one to touch a hair on the head of the vanquished. Out of the modicum available for the subsistence of my soldiers, I fed the 60,000 Turkish prisoners and many thousands of starving wretches belonging to the Mussulman population. All these facts are known to Choukri Pasha, to the foreign consuls and to the 3,500 Turkish officials, whom I sent to Constantinople with their families in prosecution of a measure entirely honorable to the Bulgarian occupation. Dr. Behaeddine-bey, friend of Talaat-bey, also knows the truth on this point. This intelligent Turk and many of his friends certainly remember that in my capacity as governor of Thrace I did what I could to help them in their misfortune.

Order of the Day of General Vasov to the Adrianople Garrison

Adrianople, March 29, 1913.

In order to arrest the progress of the cholera epidemic which is raging among the prisoners of war, and among the soldiers of certain parts of the garrison, and in order that precautions be taken to prevent bodies of prisoners from infecting the population of the town and neighborhood with their disease, I order the following measures to be taken:

1. The authorities in places to which prisoners have been sent are to take care that they are lodged either in houses, or under tents, or in barracks quitted by our soldiers and near at hand. If necessary, new lodgings may be constructed.

2. The prisoners are to be distributed into small groups, so that overcrowding may be as far as possible avoided.

3. Steps are to be taken to secure that the quarter in which the prisoners are lodged is not infected. For this purpose deep troughs are to be dug for sanitary purposes, watered with petrol every day; and the smaller troughs are to be covered with earth every day.

4. The authorities responsible for feeding the prisoners are to see that bread and other food stuffs are supplied regularly at stated intervals; a warm soup of a hundred grammes of rice and two hundred grammes of meat to be supplied per head.

5. Boiled water is to be supplied for drinking, and the Turkish *kazanes* taken in the Turkish encampments may be used for this purpose.

6. The prisoners' sentries are to be changed every day, or if that be impossible, at least every two days. These sentries are to be regarded as suspected of infection and lodged in houses or tents at a sufficient distance from the army.

7. * * *

8. To prevent the epidemic from spreading, the employment of prisoners in any form

of work is to be avoided. If it should be necessary to employ them, particularly in the town of Adrianople, they afe to be employed only after a quarantine of six days. They are to be lodged in separate barracks and fed like the soldiers.

9. All prisoners sick with cholera are to be sent to a place removed from the Turkish hospital, to the Italian school at Karagatch, and to the isolation ward in the "Merquez" Central hospital at Yanyk-Kychlm.

10, 11, 12. * * *

13. Every facility is to be given to the American mission for assisting poor or sick soldiers, whether by medicines, or food or treatment for the prisoners.

14. Those responsible for the care of the prisoners are to inform the head of the Anti-Epidemic service of the number of Turkish doctors, apothecaries and members of the ambulance service, and of the number of prisoners, in each group, in order that the sanitary *personnel* may be increased wherever it is necessary.

Signed: GENERAL MAJOR VASOV, head of the garrison.
VOLKOV, head of the general staff.

4. REPORTS OF THE SPECIAL DELEGATION SENT TO RODOSTO BY THE ARMENIAN PATRIARCHATE

The Disaster of Malgara

On July 1/14, in the morning, three officials and ten Bulgarian policemen gave back Malgara to Cheigh Ali Effendi, and then left the city which thus remained, as did the surrounding country, without any public defense and without authority, until noon on the following day.

This anarchial situation, as well as the danger threatened by the animosity of the Mussulmen and Christians, decided nearly sixty Armenians to emigrate hastily into Bulgaria. Several young girls obtained their parents' consent to join this company of emigrants on foot.

Following reports sent by Ali Effendi concerning the situation of the town, on Tuesday, July 2/15, at four o'clock, Turkish time, a part of the Ottoman troops advanced from Oludja and Kechan toward Malgara.

The Greek and Armenian clergy, several prominent people and a great crowd of the inhabitants hastened to meet the troops. Ali Effendi addressing the commander, expressed his joy at the return of the Ottoman army, which he welcomed warmly. The commander then called out in a very harsh voice to the crowd, "Get back, you cowards," instantly producing a very unpleasant impression upon the townspeople of Malgara.

Before the entry of the troops, there had been no sign of the populace, but now an ever increasing crowd accompanied the battalions as they advanced, to the growing anxiety of the Armenians.

According to information received, a third of the military force sent to Malgara belonged to the fourth corps of the army, and the whole force could not have numbered less than 35,000 men.

The populace began to excite the soldiers by repeating that the Bulgarians had done nothing, and that the people who had crushed the country were the native *giaours*—infidels. And several officers led by the *bashi-bazouks* penetrated into the Armenian quarters and made observations on their own account. Monday and Tuesday passed without event, except one or two petty thefts. But on the morning of Wednesday, July 3/16, the attitude of the populace had become more menacing and aggressive. The market was almost entirely closed. At Bazirguian-Teharchi, several small Armenian shops were sacked.

Although, under protest of the shop keepers, the military authorities had forbidden pillage, yet no authoritative proclamation against it, capable of inspiring confidence among the Armenians, had been published, and no severe penalty attached to such acts. On the contrary, following the instructions of the commandant, on Tuesday and Wednesday the public criers twice called through the Armenian quarters that "those who had stolen objects belonging to the Mussulmen or who were in possession of arms were to give them up."

The military commander of the place, Mahmoud-bey, had the prominent Armenians brought before him, and shouted violently to them, "Armenian traitors, you have possessions and arms stolen from the Mussulmen." Furthermore, on the evening of the fourth day a sub-lieutenant declared openly to the Armenian soldiers, "You Armenians have helped the Bulgarians finely, and today or tomorrow you shall be rewarded."

Naturally all these things on the part of the officials added to the already intense excitement, and the proclamations of the criers incited the populace to the grossest misdeeds.

Terror stricken by these sinister indications of the catastrophe about to overtake them, the Armenians withdrew into their own quarters, expecting from moment to moment that the storm would burst.

On Wednesday at midnight, a part of the troops left the city. On Thursday morning, July 4/17, some soldiers commanded in violent and rough words that Bedros, of Rodosto, and Garaleet Minasian, of Malgara, should show them the way to Ouzoun-Kenpru. Garaleet, greatly alarmed, hid himself in his house. The pretext was found. Immediately a number of soldiers accompanied by a company of *bashi-bazouks* went up to Minasian's house, and Ali Tchavoucheov Malgara set fire to it by means of torches soaked in petrol. He then set fire to the priest's house.

The officer second in command, Mustapha Pasha, appeared on the scene and asked what was the reason of the fire. He was told that the "Armenian refused to show the soldiers the way to Ouzoun-Kenpru." He gave vent to a burst of rage and called the Armenians by every vile name, "Race of scoundrels and rogues, swine like the Bulgarians, traitors," and so on.

While houses were burning in one quarter of the town, at the other end, in the market, towards eleven o'clock, murders were being committed with scarcely a pretense of excuse, and the people were plundering freely. The fire naturally gathered most of the Armenians together in that place, and may have been purposely meant to divert them from the further atrocities that were beginning. At this very time Yervante Pejichkian, Hadji Vartérès, Tartar Oghlou Kévork, Toros Mamélédjian, and others, were assassinated by Sououlon Osman Ogha, Emine Pehlivan Oghlon Hassan, Hassan Hodja, Mehmed Ali, etc. This fact is attested by Hadji Manuél and others, who were dangerously wounded in the course of this butchery. The wounded affirm, furthermore, that the order to kill was in the first instance given by an officer.

An Armenian covered with blood passed before Heldhed Ali Pasha, who appeared completely indifferent to the sight. The soldiers and the Mussulman population forced their way into the Armenian houses, situated on the outskirts of the town, and sacked them.

Thanks to the efforts of the Armenian soldiers in the army, the fire was got under control after twenty-three houses and all their contents had been destroyed, but the opportunity awaited for three days had now arrived.

The town was surrounded by a very considerable number of troops, and by several thousand *bashi-bazouks*. Towards ten o'clock, Turkish time, fire broke out again in several different quarters of the market, and owing to the high wind, this new disaster had in a very little time assumed terrible proportions. Suddenly there was a noise of explosion and the Armenians imagined that the city had been bombarded by the Turks, who were thus exterminating the inhabitants, and on their side the Turkish population and the soldiers believed that the noise was caused by the explosion of bombs hidden in the Armenian shops. As a matter of fact, the fire had spread to the depots, where barrels of benzine, alcohol and other spirits were stored with the most appalling results.

The commission of inquiry sent by the Kaimakam and the Minister of the Interior, Talaat-bey, tried to explain these explosions by the bursting of bombs left by the Bulgarians. But no one has dared to assert that the Armenians employed bombs, and if the explosions had been caused by such things, the mosque situated close to the place would have been blown up, and half the town destroyed. And another significant fact omitted in the report of the commission is, that not even a wall was cracked by the force of these explosions.

Panic stricken by this new calamity, the Armenians, threatened by both fire and sword, rushed towards the gardens outside the town and there took refuge. The screams and terrified lamentations of the women and children were heart rending, and they huddled together in the open air, not knowing what impending horror might yet overtake them, victims of unspeakable anguish. Fortunately there were two military doctors and a few detachments of soldiers, who were able to be of some assistance to the wretched people.

It must not be forgotten that the Kaimakam, accompanied by the chief of police and a policeman, arrived the same day at Malgara, at eleven o'clock in the evening, Turkish time, and made some effort, useless however, to put out the fire. That night he appealed to the Armenian people to help extinguish the fire, but the women and children refused to be separated from the men and clung to their husbands and fathers and brothers. The Kaimakam then turned to the troops for assistance, but the commanding officer replied, "What does it matter to us, if the people most concerned are indifferent?" Here a soldier raised his hand against the Kaimakam whom he did not recognize.

The ruin made dreadful headway. Soldiers and *bashi-bazouks* rushed into the houses and plundered them freely. A few Armenians who had the courage to approach their dwellings, to try to save a few of their belongings from the fire, were prevented from entering by the soldiers who called out, *Yassak* ("It is forbidden").

We even hear that several Armenians were arrested for this very natural act and are still detained under military authority.

At six o'clock in the evening, Turkish time, the Kaimakam returned to the Armenian refugees in the garden, and exhorted them again to lend their assistance in stopping the fire, himself guaranteeing their safety. Fifty or sixty young men volunteered at the risk of their lives to go, and thanks to their efforts the fire was finally subdued.

The unfortunate people, of course, passed the night in the open air. The next day the bodies of the victims killed in the market place were deposited in the church yard.

Eight days after the catastrophe, no Armenian dared to venture near the places devastated by the fire. The ruins were still smoking and the Mussulman children were digging out various objects belonging to the Armenians and running off with them.

A week later the body of a well known Armenian of Malgara, called Bared Effendi Adjémian, was brought back to the city from a place about two and a half hours distant. The body shockingly mutilated had become almost unrecognizable.

We add to our report a list indicating the names of the twelve Armenians killed at Malgara, of the ten Armenians wounded, the eight lost and seven taken prisoners. The number of shops burnt was 218 and the number of houses eighty-seven.

The entire material loss amounts to £T80,000.

This catastrophe has totally ruined the Armenian population of Malgara. The refugees are camping on the heaps of rubbish and debris, and in their despair their one desire is to go as far away from their native land as possible.

July 17/30, 1913.

5. Thrace

Deposition of Mr. Kristo M. Bogoyev, Head of the Administrative Section of the Military Government of Thrace

The residence of the governor was at Kirk Kilisse (Lozengrad) up to March 15 (old style). From March 19 on, it was transferred to Adrianople. Mr. Bogoyev remained at Adrianople down to the end of the Bulgarian occupation, leaving it in the last train. His evidence is concerned throughout with the last days of the occupation and the departure of the Bulgarians—July 7 and 8 (old style).

On July 6 at 6.30 p.m., the Turks having reached Ourli, I telegraphed to the ministry and the staff office for permission for the officials, refugees and such of the inhabitants as wished to do so, to leave Adrianople. Permission was received at 11.30. To avoid disturbing the population, we did not spread the news, and at midnight the cinematographs were still open in the Rechadie gardens and people went quietly home. Leaving on the morning of Sunday, July 7, between three and four in the morning with the chief of the finance section and the head secretary, we passed the night at Karmanly. I then learned that the Turks had not yet entered the town. We received by telegraph the order to return. On July 8, we were once more in Adrianople. As we returned I counted at Marache, from the window of my carriage, ten corpses of Turkish prisoners, a sight which made a deep impression on me. When I arrived at Karagatch, I inquired of the Captain Mihailov, in charge of the station, the cause of the massacres. Mihailov explained to me that a body of prisoners, fifty to sixty strong, was employed in the station as laborers on transhipment work, and lived in the barracks near the Arda bridge. The other prisoners, the larger number of those who had not yet been dispatched to Bulgaria, were housed in the place of the Ali-Pasha mosque, on the Tcharchi. After they had been left there up to two or three o'clock, they had been sent to Yambol. The group in question must have been sent to Mustapha Pasha, under the escort of the militia (*Opoltchenie*). Under the supposition that the Turks had reached Adrianople, they endeavored to escape. The escort fired upon them.

After our departure on July 7, order was maintained by Major Morfov, who took the place of the commandant of the town, and by Lieutenant Colonel Manov. Eye witnesses have told me that even while the last trains were starting (there were eight of them on July 7), the Greek inhabitants began pillaging the depots. The number of the pillages grew rapidly. Firing on them was begun from the carriages of the last train but one, and two persons were killed with their spoil of caps, trousers, etc. Throughout the day of the 7th, Karagatch was without military or civil authorities. On July 8, the authorities reappeared and undertook a general search in the houses at Karagatch and the neighboring quarter of Adrianople. I learned that stolen arms and ammunition were found in various houses and that the thieves, the owners of the said houses, were shot to the number of twenty or thirty. This story was told me at the station on July 8, and confirmed by Mr. Morfov, whom I met on returning thither after an excursion in the town. I have no knowledge of the drowning affair. I do not say it is impossible but I am ignorant of it.

As to the period preceding our administration in Adrianople, I can say that we did regularly meet the demands of the mufti, who very frequently addressed himself to us. Ten days before our departure, the mufti asked us to restore the Sultan Selim mosque to the Mahometans. I replied: "The mosque is yours, but it will be difficult for us to safeguard it, and the moment for opening it has not yet come." We then telegraphed to the Tsar. Mr. Danev replied by ordering me to open the mosque so soon as it appeared to be possible to do so. I promised to do it on a date indicated by the Turks, that of the Ramazan festival, but when the permission had been given, I learned that the festival was over two days ago. On July 2, I was again asked to open the mosque to celebrate the festival. I refused, because the Turks were by that time approaching the Midia-Enos frontier. On July 3 or 4, the mufti again came to see me. I assured him that the mosque would be handed over to them, and that the Bulgarians would not destroy it. Thereupon the mufti said that after witnessing what the Mussulmen had suffered at the beginning of the Bulgarian occupation, he had thought the Bulgarians incapable of watching over the security of the Mussulmen. He was then on the point of departing for Constantinople. "But," he added, "thanks to you I have remained here. When you summoned me for the first time after your arrival from Kirk Kilisse, I was sure that you would receive me standing. But you made me sit down; you conversed with me for a whole hour and you told me that although you could not yourself do all that you would wish, you would nevertheless remain in order to fulfil your duty, and you invited me to follow your example. I remained. I find at present that you have really known how to take care of us. I have written in that sense to the Grand Vizier."

I know that Mr. Veltchev summoned the notables, and I am aware that he threatened them in the event of an insurrection breaking out. That was natural, in view of the insignificant number of our troops, lost in the midst of 50,000 Mussulman inhabitants.

As for the Greek bishop, his deposition (in the Machkov report) is given in bad faith. I have, personally, only had two letters from him: (1) He stated that an official had taken upon himself to pronounce a divorce between a husband and wife at Baba-Eski. As a matter of fact the case was that of a young man who was driven out of the house of his fiancee, after being entertained there for six months. The civil authorities intervened. (2) The Bulgarian priest by the Hildyrym quarter was accused of having forced children, by means of threats, to attend the Bulgarian school. This accusation was investigated and found to be false. I ought on the other hand to mention that six Ongarian rifles and a military costume were found in the Greek church at Keviche-have. An incident which shows the state of mind of the Greek is that seven or eight days before the Bulgarian retreat, the lines of communication between Karagatch and the military administration were cut, and the culprits discovered to be Greeks disguised as Bulgarian soldiers.

Deposition of Major (Afterward Lieutenant Colonel) Mitov

He was appointed major by General Vasov, on the very day of the entry into Adrianople. At the end of four or five days he was promoted to be lieutenant commander and finally commander. He remained in the town down to June 14 (old style).

The explanation of the defective commissariat was that the bridge had been destroyed and the depots burned. The Bulgarian soldiers themselves only got one loaf per day. General Vasov ordered a quarter of this ration to be deducted, and this was done by Commander Tsernowsky. The quarters were distributed during the first three days; the prisoners being divided into several bodies. I made a tour of inspection myself in the morning. People were not eating the bark of trees. Some bark had actually been cut off, but in order to make a fire; such was the origin of the legend. As a matter of fact after March 13, which was a fine day, we had a tempest in the night and floods of rain. I saw fires lit with my own eyes, and a shell, which happened to be too near, went off.

On the day of the entry of the troops, I witnessed touching scenes of the soldiers sharing their bread with the people. I even saw, indeed, men falling down in the roads from sheer weakness; during the last days of the siege the bakers sold bread only to the few rich people who could afford to buy it. It is true that on the island of Sarai the folk were so weak they could not even stand upright, and appeared the shadows of their former selves. People died but not by hundreds; there were thirty deaths on the first morning.

As to pillage, the following is what I saw of it: At the moment of the entry of our troops, on the morning of the 13th, I passed by the Young Turk club (in the house of

Abouk-Pasha) and found there two carts, full of furniture; among other things there were brass bedsteads worth some thousand francs, mirrors, wardrobes and valuable articles of furniture. I drew my sword and tried to speak to the people, but as they spoke Greek we did not understand one another. Finally I drove them off. In a street a little further down a watchmaker was being pillaged. He cried out to me, "They are pillaging indoors." I ordered them to come out; three men came out and I struck one of them with the flat of my sword. The Turks cried out to me, "Bravo, *aferim, sfendim,* these are the 'Greeks'!" But there was no way of stopping the pillage. All the streets, the Sultan Selim mosque, the Konak were full of people, women, old men and children; everybody was carrying off his spoils, here a quilt, there something else. My order for the stolen goods to be thrown down was obeyed, but as soon as I had gone they were picked up and carried off again. I put a sentry at the Municipal Council house and there nothing was taken. On several occasions I entered the house of Turkish officers and saw civilians coming out; I was shot at three times. I sent out numerous patrols, but they were lost in the labyrinth of alleys. I then ordered the inhabitants to whistle to warn and summon the patrols. An instance will show the difficulty of putting a stop to pillage. I knew one of the Turkish officers who had been made prisoner, a certain Hasib-Effendi. A Greek, Yani by name, pillaged his house and stole his horses. In the same house another Turk was found with his head broken open. I ask, "Who has done this?" "A Greek from Kaik." "Who?" "I dare not say, I am afraid of being killed." "But I guarantee that no one shall injure you." "Unfortunately you can not concentrate all your attention on me alone." I assigned a sentinel to the family of Hasib-Effendi and they went to live elsewhere, in the *baptches* (gardens). Even there, a Greek occupied the same house and found means of carrying off all their coats. Quantities of pillaged goods were found in all the Greek houses. Among these were the effects of Dolaver-bey, including his piano. Any number of people came before the Municipal Council to get certificates from the commandant that such and such goods had been *purchased,* but the price, far too low, proved clearly that the goods in question had been stolen by Greeks and Jews and re-sold.

When making my tour of the town, after the entry of the troops, I stopped before the Sultan Selim mosque. At the very entrance there were two female corpses. I placed a sentry at the entrance. Some Turkish families had taken refuge in the interior; I was told that there were as many as 4,000. They had brought their goods with them and bedding; "braziers" filled part of the mosque. They sent to ask me whether they could come forth. I gave permission and had them escorted to their homes by soldiers. When they left they put their belongings on carts. Among them I saw some carpets. In reply to my formal question they stated that all the objects belonged to them. At this stage I was not aware that there was a library attached to the mosque. On the next day I learned that a second entry of the mosque led to this library. I immediately betook myself thither, found the drawers open, and all the books lying about pell mell. Some of the bindings were empty, the books having been torn out of them. I was told that all this was the work not only of Greeks and Jews, but even of Turks. The priests asked me to be allowed to keep the books, but I refused. It is said that some strangers took advantage of the opportunity of striking some excellent bargains. A very valuable Koran, among other volumes, is said to have been secured. Some days later, an officer, Pocrovsky, brought me some Turkish books in a sack, but they were ordinary ones whose origin I failed to discover. I had the Sultan Selim mosque shut and ordered that it was only to be open to the public from three to five daily.

I know nothing of the case of the captive Turkish officer, but I have seen a Bulgarian soldier supporting an enfeebled Turkish prisoner and helping him to walk. Nor do I know anything of the story of the pillage of a watchmaker's shop, but I did assign a sentinel to an Armenian optician who was afraid of being robbed, with successful results so far as he was concerned. In the same way I had Ali-pasha's bazaar shut for fifteen days, to prevent it being pillaged.

Finally I set a patrol there and the bazaar was as a matter of fact safeguarded. If some Turkish officers' houses were plundered, the local population is to blame, not the army. The owners of Turkish houses begged me on their knees to give them Bulgarian officers as lodgers, and I sent them several. On the other hand the Greek population of the "new quarter" refused to put up any officers, and it was there that disorders took place.

I know Greek houses where the owners gave money and wine, and where the women offered themselves to the Bulgarian soldiery in return for their protection against pillage, and in some cases with success. I know too that a Greek of the Kaihm quarter put on Bulgarian uniforms to go pillaging in. I ordered the thieves to be arrested, but during my stay in Adrianople, not a single one was caught. There was to my knowledge one case of outrage, that of a *gamin* by a Greek on the Karagatch bridge. The culprit was arrested and punished. No outrage was committed by our soldiers.

In order to facilitate the feeding of the poor, I called the head of the *fournadjis* (bakers) before me on the second day and supplied him with meal, ordering him to make bread and sell it at fifteen centimes the loaf. Meal was distributed free to the poor; I myself assisted therein. I caused a list of the families of Turkish officers to be drawn up and sent meal and money to their houses.

6. ADRIANOPLE

Mr. Chopov, Head of the Police at Adrianople

Mr. Chopov was accused by the "Russian official," Mr. Machkov, of having himself sent to Sofia, through a Russian subject, three bales of stolen carpets. He came before the Commission personally and made the following deposition with regard to the pillage of Adrianople and the particular facts as to which he was accused:

On March 14, two days after the capture of Adrianople, Delaver-bey, a rich Turk, ex-mayor of the town, appeared before me and lodged a complaint on the score of the pillage of his house. I caused investigation to be made, and restored him the whole of his furniture which was discovered in Greek houses. The Greeks complained of the domiciliary visits undertaken at the request of Delaver-bey. Other beys— Berkham-bey, Derghili Mustapha, Hadji Abram, etc., told me that the cattle of their *tchifliks*, near Adrianople, had been stolen and that they feared the attempted destruction of the houses in the villages and of the crops. I sent soldiers to guard them and they collected the stolen cattle, discovered in the neighboring villages, Greek and Bulgarian. Delaver and Berkham complained of disturbance in the night. I provided them with watchmen. I visited the Turks in their houses to restore their confidence, told them they might wear the fez and continue to move about freely. I did everything in my power to restore Adrianople to its normal aspect in three days. I assembled Greeks, Turks and Jews, to bid them be at ease.

As to the "stolen" carpets, I did as a matter of fact buy some *sedjade* (carpets) of small size, in the shop of Fethi-Aga at Roustein-Pasha-Khan, and paid fourteen Napoleons for them. I also bought some from Osman (Roustein-Pasha-Khan) for sixteen Napoleons, and from a Jew of Besistein for eleven Napoleons. I made one package of all these carpets and had them taken straight from Fethi-Aga's shop to the counting house of Demetriadis. Witnesses to these facts are Isaac Demetriadis, George Doukidis, Avigdor Abraham Effendi, Patchavre Djemoise, all of them bankers or business men of Roustein-Pasha-Kahn, and present when I made my purchases. I bought the carpets as presents, and gave them to my friends at Sofia. When I heard that I was being accused in Adrianople of having stolen some carpets, I went there to call for an inquiry. I went to the *Juge d'Instruction* at the Court of Appeal in Philippopoli. An inquiry was held, and the charges dismissed.

At the Hotel de Ville I opened a depot for things stolen by the Greeks. Carts full of stolen goods were brought thither. For example, I saw two stolen pianos being brought. While safeguarding the property of the inhabitants of Adrianople, I refused the request of the Bulgarian consul, Kojouharov, for an inquiry on the property stolen from him, simply because he being a Bulgarian, I was afraid we should be accused of partiality. I carried out the order issued by Savov and Danev, permitting high Turkish officials to leave Adrianople to go to Constantinople. In this connection I went to the Vali, Chalil-bey, and asked him to draw up a list of officials. I had them divided into groups, and gave them an escort as far as Dedé-Agatch. Khalil thanked me politely and the Turkish press recognized the humanity of our conduct to the Turks. In the end it was actually made the subject of reproach that I let the officials go instead of keeping them as hostages, whereas I simply carried out the orders of the general quarter.

Some days after the capture of the town, I acceded to the request of the mufti that three or four mosques should be opened for worship. I placed sentries, in order that the prayers might not be disturbed, for about two hours after dinner time. The commander Mitov drove off some two or three Servian officers, who began burning and destroying fine Korans in the Sultan Selim library. After that the mosque was shut, only opening after four o'clock in the afternoon. All the carpets were collected and rolled together. They remained intact throughout the time of my being in Adrianople. A fire broke out in a minaret, after which I allowed no one to go up.

Statement of the Chairman of the Bulgarian Committee at Adrianople

Among the charges not mentioned in printed articles is one against the Bulgarian committee which had to distribute the loads of merchandise among the wholesale dealers. In Adrianople, "jars of wine," abstracted by members of the committee, were talked of. A member of the Commission informed the persons responsible for the government of Adrianople of this accusation, and the head of the said committee, Mr. Lambrev, an advocate, appeared before us and made the following deposition:

I was Chairman of the Committee for distributing the loads of merchandise over the whole area of the newly conquered territory. The other members associated with me were Professors Boutchev and Chichov. I defy anyone who accuses us of having appropriated a cent to appear, in order that I may sue him for libel. It was our business to study the needs of the population of the whole zone of Adrianople, Xanthry, Tchataldja, Kirk Kilisse. We went to all the villages on the railway line and here we sent for the merchants and in their presence commandeered the necessary wagons and goods of different kinds (petrol, sugar, salt, groceries, etc.). At first we only had ten, afterwards fifteen wagons. As stated above, we commandeered them in the presence of all the merchants, without distinction of nationality or religion. An exception to the general rule was made at Dedé-Agatch. We made an arrangement of sale and return, according to which we could sell the goods to the best advantage. In this way we were able to secure the people a supply of sugar at forty-five centimes per ancient *oka* (1 kil. 280 gr.). From the beginning of March on, we issued a license at the rate of fr. 500–1,000 per wagon; 2,000 at Kirk Kilisse. This license served as a guarantee of the strict fulfilment of undertakings and secured the right of reselling the merchandise at a fixed price. The money was deposited and receipts given at the central offices in Kirk Kilisse, Dedé-Agatch and Adrianople; it was repaid on presentation of certificates granted by the commanders and mayors of the towns to the effect that the conditions had been fulfilled. There was only one case in which the license had to be confiscated after an inquiry, and there the wholesale merchant had sold the goods exclusively to his friends without notifying the mayor. We telegraphed to the mayors to regulate the selling price, allowing fifteen per cent profit, and the quantity to be sold, and to prevent cornering by a few buyers. The retail price lists were fixed in the same way. For example, a wholesale price of forty-seven cents corresponded to a retail price of sixty cents. About June 20 (old style), when military operations recommenced, there were seven or eight wagon loads of meal to distribute between three and four Greek and Bulgarian merchants, destined for Serres and Drama. The licenses were issued, but three days later all traffic was interrupted. A period of eight days elapsed before it was resumed, during which the licenses remained in the *mairie* under the charge of Mr. Neutchev, secretary to the mayor of Adrianople; the money to be refunded on presentation of the receipts. A single case of attempted corruption came under our notice. About the month of March, someone sent in a postal packet a sum of fr. 1,000. Mr. Boutchev threw the package and the money out of the window of the carriage with a forcible expletive. The attempt was not repeated; the system of distribution in fact made it impracticable. The system was as follows: We had, for example, six wagons to divide among 130 persons. We discovered at the *Tchardu* what goods were at the moment most needed. Next we ruled out all the dealers who were not merchants. Suppose there were eighty persons left. We divided the wagons among them equally, by making each group, composed of some seventeen to twenty persons, select one to three representatives, who then undertook to make the purchases for all. The procedure was recorded in an official document signed by all the members of the Committee.

Documents Relating to Chapter III

THEATER OF THE SERVIAN-BULGARIAN WAR

I. SERVIAN DOCUMENTS

Mutilation of officers and soldiers by the Bulgar army.

1. Reports addressed to the Staff-Office of Uskub, in reply to circular No. 7,669, of June 20.

(1) The commander of the first Moravian division, of the first reserve, relates the following facts in his report, No. 3,310, of the 20th inst.

The first regiment of infantry relates that in the course of the battle near Trogartsi, our dead were found with the organs cut out. Several were mutilated, and the son of the treasurer of the regiment, Vekoslay Zuvits, had been cut to pieces with knives.

(2) The second regiment of infantry recounts, that after the fight of the 18th, on height 650, after the first Bulgar attack, our wounded soldiers on the battlefield were mutilated and stabbed by the Bulgars. It has been learned that all the following were stabbed; the second lieutenant of reserve, Milan Ristovits, sergeant Milovan Laketits, corporals Stevan Peshits and Echedomir Dimitrijevits, soldiers Radomir Georgevits, Mitar Milenkovits, Tsvetan Dikits, Milan Mitkovits, George Mihailovits, Boshko Limits Randjel Marinkovits, Antonie Georgevits, Dragntin Georgevits, and the corporal Obrad Filipovits.

(3) Of the third regiment, the wounded were all on our side of the battlefield, therefore none of them were either mutilated or stabbed.

(4) In the fifth regiment, it has been proved that those wounded in the course of the battle on the 17th and 18th, on height 650, were mutilated by the Bulgarians. This was reported to the commandant of the Drina division, first reserve.

(5) The sixteenth regiment of infantry recounts that near the village of Dobrsham, during the retreat of the 17th instant, the Bulgarian *comitadjis* threw themselves on the wounded, robbed and killed them.

No. 3,595. (Telegram sent from Chtipe, June 30.)

By order of the Chief Staff Officer commanding, Colonel Dushan J. Peshits.

2. On account of certain movements and combats in which certain divisions are engaged, the only replies received are those of the commandant of cavalry, and of the commandant of the Drina division: first reserve: Milesh Veliki. Knowing that this information is necessary to the Minister for Foreign Affairs, we shall forward it as soon as received to the General Staff Office. The commander of the cavalry, as well as his staff major, were not witnesses of any mutilation of the dead, or of the wounded, by the Bulgars, but infantry officers have given them terrible details. The commander of the Drina division sends the following reply, No. 875, dated 23d instant:

In reply to order No. 3,310 of the Commandant of the Third Army Corps, I have the honor to affirm that, during the combats of the 17th and 18th instant, the Bulgars mutilated our wounded. Andjelko Yovits of the quick firing section of the regiment of infantry, "King Milan," had his head opened, his ears and nose cut off, then he was set at liberty and is still living. Miloye Nikohts, of the second company, fourth battalion, fifth regiment of infantry, who was wounded in the thigh, received a sword thrust in the neck and in the arm. Stanislas Aleksits, of the same company, who was wounded in the foot, was struck in the neck and in the cheek. These last two were still alive when they were taken to the field hospital, where they recounted what had happened. A wounded captain, George Mandits, was also wounded by a knife thrown at his head. Captain Yovan Gyurits, commanding company two, fourth battalion, who was buried under a pile of stones by a howitzer and remained on the battlefield which the Bulgars occupied for a time, affirms personally that he heard the Bulgar soldiers disputing among themselves whether or not they would kill our wounded. Then a Bulgar officer came up and said to kill them. I have not received any other report from the commander of the sixth regiment, where certain like occurrences have certainly taken place. I send these reports at once on account of their urgency, not waiting for the report of the sixth regiment, which I shall send as soon as received.

Commanding Staff Officer, Third Army,
General Bozsha Yankovits.

No. 3,403. (Telegram sent from Hamzéli, July 24/August 2.)

3. A soldier of our company, Lioubomir Spasits, of the village of Kievats district of Masuritsa, department of Vranie, recounts the following:

On June 17, in the course of the battle against the Bulgars, on the height which overlooks the military huts of Gorni Nogartsi, towards six o'clock in the afternoon when our troops were retiring, I did not see them firing, being behind a rock. Suddenly, I found myself surrounded by Bulgarian soldiers, who seized me, snatched away my carbine, and led me before their commander. He and another officer questioned me about our troops, our fortifications, where they were placed, etc. I replied that I knew nothing. Then they led me away. In the evening, the same officer came again and asked me the same questions about the Servian army. As I replied again that I knew nothing, he began to beat me, to jump at my throat with gross language. Then he searched me and took twenty francs and continued to beat me about the head till I lost consciousness.

Next day, the 18th, they gave me a rifle and some cartridges, and ordered me to fire on our troops. As I refused, the officer again struck me. To escape this, I fired, but in the air. When he saw this, he hit me again about the head, abusing me, then obliged me to stand within range of our own guns, so that I should be killed by our soldiers. By an extraordinary piece of luck, I was not struck. The same afternoon, when they saw our troops advance, the Bulgars began to flee. They took me, and I remained all the time with them, till a shrapnel burst beside me. Then my guards took to flight, and I remained stretched in the corn. When they saw from a distance that I was still alive, they fired at me, but I succeeded in escaping. I have forgotten to say that at the time I was made prisoner, there was a soldier of our company near me, Peter Radovanovits, of Masuritsa, district of Masuritsa, department of Vranie. He was wounded in the leg. The Bulgars gashed him with knives, insulted him and said it was better worth while to kill that Servian dog than drag him behind them.

Commandant Captain Sheten Petrovits,
By order of Commanding Staff Officer,
Colonel Dushan J. Peshits.

No. 3,667. (Telegram sent to Sokolartsi, 7 July.)

4. Received from Commanding Officer, Timok Division, Second Reserve, report following No. 1,057, dated 21st instant:

In reply to order No. 4,100 of the 19th instant, I have the honor to relate the following concerning the atrocities committed by the Bulgar army:

(1) In our division.

(a) Thirteenth regiment: Arandjel Zivkovits, of Metovitsa, district of Zaietchar, department of Timok, soldier of the second company, fourth battalion, recounts that while his regiment gave up its position close to the military huts of Shobe, June 21, thirty soldiers of this regiment were surrounded by Bulgars. The leader, a sergeant of the Bulgar troops, wished to kill them then and there, after taking their watches and money. But he at last in response to the prisoners' entreaties, let them go, but gave the order to fire upon them as they ran, so that half of them fell dead and the rest were wounded.

(b) Fourteenth regiment: The commander of the second battalion heard from wounded soldiers, eye witnesses of the facts, that at the battle of Krivolak, the Bulgars wounded our second lieutenant, Voislav Spirits, who was lying dangerously wounded.

Marian Dimts, soldier of the first company, third battalion, reports that on June 19, at the battle of Pepelishte, he saw the Bulgars cut off the head of a wounded Servian soldier.

Milan Matits of the fourth company, same battalion, recounts that he saw a Bulgarian soldier transfix one of our wounded with a bayonet.

Randjel Nikohts, of the first company, third battalion, saw a Bulgar soldier strike a badly wounded Servian soldier on the head and crush it in.

Stoian Aleksits of the second company, third battalion, saw a Bulgar hit the wounded Aleksa Nikolits with a sword, until he died.

Svetozan Miloshevits, second company, fourth battalion, taken prisoner at the battle of Pepelishte, but who later succeeded in escaping, saw the Bulgars pierce twenty of our men with knives.

Aleksa Ristits, second company, fourth battalion, says that at the battle of Krivolak, June 21, he saw a Servian volunteer who had been badly hurt and whose eyes had been put out.

Milivoie Niloikovits, second company, fourth battalion, says that June 21, at the extremity of our right wing, he saw the Bulgars striking a wounded Servian officer with their muskets. Then they struck him with knives.

Marko Milanovits, third company, third battalion, recounts that on the morning of June 20, after the battle of Pepelishte, the Bulgars forced the commander of the fourth company, third battalion, Zivoin Budimirovits, captain of reserve, who had been taken prisoner, to give the order to six men to take off their uniforms. The uniforms and the money they had with them, were seized by the Bulgars. Then the men were led, bare-foot and shivering with cold, to the firing-line. Three were killed; all the others were found injured.

(c) Fifteenth regiment:

Zivoin Miloshevits, first company, first battalion, relates that on June 21, he and twenty others were taken prisoners at Shobe. They were handed over to a Bulgar sergeant and six soldiers. The sergeant asked them for money in exchange for their liberty, and those who had any were allowed to go. Zivoin Miloshevits and Bozidar Savits, both from Rashevitsa, had no money. Their tongues were cut. The other men were cut to pieces. They were found dead.

Tchedomir Bogdanovits was tied, then cut in pieces.

Sergeant Kosta Damianovits, fifth company, fifth battalion, taken prisoner at Shobe on June 21, bought his liberty from a Bulgar sergeant. He saw two Bulgar soldiers stab and beat the following Servian prisoners, all of the same battalion: Svetozar Stanishits of Obredja, Adam Ioksimovits of Sovinovo and Alexandre Matits of Katuna.

Sergeant Padovan Radovanovits, military intendant, reports that on June 21, at the battle of Krivolak, he saw Bulgar soldiers pierce a wounded Servian with their bayonets and fire upon another badly wounded man.

Milan Miloshevits, second company, third battery, reports that on June 21 he was taken prisoner at Shobe by the Bulgars, and that after he and some others had bought their liberty by giving money to a Bulgar officer of low rank, they had been permitted to go free, but had been fired upon as they fled, and several had been killed.

Zivko Pantits, fourth company, third battalion, reports that on June 17, he saw Bulgars stabbing a wounded Servian soldier with their bayonets.

Lioubomir Milosavevits, fifth company, same battalion, relates that when the Servian troops retreated, he remained in hiding. He was two days crouched in a ditch, where he saw a dead Servian whose eyes had been torn out.

Corporal Zivadits Milits, of the first company, same battalion, relates that above the village of Dragovo, as our troops advanced, he saw beside a hut a dead Servian soldier, who had been tied to a stake with wire and roasted.

Sheten Mikolits, same company, same battalion, reports that on June 19, he saw lieutenant of reserve, Michel Georgevits, lying dead by the roadside, completely naked, with four wounds in the breast and one in the jaw.

Arsenie Zivkovits, third company, same battalion, reports that on June 17, he saw Bulgar soldiers tossing a Servian prisoner in the air on their bayonets, and when he fell on the ground they shot him with their rifles.

The captain of reserve, Pera Tutsakovits, commanding second company, fourth battalion, reports that on June 18, he saw a Servian soldier who had been tied to a stake and roasted.

(d) Half battalion of engineers:

Milivoie Vasits, engineer, reports that on June 21, at the right wing of the position close to the Shobe manufactory, the Bulgars took him prisoner with twenty other soldiers and two officers of the fourteenth regiment. The officers were placed apart, while the soldiers were led in front of the army and fired upon. Many prisoners fell dead. He and three others were seriously wounded.

(2) Montenegrin Division.

The commander of this division reports that Lieutenant Iovan Trehishianin, of Lopushima, who fell on the 9th instant at Godevari, was found on the 18th with a ball in the left side of his breast, his throat gashed, and his stomach pierced with a a bayonet. The Bulgarians had taken his boots, socks, gaiters, and trousers.

By order of the Commandant,
Assistant Chief-of-Staff,
Lieutenant-Colonel Milan Gr. Milanovits.

No. 4,147. (Telegram sent from Sokolartsi, July 22.)

5. From the commander of the army cavalry, I have received the following report, dated 19th instant:

Conforming to order 04° 4,100 of the commandant, dated 19th instant, I have the honor to transmit the following information:

(1) Cavalry-captain Dushan Dimitrijevits, acting-commandant of the second reserve of cavalry of Timok, affirms that on the 17th, he saw with his own eyes, Bulgars on the fortifications of Garvanski, tossing a wounded Servian soldier on the points of their bayonets, crying "Hurrah," when the wretched man howled and writhed in agony. The same fact is confirmed by the commandant of the first squadron, Captain Miliya Veselinovits, and his sergeant, George Popovits.

(2) The commandant of the second squadron of cavalry, Captain Spira Tchakovski, swears to having seen the roasted body of a Servian soldier, on June 25, north of the village of Kara Hazani.

(3) The commander of cavalry, quick-firing section, Captain Dimitriye Tchemirikits, swears to have seen two roasted bodies, one near the camp of Shobe, the other near the village of Krivolak. Whose bodies they were or who had burnt them, he could not say. Farther on, he affirms that four of our wounded of the fifteenth regiment had their wounds dressed by Bulgarian doctors and were then taken to a Bulgar hospital, where there were four healthy soldiers, forgotten, who had been condemned to death by the Bulgars. Thanks to a Bulgar sergeant, the wounded men succeeded in escaping. They relate that during the time they were in hospital, the wounded Bulgars used to show their wounds and say: "Look at the work of your bombs." Nothing else to point out in this section.

From the commandant of the Moravian division, cavalry, first reserve, nothing noted concerning Bulgarian cruelties.

(4) The commandant of the Moravian division, cavalry, second reserve, reports that the patrols found the mutilated bodies of our soldiers in several localities. The hands were cut off, the skin flayed off the back, the head and legs removed. All the preceding is forwarded as the continuation of the reports sent in earlier.

The Commandant,
General Bozsha Yankovits.

No. 9,206.
No. 4,111. (Telegram sent from Sokolartsi, July 20.)

6. The commandant of Moravian division, first reserve, sends the report No. 924, dated June 29, as the continuation of report No. 852 of June 26. The following reports have been sent by the first regiment of infantry:

(1) In passing the positions where the combat took place between the Bulgar and the Timok division, second reserve, we found the mutilated bodies of some of our soldiers. One of them had his head cut off, the body was buried under a pile of stones and we could not find the head. The face of another had been completely skinned. Another had his eyes torn out, another was roasted.

(2) On the positions between the camps of Shobe and Toplika, where the first battalion had marched in advance on June 24 and 25, we encountered frightful examples of mutilation of Servian soldiers, killed or wounded during the battle. Some had their eyes put out, others the nose and ears mangled, and the mouth slit from one ear to another. Others were shamefully mutilated, the stomach cut open and the entrails outside.

By order of the Commander General Staff,
D. J. Peshits.

No. 3,594.   (Telegram sent from Chtipe, July 30.)

7. The Commander of the Danube division, first of the reserve, reports the following:

The commander of the seventh regiment of infantry affirms: Occupying the positions Retki Buki, I found that the soldiers of the third regiment, second reserve, had been massacred. There were more than twenty corpses with the head split in two.

The commander of the eighteenth regiment of infantry of the first reserve, sends the report of the commander of the second company, fourth battalion, same regiment, which runs as follows:

On the 19th of this month I met Voeslhav Markovits, second lieutenant of the third regiment, seriously wounded. I am not sure of his first name, but the family name is correct.

Description: Dark, thick mustache and black beard, blue eyes; wounded in the breast; he was found stretched on a hand-cart. In reply to my questions, he related as follows: I was wounded three days ago. I fell on the battlefield in the wood. Very soon an ambulance patrol of Bulgars came up, took my watch out of my pocket, my revolver, my field glasses, all my money, and my epaulettes. Two other Bulgar ambulance men came up afterwards, and they also searched me. I begged both parties to take me to their surgeons, but they refused. This officer states that the Bulgars killed four wounded soldiers that they saw on the road, and that they did the same with the Servian prisoners.

The commandants of the other regiments, have had no cases of our men killed, wounded, or maltreated by the Bulgars.

By order of the Commandant,
Colonel Peshits.

No. 1,408.   (Telegram from Gradichté, July 19.)

8. Report of the commission named by order of the commandant of the first company, third battalion, first regiment of infantry, regiment of Prince Nilosh the Great:

The undersigned members examined the carbonized body of a soldier, at five o'clock in the afternoon, on the Tcheska positions. They swear to the following:

(1) The man was a Servian soldier; this was confirmed by the remains of a Servian uniform found near the corpse, a sword, a cartridge box, ammunition, a coat very much burned, and a fragment of tunic.

(2) Close to the carbonized corpse, we found a bloody bandage, proving that the man was wounded when he fell into the hands of the Bulgars, and was thus burnt.

(3) In examining the ground where the man had been burnt, the commission noticed that it had been trampled and dug up, a proof that the unfortunate man had struggled desperately against his murderers.

(4) Half burnt letters found near the body, informed us that the name of the victim was Marin, of Raduivatz, that he belonged to the first company, third battalion, thirteenth

regiment, second reserve. All his body with the exception of the heels was absolutely charred.

There are other equally dreadful facts. The Bulgars in many cases tore out the eyes of Servians who fell into their hands.

June 25, 1913. Signed by four members of the commission, three officers and a soldier, general staff, third army.

No. 3,665. By order, Commandant Chief-of-Staff,

Colonel Dushan J. Peshits.

(Telegram sent from Sokolartsi, July 4.)

9. The commandant of the Danube detachment of cavalry, first reserve, tells us that one of the men killed during the battle, or assassinated after it, had his eyes torn out.

Kosta Petchanats, second regiment of infantry, second reserve, reports that a second lieutenant, a Bulgar, judge in his profession, struck a wounded soldier on the head with his sword. He ordered that the man's hands should be broken, and the fingers crushed between stones. Personally, I have not been a witness to a single one of these cruelties. The arbitration doctor, Dr. Petrovits, reports the preceding, conforming to order No. 7,569.

By order of the Commandant,

Dr. Vladisavlievits.

(Telegram sent from Tsrni-Vrh, July 9.)

10. Collected July 24, 1913, in the ambulance offices of the Danube company, first reserve of Konopnitsa:

The second lieutenant of reserve, first company, second battalion, seventh infantry regiment, second reserve, Mihailo Stoyanovits, just brought in today wounded, reports the following:

> On June 21 during the battle, I was struck in the left leg and heel, by a ball. Unable to move, I had to stay where I was. Then some Bulgar soldiers came, and two of them began to rob me. They took from me a leather purse containing 115 francs, a watch worth forty-eight francs, a leather pouch, an amber cigarholder, an epaulette, a whistle, a box of matches, my cap and its cockade. Having taken all these, they made ready to go, but one of them said, "Let us kill him now!" Then he sharpened his knife against his gun and gave me three gashes, two on the left, one on the right. The other gave me a strong blow on the leg and in the right ribs. A third Bulgar came up and hit me with his musket in the chest. Then they departed.
> Received by Lieut. Colonel Zarko Trpkovits.

II. THE MEDICAL REPORTS

1. *Procès-verbal* of the inquiry concerning the body of Radomit Arandjelovits, lieutenant-colonel fourth infantry regiment (supplementary) killed on the 9th instant, fighting the Bulgars in the place called Velcki Govedarmik.

The inquiry took place under the porch of St. Nicholas church at Kumanovo, in the presence of the district prefect, Mr. Ranko-Trifunovits, Mr. Henri Barby, correspondent for the Paris *Journal,* Mr. Kutchbach, correspondent of the *Leipziger Zeitung* and the *Berliner Tageblatt,* and of Dr. Réverchon, surgeon at the military hospital of Val-de-Grâce at Paris. The corpse has been photographed.

A. External Examination

(1) Body measuring 1.87, very swollen from decomposition, rigidity of death absent, head blackening, greenish-yellow from decomposition.

(2) Right ear crushed, superior side, disclosing wound about two cent. in diameter, with irregular edge. Wound has penetrated to the skull, also crushed at this spot. The wound has no second opening.

(3) The head almost completely bald, the few remaining hairs fall if skin is touched.

(4) Below the right eyebrow, an irregular round spot about seven cent. in diameter, where the skin has dried up, beneath it traces of hemorrhage.

(5) On the line of the third rib, left side, five cent. from the sternum, an oblique wound, four cent. by five cent., edges fine and clean, soaked with blood; if the edges of the wound are cut, a flow of blood in the pectoral tissue is disclosed. In depth this wound extends to the third rib which is crushed.

(6) Right, two cent. below the elbow, two wounds with clean fringed edges, three cent. by two cent. If edge is cut across, signs of hemorrhage beneath the skin. Both wounds connect by a large canal; a quantity of blood in the tissue.

(7) Inferior region of the stomach, four cent. below the symphysis, one cent. to the right of the median line, an opening almost circular, with flat edges, going deep into the flesh. Round this opening, a black circle, two cent. wide, full of blood.

Right of the back, below the eleventh rib, a round wound one cent. in width, flat edges, round which three cent. of skin have dried off, showing hemorrhage. The wound penetrates to the eleventh rib, which is crushed. Six cent. below the left hip, a corresponding wound.

On the right side of the axis of the back, level with the eighth rib, an oblong sore, one by one and one-half, surrounded by a black ring, in which section reveals hemorrhage. The edges crushed. Left side, along the line of the back, beneath the omoplate, a wound more or less round, one cent. long, going deeply into the flesh. Fifteen cent. below, another, level with the thirteenth rib.

B. Conclusions

The colonel bears traces of four balls, and two bayonets and daggers.

Three of the shots have been fired at long range, causing serious wounds, but none of them mortal.

The fourth ball, fired with the rifle, or more likely revolver, directly touching the ear, caused grave lesions in the heart. This was a mortal wound.

The two bayonet wounds seem to have been made by one blow.

(a) In the pericardiac region, a violent blow.

(b) In the forearm at the height of the third rib.

The colonel's right arm was as if nailed to his breast, by a violent bayonet thrust. Scientifically it may be affirmed that the colonel, grievously wounded but living, was killed by a shot fired close to his head, and by a bayonet thrust in his heart.

Kumanovo, July 15/28, 1913.

Signatures.

2. *Procès-verbal* of the examination held in the place where nine of our soldiers are buried, at the foot and behind Talambas.

Conforming to order No. 2,501, dated July 14, of the commandant of the second army, a commission came today to examine the localities, to discover signs of the massacre and mutilation of our soldiers of Chuka and Gorina, massacres committed by the Bulgars upon those of our wounded who fell during the engagement which lasted from the 9th to the 12th instant, and who were unable to fight in retreat.

At eight o'clock in the morning, the order was given to exhume nine of our soldiers buried at the foot of Talambas. According to the staff surgeon Yovan Tsvakovits, eight of these soldiers had been buried on the 13th instant, and another on the 14th. After the exhumation, the commission examined each of the nine corpses. The results of this examination are given below:

(a) Swko Tsvaits, of Ponora, Nishavski district, department of Pirot, soldier of the second company, second battalion, third infantry regiment, third reserve, wounded at Chuka during the engagement of the 9th instant, has the following wounds: a shot in the left side, two fingers below the line of the abdomen where the entrance of the ball may be seen. The wound traverses the muscles and comes out at the back.

(b) There are two bayonet wounds, one at the right across the pupil and the skin of the arch of the left eyebrow to the forehead, four by five, the second, which begins at the left nostril, cuts across the whole left side of the upper lip and penetrates the mouth.

(c) Five wounds. All the left side of the head scalped; the skin of the cheek, ear and neck, burnt; burnt hair still to be seen.

Wound (a) was not mortal and could have been cured; (b) and (c) mortal and of frightful violence, because the shot fired from a distance made the man incapable of self-defence. So the wounds (b) and (c) must have been made at very close range, (b) with a military knife, (c) by setting fire.

Yanko Milenovits, of Aldinats, Zaglasvki district, department of Timok, served in the third company, second battalion, third infantry regiment, third reserve. Wounded at Chuka during the engagement of the 9th instant. The following wounds were found on his body:

(a) A rifle bullet had entered the middle of the thigh, had broken the bone and come out behind, below the knee.

(b) A wound made on the right side, outside the femur, wound ten by three. Here the skin was only torn, as also the flesh close to the skin.

(c) Wound of the gonar. Torn by a sharp instrument, wound three cent. by one-half cut.

(d) Wounds caused by the butt of a rifle on the left omoplate. The bruises two cent. wide. Head disfigured by blows of the same kind, several bones of the skull crushed.

Wound (a) serious, leaving the man defenceless, but not mortal, (b) a wound inflicted violently at close range, (c) a violent blow. The wounds in the head were by themselves mortal, and had killed the man.

Milosar Andjelkovits, of Gortchintsa, Luinitcha district, Pirot department, served in the third company, second battalion, third infantry regiment, third reserve. Fell wounded during the Chuka engagement, on the 9th instant. The following wounds were found on him:

(a) On the lower part of the right thigh, in front, a wound three by five. The bone not reached. It is possible that this wound was caused by a ball from a gun or by shrapnel.

(b) Burns; the right half of the head burnt, as well as the hair and skin of the left cheek, nose and eye torn out.

Wound (a) was not mortal, and could have been cicatriced, but it prevented the man from making any movement. The other injury (b) was inflicted after (a) and must have been violent.

Peisha Stankovits, of Velcki Boninats, Luinitchki district, Pirot department, serving in the third company, second battalion, third infantry regiment, third reserve, wounded during the Chuka engagement, 9th instant. The following wounds were found on him:

(a) Below the omoplate, in front, a wound 1½ by 1½, with no second issue. This wound could have been caused by a ball from a rifle of powerful calibre, or by shrapnel. This wound prevented the man from moving.

(b) About four fingers above the right eyebrow going towards the right, across the whole head, a deep wound, ten by one, touching the brain, the skull being crushed. This wound was produced by a violent blow with some blunt instrument, and was mortal.

Stanko Dimitrievits, of Linova, Luinitchki district, Pirot department, served in the third company, second battalion, third infantry regiment, third reserve, was wounded in the Chuka engagement, 9th instant. The following wounds were observed:

(a) On the right femur, a wound caused by a gun cartridge, with an issue twelve cent. lower down. This wound was slight, only the muscle being touched, but it prevented any movement.

(b) The skull nearly entirely crushed, even the part above the brain knocked out; it may be inferred that this wound was caused by the butt of a gun or similar weapon because the edges of the wound were stuck with scraps of bone and scraps of skin.

There was no trace of wounds caused by violence on the other four bodies which had been exhumed.

After the examination, it was unfortunately impossible to get good photographs of the bodies, on account of the fog and rain. It was attempted, but without success.

In conclusion, I may be permitted to state that we have learned from the commandant of the Talambas section, the doctor Major Yovan Tsvetkovits, and Yovan Popovits, chaplain of the third regiment of infantry, third reserve, that the persons 1, 2, 3, 4, 5, remained in the hands of the enemy during our retreat.

Signatures.

The whole of this *Procès-verbal* has been translated into German before being signed, and submitted to the doctor of the Swiss mission, Lieut. Colonel Doctor Yervin, who signed the German text.

Talambas, July 15/28, 1913.

III. Destruction of Towns and Villages

General Staff, Third Army.

Telegram from Sokolartsi, No. 4,137, Uskub, July 21, 1913, to the general staff:

I have received from the commandant of the Moravian division, second reserve, the following report, No. 2,427, dated 20th instant:

1. The villages of Kletovo, Tursko, Rudare, Neokazi, Bunesh, Raitchani, Spantchevo, Gorantse, Rotchane, Oridare, Grdovtse, Yakimova, Vinitsa, Vsti Bania and Tsrni Kamen, are almost all burnt, and the houses are in ruins. All property has been destroyed or robbed, so much so that the fugitives returning to their villages find nothing there. All this has been occasioned by the Bulgars, in the course of their retreat.

2. All the Moslem population who succeeded in escaping from the Bulgar swords and bullets, have fled into the mountains. They are returning now, little by little, to the ruins of their former domiciles. The Christian population, which was not able to withdraw with the Bulgar army, fled into the woods and mountains also, and is beginning to return in the same way.

3. All the crops which were almost ripe have been destroyed or burnt or trampled down. Certain foods, such as flour, were soaked in petrol by the Bulgars.

4. They robbed and killed our wounded, and left others to die of starvation on the battlefield. The bodies of those massacred were left to rot, although they were in the immediate vicinity of the Bulgars. These things were reported to the Bulgar officers when our line of demarcation was fixed.

5. Lieut.-Colonel Kosta Mihailovits, who was killed on the 11th and remained on the battlefield, was robbed by the Bulgars, who first stole his money and everything he had about him, then all his clothing. He was found thus despoiled, on the 18th, and buried by our soldiers.

When the Bulgar officers were asked why they had not buried our dead officers and soldiers, they replied that it was because of the fire from the Servians. When they were asked how they could rob and despoil the dead, they replied sometimes that it had not been done by the Bulgars, sometimes that it was impossible.

6. Second Lieutenant Bogin, a Bulgar, who was taken prisoner by the third regiment of infantry, at Zletovo River, killed Dragits Valjarevits, one of the second company, second battalion of the second regiment. He has acknowledged it himself and his bloodstained sword is in the possession of the second regiment.

7. On the 6th after the engagement of Kalimanska Tchouka, the wounded Servians who remained in the village of Doulitsa, were cut with knives. Their ears and noses were cut off and their eyes torn out by the Bulgar officers and soldiers. A gunner, Rasha Nilitchevits, had his two hands cut off and died as the result.

The preceding is reported conformably to the order No. 41,111 of the 20th instant.

By order of the Commandant,

Chief Aide General Staff,

Lieut. Col. Mil. G. Milovanovits.

DESTRUCTION OF KNJAZEVAC

Official Servian Report

Prefecture of the Timok Department,

No. 4,363, July 3, 1913. Zaietchar.

To the Minister of the Interior:

Conformably to instructions received by telephone from the government office, on the 29th of last month, I left for Knjazevac on the 30th of last month, at six o'clock in the evening.

From Zaietchar, as far as the road which breaks off before Vratanitza in the direction of Grlishte, nothing is altered, because the Bulgar army did not pass beyond this limit. If the road is followed in the direction of Vratanitza, the common tomb of seven of our men of the third reserve, is to be seen. These men were found dead outside of the town hall, after the Bulgar army had left the village. They were buried by the authorities. They bore no wounds made by bullets, but had been wounded by bayonet thrusts and rifle butts. They were prisoners taken by the Bulgars and put to death when the latter had to beat a retreat on the 26th of last month.

The identity of the victims could not be established, but it can be seen from their clothing, that six of them were from the department of Kramski, and the other from the vicinity of Paratchin. All that could be transported was carried away from the two inns at Vratanitza. What remained was broken, or damaged, or smashed to pieces. All the houses in the village were sacked. I notice that a great number of houses on the line of march had their windows and doors broken, so that the owners now have to fasten them with cords.

Chaos reigns in the inn at Mali-Izvor, which is on the line of march. Chairs and some tables, mirrors and pictures and pottery are broken, and in the bedrooms the same disorder and devastation is to be seen. The hangings, mattresses and all the bedclothes have been carried away. The other things have been torn up and flung into disorder. All the drinks were consumed on the premises or carried away. Most of the haystacks were stolen, two were burnt. On the road between Mali-Izvor and Kralievo Selo the crops were trampled down as if the soldiers had camped there.

At Kralievo Selo, in the city hall of the district, where there were besides the offices, the private rooms of the police officials and the district doctor, nothing can be seen but destruction. All the papers have been thrown to the winds, many of them torn up. The district safe is on the floor, smashed to bits.

In the apartments of the prefect and the doctor, everything has been broken and destroyed and flung about in a way that defies description. The doctor's medicine chest has been completely destroyed. The state of affairs in the house of Jivoin, the priest, is equally dreadful. The linen, the best of the clothing, and the hangings have all been carried away. The rest of the things have been broken and destroyed, to such an extent that nothing remains which could be used. At the priest's house, as at the city hall, even the ovens have not been left in their places, but are taken to pieces and broken. I visited several other houses of Kralievo Selo, and everywhere I found the same thing.

Violent acts were committed in the neighboring villages of Selatchka, Novo-Korito, Nrenovats and Vrbitsu. The wooden bridge was set on fire and completely burnt, as well as the bridge across the Jeleshnitza river, on the great road from Kralievo Selo to Knjazevac, near the village of Jeleshnitza. Under all these bridges, the Bulgars had piled up the tables, chairs, cupboards, and other wooden objects taken from the city hall. They were sprinkled with gasoline and set on fire.

The barracks of the fourteenth regiment of infantry were near the entrance to Knjazevac, on the left of the main road. They consisted of four pavilions, of a two-story edifice with other lateral buildings. Hayfields were close beside the barracks. These were set on fire and, as a result, three of the pavilions and the two-story building were destroyed by fire too. One pavilion only, had nothing but the interior, the door, and the windows destroyed. A great many rifles were burnt.

All the ammunition found in the barracks was collected and carried to where the new iron bridge was above the Tzgovishki Timok, at the entrance to the city. The soil beneath the bridge was dug out and mines were laid, which were exploded by means of electricity. The bridge was blown into the air, and its iron framework completely destroyed. The greater quantity of the ammunition which did not explode was thrown into the river, from which it is now being retrieved and dried.

Upon entering Knjazevac, from both sides of the lower town, and on the street as well that crosses the river and leads to the post-office, several burnt houses and shops may be seen. Everything was completely destroyed by fire, but the ruins still remain. Twenty-six houses and twenty proprietors were ruined in this way.

As far as private houses go (I visited personally about fifty shops and houses), I can assert briefly, that not one was spared. Everyone was entered and pillaged more or less. All the private safes were broken open; the Bulgars searched everywhere for money, and stole whatever they found. Not a drawer or box remained, that was not forced open. It is amazing what they were able to do in so short a time, when it is recalled that there were only 10,000 of them, or at least so the inhabitants think.

The shops suffered the most. All that could not actually be carried away, was torn and destroyed and messed. All the debris are scattered about and you sink up to your knees in it. Wherever they could find any sort of liquor, the Bulgars drank it or carried it off. Now you could not find even a small glass of cognac, in all Knjazevac.

According to international law, private property should be respected during war, more especially in towns which are not protected, which was the case with Knjazevac. The Bulgars absolutely defied this principle, and plundered private property everywhere. What they could not eat or drink, they destroyed. In certain places they poured petrol over the flour, corn and other provisions. Mr. Kutcher's dispensary and his house offer the most deplorable spectacle of Bulgar vandalism. The foreign correspondents who came as far as this town, have certainly found something to look at. They have taken any number of photographs of the traces of the Bulgar invasion. In short, it is difficult to describe the devastation of private property in Knjazevac, more especially in an official report of this kind, as an entire book would not suffice.

The damage to the principal buildings is given below:

1. *District Offices.* The damage is considerable. The Bulgars pillaged the criminal section, various documents were torn up, or misplaced in other offices. Some were even found among the ruins of the bridge over the Timok. The *Bureau des Depots* was searched and the district safe broken open. The instruments used for this purpose were found beside the safe. The typewriter was broken, and all the cupboard drawers smashed.

2. *Office of Taxes.* Only the documents found in the office of the chief of the department were destroyed or carried away. The rest were left. All the bottles of ink were thrown against the walls, and many of the books were soaked in ink. The Bulgar soldiers and non-commissioned officers had covered them with signatures, or coarse remarks.

3. *Post and Telegraph Offices.* These suffered more than any other public building. All the telegraphic and telephonic apparatus was destroyed, either twisted or broken in pieces. The four safes were broken. All the postal packets were opened and the contents stolen or scattered.

4. *Artillery Barracks.* These buildings have not suffered, but a great deal of public supplies, linen, quilts, boots, were carried away. Xanatchko T. Tsveits, a manufacturer of arms, retired from business, who was slightly deaf, was killed by the Bulgars. They said they killed him because he did not retire quickly enough to the roadside when they called behind him to do so. According to news received by telephone, the commission of doctors, at Knjazevac, saw twenty women who had been assaulted in the neighboring villages, and at Kralievo Selo, three of them were brought before the commission. It was absolutely impossible to bring all the violated women before the doctors in so short a time, chiefly because most of them keep themselves hidden, and because the parents in view of the future, are ashamed to speak of their injured daughters and try to hide their dishonor.

Commission Report

Addressed to the Commandant of the Timok Division.

Mr. Jacob Osipits Kapoustine, a Russian who had taken a long cure at Soko Mania, visited Knjazevac after the Bulgar pillage, to inspect the results, and he has placed his notes at my disposition. I add them to the rest. The damage suffered by the district on account of the pillage, amounts to about twenty-five or thirty million francs. Agriculture suffered especially.

The Prefect of the Military Post,

Jov. S. Milétits.

Thanks to the courtesy of the prefect of Soko Mania, I was able to leave early in the morning of June 28 to visit the town of Knjazevac with him, devastated by Bulgar vandals. At Ichastantsi, about three kilometers distance from Knjazevac, I heard of violent acts committed by the Bulgars in the neighboring villages.

Accompanied by a notable of Knjazevac, I at once set about verifying these reports. I ascertained as follows:

For three days the Bulgars in detachments of fifteen or twenty, went through the villages, pillaging houses and buildings, searching for money and taking all they could find, even to fifty centime pieces, and outraging women, no matter what their age or condition. Thus, in the village of Bulinovats, seven women, two only sixteen years old, were violated; at Vina, nine women—one pregnant—at Statina five women, one a girl of thirteen.

It was difficult to discover the names, the people shrinking ashamed from giving them.

Having ascertained all these facts, I left for Knjazevac. When I arrived there, my first impression was that it had the appearance of an ordinary town. If it had not been for the nine or ten edifices destroyed by fire and the wooden bridges half burnt down, I should never have guessed that only a few days before, the enemy had passed through it. Because of that, the interior aspect of the houses, shops and courtyards, when I saw them, seemed to me the more stupefying.

I entered a hundred houses, and in each I saw the same spectacle. It was the result of no ordinary pillage, but of something much more shocking. All the mirrors were broken, for example, all the cupboards, drawers, boxes, furniture, everything wooden, had been chopped to pieces with a hatchet. The doors were smashed. The upholstery was torn off the chairs and sofas, and scattered about the room. The photographs had been torn into little bits and the books destroyed. All the men's clothing had been taken, and disgusting uniforms left in its place. All the women's clothing had been deliberately torn, so had the curtains, bed linen and dish cloths. They were flung about everywhere, covered with excrement, and in some cases soaked in petrol.

In the shops, it was the same thing. The most valuable things had been carried off, and such confusion made of the rest that it was impossible to distinguish the objects. Everything had been done with the express purpose of destroying all that could not be carried away. For example, the sugar and sweets had been thrown down the closets or covered with paint and the flour had been soaked in petrol.

In the course of the search for money, all the safes had been blown up with dynamite. But the most dreadful sight of all was the pharmacy. Not a bottle or jar remained whole. The bandages and lint had been set on fire, then spread over the floor, which was in a state of indescribable dirt and chaos. They had mixed up all the drugs, and the deleterious gases from them, made it dangerous to remain long in the place.

Eye witnesses assert that the Bulgars insisted on entering the officers' and soldiers' houses and devastating them in a horrible way. The Bulgar army, after three days at Knjazevac, reached such a pitch of demoralization (on account of the wine taken from all the cellars) that an entire battalion had to be disarmed and conducted by a strong escort outside the town. There is some talk also of cruelty inflicted upon little boys, but I had too short a time in the town, to confirm these rumors.

Jacob Osipits Kapoustine,
Russian subject.

IV. Bulgarian Documents

Depositions of Bulgarian Refugees at Kustendil

1. Village of Sletovo. (Canton Kratovo.)

Twenty-four families from Sletovo fled to Kustendil, seventy-six persons in all, twenty-five men, eighteen women and thirty-three children. In the month of March, the Servians began molesting the people; they did not allow the villagers to meet together, to go to the neighboring villages or to the mill, or even to work in the fields. Under diverse pretexts they began collecting money. The priest Hadji pop Constantinov was ordered by the officer Rankovits to pronounce the name of King Peter and the Metropolitan of Belgrade at mass, and he submitted. One evening two policemen took the priest to the convent of Lesnovo to a room with a deacon; he found there Rankovits and another officer. Turning to the priest Rankovits said to him brutally, "Why do you not pronounce the names of King Peter and the Metropolitan of Belgrade at the church?" Seizing him by the beard, he drew his sword and threatened to massacre him.

The priest was let go, but foreseeing he could not go on living with the Servians, fled to Kotchani and thence to Kustendil. After his flight the authorities sacked his house and carried off his wife, his two sons, Trifound aged seven and Lazar, one and a half, and his two daughters, Victoria, seventeen, and Stoika, one. No one knows where they were sent; it was said that they were massacred. The other villagers fled because their houses had been burned and laid waste.

The Dolna quarter at Sletovo was entirely burnt on July 13/26 by the Servian soldiery and many families were carried off. We may mention one or two: The priest Hadji pop Constantinov, Slavtcho Abazov (two houses and a bakery burnt and his family carried off as hostages); Ivan Stoikov (his house was burnt); Sazdo Natzev and Miche Sredzima (their houses were burnt); Pantcho Dimitrov and Vassil Domaset (their families taken as hostages); Mite Bassoto (his shop was sacked), etc.

The families of all volunteers in the war against Turkey were carried away, no one knew whither, their houses laid waste and burned. Here again one or two may be given. Stefan Pavlov (his wife and children were taken prisoners); Stanko Gheorghiev (his two boys and his girl suffered the same fate); Kolé Dossev (his wife and children the same); Arso Domeset (his family the same); Stoyan Ivanov (the same). In a word there was no refugee who did not suffer from the Servian soldiery.

In the flight from Kustendil, many persons were worn out with fatigue and had to be abandoned on the way. Thus Basdo Petrov left his brother, his wife and his children at the Pantaley convent; Naoun Yakov left his wife and his three children at the village of Nifithitchani. The two brothers Straché and Stoyan Phillipov saw their father disappear near the Pantaley convent.

2. Village of Globets. (Kratovo.)

Kotzé Lasarov, being an ancient *comitadji*, was persecuted by the Servians. He was threatened with death and therefore resolved on flight. He took with him his family, consisting of two women, three men and three children, because he knew that the Servian officials imprisoned the families of the refugees and outraged their women.

After walking fifteen days over mountains and streams the family arrived at Kustendil. They are now living at the asylum of Mina. On their departure the Servians sacked everything. The brother and son-in-law of Kotzé remained in the village. The village of Spantchevo is said to have been burned by the Servians, the mayor and the priest killed, and many women outraged. At the village of Koutchitchino the men were imprisoned and their wives outraged by the Servian soldiers. The daughter of Alix Hadjiev, Sletovo, was outraged and died. A Wallachian, Georghi Steriov, was killed.

3. Vinitza. (Kotchani.)

The Servian troops occupied Vinitza about two o'clock on June 24. On their entry the soldiers began breaking the doors of the houses and seizing all the inhabitants of the village, men, women and children. The Turkish population was not molested, since the Servian soldiers behaved perfectly to the Turks. After collecting the peasants the soldiers made them stand in rows and began questioning them one after the other, asking whether they were Bulgarians or Servians. Anyone who dared to say he was a Bulgarian was cruelly beaten. The largest number of blows was received by Gherassim Arsov. This done, the commander of the troops chose out seventy peasants, ranged them in a line and gave the order for them to be shot. The women and children who were near began to cry out, to weep and to entreat. A horseman carrying an order arrived before the shooting began and the commander changing his mind, the seventy peasants were sent to Kotchani. Their fate is unknown. On June 27, the Bulgarian troops advanced and the Servians retired from the village. On the same day the Bulgarians left the village, the Servians took their place. Thereupon the whole population, maddened with terror by the prospect of new tortures, took flight. Only the old people remained in the village. All the refugees went to Kustendil, passing by Tzarevo-Selo.

On the way there died Sokolitza, the son of Vladimir Panov, aged fifteen, and the child of Yourdan Gotchev, who died at the age of three in the Bulgarian village of Tzarvaritza.

At Vinitza, the Servian soldiers pillaged all the shops and all the houses.

The names of some of the inhabitants of Vinitza whose shops were sacked are: Gherassim Arsov, Palikrouchev, Lazar Christov, Yane Dinov, Spiro Koujinkov, Vassil Vessinkov, Mito Todorov, Gheorghi Donev, Kotzé Arsov, Thodor Ivanov. But fifty or sixty victims of pillage might be cited.

In the same village of Vinitza, the Servians put to death Nicolas Athanasov and Stoyan Vodenitcharov. The father, aged eighty, and the mother of Todor Ivanov, were put in a barrel and rolled up and down by the Servian soldiers, who did not let them out until they paid ten *louis d'or*. Marie Arsova was also tortured by the soldiers to extract money from her. Anna Kosteva, Toevitza, Mitka Palena and other women were outraged.

(Another deposition.)

When the Bulgarian troops left Kotchani and Vinitza, Servian cavalry were said to be approaching the latter village. All the inhabitants were terror struck. Many peasants hid themselves in their houses; others, more numerous, fled towards the Bulgarian frontier. Mitko Arsov remained in his house to collect some goods, while his wife and his five children joined the band of fugitives. On the morrow, Arsov caught the band up and said that the Servian troops had seized and taken away sixty to seventy peasants. He himself was tortured and cruelly beaten by a Servian soldier who asked him for money. He would have been killed if a Turk whom he knew had not happened to ask him to restore him to liberty. Set free, he fled during the night and caught up the group of fugitives, but four or five days later he died, worn out by the blows and torture he had endured. It is said that his brother, Sando Arsov, was dragged away and maltreated by the Servians, who sought to compel him to betray where the peasants were hidden. He went mad with terror and was left alone. After wandering for a long time in the solitudes of Mount Brigla, he died of hunger and fatigue.

On the bridge of Vinitza itself, the Servian troops massacred Georghie Kovats, his wife Nata and their children, Todor, seven, Vassa, thirteen, and Lazar, a year and a half old.

4. Blatetz. (Notchani.)

The Servian troops occupied the village of Blatetz on July 1. The soldiers began their excesses immediately on their entry; they were assisted by the Turkish population of the place, who took part in all the outrages, pillage and massacres committed by the Servians, and were spared by them on account of their complicity.

Thus, for example, Turks denounced the suspected Bulgarians to the Servian soldiers.[1] Twenty persons were immediately imprisoned and then, aided by the Turks, the Servian soldiers entered the houses. All the Bulgarian houses were rifled, not even the windows and the door being left; they were carried off by the Turks and used by them in their own houses. After this regular pillage the Servians burned the quarters (*Mahalas*) called "Samardjinska," "Vatchkovska," "Dulgherska," and the school of St. Cyril and St. Methodius. The following are the names of some peasants whose houses were burnt. Athanase Petzov, Konstandi Damianov, the priest Pavle Dimitrov, Philippe Petrov, Trandaphil

---

[1] We read in another deposition, "The Turks pointed out to the Servians those who were or who were believed to be rich. A young boy called Dane had his eyes gouged out to compel him to say where his people's money was. Another, Alexa, was burned alive for the same reason. Some fifteen houses were burnt."

Stoytchev, Ivan Gheorchev, Pafle Kostov, Yordan Kostov, Simeon Damianov, Erotei Damianov, Ivan Anatonov, Bogdan Antov, Cavril Antov, Grigor Bogdanov, Zaphir Bogdanov, Yani, Christo and Seraphim Petzov, etc.

The Servian officers decided to kill the Bulgarians who had been taken. All the prisoners were accordingly led outside the village. Then a halt was called and one of the officers shouted to the wretched people: "Save himself, who can." While they were going away the Servian soldiers fired upon them and all the Bulgarians were killed. One man alone, Zaphir Traitchov Klukachki, succeeded in escaping, but not without being wounded; a finger was carried off by a bullet. For several days he wandered in the forest and then came back to the village. Another Bulgarian, Done Temovski had his face mutilated; after tearing his eyes out they killed him. Alexo Tomev was thrown alive into the fire and burnt.

The following are the names of the peasants who were shot by the Servian soldiers:[1] Triphon Mitrev, aged fifty-two, his wife and his child aged three; Anghel Miretchev, aged forty-six, his wife and his daughter; Nicolas Lazorov, forty-eight, who leaves a widow and three children; Simeon Stoimenov, nineteen, scholar at the Pedagogic school of Uskub (third course), he was in bed sick, but was dragged out by force; Ivan Zahov, forty-two, who leaves a widow and three children; Pavle Sinadinov, nineteen, who leaves a widow; Andon Sinadinov, sixty-five, his daughter, Paraskeva Andonova, a governess and one of the refugees is now in Sofia; Vladimir Avksentiev, thirty, who leaves a father, a mother— a widow—and two children, destitute; Athanasius Yanakoev, seventy, who leaves two sons and two grandsons; Mite Gheorghiev, thirty-five, who leaves a wife and two children; Danial Petzov, fifty, who leaves a wife.

Before they were killed all these wretched people saw their goods pillaged and carried off. Their families are left in the most miserable condition. The corn was carried off by the Turks in the place; all the cattle by the Servian soldiers. In the pillage, burning and massacre, the Servian soldiers were assisted by Turks well known in the country, whose names are set down: Mohamed Hadjiev, Osman Tchaouch Afouzov, Boudan Moustapha Tchaouch Redjebov, Riza Kordeveski, Ismail Tchipev, Adem Nalbansko and his sons, Soulio Tarskine, Ousso Kossevki and his son.

The Servians made a Turk, Kel Assan Effendi, a Turkish ex-advocate, at Kotchani, commander at Blatetz.

5. Canton of Kotchani.

(1) *Bezikovo.*

The Servian army entered in July 5/18, and put to death the following individuals: Pecho Antov, thirty-five (all his cattle was carried off); Gavriel Arsov, thirty-eight; Anghel Arsov, thirty-five; Nicolas Anghelov, forty; Stoiemen Vanakov, thirty-seven; Gheorghi Arsov, thirty-eight; Theodosi Christov, forty; Mitko Christov, thirty; Manassia Stoyanov, fifty; Anastas Stoyanov, fifty; Ivantcho Karanfilov, thirty-eight; Paranfil Petzov, sixty-six; Stoimen Ivanov, thirty-eight; Lazar Tassev, thirty-three; Sophia Kolibarska, seventy; Stephane Ivanov, thirty-four; Mara Galevska, seventy; Anghel Stoyanov, fifty; the son of Lazar Stoyanov Spassev, aged one year and a half, was thrown into the flames. The following women were outraged: Svezda Temilkova, twenty-three; Atahanaska Anghelova, thirty, who died afterwards; Alane Markova, thirty, who also died. The Servians put fire to sixteen houses and to the crops; the cattle were driven off.

---

[1] Some of the Bulgarians who were killed may be added to this list. Vladimir Yanev, twenty-seven; Trifound Dimov, sixty; Trifoun Samardjiev, forty-six; Anghel Stoiemenov, thirty-two; Momtchil Moutaftchiev, fifty-five; Sv. Pavel Dimitriev, fifty.

(2) *Isti-Bania.*

Christo Marin, fifty; Tryanka Simeon Ova, twenty-five; Nicolina Lazarova, twenty-eight, were killed.

(3) *Pressef.*

One hundred and seventy houses were burned.

(4) *Lyki.*

The Servian troops killed Dedo Marko, eighty years old, and his sons, Athanasius, forty-five, and Todor, forty; Alexander Bilianov, aged seventy (his sons, Gherassin, forty, and Stoyan, thirty-five, were taken no one knew whither). Ivan Mitzov, Gale Dimitrov, fifty; Nico Mitzov, thirty; Evda Andonova, fifty; Gheorghi Athanassov, sixty; Ampo Mitev, twenty-five; Spasse, thirty; Andon Stoitchev, fifty; Seraphin Alexov, thirty; Ilia Oulezov, sixty; Peter Angelov, sixty; Seraphim Gheorghiev, forty-five; Gheorghi Yovev, ninety. Those taken away by the Servians: Stoiko Mitev, twenty; Nicolas Lazarov, twenty; Eftim Temelkov, forty; Miladine Eftimov, twenty-five; Miche Yanev, sixty; Ilia Nicov, forty; Mite Tzonev, forty.

The Servians also carried off 10,000 sheep, 300 oxen, sixty horses, 100 pigs and twenty asses; ninety-four houses and 150 cabins were burned, and nineteen sacked within the village area. The whole of the corn was carried off. Stefan Petzov was robbed of ten louis, Nako Mitzov, seven Turkish pounds, and so on. Efrem Nazlymkine, Pecho Danev and Grigor Kartchev were only released on payment of nine Turkish pounds.

6. Sokolartsi. (Events of August 17 and following days.)

All the Wallachians were named Administrators, and took possession of the Municipal building, with Gheorghi Naoumov at their head. The Wallachians thus become masters and calling themselves "brothers" to the Servians, thought that an opportunity of becoming rich easily had presented itself: they accordingly made heavy impositions from the Bulgarians of Sokolartsi and the neighboring villages. Thus in Sokolartsi they collected 300 *louis d'or* as the price of escape from death. With the aid of the Servian authorities the Wallachians said, "Hitherto you were masters and pillaged our goods. Now it is our turn to pillage yours," and they were as good as their word. They forbade the women to wear their *"chamia"* (scarf or handkerchief which they wear on their head), saying, "You will not be Bulgarians any more, and since you are Servians in future you must wear nothing on your heads."

7. Lipetz. (Kotchani.)

Here the Servians killed about seventeen persons. Here are the names of some of the victims. The three brothers Antonia, Philip and Trifon Timov; the three brothers Zachary, Todor and Trifon Postolov; Simo P. Athanasov; the wife of S. P. Athanasov died of fear, while her husband was being murdered. The mother of the Postolov brothers was outraged after sixteen *louis d'or* had been taken from her. The wives of Zachary and Trifon Postolov suffered the same fate.

8. Yakimovo.

Yakimovo was also pillaged by the Servian soldiers and some houses burned.

In this village the Servians put to death Anton Phillippov and Christo Priptchenez.

9. Zarnovez.

At Zarnovez seven persons perished; the following names may be given: Ivan Pavlev, Ivan Mitev, and the priest, Tomo Triphanov.

10. Gradets. (District of Tikvich.)

On June 19, the witness to whom we are indebted for this story was in his house and heard there cries coming from the village: "Save yourselves! Our army has retired and the Servians are burning or killing everything they meet upon their way." He ran down to the village to find his children, but only found his father, aged ninety. Leaving the house of the latter he succeeded in rejoining his children and the other fugitives and hiding with them in the forest above the village. Some ten Servian horsemen then arrived and sent a peasant to them to tell them that they were going to establish order and security. Fifty or sixty peasants trusting their word returned to the village, and the witness and one of his friends drew near to spy out what happened. From afar they saw some corpses near the house of Constantine the tailor. The witness' companion returned to the village to see things more near at hand, while he himself went back to his children. At nightfall this companion returned, and told how the priest Christo and Dimitri Michkov bound back to back had been slain at the bayonet's point, as well as thirty-six other inhabitants, and that the houses had been pillaged. On the next day the village was given over to the flames.

On the third day Servians and Turks came to the forest in pursuit of the fugitives, on whom they fired from a distance. The witness then saw Traiko Curtoich, Lazar Nicolov and Athanasius Iliev fall dead before his eyes. Thanks to the night the fugitives scattered and made their escape in the direction of the villages of Lipopic and Dedino. On June 25, the witness lost his children and went to look for them at Radovitch. The Servians were already here as well as a large number of fugitive inhabitants. At this stage the invaders had not yet surrounded the little town with a cordon of troops, but shortly afterwards they encompassed it with the assistance of Servian and Turkish soldiers, and began to make a return of the population by villages and by families.

Searching for his children our witness entered a street where he saw the heads of four men rolling about on the ground. He fled, terror struck, and hiding in the middle of a company, managed to pass through the cordon of soldiers and make his escape with other fugitives. They turned their steps towards the village of Smiliantzi. Servian horsemen once again stopped them on the way. The officer after questioning them directed them towards the village, where there was some infantry. A large quantity of cattle and pigs were guarded by the soldiers, probably with a view to eating them. They took sixty-five pounds from one of the dead, whose name was unknown to witness. They sent the fugitives to pass the night in the neighboring village where the commander was to arrive the next day to question them. Instead of going to this village they went towards the mountains and crossing Pehtchevo, Saravo-Selo and Tcherna-Skala entered Bulgarian territory. At Kustendil the witness found his children.

The following story was told by a woman, Maria Constantinovo, belonging to a body of thirty-four fugitives, men, women and children, who arrived at Kustendil after the fall of Gradets: Some ten Servian horsemen accompanied by more than a thousand *bashi-bazouks* entered Gradets. The entire village was swept by an appalling panic, on the news that the Turks and Servians were killing any Bulgarian who appeared before them. The larger part of the population, men, women and children, took flight before the Servians entered. Only the old people, and those who had not succeeded in escaping, were left. "Go, fly, you young people at any rate," the old cried out. "If the Servians spare us we will let you know, but for Heaven's sake save yourselves, and let God's will be done to us." When the Servians and the Turks entered the village the old people came out to receive them and appealed to their pity. When he heard the population had taken flight, a Servian horseman sent a peasant to tell them that if they did not return all their goods would be pillaged and their houses burnt. In accordance with this announcement most of the fugitives did return. The Servian horseman then ordered the Turks to seize all the men. The Turks then threw themselves into the houses and an appalling scene followed. Some Turks invaded the witness' house and seized the head of the family. He had hardly crossed the threshold of the house when he was stabbed and fell dead on the spot. From every house came cries of distress and shots were fired. The witness who went out of her house saw the Servians seize sixty to seventy men and lead them out of the village. All the women followed them, pleading for their husbands. Once outside the village the Servians seized the younger men and began stabbing them, while the women cried out in despair and wrung their hands, without anybody showing any pity for them.

The witness, terrified by this horrible scene, fled, taking the road back to her house. During the whole time the Turks went on killing and pillaging, carrying off even the young girls. Another witness from the same village saw them with his own eyes seize Maria Pezova, aged seventeen, Minka Athanazova of the same age and Neda Panova, take them on horseback and carry them away, singing and crying towards the Turkish villages of Kocharka, Golelia and Arsalia. The witness then made his escape: near the village he rejoined other fugitives come from the same place and further on joined yet another group, the total numbers thus being about 300 persons.

While all these fugitives were going away, *bashi-bazouks* pursued and fired upon them. Bullets fell like hail: men, women and children fell dead in great numbers. Moreover, the Turks three times lay in ambush for them and so slew many more. On the third occasion the wretched people were nearly all exterminated, and were only saved by the night. Out of the whole group only nine families reached Kustendil; the larger part of these poor people were scattered. Many died, some reached Radovitch, and others finally disappeared. During the journey they were joined by fugitives from Kontché and Loubnitza who told them that the Servians and the Turks had burned and massacred everything Bulgarian, that they themselves had seen the village of Kontché in flames and heard the shots.

(Another deposition on the same facts.)

On June 24/July 7 the entire village of Gradets was set on fire by Servian troops, who killed fifty-one men and nine women of the village and carried off three young girls. The names of the men killed were: Kostadine Gounov, Yato Nicolov and his son, Lazar Petre Poreklato, Velko Gheorghiev. Constantin, Stoyanov, Anghel Zaycov, Spasso Moskovski, Trayko Daphinine, Spasse Gheorghiev Athanese and Nicolas Gheorghiev, Dino Petkov, Gheorghi Stoycov, Micho, father and son, Thanas Andov, Pavle Kotchev, the priest Christo Pavlevski, Karanfila Pavleska, Stoyan Pavlevski, etc.

Names of the women slain: Zoyia Filea and her daughters Mitra, aged fourteen years, and Ghina, two years; Tana Dintcheva, Yana Gounovska, Maria Trayanova, and her daughter-in-law Sovka Pepova, Maria Lazeva, Bojana Christova. The following were thrown to the flames: Nicolsa Stoyanov, aged ninety; Gheorghi Choumkar, eighty, and Temelko Nenkov, seventy. Those carried off: Maria Nedina, eighteen; Nenka Taneva, eighteen; and Neda Panova, seventeen.

Andrea Constantinov, aged twenty-two, was disfigured by a Servian officer who struck him with his sabre: he succeeded in escaping, but his father and his companion, Christo Vasov, aged fifty, were cut in pieces.

11. *Village of Lipa (Tekvech).* Evidence of Efrew Kamtchev and Dimo Stoyanov.

The village of Lipa was pillaged and burnt by Servian regulars, who took twelve boys, aged about 12 years, and three women, and conducted them to the village of Iberlia. Nothing is known of their fate. The rest of the population fled towards the village of

Loubnitza where they were surrounded by Servian soldiers who fired upon them and treated them with violence. The schoolmaster, Kotzé Danev, and his daughter were thus killed, and his brother was taken and led away by the Servians. The latter killed two children besides, whose names are not known. They tortured the wife of Thodor Kamtchev to force her to give them money. As she had not any, the Servian soldiers stabbed her four-year-old child to death in her arms. The other women and children were led by them into the Turkish houses, and nothing is known of their fate. In the same village, Dinep Barsovetsa of Negotino, and Kreston of Dissan were killed. The mother of Nicholas Constantinov, aged eighty years, perished as well.

12. *At Radovitch and in the vicinity.* The Servians entered Radovitch the day after June 29. For a day or two the inhabitants, of whom some had fled when the Bulgar army retreated, did not leave the town. As soon as they arrived, the Servians began to search the Bulgar houses, and to take anything they could lay their hands on. The Albanian Captain Yaa, formerly a *cavass* of the Servian Agency at Vélès, accompanied them. Before war was declared, he was already wandering about in the vicinity of Tikvech with a band of followers, causing great damage to the Bulgar population.

The Servian officers collected a great deal of money at Radovitch. Under the form of gifts to the Red Cross, the country people poured out fifteen, or thirty, or forty gold louis, to avoid the tortures which awaited them.

The Servian cavalry arrived first at the village of Novo-Sélo, where they were given bread and milk. Then came the infantry and then the soldiers began to force their way into the houses. Clothes, money, everything, was stolen. They did not, however, assault the women. No doubt they would have, but for the vigorous intervention of the people, which permitted the young women and girls to run away and hide in the forest. In the neighboring village of Varcheska, all the women were violated, and the men killed by the Turks of the nearby villages, accompanied by three Servians. The entire village was sacked. At Chipkovitza the people were terribly ill-treated. The Servian army was followed by Turks who aided them in their cruelties. No life was spared unless paid for by money. The women were violated, and some of them taken outside the village by the soldiers from whom they were rescued later on. They, too, were asked for money. Kalia, wife of Traiko Andonov, a notable of Chipkovitza, was undressed, robbed of the money she had about her, then assaulted. The daughter-in-law and the daughter of Kostadine Ghigov were also violated, while Ghigov himself was beaten. Every one of these brutalities was the work of Servians.

Goods and cattle, both were plundered at Chipkovitza, as at Novo-Sélo. From the house of the witness from whom these details have been obtained, everything was stolen that could be taken, including eight gold louis. His brother was seized and searched, and when they found fr. 40 on him, they led him into the house to see if he could not find some more money there. The Servians wanted to murder him with a hatchet, but he threw himself from a window, and in this way saved his life. At Smilentzi the famous Captain Yaa killed Gogué Kripilski and three other inhabitants, Zacharie Arsein, young Aughel and another boy. The wife and daughter-in-law of the Voïvode of Radovitch, Stamen Temelkov, himself originally of the village of Orahovitza, were cruely ill-treated. The Bey of Radovitch, Yachar-bey, arrived at Orahovitza accompanied by Servian soldiers. They seized the women, extracted money from them, burnt their hands, searched the houses, and found revolvers, sabres and watches which they carried off.

At Boislavtsi the Bulgars whose names follow were robbed. Sv. Stephen Athanassov who lost seven louis; Todor Ivanov who lost thirty-five louis; Gligor Iliev from whom three louis were taken, a watch, and a pair of shoes; Traiko Domazetov robbed of £T5;

and the widow Trayanka Eftimova, robbed of £T3. The locality of Kontché was burnt by the regular Servian army. The sons of Dana Dontcheva, Athanas, aged twenty, and Efting, aged seventeen, were taken no one knows where.

Loubnitza was also burnt by the Servian troops who caused the death of Philippe Stoimenov (sixty years), Dona Kotzeva, school teacher (sixteen years), Gheorghi Stefanov (thirty years), Dimitrouche Christov (ten years), Efa Kotzeva (thirty years), Ilia Stephanov (twenty-five years) and Kotze Stephanov. As to the women, some were carried off, such as Rossa Iliev, Nevenka Trayanova, Yordana Stephanova, Gouna Stoyandva, Soultana Gheorghieva, and others were killed, as was Zlata Mihalova.

13. *Protocol of the Inquiry of the Bulgarian Commission upon the Massacres of Bossilegrad.*

The Commission named by order of the Commandant of the fifth actual army (No. 1764) composed of Colonel Tanev Alexandre, chief of the Brigade of United Cavalry, President; Mr. M. Eschenkov Nicola, Chief of the District of Kustendil; Dr. Petrov, Lieutenant of the Health Department; Tochko, Chief of the Sanitary Section of the Fifth Army; Rev. Father Anastase Poppe Zacariev, acting as Bishop; Sotir Iltchov, Municipal Town Councilor, members:

Met today, July 2, 1913, near the fulling mill of Dimitri Doitchinov, situated about one kilometer on the road from Bossilegrad to Lubalité, at the place where on June 28 last, towards nine o'clock in the morning, were shot and buried by the Servian army, to whom they had given themselves up, Colonel Tanev Ilarion, chief of the Sixth Regiment of Cavalry; Lieutenant Stefanov Stefan, commissary of stores in the same regiment; the Lieutenant of Sanitary Service, Cautev Stefan, veterinary doctor of the same regiment; Cavalry Sergeant Vladev Christo, trumpet major, and Lieutenant Minkov Assen of the 111th Regiment of her Imperial Highness the Grand Duchess Maria Pawlowna; in order to establish the identity of the dead, to investigate the circumstances in which they were shot, and to draw up the necessary act upon the subject.

According to the disposition of the Captain of the Sanitary Service, Dr. Koussev Pantelei, taken prisoner like his companions but left at Bossilegrad on account of the serious wound he had received in his breast; of the old woman, Elena Mitreva, eye witness while she was at the fullery of the fusillade which killed the above named; of the fuller Sotir Bogilov, and of the miller Mito Simionov, who buried the dead in the garden of the fullery; as well as according to the report of the Captain of Cavalry, Captain Vesselinov, Chief of the Squadron of the Sixth Regiment of Cavalry, it is established:

1st. That by the sudden appearance at dawn of the Tenth Regiment of Servian Infantry at Bossilegrad, the aforementioned officers and the trumpet major, as well as the Captain of the Sanitary Service Koussev, were surrounded in the street and taken prisoner. Then a Servian soldier fired at a distance of two feet, piercing the breast of Captain Koussev. The capture of the Bulgar officers once assured, the Servian commandant proposed to Colonel Tanev, to send an order to the second and third squadrons to give themselves up. Under the threat of being shot, Colonel Tanev wrote the required letter and sent it to the superior commandant of the squadrons, Cavalry Captain Vesselinov. In the meantime, the shots became more frequent. The machine guns of the regiment were brought out, and these opened fire at forty feet. Then the Captains of Cavalry, Vesselinov and Mednicarov, who were commanding the Bulgar squadrons, led the latter with fixed bayonets against the hostile foot soldiers, drove back the Servians and put them to flight, while the imprisoned officers and the drum major were conducted to the first mill on the road leading to Lubalité. Once there, the order was a second time given to Colonel Tanev to send a second command to the squadrons to give themselves up. He did this, but without result. It was then that our infantry appeared on the height, which forced the Servians to leave the town to reach the neighboring hills, and to send the prisoners, with the exception of Captain Koussev, on the road to Lubalité.

2d. That the old woman Elena Mitreva, says that she kept close to the fullery, and saw when the officers were led off. They were marching in front, and behind them, at a short distance, about ten Servian soldiers followed. When they came near the fullery, the Servian soldiers put up their rifles and fired at the officers who fell dead on the road, one of them even rolling into the river. After that the Servian soldiers plundered them and stole their boots.

3d. That the fuller Sotir Bogilov, and the miller Mitse Simeonov, being in proximity to the fullery, carried the bodies of the dead men into the garden of the aforesaid building, with the aid of the Servian soldiers, and having dug a common trench, buried them. While the burial was taking place, one of the Servian soldiers said that among the dead there were some Swabians and a Turk, so that the Servians obliged Mitse Simeonov to examine the latter to ascertain if he were circumcised.

4th. That the commission has ordered the opening of the trench to establish the identity of the deceased. This has been done. The faces were black and swollen, but the features could be recognized, and it was proved that the bodies were undoubtedly those of the aforesaid victims, as indeed their uniforms, still decorated with their epaulettes, attested.

The result of the examination of the Doctor Lieutenant Petrov, establishes that Colonel Tanev was struck in the temple, and that the ball came out at the top of the skull, scattering the brains. As to Lieutenant Minkov and the drum major, they were struck on the nape of the neck, the ball in the first case emerging through the left eye, and in the second case, by the right eye. The veterinary, Contev, was struck by three balls; one penetrated the back and pierced the middle of the stomach, the second crossed the kidney; the third struck him in front, below the left shoulder. Lieutenant Stefanov was struck by two balls, one which entered the back and went through the chest, the other entering the kidney.

The commission ordered that the bodies of the defunct should be transferred to the cemetery of the church and buried there, which was done the same day.

In testimony of which the present process has been drawn up

Signed: COLONEL TANEV ALEXANDRE,

Chief of the Double Brigade, President of the Commission.

Members:

FSCHENKOV,

Chief of the District of Kustendil.

DR. PETROV,

Chief of the Sanitary Section, Fifth Army.

REV. FATHER ANATASE POPPE ZACHARIEV,

Acting as Bishop.

SOTIR ILTCHEV,

Municipal Councilor.

Certified confirmed from the original.

DR. G. FZENOV,

Secretary to the Minister of War.

APPENDIX I

Bulgaria

Table of Officers and Soldiers Wounded During the Wars of 1912–1913

Sent in by Major General Clement Boyadjiev, Minister of War in Bulgaria

	Killed	Wounded	Disappeared	Remarks
War against the Turks.				
Officers	313	915	2	Figures have been verified.
Soldiers	29,711	52,550	3,193	Figures have been verified.
War against the allies.				
Officers	266	816	69	Figures have been verified
Soldiers	14,602	50,303	4,560	Approximate figures.
Totals:				
Officers	579	1,731	71	
Soldiers	44,313	102,853	7,753	

Cost of the War of 1912–1913

(June 25, 1913)

1. *Maintenance of the army*

(a) Food of the army, *i. e.,* 563,076 effectives at fr. 1.40 per day, and 211,431 animals (beasts of transport, horses, remount mules) at fr. 2.20 a day, from September 17, 1912, to June 1, 1913 . . . . . .   fr. 322,137,832.20

(b) Pay of reserve officers, together with the indemnity on the opening of the campaign and supplementary war pay   89,793,490

(The sums paid to officers in time of peace, due under any circumstances, being deducted.)

2. *Equipment of the army*

(a) Clothing of the army in the field, *i. e..* 563,076 men at fr. 100 per head (uniform, cap, linen and boots)   56,307,600

(b) Equipment of the army in the field, *i. e.,* 450,000 men at fr. 60 per head (haversack, can, nosebag, etc.) 27,000.000

3. *Material of war and ammunition*

(a) *Artillery.*

Batteries of mountain cannon. Batteries of field cannon. Batteries of siege cannon, including shells, shrapnel, etc., which according to the statement put in by the War Minister amounted to fr. 126,612,926. Allowing fifty per cent for destruction or loss of the original value, there remain.............................. fr. 63,306,463

(b) *Infantry.*

330,000 muskets (Mannlicher system) at fr. 80 each..	fr. 26,400,000
100,000 muskets (Mannlicher system) supplied at the beginning of the war at fr. 100 each..........	10,000,000
With 1,000 cartridges at fr. 140 for each of the 430,000 muskets	60,200,000
51,328 muskets—Berdan—at fr. 60 each............	3,079,680
50,000 muskets (Three line system) at fr. 80 each...	4,000,000
With 500 cartridges per musket at fr. 90 a thousand..	2,250,000
232 machine guns (Maxim system) at fr. 13,850 each	3,213,200
With 40,000 cartridges per machine gun or 9,280,000 cartridges, at fr. 140 per thousand, *i. e.,*..........	1,299,200
Delivered during the war	
24,000,000 cartridges, 8mm., Mannlicher system, ninety-five supplied by the firm of Erhardt, *i. e.,*..	2,302,800
Mannlicher outfits supplied by the firms of Weiss, Hirtenberg, Erhardt, Gutt and the *Société Français*	4,926,780
Miscellaneous items	813,091

fr. 118,484,751

Since the war lasted more than six months at least half of this material and ammunition was lost or used up, leaving half, *i. e.,* fr. 59,242,375.50.

(c) *Cavalry* 1,500,000

(d) *Engineers* 18,000,000

Approximate value of the loss of portable works and artillery parks.

Loss of bridge construction material and purchase of material for temporary bridges, etc.

Explosives.

Construction of roads and bridges during the war.

Trappings for animals.

Deterioration of aeroplanes, of telegraphic wires, of signalling apparatus, of bicycles.

Cantonments, conversion of barracks into hospitals in the occupied territories and repair of the existing barracks.

Extraordinary hiring of stables, depots, hostels, houses, etc., and indemnity for their destruction.

Deterioration of motors and indemnity for them.

Sanitary service 12,000,000

4. *Cost of transport. Requisitions. Service horses*

(a) During the period of hostilities there was no transport on the Bulgarian railway lines except that of soldiers, ammunition, provisions, and the sick.

The loss to the Bulgarian treasury is the total receipts from the railways received in this period in time of peace.

The receipts for 1911 amounted to fr. 25,645,973. Allowing in round figures a minimum loss of two million francs a month, the total for six and a half months is........................ fr. 13,891,566

(b) The service of the Bulgarian army comprised 116,731 horses and 100,000 oxen, some belonging to the army, others subsequently requisitioned, representing a total of 216,731 animals at fr. 500 a head, or fr. 108,365,500.

Half these animals were killed and lost. To the accounts there must be carried, therefore, fifty per cent of their value or...... 54,182,750

Attached to the army there were 50,000 carriages at fr. 300 each, a value of fifteen million francs. Thirty per cent at least of these are absolutely unusable; there is thus a loss of................. 4,500,000

Before, or at the beginning of the war, the War Minister purchased 7,350 horses for the army at a cost of fr. 6,972,681.80

It is estimated that 7,893 horses were killed or rendered useless; at a thousand francs each, this represents a loss of............... 7,893,000

5. *Cost of maintenance of the sick*

Provision of hospital accommodation in various establishments for the sick and wounded. Allowing two francs per day per soldier, and allowing for each soldier of an army of 563,076 men an average period, during the war, of thirty days of sickness, the total expense between September 17, 1912, and January 1, 1913, is.... 33,784,560

6. *Miscellaneous losses*

Loss and damage to war material, and other miscellaneous losses.. 2,000,000

Total... fr. 824,782,012.20

Net cost of the clothing and equipment of the Bulgarian soldier

(a) *Clothing*

Soldier's greatcoat	fr. 24
Coat.	13.85
Trousers	8
Cap	2.25
Shirt, in the shape of a coat for summer wear.....................	3.60
Boots	23
Knickerbockers (summer trousers).................................	3
Summer cap	2.15
Cover for the cap..	.70
Shirt	1.50

Knickerbockers . .   . .   fr. 1.50
National shoes of leather. 3.70
Cloth band for the national shoes. 4.50
Ties for the national shoes. 45
Hood for use in cold weather.   3
Gloves 50
Flannel 4.50
Puttees 70
Cravat 35
                                                                                                    _____
                                                                                                    fr. 101.25

(b) *Equipment*

Haversack . . . .   fr. 20
Tent 7.85
A pair of cartridge boxes.   12
Shoulder cartridge boxes   6
Straps 1.80
Banderole 1.30
Strap for cap 40
Strap for bayonet 50
Portable shovel 1.27½
Portable spade   2
Covering for the spade. 82½
Covering for the shovel. 90
Fork 3.50
Porringer 75
                                                                                                    _____
                                                                                                    fr. 59.10

(c) *Bedding*

Woolen quilt . . . .   fr. 15.50
Mattress   3
Pillow 40
Pillow case 50
Sheets   2
                                                                                                    _____
                                                                                                    fr. 21.40

Possessions and goods belonging to the company carried by certain soldiers,
   utensils, instruments, drums, trumpets, flags, bags, belts and leathers for
   revolvers, razors, scissors for hair cutting, per man. . . . . fr. 20

Pensions to be granted

Pensions to families of soldiers killed in the war at the rate of fr. 500 per
   family for twenty years, for 29,711 families of soldiers killed or dead
   as the result of their wounds equals fr. 14,855,500 per year, the value
   of which at 5 per cent per year or 2½ per cent per half year,
   amounts to . . . . fr. 372,919,199

Pensions to families of officers at the rate of 3,000 francs per family for twenty years, for 303 families of officers killed or dead as the result of their wounds,=939,000 per year, the actual value of which, at the rate of 5 per cent a year or 2½ per cent per half year, amounts to...   fr. 23,571,501

Pensions to invalided officers or soldiers at fr. 300 a year on 10 per cent of the total number wounded, *i. e.,* 8,668 men for thirty years= 2,600,000 francs per year, the actual value of which at 5 per cent per year or 2½ per cent per half year amounts to..................   75,379,953

These are the figures given to the Financial Commission in June, 1913. They certainly ought to be increased, since the note of the numbers of killed and wounded given to the Commission by the War Minister in the middle of September, 1913, were soldiers killed 44,313, officers 313, invalided 10,458.

Cost of maintenance of prisoners of war

Food and treatment

77,333 non-commissioned officers and soldiers for 907,393 days at fr. 140..   fr. 12,704,150.30
Eight generals for 750 days at fr. 20 a day.............................   15,000
149 officers of the general staff for 16,625 days at fr. 11...................   182,985
1,796 superior and other officers for 187,533 days at fr. 7.................   1,312,731

Total on June 1, 1913.......................................   fr. 14,214,866.30

Miscellaneous expenditure

Cost of lodging, heating and lighting....................................   fr. 1,093,879
Cost of clothing 141,298.54
Cost of barrack construction...   136,102.44
Miscellaneous (medicines, clothing for the sick, and burial expenses), etc...   406,637

Total on March 25/April 8, 1913...........................   fr. 15,992,783.28

The Public Debt of Bulgaria

On January 1 of the year	Consolidated debt in circulation	Floating debt	General total
1905	fr. 349,645,000	fr. 10,150,880	fr. 359,795,880
1906	363,086,000	17,232,599	380,318,599
1907	359,678,209	46,969,996	406,648,205
1908	446,583,209	38,402,187	484,985,396
1909	440,976,000	44,171,581	485,147,581
1910	516,281,700	52,118,675	568,400,375
1911	610,199,410	27,776,620	637,976,030
1912	603,799,618	29,493,524	633,293,142
1913	625,005,286	107,615,521	732,620,807

Bulgarian Post-Office Savings Bank

1912

Month	New accounts	Deposits Numbers	Value	Withdrawals Numbers	Value
January	4,672	27,112	fr. 3,624,773	15,425	fr. 2,600,961
February	3,373	29,361	3,609,593	15,921	3,131,083
March	3,228	30,702	4,058,352	15,840	2,962,828
April	2,950	19,227	3,136,514	17,185	3,156,850
May	3,000	21,350	3,275,377	16,604	2,931,487
June	2,830	23,343	1,155,665	15,470	2,746,104
July.	2,841	22,834	3,167,645	15,791	2,655,623
August	2,257	19,914	2,889,400	16,829	3,123,244
September	1,376	10,566	2,020,723	27,203	4,210,244
October	731	3,637	1,193,656	7,798	752,615
November	1,398	5,947	1,901,140	6,631	688,863
December	714	5,433	1,116,275	7,797	834,725

1913

Month	New accounts	Deposits Numbers	Value	Withdrawals Numbers	Value
January	2,294	12,811	fr. 2,391,742	9,110	fr. 956,660
February	1,873	13,359	2,562,444	8,945	1,035,684
March	1,725	12,862	2,667,255	10,437	1,281,017
April	2,150	13,643	2,992,408	11,444	1,494,575
May	2,260	13,911	3,190,410	11,034	1,443,849
June			2,831,532		1,218,740
July			1,209,522		1,573,196

Bulgarian Industries

An industrial inquiry made in 1909 showed that there were 261 private industrial establishments and five State industrial establishments profiting by the law for the encouragement of native industries.

The 261 private establishments are divided as follows:

	Number of establishments	Number of workpeople	Capital invested
1. Mines and quarries.	4	675	fr. 2,433,366
2. Metal trades	!6	816	2,331,074
3. Pottery trades	10	593	5,446,099
4. Chemical industries	25	497	2,583,688
5. Food and drink trades.	100	2,647	26,490,397
6. Textile trades	61	3,971	12,608,388
7. Furnishing and woodworking trades.	18	939	3,296,756
8. Leather trades	22	434	1,836,344
9. Paper trade	3	185	1,182,224
10. Production of physical forces.	2	50	6,257,450
Total	261	10,807	fr. 64,465,786

The five industrial establishments belonging to the State are as follows:

1. Mines and Quarries............................	2	1,360	fr. 1,646,654
2. Metal trades (repairs of carriages and loco- motives)	3	786	
Total	5	2,146	fr. 1,646,654

These industrial establishments may be grouped as follows according to the date of their foundation:

Number founded from 1830 up to 1879..			20
" 1880 1884...			23
" 1885 1889...			33
" 1890 1894...			54
" 1895 1899...			36
" 1900 1904...			30
" 1905 1909...			70
Total			266

During the period 1909 to 1912 the following industrial houses have been registered, as industries encouraged by the State:

Textile factories	15
Manufacture of felt and straw hats....................................	1
Metal trades	18
Manufacture of stoneware, bricks, etc................................	14
Chemical industries (soap, candles, oleaginous products, etc.).........................	11
Manufacture of sugars (sweets, chocolates, etc.)......................................	6
Cakes and biscuits	12
Glass	1
Wood and furniture	6
Tanneries	8
Paper and cardboard...	3
Cement	2
Stone and marble quarries	2
Shipbuilding (Varna)	1
Medical supplies (Sofia)	1
Electricity	1
Total	102

The Refugees

The following table gives the approximate distribution of the refugees in Bulgaria, on September 15, 1913:

1.	The town of Sofia...........	9,000	15.	Canton of d'Aitos	400
2.	Canton of Samokov..........	6,200	16.	" Anchialo	200
3.	" Doubnitza	10,000	17.	" Bourgas	6,500
4.	" Kustendil	4,900	18.	" Karnobat	1,400
5.	" Pechtera	12,000	19.	" Narmanly	1,600
6.	" Stanimaka	500	20.	" Eski-Djouma	200
7.	" Borissovgrad	1,900	21.	" Varna and Provadia	900
8.	" Tchirpan	1,200	22.	" Radomir	350
9.	" Naskovo	8,200	23.	" Ihtiman	450
10.	" Nova-Zagora	1,100	24.	Town and canton of Philippoli	6,230
11.	" Stara-Zagora	7,800	25.	Razardjik	4,500
12.	" Kazanlik	500	26.	Kotal	30
13.	" Yambol	2,900	27.	Paschnakly	2,500
14.	" Sliven	2,900	28.	Corna-Djoumaia	10,000

Total..................... 104,360

Greece

Table of the Losses of the Greek Army.

We have not been able to obtain the information necessary to draw up this table. Upon the date of 1/14 December, 1913, the Minister of Foreign Affairs for Greece replied in the following terms to a request which we had addressed to him: "I greatly regret that I am unable to give a satisfactory reply to your request of the 17th of this month. The Minister of War informs me that the General Staff, not having yet completed its statistics, nor collected all its reports, is in the meantime not prepared to give the exact figures of the numbers wounded in our two wars, nor of those likely to be invalided for life."

Cost of the War of 1912–1913

(June 1, 1913)

I. Maintenance of the army

(a) Food of the army, 215,000 effectives at fr. 2 a day, 257 days .... fr. 110,510,000

(b) War animals (45,064 animals requisitioned, 2,587 horses and mules for remounts, 4,000 army horses at fr. 2.50 a day, total 51,651 animals), 257 days... 33,185,767

(c) Pay of reserve officers, together with the indemnity on the opening of the campaign and supplementary war pay 17,073,000

fr. 160,768,767

II. *Equipment of the army*

(a) Clothing of the army in the field, 215,000 men at
     fr. 92.45 .... fr. 19,876,750
(b) Equipment of the army in the field, 215,000 men
     at fr. 42.80 ....·............   9,202,000
                                                                              fr. 29,078,750

III. *War material and ammunition*

(a) *Artillery.*
     Full supply of cartridges for the heavy artillery..   fr. 2,200,000
     Shot for quickfiring mountain cannon, to the
       number of 200,000   9,660,000
     Deterioration of the material of mountain cannon   2,720,000
     Deterioration of the material of mountain cannon   510,000
     Deterioration of the material of heavy artillery
       cannon   850,000
     Deterioration of the harness, etc., of field
       artillery   1,200,000
     Deterioration of the harness of the mountain
       artillery   525,000
     Loss and deterioration of equipment for groom-
       ing horses, etc.   530,000
                                                                              fr. 18,195,000

(b) *Infantry.*
     Consumption of cartridges to the number of
       sixty-five million ....   fr. 6,825,000
     Loss and deterioration of 180,000 musket bar-
       rels at fr. 16........................   2,880,000
     Loss and deterioration of 18,000 complete mus-
       kets at fr. 90..............................   1,620,000
     Loss and deterioration of transport vehicles......   950,000
     Deterioration of machine gun material...........   100,000
                                                                              12,375,000

(c) *Cavalry.*
     Deterioration of harness........................   fr. 850,000
     Loss and deterioration of equipment for groom-
       ing horses   75,000
                                                                              925,000

(d) *Engineers.*
     Approximate loss of portable works and artil-
       lery parks   300,000
     Loss of bridge apparatus and purchase of mate-
       rial for the construction of temporary bridges..   150,000
     Explosives   300,000
     Construction, repair of roads and bridges during
       the war   1,000,000

Harness for animals ....   fr. 300,000
Deterioration of wireless telegraphy, signaling
    apparatus, bicycles, etc.   900,000
Cantonments, conversion of barracks into hos-
    pitals in the occupied territories and the repair
    of existing barracks   550,000
Extraordinary hire of stables, depots, hostels,
    houses and indemnity for damage done to them   300,000
Deterioration of and indemnity for motors......   2,800,000
Repairs of motors and running expenses........   2,765,787
                                                    —————————   9,365,787

(e) *Sanitary service.*
Construction of barracks for the wounded......   150,000
Sanitary material imported from abroad.........   3,200,000
Sanitary material bought at home...............   450,000
Medicines imported from abroad.................   1,100,000
Hospital installation in trains and boats..........   700,000
                                                    —————————   5,600,000

IV. *Cost of transport, requisition, and horses for the war*

(a) Railway transport, six million francs, and sea trans-
    port, thirty million francs.......................   fr. 36,000,000
(b) Requisition of 45,064 animals, 6,081 carriages and
    4,147 boats   30,370,000
(c) Remounts: 1,164 horses from Hungary, eighty-five
    from Algeria, 1,338 from France and 800 mules
    from Italy   3,897,797
                                                     —————————   fr. 70,267,797

V. *Cost of maintenance of the sick*

Various hospital installations for the wounded and
    the sick to the end of May, 1913.................   fr. 4,240,000

VI. *Miscellaneous*

Loss and deterioration of war material and miscel-
    laneous losses   7,000,000

                                                    —————————
Grand total.................................   fr. 317,816,101

Naval expenditure

From September 18, 1912, to May 31, 1913 (old style), regular peace expenditure being deducted

Maintenance of the fleet

(a) *Movement material.*   Tons.

Coal	235,000	at	49.52	fr.	11,637,200
Petrol for scouts.	8,250	"	107.02		882,915
Petrol for submarines.	1,250	"	147.50		184,625
Lubricating oil for machinery.	475	"	700		332,500
" for cylinders	25	"	1,300		32,500
" for bulkheads	250	"	700		175,000
" special	9	"	1,200		10,800
" for submarines . . .	19	"	300		5,700
" for stimoilne	5	"	720		3,600
" ordinary	180	"	1,000		180,000
Tow	205	"	1,500		307,500
Miscellaneous.					12,460
				fr.	13,764,800

(b) *Maintenance material.*

Petrol	45	at	1,000	fr.	45,000
Alkaline salt	16	"	200		3,200
Alcohol	6	"	820		4,920
Seeds	4.65	"	1,500		6,975
Naphtha	4	"	1,750		7,000
Linseed oil	30	"	1,400		42,000
Red lead	19	"	1,000		19,000
Stucco	4½	"	800		3,600
Paint	35	"	1,000		35,000
Miscellaneous.					45,805
				fr.	212,500

(c) Excess in wages   3,925,000
(d) Excess on commissariat   6,991,000
(e) Clothing for reservists   1,705,000

Cantonment

Mackintoshes, hammocks, greatcoats, beds, tables and chairs, kitchen
and ship utensils . . . .   fr.   115,000

War material

(a) Ammunition   4,670,000
(b) Wear and tear of

Two quick firing cannons, Averov.	fr.	90,000
One Averov cannon, nineteen		200,000
Warship cannon after battle.		2,000,000
War material destroyed on the man of war *Macedonia*. . . .		125,000
Conversion of powder, resulting from the overheating of		
the vessels		1,000,000
Torpedoes		1,200,000
Automatic torpedoes		150,000
		4,765,000

(c) Sanitary service and hospital boats.   550,000

Boats requisitioned for the service of the fleet

Indemnity to packets..	fr. 7,226,600	
" to cargo boats....................................	3,431,943	
" tugs	233,400	
" to deteriorated lighters and tugs....................	266,000	
" to lighters	115,670	
" for loss and deterioration resulting from extraordinary use	2,000,000	
" damage to the transatlantic steamer *Macedonia*......	4,000,000	
Destruction of the steamer *Loros*............................	450,000	
		fr. 17,723,613

Establishment of bases of operation

Installation of wireless telegraphy.............................	fr. 400,000	
Installation for debarkation and the supply of water and light....	150,000	
Setting up of instruments and workshops at Oreons...........	150,000	
		fr. 700,000

Loss of and damage to steamboats

Damage on the armored cruiser *Ameroff*......................	fr. 650,000	
Damage on scouts	450,000	
Damage on other boats......................................	570,000	
Damage to machinery and furnaces	550,000	
Miscellaneous damage	1,000,000	
Reduction in the value of the units of the fleet................	17,000,000	
		fr. 20,220,000

Grand total .... fr. 75,341,913

Pensions

The departments concerned estimate the sum required to secure the pensions, provided by law, to the families of officers, soldiers and marines killed during the war, and to those who are invalided at

fr. 50,000,000 for the land army, and
fr. 4,000,000 for the fleet.

Prisoners of war

(a) Food and maintenance of 53,811 soldiers and non-commissioned officers from their capture up to March 31, 1913 (food being reckoned at the rate of fr. 0.40 per day)............................ fr. 11,213,236.24

(b) Pay to captive officers up to March 31, 1913 (1,430 officers).......... 726,732.94

(c) Cost of transport and removal of prisoners by land and sea up to March 31, 1913 .... 382,654.13

(d) Between April 1, 1913, and June 30, 1913, an average of fr. 58,430 per day was spent on soldiers, and fr. 9,359.30 on the officers, totaling 6,168,826.30

(e) Cost of assistance given to liberated prisoners, expense of burying the dead and other general charges............................ 1,508,550.39

fr. 20,000,000.00

Damage caused by the detention of ships

Ships detained at Constantinople:

Ten packets	fr.	5,404,500
Thirteen cargo boats		6,274,200
Twenty-three tugs		5,195,700
Forty-one sailing ships, lighters, barques, etc.............		1,211,966

fr. 18,086,366

Ships detained and afterwards released on the intervention of
    interested individuals of foreign nationality:

Six packets	fr.	337,200
Fifty-two cargo boats		3,621,322

fr. 3,958,522

Ships compelled to remain shut up in the Black Sea to escape
    the danger of being detained at Constantinople (loss
    of cargo):

Twenty-three cargo boats .... fr. 4,511,014

fr. 26,555.902

Public Debt of Greece

Capital to be amortised—January 1, 1913

drs. 5%	1881	120 millions	drs.	92,681,000
" 5%	1884	170 millions	"	80,905,000
" 4%	1887	Monopolies	"	121,930,000
" 4%	1889	Rents	"	138,787,000
" 5%	1890	Larissa	"	53,496,000
" 5%	1893	Funded	"	8,706,000
" -2½%	1898	Guaranteed	"	130,870,000
" 4%	1902	Hellenic railways	"	55,782,000
" 4%	1910	110 millions	"	110,000,000
" 5%	1907	20 millions	"	19,578,000
" 5%	1907	15 millions	"	14,490,000
" 1%		Maritime allocations	"	17,139,000

844,364,000

drs. 5%	1898	Unified	drs.	74,930,000
" 5%	1900	Meligala railways	"	11,470,000
		Patriotic	"	1,828,500
Circulation of bank notes on account of the Greek treasury				61,779,575

150,008,075

Total . . . . drs. 994,372,075

Savings Bank

Of all the Athenian Banks

1900.	December 31	drs.	3,598,000
1912.	June 30	"	40,257,000
1913.	June 30	"	59,365,000

Loans on securities in all the Athenian Banks

1900.	December 31	drs.	39,885,000
1911.	December 31	"	146,858,000
1912.	December 31	"	150,841,000

Loans on guaranteed merchandise and general depot in all the Athenian Banks

1900.	December 31	drs.	6,901,000
1911.	December 31	"	99,314,000
1912.	December 31	"	85,970,000
1913.	June 30	"	84,120,000

Greek Emigration to the United States

Year	Greek emigration	Total immigration to the United States
1885	172	395,346
1886	104	334,203
1887	313	490,109
1888	782	546,889
1889	158	444,427
1890	524	455,302
1891	1,105	560,319
1892	660	579,663
1893	1,072	493,730
1894	1,356	285,631
1895	597	258,536
1896	2,175	343,267
1897	571	230,832
1898	2,339	229,299
1899	2,333	311,715
1900	3,771	448,572
1901	5,910	487,918
1902	8,104	648,743
1903	14,090	857,046
1904	11,343	812,870
1905	10,515	1,026,499
1906	19,489	1;100,735
1907	36,580	1,285,349
1908	21,415	782,870
1909	14,111	751,786
1910	25,888	1,041,570
1911	37,021	878,587

Money sent in Postal Orders from Greece to America and from America to Greece

Year	Postal orders sent from Greece to America		Postal orders sent from America to Greece	
	Number of Orders	Value	Number of Orders	Value
1902	42	drs. 1,494.67	409	drs. 66,475
1903	49	2,637.62	1,676	267,364.75
1904	110	8,022.55	4,477	701,943.55
1905	124	7,602.84	10,007	1,734,967
1906	150	14,673.98	34,211	7,485,685.60
1907	156	15,548.37	59,840	13,956,494.35
1908	499	88,526.34	47,079	9,555,209
1909	239	35,012.63	61,245	13,727,693
1910	241	36,283.64	88,463	20,427,062.65
1911	336	58,085.09	92,105	19,579,887.65

Deposits in the banks of moneys sent from America

1910

National Bank	drs. 18,265,808
Bank of Ionia	10,186,103
Bank of Athens	9,405,610
Bank of Mitylene	2,141,980
Popular Bank	412,693
Commercial Bank	11,406,084
Bank	2,018,182
	————— drs. 53,836,460

1911

National Bank	drs. 17,269,317
Bank of Ionia	11,216,615
Bank of Athens	4,068,000
Orient Bank	1,031,250
Commercial Bank	11,250,000
Popular Bank	111,035
Bank	2,376,842
	————— drs. 47,323,059

Deposits in the National Bank of Greece, before and during the War

1912.

June 30	drs. 198,705,000
September 30	" 197,785,000 (Declaration of war.)
October 31	" 201,870,000
November 30	" 213,233,000
December 31	" 217,555,000

1913.

January 31	" 222,985,000
February 28	" 226,596,000
March 31	" 229,625,000
April 30	" 233,893,000
May 31	" 240,321,000
June 30	" 243,476,000
July 31	" 249,046,000

Deposits in all the Athenian Banks

1900.	December 31	..................................drs.	92,755,000
1912.	June 30	.... "	352,762,000
1913.	June 30	.... "	441,681,000

Capital of Banks and Industrial Joint Stock Companies

	Capital	Value on the market on December 31, 1912	Capital in 1904
Banks.			
Shares ....drs.	115,000,000	drs. 180,500,000	drs. 124,240,000
Debentures	123,216,400	134,222,000	107,663,000
Railways.			
Shares	62,000,000	59,000,000 }	65,526,000
Debentures	16,000,000	13,000,000 }	
Electricity, public works.			
Shares	19,500,000	25,000,000 }	22,000,000
Debentures	16,000,000	14,000,000 }	
Industrial companies	19,000,000	23,000,000	7,790,000
Engineering companies.			
Shares	21,000,000	16,000,000 }	16,000,000
Debentures	5,000,000	5,000,000 }	
Various companies.			
Shares	50,000,000	39,000,000 }	1,650,000
Debentures	9,000,000	9,000,000 }	
	455,716,400	517,722,000	344,869,000

Mercantile Marine—Sailing Ships

Year	Number of sailing ships	Tonnage
1903.	1,035	145,361
1911.	760	101,459

Comparative table showing the growth in tonnage of the steamships of the Hellenic Mercantile Marine

Year	Number of steamers	Net tonnage
1886	78	32,127
1892	93	58,522
1903	209	201,651
1907	258	256,474
1909	300	296,354
1911	347	384,446

The Refugees

The government has nominated a special commission to study the arrangements made for the refugees from Thrace and Macedonia. The members of this Commission were Messrs. Chomatianos, Administrative Commissioner at Kozani; Panayotopoulos, Director of the Thessalian Department of the Agricultural Bank in the Finance Ministry; Dimitriopoulos, Departmental Engineer, and Karaghinis, an official in the Department of Agriculture. The questions put to this Commission by Mr. Repoulis, Minister of the Interior, are as follows:

(1) Number of the refugees.

(2) Place from which they came.

(3) Did they possess property which they have sold or abandoned; are they peasant proprietors or simple day laborers?

(4) Are other occupations or professions represented?

(5) Specification of the crops cultivated (cereals, tobacco, vines, silk, etc.).

(6) Pecuniary position of the refugees. Have they ready money with them?

(7) The Commission shall examine the refugees to see which among them could find work as peasant proprietors or day laborers, and which ought to have land granted to them by the State, as being former owners.

(8) Which demesne lands could be parcelled out for this purpose; which individual properties could be utilized in the same way and under what conditions?

(9) The Commission shall consider the state of centers abandoned by their inhabitants to determine how they would be affected by the installation of refugees in them.

These questions afford some indication of the work of the Commission, which may extend its inquiry to cover any points which it may judge to be desirable. The Commission is controlled by Mr. Dragoumis.

Montenegro

Cost of the War of 1912–1913

1. Maintenance of the army

(a) Food of the army mobilized in Montenegro in the Sandjak, at Berana and Ipek, and of volunteers...................................... fr. 27,839,500

Horses and mules requisitioned and attached to the army........... 4,505,600

Subventions in money and meal given to poor families during the war, after mobilization of all able bodied men, without any age limit..... 5,000,000

(b) Pay of officers including indemnity at the start of the campaign and supplementary war pay 5,500,000

2. Equipment of the army

(a) Clothing of the army in the field.................................... 7,250,000

(b) Equipment of the army in the field.................................. 4,350,000

3. *War material and ammunition*

Artillery.

    Batteries of mounted cannon, batteries of field cannon and batteries of siege cannon with their respective ammunition.

Infantry.

    Quick firing machine guns, cartridges, cartridge boxes and muskets. Cost of ammunition, the loss and deterioration of the said material.

Engineers.

    Loss of portable works and artillery parks; purchase of material for the construction of temporary bridges.

    Explosives, construction, repair of roads during the war. Deterioration of telegraphic and signaling apparatus, projectors.

    Barracks, hiring of houses, stables, depots, etc., and indemnity for damage sustained.

fr. 25,436,000

    Purchase, hire, deterioration and maintenance of motors, carriages and carts 2,800,000

Sanitary Service.

    Cantonments, sanitary appliances purchased at home and abroad. Medicines, hospital installations and ambulance wagons............ 4,300,000

4. *Cost of transport, requisitions, war horses*

(a) Transport, by railway, water and road............................... 2,900,000
(b) Requisition of animals, carriages and other means of transport........ 4,100,000
(c) Various remounts, horses and mules................................ 300,000

5. *Cost of maintenance of the sick*

Hospital installations for the sick and wounded, fixed or temporary ambulances 4,350,000

6. *Miscellaneous*

Indemnities for burned villages; other losses and damage............. 2,000,000

Total.. fr. 100,631,100

This account does not include indemnities payable to the families of dead soldiers and to invalided soldiers, or the cost of prisoners of war.

Servia

Under the date of February 13, 1914, the Servian Minister of War has communicated to the Skupshtina the following figures of the losses of the Servian army during the two last wars:

    Serbo-Turkish war: Dead, 5,000; wounded, 18,000.

    Serbo-Bulgarian war: Dead, 7,000 to 8,000; wounded, 30,000.

    Two thousand five hundred soldiers died as a result of their injuries. Between 11,000 and 12,000 from sickness, and 4,300 from cholera. Among the latter, 4,000 died during the Serbo-Bulgarian war.

Cost of the War of 1912–1913

(June 1, 1913)

The following account was presented to the Financial Commission on Balkan Affairs, on June 25, 1913:

1. Maintenance of the army

(a) Food of the army .... fr. 226,324,000

(b) Pay of reserve officers, indemnity at the opening of the campaign and supplementary war pay.................................... 26,595,500

2. Equipment of the army

(a) Clothing for the army in the field................................ 40,254,000

(b) Equipment for the army in the field.............................. 24,152,000

3. War material and ammunition

Artillery. Charges for quick firing mountain cannon and heavy artillery; deterioration of mountain cannon and heavy artillery material; deterioration in harnesses, grooming accessories, etc.

Infantry. Consumption of cartridges, loss and deterioration of muskets, etc.

Cavalry. Deterioration of harness, loss and deterioration of grooming accessories, etc. .... fr. 118,030,000

Engineers. Deterioration and loss of portable works and artillery parks; explosives, grooming accessories, aeroplanes, automobiles, bicycles, bridges, signalling apparatus, wireless telegraphy, etc.

Sanitary Service. Medicines and instruments, tents and barracks, hospital installation, ambulance trains, etc.

4. *Cost of railway transport*.. 32,029,000

5. *Requisition of animals, carriages, remounts of different kinds*......... 87,969,000

6. *Cost of maintenance of sick and wounded*.......................... 9,462,000

7. *Miscellaneous* 10,000,000

Total... fr. 574,815,500

Observations

The expenditure enumerated above does not include:

(a) Pensions to the families of officers and soldiers killed during the war or dying after it.

(b) Cost of maintenance of prisoners.

(c) Expenses necessitated by the conquest of Albania.

(d) Indemnities claimed by the Oriental Railroad Company.

(e) Indemnities due in respect of events previous to the outbreak of hostilities, responsibility for which has been accepted by the Ottoman Government (*e. g.,* seizure of cannon and wagons).

(f) Cost of repatriating troops.

Another estimate of the cost of the war was given us on September 30, by Mr. Stefano-vits, Secretary to the Servian Minister of Foreign Affairs, as follows:

Losses incurred by Servia in the Serbo-Turk War (1912-1913)

I. Loss of material

1.	Expenditure on ammunition	fr. 28,849,060.80
2.	Value of material rendered quite unusable:	
	(a) Clothing equipment and harness...........................	49,502,698.17
	(b) Garrison expenses	14,841,530
	(c) Sanitary expenses	728,150
	(d) Engineers..	1,255,050
	(e) Artillery...	11,242,220
	Total...	fr. 77,569,648.17

3.	A certain portion of the unusable material may be regarded as lost:	
	(a) Sanitary...	fr. 1,678,370
	(b) Engineers..	194,368
	(c) Artillery...	43,468,732
	Total...	fr. 45,341,470

4.	Loss of animals, expenditure on requisition and purchase of animals, cost of transport	71,528,867.66
5.	Food for men	133,932,420.66
6.	Food for animals	67,168,530
7.	Pay of officers, non-commissioned officers, etc.......................	9,516,988
8.	Mobilization expenses	1,191,609
9.	Cost of the occupation of Albania and the siege of Scutari............	9,177,625

II. Prisoners of war

Maintenance of 393 officers and officials and of 16,155 non-commissioned officers and soldiers .... fr. 1,604,638.75

The various totals amount to 445,880,858.04, or 128,934,641.96 *less* than the total submitted by Servia to the Financial Conference on Balkan Affairs, on June 25, 1913. It should further be noted that this only includes expenses up to that date, a final statement is still to be presented which should further include the cost of maintenance of prisoners and the expenditure necessitated by the conquest of Albania.

Servian Public Debt

Loans

1881.	Twenty shares	fr. 21,920,000
1888.	Tobacco shares	8,930,000
1895.	4% Rent	333,520,000
1902.	5% Loan	55,651,000
1906.	4½% Loan	91,325,000
1909.	4½% Loan	147,709,500
		fr. 659,055,500

Recapitulatory Table of the Claims for Pecuniary Compensation Made by the Balkan States as the Result of War Operations

Heads of Claims	Bulgaria	Greece	Montenegro	Servia	Total
I. *Claims relative to military expenditure.*					
1. Expenditure on the army	fr. 824,782,012.20	fr. 317,816,101	fr. 100,631,100	fr. 574,815,500	fr. 1,818,044,713.20
2. Expenditure on the navy		75,341,913			75,341,913
3. Pensions	471,870,653.00	54,000,000			525,870,653
4. Damage caused by the cruiser "Hamidieh"		504,600			504,600
Totals	fr. 1,296,652,665.20	fr. 447,662,614	fr. 100,631,100	fr. 574,815,500	fr. 2,419,761,879.20
II. *Other claims presented by the States as States.*					
1. Repatriation of refugees and Ottoman subjects		fr. 2,000,000		fr. 2,000,000	fr. 4,000,000
2. Maintenance of prisoners of war	fr. 15,992,783.28	20,000,000	fr. 2,500,000	16,000,000	54,492,783.28
3. Indemnity for wagons seized				879,668.33	879,668.33
4. Indemnity for material of war seized				5,287,759.80	5,287,759.80
Totals	fr. 15,992,783.28	fr. 22,000,000	fr. 2,500,000	fr. 24,167,428.13	fr. 64,660,211.41
III. *Pecuniary compensation claimed on account of damage caused to individuals.*					
1. Damage caused to the inhabitants of Epirus		fr. 10,996,370			fr. 10,996,370
2. Damage caused to Balkan subjects		41,000,000		fr. 2,000,000	43,000,000
3. Restitution of the funds to the branches of the Agricultural Bank					
4. Damage resulting from the detention of vessels		26,555,912			26,555,912
Totals		fr. 78,552,282		fr. 2,000,000	fr. 80,552,282
General Totals	fr. 1,312,645,448.48	fr. 548,214,896	fr. 103,131,100	fr. 600,982,928.13	fr. 2,564,974,372.61

ANALYSIS OF THE REPORT

CHAPTER I

Origin of the Two Balkan Wars

1.—Ethnography and National Aspirations

Before the advent of the Turks in Europe, the two Balkan peoples already aspired to leadership in the peninsula.—From the tenth to the sixteenth century, the Bulgarians, the Servians and the Byzantines usurped this leadership in turn, without accomplishing the fusion of the races.

How the Turks stamped out the differences between the nationalities by exterminating the warrior class and by the subordination of the orthodox cults to the Greek church, which had its See at the Phanar (Constantinople).—The raïas and the Greek Patriarchy.—The Roum-mileti.—The predominance of the Greek church was consummated in 1765–1767, leaving the Slav dissatisfied and the Greek priest in foreign environments.......... 21

First Manifestations of the National Idea

2.—THE STRUGGLE FOR AUTONOMY

FROM THE BEGINNING OF THE NINETEENTH CENTURY, TWO PARALLEL AND RIVAL IDEAS MANIFEST THEMSELVES: AUTONOMY AND THE PARTITION OF MACEDONIA

3.—THE ALLIANCE AND THE TREATIES

4.—CONFLICT BETWEEN THE ALLIES

CHAPTER II
Greeks and Bulgarians

1.—POSITION OF THE MACEDONIANS DURING THE FIRST WAR

2.—CONDUCT OF THE BULGARIANS DURING THE SECOND WAR

3.—THE BULGARIAN PEASANT AND THE GREEK ARMY

CHAPTER III

Bulgarians, Turks and Servians

1.—ADRIANOPLE

3.—THE BATTLE GROUND OF THE SERBO-BULGARIAN WAR

CHAPTER IV
The War and Nationalities

3.—GREEK MACEDONIA

CHAPTER V

The War and International Law

5.—THE USE OF FORBIDDEN BOMBS AND EXPLOSIVES

6.—VIOLATIONS OF THE FLAG OF TRUCE

7.—FATE OF THE SICK AND WOUNDED

8.—ATTACK AND PILLAGE OF NONCOMBATANTS

9.—TRIBUTE AND ARBITRARY REQUISITIONS

10.—ASSAULTS AGAINST PERSONS, PROPERTY AND RELIGIOUS BELIEF

CHAPTER VI
Economic Consequences of the War

CHAPTER VII

Moral and Social Consequences of the War
Conjectures About the Future of Macedonia

1.—MORAL AND SOCIAL CONSEQUENCES

2.—CONJECTURES IN REGARD TO THE FUTURE OF MACEDONIA

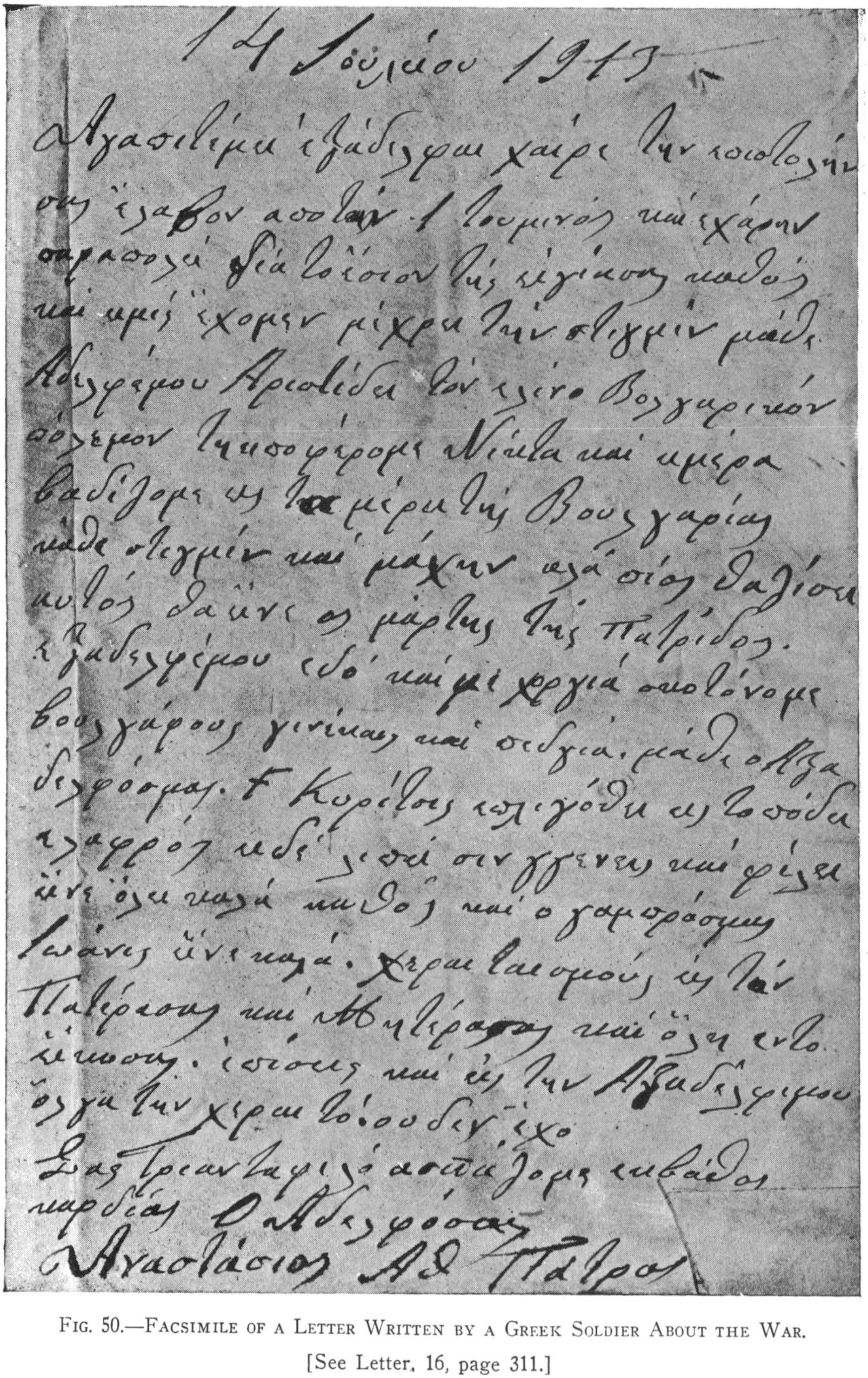

FIG. 50.—FACSIMILE OF A LETTER WRITTEN BY A GREEK SOLDIER ABOUT THE WAR.

[See Letter, 16, page 311.]